THE BEST PLAYS OF 1971–1972

THE
BURNS MANTLE
YEARBOOK

THE
BEST PLAYS
OF 1971-1972

EDITED BY OTIS L. GUERNSEY JR.

*Illustrated with photographs and
with drawings by* HIRSCHFELD

DODD, MEAD & COMPANY

NEW YORK · TORONTO

EDITOR'S NOTE

THE 1971-72 theater season in New York was a national and international festival instead of the local event it used to be. The Best Plays list includes one French and two British plays; many American regional theater hits were brought to the local playhouses; off-Broadway hits moved uptown and played Broadway. In one case, an American musical staged its Broadway tryout production in London. In another, an American script premiered in London and then was produced in Washington, D.C. before moving to New York, thus linking a good part of the English-speaking stage.

It is both a duty and a pleasure for the *Best Plays* series of theater year-books to reflect the basic developments in the theater of its time, and *The Best Plays of 1971-72* mirrors this nationalization and internationalization. Internationally, we have expanded our coverage of the London season, viewing it in the perspective of two articles, one by John Spurling on the underground, off-beat theater and one by our European Editor, Ossia Trilling, on the season in the West End. Mr. Trilling's listing of the major shows of the London season is ever more detailed and comprehensive (with the invaluable assistance of Ann Engel and with much-appreciated help from the editor of the British weekly *Time Out*) and includes this year more than 400 entries. As always, Mr. Trilling's coverage of the theater on the European continent in his annual essay, and of the Paris theater in his listings, is incomparably thorough and informative.

Nationally, Ella A. Malin's Directory of Professional Regional Theater is the definitive catalogue of coast-to-coast play production and includes full cast listings of American and world premieres. It is augmented this year by special reports on other than regional theater production in Los Angeles (by Rick Talcove) and in Washington (by Jay Alan Quantrill), two increasingly important centers of legitimate stage creativity.

In the New York lists of Broadway and off-Broadway shows our policy is the widest possible inclusion consistent with professional standards of theater work. The Broadway list includes the major repertory productions and such "limited" and "middle" shows as appeared. The off-Broadway list takes in not only all productions technically fitting the classification, but quite a few that don't but were brought into the off-Broadway limelight in commercial-theater lists like those in *Variety* and *Theater Information Bulletin*. With the addition of factual data on the more important off-off-Broadway productions, ours is a virtually complete record of the 1971-72 professional and semi-professional New York theater.

Stanley Green, author of *Ring Bells! Sing Songs!* (a history of Broadway musicals in the 1930s) and the forthcoming *Starring Fred Astaire,* keeps *Best*

Plays readers informed on all major acting assignments with his comprehensive listing of the year's cast replacements in New York shows in long first runs or on first-class tours here and even in London. Bernard Simon, editor of *Simon's Directory,* and Joseph Felician of American Theater Productions, Inc. provided the information on bus-truck tours. The necrology and listing of publication of plays and musicals in books and on records were prepared with her customary care and expertise by Rue Canvin. Other stars of the *Best Plays* editing team include the editor's patient and extremely durable wife, and Jonathan Dodd of Dodd, Mead and Company.

We have many to thank for the acquisition and preparation of material in these pages: Henry Hewes of *The Saturday Review,* Mimi Horowitz of *Playbill,* Hobe Morrison of *Variety,* Clara Rotter of the New York *Times,* Ralph Newman of the Drama Book Shop, as well as literally hundreds of people in theater production and communications who generously assisted our editors in the compiling of detailed information. We are most grateful also to the authors of the Best Plays and their agents and publishers who have made extensive quotation available in our synopses; to Al Hirschfeld for his drawings which as always give a theater season its official "look"; to the stage designers whose work is displayed in the photo section as examples of the year's best; and to the photographers in New York and across the country whose cameras preserve the visual record of a year's activity on our stages, including Joseph Abeles, Bert Andrews, Fletcher Drake, David H. Fishman, Sy Friedman, Henry Grossman, Andy Hanson, Nat Messik, Martin Selzer, William L. Smith, Martha Swope, Alan B. Tepper, John Timbers, UPI Photos, John Veltri and Van Williams.

Peripherally but emphatically, we are grateful to Clive Barnes for his WQXR radio review of our *Best Plays* volumes and our recently-published *Directory of the American Theater, 1894-1971,* a complete listing of play titles and authors indexed to the whole *Best Plays* series. We do not *thank* Mr. Barnes (it's bad manners to thank a critic for doing his thing) but we are grateful for his sensitive perception of our "very valuable series" with its "magnificent documentation" and its "tart, astringent and yet affectionate" commentary from a "fine critical perspective" on the season in New York, in a book which in the stated opinion of Mr. Barnes is "a theater-lover's must."

OTIS L. GUERNSEY Jr.

June 1, 1972

CONTENTS

Drawings by HIRSCHFELD

SUMMARIES
OF THE
SEASONS

THE SEASON IN NEW YORK

By Otis L. Guernsey Jr.

LOOKING back on the New York Theater season of 1971-72, we can see splashes of bright color all over the place; but we have to admit that the predominant hue was gray. This was a season of gray subject matter and gray, half-realized achievement. Its best work, the imported full-length Harold Pinter play *Old Times,* was a misted memory of Paradise lost performed in a bleak white-on-white setting so that if you missed the point intellectually you'd be sure to grasp it visually—if you were one of the relatively few Broadway theatergoers who went to see it. The season's best musical, *Ain't Supposed to Die a Natural Death,* was a grim reminder of conditions in the black ghetto done as a series of chants, with a poetic but songless score. The season's most lavish showcase musical, *Sugar,* was based on an old movie. Its biggest musical hit, *Jesus Christ Superstar,* was a nightmare version of the passion and crucifixion.

In April the New York *Times* was able to announce "All Broadway Stages Occupied or Booked"—wonder of 1972 wonders, all 30-odd Broadway theaters were full of shows in the waning weeks of the season. Unfortunately, grayly, they weren't also full of audiences. Only one show was selling out, Neil Simon's *The Prisoner of Second Avenue* (a comedy about the frustrations of high-rise living, admittedly funny, but focused on a man having a nervous breakdown within four gray walls of a drab modern apartment).

At first glance, one could suppose that off Broadway had enjoyed an almost purple year. For the first time in the 53-year history of the *Best Plays* volumes, off Broadway captured half the ten Best Play citations, including the best American play of the season: *Sticks and Bones* by David Rabe, the Tony Award-winning drama of a returning Vietnam War veteran. The other four off-Broadway Best Plays were Jason Miller's *That Championship Season,* winner of the Critics Award; Tennessee Williams's *Small Craft Warnings,* bringing back into the contemporary theater one of our greats; Terrence McNally's *Where Has Tommy Flowers Gone?,* a portrait of a modern young rebel; and Jean Genet's *The Screens* in its American premiere at the Chelsea Theater Center over in Brooklyn. What's more, off Broadway was the place of origin of the Tony and Critics Award-winning musical *Two Gentlemen of Verona.* This outstanding record was smudged, however, by dreary economic problems in a season of high off-Broadway production costs and sluggish audience re-

3

The 1971-72 Season on Broadway

PLAYS (19)

The Trial of the Catonsville Nine (transfer)
Solitaire/Double Solitaire
The Incomparable Max
Unlikely Heroes
THE PRISONER OF SECOND AVENUE
Twigs
Fun City
The Love Suicide at Schofield Barracks
MOONCHILDREN
Night Watch
STICKS AND BONES (transfer)
Children! Children!
Voices
Elizabeth I
Promenade, All!
All the Girls Came Out to Play
Ring Round the Bathtub
An Evening With Richard Nixon And . . . ;
Tough to Get Help

MUSICALS (13)

Jesus Christ Superstar
AIN'T SUPPOSED TO DIE A NATURAL DEATH
The Grass Harp
Two Gentlemen of Verona (transfer)
Wild and Wonderful
Inner City
Grease
The Selling of the President
Sugar
Different Times
Hard Job Being God
Don't Play Us Cheap!
Heathen!

REVIVALS (12)

You're a Good Man, Charlie Brown
No Place to Be Somebody
On the Town
Lincoln Center Rep
Mary Stuart
Twelfth Night
The Crucible
There's One in Every Marriage
The Sign in Sidney Brustein's Window
The Country Girl
A Funny Thing Happened on the Way to the Forum
Captain Brassbound's Conversion
Lost in the Stars

REVUES (2)

That's Entertainment
Don't Bother Me, I Can't Cope

SPECIALTIES (1)

Black Light Theater of Prague

HOLDOVER SHOWS WHICH BECAME HITS DURING 1971-72

Bob and Ray, the Two and Only
Coco
Lenny
The Me Nobody Knows
No, No, Nanette
Two by Two

FOREIGN PLAYS IN ENGLISH (9)

To Live Another Summer,
To Pass Another Winter
Narrow Road to the Deep North
OLD TIMES
Only Fools Are Sad
Murderous Angels
Anne of Green Gables
VIVAT! VIVAT REGINA!
Wise Child
The Little Black Book

Categorized above are all the plays listed in the "Plays Produced on Broadway" section of this volume.

Plays listed in CAPITAL LETTERS have been designated Best Plays of 1971-72.

Plays listed in **bold face type** were classified as hits in *Variety*'s annual list of hits and flops published June 7, 1972, or judged imminently likely to become hits.

Plays listed in *italics* were still running June 1, 1972.

sponse. Runs were short, success was limited, and as of season's end none of the 1971-72 productions could be called a ringing hot-ticket hit.

Pinter, Simon and Melvin Van Peebles's *Ain't Supposed* were joined on Broadway's half of the Best Plays list by Robert Bolt's colorful historical play *Vivat! Vivat Regina!* and by Michael Weller's *Moonchildren,* an affectionate report on college students' escape fantasies in the troubled 1960s. Therefore the makeup of the 1971-72 Best Plays list is one musical and nine straight plays; three foreign plays (two British and one French) and seven American (one of these, *Moonchildren,* came by way of London and Washington, where it was a big success, to New York where, characteristically and grayly in this difficult season, it was a 16-performance flop); six by "established" and four by new writers. If it was reassuring to find favorites like Harold Pinter, Neil Simon, Terrence McNally, Robert Bolt, Jean Genet and Tennessee Williams on the year's best list, it was also reassuring to find in their company new playwriting talent of the calibre of David Rabe, Melvin Van Peebles, Jason Miller and Michael Weller—as well as Phillip Hayes Dean (*The Sty of the Blind Pig*), Richard Wesley (*The Black Terror*), J.E. Franklin (*Black Girl*), Conor Cruise O'Brien (*Murderous Angels*), Romulus Linney (*The Love Suicide at Schofield Barracks*), David V. Robison (*Promenade, All!*), David Wiltse (*Suggs*) and "Lee Barton" (a pseudonym for the author of *Nightride,* if he is a new playwright) who were not far behind.

The number of shows produced on Broadway—most in first-class, a few in "limited" or "middle" productions—held steady at 56 in 1971-72 (see the one-page summary accompanying this report). This was the same number as last year, after a dropoff from 68 the year before, 76 the year before that and 84 in 1967-68. Some encouragement can be drawn from the rise in the number of American straight play programs produced on Broadway this season to 19 from last season's all-time low of 14; and in the slight rise in the number of American musicals from 11 to 13 in 1971-72. This overall production statistic in 1969-70 was 21 plays and 14 musicals, 24-12 the year before that and 25-10 in 1967-68. Off Broadway the American straight play number was higher, too, with 43 programs as compared to 39 last year. With musical production steady and straight plays reversing their previous downward curve, there is certainly some cause, if not for rejoicing, or even for guarded optimism, at least for renewed determination.

It was the other numbers that took on overtones of gray this season—the relatively few people on the streets of the Broadway area at show time (and the far from festive mood of those who were showing up), the prohibitively high cost of a top ticket, the soaring price tag on every aspect of production. On Broadway, the going rate for fifth row center on Friday night at *Jesus Christ Superstar* was $15, and the same every night at *Sugar.* It cost $9 for the best seat at the new Neil Simon on weekends, $8.50 week nights; $8 and $6 at *Sticks and Bones* on Broadway. Weekend matinee top for plays was running around $8, for musicals $8-$10. Off Broadway, Joseph Papp was playing his hits for $5 weekdays, $6 weekends, but an expensive $7.50 was more like what you would be asked to pay for a good seat at an off-Broadway success on a preferred night.

According to *Variety* estimate, the average production cost of a Broadway musical had risen to $534,000 (and this is an *average,* the big ones couldn't open for anything like that sum). For straight plays the average had reached $141,000. Off Broadway, costs for a musical ran from $100,000 up and for a play $40,000 up. At these prices, New York producers began to look enviously in the direction of London (where this season the West End actors were negotiating a raise in the weekly minimum from $43 to $72, while Equity's weekly Broadway minimum is now $185). In October, the American musical *Ambassador* was produced in London for $240,000 as a sort of tryout for Broadway. It wasn't a success, but it would have cost three times as much to find this out on Broadway. In April London saw a $450,000 musical version of *Gone With the Wind,* reputedly London's most expensive musical ever, but a half-price bargain compared to the estimated Broadway cost.

In this context, *Variety's* summary of the season gives no great cause for rejoicing—nor any significant jolt of alarm. The total Broadway gross for 1971-72 was $52.3 million, off from last year's $54.9 million and way under 1967-68's record $59 million but still a sizeable sum. Touring Broadway productions grossed $49.7 million in 1971-72, so that the season's total take was well over $100 million. In the matter of playing weeks (if ten shows play ten weeks that's 100 playing weeks) Broadway registered 1,092 (plus 65 previewing weeks) this season as compared with 1,099 last year, 1,047 the year before that and 1,200-odd in the four previous years. More significantly and somewhat less hopefully, there was only one Broadway "hit," one show which had recouped its cost as of June 1: the touring *Captain Brassbound's Conversion.* If prices are higher and runs are longer nowadays, so are costs, so that it takes much longer to reach the break-even point, the "hit" level (and as of June 1 it looked as though *Jesus Christ Superstar* and *The Prisoner of Second Avenue* would soon become the first two 1971-72 shows to break through the overcast into the profitable sunlight).

There were a few patches of blue in the gray overcast. According to *Variety* estimates, *Fiddler on the Roof's* net profit on its $375,000 investment reached $7,215,000 as it climbed toward the top of the heap to become the longest-running show in Broadway history at its 3,225th performance on June 17, 1972. As *No, No, Nanette* reached the break-even point on its $650,000 investment, it had an additional near-$1 million advance sale already in hand. *Sleuth* has netted more than $1 million on its $150,000 investment; *Promises, Promises* and *1776* about $1.5 million each on $500,000; *Oh, Calcutta!* $310,000 on $100,000.

Perhaps the most remarkable 1971-72 success story of them all was that of Jerome Lawrence and Robert E. Lee's *The Night Thoreau Spent in Jail,* the subject of an article by its authors in *The Best Plays of 1970-71. Thoreau* never got to New York, as planned—it is still on the way—but it scarcely needed to. By the time its American Playwrights Theater circuit production option expired on Jan. 1, 1972, it had received 141 productions by member groups of this cross-country resident and university theater organization—not a tour, but 141 *separate* productions with 141 different casts, directors, designers, etc.

Unhappily, there were also the patches of blacker significance drifting through the weeks of production. *Old Times,* the season's best play, was mounted for $100,000 and lost $120,000 in a Broadway run of 119 performances. *The Rothschilds* was still in the red for $650,000 of its $850,000 production cost when it closed after a run of no less than 507 performances. *Follies,* last season's best musical and indeed one of the outstanding theater works of the decade, eked back about $160,000 of its nearly $800,000 production cost until, in midwinter, the sands began to flow the other way and the gap to widen again.

In the gloom, stars and near-stars twinkled all the more brightly because of the contrast. Flashes of light included Robert Shaw, Rosemary Harris and Mary Ure pausing Pinteresquely in *Old Times* . . . Richard Venture establishing a New York reputation in the two leading roles of *Solitaire/Double Solitaire* and as the Belgian industrialist of *Murderous Angels* . . . Peter Falk, Lee Grant and Vincent Gardenia in *The Prisoner of Second Avenue* . . . Raul Julia, Clifton Davis, Jonelle Allen and Diana Davila brushing up on John Guare's and Mel Shapiro's version of Shakespeare in *Two Gentlemen of Verona* . . . Barry Bostwick mimicking a 1950s James Dean saunter in *Grease,* aided and abetted by Adrienne Barbeau and Timothy Myers . . . Phil Silvers and Larry Blyden, great individually and as a pair in the Burt Shevelove revival of *A Funny Thing Happened on the Way to the Forum* . . . Sada Thompson's display of virtuosity as three middle-aged women and their mother in *Twigs* . . . Robert Drivas, alienated and adrift but alive in the big city in *Where Has Tommy Flowers Gone?* . . . Eileen Atkins's perfect Elizabeth in *Vivat! Vivat Regina!,* with Lee Richardson's Bothwell . . . Tom Aldredge's Ozzie and Elizabeth Wilson's Harriet, trapped in their Consciousness I lifestyle in *Sticks and Bones,* and Cliff DeYoung's reptilion teen-ager in the same play . . . Mercedes McCambridge's staunch bit in *The Love Suicide at Schofield Barracks* . . . Lester Rawlins's witty and affectionate portrayal of a most distinguished living American playwright in *Nightride* . . . Jason Robards, a pro playing an old pro in *The Country Girl* . . . Hume Cronyn as a nonagenarian who still *can* in *Promenade, All!* . . . Eugenie Leontovich in her own free adaptation of Tolstoy, *Anna K* . . . Robert Morse dressed in women's clothes and sharing an upper berth with the irresistably beautiful Elaine Joyce in *Sugar* . . . Brock Peters in *Lost in the Stars* and Bernadette Peters in *On the Town* . . . Clarice Taylor and Adolph Caesar as indomitable black brother and sister in *The Sty of the Blind Pig* . . . Ingrid Bergman as a handsome Lady Cecily in *Captain Brassbound's Conversion* . . . The entire acting ensembles of *That Championship Season, Moonchildren, Ain't Supposed to Die a Natural Death, Small Craft Warnings, And They Put Handcuffs on the Flowers* and *The Real Inspector Hound.*

Other luminaries had not much luck with their vehicles and twinkled pretty much in vain, including Richard Kiley giving two of his telling performances in short-lived plays, *The Incomparable Max* and *Voices,* the latter in company with Julie Harris . . . Donald Pleasence, George Rose and Bud Cort handling with great skill the murky nonsense of *Wise Child,* a trick play imported from England . . . Lou Jacobi as an unlucky lover, David Ackroyd as a tough Army sergeant and Michael Tolan as an embattled suburban lawyer in *Unlikely Heroes* . . . Pat Hingle as a Presidential aspirant in *The Selling of the President* and George S. Irving in the title role of *An Evening With Richard Nixon And* . . . Barbara Cook and Ruth Ford in *The Grass Harp* . . . Bill Hinnant as a suicidal life guard in *God Bless Coney* . . . Richard Benjamin and Delphine Seyrig struggling with bleak situation comedy in *The Little Black Book* . . . Hal Linden as Sidney Brustein in the revival of the Hansberry play . . . Gwen Verdon flashing in and out like a subliminal image in the one-performance run of the melodrama *Children! Children!* . . . Incidentally, there were five of these single-performance flops this season on Broadway. The others were *Wild and Wonderful,* a musical about the big city youth movement; *Ring Round the Bathtub* about an Irish-American family in Chicago during the Depression; *Tough to Get Help,* a suburban situation involving a rich liberal and the black couple who work for him; and *Heathen,* the Robert Helpmann-Eaton Magoon Jr. musical about Hawaii in 1819 and 1972. Off Broadway there were ten: *Drat!, Memphis Store-Bought Teeth, Two if by Sea* (musicals), *In the Time of Harry Harass, Brothers, Whitsuntide, Cold Feet, Masquerade* (the latter a part of the 1972 Elizabeth I canon, dramatizing her relationship with the Earl of Oxford), the Roundabout Repertory's American premiere production of the late John Whiting's 1947 play *Conditions of Agreement,* and *The Soft Core Pornographer,* for which the New York *Times's* Clive Barnes produced the following tag line for his unfavorable review: "What less can I say?"

Few of our so-called "established" playwrights ventured out into the threatening overcast of 1972. Of those who did, only a handful distinguished themselves. Among those who missed a hold on Broadway were Robert Anderson with *Solitaire/Double Solitaire* and the Messrs. Lawrence & Lee with *The Incomparable Max.* Off Broadway, Ed Bullins's *The Duplex,* a slice-of-life play about an all-night party in a black California community (stylistically akin to the same author's *The Pig Pen*), fell far below the very high standard of acute observation and intensity of expression which this distinguished playwright has set in his better works. In the Broadway instances of Anderson and Lawrence & Lee it was more the form than the performance which raised difficulties. Both *Solitaire* and *Max* were one-act play programs, Anderson's a back-to-back pair of wry comments on the final victory of machines over man in the first play and the tensions of married life in the second; Lawrence & Lee's a pair of dramatized Max Beerbohm short stories about clairvoyance, sandwiched in between character vignettes of Beerbohm himself (played by Clive Revill) as a sort of commentator. Both programs were written and acted with a wit and flair worthy of the Broadway spotlight, but by their very nature as one-acters they couldn't add up to the big play, the big evening which now more than ever the Broadway theater craves from its precious Andersons,

Lawrences & Lees. George Furth's one-act play program *Twigs* made it on Broadway this season on its strength as a vehicle for a big Sada Thompson virtuoso appearance as much as on its own inner values. *Unlikely Heroes* did not, even though it was sterner stuff than either *Solitaire, Max* or *Twigs* in its three one-act episodes of the Jewish experience, adapted by Larry Arrick from Philip Roth stories: a Jewish army sergeant's efforts to be fair to a malingering Jewish recruit, a Jewish poppa's ill-fated romantic adventure with an amorous widow, and, last but warmest, a young Jewish lawyer's inner torment and outward metamorphosis as he resists the enforcement of suburban zoning laws on a Hebrew school. The episodic or stream-of-vignettes means of expression seemed to be cropping up all over the place this season in both song and story, as though life were too pungent a matter to taste in any but little bites; notable shows which partook of this style included *Ain't Supposed to Die a Natural Death, Older People, Don't Bother Me, I Can't Cope, And They Put Handcuffs on the Flowers* and to some extent even *Where Has Tommy Flowers Gone?* and *Small Craft Warnings.* Even so, the one-act play program doesn't adapt easily to Broadway's high-cost, big-deal environment (*Twigs* and *Plaza Suite* to the contrary, perhaps for special reasons), or even in ever-higher-costing, bigger-dealing off Broadway these days except as an almost self-consciously non-commercial showcase for playwriting talent. The customary spate of off-Broadway one-act play programs dwindled this year to a mere trickle of five: Martin Craft's *Out of Control;* Eugene Yanni's *Friends* and *Relations; Black Visions* (a Public Theater showcase for the work of Sonia Sanchez, Neil Harris and Richard Wesley in one-acters dealing with contemporary black problems and emotions); a notable staging at American Place of Ronald Ribman's *Fingernails Blue as Flowers* and Steve Tesich's *Lake of the Woods;* and, from London, Tom Stoppard's *After Magritte* and *The Real Inspector Hound.*

The producer of the year both on and off Broadway was Joseph Papp. He brought two of his New York Shakespeare Festival Shows to Broadway—the musical *Two Gentlemen of Verona* from Central Park and the drama *Sticks and Bones* from the indoor season at the Public Theater—and carried off both major Tony awards, the first working of this hat trick since David Merrick did it with *Hello, Dolly!* and *Luther* in 1964. Papp's off-Broadway production of *That Championship Season* won the Critics Award in a hot contest with *Sticks and Bones* (and both of these were named Best Plays), while *Verona* easily ambled off with the Critics Award for best musical. Underneath this glittering tip of the Papp iceberg lay a large mass of exceptionally imaginative theater indoors and out, including *The Black Terror, Iphigenia, Older People* and a rare opportunity to see Shakespeare's *Timon of Athens* on its feet. Moreover, Papp had the audacity to suggest publicly that his New York Shakespeare Festival should be subsidized Federally to take over the legit program at the John F. Kennedy Center in Washington, D.C. and establish a national theater whose productions might commute between New York and Washington. He also suggested that the government set aside a special fund to subsidize new American plays on a national scale, in cross-country as well as big-city theater. Roger L. Stevens, previously the wellspring of Federal subsidy and currently the boss at Kennedy Center, quickly characterized Papp's suggestions as "ephemera." They may have been intended, indeed, as a sort of conversational prank, agitating the smooth surface to see what could be set into reaction.

As for the redoubtable David Merrick, he deserves a cheer from the New York theater for staying with it, for producing show after show in a variety of genres. He was a sign of life in an entertainment form showing too many patches of barren ground, from which too many of the Harold Princes were temporarily absenting themselves, and in which Richard Barr's Theater 1972 was having bad luck with short-lived shows. Merrick produced two Best Plays, *Moonchildren* and (with Arthur Cantor) *Vivat! Vivat Regina!;* a big musical, *Sugar;* and the Canadian adaptation of Feydeau's farce *There's One in Every Marriage,* which was a *succes d'estime.* Another 1971-72 production activist was Roger L. Stevens who imported the distinguished *Old Times* from London and a revival of Odets's *The Country Girl* from Kennedy Center. T. Edward Hambleton's Phoenix Theater covered some of the gray with themes of contemporary relevance in bringing to Broadway *The Trial of the Catonsville Nine* and Conor Cruise O'Brien's *Murderous Angels,* about the Hammarskjold-Lumumba collision.

In spite of all the talk in recent seasons about a new era of directors' theater, there was little sign of directorial exaltation over playwriting in 1971-72. The year's best direction of a straight play was Peter Hall's of Pinter's *Old Times,* yet not for a moment would anyone consider him the *auteur* of the evening. In the case of top musical direction, Burt Shevelove's of the *A Funny Thing Happened on the Way to the Forum* revival, the director was indeed the *auteur* both literally and figuratively, since he both directed and rewrote his own book for the occasion. The scripts were outstandingly well served in directorial stints like Alan Schneider's of *Moonchildren,* Gilbert Moses's of *Ain't Supposed to Die a Natural Death,* Jacques Levy's of *Where Has Tommy Flowers Gone?,* Nathan George's of *The Black Terror,* Fernando Arrabal's of his own *And They Put Handcuffs on the Flowers,* Joseph Hardy's of the Stoppard one-acters, A.J. Antoon's of *That Championship Season,* Gower Champion's of *Sugar* and Mike Nichols's of *The Prisoner of Second Avenue* (the Tony Award winner, and in his acceptance speech Nichols took pains to acknowledge Neil Simon as the *auteur* of this popular comedy).

The conspicuous exception to this deferent directorial attitude was Tom O'Horgan, whose garishly imaginative wonder-boy approach to theater is bound to elbow the playwright to one side. Certainly O'Horgan was the *auteur* of last season's *Lenny* and to a great extent of this season's *Jesus Christ Superstar;* and to a lesser but some extent in his staging of the Eve Merriam musical *Inner City.*

With such talents and excitement going for it, how could the New York theater find itself trapped in a gray season? One reason may be that very few of the most skilled of both younger and older generations of American playwrights saw fit to offer any script at all in New York this year. There was no

Miller, no Albee, no van Itallie, no Feiffer play this season; we must thank
our lucky stars that we had a Simon, a Guare, a McNally, a Williams. In the
1971-72 environment of economic strain, social upset and esthetic dichotomy,
the playwrights, it seems, are hanging back.

Audiences are hanging back, too, and perhaps for much the same reasons.
The strange behavior of audiences and playwrights may be two sides of the
same coin. Consider first the economic strain: the price of a ticket, high as it
is, is only a small part of the onerous cost of theatergoing, which is now
scaled at the level of the special occasion rather than of casual drop-in entertainment. It piles up all the extras that a special occasion demands: cocktails,
dinner, taxis, dress, etc. Nowadays even the off-Broadway theater has priced
itself out of range of casual pleasure. Even in this era of inflation, $7.50 (the
usual off-Broadway top) is a lot of money for admission to anything and too
much for careless mild rapture, even when that is available at an off-Broadway
show. No wonder a large part of the audience, particularly the less affluent
young section, is hanging back—and it is obvious that this economic strain
also has an inhibiting effect on the playwright. The box office won't give you
your money back if you don't like the show, so the advance shopping information services—that is to say, the daily drama reviewers in general and the
daily reviewers of the New York *Times* in particular—have more and more
power over the life or death of plays on and off Broadway, in proportion as
costs rise. Many playwrights are reluctant to submit their scripts to the judgment of one man, however dedicated and qualified this one man may be. They
hold their scripts back waiting for the situation to improve, which it shows no
signs of doing. Thus economic strain is a blade which slashes at the theater
both ways, at both audience and dramatist.

So does the spiky bludgeon of social unrest. The legitimate stage has done
much to enhance the quality of New York life over eight or nine decades, and
vice versa, but it is now getting a bad name by association with the city to
which it has contributed so much. Sensational bad news travels fast, and New
York's crime-in-the-streets publicity is offered up daily not only to theater
audiences in the city and its suburbs but also to those many ardent fans of
New York theater across the country who customarily make an annual pil-
grimage to Broadway. The extent and frequency of crime in New York's
streets are exaggerated in these reports, of course, and small mention is ever
made of countermeasures such as increased police visibility and scrutiny in
key theater areas, especially Times Square, and other admirable programs
organized by the city and the theater committees to meet the problems of civil
disorder without turning the world's most interesting city into a police state.

It is almost never emphasized that the centers of legitimate stage activity
are the objects of special supervision. The theatergoer's attention may be captured by some weird-looking specimens of humanity on his way to and from
the theater (*everybody* comes to New York) in a free street show often more
colorful than the one he is on his way to see at $9.90 per, but the activity
of theatergoing is an almost entirely safe recreation even in permissive New
York. The peace is being kept, and perhaps the next step will be to improve

the atmosphere. The threat of culture shock in a visit to the Times Square, Lower Second Avenue or Sheridan Square areas, let alone violence, is enough to scarce off many members of the audience. Certainly there is today a freaked-out atmosphere over what should be the Gay White Way of imagination and excitement, inhibiting the playwright's drive to make the scene as well as the audience's, tempering his satisfaction in a success by making him wonder if anybody really cares about his painstakingly hand-made work of art in this swirl of stamped-out divertissements and stamped-down humanity.

Writing about the Tony Award ceremonies in the New York Sunday *News,* the columnist Rex Reed touched on these matters as follows: "People stay home in front of their TV sets because it's cheaper and safer, or they go to movies because even the worst movie in town is usually more interesting than nine out of ten Broadway plays . . . You'll pay $12 a seat to wear torturous clothes and suffer through something that will bore you to death for the same length of time you could have been home watching the Movie of the Week in your pajamas for nothing."

Reed went on to characterize some of the major Tony contenders. To him, *Follies* was a combination of "an atrocious book and a really fine score;" *Sticks and Bones* "a sophomoric piece of drivel that would be rejected by a college creative writing class;" *Old Times* "a Harold Pinter play which put a lot of people to sleep and got out of town fast;" *The Prisoner of Second Avenue* "mindless."

I am at pains to quote Reed in these pages not because I consider him a useful authority on the theater but because I consider him an articulate authority on his own likes and dislikes and at the same time a mirror-image of the attitudes of a segment of the New York audience. Listen again to some of his key phrases: "$12 a seat," "torturous clothes," "in our pajamas"—economic strain *and* comparative inconvenience. "Safer" to stay home—social upset and the threat of personal danger.

Finally, Reed reflects the third and most problematical issue: the issue of esthetic dichotomy within our contemporary stage art. In his comments on *Follies, Sticks and Bones, Old Times,* and *Prisoner,* Reed is operating on a level of perception far removed from that of a major segment of today's theater audience. The trouble is—and this is the rub—he's not alone there on his plateau. He has plenty of company including many of the ladies in hats at matinees and the gentlemen in black ties at evening benefits whose enjoyment of and loyalty to the stage has endured and sustained it for decades.

There was a day when the New York theater audience was one big, admiring unit of homogenized taste, and the theater art grandly homogenized in form and style to suit the massive majority. Over the last decade, however, American theater artists have been struggling to emerge from this cocoon. They have been experimenting—often successfully—with new forms, new means of expression, a new theatrical language. In doing so, they have divided the audience, carrying some along with them on the adventure of change but repelling others. Today there are two separate theaters existing side by side in New York, with—to some extent—separate audiences for each. Here is another two-edged sword; with this esthetic dichotomy, any given play has only a portion of the potential audience it had before, not because the theater audience is smaller (it isn't) but because it has been split into partisan sections.

There is no doubt in my mind and heart that *Follies*—book, lyrics, the whole thing—is one of the great musicals of the decade if not of the century; that *Sticks and Bones* is a highly sophisticated work of new theater expressed on at least three levels; that *Old Times* is a masterpiece of the new subliminal form of theater expression; that *The Prisoner of Second Avenue* (which doesn't belong in this group but, more properly, to the old form) is only "mindless" if one considers Molière's comic fancies mindless. What I doubt is that the first three of these shows will ever find it possible to reach, or are even designed to reach, that portion of the theater audience which is the esthetic constituency of the columnist quoted above. As that esteemed philosopher Wally Schirra has noted so often, "A great spacecraft makes a lousy boat."

One Wednesday afternoon last season I dropped in at two Broadway matinees to check replacement performances. I went to the first act of *Vivat! Vivat Regina!*, and the ladies who made up most of the audience were clearly loving the spectacle. They were spellbound, and as I left the theater at intermission I heard them discussing the play itself rather than irrelevancies, a sure sign of involvement. They could hardly wait for the second act to begin.

Around the corner at the matinee of *Sticks and Bones* it was another story. The house was nearly full and you could feel the tension, all right—but it was the wrong kind. This audience was not gripped by the play, as the off-Broadway audience had been, it was in a state of esthetic alarm. It was afraid of what was going to happen next, not in empathy for the characters, but in self-defense. When the Vietnam veteran in this play decides to cut his wrists (it is one of his delusions, I think, but is presented on the stage as though it were actually happening, with a straight razor and a lot of red fluid), the audience was horrified. If there had been an easy way out they would have poured into the street seeking the womb-like reassurance of their special buses. When the curtain went down, about a third of the audience pressed for the exits without waiting for the actors to take their bow (and yet I must also report that I was astonished at the volume and enthusiasm of the applause of those who remained in their seats).

This is what can happen when an audience is mismatched to a play in our era of esthetic dichotomy. It's the job of the theater's institutions to solve the problems of economic strain, whether through organized subsidy or restructuring the economy of production or both. It's ultimately New York City's job to keep the problems of social unrest from polluting the experience of theater-going or enjoying any other art, because there is everything to lose—without the stabilizing environmental influence of its powerful arts contingent, New York would become just another city, just another desert on the edge of a jungle. But the theater's third major problem, that of esthetic division, is a highly personal matter between the playwrights and their audiences.

Here is where the theatergoer must play his major part in the development of the art form. First and foremost, he must understand that there are at least two and probably several kinds of theater nowadays, not just one, and that one kind is not easily judged by the standards of the other. Of course he has every right to ensure his enjoyment, which is what the theater is all about, by taking extra pains to find a show to match his personal taste (that's what keeps the critics powerful). But occasionally he should take a chance just for the hell of it, or maybe for the love of the theater. You *Sticks and Bones* people—stop turning up your nose at *Vivat,* it's a colorful and entertaining *coup de théâtre.* You *Vivat* people—come on over to see a challenging play like *Sticks and Bones* once in a while. Do it in the spirit of adventure, and don't be afraid to hate it if you do, or give in to it if you can; but don't give up on the theater because some evening you find yourself attending a show that's not for you. Your kind of show is almost certainly playing just around the corner.

Broadway

A "hit" in the true Broadway meaning of the word isn't merely a show that is hard to get into on a Friday night in December, but a show which pays off its production cost (it may be easy to get into but become a "hit" by virtue of a movie sale or a profitable road tour). In recent seasons, however, the word "hit" has been losing a lot of its magic. With higher costs hopefully compensated by longer runs, few productions, however popular, reach the break-even point in the season in which they opened. And very often Broadway doesn't have either the first or the last word on a playscript as it once did. Plays now come to Broadway from previous regional or foreign production which has already established their position in world theater. A good script ignored on Broadway for some special reason may take on an illustrious life of its own elsewhere on world stages or in other media. So we make no special point in this resume about which 1971-72 offerings were "hits" and which were "flops" except that this information is recorded in the one-page summary of the Broadway season accompanying this article.

The ultimate insignia of New York professional theater achievement (we insist) is not the instant popularity of the hit list, but selection as a Best Play in these volumes. Such selection is made with the script itself as the primary consideration, for the reason (as we have stated in previous volumes) that the script is the very spirit of the theater, the soul in its physical body. The script is not only the quintessence of the present, it is most of what endures into the future.

So the Best Plays are the best scripts. As little weight as is humanly possible is given to comparative production values. The choice is made without any regard whatever to a play's type—musical, comedy or drama—or origin on or off Broadway, or popularity at the box office or lack of same.

The Best Plays of 1971-72 were the following, listed in the order in which they opened (an asterisk * with the performance number signifies that the play was still running on June 1, 1972):

Where Has Tommy Flowers Gone? (off Broadway; 78 perfs.)	*The Screens* (off Broadway; 28 perfs.)
Ain't Supposed to Die a Natural Death (Broadway; 256* perfs.)	*Vivat! Vivat Regina!* (Broadway; 116 perfs.)
Sticks and Bones (off B'way & B'way; 225* perfs.)	*Moonchildren* (Broadway; 16 perfs.)
The Prisoner of Second Avenue (Broadway; 229* perfs.)	*Small Craft Warnings* (off Broadway; 67* perfs.)
Old Times (Broadway; 119 perfs.)	*That Championship Season* (off Broadway; 34* perfs.)

The bests of 1971-72 straight plays were, in the opinion of the *Best Plays* editor, two which by a coincidence carried the imprimatur, if not the byline, of Master Will Shakespeare. These trans-Atlantic rivals were Harold Pinter's *Old Times,* first produced by London's Royal Shakespeare Company, and David Rabe's *Sticks and Bones,* first produced on the indoor program of the New York Shakespeare Festival and later brought uptown to Broadway. Pinter's third full-length play (the other two were *The Caretaker* and *The Homecoming,* both Best Plays of their seasons) was like his others a comment on the human condition in general, rather than a headline-relevant work like Rabe's. As far as external reality is concerned, *Old Times* had a deceptively simple subject: a movie director and his wife receive the wife's former London roommate (herself married and living in Sicily) for a weekend visit to their farmhouse home in England, near the coast. This pale concept was further washed out by John Bury's white-on-white setting, often with white furniture blending into the white walls, in a design statement subtly harmonized to the play. The weekend visit is a white-on-white excuse for a situation, in a play which was not concerned with present reality but—as its title *Old Times* implies—with the half-seen, half-heard, almost subliminal events of the past, existing only in memory and nearly drowned in it. In contrast to *Rashomon* in which a single episode is remembered differently in sequence, *Old Times's* stream of past incidents is remembered simultaneously by its three characters, but differently, like a musical composition performed by an instrumental trio who do not play long in unison but break into scintillating harmonies and discords. Hard facts are as fleetingly experienced as single musical notes: is this really the first time the husband (Robert Shaw) and the roommate (Rosemary Harris) have met, or did they in fact once spend an evening together in a London bar, while he "gazed" (Pinter lays special stress on the word) up her skirts at underwear borrowed from her roommate, his future wife? Did this wife (Mary Ure) share a very strong emotional attachment with the other woman while they were roommates in London? Did the husband try to make love to both women on a single evening, and does he now regret he married the one instead of the other? Acted with uniform sensitivity and directed like-wise by Peter Hall, *Old Times* never supplied direct answers but was entirely fascinating as it asked the questions. At the end, when the husband suddenly weeps for a few moments and then as suddenly ceases, you perhaps did not know exactly why, but you couldn't help feeling sad along with him, in an in-tuition of Paradise somehow lost. *Old Times,* our choice for best of bests, never quite caught on with New York audiences, though it was a close runner-up in the Critics Circle voting for best foreign play and was awarded a special citation; nor was it originally produced in the commercially-exposed side of the London theater, but in the shelter of the Royal Shakespeare Company's organization and subsidy, as was *The Homecoming* and other Pinter works. Their existence ahead of their time in the spotlight of public attention is a powerful argument for subsidy and strong evidence of its potential rewards.

The best American play of the season was David Rabe's *Sticks and Bones.* Rabe is a Vietnam war veteran who made his professional playwriting debut last season at Joseph Papp's Public Theater with *The Basic Training of Pavlo Hummel* (the New York Shakespeare Festival's longest-running show to date, 363 performances before it closed this season). In that first play Rabe's pro-tagonist is a soldier finally killed in Saigon; in his second, *Sticks and Bones,* his Vietnam war veteran comes home, wounded and blind, to a Henry Al-drich-type American family that remains as stubbornly blind to his spiritual despair as he is to the physical world around him.

There are at least three separate levels of action in this play. First, there is the veneered middle-class American home life with the family resisting any emotional intrusion by their veteran or his memories of war; a teen-aged son's excruciatingly cheery "Hi mom, hi dad" loses not a shade of its day-glo brightness because his blinded brother is home from a cruel war, agonizing in the room upstairs. The soldier is alone on his own private level of experience, haunted by dreams of killing and of love. The living memory figure of the Vietnamese girl he left behind him follows him around the house, and he is often unable to distinguish between the real and the hallucinatory. He's ready to believe that his family would quite casually recommend that the best solu-tion for him would be to cut his wrists, when in reality—or apparent reality—they are only talking about some TV show they saw the night before.

The third level of *Sticks and Bones* is a sort of mezzanine between the two, where they sometimes meet and set off explosions like a contact of matter and anti-matter. Caught on this split-level, neither completely comfortable either with the family or with the veteran, is the father, played by Tom Aldredge in the season's best performance by an actor. His wife (played by Elizabeth Wil-son in the year's best supporting performance by an actress) is comfortably secure in her conviction that a little snack of fudge and milk cures any but the most major upset, in which case you call in the priest. But the husband is at the center of the storm, trying to cope, but buffeted by self-contradicting winds, in a play we have all been waiting for; a play which explores some of the deeper cracks in the American spirit caused by the Vietnam war. *Sticks and Bones* was the close runner-up for the Critics Award (and like *Old Times* won a special citation) as well as the Tony winner, a credit to the theater and to David Rabe who newly but surely joins the ranks of our leading young playwrights.

The man who produced *Sticks and Bones* off Broadway and then brought it into the more intense limelight of the West Forties, Joseph Papp, was widely quoted in the press this season as having declared that Broadway can no longer muster an audience for serious drama. I've always been uneasy about that phrase "serious drama" as a possible redundancy, but it has a certain usefulness. Drama may imply serious, if not tragic, themes, but in our contemporary theater it often uses the moods and devices of the human comedy to frame its tragic implications. Plays like *Old Times* and *Sticks and Bones* probably ought to be called dramas (if a classification is demanded) because they are only comedic when their winds are blowing nor'-nor'-west; the pathos, even the agony at times, is stronger than the irony. They are black comedy-dramas, or something like that; dramas if you will, but not "serious drama" in the straightforward, pike-thrusting sense of that phrase.

Neither is Robert Bolt's *Vivat! Vivat Regina!,* another Best Play imported from the London stage. Any story in which one of the two leading characters has her head cut off in the last scene is probably going to be called a drama; but there is a romantic light touch in the handling of this series of queenly vignettes, with only a whiff of pentameter. Bolt presents his queens as young women who must make a choice between reigning and loving, of growing to maturity either as monarch or as woman but not both. Elizabeth opts for England, Mary for romance, and such is the story of their lives in this play. Elizabeth becomes vividly a queen, Mary vividly a woman; and, at last, each envies the other's lot. The spectacle was enhanced by the excellent designs of Carl Toms both in costumes (rich and elegant) and in scenery (simple, spare, versatile), and the drama was powered by a dominating Eileen Atkins performance as Elizabeth, memorable even in a year of many Elizabeths on stages and screens. The Virgin Queen and her reign received much dramatic attention in every medium this season, even twice more on Broadway, once in the revival of Schiller's *Mary Stuart* at Lincoln Center and again in Paul Foster's *Elizabeth I,* an historical cartoon with the events of the reign and the ideas and ambitions underlying it presented through a company of 16th century street actors.

Two wholly serious Broadway dramas added interest and dimension to the season. Romulus Linney's *The Love Suicide at Schofield Barracks* took the shape of an Army inquiry into the suicide of a commanding general and his wife in full public view at a barracks Halloween party. Gradually the investigation discloses that the suicide was an act of protest against the Vietnam war, with Mercedes McCambridge and William Redfield in standout performances on the witness stand. *Murderous Angels,* a play by Conor Cruise O'Brien staged at the Mark Taper Forum in Los Angeles before coming to New York under Phoenix Theater auspices, was another script that brought some thunder to the atmosphere in a dramatization of the Dag Hammarskjold-Patrice Lumumba confrontation in the Congo in the 1950s, which ended fatally for both. The Irish author of the play was the Secretary-General's representative in Katanga at the time of these events, but in his effort to write a play instead of an historical tract he juggled the facts and characters to suit his purpose. This brought a flood of criticism down upon his work in New York by those who resented what they considered a demeaning characterization of Lumumba, and equally by friends of Hammarskjold who didn't approve of the way he was presented. But viewed as an invention for the stage, *Murderous Angels* had a strong premise: since it was Lumumba's responsibility to arouse his compatriots to effective rebellion against their oppressors, and Hammarskjold's responsibility to keep them cool in order to avoid a confrontation of great powers over the issue, there arose an almost tragic conflict of interests which forced two "angels" to murder each other in their holy causes, inevitably, as a tragic mutual duty. It is a pity that O'Brien had to use real names in his drama, which might well have stood on its own feet without historical buttressing, avoiding odious historical comparisons. *Murderous Angels* didn't find an audience on Broadway, nor did *The Love Suicide at Schofield Barracks,* nor even the off-Broadway hit *The Trial of the Catonsville Nine* when it transferred to Broadway for a brief visit in June. These experiences and Mr. Papp's observation to the contrary notwithstanding, this doesn't prove that the audience isn't there.

That popular form of not-wholly-"serious" drama, the thriller, was variously represented this season. Besides the short-lived *Children! Children!,* there was *Night Watch* by Lucille Fletcher, author of the famous radio play *Sorry, Wrong Number.* In the new play she presented yet another menacing husband and agonizing wife (played by Len Cariou and Joan Hackett under Fred Coe's concise direction) in a cat-and-mouse game which held quite a few chills and a fair share of surprises. Richard Lortz's ghost story *Voices* had the makings of a memorable one-act play about a couple seeking refuge in a gloomy, empty house in a snowstorm, only to find the place haunted. As a full-length play it spread itself too thin, despite consistently strong performances by Richard Kiley and Julie Harris as the couple and the other-worldly atmosphere enhanced by Peggy Stuart Coolidge's ghost-music score.

Returning to the Best Plays list, the best comedy of the year was Neil Simon's ninth straight Broadway success (most of which were also hits in the *Variety* sense of the word) and sixth Best Play, *The Prisoner of Second Avenue.* As the Molière of our era, Simon takes the position of a fellow-sufferer mindful of our woes—with a streak of anger that has broadened almost consistently since the happy times of *Barefoot in the Park.* Simon's prisoner in the new play is a high-salaried adman who has all the modern inconveniences money can buy in his 82d Street high-rise: failing plumbing, hostile neighbors, garbage smells, burglar risk as high as the rent and a couple of German airline hostesses living it up on the other side of the thin wall. When he loses the job that pays for all of this luxury, the adman goes over the edge into a nervous breakdown. Life has insulted him one too many times, and he insults it back by blowing his mind. His wife takes over the breadwinning chore and his brother and three sisters, who haven't paid him a visit in nine years, gather self-righteously to help their baby brother who has lost touch with reality. This family scene, with Vincent Gardenia as the brother trying to herd his sisters into some kind of line of practical support, is worthy of Molière in its cartoons of avarice, role-playing, hypocrisy, sibling rivalry, etc. Mike Nichols's Tony Award-winning direction drew every bit of sense and nonsense into the open and helped evoke excellent performances from Peter Falk and Lee Grant as the beseiged husband and wife. That's how Neil Simon views the way we live, as a state of seige under regular assault, with no help in sight from the fortress walls. The fact that a miraculously gifted playwright is still able to treat this as a subject for comedy made *Prisoner* one of the more cheering thoughts of the season.

Another outstanding comedy (self-styled a "comic play") and Best Play on Broadway this season was *Moonchildren,* the professional New York debut of its author, Michael Weller. It is about college students in the 1960s, huddling together in their dormitory and living fantasy lives by mutual agreement, shrinking from a reality which they are sure is growing increasingly materialistic, crass, hostile. In their own imaginative way they are whistling past the graveyard which they fear their planet may become. Weller's *Moonchildren* are Terrence McNally's *Tommy Flowers* ten years earlier. As college seniors in the 1960s they are lovingly and innocently reinventing themselves and their lives (one pair of youths decide they are brothers whose father is a trapper; no invention is too unlikely to be accepted without skepticism by the others). Later in the 1970s, turning 30, most of them will have sharpened a *Tommy Flowers* edge by losing their innocence without solving their problems. Not in this comedy, though; here their instinctive response to life is still affectionate. With James Woods, Kevin Conway, Edward Herrmann and Cara Duff-MacCormick heading an attractive ensemble under Alan Schneider's exceptionally skillful direction, the script's faults (repetitiousness, a confusion of destination) were minimized and its virtues (texture, imagination, insight into the motivations of contemporary youth) maximized.

Weller's play was enthusiastically received in a world premiere production in London at the Royal Court Theater (under the title *Cancer*) and at the Arena Stage in Washington before coming to Broadway, where it was boosted by accolades in both the daily and Sunday *Times.* Nevertheless, New York audiences shunned it (it lasted only 16 performances), probably because of its subject matter—most people, New Yorkers anyhow, are up to here with the distresses of youth and do not thirst for more as entertainment. In the season of 1971-72, almost no one wanted to see even a *good* play, even a good *comedy,* about the problems of youth. Well, here's a script that perhaps Lincoln Center or the Roundabout could revive in a few years.

Five other Broadway attractions billed themselves outright as comedies. David V. Robison's *Promenade, All!* was a sketchbook of an American family in transition from the late 19th century to the present, pausing at four stops along the way—1895, 1920, 1945 and now—to acquaint us with six generations of individuals facing their personal and business crises. The nine members of the Huntziger, later Hunt, family whom we meet on this trip are an appealing assortment of pleasure-loving or fortune-hunting products of their eras, played to the absolute limit by Richard Backus (all the young men), Anne Jackson (all the women), Eli Wallach (the driving or neurotic types) and Hume Cronyn (most notably as a 93-year-old who volunteers for a sex experiment). This was a fresh and comfortable patch of blue drifting across the stormy season. Another comedy, *Fun City,* by Lester Colodny, Joan Rivers and Edgar Rosenberg, projected Neil Simon's New York into a future when all services will be breaking down but we will all be used to it. Gabriel Dell, Miss Rivers and Rose Marie worked hard for the laughs in this play, which also featured the season's most distinguished bit-part casting: Paul Ford in the minuscule role of an aged mailman. A third self-styled "comedy" was the short-lived Richard T. Johnson-Daniel Hollywood script *All the Girls Came Out to Play* about a writer and his agent who seclude themselves in the suburbs to work on a show, are mistaken for homosexuals by the community and exploit this error by demonstrating to the suburban wives that they are not. The fourth was a French comedy adapted by Jerome Kilty and produced here under the title *The Little Black Book,* with Richard Benjamin as a gullible bachelor and Delphine Seyrig as a stranger who forces her way into his life and slowly begins to fascinate him, for some unknown reason; she (the character, not Miss Seyrig) was the most repellent nuisance to appear on a stage this season. Finally there was *Tough to Get Help,* a comedy about a rich advertising man's suburban household and the black couple who maintain it, unshriven even by the direction of Carl Reiner.

Gore Vidal's *An Evening With Richard Nixon And* . . . was a ponderous political satire on the President's opportunistic career and all-American style, overloaded with double and triple framing and a portentous historical perspective. Beginning as a Pro and Con argument, it soon enlists the shades of Kennedy and Eisenhower as chief advocates of either side, with George Washington as judge and everyone else in the modern history books brought into the act. It fared slightly better than the season's other political foray, *The Selling of the President,* but not much better. It made a sitting duck-type victim out of Nixon (played bravely and even admirably by George S. Irving), his entourage and even his family, so that its partisan zeal was weakened by embarrassing personal comment, blunting its point about the Nixon regime being merely the inevitable product of decades, even centuries, of instinctive American imperialism.

Among other scripts which must on balance be classified as comedies even though they didn't make a point of it in the billing was George Furth's *Twigs,* one of the season's most conspicuous successes, with Sada Thompson carrying off the year's female starring honors in a quadruple performance. *Twigs* was four playlets centering on the woman in each of them. The first is a newly-divorced, young middle-aged, middle-class housewife who succumbs gracefully to the first attractive man she meets, the mover who helps her set up the furniture in her new apartment. The second is a drudge who once had a chance in the movies but is now married to an insensitive boor. The third is happily married in a suburban sort of way and enjoys a playful relationship with her husband. The fourth—and this is the punch line of the collection of playlets—is a bent, aged but verbally active old crone who is the mother of all the previous three and detests any hint of sentiment in her relationship with her offspring. She is a handful (I don't want to usurp the playwright's prerogative by saying more about her specific goals) and she is also a sort of summing-up of her three daughters, as Miss Thompson made abundantly clear in her virtuoso performance.

A pair of English black comedies turned out not to travel very well, but at least they added an extra taste to the season. Simon Gray's short-lived *Wise Child,* about a criminal on the lam disguised in women's clothes, was an attenuated joke about sexual identity. Its acting was more sustaining than its subject, however, with Donald Pleasence snarling in his female get-up, Bud Cort as his youthful accomplice and especially George Rose as a smirking pervert who runs the hotel in which the other two are hiding out. Lincoln Center Repertory tried Edward Bond's *Narrow Road to the Deep North,* a batch of sprawling, episodic comments about fascism, colonialism, idealism and other conceits of human beings in the mass. Bond's play is set in the 17th, 18th and 19th centuries in Japan, where and when, presumably, submission was a habit and violence a way of life. It was one of the meatier offerings of 1971-72, and Dan Sullivan staged its tumultuous, if somewhat obviously symbolical, episodes with clarity and fluidity on the Vivian Beaumont's thrust stage.

On the musical scene, Melvin Van Peebles arrived in town and started putting out Broadway musicals as though he planned to do Neil Simon's thing, except that he produced them, wrote the music as well as the words and directed one of them himself. 1971-72 was a year in which several Broadway musicals had something but none everything, and Van Peebles's *Ain't Supposed to Die a Natural Death* emerged onto the list of Best Plays by virtue of its originality and its power. The author has practically invented his own form to present ironic, impassioned snapshots of the black ghetto. His subject is the agonies and the very scarce joys of life on the bottom of the scale where poverty, crime and neglect are facts of life along with love, beauty and charity. Van Peebles's music was an unobtrusive accompaniment to lyrics which were not sung, but spoken in a rhythmic continuity something like a poem, something like a recitative, something like narration. *Ain't Supposed to Die a Natural Death* is a strange mutation of musical theater, using the idiom and imagery of the musical stage to great effect under the direction of Gilbert Moses, with an acting ensemble to uniformly gifted that it seemed almost unnecessary to single out one of them, Beatrice Winde, for a Tony nomination. For its finale, the musical confronts the audience and declares "Put a curse on you!" for even passive complicity in events depicted on the stage. I could have done without the Van Peebles curses, but nevertheless I admired his most inventive use of the musical theater.

Having gathered his Broadway momentum, Van Peebles coasted in with *another* interesting musical this same season, *Don't Play Us Cheap!,* an antithesis of his previous work, without a mean bone in its body; without a curse or even a sneering "the man" in its dialogue. This one was a warm, friendly fantasy about a couple of would-be evil spirits disguising themselves as humans and trying to break up a family party in Harlem on a swinging Saturday night. These are just folks enjoying themselves and each other, expressing themselves in song when the spirit or spiritual moves them (the music for this show is happier, more folk-songey, and the lyrics are almost conventionally styled). The party goers include an enchanting young girl (Rhetta Hughes), her wise and unfailingly benign aunt (Joshie Jo Armstead), a needle-shaped neighbor (Avon Long) and a handsome young evil spirit (Joe Keyes Jr.) who discovers to his shame that he isn't really so evil after all. With his two musicals, Van Peebles poisoned Broadway with hate and then brought forth the antidote love, all in the same season, in a remarkable display of musical energy and virtuousity.

The year's most popular musical was the Tom O'Horgan staging of *Jesus Christ Superstar*. Like *Ain't Supposed to Die a Natural Death,* this was a visualization of material previously published on records, a rock concert version of the Gospel story with music by Andrew Lloyd Webber and lyrics by Tim Rice which had already gained international renown in a best-selling LP record album. In O'Horgan's hands, this material became *Lenny* with Biblical overtones; *Hair* in Galilean dress. The character of Jesus in the last seven days of his life was almost submerged under the fantastic (and undeniably colorful) scenery by Robin Wagner and costumes by Randy Barcelo, with the crowd scenes as full of monstrous and unexplained images as the corners of a Hieronymus Bosch painting. Herod camping across the stage on his wedgies . . . Caiaphas and his priests suspended in air on a framework of dinosaur bones . . . Jesus having a tantrum as he drives the money-changers from the temple . . . the soul of Judas (played by Ben Vereen, a black actor) in space on a trapeze decorated with pretty girls and peacock feathers . . . this was an evening of raw, often indigestible, stage imagery, sometimes in questionable taste but as unstoppable as a circus. The lyrics are rock-opera streamlined, and yet respectful of the subject (for example, in the Last Supper scene, Jesus reproaches his friends with indifference: "For all you care, this bread could be my body/For all you care, this wine could be my blood"). But unlike last season's *Godspell, Superstar* had no reverential tone. The American Jewish Committee and the Anti-Defamation League of B'nai B'rith protested the show because it represents Caiaphas and his henchmen as prime movers of the crucifixion, "unambiguously lays the primary responsibility for Jesus's suffering and crucifixion to the Jewish priesthood. The priests are portrayed as hideously inhuman and Satanically evil; contemptuous, callous and bloodthirsty. There is no warrant in the New Testament either for the attribution of primary guilt or for the caricatured characterization." The protest implied for *Superstar* a significance which otherwise seemed hard to find in its comic-strip versions of villainy. The show's producer, Robert Stigwood, stated in rebuttal that these incidents were "confrontations of a reformer and the Establishment which continually recur in the history of man." *Superstar* had very little religious meaning, nor would it win prizes for artistic taste, but it was a prime example of the Tom O'Horgan beaux-arts-ball type of musical extravaganza.

O'Horgan's second musical of the season, *Inner City,* was sterner stuff but unable to find an audience on Broadway, possibly because it existed in the shadow of the Van Peebles material. This was a series of fairy tale-parodying musical takeoffs on the outrages of the black ghetto, based on Eve Merriam's book *The Inner City Mother Goose,* with song titles like "You'll Find Mice" and "Twelve Rooftops Leaping." Linda Hopkins won a Tony for her efforts in this show, conceived and directed by O'Horgan, which suffered, perhaps unfairly, from being the second of two Broadway musicals and one of many 1971-72 stage works about the black condition.

It was David Merrick's prerogative to supply Broadway with a big showcase musical, the kind that attracts expense account customers and stimulates the pulsebeat of show business all over town. *Sugar* filled this bill admirably. Peter Stone's book recreated 101 per cent of the fun of the Marilyn Monroe movie on which it was based, *Some Like It Hot,* about two musicians hiding out from menacing Prohibition-era gangsters by disguising themselves as women and joining an all-girl orchestra. Jule Styne and Bob Merrill provided a happy jazz-era score and Merrick found an absolutely gorgeous and talented comedienne, Elaine Joyce, to play the Monroe part (Miss Joyce has none of the voluptuousness of a sex goddess, but she is so well proportioned that her beauty is a joke at other women's expense). Robert Morse clearly had a wonderful time with the Jack Lemmon role, playing all the double and even triple entendres of a masquerade in which the costume gradually gains dominance over its wearer until he becomes confused about his identity. Gower Champion put it all together very adroitly indeed as director and as choreographer. Even the designs by Robin Wagner and Alvin Colt were fun. *Sugar* was an entertainment in the most cheerful sense of the word, welcome as the flowers in early April when it finally appeared on the New York scene.

Two other musicals helped lift the spirits of the season, both originating far from the Times Square area but both finally making it there. Joseph Papp's production of *Two Gentlemen of Verona* (dropping Shakespeare's *The* from the title on Broadway) originated in Central Park as a New York Shakespeare Festival summer giveaway but proved so popular that it moved to Broadway in the fall at a $15 top. This was Galt MacDermot's first Broadway score since *Hair*—masterful stage music, if less than a masterpiece—and the John Guare-Mel Shapiro adaptation kept Shakespeare's lovers revolving like hurrying planets around the wisp of a tale. The attractive cast was headed by Raul Julia and Diana Davila as one of the couples and Clifton Davis and Jonelle Allen as the other, the latter pair stopping the show with a lively duet called "Night Letter." *Two Gentlemen of Verona* was warmly received by the critics, but coolly by the public at first; evidently the audience was reluctant to shell out hard cash for a show that had been given away free only a few weeks before. This block soon dissolved, however, and *Verona* went on to become a success and win the Critics Award for best musical as well as the Tony.

Another high-spirited session was *Grease,* which managed to whip up some quite genuinely appealing nostalgia for the Elvis Presley-James Dean, rock musical tempest-in-a-teapot era of the 1950s. This show written by Jim Jacobs and Warren Casey opened downtown at the Eden Theater on Second Avenue, but it was operating on first-class Broadway contracts and thus was classified as a Broadway production. It was easily worthy of the name, with a very bright book and score and Barry Bostwick (lapsing into a James Dean saunter whenever threatened or embarrassed, as protective coloration), Adrienne Barbeau and Timothy Meyers heading a cast which bore down hard on the humor of high school characters with grease slicking down their hair and mischief in their hearts. Facetiously billed as the *No, No, Nanette* of the 30-year-olds, *Grease* was fun for all ages and moved uptown to the Times Square area at season's end.

Among the shorter-lived Broadway musical efforts were an adaptation of Truman Capote's *The Grass Harp,* highly praised in some quarters for its Claibe Richardson-Kenward Elmslie score, and the effort to make a musical out of Joe McGinnis's book *The Selling of the President,* about the merchandizing, Madison Avenue-style, of Richard Nixon's 1968 campaign (in the show the date was put forward and the candidate was a fictional senator, played by Pat Hingle). Micki Grant's bright and lively *Don't Bother Me, I Can't Cope* came to Broadway in a middle theater production of topical musical diversion, some of its score based on calypso, Gospel and other folk sources, with even the ghetto themes traced out with wit and style under Vinnette Carroll's driving direction. This was an Urban Arts Corps production which had originally appeared in New York and elsewhere in a slightly different form.

A Howard Dietz-Arthur Schwartz musical revue *That's Entertainment* was a collection of song numbers from their distinguished past shows, but it lacked any point of view or other *raison d'être* over and above the music itself. A new musical written and directed by Michael Brown, *Different Times,* was only tenuously premised on an episodic story line about several generations of an American family, and the score wasn't one of Brown's best. The Supreme Being Himself found his way onto the stage in Old Testament episodes musicalized in *Hard Job Being God* which, like the Creation, ran for only 6 performances.

Three foreign musicals visited Broadway in 1971-72. The Israeli production *To Live Another Summer, To Pass Another Winter* was a topical musical revue mostly about Israel's emergence as a nation; an image of a forthright, self-possessed, determined—and when driven to it, arrogant—new society expressed in songs, sketches, a sense of humor and the appealing performances, in English, of a young Israeli cast. A second import from Israel, *Only Fools Are Sad,* was a paean to the simple, pious life expressed in an anthology of Hassidic songs and stories translated into English. A third import was *Anne of Green Gables,* a Canadian musical version of the novel about an orphan girl's childhood. Also touching at these shores was the Black Light Theater of

Prague, a vaudeville of trick staging with fluorescent shapes animated by black-clad actors in a black setting.

So this was a Broadway season dominated by the powerful invaders from England and Lafayette Street. A gray year for the Broadway stage as an institution, it was nevertheless splashed with the color of individual achievement. Here is where we list the *Best Plays* choices for the bests among the individual contributions of 1971-72. In the category of so-called "supporting" performances, clear distinctions cannot possibly be made on the basis of official billing, in which the actor's agent may bargain him into a contract as a "star" following the title (which is not true star billing) or as an "also starring" star, or any of the other typographical gimmicks. Here in these volumes we divide the acting into "primary" and "secondary" roles, a primary role being one which carries a major responsibility for the play; one which might some day cause a star to inspire a revival in order to appear in that role. All others, be they vivid as Mercutio, are classed as secondary.

Here, then are the *Best Plays* bests of 1971-72:

PLAYS

BEST PLAY: *Old Times* by Harold Pinter
ACTOR IN A PRIMARY ROLE: Tom Aldredge in *Sticks and Bones*
ACTRESS IN A PRIMARY ROLE: Sada Thompson in *Twigs*
ACTOR IN A SECONDARY ROLE: Vincent Gardenia in *The Prisoner of Second Avenue*
ACTRESS IN A SECONDARY ROLE: Elizabeth Wilson in *Sticks and Bones*
DIRECTOR: Peter Hall for *Old Times*
SCENERY: John Bury for *Old Times*
COSTUMES: Carl Toms for *Vivat! Vivat Regina!*

MUSICALS

BEST MUSICAL: *Ain't Supposed to Die a Natural Death* by Melvin Van Peebles
ACTOR IN A PRIMARY ROLE: Robert Morse in *Sugar*
ACTRESS IN A PRIMARY ROLE: Elaine Joyce in *Sugar*
ACTOR IN A SECONDARY ROLE: Larry Blyden in *A Funny Thing Happened on the Way to the Forum*
ACTRESS IN A SECONDARY ROLE: Jonelle Allen in *Two Gentlemen of Verona*
DIRECTOR: Burt Shevelove for *A Funny Thing Happened on the Way to the Forum*
SCENERY: Robin Wagner for *Jesus Christ Superstar* and *Sugar*
COSTUMES: Alvin Colt for *Sugar*
CHOREOGRAPHY: Gower Champion for *Sugar*
LYRICS: Tim Rice for *Jesus Christ Superstar*
MUSIC: Andrew Lloyd Webber for *Jesus Christ Superstar*

Revivals on and off Broadway

It was a small but healthy year for revivals, with only a dozen each on Broadway and off, (11 fewer than last year's total), but with several notable accomplishments in the list. Burt Shevelove updated his and Larry Gelbart's book for *A Funny Thing Happened on the Way to the Forum,* staged it in Los Angeles and finally brought it to Broadway with Phil Silvers as Pseudolus and Larry Blyden as Hysterium, a new comedy team honored by both Tony Awards for actors in the musical category. Blyden is too good an actor to settle for a career as a straight man; but on the basis of his performance here he is much too good a straight man not to make the most of this exceptional opportunity, playing the house slave with a myopically persistent belief that his world is the best of all possibles, even though angels might fear to tread in it. Under Shevelove's direction the jokes seemed fresh and very, very funny, and the Stephen Sondheim score included two numbers that weren't in the original production: "Farewell" in the first act and "Echo Song" in the second. Last year Shevelove came up with the season's biggest hit, the revival of *No, No, Nanette,* while Sondheim was creating the brilliant *Follies.* This year, together, they have again lit up the Broadway sky, and I suspect that if Plautus had it this good in the 1961-62 production, he certainly couldn't have had it any better.

The Maxwell Anderson-Kurt Weill musical *Lost in the Stars* also received a first-rate revival production mounted at Kennedy Center in Washington and brought to New York after a couple of stopoffs. Based on Alan Paton's *Cry the Beloved Country,* and originally billed as a "musical tragedy," this is a book show with musical interpolations, about two South African families, one black and one white, brought together in an ultimate agony of social malaise, an almost senseless murder. The performance of Brock Peters as the black country minister whose son turns to crime was a standout in this context, a late 1940s poetic design in which brotherly love seems to shine somewhere behind the dark clouds of racism in a more heartbreaking but less cynical view than we are used to in these darker days. A similar effort to mount a revival of the ebullient Betty Comden-Adolph Green-Leonard Bernstein musical *On the Town* in a full-scale Broadway production fizzled out expensively, leaving little more than the memory of another Bernadette Peters acting coup in the role of Hildy the lady taxi driver. Likewise, the durably popular *You're a Good Man Charlie Brown* failed to attract an audience with a Broadway revival production early in the season.

Neither did there seem to be much of an audience for the uptown restaging of the recent Pulitzer Prize drama *No Place to Be Somebody* by Charles Gordone, but two more venerable scripts attracted attention with the alluring twinkle of their starring performances. Clifford Odets's *The Country Girl* and George Bernard Shaw's *Captain Brassbound's Conversion* both jumped from the Kennedy Center to Broadway, the former for a run, the latter for an engagement limited to two weeks. With Jason Robards, Maureen Stapleton and

George Grizzard as the backstage characters in the Odets play about an aging but talented star and his apparently man-eating wife, *The Country Girl* proved to be a still-valid comment on the nature of emotional commitment. Ingrid Bergman was the big attraction in *Brassbound* (which she had just previously done in London), adding her personal grace to the indomitable character of Lady Cicely in the Shaw comedy.

Off Broadway, Sean O'Casey's *The Shadow of a Gunman* alone among the revived straight plays was able to make a run for it, probably because it played upon already-tingling emotions with its drama of violence in the Dublin "troubles" of the 1920s, now echoing tragically through streets of Ulster. Mid-20th century scripts which tried unsuccessfully to stage comebacks this season were Saul Bellow's *The Last Analysis,* Sidney Michaels's *Dylan* and, uptown, Lorraine Hansberry's *The Sign in Sidney Brustein's Window.* David Merrick deserves applause for bringing in the Stratford, Canada version of the Georges Feydeau farce *There's One in Every Marriage* in an adaptation by Suzanne Grossman and Paxton Whitehead, in a production whose acting and direction left little to be desired and therefore indicated that in the present, problematical Broadway commercial context there's not much of an audience for the ephemeral frivolities of Feydeau, even when well executed. Still another echo of the theater's glorious past, the drama *Rain,* made a short-lived appearance downtown. Last season's *Alice in Wonderland,* on the other hand, came right back this season and once again was warmly embraced by both critics and audiences.

In organizational production of revivals, the New York Shakespeare Festival's summer program outdoors at the Delacorte gave New Yorkers the opportunity to see two very seldom-produced Shakespeare plays: *Timon of Athens* (with Shepperd Strudwick in the title role) and *Cymbeline* (offered under the title *The Tale of Cymbeline*). According to the *Directory of the American Theater, 1894-1971,* which lists all plays, authors and sources of Broadway, off-Broadway and off-off-Broadway shows named in all the 56 *Best Plays* yearly and retrospective volumes, this was the first *Timon* produced professionally in New York (it's about a rich man who tries to buy friendship and suffers a King Lear-like rejection when his money runs out). The third offering of Joseph Papp's outdoor season was the musical *Verona* which went on to become a Broadway success.

Another major revival-producing group, Gene Feist's Roundabout, mounted creditable productions of Ibsen's *The Master Builder,* Shakespeare's *The Taming of the Shrew* and Shaw's *Misalliance.* Over in Brooklyn, the Chelsea Theater Center took a breather in the midst of a season of challenging new plays and put on a revival of John Gay's *The Beggar's Opera,* with "musical realization" by Ryan Edwards. The show not only delighted audiences in Brooklyn but later moved into the McAlpin Rooftop Theater, hopefully settling in for a run.

This brings us finally to the subject which we must inevitably confront in these yearly summaries of revival activity in New York: The Lincoln Center Repertory Company in its glittering facility, the Vivian Beaumont Theater.

Its finest hour this season was the revival of Arthur Miller's *The Crucible* with Robert Foxworth in the pivotal role of the drama about Salem witch-hunting, written at the time of the Sen. Joseph McCarthy Communist-hunts of the 1950s but acquiring a broader relevance with the passage of time. A criticism by Arthur Miller of the Lincoln Center board of directors was first printed in the spring of 1972 in the playwrights' own publication the *Dramatists Guild Quarterly* and later received a wider circulation in the *Times* and *Variety*. Miller's point—made in connection with an effort to prevent the demolition of the Forum Theater and the Beaumont's repertory storage space to make room for some kind of movie program—was that it's futile for critics and other commentators to confine their remarks to the material presented on the Beaumont's stage or even the efficacy of Jules Irving's artistic directorship, when the problem begins with the Lincoln Center board of directors' apparent ignorance of and indifference to what is required in dedication and currency to start and maintain a repertory theater. The decision to revive *The Crucible* had no connection with Miller's comments; the necessary permission for a revival production was acquired through channels before Miller's criticism appeared. But the decision was a good one; revivals of American plays like *The Crucible* are what Lincoln Center should be all about. And if the organization had maintained Elia Kazan's and Robert Whitehead's original momentum toward creating an American repertory company, they might possess two other Miller plays, *After the Fall* and *Incident at Vichy,* in their permanent repertory today, because the Lincoln Center company was the first to produce them.

Wishing won't make it so, however, and the fact is that the Lincoln Center board, or somebody up there, did arrest the Kazan-Whitehead development; and if there has been purpose or progress in the work of Lincoln Center since then, it cannot be seen by the naked eye (occasional excellence, yes, now and then an imaginative or challenging single production—a company in being, perhaps, but without any sense of *becoming*). On Lincoln Center's 1971-72 Beaumont schedule, Edward Bond's *Narrow Road to the Deep North* was stimulating theater and Schiller's *Mary Stuart* was right in step with this season's parade of Elizabeth I-Mary Queen of Scots plays. But neither the production of British scripts nor the pursuit of trends would be found among the mandates extended to Lincoln Center Repertory by that part of the theatergoing public which hoped—and maybe somewhere, faintly, still hopes—that it would some day become an American company along the lines of the Old Vic or the Comédie Française. The fourth program on this year's Beaumont schedule, a revival of Shakespeare's *Twelfth Night,* was a wholly competent exercise in station-keeping, in schedule-filling. It's not Lincoln Center's lack of performance that is mainly in question, it is its lack of policy. Arthur Miller said it all when he wrote: "The first order of business now is to get clear in our own minds what (a repertory) theater is, what it can do and what is financially needed to do it. Then if we are convinced of its value, a considered, serious attempt must be made to transform Lincoln Center into such a theater."

Off Broadway

When in mid-year *Variety* characterized the 1971-72 off-Broadway season as "possibly the worst in a decade," the newspaper was speaking of the drab performance of even the more prominent shows at the box office. Once a blissfully carefree, artistically because financially liberated, often experimental Elysian Field of New York play production, the off-Broadway theater is now being made heir to all the cost and other commercial and social problems that have beset its big brother to the north, including ever-expanding demands from the theatrical unions and guilds. By the term "off Broadway" in this volume we mean those productions offered in houses of 299 seats or less, usually under the organizational umbrella of the League of Off-Broadway Theaters, which have Equity casts, plan to play regular schedules of performances open to the public and to public scrutiny by means of reviews. A few others which don't qualify technically are included at the editor's discretion, usually because they are visitors from abroad or have found their way onto other major but less precise lists of "off-Broadway" shows and therefore would be expected to appear on this one.

The rising cost of off-Broadway production ($100,000 average for musicals, $40,000 for straight plays according to *Variety* estimate) seems to have inhibited musical production more than play production in 1971-72. This may be partly because many of off Broadway's plays are produced by organizations like Joseph Papp's New York Shakespeare Festival which are partly subsidized and partly supported by subscription lists. There were only ten musicals produced off Broadway this season, as compared to 13 last year and 16 in 1969-70. In contrast, there were 52 new straight play programs in English as compared to 45 last year, reversing direction toward the total of 64 in 1969-70.

Of these 1971-72 straight play programs, 43 were new American scripts, again reversing direction from last year's 39 toward the spate of 53 in 1969-70 and 55 in 1968-69. But *Variety's* "worst season in a decade" comment was applicable to audience response if not to production volume. 1971-72 was a season in which off Broadway's top attractions suffered neglect at the box office. A contributing factor might be that the going top for most off-Broadway offerings was $7.50 with some exceptional draws priced as usual up to $10—much too expensive for the casual but stimulating evening out which has been off-Broadway's thing, particularly when compared to the price of admission to other casual entertainment like the movies; and only a couple of dollars cheaper than the price of the exceptional evening on Broadway, with its sense of special occasion. If there ever has existed an off-Broadway theatergoing "habit," particularly among the adventurous young people in the audience, surely it was threatened by these high admission prices, and exacerbated by the geographical diffusion of off-Broadway theaters in all corners, some of them dark, of a city whose state of social unrest inhibits many entertainment-hungry citizens from leaving their homes for any reason.

The 1971-72 Season off Broadway

PLAYS (43)

The Justice Box
Charlie Was Here and Now He's Gone
Public Theater 1971
Dance Wi' Me
Black Girl
Georgie Porgie
Out of Control
WHERE HAS TOMMY FLOWERS GONE?
Friends & Relations
A Song for the First of May
A Gun Play
In the Time of Harry Harass
Public Theater 1972
STICKS AND BONES
The Black Terror
Iphigenia
Black Visions
THAT CHAMPION-SHIP SEASON
Older People
The Hunter
Lincoln Cent. Forum
The Duplex
Suggs
Negro Ensemble
The Sty of the Blind Pig
Frederick Douglass

Masquerade
El Hajj Malik
Kaddish
American Place
Fingernails Blue as Flowers &
Lake of the Woods
Sleep
The Chickencoop Chinaman
Nightride
22 Years
Rosebloom
Brothers
The Web and the Rock
Whitsuntide
In Case of Accident
SMALL CRAFT WARNINGS
The Soft Core Pronographer
God Says There Is No Peter Ott
Cold Feet
The Divorce of Judy and Jane
Anna K
The Silent Partner
Jamimma

MUSICALS (10)

The Two Gentlemen of Verona
Leaves of Grass
Drat!
F. Jasmine Addams
Richard Farina
Memphis Store-Bought Teeth
Wanted
Two If by Sea
God Bless Coney
Sweet Feet

REVUES (3)

Look Me Up
Uhuruh
Hark!

REVIVALS (12)

The Last Analysis
N.Y. Shakespeare
Timon of Athens
The Tale of Cymbeline
Roundabout
The Master Builder
The Taming of the Shrew
Misalliance
Dylan
The Shadow of a Gunman
Alice in Wonderland
The Beggar's Opera
Rain
One for the Money

SPECIALTIES (6)

The James Joyce Memorial Liquid Theater
Baird Marionettes
The Wizard of Oz
Peter and the Wolf
Kumquats
JFK
Walk Together Children

FOREIGN-LANGUAGE PRODUCTIONS (2)

Szene 71
Kabale Und Liebe
Der Prozess

FOREIGN PLAYS IN ENGLISH (11)

Lincoln Cent. Forum
Play Strindberg
People Are Living There
The Ride Across Lake Constance
Love Me, Love My Children
Chelsea Theater
THE SCREENS
The Water Hen
A Ballet Behind the Bridge
Theater: Fair of Opinion
And They Put Handcuffs on the Flowers
The Real Inspector Hound & After Magritte
Conditions of Agreement

Categorized above are all the plays listed in the "Plays Produced off Broadway" section of this volume.
Plays listed in CAPITAL letters have been designated Best Plays of 1971-72.
Plays listed in *italics* were still running June 1, 1972.

Certainly the *Variety* comment isn't applicable to the esthetics of off Broadway in 1971-72. Unprecedentedly, it won half the Best Play citations with *Sticks and Bones, That Championship Season, Where Has Tommy Flowers Gone?, Small Craft Warnings* and *The Screens*. It carried off all three Critics Awards for best play, best foreign play and best musical and, in raids uptown, both major Tony Awards. Its deepest gloom was the failure to command strong support for *Tommy Flowers* or the Al Carmines musical *Wanted;* its brightest hours were its hospitable reception of a new play by Tennessee Williams, and the emergence of what is certainly a major new playwriting talent in David Rabe, who not only won major prizes with *Sticks and Bones* but also set the present long-run record at Joseph Papp's Public Theater with *The Education of Pavlo Hummel's* 363 performances.

The Williams play *Small Craft Warnings* was a fine theater piece, unstructured but communicative. An inner flame of poetry is what warms it up, not its outward energies. It takes place in a third-rate but tolerantly hospitable bar and grill on the California coast, and as in Saroyan's *The Time of Your Life* it is what the characters are, not what they do, that tells the tale. Its patrons are small souls, not great ones, come to grief; character rejects, if you will, from the great Williams works of the past. The stud is a degraded Stanley Kowalski trying to work the men's room; the nymphomaniac is a Blanche Dubois without the slightest pretense of refinement. A talkative frump romanticizing her long-dead younger brother could be Laurette Taylor's beautician, while the bartender is an Eddie Dowling-like observer of the passing scene which he neither approves nor disapproves, but tolerates. A homosexual played by Alan Mixon is the only commanding presence; all the others, including a drunken doctor, have long since admitted defeat and learned to live with it. The director of an obviously dedicated cast, Richard Altman, kept the Williams brilliance shining through the melancholy haze of the subject matter, in a very good play by a great playwright.

Another highlight of the off-Broadway season was Terrence McNally's *Where Has Tommy Flowers Gone?* with Robert Drivas as a 30-year-old child of the 1950s adrift in the stormy sea of New York in the 1970s, living by his larcenous ingenuity, looking for warm patches in a cold, cold world. McNally's first full-length play, presented on Broadway in the 1964-65 season, was a very black comedy about such symptoms of end-of-the-world malaise as homosexuality and sadism, with no sentimentality, entitled *And Things That Go Bump in the Night.* It was maybe the first really cool play, years ahead of its time; a Broadway flop which has since been produced successfully all over the world, reviewed in New York with myopic distaste by such heavy-lidded critics as Otis L. Guernsey Jr. poking at it with a stick in his comments published in *The Best Plays of 1964-65.* Well, the times and maybe even the critics—some of them breathing a little hard—have finally caught up with McNally. His *Tommy Flowers* is a cool portrait of disillusioned youth viewed without a trace of sentimentality or extra affection, without any special pleading for his cause, no quarter asked and none given, in a string of episodes in which the Jacques Levy direction helped unify the style and point of view.

What does Tommy Flowers—30, rootless, jobless, unfulfilled—want? He has grown up in a world in which the movies, TV, comic strips and especially Holden Caulfield have exposed him to everything, so of course he wants *everything*. He has no means or will to pay for it, and his response to frustration becomes a game of ripping off Bloomingdale's and Howard Johnson's. His grin is a Robin Hood grin; his merry men are an old man, a young girl and a dog named Arnold who luckily does not expect too much out of life. As his world grows colder and colder, Tommy Flowers still grins, but now it's a *risus sardonicus* and he has a home-made bomb in his knapsack. Tommy (played by Robert Drivas with perfect clarity through all his sudden changes of mood and key) isn't a hero, an anti-hero or a villain. You don't have to make a standard emotional response to him, but you'd better take him into consideration as McNally does with consummate playwriting skill, and stand out of the way when the bomb goes off.

Another of off-Broadway's distinguished Best Plays was *That Championship Season,* a reflective drama cast in the conventional realistic theater mold by its author Jason Miller and directed by A.J. Antoon to squeeze every drop of gall from its gradually contracting circumstances. In it, members of a 1952 state basketball championship team, now in their 30s, gather for an annual reunion at the house of their former coach, now retired. They are here to remind each other and themselves of their triumph, relive it with jokes, backslapping and beer busting among hale fellows well met. The trouble is that their lives have gone sour. Somehow the qualities that won them the championship are losing them the game of life, even though they still have the outward insignia of lettermen. One of them is mayor—but he will almost certainly lose the next election to someone he considers a nonentity. Another is a captain of industry—but a polluter who in his own view is respected for his money alone. Another is a school official—but he feels the others have held him back from further advancement. The fourth is a self-taught alcoholic, and proud of it. Only the Coach still believes that they won something of value back there in 1952, and if they will all stick together and remain true to the old values of aggressive elitism it will all somehow come out right (even though one of his "boys" vomits into the precious silver trophy).

The ensemble portraying these desperate loser-winners was truly a championship team whose members were Walter McGinn (the drunk), Charles Durning (the mayor), Michael McGuire (the teacher), Paul Sorvino (the tycoon) and last but certainly not least, Richard A. Dysart as the Coach. Since a basketball team consists of five members, it is obvious that someone is absent from this play. They talk about him a lot—his name is Martin and he shuns these reunions because he feels they won the championship by foul and ruthless means urged on them by the Coach, and should have given the trophy back. Martin doesn't show up at this reunion, either, so we will never know whether he messed up his life like the others, or was saved by his recognition of the hollowness of their competitive values. In any case, *That Championship Season* was a most effective work of conventionally-oriented theater, the winner of the Critics Award, scheduled as of this volume's press time to follow in the footsteps of *Sticks and Bones* and move from the Public Theater uptown to the Broadway area early in the fall of 1972.

Still another off-Broadway Best Play was *The Screens,* Jean Genet's script using colonialism in Arab countries as a stark symbol of human behavior at its worst, written in 1959 but never produced in its entirety in Paris until 1966 because of the sensitivity of the Algerian question, presented here this season in its American premiere in an English translation by Minos Volanakis at the Chelsea Theater Center. The Chelsea is a production and performance group whose activities are centered across the river from Manhattan in the Brooklyn Academy of Music, a long way off Broadway. It has nevertheless acquired over the past few seasons a courtesy off-Broadway classification in all lists because of its presentation of consistently challenging theater season after season in premieres of plays like LeRoi Jones's *Slave Ship* and Heathcote Williams's *AC/DC.* Now the Chelsea has topped its previous achievement with Genet's long (over 5 hours), crowded (more than 40 players), episodic but virulent play about society's drive toward self-destruction, exposed in suicidal colonial policies in Africa and in a masochistic native anti-hero named Said who marries the ugliest girl he can find and steers their lives into crime toward an apocalypse of deliberate and total disaster. *The Screens* is written in the absurdist style, unleashing Genet's imagination in sudden, almost unbearable purple bursts of brutality and degradation (but seldom suffering; looked at through Genet's tinted glasses, evil and pain are not suffered, they are merely lived and sometimes even enjoyed). *The Screens* gained no strength from its structure, which is non-existent, but from its tragic mood expressed in poetic symbols of nihilism in its happiest moments, horror in its unhappiest. The designs by Robert Mitchell and Willa Kim, the direction by the translator, Volanakis, and the performances of a large company on its mettle combined with the 5-hour Genet script to produce a massive experience of theater which won the Critics Award for best foreign play over the formidable competition of the new Harold Pinter script.

The Chelsea Theater Center continued its most distinguished season to date with the unusual *Kaddish,* a visualization and dramatization of the Allen Ginsberg poem about his mother, a glowing and poignant memoir which transferred to Circle in the Square for an extended run in Manhattan. A bouncing revival of John Gay's *The Beggar's Opera* was also moved to Manhattan after its regularly-scheduled run in Brooklyn. For its season's finale, Chelsea turned once again to the American premiere of a European work, in English: *The Water Hen,* a play by Stanislaw Ignacy Witkiewicz, a Polish playwright who committed suicide in 1939 and whose plays have only recently been produced and appreciated. Written in 1921, *The Water Hen* is a comedy which seems to anticipate the theater of the absurd by decades in a wild, symbolic fantasy about a timeless seductress (a "water hen") who enchants several generations of a family.

A recurrent theme this season off Broadway as well as on was the black condition. While Broadway mounted its images musically in *Ain't Supposed to Die a Natural Death, Inner City, Lost in the Stars, Don't Play Us Cheap!*

and the revue *Don't Bother Me, I Can't Cope,* off Broadway posed its questions dramatically. The best of these plays was the Negro Theater Ensemble's production of Phillip Hayes Dean's *The Sty of the Blind Pig* taking place, not in the kaleidoscopic 1970s, but in the 1950s just before the civil rights movement. It painted a picture of black family life in Chicago in primary colors. Mother (Clarice Taylor, her elbows as sharp as her principles) and her gambler brother (jaunty Adolph Caesar) are proud members of an older generation which would scorn to suffer identity problems. Somehow, however, the daughter senses that she is not what she will become, and her association with a blind street singer looking for his lost love sharpens her perceptions even more. She is like Tony in *West Side Story,* vibrating with an inner knowledge that "something's coming." She and her family seemed to be real rather than symbolical black personalities caught accurately in their small and special segment of time.

Another matter of special relevance raised this season on the Negro Ensemble Company's program was the career and writings of Frederick Douglass, a onetime slave who became a noted abolitionist, recapitulated in *Frederick Douglass . . . Through His Own Words.* The company also presented Lennox Robinson's *A Ballet Behind the Bridge,* as well as a full schedule of less formal work-in-progress stagings.

Still another effective off-Broadway dramatization of the black condition was J.E. Franklin's *Black Girl,* produced by the New Federal Theater at the Theater de Lys, about an upward-mobile family in a small Texas town. Some of its members drag it down with unhappy gravitational forces of cynicism and selfishness, but there is vision here, and an energy which impels others into an escape velocity toward a more fulfilling life. Also prominent on the off-Broadway list was *El Hajj Malik,* an intense reenactment of the life of Malcolm X, with different actors playing Malcolm in succeeding episodes, a technique which proved both a strength and a weakness to the play. It emphasized the universality of the black leader's appeal, but it tended to blur the human focus in a script which already was determined to sacrifice intimacy of personal detail in favor of volume of protest.

Vinie Burrows returned to town in her distinguished one-woman show *Walk Together Children,* with its cavalcade of black imagery in folk songs and other writings from slave days to the present. The abovementioned New Federal Theater moved from Henry Street to the Ellen Stewart Theater (renamed the New Federal) in May, bringing with them *Jamimma,* the Martie Evans-Charles play which had received a workshop viewing earlier in the season. This was a sensitive study of a black girl prepared to bear the illegitimate child of a lover who isn't worthy of her, facing life in today's Harlem.

The black condition was also brought into concern within Joseph Papp's indoor schedule of productions at the Public Theater. Richard Wesley's *The Black Terror* was an explicit play about an executioner for a group of black activists. Though this human paradox functions most efficiently as a killer, still he doubts the final worth of violent methods as a means of changing society. This was a strong play, tautly directed by Nathan George, explosive, brutal, melodramatic. Its author Wesley was produced a second time this season by the Papp organization, as his one-acter *Gettin' It Together* was part of the four-play program *Black Visions*. Other programs which filled the Public Theater's stages during a busy and conspicuous year were *Dance Wi' Me,* a former Cafe La Mama experimental comedy-with-music about an attractive loser, and *Iphigenia,* a free rock-musical adaptation by Doug Dyer, Peter Link and Gretchen Cryer of the Euripides dramas in Aulis and Tauris. Then there was *Older People,* a rueful but sympathetic study of old age in various poses, many humorous, of regret, arrogance and failing powers, especially sexual, by John Ford Noonan, a member of the new generation of playwrights. This was a pungent, if uneven, piece which had its place in Papp's well-rounded season (with a list of seven productions, they can't all be prize winners). Finally among Papp's full-length programs came Murray Mednick's *The Hunter,* a murkily symbolical drama of two soldiers in Civil War uniform who capture a passing hunter, crucify and then kill him, in an enigmatic puzzle of hostilities.

Over at Lincoln Center, no sooner had the furore over the possible demolition of the Forum Theater (about which more hereinunder, in the "Off-stage" chapter of this report) died down than the Forum was right back in the news again with a controversial production of the distinguished black playwright Ed Bullins's *The Duplex;* controversial because Bullins objected strenuously and publicly to the Forum's production concept of his play (a rambling and indifferent slice-of-black-life string of episodes, very minor Bullins). Elsewhere on the Forum schedule this season the Lincoln Center company chose to present a series of scripts by foreign authors: Friedrich Duerrenmatt's *Play Strindberg,* a somewhat camped black-comedy rewrite of *The Dance of Death;* Athol Fugard's *People Are Living There,* a conversational review of social conditions in South Africa; and a translation of *The Ride Across Lake Constance,* an unstructured collage of words and characters by the Austrian playwright Peter Handke. For those who conceive the Forum's purpose, as Lincoln Center Rep's experimental arm, to be the stretching of the company's muscles and the audience's mind in avant garde works of *American* theater, the final program was more relevant: *Suggs,* a play about a romantic youth from the sticks who plunges eagerly into city life and is gradually disillusioned by its crushing imperatives, written by a noteworthy new American playwright, David Wiltse. The Forum has known its finest hours in the introduction to its public of such as Wiltse, Ron Cowen (*Summertree*) and John Ford Noonan (*The Year Boston Won the Pennant*), representative as they are of healthy new growth and evolution within the domestic genus of playwrights.

1971-72 proved to be a disappointing year for devotees of the American Place Theater, the organization which has encouraged so many talented new writers and offered such fascinating theater under the groined ceiling of St. Clement's Church on a side street over west of Ninth Avenue. This year American Place moved to a fine new installation at the bottom of a skyscraper near Sixth Avenue, and it was as though their familiar energy had been absorbed in the move, with too little remaining for the stage. Their first program in the new facility was a portmanteau of the one-acters *Fingernails Blue as Flowers* and *Lake of the Woods,* telling comments on our maladjusted society but certainly lesser Ronald Ribman and Steve Tesich than American Place has presented before. Jack Gelber's *Sleep* was a mildly entertaining comedy about the fantasies of a guinea-pig volunteer in a pompously scientific experiment on the nature of sleep. American Place's final production had a somewhat wider grasp: *The Chickencoop Chinaman* by Frank Chin, a cry from the heart of the yellow minority victimized in 20th century America as faceless, identityless exotic cultural stereotypes, but individualized in the play's Chinese-American hero, a talented and suffering loner who once had a childhood daydream that perhaps the Lone Ranger was an Oriental good guy wearing a mask to conceal the shape of his eyes. The play shares a general tendency this season to ingest emotions and conflicts in little bites instead of big ones, but its production did credit to Wynn Handman's American Place Theater, which we hope will enjoy a rapid acclimatization and an inspired season in its new quarters in the coming year.

Among the rest of off Broadway's 1971-72 straight plays the subject matter was far-ranging and variegated in style. *Nightride* by Lee Barton (a pseudonym) contrasted old and new homosexual attitudes, in a confrontation between a distinguished but now over-the-hill playwright who has never openly acknowledged his homosexuality either in plays or in private life, and a young rock star who boasts of it proudly. This was darkish comedy which benefited greatly from the performance of Lester Rawlins as the playwright whose flaming intelligence and sense of the ridiculous carries him through the most awkward, even violent, situations. Another script which addressed audiences on the subject of homosexuality was George Birimisa's *Georgie Porgie,* a study of a homosexual's relationship with his wife, mother and lovers which opened in midsummer to mixed notices but ran well into the fall. *The Divorce of Judy and Jane* peered at the subject from yet another angle in a short-lived and short-focused study of a group of Lesbian types.

The convicted killer Charles Manson was viewed as an innocent victim of society in *22 Years,* and Yale M. Udoff's *A Gun Play* also contemplated the violence of our times, in the setting of a once-chic restaurant. Harvey Perr's *Rosebloom* considered the uses and nature of violence in a dark study of intensifying passions among a cripple and his wife and mother awaiting the return from prison of his father. Originally produced at the Mark Taper Forum, it deserved a longer run than its scant 23 performances.

Tolstoy's *Anna Karenina* provided Eugenie Leontovich with a theatrical springboard: take a group of actors rehearsing a stage version of *Anna Karenina* and switch back and forth between old Russia and modern New York, commenting on the tragic love story—and other pertinent matters—even as the love story unfolds. As written, acted and directed by Miss Leontovich *Anna K* was salty theater, episodic like so much of the season's works but certainly one of its off-Broadway highlights.

A foreign play that added a new flavor to the 1971-72 brew was Fernando

Arrabal's *And They Put Handcuffs on the Flowers,* which had previously made its American premiere in an off-off-Broadway experimental staging. It is a script of great power about political prisoners degraded to the lowest levels of physical and mental suffering by the very fact of their incarceration as well as the cruelty of their captors. It was written in French by the Spanish playwright Fernando Arrabal (who was once jailed by Franco), translated by Charles Marowitz and presented here under Arrabal's own direction. This included arranging for the audience to grope its way into a darkened theater with irregularly-arranged seats to give an impression of confinement before the play even began. The gruesome episodes (this work is episodic *too*), often charged with shock, culminate in an execution by garroting simulating all the horrible physical details including the emptying of the naked victim's bladder after "death," a noteworthy feat of performance, if not of esthetics. Powerful as it is, this Arrabal protest play is nevertheless like Lewis Carroll's grin without the cat: a violent play without developed characters, physical horror disoriented from humanity, disgust almost without pity, monstrously imaginative but insubstantially human.

No less flavorful at the other end of scale was another foreign program, Tom Stoppard's entertaining exercises in the absurd in his one-acters *The Real Inspector Hound* and *After Magritte.* In the latter, he sends up a Scotland Yard inspector, satirizing all investigative gravity with a farcical construction of preposterous circumstantial evidence, all pointing toward a totally wrong conclusion. The longer piece, *Inspector Hound,* manages to draw its cartoons in depth, and in double projection, taking off a typical murder play at the same time as it exposes the vanities, petty jealousies and propensities of critics covering the play's opening. These works were slight as well as short, but the balancing skill of the author of *Rosencrantz and Guildenstern Are Dead* was fully evident in them. Also from abroad, John Whiting's 1947 play *Conditions of Agreement* was given an American premiere production at the Roundabout. It was a play of sinister implication stopping short of action, with politely British characters abrading each other with memories of an accidental death, menacing each other with threats of unnameable evil but never quite bringing themselves to touch each other.

Other than *Two Gentlemen of Verona, Wanted* was the only moderately successful American book show of the off-Broadway season. David Epstein's libretto viewed the bad guys of American history in a new light, as honored rebels against the oppressive law-and-order forces of their day. This amiable cur-bites-Rin Tin Tin reversal of identities took an added lyric bounce from the Al Carmines score. Here again was a show which merited a wider audience than it could gather in its 79 performances, but this was that kind of a season. The American past turned up more than once more as the subject for off-Broadway musical treatment; even Walt Whitman got into the act in a musical adaptation entitled *Leaves of Grass.* A Canadian import, *Love Me, Love My Children,* exploring the big city youth counter-culture, was an attractive visitor which freshened the off-Broadway musical scene for most of the season.

A spirit of youthful energy invigorated *Hark!* with an ensemble of attractive performers singing songs about almost everything relevant to today's living. It came along in late spring and also freshened the scene with its music by Dan Goggin and Marvin Solley and lyrics by Robert Lorick. A topical cabaret revue, *Look Me Up,* settled in at Plaza 9 for a long run, while a visiting revue from San Francisco, *Uhuruh,* stayed only a week. A foreign-language visitor was the Szene 71 group from Schweinfurt with a Schiller play and a new dramatization of Kafka's *The Trial,* presented in German. Standout specialty programs were the perennially favorite Bil Baird Marionettes and an experience entitled *The James Joyce Memorial Liquid Theater,* an evening of audience participation in fun, games and physical sensations up to and including a couple of respectful kisses. Jeremiah Collins appeared in *JFK,* adapted from the records of the late President's administration. Finally, there was *Kumquats,* a trifle whose subtitle says it all: "The World's First Erotic Puppet Show."

In sum, it was a difficult year off Broadway—but the difficulty was less often artistic than financial; the art form itself was less often guilty than victimized. That preoccupation with nakedness and perversion so conspicuous in recent seasons seems to have pretty much disappeared (or maybe we're noticing it less). Light shone in the gloom, reflecting from the coppery newness of David Rabe and from the deeply glowing patina of Tennessee Williams. If you wanted to select a single symbolic incident among all that happened off Broadway in 1971-72, you'd probably pick the closing of John Guare's distinguished long-run prizewinner *The House of Blue Leaves* after 337 performances on Dec. 3, 1971, following a fire which broke out in the middle of the night and gutted the theater. Circumstances were tough all over for off-Broadway productions in this season of 1971-72, but this was the one that was clearly impossible.

Offstage

Offstage as on, theater activity tended to come in shades of gray, with very few flashes of lightning. There wasn't even a really rancorous controversy over a critic (the best ones were *between* critics), not even involving David Merrick. Merrick let everybody know he was still a law unto himself by switching his shows to an 8 p.m. curtain when everybody else on Broadway was opening at 7:30, but this was little more than a muscle-stretching exercise. There was one brief flurry over the use of quotations from critics' reviews in promotional material. The city's watchdogs made a move to regulate the use of "false and misleading" quotations used out of their context. The city soon mitigated its attitude, however, when various organizations including the Authors League pointed out that quote-ad surveillance would constitute a violation of freedom of the press and "the rights of authors, publishers and producers under the First and Fourteenth Amendments," placing such ads at the mercy of "the varying subjective judgments of many officials."

On one occasion, theater folk *did* rise up in wrath like a parent protecting a menaced cub. The existence of Lincoln Center's little Forum Theater and the "waste" storage space at the Vivian Beaumont, designed to accommodate the productions of a repertory company which has never come into being, was threatened in early fall by a takeover plan suggested and approved by City Center's Richard Clurman and Lincoln Center's Amyas Ames. A substantial portion of Lincoln Center Repertory's deficit is attributed to the cost of maintaining its theaters year-round even when dark. The plan was to have the city lease the Beaumont, turn it over to City Center, put up $5.2 million to turn the Forum and the Beaumont storage area into three movie theaters (this plan was approved by two city agencies). Clurman and Norman Singer —who after Morton Baum's death had demonstrated their faith in the legitimate stage by abandoning the presentation of plays and musicals at City Center—were going to "rescue" Lincoln Center with a similar policy. All possibility of a repertory theater was to be abandoned in order to mount still another movie showcase in a city already overstuffed with them.

Theater folk, their anger aroused, came galloping to the rescue. An Ad Hoc Committee to Save Theater at Lincoln Center was formed under Dore Schary's chairmanship. Its members included Joseph Papp, Jo Mielziner (co-designer of the Beaumont), Clive Barnes, Henry Hewes, John Simon, John Guare, Frank D. Gilroy, Arthur Miller, Edward Albee, Robert Anderson, Abe Burrows, Paddy Chayefsky, Ossie Davis, Jerome Lawrence, T. Edward Hambleton, Joel Schenker, Cheryl Crawford and Stuart Ostrow. They held discussion meetings, they kept at the city agencies and the City and Lincoln Center boards until they chased away the marauders. The City Center withdrew its interesting proposal—but the beat of the deficits and the unmet need for a functioning repertory company in New York goes on.

A citizens' committee of 19 persons under the chairmanship of Eugene R. Black Jr., sponsored by the New York State Council on the Arts and the New York City Cultural Council, financed with the help of New York State and the Rockefeller Brothers Fund, with a research staff headed by the same William J. Baumol who put out a report on the performing arts five years ago, made a close study of the theater and came to the surprisingly rose-colored conclusion that "The extent of decline of activity on Broadway has sometimes been exaggerated in the press . . . . . Broadway has been the base and bulwark of the American stage, in spite of the profit incentive. Most of what is good and enduring in our theatrical heritage has emerged from the hard trial-and-error of Broadway-type presentations and our best new works will probably continue to come from this source."

The Black Committee's report contained a list of 19 recommendations which are worth placing on the *Best Plays* record as a summary of the many tangible efforts being made in the 1970s by the theater to acclimatize to the changing environmental pressures. Here are the 19 points:

1. Repeal of regulations inhibiting the sale of theater tickets.
2. Establishment of a program of last-minute distribution of tickets that might otherwise go unsold.

3. City financial support to selected theatrical companies.

4. Setting up a program under which a portion of taxes be applied to theatrical activity devoted to betterment of theater.

5. Continued support of selected theater groups by the State Council on the Arts, the National Endowment for the Arts and private foundations.

6. Establishment of a national playwriting contest.

7. Publication of a weekly theatrical newsletter.

8. Setting up experiments in pricing and performance time related to the fluctuations of current demand.

9. Supplementing of private funds to the Theater Development Fund by the arts councils and foundations.

10. Formation of a Youth Incentive Program underwriting the distribution of tickets to students.

11. Expansion of the League of New York Theaters' current program of providing tickets to students.

12. Pooling of resources by the League of New York Theaters, the Off Broadway Association and Actors Equity for overall helpful theater programs.

13. Combining the Tony and Obie Award groups.

14. Cooperation by the Police Department and the Office of Midtown Planning and Development in the curtailment of crime in the theater district.

15. Organization of a program of data under the auspices of the American National Theater and Academy.

16. Appointment by Mayor Lindsay of an individual on his staff to serve as liaison to the theater.

17. Encouragement by city departments and agencies as well as Actors Equity of the production of plays in New York City.

18. Consideration by the Office of Midtown Planning, the City Planning Commission and other appropriate city agencies of new incentives to encourage builders to include legitimate theaters in their prospective buildings.

19. Transportation of theatergoers and tourists to the Times Square area at city expense from East Side locations.

The word "subsidy" was on the tip of every theater tongue, with economic pressures mounting, with the object lesson of Harold Pinter's *Old Times*—originally produced in the subsidized shelter of the Royal Shakespeare Company—staring Broadway in the face, and with Joseph Papp demonstrating with play after play in the Public Theater how much subsidy can accomplish when it links arms with imagination. For the live performing arts, subsidy is no longer a matter of whether but of when and how much, to whom and under what circumstances. In 1971-72 as in previous seasons, the Theater Development Fund was doing its helpful thing, supporting the commercial-theater shows its committee deemed worthwhile by purchasing blocks of tickets to strengthen a show's economic position after it has been produced but before it has caught on, and distributing those tickets to audiences who might otherwise not be motivated or able to attend a live theater performance. TDF had $250,000 available for subsidy purchases this season. Among shows which received a portion of this benefice were *Old Times* ($30,000), *James Joyce*

Memorial Liquid Theater ($5,000), *The Love Suicide at Schofield Barracks* ($25,000), *El Hajj Malik* ($5,000) and *Ain't Supposed to Die a Natural Death* ($10,000).

Congress voted $29,750,000 to the National Endowment for the Arts for 1971-72. Major grants to theater organizations across the country amounted to somewhere near 10 per cent of this total Federal money for the arts. Among New York theater organizations, Joseph Papp's received $125,000, the Phoenix Theater $50,000, American Place $25,000 (for administrative staff development), Chelsea Theater Center $50,000, La Mama Experimental Theater Club $75,000, Negro Ensemble Company, $75,000, Repertory Theater of Lincoln Center $25,000 (for Forum productions). Lesser sums were granted to companies like the Open Theater, Cubiculo, Ridiculous, Roundabout, New Dramatists, etc. With this Federal subsidy administered by Nancy Hanks more than double last year's, the bottom of the huge empty bucket was moistened, at least.

New York State appropriated $14,000,000 this season to its Council on the Arts, and some of this was expected to filter through to the legitimate stage. New York City, which spends $23,000,000 a year on museums, zoos, gardens, etc., limits its performing-arts aid to a paltry $1,200,000 of which Joseph Papp gets a well-deserved $350,000 share. ANTA had planned to subsidize selected Limited Gross productions at the ANTA theater to the tune of $40,000 each during their first five weeks providing they played to a $3.50 top, but this plan never materialized.

Only one 1971-72 production—*Solitaire/Double Solitaire*—availed itself of the Limited Gross arrangement, in which the Broadway producer agrees to limit his potential weekly gross to $25,000 by cutting ticket prices and/or roping off part of the theater, in exchange for certain salary and royalty concessions by the theatrical unions and guilds. This experiment wasn't a success. The theatergoing public actually tended to become suspicious of the lowered prices, for one thing; and for another, those connected with the show reported a prevailing feeling of "lacklustre" because of their second-class financial status. The whole Limited Gross scheme was being re-evaluated as the season ended. The idea of Middle Theater, with special contractual arrangements for shows playing in theaters whose capacities fall between the two stools of Broadway and off-Broadway, was seldom implemented.

Old and new theater organizations were busy doing their thing in 1971-72. The Research Library and Museum of the Performing Arts, often known as the "Theater Collection" of the Public Library, was pressing forward against great financial difficulties. It was nearly forced to close its doors to the public midway in the season when anticipated support failed to come through, but the library raised enough from private sources to stay open at least through the season (the Theater Collection, contrary to popular belief, is *not* publicly funded, but is supported—at least sufficiently to maintain a caretaker staff behind closed doors if all else fails—by a merger of the previously-endowed Astor, Lenox and Tilden libraries). Over at the Dramatists Guild, after years of study and preparation a committee came up with a proposed new Minimum Basic Agreement for recommended use by off-Broadway play-wrights and managers in the same way as the Guild's long-standing Broadway agreement is used. The American Educational Theater Association (AETA) found itself diversifying beyond the confines of education-oriented activity and consequently dropped the word "Education" from its name and became ATA. Actors Equity negotiated a new three-year contract with Broadway in which the minimum rose from $164.45 to $185 weekly, escalating to $210 in the final year of the contract. The press agents re-elected Merle Debuskey president of their Association of Theaterical Agents and Managers.

Henry Hewes moved up to succeed George Oppenheimer as president of the New York Drama Critics Circle at the end of Oppenheimer's term of office. Clive Barnes was named vice president of the organization, which was enlivened by a couple of internecine differences of opinion. William Glover of the AP complained that producers were shifting opening dates to suit the special convenience of Barnes, and as a public protest he refused to cover the opening of *Older People*. More private but even more heated was a confrontation at a Critics Circle meeting between Brendan Gill and John Simon over a matter of semantics, with Simon clarifying his position with the admonishment that he would "kick in the head" of the *New Yorker* critic. The Circle as a group voted against admitting their broadcasting brethren to membership, arguing that this would make the group even more unwieldy that its present 22-member state, and that the frequent changes of TV and radio drama-critic personnel would lead to confusion. Toward the end of the season, Allan Wallach took over *Newsday's* daily reviewing stint from George Oppenheimer, who like Walter Kerr of the *Times* will devote himself to Sunday coverage.

A former distinguished editor of these *Best Plays* volumes, John Chapman, celebrated his 50th anniversary with the New York *Daily News* in the spring of 1971. Then about a month later, on July 1, 1971, he announced his retirement from the post of drama critic which he had held for so long, and he was succeeded by Douglas Watt. Illness, not disaffection, was the cause of his retirement, and his death in mid-winter deepened the gloom of this gray season. John Chapman loved all kinds of theater (he always thought it strange that his colleagues would never join him in classifying grand opera as "theater" in its truest sense) and he was beloved by its practitioners. He leaves bright memories of warm friendships and a distinguished career as the drama critic who succeeded Burns Mantle on the *News* and in the editorship of five of these *Best Plays* volumes, 1947-48 through 1951-52.

Among the producing organizations, off-off-Broadway groups were joining together for unified action, and so were eight of the city's black-theater troupes. The Black Theater Alliance, which will try to attract more aid from Federal and other sources, is made up of The Bed-Stuy Theater Inc., the Afro-American Studio for Acting and Speech, the Afro-American Total Theater, the New Heritage Repertory Theater, the Brownsville Laboratory Theater, the Afro-American Singing Theater, the New World Workshop and Theater Black. Delano Stewart of Bed-Stuy was named Black Theater Alliance's first president. American Place Theater moved from St. Clement's Church to gleaming new quarters in a new theater and allied facilities built into the bot-hom of an office skyscraper on 46th Street east of Broadway. The 300-seat house is the first new Broadway-area theater built expressly for the legitimate stage in 38 years.

Even the actors got into the producing act. A group of 30 performers, most of them stars, banded together in a producing organization first called Solar (Society of Loose Actors Revolving) Theater Inc. and later Larc, Inc. for the purpose of establishing "a New York-based theater production company which can deliver a quality theater product without financial sacrifice on the part of the participating actors." Larc's first step was the co-production of *Promenade, All!* starring three Larc members—Hume Cronyn, Eli Wallach and Anne Jackson—and they hope to expand and become self-sustaining. Among Larc members are Martin Balsam, Anne Bancroft, William Daniels, Blythe Danner, Colleen Dewhurst, Keir Dullea, Al Freeman Jr., George Griz-zard, Barbara Harris, Julie Harris, Eileen Heckart, Pat Hingle, Dustin Hoff-man, Ken Howard, Richard Kiley, Frank Langella, Robert Loggia, Salem Ludwig, Liska March, Burgess Meredith, George C. Scott, Maureen Stapleton, Rod Steiger, Jessica Tandy, Jo Van Fleet, Jon Voight and Fritz Weaver.

A good deal of energy was expended behind the scenes this season on ways to make theatergoers happier and theatergoing more convenient and satisfy-ing. An experiment in the use of the American Express credit card to buy Broadway theater tickets was put into effect in March. Once again the Tony Award ceremonies focused the TV spotlight on Broadway theater in a coast-to-coast network program, and again this was the best of the annual award shows on TV, thanks to the expertise of Alexander H. Cohen who produced it. Locally, first steps were taken toward establishing a Theater Hall of Fame in the Broadway area, in the Grand Gallery of the new Uris Theater built into an office tower at Broadway and 50th Street. A committee has selected 90 theater celebrities from 1860 to 1930 whose names will be inscribed on indi-vidual plaques, as will those to be elected in the future. All practitioners of theater arts whose careers span at least 25 years with at least five major Broad-way credits are eligible. There will be special exhibits from time to time hon-oring such individuals as Helen Hayes and George Gershwin. Among those elected to the Hall of Fame in the first go-round were Noel Coward, Ruth Gordon, Oscar Hammerstein II, Lorenz Hart, Howard Lindsay, Cole Porter and Richard Rodgers.

Then there has been the continuing effort to arrange the curtain time to suit the customer. David Merrick's iconoclastic 8 p.m. scheduling to the contrary, a *Playbill* survey of theater audiences indicated that the majority approve the 7:30 p.m. curtain, with the reservation that one night a week, on Saturday perhaps, there could be a later 8:30 or even 9 p.m. curtain as a city dwellers' special. Off Broadway has long since established two-performance scheduling on Friday and Saturday nights, with the second show starting anywhere be-tween 9 and 10:30 p.m. Also off Broadway, American Place set a 6:15 p.m. curtain on Tuesdays for those who want to proceed straight from the office to the theater, with snacks available in a cafe on the premises.

Just as the season ended, Merrick came up with a gimmick long employed by restaurants in the Broadway area but new to show business: free parking for *Sugar* orchestra and mezzanine ticketholders Monday through Friday evenings by arrangement with a nearby garage. At going parking rates, this would represent a saving of about $3 for those who come to the theater in their own cars. Merrick announced it as the beginning of an ongoing effort "to make Broadway theatergoing more pleasant and convenient." As the earth continued on around the sun and headed into the warm summer months, theater folk were keeping an eye on this and all the other customer-serving experiments to see what effect if any they might have on the box office and/or the temper of the theatergoers.

Stepping back from the 1971-72 New York theater season to take a long view before it disappears over the horizon, you can see both the stigmata of invalidism and the insignia of fabulousness. The farther away we get, the more the gray predominance blends into the grayness of everything else, while the slashes of bright color are visible for a long time in the rays of memory. The theater's best work is well worth saving and remembering, and there seems to be no internal stunting of its growth as an art form. Why then is its very existence called to judgment in each passing season? Why is it so extremely sensitive to every disturbance of the economic and social environment? Why are we so relieved every June when the first report of that new musical going into production or this famous playwright's new work to be produced in the coming fall promise us that once more, at least, there will be a new theater season in New York?

Looking at 1971-72 from afar, one might conclude that the theater is in an all-out struggle to maintain its position as a popular art instead of permitting itself to fade into a closet art. No one (or at least no one I know) talks of a crisis in chamber music, nor is its vigorous existence as a closet art form much affected by the increase of crime in the streets. If in the late 20th century the theater became a closet art as it has in some periods of its history, you would be hearing only about its fabulousness and nothing about invalidism. It would become a cultural imperative to attend a play or two a year at a university, or museum, or theater club, or as a subscriber to a touring attraction. A few students would still study playwriting, and there might still be a group of ardent diehards—comparable, say, to the fans of Irish football—who would amuse themselves by putting on plays in some dark corner of New York City, managed, no doubt, by Joseph Papp.

In this decade, though, the theater is anchored much too firmly to the popular scene—if only by means of its musical stage—to be led off into the closet. The hardy hit musicals account for a large portion of those $100 million dollar grosses, and they keep reminding the public in the West Forties how satisfying and thrilling a good live entertainment can be. The situation, then, seems to clarify in the long view: a fadeout is not really available to the theater as we know it, not while it continues to show vigorous signs of life and growth. The theater must remain a popular art, and those precious portions of it which have economic difficulty must be sustained by popular subsidy. The American culture must ask itself not what the theater costs or what it might bring in, but what it is *worth*. The answer to this comes in huge superlatives; from every point of view, the theater is hugely worth America's support. We must respond accordingly, and soon, if we are to have dramatic art in the 1970s and 1980s as well as anodyne, a culture as well as media, a life as well as an economy, human beings as well as a society.

O
O
O

THE SEASON AROUND THE UNITED STATES

with

A DIRECTORY OF PROFESSIONAL REGIONAL THEATER

O
O
O

Including selected Canadian programs
and selected programs for children

Compiled by Ella A. Malin

Professional 1971-72 programs and repertory productions by leading resident companies around the United States, plus major Shakespeare festivals including that of Stratford, Ontario (Canada), are grouped in alphabetical order of their locations and listed in date order from late May, 1971 to June, 1972. This list does not include Broadway, off-Broadway or touring New York shows, summer theaters, single productions by commercial producers or college or other non-professional productions. The directory was compiled by Ella A. Malin for *The Best Plays of 1971-72* from information provided by the resident producing organizations at Miss Malin's request. First productions of new plays—American or world premieres—in regional theaters are listed with full casting and credits, as available. Figures in parentheses following titles give number of performances and date given is opening date, included whenever a record of these facts was obtainable from the producing managements. A plus mark (+) with the performance number signifies the show was still running on June 1, 1972.

Augmented reports on other than regional theater production in Los Angeles by Rick Talcove and Washington, D.C. by Jay Alan Quantrill are included under those cities' headings in this listing.

Summary

This Directory lists 325 productions (including programs of one-acters and workshop productions) presented by 38 groups in 56 theaters in 36 cities (31 in the United States and 5 in Canada) during the 1971-72 season. Of these, 156 were American plays in 118 full productions and 38 workshop productions. 56 programs were world premieres, 13 were American or North American continental premieres.

Frequency of production of individual scripts was as follows:

   4 plays received 5 productions (*The Glass Menagerie, The Price, The House of Blue Leaves, The Taming of the Shrew*)
   2 plays received 4 productions (*Dracula, The School For Wives*)
   6 plays received 3 productions (*Child's Play, The Matchmaker, The Trial of the Catonsville Nine, Our Town, What the Butler Saw, Much Ado About Nothing*)
  27 plays received 2 productions.
 239 plays received one production (this includes groups of one-acters produced together.)

Listed below are the playwrights who received the greatest number of productions. The first figure is the number of productions; the second figure (in parentheses) is the number of plays produced, including one-acters.

Shakespeare	29 (16)	Simon	4 (3)
Williams	7 (3)	Orton	4 (2)
Miller	7 (2)	Allen (Jay)	4 (2)
Shaw	6 (6)	Chekhov	3 (4)
Molière	6 (2)	Albee	3 (3)
Wilder	6 (2)	O'Neill	3 (3)
Feydeau	5 (5)	Pinter	3 (3)
Guare	5 (1)	Coward	3 (2)
Ibsen	4 (3)		

ABINGDON, VA.

Barter Theater

I DO! I DO! (26). By Tom Jones and Harvey Schmidt; based on *The Fourposter* by Jan de Hartog. June 1, 1971. Director, Owen Phillips; musical director, Byron Grant; scenery, Frank Moss; lighting, Bryan H. Ackler; costumes, Martha Kelly. With Jeffrey Dalton, Ellen March.

FORTY CARATS (48). By Jay Allen; adapted from a play by Barillet and Gredy. June 15, 1971. Director, Michael Norell; scenery and lighting, Bennet Averyt; costumes, Martha Kelly. With Ann Buckles, Milton Tarver, Jerry Oddo.

DON'T DRINK THE WATER (20). By Woody Allen. June 29, 1971. Director, Owen Phillips; scenery, Don Drapeau; lighting, Bryan H. Ackler; costumes, Martha Kelly. With Michael Norell, James Sargent, Robert Foley, Milton Tarver, Liz Ingleson, William Schilling.

TOO YOUNG FOR SPRING (16). By Jasper Oddo. July 20, 1971. Director, Owen Phillips; scenery and lighting, Frank Moss; costumes, Martha Kelly. With Milton Tarver, Marilee Sennett, Robert Foley, Cynthia Shallat, James Sargent.

A STAND IN THE MOUNTAINS (4). By Peter Taylor. August 3, 1971. Director, Michael Norell; scenery, Kathrin Moore; lighting, Frank Moss; costumes, Martha Kelly. With Dale Carter Cooper, James Sargent, Milton Tarver, Jerry Oddo, Liz Ingleson.

MUCH ADO ABOUT NOTHING. (21) By William Shakespeare. August 6, 1971. (Reopened, April 12, 1972.) Director, Owen Phillips; scenery, Bennet Averyt; lighting, Bryan H. Ackler; costumes, Martha Kelly. With Robert Foley, Jerry Oddo, Milton Tarver, John Milligan, William Schilling, Ginger Bowen, Liz Ingleson.

THE GLASS MENAGERIE (24). By Tennessee Williams. September 14, 1971. Director, Owen Phillips; scenery, David Murphy; lighting, Bryan H. Ackler; costumes, Martha Kelly. With Dale Carter Cooper, Michael Norell, Liz Ingleson, James Sargent.

ANGEL STREET (25). By Patrick Hamilton. October 5, 1971. Director, Owen Phillips; scenery, David Murphy; lighting, Bryan H. Ackler; With Liz Ingleson, Michael Norell, Dale Carter Cooper, Marilee Sennett, James Sargent.

OUR TOWN (29). By Thornton Wilder. April 27, 1972. Director, Owen Phillips; designer, David Murphy; costumes, Evelyn Moricle. With Rex Partington, Susan Kingsley, John Milligan, Robert Foley, Dorothy Marie, Milton Tarver, Kristina Callahan.

DRACULA (24). By Hamilton Deane and John L. Balderston; based on the novel by Bram Stoker. May 23, 1972. Director, Kenneth Frankel; scenery, Bennet Averyt; lighting, Stuart Richman; costumes, Evelyn Moricle. With Woody Romoff, Sarah Burke, Richard Sanders.

Barter Playhouse

SPOON RIVER ANTHOLOGY (11). Conceived, adapted and arranged by Charles Aidman from Edgar Lee Masters's *Spoon River Anthology*. July 20, 1971. Director, Michael Norell; lighting, Sally Hassenfelt; costumes, Martha Kelly. With Marianne Clarkson, Carolyn Canonico, Jeffrey Dalton, James Gillespie, Michael Norell, Cindy Tarver, Rick Vaughan, Margaret Zajone.

THE RIVALRY (13). By Norman Corwin. August 2, 1971. Director, Michael Norell; lighting, Bryan H. Ackler; costumes, Martha Kelly. With Marilee Sennett, William Schilling, Michael Norell.

Barter Children's Theater: Barter Playhouse

DICK WHITTINGTON AND HIS CAT (11). By Ellen Stuart. July 1, 1971.

REYNARD THE FOX (8). By Arthur Fauquez. July 21, 1971.

ANN ARBOR, MICH.

The University of Michigan Professional Theater Program:
New Play Project—Mendelssohn Theater

LAST RESPECTS (8). By Danny Lipman. February 22, 1972. Director, Harvey Medlinsky; scenery, Ursula Belden; lighting, Joe Appelt; costumes, Brent Ramsey.

Moe	Ben Hammer
Phyllis	Irene Connors
Lt. Fish	Homer Foil
Henny	Kathleen Perkins
Sylvie	Glenn Crane
Claudia	Priscilla Lindsay
Earle	William Becze
Announcer	Jim Harris
Scruffy	Ian Stulberg
Joel	Randall S. Forte
Sophia	Lisa Goodman

Two acts.

ASHLAND, ORE.

Oregon Shakespearean Festival: Outdoor Theater

HENRY IV, PART 1 (29). By William Shakespeare. June 19, 1971. Director, Pat Patton; scenery, Richard L. Hay; lighting, Jerry L. Glenn; costumes, Jean Schultz Davidson. With Philip Davidson, Tom Donaldson, Richard Allan Edwards, Ric Hamilton, Diana Bellamy, Christine Abbott.

MUCH ADO ABOUT NOTHING (29). By William Shakespeare. June 20, 1971. Director, Larry Oliver; scenery, Richard L. Hay; lighting, Steven A. Maze; costumes, Jean Schultz Davidson. With Ric Hamilton, Fredi Olster, Martha J. Tippin, Will Huddleston.

MACBETH (28). By William Shakespeare. June 21, 1971. Director, Philip Davidson; scenery, Richard L. Hay; lighting, Steven A. Maze, costumes, Jean Schultz Davidson. With Raye Birk, Martha J. Tippin, Len Auclair.

A MIDSUMMER NIGHT'S DREAM (42). By William Shakespeare. June 27, 1971. Director, Raye Birk; scenery, Richard L. Hay; lighting, Steven A. Maze; costumes, Jean Schultz Davidson. With Shirley Patton, Fredi

Olster, Larry Martin, Candace Birk, Will Huddleston, David Williams, Michael Winters, J. Steven White.

THE GLASS MENAGERIE (18). By Tennessee Williams. June 28, 1971. Director, Larry Oliver; scenery, Peter Maslan; lighting, Steven A. Maze; costumes, Jean Hartman. With Diana Bellamy, Ric Hamilton, Fredi Olster, Michael Winters.

A MAN FOR ALL SEASONS (18). By Robert Bolt. June 29, 1971. Director, Pat Patton; scenery, Richard L. Hay; lighting, Steven A. Maze; costumes, Jean Schultz Davidson. With Raye Birk, Diana Bellamy, Martha J. Tippin, Tom Donaldson, Garry Moore.

Oregon Shakespearean Festival: Angus Bowmer Theater

ROOM SERVICE (12). By John Murray and Allen Boretz. March 10, 1972. Director, Laird Williamson; scenery, Richard L. Hay; lighting, Steven A. Maze; costumes, Kendra S. Phipps. With Byron Jennings, James Barton Hill, Michael Winters, Timothy D'Arcy, Elizabeth McAninch, Kathryn Martin.

THE PLAYBOY OF THE WESTERN WORLD (11). By John Millington Synge. March 11, 1972 (matinee). Director, Jerry Turner; scenery, Richard L. Hay; lighting, Steven A. Maze; costumes, Jean Schultz Davidson. With Will Huddleston, Philip Davidson, Elizabeth Cole, Stephanie Voss.

UNCLE VANYA (11). By Anton Chekhov; adaptation by Larry Oliver. March 11, 1972 (evening). Director, Larry Oliver; scenery, Richard L. Hay; lighting, Steven A. Maze; costumes, Jean Schultz Davidson. With Michael Winters, Laird Williamson, Elizabeth Cole, Mary Turner, Shirley Patton, William Roberts.

THE CRUCIBLE (11). By Arthur Miller. March 12, 1972. Director, Pat Patton; scenery, Richard L. Hay; lighting, Steven A. Maze; costumes, Jean Schultz Davidson. With Garry Moore, Elizabeth Cole, Laird Williamson, Stephanie Voss, Diana Bellamy.

BALTIMORE

Center Stage

THE TRIAL OF THE CATONSVILLE NINE (23). By Daniel Berrigan; adapted by Saul Levitt. October 31, 1971. Director, John Stix; scenery, lighting and costumes, Eldon Elder. With Ward Costello, John Newton, Roger DeKoven, Earle Hyman, Barbara Frank, Judith Jordan.

THE SEAGULL (24). By Anton Chekhov; English translation by Stark Young. November 28, 1971. Director, Robert Lewis; scenery, lighting and costumes, Leo Kerz. With Kay Doubleday, Earle Hyman, John Costopoulos, Judith Jordan.

THE BEAUX' STRATAGEM (30). By George Farquhar. January 2, 1972. Director, John Lithgow; scenery and costumes, Eldon Elder; lighting, John Sichina, Peter W. Culman. With Wil Love, John Costopoulos, Fran

Brill, Barbara Frank, Vivienne Shub, Henry Strozier.

ANDORRA (23). By Max Frisch. February 6, 1972. Director, John Stix; scenery, lighting and costumes, Leo Kerz. With Mathew Anden, Margaret Ramsey, Alfred Ryder, Elaine Aiken.

STAIRCASE (23). By Charles Dyer. March 12, 1972. Director, Alfred Ryder; scenery, lighting and costumes, Leo Kerz. With Alfred Ryder, Arthur Mallet.

DEATH OF A SALESMAN (23). By Arthur Miller. April 9, 1972. Director, Lee D. Sankowich; scenery, Marjorie Kellogg; lighting, John Sichina, Peter W. Culman; costumes, Mary Strieff. With Richard Ward, Barbara Clarke, Dennis Tate, Terry Alexander, Stanley Greene.

Center Stage: Guest Production

AN EVENING OF MIME (7). March 1,   1972. With Bert Houle, Sophie Wibaux.

BUFFALO

Studio Arena Theater

THE GINGERBREAD LADY (32). By Neil Simon. October 7, 1971. Director, Arthur Storch; scenery, Larry Aumen; lighting, David Zierk; costumes, James F. Frank. With Jo Van Fleet, Dean Dittmann, Virginia Kiser, Alex Colon, Carol Williard, Kurt Garfield.

BUYING OUT (24). By Lawrence Roman. November 4, 1971 (world premiere). Director, Warren Enters; scenery, Karl Eigsti; lighting, David Zierk; costumes, June Gaeke.

Ben Sky ....George Voskovec
Rachel Hermann ....Irene Dailey
Nathan Sky ....Harold J. Stone
Grace Sky ....Joanna Roos
Raymond Sky ....Harold Gould
Tish Sky ....Sylvia Gassell
Donnie Hermann ....Nicolas Surovy
Myra Sky ....Charlotte Jones
Joby Sky ....Paul Vincent
Nurse ....Lois Avery
    Time: August 1961. Place: Los Angeles. The action takes place in the homes of the characters, in the office of a supermarket called "Five Star Mart," and in a hospital. Two acts.

THE ME NOBODY KNOWS (31). Adapted by Robert H. Livingston and Herb Schapiro from the book by the same name; music, Gary William Friedman; lyrics, Herb Schapiro. December 9, 1971. Director, Gerri Dean; scenery, Douglas Lebrecht; lighting, David Zierk; costumes, James F. Frank; musical director, Neal Tate. With Nancy Lee Baxter, Sandra Wypych, Jonathon Brooks, John Charles, Cynthia Hamilton.

MAMA (33). Book by Neal Du Brock; music and lyrics by John Clifton; based on Kathryn Forbes's book *Mama's Bank Account* and John van Druten's play *I Remember Mama*. January 6, 1972 (world premiere). Director, Warren Enters; scenery, Robert Randolph;

lighting, David Zierk; costumes, Patton Campbell; musical director, John L. DeMain; musical numbers staged by Tom Panko.

Katrin ....Jill O'Hara
Papa ....Wesley Addy
Nels ....Bruce Detrick
Christine ....Marilynn Scott
Dagmar ....Eva Grant
Mr. Hyde ....Nelson Welch
Mama ....Celeste Holm
Aunt Trina ....Pamela Saunders
Aunt Jenny ....Charlotte Jones
Aunt Sigrid ....Lois Holmes
Uncle Chris ....Michael Kermoyan
Doctor Johnson ....Leslie Barrett
Mr. Thorkelson ....Curtis Wheeler
Arne ....Todd Dorfman
Nurse; Woman ....Lee Daniels
Florence Dona Moorhead ..Marijane Maricle
    Time: 1910. Place: In and around San Francisco. Two acts.

THE TRIAL OF THE CATONSVILLE NINE (24). By Daniel Berrigan; adapted by Saul Levitt. February 3, 1972. Director, Robert W. Tolan; scenery, Douglas Lebrecht; lighting, Peter J. Gill; costumes, Pearl Smith. With Marion Belcher, Jake Dengel, Barry Ford, Bill Herndon, Jack Landron.

ROMEO AND JULIET (31). By William Shakespeare. March 2, 1972. Director, Warren Enters; scenery, Douglas Lebrecht; lighting, David Zierk; costumes, Pamela Scofield. With Susan Sharkey, Kristoffer Tabori, Charlotte Jones, David Birney.

MAN OF LA MANCHA (33). By Dale Wasserman; music by Mitch Leigh; lyrics by Joe Darion. May 4, 1972. Director, Antony De Vecchi; scenery, Larry Aumen; lighting, David Zierk; costumes, Jean Webster; musical director, Lawrence J. Blank. With Stephen Arlen, Martin Ross, Gloria Zaglool.

Studio Arena Theater: Guest Production

PLAY STRINDBERG (24). By Friedrich Durrenmatt; translated by James Kirkup. April 6, 1972. The Repertory Theater of Lin-

coln Center production with Robert Benson, Ray Fry, Priscilla Pointer, Robert Symonds.

Note: Studio Arena Theater also presents The Now Theater Repertory Company during the school year. Productions included *The Present, The Country, The Proposition, The Proposition Circus* and *The Hut.*

BURLINGTON, VT.

Champlain Shakespeare Festival: University of Vermont
Arena Theater

THE TAMING OF THE SHREW (20). By William Shakespeare. July 20, 1971. Director, Anthony Wiles; scenery, William M. Schenk; lighting, Gregory MacPherson; costumes, Margaret Spicer. With David Darlow, Jeanne De-Baer, Carlton Berry.

JULIUS CAESAR (20). By William Shakespeare. July 23, 1971. Director, Edward J. Feidner; scenery and lighting, William M. Schenk; costumes, Margaret Spicer. With Dennis Lipscomb, Randy Kim, David Darlow.

CHICAGO

Goodman Resident Theater Company: Goodman Memorial Theater

ASSASSINATION, 1865 (30). By Stuart Vaughan. October 30, 1971 (world premiere). Director, Stuart Vaughan; scenery, Sandro La-Ferla; lighting and special effects, Bengt Nygren; costumes, Virgil Johnson.

Col. Burnett	Dalton Dearborn
Gen. Holt	Maurice D. Copeland
Gen. Ewing	Jonathan Farwell
Maj. Doster	Tom V. V. Tammi
Hon. Bingham	Donald Woods
Maj. Gen. Hunter	Vincent Park
Maj. Gen. Wallace	Lee Young
Brig. Gen. Harris	Will Cleary
Brig. Gen. Foster	Robert Morgan
Lt. Col. Glendenin	William Rosenheim
Reverdy Johnson	Shepperd Strudwick
J. P. Furgeson	Ray Rayner
Maj. Rathbone; James Lamb	Roy Sorrels
Dr. Stone	Dennis Kennedy
Charles A. Dana	Jim Stephens
Isaac Jacquette	Jose Borcia
J. A. Ritterspaugh;	
William Evans	Paul Tomasello
Peanuts Burroughs	Nick Polus
William Bell	Leonard Kelly
John M. Lloyd	Art Kassul
Alexander Lovatt	Frank Miller
Lt. Col. Conger;	
Dr. George Mudd	James O'Reilly
Sgt. Boston Corbett;	
Sanford Conover	Ralph Foody
Louis J. Weichmann	Mark Lamos
Mrs. Hudspeth	Marji Bank
Charles Duell	Leonard Kelly
Robert Morgan	Jose Borcia
John Ford	Art Kassul
Betty Washington	Melva Williams
Margaret Branson	Anne Thompson
Dr. Charles H. Nichols	Ray Rayner
Anna E. Surratt	LuAnn Post

Goodman Theater: Guest Production

A PLACE WITHOUT DOORS (21). By Marguerite Duras. September 21, 1971. Long Wharf Theater Production. Director, Brian

Clerk	Allan Carlsen
Soldiers	David Moore, Mark Petrakis

Time: May and June, 1865. Place: An upstairs room in the Old Penitentiary, Washington City. Two acts.

THE IMPORTANCE OF BEING EARNEST (35). By Oscar Wilde. December 20, 1971. Director, Douglas Seale; scenery and costumes, Alicia Finkel; lighting, G. E. Naselius. With Philip Kerr, Russell Nype, Brenda Forbes, Anne Meacham, Nancy Coleman, LuAnn Post.

THE ROYAL FAMILY (35). By George S. Kaufman and Edna Ferber. January 25, 1972. Director, Douglas Seale; scenery, James Maronek; lighting, Jerrold Gorrell; costumes, Virgil Johnson. With Cathleen Nesbitt, Mary Best, Rebecca Balding, Allan Carlsen, Mike Nussbaum, Marrian Walters, Dalton Dearborn.

THE RULING CLASS (34). By Peter Barnes. March 7, 1972. Director, Patrick Henry; scenery, Sandro LaFerla; lighting, Wayne Tignor; costumes, Virgil Johnson. With Murray Matheson, Maurice D. Copeland, Eric Brotherson, Dale Benson, Pauline Brailsford, Laurence Guittard, Dalton Dearborn.

THE BOYS FROM SYRACUSE (34). April 18, 1972. Book by George Abbott; music by Richard Rodgers; lyrics by Lorenz Hart; based on William Shakespeare's *The Comedy of Errors*. Director, Christopher Hewett; scenery, James Maronek; lighting, G. E. Naselius; costumes, Alicia Finkel; choreography and musical staging, Bob Herget. With Bill Ross, Rudy Tronto, Kenneth Cory, Danny Carroll, Lonnie Burr, Gale Gill, Jana Lapel.

Murray. With Mildred Dunnock, Alvin Epstein, Hiram Sherman

Goodman Children's Theater Company: Goodman Memorial Theater

THE PIED PIPER OF HAMELIN (25). By William Glennon. October 10, 1971. Director Kelly Danford; scenery, Jim Reed; lighting, Jim Hegwood; costumes, Sandra Tignor; choreography, Jerry Tullos. With Allan Almeida, Mark Ganzel, David Coleman, Maryann Kohler.

THE SNOW QUEEN (32). By Surgio Magito and Rudolf Weil; based on the story by Hans Christian Andersen. November 27, 1971 (re-opened January 8, 1972). Director, Bella Itkin; scenery, Beverly Sobieski; lighting, Robert Shook; costumes, Dunja Ramicova.

THE MAGIC ISLE (16). By Wesley Van Tassel; music and lyrics by Mark Ollington. December 26, 1971. Director, Kelly Danford; scenery, Joseph Nieminski; lighting, John M. Hickey; costumes, Sandra Tignor. With Adrian Marks, Stan Haze, Robert Neu, Merrell Jackson, Tom Long, Robert Gibson, Angel Menzie, Bruce Boxleitner, Alice Bauman, Kevin L. Connolly.

STARMAN JONES (28). By Douglas L. Lieberman; based on the novel by Robert A. Heinlein. February 12, 1972 (world premiere). Director, Douglas L. Lieberman; scenery, Michael O'Kane; lighting, Paul Thompson; costumes, Pepper Ross.

Travelogue Voice	Jack Jones
Maw; Crew Woman 1	June Kaplan
Monty; Crew Man 1	Joseph Wilson
Sam Anderson	Mitch Maurer
Secretary	Denise Latella
High Secretary;	
Crew Man 2	David Kent
Aunt Becky; Crew Woman 2	Linda Taccki
Bernie; Mr. Simes	Yancy Bukovec
Mr. Kuiper	Howard Mandel
Crew woman 1	June Kaplan
Eldreth Coburn	Sarah Frutig
Captain Blaine	Gerald Walling
Dr. Hendrix	James Dunbar
Miss Kelly	Denise Latella
Mr. Giordano	Steven Sodaro
Maximilian Jones	Charles Fleischer

The play takes place in the Future, on a farm on Earth and elsewhere in the Universe. Two acts.

THE THIRTEEN CLOCKS (30). By Elaine Berman; based on the book by James Thurber. April 1, 1972. Director, Reggie Schwander; scenery, William Schmiel; lighting, Kenneth Peters; costumes, Dunja Ramicova. With John Bannick, Robert Kallus, Maryann Kohler, Mark Ganzel, Stephen Sodaro, Angeliki Stathakis.

Note: The Goodman Theater's Studio Theater Company presented *Saved, Gas I and II, Jamie and the Nine 300, Subject to Fits, Kaspariana* between December 11 and May 21, 1972. The Touring Company presented *The Thwarting of Baron Bolligrew* by Robert Bolt; *The Hide-and-Seek Odyssey of Madeline Gimple* by Frank Gagliano, and *The Magic Isle*, during the 1971-1972 school year.

CINCINNATI

Playhouse in the Park: Robert S. Marx Theater

CARAVAGGIO (40). By Michael Straight. July 1, 1971 (world premiere). Director, Word Baker; scenery and lighting, Jo Mielziner; costumes, Caley Summers.
Musicians:

Ambrogio	Tom Margolis
Ippolito	Luigi
Andres	Dave Holbrook
Allesandra	Tom Burke
Pages	Steve Buck, Steve O'Banion, Steve Burdick, Reginald Valentine
Cardinal Del Monte	Michael Flanagan
The Prince	John Ventantonio
Caravaggio	Cal Bellini
Father Firmo	Jerry Cunliffe
Tresigini	Tom Belleville
Longo	Arthur Morey
Pietro	Tony Gaetano

Baglione	J. Frederick Jones
Baglione's Page	Bill Burnett
Magistrate	Max Hager
Clerks	Dave Holbrook, Paul Forste
Corporal of the Guard	Pat King
Guards	Dean Builter, Steve Buck
Pasqualone;	
Old Friar	William Duff-Griffin
Dead Woman	Prue Warren
1st Fisherman	Jim O'Connor
2d Fisherman; Prior	Dudley Sauve
Giorgio	R. A. Dow
Ferdinand	Paul Forste
Dominic	Gene Wolters
Father Peter	Paul Milikin
Lord President;	
Grand Inquisitor	Jack Gwillim
Grand Master	William Larsen

Robert Shaw as Deeley, Mary Ure as Kate and Rosemary Harris as Anna in Harold Pinter's *Old Times*

Sada Thompson as Celia in *Twigs*

Ben Vereen as Judas in *Jesus Christ Superstar* (FAR RIGHT)

Elizabeth Wilson as Harriet (FAR LEFT) and Tom Aldredge as Ozzie in *Sticks and Bones*

Larry Blyden as Hysterium in *A Funny Thing Happened on the Way to the Forum*

Bernadette Peters as Hildy in *On the Town* (FAR RIGHT)

Lester Rawlins as Jon Bristow in *Nightride* (FAR LEFT)

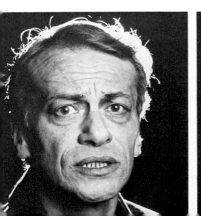

Richard Venture as Sam Bradley in *Solitaire*

Robert Morse as Jerry in *Sugar*

Barry Bostwick as Danny Zuko in *Grease* (FAR RIGHT)

Vincent Gardenia as Harry Edison in *The Prisoner of Second Avenue* (FAR LEFT)

Eileen Atkins as Elizabeth I in *Vivat! Vivat Regina!*

Jonelle Allen as Silvia in *Two Gentlemen of Verona*

Robert Drivas as Tommy Flowers in *Where Has Tommy Flowers Gone?* (FAR RIGHT)

Ingrid Bergman as Lady Cicely in *Captain Brassbound's Conversion* (FAR LEFT)

Hume Cronyn as Willie in *Promenade, All!*

A soldier's homecoming from Vietnam is portrayed in this family scene from David Rabe's Tony Award-winning *Sticks and Bones*, with Drew Snyder as the blinded veteran, Hector Elias as his escort, Cliff DeYoung as his teen-aged brother, Tom Aldredge (holding paper) as his father and Elizabeth Wilson as his mother

Above, two queens in Carl Toms's costume sketches for *Vivat! Vivat Regina! At left*, Elizabeth I as an old woman in Act II; *at right*, Mary Queen of Scots as a young girl in Act I

Young Elizabeth I (Eileen Atkins) in council in Robert Bolt's *Vivat!* is flanked by Walsingham (John Devlin), Cecil (Douglas Rain), de Quadra (Dillon Evans) and Dudley (Robert Elston)

Above, Lee Grant, Vincent Gardenia, Florence Stanley, Dena Dietrich and Tresa Hughes in a family discussion of the troubles of Peter Falk (*left*), in the new Neil Simon comedy *The Prisoner of Second Avenue*

Right, Joan Hackett and Len Cariou as husband and wife in the thriller *Night Watch*

Left, Robert Donley and Sada Thompson in the *Ma* episode of *Twigs*

Below, Louis Zorich, Christopher Guest, Cara Duff-MacCormick (under table) and Kevin Conway in *Moonchildren*

Left, Tina Chen, Robert Burr, Frank Geraci and Michael Landrum in *The Love Suicide at Schofield Barracks*

"REAL" PEOPLE—*Right*, Jean-Pierre Aumont as Dag Hammarskjold and Lou Gossett as Patrice Lumumba in *Murderous Angels*; *below,* George S. Irving as Richard M. Nixon with five of his best-known contemporaries (played by George Hall, William Knight, Robert Blackburn, Alex Wipf and Chet Carlin, wearing masks) in *An Evening With Richard Nixon and . . .*

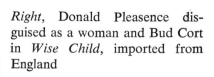

Above, Hume Cronyn, Anne Jackson and Eli Wallach in *Promenade, All!*

Right, Donald Pleasence disguised as a woman and Bud Cort in *Wise Child*, imported from England

TWO-SHOTS IN BROAD-
WAY ONE-ACTERS — *At
top*, Richard Venture and
Joyce Ebert in *Double Solitaire; above*, Michael Tolan
and Lou Jacobi in the *Eli, the
Fanatic* segment of *Unlikely
Heroes*; *right*, Richard Kiley
and Clive Revill (as Max Beerbohm) in the Enoch Soames
episode of *The Incomparable
Max*

Jonelle Allen aloft in a scene from the Critics and Tony Award-winning musical *Two Gentlemen of Verona*

Caiaphas (Bob Bingham, *top center*) watches Jesus of Nazareth (Jeff
Fenholt, *center*) in the midst of the people in the Tom O'Horgan
stage version of the rock opera *Jesus Christ Superstar*

Randy Barcelo's costume design for Herod in *Jesus Christ Superstar* is shown in the sketch *above* and the onstage photo *above right*. Other Barcelo designs pictured here are those for Jesus (*above left*) and *below* the Tormentors, the Priests and the Soldiers

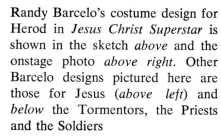

Above, the railroad station scene in *Sugar* with Sweet Sue (Sheila Smith, *left,* holding baton) and her all-girl orchestra and Tony Roberts and Robert Morse (*center,* in foreground) as Joe and Jerry, disguised in women's clothes. *Below,* Alvin Colt's sketches of costumes designed to make the two leading men look like women, with the railroad station scene dresses at *left* and the Miami arrival scene costumes at *right*

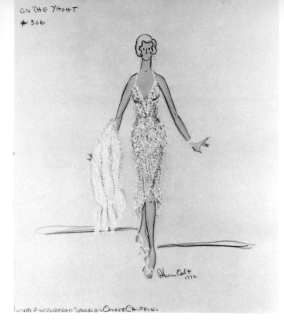

Elaine Joyce in the title role of *Sugar*,
with a sketch of one of her costumes

The cast of *Grease* in a musical parody of the rock 'n' rolling 1950s

Above, the ensemble of Micki Grant's revue, *Don't Bother Me, I Can't Cope*

Right, Carl Hall, Larry Marshall and Allan Nicholls in a scene from *Inner City*

Left, Phil Silvers as Pseudolus on the backs of The Proteans (Joe Ross, Bill Starr, Chad Block) in Burt Shevelove's restaging of *A Funny Thing Happened on the Way to the Forum*

Marco St. John, Michael Dunn and Shepperd Strudwick in Joseph Papp's production of *Timon of Athens* outdoors in Central Park

DUETS—*Above,* Paul Sparer and Jill O'Hara in Roundabout's *The Master Builder*; *right,* Martha Henry and Robert Foxworth in the Lincoln Center Repertory production of Arthur Miller's *The Crucible*; *below,* Marilyn Gardner and Jack Creley in a scene from the Feydeau farce *There's One in Every Marriage*

Brock Peters (*foreground*) in a scene from *Lost in the Stars*

Alice (Angela Pietropinto, *center*) and her friends played by The Manhattan Project in *Alice in Wonderland*

Walter McGinn, Paul Sorvino, Richard A. Dysart, Michael McGuire and Charles Durning toasting a victory of yesteryear in Jason Miller's *That Championship Season,* the Critics Award winner

Above, Brad Sullivan, Gene Fanning, Bill Hickey, Helena Carroll and David Hooks in Tennessee Williams's *Small Craft Warnings*

Below, Robert Drivas and Kathleen Dabney in the Bloomingdale's scene of Terrence McNally's *Where Has Tommy Flowers Gone?*

CHELSEA THEATER CENTER—
Above, the Brooklyn-based troupe's
American premiere production of
Jean Genet's *The Screens*, with (in
foreground) Joseph Della Sorte as Ha-
bib, Osceola Archer as Ommu and
Robert Jackson as Said; *right*, James
Cahill in Witkiewicz's *The Water
Hen*, another U.S. premiere of a for-
eign work

N.Y. SHAKESPEARE FESTIVAL PUBLIC THE-ATER—The throng on Joseph Papp's indoor stages during 1971–72 included (*right*) Earl Sydnor and Susan Batson in *The Black Terror* and (*below*) Will Hare, Bette Henritze, Stefan Schnabel (*top*), Polly Rowles, Barnard Hughes (*top*) and Madeleine Sherwood in *Older People*

NEGRO ENSEMBLE COMPANY — *Below*, Clarice Taylor, Moses Gunn and Frances Foster in *The Sty of the Blind Pig*

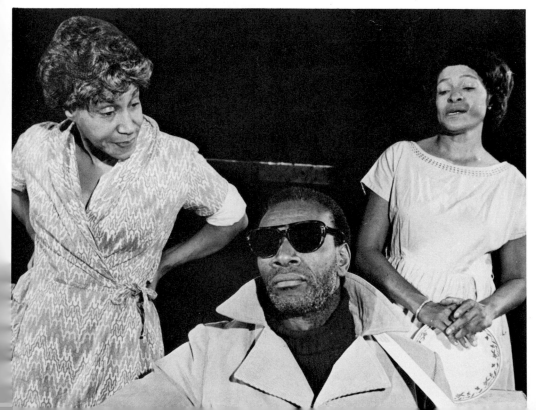

AMERICAN PLACE — *Right*, Sab Shimono and Andy Kim swing Anthony Marciona in *The Chickencoop Chinaman*

LINCOLN CENTER FORUM THEATER— *Left,* William Atherton in *Suggs*; *below,* Marie Thomas, Mary Alice, Phylicia-Ayers Allen, Norma Donaldson, Carl Mikal Franklin, Albert Hall and Johnny Hartman in Ed Bullins's play *The Duplex*

Right, Gloria Edwards, Kishasha and Loretta Green in *Black Girl*

Below, Ron Faber, George Shannon and Peter Maloney in Arrabal's *And They Put Handcuffs on the Flowers*

Chandler Hill Harben and Jeremy Stockwell in *Nightride*

James Harris and Norman Butler in *El Hajj Malik*

Boni Enten, Edmond Genest, Carrie Nye, Jane Connell and Remak Ramsey in Tom Stoppard's *The Real Inspector Hound*

Above, members of the audience have joined *James Joyce Memorial Liquid Theater* cast members in an encounter session in one of the audience participation activities in this entertainment

Grandpa, the Cat and Peter in the Bil Baird Marionette production of *Peter and the Wolf*

A SAMPLING OF NEW PLAYS

IN REGIONAL THEATERS

NEW HAVEN—*Above*, Andy Robinson, Kitty Winn and Fritz Weaver in *Patrick's Day* at the Long Wharf Theater

MILWAUKEE—*Below*, John Hancock in the role of God in Milwaukee Rep's production *The English Mystery Plays*

LOS ANGELES—The Mark Taper Forum schedule included an "uninhibited" new adaptation of *Volpone* (*above*, with Avery Schreiber as Volpone and Sam Waterston as Mosca) and the New Theater for Now experimental staging of *Ten Com. Zip Com. Zip* (*right*, with Barbara Colby as a disillusioned modern rebel)

CHICAGO—Dalton Dearborn, Frank Miller and Maurice Copeland in Stuart Vaughn's *Assassination—1865* at the Goodman Theater

CLEVELAND — *Left*, Jonathan Bolt in the Play House production of *Woman in the Dunes*

DALLAS—*Below,* Jim Lipka and Jim Progar in *I'm Read, You're Black* at Dallas Theater Center

ANN ARBOR—*Above*, Ben Hammer and Irene Connors in Michigan University's New Play Project, *Last Respects*

WINNIPEG, CANADA—*Right*, P. M. Howard (with guitar), Abraham Alvarez, Alan Jones and Margaret Bard in *Head 'Em Off at the Pas* (sic) at Manitoba Theater Center

PROVIDENCE, R.I.—*Above*, James Eichelberger and Richard Kneeland in *Down by the River Where Waterlilies Are Disfigured Every Day* at Trinity Square Playhouse

WASHINGTON, D.C.—*Above*, Gary Bayer and Paul Benedict in the American premiere of Gunter Grass's *Uptight* at Arena Stage; *below*, Lucy Lee Flippen, Jack Halstead, Ronn Robinson and Edmund Day in *The Deadly Delilah* at Washington Theater Club

Grand Master's Page ......Michael Mullins
Antonio ....Roger Kozol
Fisherman's Wife ....Lieux Dressler
Takes place in various cities and places in
Italy, 1594-1610. Act I: 6 scenes. Act II: 5
scenes.

HAMLET (39). By William Shakespeare;
text edited by Michael Flanagan. September
1, 1971. Directors, Word Baker, Dan Early;
scenery, Stuart Wurtzel; lighting, John Mc-
Lain; costumes, Caley Summers. With Daniel
Davis, Frank Raiter, Jack Gwillim, Gastone
Rossilli, Ann Kinsolving, Marsha Wishusen.

LIFE WITH FATHER (76). By Howard

Lindsay and Russel Crouse; based on the
book by Clarence Day Jr. November 1, 1971.
Director, Michael Flanagan; scenery, Stuart
Wurtzel; lighting, John McLain; costumes,
Caley Summers. With Laurence Hugo, Ludi
Claire, Gary Dontzig, Tom Burke, Nancy
Foy.

THE INNOCENTS (24). By William Archibald; based on Henry James's *The Turn of
the Screw*. May 4, 1972. Director, Michael
Flanagan; scenery, Peter Harvey; lighting,
John McLain; costumes, Caley Summers.
With Carol Thomas, Pamela Simpson, Patricia O'Connell, David Elliott.

Playhouse in the Park: Robert S. Marx Theater—Guest Production

THE SCHOOL FOR WIVES (24). By Molière. April 6, 1972. Trinity Square Repertory

Company production.

Playhouse In the Park: Shelterhouse Theater

THE LAST SWEET DAYS OF ISAAC (48).
Book and lyrics, Gretchen Cryer; music,
Nancy Ford. June 1, 1971. Director, Word
Baker; scenery, Ed Wittstein; lighting, David
F. Segal; costumes, Caley Summers. With
Austin Pendleton, Alice Playten, David Ly-
man.

RAIN (38). By John Colton and Clemence
Randolph; from the story by W. Somerset
Maugham. August 1, 1971. Director, Michael

Flanagan; scenery, Stuart Wurtzel; lighting,
Leo Bonamy; costumes, Patrizia Von Bran-
denstein. With Carol Keefe, Madeleine le
Roux, James Cahill.

WHY HANNA'S SKIRT WON'T STAY
DOWN (42). By Tom Eyen. October 1, 1971.
Director, Neil Flanagan; scenery, Stuart Wurt-
zel; lighting, Jay Depenbrock; costumes,
Caley Summers. With Helen Hanft, Steven
Davis, Karole Kaye Stevenson.

Playhouse in the Park: Shelterhouse Theater—Guest Production

DEAR LIAR (10). By Jerome Kilty. Actors

Theater of Louisville production.

Note: Playhouse in the Park will continue the 1972 season with SHELTER, a new musical by
Gretchen Cryer and Nancy Ford; THE PLAY'S THE THING by Ferenc Molnar; SENSA-
TIONS OF THE BITTEN PARTNER, a new play by Milburn Smith; THE RIVALS by Richard Brinsley Sheridan; THE MERCHANT OF VENICE by William Shakespeare; GODSPELL
by John-Michael Tebelak and Stephen Schwartz. June through October, 1972.

CLEVELAND

Cleveland Play House: Euclid-77th Street Theater

PLAZA SUITE (19). By Neil Simon. September 8, 1971. Director, Jonathan Bolt; scenery, Paul Rodgers; lighting, Jeffrey Dallas;
costumes, Joe Dale Lunday. With Jean Barrett, John DeVenne, David O. Frazier, June
Gibbons, Vivienne Stotter, Robert Thorson.

DARK OF THE MOON (29). By Howard
Richardson and William Berney. October 8,
1971. Director, J. J. Garry, Jr.; scenery, Richard Gould; lighting, Jeffrey Dallas; costumes,
Joe Dale Lunday. With Paula Duesing, Douglas Jones, Bob Moak, Mary Shelley.

THE BIRDS (12). By Aristophanes; adapted

by J. J. Garry Jr. from a version by Walter
Kerr. November 12, 1971. Director, J. J.
Garry Jr.; scenery, Richard Gould; lighting,
Jeffrey Dallas; costumes, Joe Dale Lunday.
With Eric Conger, Bob Moak, Paula Duesing,
Stephanie Lewis, Robert Thorson.

CHILD'S PLAY (35). By Robert Marasco.
December 17, 1971. Director, Bertram Tanswell; scenery, Richard Gould; lighting, Jeffrey Dallas; costumes, Joe Dale Lunday. With
John Bergstrom, Jonathan Bolt, Allen Leatherman, Robert Snook.

MOBY DICK, REHEARSED (8). By Orson

Welles; adapted from the novel by Herman Melville. February 11, 1972. Director, Eric Conger; scenery, Richard Gould; lighting, Jeffrey Dallas; costumes, Joe Dale Lunday. With Andrea Danford-Baylor, Jonathan Bolt, Richard Oberlin, Mark Taylor, Robert Thorson.

THE PRIME OF MISS JEAN BRODIE (37). By Jay Allen; adapted from the novel by Muriel Spark. February 25, 1972. Director, Bertram Tanswell; scenery, Richard Gould;

Cleveland Play House: Drury Theater

A DOLL'S HOUSE (19). By Henrik Ibsen; translated by Eva Le Gallienne. October 15, 1971. Director, Douglas Seale; scenery, Richard Gould; lighting, Jeffrey Dallas; costumes, Joe Dale Lunday. With Carolyn Younger, Brenda Curtis, John Bergstrom, David O. Frazier, Richard Halverson.

WOMAN IN THE DUNES (19). By Peter Coe; adapted from the Kobo Abé novel. November 19, 1971 (world premiere). Director, Peter Coe; scenery, Richard Gould; lighting, Jeffrey Dallas.
Woman .... Julia Curry
Man .... Jonathan Bolt
1st Voice .... John DeVenne
2d Voice .... Larry Tarrant
    Two acts.

FRANK MERRIWELL, OR HONOR CHALLENGED (36). Book by Skip Redwine, Larry Frank, Heywood Gould; music and lyrics by Skip Redwine, Larry Frank. December 25,

lighting, Jeffrey Dallas; costumes, Joe Dale Lunday. With Sheila Russell, Carolyn Younger, Stephanie Lewis, Jon Beryl, John Buck Jr.

FORTY CARATS (31). By Jay Allen; adapted from a play by Barillet and Gredy. April 14, 1972. Director, Jonathan Bolt; scenery, Richard Gould; lighting, Peter Shokalook. With Julia Curry, William Watson, John Buck Jr., Allen Leatherman, Edith Owen, Eleanor AuWerter.

1971. Director, George Touliatos; scenery, Robert Gould; lighting, Jeffrey Dallas; costumes, Estelle Painter; musical director, Donna Renton; choreographer, Anne McCluskey. With John Everson, Robert Allman, Kathleen Krizner, William Watson, Stephen Randolph, Mary Shelley.

THE HOUSE OF BLUE LEAVES (24). By John Guare. March 3, 1972. Director, Bob Moak; scenery, Richard Gould; lighting, Jeffrey Dallas; costumes, Joe Dale Lunday. With Richard Halverson, William Watson, Mary Shelley, Evie McElroy.

THE LIAR (17). By Carlo Goldoni; translated by Tunc Yalman. April 7, 1972. Director, Tunc Yalman; scenery, Richard Gould; lighting, Jeffrey Dallas; costumes, Joe Dale Lunday. With Robert Snook, Brenda Curtis, Kathleen Krizner, Richard Halverson, Robert Allman.

Cleveland Play House: Brooks Theater

WHAT THE BUTLER SAW (47). By Joe Orton. December 10, 1971. Director, Andrew Lack; scenery, Richard Gould; lighting; John Rolland; costumes, Harriet Cone. With Richard Halverson, Jean Barrett, Brenda Curtis, Douglas Jones, Norm Berman, Liam Smith.

THE PRICE (31). By Arthur Miller. March 10, 1972. Director, Jonathan Bolt; scenery, Richard Gould; lighting, John Rolland; costumes, Joe Dale Lunday. With David O. Frazier, Myrna Kaye, Norm Berman, Allen Leatherman.

DALLAS

Dallas Theater Center: Kalita Humphreys Theater

THE APPLE TREE (23). Book, music and lyrics by Sheldon Harnick and Jerry Bock; additional book material by Jerome Coopersmith; based on stories by Mark Twain, Frank R. Stockton and Jules Feiffer. June 3, 1971. Director/choreographer, Lee Theodore; scenery, Mary Sue Jones, Lynn Lester; lighting, Randy Moore; costumes, John Henson; musical director, Raymond Allen. With Randolph Tallman, Synthia Rogers, Norma Levin, John Figlmiller, Chelcie Ross, Deanna Dunagan.

PRIVATE LIVES (25). By Noel Coward. July 13, 1971. Director, Rocco Bufano; scenery and costumes, John Henson; lighting, Sally Netzel. With Carole Cook, Chelcie Ross, Mona Pursley, Ken Latimer, Sally Netzel.

THE NIGHT THOREAU SPENT IN JAIL (12). By Jerome Lawrence and Robert E. Lee. September 10, 1971. Director, Paul Baker; scenery, David George; lighting, Randy Moore; costumes, John Henson. With

Randolph Tallman/Steven Mackenroth, Michael Dendy, Mary Sue Jones, Judith Davis.

THE LION IN WINTER (28). By James Goldman. October 12, 1971. Director, Don Eitner; scenery, Dale Barnhart; lighting, Robyn Flatt, Sam Nance; costumes, Kathleen Latimer. With Carole Cook, Tom Troupe, Steven Mackenroth, Randy Moore, Randolph Tallman, Pam Gorham.

DRACULA (6). By Hamilton Deane and John L. Balderston; adapted from the novel by Bram Stoker. October 22, 1971. Director, Judith Davis; scenery, Yoichi Aoki; lighting, Larry Kennedy, Walid Khaldi; costumes, Chequita Jackson. With Bennie Mathews, Chequita Jackson, Carlos Gonzales, Clyde Evans, Mike Gomez, Charles Jones.

THE SCHOOL FOR SCANDAL (28). By Richard Brinsley Sheridan. November 16, 1971. Director, Campbell Thomas; scenery, Lynn Lester; lighting, Margaret Yount; costumes, Carolyn Frost. With Ken Latimer, Chelcie Ross, Randy Moore, Mary Sue Jones, Sally Netzel, Michael Wray.

SNOW WHITE, AND FAMOUS FABLES (18). Script arranged by Stephanie Rich. December 17, 1971. Directors, Stephanie Rich, Robyn Flatt; scenery, Linda Blase; lighting,

Sam Nance; costumes, Joan Meister. With John Stevens, Margaret Yount, Peter Madison, Robyn Flatt, Marian Smith-Martin, Carol Frost, Norma Levin and other members of Dallas Theater Center Company.

J.B. (35). By Archibald MacLeish. January 18, 1972. Director, C. Bernard Jackson; scenery, Marshall Kaufman; lighting, Randy Moore; costumes, Mary Ann Colias and Patricia Lobit. With Steven Mackenroth, Reginald Montgomery, Tim Green, Norma Levin, Carlos Gonzalez, Yoichi Aoki, Chelcie Ross.

LYSISTRATA (35). By Aristophanes; translated by Patrick Dickinson; original music by Manos Hadjidakis; lyrics translated and adapted by N. C. Germanacos. March 7, 1972. Director, Takis Muzenidis; scenery, Yoichi Aoki; lighting, Randy Moore; authentic Greek costumes from National Theater of Greece. With Molly McGreevy, Judith Davis, Robyn Flatt, John Henson, Randy Moore, Jacque Thomas.

OUR TOWN (35). By Thornton Wilder. April 18, 1972. Director, Ken Latimer; scenery, Sam Nance; lighting, Linda Blase; costumes, Noel Noblitt. With Mary Sue Jones, Ryland Merkey, Michael Wray, John Logan, Synthia Rogers, Toni Zbranek.

Dallas Theater Center: Down Center Stage

THE DIARY OF A MADMAN (45). By Nikolai Gogol; translated by Rodney Patterson; adapted by Don Eitner and Tom Troupe. June 16, 1971. Director, Don Eitner; scenery and costumes, Dale Barnhart; lighting, Paul John Smith. With Tom Troupe.

THE PRICE (30). By Arthur Miller. October 19, 1971. Director, Bryant J. Reynolds; scenery, Marian Smith-Martin; lighting, Steve R. Smith; costumes, Nancy Jones. With Preston Jones, Louise Mosley, Michael Dendy, Barnett Shaw.

EXIT THE KING (30). By Eugene Ionesco. December 21, 1971. Director, Michael Dendy; designer, Johanna Stalker; lighting, Allen Hibbard. With Kerry Newcomb, Cecilia Flores, Judith Davis, Barry Hope.

DEAR LOVE (40). By Jerome Kilty. February 8, 1972. Director, Preston Jones; scenery, Russell Guinn; lighting, Marshall Kaufman; costumes, Noel Noblitt. With Marian Smith-Martin, Howard Renensland, Jr.

A TRIO OF ORIGINALS: I'M READ, YOU'RE BLACK by Lewis Cleckler, directed by Barry Hope; FEATHERS by Kerry New-

comb, directed by Jim Bennett; SALOON by Sally Netzel, directed by Pam Gorham (15). April 13, 1972 (world premiere). Scenery, Johanna Stalker; lighting, John Black; costumes, Charles Jones.

I'm Read, You're Black
Link ....Jim Lipka
Mac ....Jim Progar
Albert ....Sam Nance
Whirlaway ....James Crump
Man ....Kevin Kelley
Mama ....Sherry Renolds
  Place: The interior of a gas station in a small West Texas town. Time: The present, summer.

Feathers
Nurse Malfi ....Denise Chavez
Logan ....Steve R. Smith
Roger ....Bob Dickson
Cap ....Herman Wheatley
  Place: The interior of a cardboard box. Time: Any time.

Saloon
Hero ....Allen Hibbard
Heroine ....Lynn Lester
  Place: A saloon. Time: The present.

Dallas Theater Center: The Janus Players in the Lay Studio

DAY OF ABSENCE (25). By Douglas Turner Ward. July 27, 1971, reopened September 7, 1971. Director, Judith Davis; designer, John Henson; lighting, Linda Blase. With Carlo Gonzalez, Johanna Clayton, Charles Jones, Bennie Mathews, Chequita Jackson, Donna Medcalf, Reginald Montgomery, Eddie Laurie, Kevin Kelley.

SHADES OF BLACK AND BROWN (10).

Musical written by the Janus Players. March 14, 1972 (world premiere). Director, Reginald Montgomery; designer, Judith Ann Cuesta; lighting, Mike Gomez, Rick Hernandez. With Xocia Armstrong, Gloria Bernal, Johanna Clayton, Chequita Jackson, Pat Maxie, Ruby Walker, Mike Gomez, Rick Hernandez, Charles Jones, Larry Kennedy, Agapito Leal, Bennie Mathews. 10 musical numbers and finale.

HARTFORD, CONN.

Hartford Stage Company

NO PLACE TO BE SOMEBODY (44). By Charles Gordone. October 15, 1971. Director, Richard Ward; scenery and costumes, Lawrence King; lighting, Lawrence Crimmins. With Rod Perry, Tana Hicken, Paul Rudd.

HENRY V (44). By William Shakespeare. November 26, 1971. Director, Paul Weidner; scenery and costumes, Santo Loquasto; lighting, Lawrence Crimmins. With Harris Yulin, Jack Murdock, Diana Kirkwood, Darthy Blair, Geddeth Smith, Bernard Frawley.

ROOTED (44). By Alexander Buzo. January 7, 1972 (American premiere). Director, Paul Weidner; scenery and costumes, Lawrence King; lighting; Lawrence Crimmins.
Gary ....David H. Leary
Bentley ....Jack Murdock
Sandy ....Barbara Caruso
Richard ....David O. Petersen
Diane ....Veronica Castang

Place: The living room of Bentley's and Sandy's home unit in Sydney. Three acts.

CHARLEY'S AUNT (44). By Brandon Thomas. February 18, 1972. Director, Jeremiah Sullivan; scenery, William Wall; lighting, Lawrence Crimmins; costumes, Linda Fisher. With Robert Moberly, Gary Dontzig, Paul Rudd, Sandra Thornton, Kathleen Miller, Tana Hicken.

TINY ALICE (44). By Edward Albee. March 31, 1972. Director, Paul Weidner; scenery, Lawrence King; lighting, Lawrence Crimmins; costumes, Victoria Ziessin. With Jordan Christopher, Charlotte Moore, Edward Hall, Donald Ewer, David O. Petersen.

LOOT (44). By Joe Orton. May 12, 1972. Director, Ted Cornell; scenery, John Conklin; lighting, Peter Hunt; costumes, Whitney Blausen. With Jack Murdock, Bernard Frawley, Charlotte Moore, David O. Petersen.

Hartford Stage Company: Guest Production

I AM A WOMAN (2). Compiled and performed by Viveca Lindfors. December 4, 1971.

HOUSTON

Alley Theater: Large Stage

CAMINO REAL (38). By Tennessee Williams. October 21, 1971. Director, Nina Vance; scenery and costumes, Jerry Williams; lighting, Richard D. Cortright; music, Bernardo Segall; choreography, Carolyn Franklin. With William Trotman, William Glover, Lillian Evans, Anne Shropshire, Rick Lieberman, Lauren Frost.

A FLEA IN HER EAR (46). By Georges Feydeau. December 2, 1971. Director, R. Edward Leonard; scenery and costumes, Jerry Williams; lighting, John Hagen. With Nancy Leonard, William Glover, Russ Marin, Lillian Evans, William Hardy.

SPOON RIVER (38). January 20, 1972. Conceived, adapted and arranged by Charles Aidman from Edgar Lee Masters's *Spoon River Anthology*. Director, William Trotman; lighting, John Hagan; costumes, Jerry Williams. With George Ebeling, Clint Anderson, Bettye Fitzpatrick.

HADRIAN VII (38). March 2, 1972. By Peter Luke; based on the novel and other works by Fr. Rolfe (Baron Corvo). Director, William Trotman; scenery and costumes, Jerry Williams; lighting, John Hagan. With Robert Casper.

THE TAMING OF THE SHREW (39). By William Shakespeare. April 21, 1972. Director, R. Edward Leonard; scenery, Jerry Williams; lighting, Jonathan Duff; costumes, Ferruccio Garavaglia. With Lillian Evans, Woody Eney, I. M. Hobson, Nancy Leonard, Woody Skaggs, Bettye Fitzpatrick.

Arena Theater: Arena Stage

U.S.A. (1). November 15, 1971. By John Dos Passos and Paul Shyre; from the triology by John Dos Passos. Director, Jack Westin; lighting, John Hagen. With Timothy Casey, Woody Skaggs, Joel Stedman, Karen Shallo, Justine Wasieleuski, Marifran Yoder, Lauren Carner.

WHAT THE BUTLER SAW (36). By Joe Orton. December 23, 1971. Director, Beth

CHILD'S PLAY (38). By Robert Marasco. May 25, 1972. Director, Beth Sanford; scenery, Jerry Williams; lighting, John Hagan, William Trotman. With William Trotman, George Ebeling, Timothy Casey, Rutherford Cravens, Michael Hall, David McCarver.

Sanford; scenery, Paul Prentiss; lighting, Jonathan Duff, Ferruccio Garavaglia. With William Hardy, Justine Wasielewski, Donna O'Connor, I. M. Hobson, Woody Skaggs.

MY SWEET CHARLIE (13). By David Westheimer. February 3, 1972. Director, William Glover; scenery and costumes, Jerry Williams; lighting, John Hagen. With Charles Robinson, Lauren Carner.

KANSAS CITY, MO.

Missouri Repertory Theater

MEASURE FOR MEASURE (17). By William Shakespeare. July 1, 1971. Director, John Houseman; scenery, Jack Montgomery; lighting, Charles Weeks; costumes, Richard Hieronymus; music, Virgil Thomson. With Art Ellison, Alvah Stanley, Robert Scogin, Vivian Ferrara, Valerie von Volz, LoElla Deffenbaugh.

THE SUBJECT WAS ROSES (12). By Frank D. Gilroy. July 8, 1971. Director, Robin Humphrey; scenery and costumes, Jack Montgomery; lighting, Charles Weeks. With Al Christy, Ronetta Wallman, Robert Elliott.

THE WALTZ OF THE TOREADORS (15). By Jean Anouilh; translated by Lucienne Hill. July 15, 1971. Director, John O'Shaughnessy; scenery, Jack Montgomery; lighting, Charles Weeks; costumes, Barbara J. Costa. With Richard Halverson, Harriet Levitt, Ronetta Wallman.

THE NIGHT THOREAU SPENT IN JAIL (15). By Jerome Lawrence and Robert E. Lee. July 22, 1971. Director, Rod Alexander; scenery, J. Morton Walker; lighting, Charles Weeks; costumes, Richard Hieronymus. With Art Ellison, Ronetta Wallman, Alvah Stanley.

THE SCHOOL FOR WIVES (15). By Molière; translated by Donald Frame. August 5, 1971. Director, John O'Shaughnessy; scenery, Jack Montgomery; lighting, Charles Weeks; costumes, Richard Hieronymus. With Alvah Stanley, Richard Halverson, Valerie von Volz, Art Ellison.

AN ENEMY OF THE PEOPLE (15). By Henrik Ibsen; translated by Allen Fletcher. August 12, 1971. Director, Patricia McIlrath; scenery, Max Beatty; lighting, Charles Weeks; costumes, Richard Hieronymus. With Alvah Stanley, Harriet Levitt, Al Christy, Robert Elliott.

LAKEWOOD, OHIO

Great Lakes Shakespeare Festival

OTHELLO (20). By William Shakespeare. July 9, 1971. Director, Lawrence Carra; scenery, Milton Howarth; lighting, Frederic Youens; costumes, William French. With Roger Robinson, Charles Berendt, Norma Joseph, Judith Shogren, Bruce Gray.

YOU NEVER CAN TELL (15). By George Bernard Shaw. July 14, 1971. Director, Law-

rence Carra; scenery and lighting, Frederic Youens; costumes, William French. With Brenda Bergstrom, John Milligan, Robert Englund, Judith Shogren, Mary Lindsay, Keith Mackey.

THE TAMING OF THE SHREW (15). By William Shakespeare. July 28, 1971. Director, Lawrence Carra; scenery, Milton Howarth;

lighting, Frederic Youens; costumes, William French. With Keith Mackey, Mary Lindsay, Norma Joseph, Bruce Gray.

GODSPELL (17). Conceived by John-Michael Tebelak; based on the Gospel according to St. Matthew; music and new lyrics by Stephen Schwartz. August 11, 1971. Director, John-Michael Tebelak; scenery and lighting, Frederic Youens; costumes, William French; music

performed and directed by Woodsmoke. With members of the Great Lakes Shakespeare Festival Company.

HENRY IV, PART 1 (7). By William Shakespeare. August 25, 1971. Director, Lawrence Carra; scenery, Milton Howarth; lighting, Frederic Youens; costumes, William French. With Robert Allman, John Milligan, Robert Denison, Keith Mackey, Juliet Shogren.

LOS ANGELES

Center Theater Group: Mark Taper Forum

THE TRIAL OF THE CATONSVILLE NINE (54). By Daniel Berrigan, S.J. June 17, 1971. Director, Gordon Davidson; scenery, Peter Wexler; lighting, Tharon Musser; costumes, Albert Wolsky. With Ed Flanders, Douglass Watson, Donald Moffat, Gwen Arner, William Schallert.

MAJOR BARBARA (54). By George Bernard Shaw. August 26, 1971. Director, Edward Parone; scenery, Romain Johnston; lighting, Tharon Musser; costumes, Noel Taylor. With Blythe Danner, Diana Webster, Norman Lloyd, David Birney, Scott Hylands.

GODSPELL (54). By John-Michael Tebelak, based on the Gospel according to St. Matthew; music and new lyrics, Stephen Schwartz. November 4, 1971. Director, John-Michael Tebelak and Nina Faso; scenery, Peter Wexler; lighting, H. R. Poindexter; costumes, Susan Tsu. With Lamar Alford, Roberta Baum, David Haskell, Lynne Thigpen.

HERE ARE LADIES (18). From the works of Irish writers. January 24, 1972. Director-designer, Sean Kenny; music, Sean O'Riada. With Siobhan McKenna. In repertory with THE WORKS OF BECKETT (18). Adapted by Jack MacGowran. January 25, 1972. Scenery and lighting, Sean Kenny; costumes, Theoni V. Aldredge. With Jack MacGowran.

VOLPONE (54). By Ben Jonson; adapted with music and lyrics by Jack Rowe, Timothy Near, Holly Near, Cordes Langley. March 9, 1972 (world premiere). Director, Edward Parone; scenery, Ming Cho Lee; lighting, Martin Aronstein; costumes, Noel Taylor.

Mosca	Sam Waterston
Girl	Kristin Helmore
1st Servant	Jack Rowe
2d Servant	Ernest Harada
3d Servant	Ronald Warden
4th Servant; Court Attendant	Ted Pejovich
Volpone	Avery Schreiber
Voltore	Herb Edelman
Corvino	John Schuck
Corbaccio	William Schallert
Canina	Joyce Van Patten
Colomba	Marian Mercer
Leone	Adam West
Police Lieutenant	Anthony Costello
Cops	Richard Doran, Herman Poppe
Judge	Ezra Stone

The action of the musical takes place in the course of one day in San Francisco, 1872, in the homes of Colpone, Corvino, Corbaccio, as well as a San Francisco courtroom. Two acts.

OLD TIMES (54). By Harold Pinter. May 25, 1972. Director, Jeff Bleckner; scenery, Santo Loquasto; lighting, Tharon Musser. With Verna Bloom, W. B. Brydon, Faye Dunaway.

Note: Center Theater Group's 1972 season at the Mark Taper Forum will also include *The Goodbye People* by Herb Gardner, August 10-September 24; and *Henry IV, Part 1* by William Shakespeare, directed by Gordon Davidson, October 26-December 10.

Center Theater Group: Mark Taper Forum—New Theater For Now

June 1, 1971 through May 31, 1972. Each program received 6 performances. All are world premieres.

AUBREY BEARDSLEY, THE NEOPHYTE, by Jon Renn McDonald. Director, Michael Montel; scenery, costumes and masks, Jeremy Railton; lighting, Donald Harris; music and musical direction, Harold Oblong.

Young Girl with a Cat	Catherine Burns
Saint Anthony	Bill Callaway
Aubrey Beardsley	David Dukes
Monther; Venus; St. Rose of Lima	Sharon Gans
Waiter; Musician	Harold Oblong
Oscar Wilde; Fat Dancer	Robert H. Rovin
John Grey; Roderick Usher	Leon Russom
Mabel; Mlle. de Maupin	Louise Sorel

James A. MacNeil;
Mephistopheles ....Clyde Ventura
Asomuel ....Paul Winfield
Two acts.

TEN COM. ZIP COM. ZIP by Matthew Silverman. Director, Edward Parone; scenery, Michael Devine; lighting, Donald Harris.
Leslie ....Barra Grant
Teddy ....Michael Pataki
Marshall ....Mark Bramhall
Blanch ....Barbara Colby
Estelle ....Helene Winston
Rochelle ....Ayn Ruymen
Rosewall ....Larry Ferguson
The action takes place in Berkeley and the upper West Side of New York City, 1970. Two acts.

A MEETING BY THE RIVER by Christopher Isherwood and Don Bachardy; based on Christopher Isherwood's novel of the same name. Director, James Bridges; scenery and costumes, Jeremy Railton; lighting, Donald Harris.
Oliver ....Sam Waterston
Mother ....Florida Friebus
Patrick ....Laurence Luckinbill
Penelope ....Susan Brown
Tom ....Gordon Hoban

Rafferty ....Jason Wingreen
Senior Swamis ..Logan Ramsey, Sirri Murad
Junior Swami; Friend;
Porter ....John Ritter
Brachmachari; Friend;
Porter ....Jack Bender
Passport Official;
Photographer ....Siri Murad
Two acts.

IN A FINE CASTLE by Derek Walcott. Director, Edward Parone; scenery and lighting, Donald Harris; costumes, Jeremy Railton.
Brown ....Georg Stanford Brown
Flag Dancer ....William Couser
Shelly ....Paula Kelly
Agatha ....Diana Webster
Oswald ....Kurt Kasznar
George ....Davis Roberts
Clodia ....Joan Van Ark
Antoine ....Marco St. John
Michael ....Anthony Sweeting
Sidney Prince ....Jason Bernard
Elizabeth Prince ....Mitzi Hoag
On the rim of the Grand Savannah in Port of Spain there is a crescent of fantastical architecture, but the castle in this fantasy is a composite, and its family is not meant to represent any previous or present owners. Two acts.

Center Theater Group: Ahmanson Theater

A FUNNY THING HAPPENED ON THE WAY TO THE FORUM (47). Book by Burt Shevelove and Larry Gelbart, based on the plays of Plautus; music and lyrics, Stephen Sondheim. October 12, 1971. Director, Burt Shevelove; scenery, James Trittipo; lighting, H. R. Poindexter; costumes, Noel Taylor; choreography, Ralph Beaumont; music and vocal director, Jack Lee. With Phil Silvers, Nancy Walker, Larry Blyden, Lew Parker, Carl Ballantine, Reginald Owen.

THE CAINE MUTINY COURT-MARTIAL (47). By Herman Wouk. November 30, 1971. Director, Henry Fonda; scenery and lighting, H. R. Poindexter; costumes, Noel Taylor.

With Hume Cronyn, John Forsythe, Andrew Prine, Joe Don Baker, Edward Binns, Paul Stewart, Bruce Davison.

SLEUTH (47). By Anthony Shaffer. January 11, 1972. Director, Clifford Williams; scenery and costumes, Carl Toms; lighting, William Ritman. With Anthony Quayle, Donal Donnelly.

RICHARD II (47). By William Shakespeare. March 7, 1972. Director, Jonathan Miller; scenery and lighting, H. R. Poindexter; costumes, Gabriella Falk. With Richard Chamberlain, Sorrell Booke, Patrick Hines, Jack Ryland, Priscilla Morrill.

The Season Elsewhere in Los Angeles

By Rick Talcove

Theater critic of the Van Nuys, Calif. *Valley News*

Any discussion of theater in Los Angeles must begin with one word: expansion. On any given week in any given month a casual browsing of the Los Angeles *Times* theater listings will offer some 50 or more productions to choose from . . . and the number is not infrequently as high as 65. Some of these productions, of course, represent community and college productions. But you're likely to find Equity workshops sprouting up anywhere, as well as commercial ventures coming and going, and occasionally staying.

Certainly the well-subsidized productions at the Music Center (the Ahmanson and Mark Taper Forum for plays; the Dorothy Chandler Pavilion for musicals) as well as the Huntington Hartford bring much prestige to Los Angeles theatergoers. They do not, however, bring the greatest number of productions. For prolific producing, you go to the Company Theater where it is not unlikely to have three or four shows going strong, sometimes in a performance schedule that defies the imagination.

Basically, the Los Angeles playgoer is either loyal or diverse. He may exclusively patronize the Century City Playhouse for Feiffer and Orton or he may stick with more conventional fare with the Civic Light Opera or Center Theater Group's Ahmanson.

From a news standpoint, the most important event during the entire season was the decision by Actors Equity to withdraw the mandatory 8 performance limit on professional workshop productions. These were presentations where actors paid dues to support their "workshop" and perform within a specifically limited time. Although theoretically any theatergoer could see these productions by making reservations, Equity's rules made it more advantageous to groups to reserve their talents for critics and people within the entertainment industry, at no cost to the audience (no admission can be charged) but virtually lost to most people.

During a special one-year trial period, workshops with fewer than 100 seats will be able to charge admission and run as long as they can; overall, a sensible and long-needed plan that hopefully will boost production even more.

As for the kinds of presentations, occasionally three community groups offer *Plaza Suite* simultaneously. Most of the time, though, it's as diverse as possible: Brecht, Shakespeare, Williams and many plays New York rejected perhaps a bit too soon, plus probably more "originals" than anyone can count.

The following list is a selection of the most noteworthy commercially-produced productions staged during the year. The list does not include the numerous touring shows nor any of the workshop offerings, nor the Center Theater Group productions at the Ahmanson and the Mark Taper (see the Regional Theater listing above). A plus sign (+) with the performance number signifies the show was still running on June 1, 1972.

Century City Playhouse: Theater Now Troupe

WHAT THE BUTLER SAW (39). By Joe Orton. September 17, 1971. Director, David Sheldon; scenery, Bill Todd; lighting and sound, Theater-tec. With Herb Armstrong, Susan Harting, Barrie Claire, Ken Smedberg, Robert Cornthwaite, Rick Hirst.

KINGDOM OF EARTH (30). By Tennessee Williams. January 7, 1972. Director, Adrienna Marsen; scenery, Barry Frost; lighting, Joseph Sculler; sound, Narda Lesher. With Bari Silvern, Michael Pataki, John McMurtry.

STEAMBATH (2+). By Bruce Jay Friedman. May 27, 1972. Director, Bari Silvern; scenery, Robin Swede; With Terrence Locke, Walter Koenig, G.J. Mitchell, Dale Baldridge Jr., Abbi Anderson.

Company Theater

THE JAMES JOYCE MEMORIAL LIQUID THEATER (10). November 13, 1971. Conceived and directed by Steven Kent in conjunction with the Company Theater Ensemble; music by Jack Rowe, Lance Larsen, Bob Walter, Daniel Sonneborn; designed by Donald Harris. With the ensemble of The Company Theater.

CALIBAN (52+). By Michael Monroe. November 26, 1971 (world premiere). Director, Steven Kent; scenery, Russell Pyle; lighting, Gladys Carmichael; costumes, Steven Kent, Marcina Motter; film sequences, William Dannevik; additional movement and musical staging, Joan Tewkesbury Maguire; music, Daniel Sonneborn, Michael Monroe, Steven Kent.

Trinculo	Gar Campbell
Stephano	Bill Hunt
Caliban	Dennis Redfield
Ariel	Barry Opper
Alonso	Larry Hoffman
Sebastian	Michael Stefani
Antonio	Richard Serpe
Gonzalo	Arthur Allen
Ferdinand	Wiley Rinaldi/Jerry Hoffman
Miranda	Trish Soodik
Prospero	Michael Carlin Pierce
Sycorax	Candace Laughlin
Michelet	J. Thomas Hudgins
Mary Mark	Barbara Grover

CHAMBER MUSIC (17). By Arthur Kopit. January 13, 1972. Director, Michael Carlin Pierce; scenery and lighting, Donald Harris. With Marcina Motter, Roxann Pyle, Bill Hunt, Lance Larsen, Polita Marks, Gladys Carmichael, Sandra Morgan, Nancy Hickey, Barbara Grover, Dennis Redfield.

THE GLOAMING, OH MY DARLING (17). By Megan Terry. January 13, 1972. Director, Steven Kent; scenery, Donald Harris; lighting, Russell Pyle; additional staging, Joan Tewkesbury Maguire; music, Steven Kent. With Candace Laughlin, Trish Soodik, Michael Carlin Pierce, Barbara Grover, Bill Hunt, Lori Landrin, Nancy Hickey, Marcina Motter, Daniel Sonneborn, Jerry Hoffman.

THE EMERGENCE (15+). A commissioned work by Ama Giesta Fleming and the Company Theater Ensemble. February 17, 1972. Director, Steven Kent; scenery and lighting, Russell Pyle; costumes, Steven Kent, Ted Shell; choreography, Roger Barnes; music, Kerri Gillette, Steven Kent, Wiley Rinaldi, Jack Rowe, Robert Walter. With Polita Marks, Barbara Grover, Arthur Allen, Larry Hoffman, William Dannevik, Jerry Hoffman, J. Thomas Hudgins, Daniel Sonneborn, Richard Vetter, Steven Kent, Elinor Graham, Lance Larsen, Sandra Morgan, Wiley Rinaldi, Bill Hunt, Michael Carlin Pierce, Barry Opper, Dennis Redfield, Trish Soodik, Candace Laughlin, Roxann Pyle, Marcina Motter, Lori Landrin, Nancy Hickey, Knut Hoff.

The Los Angeles Art Ensemble and Grill

VOLUME ONE (6). March 26, 1972. Comprising INTERSECTIONS 7 by Paul Epstein, director, Steven Kent; THE CHERUB by Michael McClure, director, Steven Kent; BALLS by Paul Foster, director, Steven Kent; PASSION PLAY by Stephen Foreman, director, Larry Hoffman; THE MEATBALL by Michael McClure, director, Steven Kent. Designers, Russell Pyle, John Sefick, Roger Barnes, Ted Shell. With Nancy Hickey, Jerry Hoffman, Candace Laughlin, Roxann Pyle, Dennis Redfield, J. Thomas Hudgins, Roger Barnes, Bill Hunt, Michael Carlin Pierce, Arthur Allen, Polita Marks, Larry Hoffman, Marcina Motter, Sandra Morgan, Barbara Grover, Lance Larsen, Richard Serpe, Steven Kent.

VOLUME TWO (3+). May 14, 1972. Comprising CRABS by Sally Ordway, director, Michael Carlin Pierce; RIDERS TO THE SEA by John Millington Synge, director, Dennis Redfield; CROSS-COUNTRY by Sally Ordway, director, Michael Carlin Pierce; THE CONQUEST OF EVEREST by Arthur Kopit, director, Larry Hoffman. Designers, Russell Pyle, John Sefick. With Larry Hoffman, Trish Soodik, Lance Larsen, Nancy Hickey, William Dannevik, Sandra Morgan, Polita Marks, Jerry Hoffman, Richard Serpe.

At Some Other Los Angeles Theaters

A CIRCLE ON THE GROUND (20). By John Groves. January 28, 1972 (world premiere). Director, Jackson Phippin; scenery and lighting, John Sherwood; costumes, Judith Grant. At the Gallery Theater.

First Actor; Gandhi	James Tartan
First Actress;	
Madeleine Slade	Jan Burrell
Director	Albert Lord
Clown	Ben Frank
Second Actor; Mahadev;	
Nehru	Larry Simpasa
Second Actress; Kasturba	Bara Byrnes

Two acts.

THE HOUSE OF BLUE LEAVES (72). By John Guare. January 18, 1972. Director, Frank Hamilton; scenery, Conrad Penrod. With Alice Ghostley, Harold Gould, Katherine Helmond. At the Huntington Hartford Theater.

THE WAKE (32). By Steve Allen. September 28, 1971 (world premiere). Director and designer, Kay E. Kuter; costumes, Kevin G. Tracey. At the Masquers Club.

Josephine Scanlon	Pat Marlowe
Margaret Scanlon	Lisabeth Field
John O'Toole	Clancy Cooper
Tommy Monaghan	Len Finney
David Considine	Gene Andrusco
Mike Scanlon	Frank Scannell
Mary McCaffrey	Opal Euard
Sarah McCaffrey	Dorothy Crehan
Rose Scanlon O'Brien	Helena Nash
Father Morrisey	Jonathan Hole
Jack Scanlon	Sean McClory
Molly Fitzgerald	Gertrude Graner
Chuck McDermott	George Riley
Matty Mulcahey	Hal K. Dawson
Belle Scanlon Considine	Dolores Quinton
Nellie Riley	Kathleen O'Malley

Three acts.

HOOTSUDIE (20+). By Lonny Chapman. April 28, 1972 (world premiere). Director, Lonny Chapman; producer, Lou Antonio; scenery, Mike Van Landingham. At the Merle Oberon Playhouse, Actors Studio West.

Hoot	Jim Antonio
Sudie	Lane Bradbury
Milly	Elizabeth Lane

Two acts.

SPOON RIVER (8+). By Charles Aidman; based on Edgar Lee Masters' *Spoon River Anthology*. May 19, 1972. Director, Charles Aidman; scenery, Donald Harris; costumes, Donald Bruce; lighting, Michael Murnane. With Philip Abbott, Charles Aidman, Betty Garrett, Hal Lynch, Joyce Van Patten, Peggy Walton. At Theater West.

LOUISVILLE, KY.

Actors Theater of Louisville

PLAY IT AGAIN, SAM (17). By Woody Allen. August 24, 1971. Director, Jon Jory; scenery, Hal Tine; lighting, Judy Rasmuson; costumes, Paul Owen. With Arnold Stang, Ken Jenkins, Katharine Houghton.

THE PRIME OF MISS JEAN BRODIE (7). By Jay Allen, adapted from the novel by Muriel Spark. September 14, 1971. Director, Jon Jory; scenery, Dusty Reeds; lighting, Geoffrey Cunningham; costumes, Paul Owen. With Peggy Cowles, Dianne Weist, Mary Michaels, Sandy McCallum, Stanley Anderson.

THE GLASS MENAGERIE (7). By Tennessee Williams. September 21, 1971. Director, Ken Jenkins; scenery, Dusty Reeds; lighting, Geoffrey T. Cunningham; costumes, Paul Owen. With Eunice Anderson, Ken Jenkins, Katharine Houghton, Stanley Anderson.

TRICKS (29). Book by Jon Jory; music by Jerry Blatt; lyrics by Lonnie Burstein; based on Molière's *Scapin*. October 14, 1971 (world premiere). Director, Jon Jory; scenery, Paul Owen; lighting; Geoffrey T. Cunningham; costumes, Kurt Wilhelm; musical director, Richard Berg.

Octave	Ted Pejovich
Sylvestre	Christopher Murney
Scapin	Eric Tavaris
Hyacinthe	Carolyn Connors
Argante	Sandy McCallum
Geronte	Max Wright
Leandre	Stephen Keep
Property Mistress	Adale O'Brien
Zerbinette	Donna Curtis

The Commedia:

Arlechino	Richard Berg
Pedrolino	Karl Kirchner
Pantalone	Stuart Paine
Scaramuccia	Larry Holt
Capitano	Tom Owen

The action takes place in and around Venice. Act I: Prologue and 8 musical numbers. Act II: 6 musical numbers.

NIGHT MUST FALL (14). By Emlyn Williams. November 11, 1971. Director, Christopher Murney; scenery and costumes, Paul Owen; lighting, Johnny Walker. With Leona Maricle, Clarence Felder, Stanley Anderson. And ANGEL STREET (13). By Patrick Hamilton. November 12, 1971. Director, Patrick Tovatt; scenery and costumes, Paul Owen; lighting, Johnny Walker. With Lynn Milgrim, Ken Jenkins, Sandy McCallum. In repertory.

A MIDSUMMER NIGHT'S DREAM (34). By William Shakespeare. December 9, 1971. Director, Jon Jory; scenery, Grady Larkins; lighting, Ron Wallace; costumes, Paul Owen. With Ken Jenkins, Adale O'Brien, Christopher Murney, John Glove, David Clennon, Donna Curtis, Lynn Milgrim, Clarence Felder.

MARAT/SADE (27). By Peter Weiss; English version by Geoffrey Skelton, verse adaptation by Adrian Mitchell. January 13, 1972. Director, Jon Jory; scenery and costumes, Paul Owen; lighting, Geoffrey T. Cunningham. With Clarence Felder, Stanley Anderson, Peggy Cowles, Judith Long.

HEDDA GABLER (14). By Henrik Ibsen. February 10, 1972. Director, Jon Jory; scenery, Grady Larkins; lighting, Geoffrey T. Cunningham; costumes, Paul Owen. With Peggy Cowles, Max Wright, Judith Long, Stanley Anderson.

MY THREE ANGELS (34). By Sam and Bella Spewack. March 9, 1972. Director, Victor Jory; scenery and costumes, Paul Owen; lighting, Johnny Walker. With George Cavey, Dale Carter Cooper, Victor Jory, Sandy McCallum, Christopher Murney.

DEATH OF A SALESMAN (34). By Arthur Miller. April 13, 1972. Director, Jon Jory; scenery and costumes, Paul Owen; lighting, Geoffrey T. Cunningham. With Victor Jory, Jean Inness, Christopher Murney, Joe Hindy.

MILWAUKEE

Milwaukee Repertory Theater Company: Todd Wehr Theater

CAT AMONG THE PIGEONS (44). By Georges Feydeau; translated by John Mortimer. October 8, 1971. Director, Nagle Jackson; scenery, Kert Lundell; lighting, William Mintzer; costumes, James Edmund Brady. With Mary Jane Kimbrough, Josephine Nichols; Charles Kimbrough, William McKereghan.

THE ENGLISH MYSTERY PLAYS (44). An original presentation compiled by Nagle Jackson. November 16, 1971 (world premiere). Director, Nagle Jackson; scenery, Christopher M. Idoine; lighting, William Mintzer; costumes, James Edmund Brady; musical arranger-director, Lorraine Greenberg.
Noah; King Gaspar . . . . Jim Baker
Gossip; Mak's Wife;
    Good Angel . . . . Candace Barrett
Lucifer . . . . Raye Birk
David; Japhet; Pharoah Soldier; Herod
    Soldier; Bad Angel . . . . Jerry Brown
Abel; 3d Shepherd;
    Good Angel . . . . Robert Ground
Cain; 2d Shepherd; Pharoah Soldier; Herod
    Soldier; Bad Angel . . . . Ric Hamilton
God . . . . John Hancock
Shem's Wife; Salome;
    Bad Angel . . . . Stephanie J. Harker
Shem; Pharoah; Mak; King Melchior;
    Good Angel . . . . Jim Jansen
Caesar Augustus; 1st Shepherd;
    Bad Angel . . . . Charles Kimbrough
Eve; Ham's Wife;
    2d Mother . . . . Judith Light
Sirinus, Herod . . . . William McKereghan
Noah's Wife; Elizabeth; 3d Mother;
    Good Angel . . . . Josephine Nichols
Gabriel . . . . Fredi Olster
Gossip; Mary;
    Good Angel . . . . Penelope Reed
Adam; Ham; Moses;
    King Balthasar . . . . Jack Swanson
Abraham, Joseph . . . . Jeffrey Tambor
Japhet's Wife; Tebell; 1st Mother;
    Good Angel . . . . Martha Tippin

Isaac; Caesar's Messenger; Herod's Messenger;
    Soldier, Good Angel . . . . Blake Torney
    Part I: 7 Plays—The Creation, The Killing of Abel, The Play of Noah, Abraham, Pharoah, David, Caesar Augustus. Part II: 5 Plays—The Annunciation, The Salutation of Elizabeth, The Shepherd's Play, The Offering of the Magi, The Flight into Egypt. Two intermissions. Note: The English Mystery Plays: An Easter Cycle, compiled and directed by Raye Birk, was presented on a special two-week tour March 27, 1972.

THE WHITE HOUSE MURDER CASE (44). By Jules Feiffer. December 31, 1971. Director, Rod Alexander; scenery, John Jensen; lighting, William Mintzer; costumes, James Edmund Brady. With Jim Jansen, John Hancock, Jim Baker, Charles Kimbrough, Robert Ground.

MEASURE FOR MEASURE (44). By William Shakespeare. February 11, 1972. Director, Nagle Jackson; scenery, Christopher M. Idoine; lighting, William Mintzer; costumes, James Edmund Brady. With Raye Birk, Jack Swanson, Charles Kimbrough, Judith Light, Candace Barrett, Martha Tippin.

A DELICATE BALANCE (44). By Edward Albee. March 24, 1972. Director, Charles Kimbrough; scenery, Christopher M. Idoine; lighting, William Mintzer; costumes, James Edmund Brady. With Josephine Nichols, Penelope Reed, Mary Jane Kimbrough, William McKereghan.

THE JOURNEY OF THE FIFTH HORSE (44). By Ronald Ribman; based in part on Ivan Turgenev's story Diary of a Superfluous Man. May 5, 1972. Director, Nagle Jackson; scenery, Christopher M. Idoine; lighting, Ken Billington; costumes, James Edmund Brady. With Robert Ground, Judith Light, Jim Baker, Fredi Olster, Jim Jansen, William McKereghan, Jeffrey Tambor, Josephine Nichols.

MINNEAPOLIS

The Guthrie Theater Company: Guthrie Theater

CYRANO DE BERGERAC (34) by Edmond Rostand; translated and adapted by Anthony Burgess. July 22, 1971 (matinee). Director, Michael Langham; scenery and costumes, Desmond Heeley, John Jensen; lighting, Gil Wechsler. With Len Cariou, Paul Hecht, Roberta Maxwell, Ken Pogue.

THE TAMING OF THE SHREW (33). By William Shakespeare. July 22, 1971 (evening). Director, Michael Langham; scenery and costumes, Desmond Heeley and John Jensen; lighting, Gil Wechsler. With Michele Shay, Len Cariou, Roberta Maxwell.

MISALLIANCE (29). By George Bernard Shaw. September 24, 1971. Director, Edward Gilbert; scenery and costumes, Peter Wingate; lighting, Kerry Lafferty. With Sandor Szabo, Betty Leighton, Paul Ballantyne, Bronia Stefan, Briain Petchey, Roberta Maxwell.

A TOUCH OF THE POET (29). By Eugene O'Neill. September 25, 1971. Director, David Wheeler; scenery, John Jensen; lighting, Kerry Lafferty; costumes, Jack Edwards. With Robert Pastene, Barbara Byrne, Penelope Allen, Betty Leighton, Ken Pogue.

THE DIARY OF A SCOUNDREL (32). By Alexander Ostrovsky; translated by Rodney Ackland. November 9, 1971. Director, Michael Langham; scenery, John Jensen; lighting, Gil Wechsler; costumes, Desmond Heeley. With Len Cariou, Robert Pastene, Mary Savidge, Ellin Gorky, Sandor Szabo, Barbara Byrne.

CYRANO DE BERGERAC (14). By Edmond Rostand; translated and adapted by Anthony Burgess. December 10, 1971. Director, Michael Langham; scenery and costumes, Desmond Heeley, John Jensen; lighting, Gil Wechsler. With James Blendick, Diana Barrington, Leon Pownall.

THE TAMING OF THE SHREW (17). By William Shakespeare. December 3, 1971. Director, Michael Langham; scenery and costumes, Desmond Heeley, John Jensen; lighting, Gil Wechsler. With Michele Shay, Len Cariou, Mary Hitch.

FABLES HERE AND THEN (8). An arrangement of myths, tales, legends, from the Chinese, Japanese, African, American Indian and contemporary sources. December 20, 1971. Director, David Feldshuh. With members of the Guthrie Theater Company.

NEW HAVEN

Long Wharf Theater

YOU CAN'T TAKE IT WITH YOU (25). By Moss Hart and George S. Kaufman. October 22, 1971. Director, Arvin Brown; scenery, Kert Lundell; lighting, Judy Rasmuson; costumes, James Edmund Brady. With Teresa Wright, William Swetland, Emery Battis, Patricia Pearcy, James Naughton, Carol Teitel.

THE CONTRACTOR (25). By David Storey. November 19, 1971 (American premiere). Director, Barry Davis; scenery, Elmon Webb and Virginia Dancy; lighting, Ron Wallace; costumes, Whitney Blausen.

Kay	John Braden
Marshall	John Cazale
Ewbank	William Swetland
Fitzpatrick	Emery Battis
Bennett	James Naughton
Paul	Christopher Hastings
Claire	Patricia Pearcy
Glendenning	Tom Atkins
Old Ewbank	John Cromwell
Maurice	Peter Brouwer
Old Mrs. Ewbank	Ruth Nelson
Mrs. Ewbank	Carol Teitel

Time: The present, late summer. Place: The lawn of the Ewbanks' house, somewhere in the North of England. Three acts.

A STREETCAR NAMED DESIRE (33). By Tennessee Williams. December 17, 1971. Director, Barry Davis; scenery, Elmon Webb and Virginia Dancy; lighting, Judy Rasmuson; costumes, Bill Walker. With Joyce Ebert, Tom Atkins, Laurie Kennedy.

HAMLET (25). By William Shakespeare. January 21, 1972. Director, Arvin Brown; scenery, John Conklin; lighting, Ron Wallace; costumes, John Conklin and Whitney Blausen. With Stacy Keach, Stefan Gierasch, William Swetland, James Naughton, Joyce Ebert, Kitty Winn.

THE WAY OF THE WORLD (25). By William Congreve. February 18, 1972. Director, Malcolm Black; scenery, David Jenkins; lighting, Judy Rasmuson; costumes, Bill Walker.

With Peter Donat, Gordon Gould, Emery Battis, Patricia Pearcy, Joyce Ebert, Roberta Maxwell, June Connell.

TROIKA: AN EVENING OF RUSSIAN COMEDY (25). Adapted by Morris Carnovsky. March 17, 1972. THE COUNTRY WOMAN (American premiere) by Ivan Turgenev, director, Morris Carnovsky, with Joyce Ebert, Mat Conley, Helen Verbit, John Braden; THE WEDDING by Anton Chekhov, director, Morris Carnovsky, with Emery Battis, Martha Schlamme, Tom Atkins, William Swetland, Will Lee, Helen Verbit; A SWAN SONG by Anton Chekhov, director, Arvin Brown, with Morris Carnovsky, Will Lee. Scenery, Elmon Webb and Virginia Dancy; lighting, Ron Wallace; costumes, Bill Walker.

THE ICEMAN COMETH (25). By Eugene O'Neill. April 14, 1972. Director, Arvin

Brown; scenery, Elmon Webb and Virginia Dancy; lighting, Ron Wallace; costumes, Whitney Blausen. With William Swetland, John Beal, George Ede, William Hansen, Emery Battis, Patricia Pearcy, Lee Wallace.

PATRICK'S DAY (25). By Bill Morrison. May 12, 1972 (world premiere). Director, Edward Gilbert; scenery, Elmon Webb, Virginia Dancy; lighting, Ron Wallace; costumes, Bill Walker.

Patrick Power ....Fritz Weaver
Myra Power ....Nancy Marchand
Watt Taylor ....Andy Robinson
Louis Molloy ....Tom Atkins
Aideen ....Kitty Winn
Eddie ....Frank Speiser
Dominic ....George Ede
Feeny ....Emery Battis
Dr. Brennan ....William Swetland
Three acts.

Long Wharf Theater: Children's Theater

ROBIN HOOD (7). By Elaine Berman. October 15, 1971. Director, Isaac Schambelan; scenery, Dennis Dougherty; lighting, Tarrant Smith; costumes, Bill Walker. With Richard Marion, Suzanne Lederer, Guy Boyd, Dan Held.

ALICE IN WONDERLAND (7). Based on Lewis Carroll's book; music by Michael Posnick. December 4, 1971. Director, Michael Posnick; scenery and lighting, Tarrant Smith; costumes, Bill Walker; projections, Arthur Howard. With Susan Merson, Dan Held, Robert Hitt, Guy Boyd.

DEPUTY ANNE (7). Created by the Long Wharf Children's Theater Company. January 29, 1972 (world premiere). Director, Isaac Schambelan; scenery and lighting, Tarrant Smith; costumes, Luise Zito; music, Richard

Marion; musical director, Lee Bissell.
Anne ....Suzanne Lederer
Doc ....Guy Boyd
Jerome ....Richard Marion
Fenster ....Dan Held
Anne's Mother; Molly ....Carol Morell
Sheriff Dick ....Robert Hitt
Sleazy Jake ....Mark Winkworth
Sleeping Dawn ....Susan Merson

HANS CHRISTIAN ANDERSEN FABLES: THE EMPEROR'S NIGHTINGALE; THE SWINEHERD; THE EMPEROR'S NEW CLOTHES (7). Story Theater adaptations by Rhoda Levine. March 25, 1972. Director, Rhoda Levine; scenery and lighting, Tarrant Smith; costumes, Sherry Morley. With Dan Held, Terrance Sherman, Mark Winkworth, Susan Merson, Richard Marion, Suzanne Lederer, Robert Hitt, Carol Morell.

Yale Repertory Theater

Fall rotating repertory:

WHEN WE DEAD AWAKEN (22). By Henrik Ibsen; translated by Michael Feingold. October 14, 1971. Director, Tom Haas; scenery and costumes, Steven Rubin; lighting, Edgar Swift. With Nancy Wickwire, Stephen Mendillo, Sarah Albertson, Carmen De Lavallade, Bill Gearhart.

THE BIG HOUSE (22). By Lonnie Carter. October 21, 1971. Director, Robert Brustein; scenery and costumes, Steven Rubin; lighting, Dennis L. Dorn; music, Maury Yeston; chore-

ography, Carmen De Lavallade. With Dick Shawn, Jeremy Geidt, Elizabeth Parrish, Tony De Santis, James Brick.

CALIGULA (22). By Albert Camus; adapted from the French by Justin O'Brien. November 25, 1971. Director, Alvin Epstein; scenery and costumes, Steven Rubin; lighting, Nathan L. Drucker. With Christopher Walken, Nancy Wickwire, James Brick, David Hurst, Jeremy Geidt, Stephen Mendillo.

Mini-season (each production runs about one week):

THE SEVEN DEADLY SINS, translated by W. H. Auden and Chester Kallman, director,

Alvin Epstein; and THE LITTLE MAHAGONNY, translated by Michael Feingold, adapted by Ellis M. Pryce-Jones, director, Michael Posnick. By Bertolt Brecht and Kurt Weill. January 20, 1972. Scenery and costumes, Santo Loquasto; lighting, Al Kibbe; musical director, Thomas Fay. With Jeremy Geidt, Elizabeth Parrish, Carmen De Lavallade, James Brick, Jack Litten, John McAndrew.

PASSION by Edward Bond. February 1, 1972 (American premiere). Director, Michael Posnick; scenery and costumes, Ellis M. Pryce-Jones; lighting, Al Kibbe.

Narrator ....James Brick
Dead Soldier ....Bill Gearhart
Old Woman ....Sarah Albertson
Queen ....Elizabeth Parrish
Prime Minister ....Paul Schierhorn
Magician ....Jeremy Geidt
Little Girl ....Rosemary Stewart
Jesus ....Herb Downer

In rotating repertory:

I MARRIED YOU FOR THE FUN OF IT (22). By Natalia Ginzburg; translated by John Hersey. February 17, 1972 (American premiere). Director, Roger Hendricks Simon; scenery and costumes, Steven Rubin; lighting, William B. Warfel.

Pietro ....Alvin Epstein
Giuliana ....Joan Welles
Vittoria ....Stephanie Cotsirilos
Pietro's Mother ....Elizabeth Parrish
Camelia ....Sarah Albertson

LIFE IS A DREAM (22). By Pedro Calderon de la Barca; English version by Roy Campbell; music by Sarah S. Meneely. February 24, 1972. Director, Jacques Burdick; scenery, Gary James Wheeler; lighting, Ian Calderon; costumes, Michelle Guillot. With Nancy Wickwire, Jeremy Geidt, Stephen Joyce, Thomas Barbour, James Brick, Carmen De Lavallade, David Hurst.

HAPPY END (22). By Dorothy Lane; American adaptation and lyrics by Michael Feingold; lyrics by Bertolt Brecht; music by Kurt Weill. April 6, 1972 (American premiere). Director, Michael Posnick; musical director, Thomas Fay; scenery, lighting and projections,

Buddha ....Jonathan Marks

STOPS by Robert Auletta. February 1, 1972 (world premiere). Director, Michael Posnick; scenery and costumes, Ellis M. Pryce-Jones; lighting, Al Kibbe.

Mattie ....Joan Pape
Jeff ....Jeremy Geidt
Irene ....Sarah Albertson
Young Man ....James Brick

JACQUES BREL IS ALIVE AND WELL AND LIVING IN PARIS. English translation by Mort Schuman, Eric Blau and the Jacques Brel Company. February 8, 1972. Director, David Schweizer; scenery, Ellis M. Pryce-Jones; lighting, Al Kibbe; musical direction and arrangements, Steven Blier. With Stephanie Cotsirilos, Bill Horwitz, Glenn J. Mure, Julie Preston and the Jacques Brel Company.

Raymond C. Recht; costumes, Michael H. Yeargan.

The Gang:
Bill Cracker ....Stephen Joyce
Jimmy Dexter ....David Hurst
Johnny Flint ....James Brick
Bob Marker ....Thomas Barbour
Sam Wurlitzer ....Jeremy Geidt
Dr. Nakamura ....Alvin Epstein
Lady in Gray ....Elizabeth Parrish
Miriam ....Rosemary Stewart

The Salvation Army:
Maj. Stone ....Nancy Wickwire
Capt. Hannibal Jackson ..John McAndrew
Lt. Lillian Holiday ....Stephanie Cotsirilos
Sister Mary Pritchard ....Joan Welles
Sister Jane Grant ....Sara Albertson
Brother Ben Owens ....Herb Downer
1st Man ....Yannis Simonides
2d Man ....Bill Gearhart
Cop ....Paul Schierhorn

The Fold: Lisa Carling, Dean Lanier Radcliffe, Yannis Simonidea. Place: Chicago. Time: 1919. Act I: Bill's Beer Hall. Act II: The Salvation Army Mission, Canal Street. Act III, Scene 1: The Beer Hall. Scene 2: The Mission.

Yale Repertory Theater: Experimental Program

THREE CUCKOLDS by Leon Katz; adapted from Italian "commedia," November 2-6, 1971; TROILUS AND CRESSIDA by William Shakespeare, December 4-8, 1971; IN GOOD KING CHARLES' GOLDEN DAYS by George Bernard Shaw, February 8-12.

Yale Repertory Theater: Sunday Night Series

EVIDENCE by Stephen Taylor, director, Steve Robman, January 23, 1972; CRUCI-   FICADO by Edgar White, February 27, 1972. Artistic director of series, Eva Vizy.

Note: The Yale Repertory Theater and Drama School also present Children's Theater, a Workshop Series, Yale Cabaret, Studio Projects and Main Stage Productions with students, members of the Repertory Theater and faculty members.

PROVIDENCE, R.I.

Trinity Square Repertory Company: Trinity Square Playhouse

CHILD'S PLAY (64). By Robert Marasco. September 21, 1971 (re-opened February 1, 1972). Director, Adrian Hall; scenery, David Jenkins; lighting, Roger Morgan; costumes, John Lehmeyer. With William Cain, James Eichelberger, David C. Jones, Richard Kneeland.

TROILUS AND CRESSIDA (48). By William Shakespeare. November 1, 1971. Director, Adrian Hall; scenery, Eugene Lee; lighting, Roger Morgan; costumes, Betsey Potter. With William Cain, Joseph Culliton, Donald Somers, Jobeth Williams.

DOWN BY THE RIVER WHERE WATER-LILIES ARE DISFIGURED EVERY DAY (40). By Julie Bovasso. December 20, 1971 (world premiere). Director, Adrian Hall; scenery, Eugene Lee; lighting, Roger Morgan; costumes, A. Christina Giannini; music, Richard Cumming.

Phoebe Snow ....James Eichelberger
Clement ....Richard Kneeland
Count Josef ....William Cain
Count Junior ....Thomas R. Mason
Constantine ....David Kennett
Herschel ....Howard London
Missy ....Timothy Crowe
Sissy ....Richard Kavanaugh
Barry Zap ....William Damkoehler
Queen Nell ....David C. Jones
King Arny ....George Martin
Prince Percy ....Jon Kimbell
The Joint Chiefs of Staff:
  General Hunt ....Donald Somers
  General Buckley ....Robert J. Colonna
  Admiral Duncan ....Alan Tongret
  Admiral Mitchell ....Bree Cavazos
  General Williamson ......Howard London
Paratrooper ....Richard Jenkins
The place is here. The action ranges back and forth from a high-rise apartment to the office of the Prime Minister, to a slum tenement. A revolution is in progress. Two acts.

THE SCHOOL FOR WIVES (80). By Molière; English verse translation by Richard Wilbur. March 1, 1972. Director, Adrian Hall; scenery, Robert D. Soule; lighting, Roger Morgan; costumes, A. Christina Giannini. With Cynthia Wells, Robert J. Colonna, Richard Jenkins, Barbara Orson.

THE PRICE (48). By Arthur Miller. April 11, 1972. Director, Larry Arrick, scenery, Robert D. Soule; lighting, Roger Morgan. With Michael Gorrin, George Martin, William Cain, Barbara Orson.

ROCHESTER, MICH.

Oakland University Professional Theater Program: Meadow Brook Theater

THE MATCHMAKER (27). By Thornton Wilder. October 14, 1971. Director, Terence Kilburn; scenery and lighting, Richard Davis; costumes, Mary Schakel. With Harry Ellerbe, Robert Englund, Bruce Gray, Elizabeth Orion, Naomi Stevens.

THE ANDERSONVILLE TRIAL (27). By Saul Levitt. November 11, 1971. Director, Charles Nolte; scenery and lighting, Richard Davis; costumes, Mary Schakel. With Booth Colman, J. L. Dahlmann, Bernard Kates, William Needles, Charles Nolte.

HEARTBREAK HOUSE (27). By George Bernard Shaw. December 9, 1971. Director, Terence Kilburn; scenery and lighting, Richard Davis; costumes, Mary Schakel. With Jack Bell, Harry Ellerbe, Christopher Ross-Smith, Angela Wood.

THE GLASS MENAGERIE (27). By Tennessee Williams. January 6, 1972. Director, Terence Kilburn; scenery and lighting, Richard Davis; costumes, Mary Schakel. With Diane Bugas, David Himes, David Little, Elizabeth Orion.

THE ODD COUPLE (27). By Neil Simon. February 3, 1972. Director, John Going; scenery and lighting, Richard Davis; costumes, Mary Schakel. With J. L. Dahlmann, Page Johnson, William Le Massena, Bradlee Shattuck.

A DOLL'S HOUSE (27). By Henrik Ibsen. March 2, 1972. Director, Terence Kilburn; scenery and lighting, Richard Davis; costumes, Mary Schakel. With Paul Ballantyne, Glynis Bell, Peter Brandon, David Himes, Gloria Maddox.

THE BOY FRIEND (27). By Sandy Wilson. March 30, 1972. Director, Joseph Shaw; scenery and lighting, Richard Davis; costumes, Mary Schakel; choreography, Geoffrey Webb. With Glynis Bell, Warren Burton, Anne Kaye, William Le Massena, Susan E. Scott.

THE PRICE (27). By Arthur Miller. April

27, 1972. Director, John Ulmer; scenery and lighting, Richard Davis; costumes, Mary Schakel. With Laurence Hugo, Macon McCalman, Elizabeth Orion, Albert M. Ottenheimer.

SAN FRANCISCO

American Conservatory Theater: Geary Theater

CAESAR AND CLEOPATRA (48). By George Bernard Shaw. October 30, 1971. Director, William Ball; scenery, James Tilton; lighting, F. Mitchell Dana; costumes, Ann Roth. With Peter Donat, Lee McCain, E. Kerrigan Prescott, Scott Thomas, M. Singer, Karie Cannon.

ANTONY AND CLEOPATRA (26). By William Shakespeare. November 2, 1971. Director, Allen Fletcher; scenery, James Tilton; lighting, F. Mitchell Dana; costumes, Ann Roth. With Ken Ruta, Paul Shenar, Herbert Foster, Michael Learned, Patrick Gorman.

THE TAVERN (17). By George M. Cohan. November 23, 1971. Directors; Ellis Rabb, Peter Donat; scenery, Jackson DeGovia; lighting, Maurice Beesley; costumes, Elizabeth Covey. With Joseph Bird, Richard Council, Deborah Sussel, Ray Reinhardt, William Patterson, Joy Carlin.

DANDY DICK (25). By Arthur Wing Pinero. December 14, 1971. Director, Edward Hastings; scenery, Robert Blackman; lighting, Maurice Beesley; costumes, Walter Watson. With William Paterson, Herbert Foster, Marc Singer, Ken Ruta, Lee McCain, Karie Cannon.

ROSENCRANTZ AND GUILDENSTERN ARE DEAD (27). By Tom Stoppard. January 11, 1972. Director, William Ball; scenery, Stuart Wurtzel; lighting, Maurice Beesley; costumes, Robert Fletcher. With Marc

Singer, Larry Carpenter, Ken Ruta, Howard Sherman, Paul Shenar, Lee Cook, F. Kerrigan Prescott, Larry Martin, Nancy McDoniel, Winifred Mann.

PARADISE LOST (24). By Clifford Odets. February 1, 1972. Director, Allen Fletcher; scenery, Robert Blackman; lighting, Maurice Beesley; costumes, Elizabeth Covey. With Deborah Sussel, Joseph Bird, Winifred Mann, Joy Carlin, G. Wood, Paul Shenar, Ray Reinhardt.

PRIVATE LIVES (26). By Noel Coward. February 22, 1972. Director, Francis Ford Coppola; scenery, Robert Blackman; lighting, Maurice Beesley; costumes, Robert Fletcher. With Deborah Sussel, Paul Shenar, Jay Doyle, Michael Learned, Karie Canon.

THE CONTRACTOR (22). By David Storey. March 14, 1972. Director, William Ball; scenery, Paul Staheli; lighting, Maurice Beesley; costumes, Julie Staheli. With Ray Reinhardt, Marc Singer, Lee McCain, G. Wood, Richard Council.

SLEUTH (11+). By Anthony Shaffer. April 4, 1972. Director, Ellis Rabb; scenery and costumes, Robert Blackman; lighting, Maurice Beesley. With Ken Ruta, Peter Donat, M. B. Gormaly, Edward Collingwood, Jay Copeland. *Sleuth* was held over through June, therefore performance count was incomplete at press time.

American Conservatory Theater: Marines' Memorial Theater

Non-repertory productions included:

MOTHER EARTH (103) performances. A rock musical about ecology by Ron Thronson and Toni Shearer. THE EFFECT OF

GAMMA RAYS ON MAN-IN-THE-MOON MARIGOLDS (77). By Paul Zindel.

American Conservatory Theater: Guest Productions

HAIR (32) by Gerome Ragni, James Rado and Galt MacDermot; HARVEY (15) by Mary Chase, with Gig Young and Shirley

Booth; THE SCHOOL FOR WIVES (16) by Molière, with Brian Bedford. September-October 1971.

SARASOTA, FLA.

Asolo Theater Festival: The State Theater Company

OUR TOWN (20). By Thornton Wilder. June 18, 1971. Director, Robert Strane; scenery,

William King; lighting, James Meade; costumes, Catherine King. With William Leach,

Barbara Redmond, Robert Lanchester, Susan Sandler, Eberle Thomas, Bradford Wallace.

INDIANS (15). By Arthur Kopit. July 16, 1971. Director, Eberle Thomas; scenery, William King; lighting, James Meade; costumes, Catherine King. With Walter Rhodes, William Leach, Robert Lanchester, Bill E. Noone.

BORN YESTERDAY (8). By Garson Kanin. Reopened, July 18, 1971. Director, Howard J, Millman; scenery, Henry Swanson; lighting, James Meade; costumes, Flozanne John. With William Leach, Walter Rhodes, Sharon Spelman.

THE FRONT PAGE (33). By Ben Hecht and Charles MacArthur. February 17, 1972. Director, Howard J. Millman; scenery, Rick Pike; lighting, James Meade; costumes, Flozanne John. With Walter Rhodes, William Leach, Kathleen Klein, Penelope Willis.

TWELFTH NIGHT (24). By William Shakespeare. February 19, 1972. Director, Robert Strane; scenery, Henry Swanson; lighting, James Meade; costumes, Catherine King. With Eberle Thomas, Kathleen Klein, Kathleen O'Meara Noone, Philip LeStrange, Robert Lanchester, Barbara Redmond.

THE BEST MAN (17). By Gore Vidal. February 25, 1972. Director, Bradford Wallace; scenery, Henry Swanson; lighting, James Meade; costumes, Catherine King. With Robert Lanchester, Bill E. Noone, William Leach, Polly Holliday.

HAY FEVER (20). By Noel Coward. March 3, 1972. Director, Eberle Thomas; scenery, Henry Swanson; lighting, James Meade; costumes, Catherine King. With Polly Holliday,

Robert Strane, Penelope Willis, Richard Hopkins.

DRACULA (23). By Frederick Gaines; adapted from the novel by Bram Stoker. March 31, 1972 (world premiere). Director, Jon Spelman; scenery, John Ezell; lighting, James Meade; costumes, Catherine King; movement styling, C. W. Metcalf.

Count Dracula	Philip LeStrange
Jonathan Harker	Walter Rhodes
Mina Murray Harker	Penelope Willis
Lucy Westenra	Kathleen Klein
Arthur Holmswood	Justin T. Deas
Dr. John Seward	William Leach
Quincy Morris	Bill E. Noone
Dr. Van Helsing	Robert Lanchester
R. M. Renfield	B. G. Ross
Rusalka	Devora Millman

THE HOUSE OF BLUE LEAVES (17). By John Guare. April 7, 1972. Director, Robert Strane; scenery, Henry Swanson; lighting, James Meade; costumes, Catherine King. With Bradford Wallace, Polly Holliday, Barbara Redmond, Richard Hopkins.

THE MATCHMAKER (31). By Thornton Wilder. May 5, 1972. Director, Robert Lanchester; scenery, James Tilton; lighting, James Meade; costumes, Catherine King. With Barbara Redmond, William Leach, Philip LeStrange, Justin T. Deas, Kathleen O'Meara Noone.

THE DEVIL'S DISCIPLE (26). By George Bernard Shaw. June 9, 1972. Director, Richard O. Mayer; scenery, Henry Swanson; lighting, James Meade; costumes, Barbara Costa. With Walter Rhodes, Polly Holliday, Penelope Willis, Robert Strane, Kathleen O'Meara Noone, Robert Lanchester.

Asolo Theater Festival: Children's Theater

THE PUPPET PRINCE (16). By Alan Cullen. July 1, 1971. Director, Jon Spelman; scenery, Rick Pike; lighting, Terry Smith; costumes, Margaret Maggard. With Rita Grossberg, James Wrynn, Ralph Allison.

THE SNOW QUEEN (18). By Suria Magito and Rudolf Weill; based on the story by Hans Christian Andersen. August 12, 1971. Director, Moses Goldberg; scenery, Rick Pike; lighting, Terry Smith; costumes, Margaret

Maggard. With Billy Gene Ross, Virginia Anderson, Ralph Allison, Rita Grossberg, Nancy Allison.

THE YELLOW LAUGH (10). By Arthur Fauquez; translated by Eberle Thomas. March 5, 1972 (American premiere). Director, Dr. Moses Goldberg; scenery and costumes, Rick Pike; lighting, Terry Smith. With Rick Pike, Charles Davis, Rita Grossberg, James Wrynn.

Note: During the 1971-72 season, Asolo toured their production of *Twelfth Night* in 16 cities in Florida; as well as sending two children's theater productions, *Cinderella* and *Just So Stories* to schools in twenty-two counties, September 3 to December 31, 1971.

SEATTLE

Seattle Repertory Theater

RING ROUND THE MOON (20). By Jean Anouilh. October 20, 1971. Director, W. Duncan Ross; scenery, Jason Phillips; lighting, William Mintzer; costumes, Lewis D. Rampino. With John Tillinger, Margaret Hamilton, Susan Carr, Robert Loper.

THE HOUSE OF BLUE LEAVES (18). By John Guare. November 17, 1971. Director, W. Duncan Ross; scenery, Jason Phillips; lighting, William Mintzer; costumes, Lewis D. Rampino. With Josef Sommer, Nancy Zala, Gwen Van Dam, John Abajian.

HOTEL PARADISO (18). By Georges Feydeau. December 8, 1971. Director, W. Duncan Ross; scenery, Jason Phillips; lighting, William Mintzer; costumes, Lewis D. Rampino. With Donald Moffat, Nancy Zala, Gwen Arner, William Young, Don Freeman.

GETTING MARRIED (19). By George Bernard Shaw. December 29, 1971. Director, Clayton Corzatte; scenery, Jason Phillips; lighting, Miles Fischel; costumes, Lewis D. Rampino. With Margaret Phillips, W. Duncan Ross, Pauline Flanagan, George Vogel, Byron Webster.

AND MISS REARDON DRINKS A LITTLE (19). By Paul Zindel. January 10, 1972. Director, Robert Loper; scenery, Jason Phillips; lighting, William Mintzer; costumes, Lewis D. Rampino. With Marian Mercer, Eve Roberts, Pauline Flanagan, Ronny Gale.

ADAPTATION by Elaine May and NEXT by Terrence McNally (21). February 9, 1972. Director, Wayne Carson; scenery, Jason Phillips; lighting, William Mintzer; costumes, Lewis D. Rampino. With Michael Keenan, Gun-Marie Nilsson, Tom Carson, Clayton Corzatte, William Young, Nancy Zala.

Seattle Repertory Theater—Guest Production

I AM A WOMAN (8). Compiled and performed by Viveca Lindfors. March 7, 1972.

STRATFORD, CONN.

American Shakespeare Festival Theater

THE MERRY WIVES OF WINDSOR (27). By William Shakespeare. June 12, 1971 (matinee). Director, Michael Kahn; scenery, Douglas W. Schmidt; lighting, John Gleason; costumes, Jane Greenwood; choreography, Anna Sokolow. With Jane Alexander, Lee Richardson, Tobi Brydon, Jan Miner, Maury Cooper, W. B. Brydon.

THE TEMPEST (33). By William Shakespeare. June 12, 1971 (evening). Director, Edward Payson Call; scenery, Ben Edwards; lighting, John Gleason; costumes, Jane Greenwood. With Morris Carnovsky, Roy Cooper, Robert Stattel, Dianne Wiest, Jess Richards, David Hurst.

MOURNING BECOMES ELECTRA (29). By Eugene O'Neill. June 16, 1971. Director, Michael Kahn; scenery, William Ritman; lighting, John Gleason; costumes, Jane Greenwood. With Jane Alexander, Sada Thompson, Roy Cooper, Lee Richardson, Peter Thompson.

SYRACUSE

Syracuse Repertory Theater

SHE LOVES ME (11). Book by Joe Masteroff; music, Jerry Bock; lyrics, Sheldon Harnick. March 3, 1972. Director, Tom Roland; scenery, Leonard Dryansky; lighting, Robert Alexander; costumes, Sue Ann Smith; musical director, Steve Metcalf. With Zoaunne LeRoy Henriot, Roberta Vatske, Hal Holden, Gerald Richards.

ONE FLEW OVER THE CUCKOO'S NEST (18). By Dale Wasserman, from the novel by Ken Kesey. March 17, 1972 and May 10, 1972. Director, Rex Henriot; scenery, Robert K. Cloyd; lighting, Robert Alexander; costumes, Sue Ann Smith. With Hal Holden, Bob Gunton, Patrick Desmond, Eve Packer.

THE SIGN IN SIDNEY BRUSTEIN'S WINDOW (11). By Lorraine Hansberry. March 31, 1972. Director, Rex Henriot; scenery, Robert Louis Smith; lighting, Robert Alexander; costumes, Sue Ann Smith. With Jack Collard, David Deardorff, Eve Packer, Susan Harney.

THE HOUSE OF BLUE LEAVES (11). By John Guare. April 4, 1972. Director, Rex Henriot; scenery, Robert K. Cloyd; lighting, Robert Alexander; costumes, Sue Ann Smith.

With Jack Collard, Zoaunne LeRoy Henriot, Fran Herbert.

HAPPY BIRTHDAY, WANDA JUNE (11). By Kurt Vonnegut Jr. April 28, 1972. Director, Rex Henriot; scenery, Robert Lewis Smith; lighting, Robert Alexander; costumes, Sue Ann Smith. With Tiffany Hendry, Tom Brennan, Jack Collard, Patrick Desmond.

WALTHAM, MASS.

Brandeis University: Spingold Theater

THE RULES OF THE GAME (9). By Luigi Pirandello. October 27, 1971. Director, Peter Sander; scenery, Michael F. Hottois; lighting, Hank Sparks; costumes, Rachel Kurland. With Gil Schwartz, Helen Butler, Frank Bara, Lucy Chudson, David A. Zucker, Richard A. Rubin, Dean Haglin, David S. Howard.

THE GLASS MENAGERIE (11). By Tennessee Williams. November 30, 1971. Director, Harold Scott. With Maureen O'Sullivan, Lucy Chudson, David Zucker.

A CRY OF PLAYERS (11). By William Gibson. February 8, 1972. Director, Glenn Jordan; scenery, Hank Sparks; lighting, Marjorie Basch; costumes, Betsy Leichliter. With

Marc Vincenti, William Countryman, Linda Varvel, David Palmer, Helen Butler.

THE RIVALS (9). By Richard Brinsley Sheridan. March 15, 1972. Director, Charles Werner Moore; scenery, Corinna Taylor; lighting, Michael F. Hottois; costumes, G. Paulette Spruill. With Virginia Feingold, Lucy Chudson, Linda Varvel, William Countryman, David Palmer, David S. Howard.

MOONCHILDREN (9). By Michael Weller. May 3, 1972. Director, Peter Sander; scenery, Charles Flaks; lighting, Ralph Dressler; costumes, Corinna Taylor. With Rex D. Hays, Laure Mattos, David Guc, David Palmer.

Note: New plays in the Laurie Premiere Theater were *Tucholsky, The Siege of Syracuse, Sex, Cold Cans and A Coffin, Wishes, The Story and the Rose, It's Your Life and You Can Have It.*

WASHINGTON, D.C.

Arena Stage: Kreeger Theater

PANTAGLEIZE (47). By Michel de Ghelderode; translated by George Hauser. October 22, 1971. Director, Gene Lesser; scenery, Santo Loquasto; lighting, William Mintzer; costumes, Linda Fisher. With Richard Bauer, Carl Mikal Franklin, Lou Gilbert, Linda Geiser, Macon McCalman, Paul Benedict.

THE HOUSE OF BLUE LEAVES (47). By John Guare. January 7, 1972. Director, Norman Gevanthor; scenery, Santo Loquasto; lighting, Henry R. Gorfein; costumes, Gwynne Clark. With Roy Shuman, Gar Bayer, Leslie Cass, Dorothea Hammond.

UPTIGHT (47). By Gunter Grass; translated by A. Leslie Willson and Ralph Manheim. March 17, 1972 (American premiere). Director, Alan Schneider; scenery, Santo Loquasto; lighting, Hugh Lester; costumes, Marjorie Slaiman; music, Michael Valenti.
The Cast:
Eberhard Stausch .... Paul Benedict

Irmgard Seifert .... Leslie Cass
Dentist .... Richard Bauer
Philipp Scherbaum .... Gary Bayer
Veronika Lewand .... Ann Sachs
The Musicians:
Keyboard and Musical
    Director .... Rich Aurich
Percussion .... Richard Levan
Guitar .... Don Scimonelli
Time: The recent present. Place: West Berlin; a dentist's office, a classroom, various living quarters, a bar, the street, etc. Two acts.

TRICKS (47). Book by Jon Jory; music, Jerry Blatt; lyrics, Lonnie Burstein; based on Molière's *Scapin.* May 19, 1972. Director, Jon Jory; scenery, Paul Owen; lighting, Vance Sorrells; costumes, Kurt Wilhelm; musical director, Tom Owen; choreography, Virginia Freeman. With Richard Bauer, Howard Witt, Gary Dontzig, Carolyn Connors, Max Wright, Adale O'Brien.

Arena Stage: Arena Theater

MOONCHILDREN (40). By Michael Weller. October 29, 1971 (American premiere). Director, Alan Schneider; scenery, William Ritman; lighting, Vance Sorrells; costumes, Marjorie Slaiman.

The Students:

Mike	Kevin Conway
Ruth	Maureen Anderman
Cootie (Mel)	Edward Herrmann
Norman	Christopher Guest
Dick	Stephen Collins
Kathy	Jill Eikenberry
Bob Rettie (Job)	James Woods
Shelly	Cara Duff-MacCormick

The Others:

Ralph	Donegan Smith
Mr. Willis	Robert Prosky
Lucky	Ronald McLarty
Bream	Howard Witt
Effing	Ted Hannan
Uncle Murry	Ben Kapen
Santa Claus	Jean Schertler
Cootie's Father	Russell Carr
Milkman	Mark Robinson
Plumber	Richard David

The place is a student apartment in an American university town around 1965-66. Act I, Scene 1: An evening in early fall. Scene 2: A few weeks later, morning. Scene 3: That afternoon. Scene 4: A November evening. Act II, Scene 1: Morning, just before Christmas vacation. Scene 2: Late spring, before graduation. Scene 3: The following afternoon.

TWELFTH NIGHT (40). By William Shakespeare. December 23, 1971. Director, Jeff Bleckner; scenery and costumes, John Conklin; lighting, Vance Sorrells. With Marc Alaimo, Margaret Linn, Robert Prosky, Maureen Anderman, Edward Herrmann, Zina Jasper, Richard Bauer, Bruce Weitz.

A CONFLICT OF INTEREST (40). By Jay Broad. February 4, 1972 (world premiere). Director, Jerry Adler; scenery, David R. Ballou; lighting, Vance Sorrells; costumes, Marjorie Slaiman.

Justice Jacob Balding	Dane Clark
Liz Balding	Joan Ulmer
Lewis Amory	Howard Witt
Robert Cutler	Richard Bauer
Pres. William Maxwell	Michael Higgins
Rep. Steven Clark	Mark Robinson
Rep. Lawrence Beagle	Richard David
Rev. Freddie Armstrong	Richard Sanders
Sen. Horace Samuels	Morris Engle
Sen. Thaddeus Jones	Glenn Taylor
Kenneth J. Smith	Bruce Weitz
Mrs. Sally Douglas	Anne Willmarth
Chief Justice Harry Griffin	Walter Abel
Bellhop	John Devine
Joe Farnswirth	Macon McCalman
Peggy Jones	Cecilia Ward

Place: Washington, D.C. Time: Spring. Two acts.

Guest Production

STATUS QUO VADIS (40). By Donald Driver. April 7, 1972. Director, Donald Driver; scenery, Rick Paul and Hugh Lester; lighting, Vance Sorrells; costumes, Georgiana Jordan. With Geraldine Kay, Otto L. Schlesinger, Max Howard, William Vines. George Keathley's Ivanhoe Theater production.

Washington Theater Club

WHORES, WARS AND TIN PAN ALLEY (30). An evening of songs by Kurt Weill. June 3, 1971. Scenery, Paul Parady; lighting, T. C. Behrens. With Martha Schlamme, Alvin Epstein, David Lewis (piano).

ADAPTATION by Elaine May and NEXT by Terrence McNally (31). September 29, 1971. Director, Joel J. Friedman; scenery, T. C. Behrens; lighting, Michael J. Rosati, costumes, Madeleine Grigg. With Armand Assante, Joseph Daly, Jamie Donnelly, Ronn Robinson, Benjamin H. Slack, Victoria Zussin.

ALL OVER (30). By Edward Albee. November 3, 1971. Director, Davey Marlin-Jones; scenery, T. C. Behrens, John H. Paull; lighting, Michael J. Rosati; costumes, Madeleine Grigg. With Carmen Mathews, Barbara Caruso, Don Lochner.

CURSE YOU, SPREAD EAGLE (38). Compiled and edited by Sue Lawless. December 8, 1971 (world premiere). Director, Leland Ball; scenery and lighting, John H. Paull; costumes, Madeleine Grigg; musical director, Herbert Kaplan. With Marshall Borden, Donna Liggitt Forbes, Marcia Lewis, Carleton Carpenter, Ann Hodapp, Joshua Mostel.

LEMON SKY (31). By Lanford Wilson. January 12, 1972. Director, Davey Marlin-Jones; scenery, T. C. Behrens, John H. Paull; lighting, Michael J. Rosati; costumes, Madeleine Grigg. With James Broderick, Michael Christopher, Trinity Thompson, Jennifer Warren.

THE PHILANTHROPIST (31). By Christopher Hampton. February 16, 1972. Director, Thomas Gruenewald; scenery, T. C. Behrens, John H. Paull; lighting, Michael J. Rosati; costumes, Madeleine Grigg. With Marjorie Lynne Feiner, Ralph Cosham, Ted Graeber, Nancy Reardon, Edward Zang, Holland Taylor, Howard Zielke.

WASHINGTON SQUARE (31). Book by Kenneth Jerome and Jerome Walman; music by Jerome Walman; lyrics by Kenneth Jerome; based on the novel by Henry James. March 22, 1972 (world premiere). Director, Davey Marlin-Jones; scenery, John H. Paull and T. C. Behrens; lighting, Michael J. Rosati; costumes, Madeleine Grigg; musical director-orchestrater, Harrison Fisher.

Catherine Sloper .... Jeannie Carson
Lavinia Penniman,
  her aunt .... Lois Holmes
Dr. Austin Sloper,
  her father .... Hurd Hatfield

Morris Townsend .... Biff McGuire
The setting of the play is the drawing room in the home of Dr. Austin Sloper at 16 Washington Square, and the memory of Catherine Sloper. Two acts.

FOUR MINUS ONE: ANIMAL by Oliver Hailey and THE DEADLY DELILAH by Raleigh Bond, directed by Davey Marlin-Jones; THE BASEMENT by Harold Pinter, directed by Bill Walton (31). April 26, 1972. Scenery, T. C. Behrens; lighting, Michael J. Rosati; costumes, Madeleine Grigg. With Lucy Lee Flippen, Edmund Day, Susan Lipton, James Brochu, Nelson Smith, Micky Hartnett, Ronn Robinson, Jack Halstead John Seitz, Eric Tavaris.

LADY AUDLEY'S SECRET (31+). By Douglas Seale; adapted from the novel by Mary Elizabeth Braddon; music by George Goehring; lyrics by John Kuntz. May 31, 1972. Director, Douglas Seale; scenery, John H. Paull; lighting, Michael J. Rosati; costumes, Alicia Finkel. With Douglas Seale, Russell Nype, Donna Curtis.

Washington Theater Club: Monday Night Staged Readings

THE DEADLY DELILAH by Raleigh Bond; A LITTLE SINGING and A LITTLE DANCING by Robert Kimmel Smith; THE KNACKERS YARD by Johnny Speight; MADAM CLEO by Warren Kliewer, CARNIVAL PARTY by Henry B. Ryand and PLAYGROUND by Louis Vuolo; MONOLITH by Jeffrey Thresher; THE WIZARD

OF SPRUCE STREET by Devorah Lundy; FIRE ON WATER by Lucy Kennedy; THE NIGHT WATCHMEN by Stratis Karras; THANKSGIVING AT AUNT BETTY'S by Robert Riche; WILD BILL by John Clifford. September 1971 through June 1972, 10 Monday night staged readings, 1 performance each.

The Season Elsewhere in Washington

By Jay Alan Quantrill

Drama critic of radio station WAVA and *Woodwind* magazine

The Washington cultural scene seems to have weathered the double-barreled impact of the openings of the Wolf Trap Farm Park and the John F. Kennedy Center. In fact, both (but particularly the Center) gave sharp focus to the theatrical activities here, so that Washington is at long last considered a good theater town and a burgeoning cultural center.

Of the theaters producing professionally, the Eisenhower, the Opera House (both at the Kennedy Center), Ford's and the National house touring shows, among other attractions. But the majority of those at Ford's and the Kennedy Center are locally generated for Washington consumption, and many have gone on to tour other cities, sometimes including New York. An important development: the pre-Broadway "tryouts" numbered only four (*The Prisoner of Second Avenue, Fun City, Sugar,* and *The Little Black Book*); but *five* Washington productions (*Moonchildren, The Country Girl, Lost in the Stars, Captain Brassbound's Conversion* and *Don't Bother Me, I Can't Cope*) have already found their way to New York, with others still hoping.

Post-Broadway touring attractions included *The Gingerbread Lady* (much praised here), *Promises, Promises,* and *Purlie* (both big draws) at the National. There was a special re-creation of Claire Bloom's *The Doll's House* for the opening of the Eisenhower Theater in the Kennedy Center. The National Theater changed hands, in May, from Louis Lotito to the Nederlander circuit and started off with a five-musical subscription series: *Company* (critically praised though very poor box office) and *1776* (which did okay), plus three for next season.

The most rewarding production of the season was Arena's Stage's *Pantagleize,* a rich blending of romantic theatricalism and tragic intellectualism unsurpassed for its force and pleasure. But then a two-performance engagement of *365 Days,* Minnesota's entry in the American College Theater Festival (at the Eisenhower), was easily the single most powerful event of the season. With nonliteral action and poetic movement, this play presented one of the most tragic aspects of the war in Vietnam in a highly compelling manner. The musical highlight was unquestionably the *Lost in the Stars* production, which starred Brock Peters and boasted direction by Gene Frankel and sets by Oliver Smith. It was moving, and grandly entertaining, *and* relevant.

Ford's Theater, after considerable legal battling, rid itself of the Circle-in-the-Square organization and set up shop on its own, presenting what was labelled its "Showcase Season" which centered on soft-rock revues and one-man shows. The National Park Service, the housekeeping organization at Ford's, lost its ability to censor productions after a controversy over the writings of H. L. Mencken in a solo show about the writer. *Godspell* opened to unanimous praise and was selling out.

The Kennedy Center's scheme for the season was to keep the halls filled, which is exactly what it did, mostly with its own revivals of American plays and musicals, plus imports from England. *Mass,* which opened the Center in September, was most controversial and is being revived for touring. Ingrid Bergman in Shaw's *Captain Brassbound's Conversion* did well at the box office.

The best effort of the season for the Washington Theater Club was a "second chance" for Albee's *All Over.* It's "new" works included a depressing musicalization of Henry James's *Washington Square,* and a deadly trio of one acts by Pinter, Hailey, and Bond. The Chicago import, *Lady Audley's Secret,* had some pleasant tunes and little else.

The Folger Library Theater group attracted a lot of attention and patrons with a four-play season, promising some fascinating things for the future. Catholic University presented two professional productions this season, neither of which got very good notices. The National Players, a professional non-Equity, classical touring troupe from Catholic University played nine months of *The Miser, The Trial* and *The Taming of the Shrew* in repertory. Olney Theater had just opened *Play Strindberg* as the season closed.

It was an exciting season in Washington, mostly, I suppose, because it was so varied and expensive. Guiding lights in the playhouses around town are reacting to the impact of Kennedy Center and Wolf Trap in a reserved and basically wary manner, though most will agree that Kennedy's opening did, in fact, help business. There is a tendency towards audience-pleasers that may be a result of wanting to compete with Kennedy, an almost frantic eagerness to get sure-fire successes onto the stage in order to get back audiences which haven't really deserted. Things are looking better for next season; and though experimental production hasn't reached the desired level, there's a healthy ferment and something is bound to surface soon.

Here is a listing of professional productions in Washington between June 1, 1971 and May 31, 1972. A plus sign (+) with the performance number indicates the show was still running on June 1, 1972. Not included in this listing are the productions of Arena Stage and the Washington Theater Club (see the Regional Theater listing above), most touring shows and packaged shows.

Olney Theater, Olney, Md.

HAY FEVER (21). By Noel Coward. June 1, 1971. Director, Leo Brady; scenery and lighting, James D. Waring; costumes, Joan Markert. With George Vogel, Roni Dengel, Grayce Grant, Peter Vogt, Halo Wines.

WHISPERS ON THE WIND (21). Intimate musical with book and lyrics by John B. Kuntz; music, Lor Crane. June 22, 1971. Direction, scenery and lighting, James D. Waring; costumes, Joan Markert. With Jay Gregory, Suellen Esty, Edmund Gaynes, Samuel D. Ratcliffe, Judy MacMurdo.

TWO FOR THE SEESAW (21). By William Gibson. July 13, 1971. Direction, scenery and lighting, James D. Waring. With James Broderick, Patricia Elliott.

THE HOMECOMING (21). By Harold Pinter. August 3, 1971. Direction, scenery and

lighting, James D. Waring. With Patricia Elliott, Sydney Walker, Edward McPhillips, James Patterson, Robert Murch, Steven Sutherland.

CHILD'S PLAY (21): By Robert Marasco. August 24, 1971. Director, Leo Brady; scenery and lighting, James D. Waring. With Sydney Walker, Michael McGuire, Steven Collins, Bryan E. Clarke, Peter Vogt.

PLAY STRINDBERG (2+). After August Strindberg's *Dance of Death;* by Friedrich Duerrenmatt; translated by James Kirkup. May 30, 1972. Director, Dan Sullivan; scenery, Douglas W. Schmidt; lighting, John Gleason; costumes, James Berton Harris. With Robert Symonds, Priscilla Pointer, Ray Fry. The Lincoln Center Repertory production, presented by the University Players.

Summer Shakespeare Festival

YOUR OWN THING (30). Rock musical suggested by William Shakespeare's *Twelfth Night;* book, Donald Driver; music and lyrics, Hal Hester and Danny Apolinar. July 13, 1971. Directed by Donald Driver; scenery,

Robert Troll; lighting, Jennifer Tipton; costumes, Jon Franz. With Igors Gavon, Emily Yancy, Michael Valenti. Ellie Chamberlain, artistic director.

John F. Kennedy Center: The Opera House

MASS (13). Specially commissioned work for the inauguration of the John F. Kennedy Center for the Performing Arts; by Leonard Bernstein; additional texts by Stephen Schwartz. September 8, 1971 (world pre-

miere). Director, Gordon Davidson; scenery, Oliver Smith; lighting, Gilbert Hemsley Jr.; costumes, Frank Thompson; choreography, Alvin Ailey; musical director, Maurice Peress. With Alan Titus and The Norman Scribner

Choir, The Berkshire Boys' Choir, The Alvin Ailey American Dance Theater. Walter Willison replaced Mr. Titus at matinees. Produced by Roger L. Stevens, associate producer Schuyler G. Chapin.

Musical Numbers: "A Simple Song," "I Don't Know," "Easy," "Gloria Tibi," "Thank You," "The Word of the Lord," "God Said," "Non Credo," "Hurry," "World Without End," "I Believe in God," "Our Father," "I Go On," "Things Get Broken," "Secret Songs."

CANDIDE (32). Musical based on the Voltaire classic; music, Leonard Bernstein; lyrics, Richard Wilbur; additional lyrics, John Latouche; adaptation, Sheldon Patinkin. October 26, 1971. Director, Sheldon Patinkin; scenery, Oliver Smith; lighting, Peggy Clark; costumes, Freddy Wittop; musical director, Maurice Peress; production numbers and choreography, Michael Smuin. With Frank Porretta, Mary Costa, Rae Allen, Robert Klein. Produced by Kennedy Center in association with the Los Angeles and San Francisco Civic Light Opera

Associations, Edwin Lester general director.

LOST IN THE STARS (29). Musical based on Alan Paton's novel *Cry, the Beloved Country;* Music, Kurt Weill; book and lyrics, Maxwell Anderson. February 19, 1972. Director, Gene Frankel; scenery, Oliver Smith; lighting, Paul Sullivan; costumes, Patricia Quinn Stuart; choreographer, Louis Johnson; musical director, Lehman Engel. With Brock Peters, Jack Gwillim, Gilbert Price, Rod Perry. Produced for the Kennedy Center by Roger L. Stevens and Diana Shumlin.

CAPTAIN BRASSBOUND'S CONVERSION (24). By George Bernard Shaw. March 13, 1972. Director, Stephen Porter; scenery, Michael Annals; lighting, William H. Batchelder; costumes, Sarah Brook; Miss Bergman's costumes, Beatrice Dawson. With Ingrid Bergman, Pernell Roberts, Eric Berry, Jay Garner, Leo Lyden. Roger L. Stevens-Arthur Cantor production, by arrangement with H. M. Tennent, Ltd. Brought to the U.S. for tour beginning at Kennedy Center.

John F. Kennedy Center: Eisenhower Theater

A DOLL'S HOUSE (24). By Henrik Ibsen; adaptation by Christopher Hampton. October 16, 1971. Director, Hillard Elkins; scenery, lighting and costumes, John Bury. With Claire Bloom, Ed Zimmermann, Patricia Elliott, Robert Gerringer. The Hillard Elkins New York production, specially remounted for this engagement.

THE COUNTRY GIRL (39). By Clifford Odets. November 16, 1971. Director, John Houseman; scenery and lighting, Douglas W. Schmidt; lighting consultant, James D. Waring; costumes, Frank Thompson. With Jason Robards Jr., Maureen Stapleton, George Grizzard. Producer, Roger L. Stevens in association with Hugh O'Brian, production supervised by Frank Cassidy.

THE TIME OF YOUR LIFE (24). By William Saroyan. January 15, 1972. Director, Edwin Sherin; scenery, Oliver Smith; lighting, Paul Sullivan; costumes, Kate Drain Lawson. With Henry Fonda, Jane Alexander, Victor

French, Strother Martin, Gloria Grahame, Bert Freed, Pepper Martin, John Crawford, Richard X. Slattery, and Lou Gilbert. The Plumstead Playhouse production presented by Kennedy Center.

RICHARD II (29). By William Shakespeare. May 3, 1972. Director, Jonathan Miller; scenery and lighting, H. R. Poindexter; costumes, Gabriella Falk. With Richard Chamberlain, Patrick Hines, Jack Ryland, Sorrell Booke. Produced for the Kennedy Center by Roger L. Stevens and J. Charles Gilbert (originally produced by Center Theater Group, Los Angeles).

THE MARQUISE (3+). By Noel Coward. May 29, 1972. Director, Roger Redfarn; scenery, Tony Abbott, Donald Taylor; lighting, Michael Northen; costumes, Alan Barrett. With Glynis Johns, Richard Todd. A Triumph Theater Production, from England (on its way to Australia).

Ford's Theater

DON'T BOTHER ME, I CAN'T COPE (32) Musical revue by Micki Grant. September 15, 1971 (world premiere). Director, Vinnette Carroll; scenery, Richard A. Miller; lighting, Bronislaw J. Sammler; costumes, Edna Watson; choreography, Talley Beatty; musical director, Danny Holgate. With Micki Grant, Alex Bradford, Hope Clarke, Arnold Wilkerson, Carl Bean, Charles E. Campbell, Bobby

L. Hill, Willie James McPhatter. Dancers: Gerald Francis, J.L. Harris, Leona Johnson, Philip A. Stamps. Produced by Ford's Theater Society in association with Arch Lustberg and Ed Padula, in the Urban Arts Corps production.

MOTHER EARTH (40). Musical revue about ecology with book and lyrics by Ron Thronson; music by Toni Shearer. October 20, 1971 (East Coast premiere). Director, Sid Grossfield; scenery and lighting, Jim McKie; costumes, Rickie Hansen, Warden Neil; choreographer, Steve Merritt; visuals, Kenneth Shearer; musical director, Toni Shearer. With Patti Austin, Christine Avila, Elaine Blankston, Ron deSalvo, Michael Devin, Joel Kimmel, Peter Jason, Tip Kelley, Carol Kristy, Arlene Parness. Produced by Ford's Theater Society in association with Steven L. Parkes.

ECHOES OF THE LEFT BANK (24). Song fest of French tunes by Brel, Monnot, Becaud, Le Grande, Aznavour. Conceived by Rhoda Roberts. January 4, 1972 (world premiere). Directors, Nick DeNoia and Ken Berman; scenery and lighting, Duane Mazey; costumes, Ruth Graves; musical supervision, Milton Rosenstock. With Jamie Thomas, Suzanne Oberjat, Harrison Somers, Ed Evanko, Danielle Odderra. Produced by Ford's Theater Society. Frankie Hewitt executive producer.

MOBY DICK (16). One-man show conceived, adapted and performed by Jack Aranson, based on Melville's novel. February 1, 1972. Director, Philip Pruneau; scenery, Stuart Wurtzel; lighting, Jim Dickson; sound, Dan

Dugan. Produced by Ford's Theater Society, Frankie Hewitt executive producer, in association with the San Francisco City Theater Company.

AN UNPLEASANT EVENING WITH H. L. MENCKEN (23). Adapted from the words of Mencken by Paul Shyre. March 8, 1972 (world premiere). Directed by Paul Shyre; scenery and lighting, Eldon Elder. With David Wayne. Produced by Ford's Theater Society in association with Frank Connelly and Gerald Roberts.

GODSPELL (54+). Musical based on the Gospel according to St. Matthew; conception, book, original direction and scenery, John-Michael Tebelak; music and lyrics, Stephen Schwartz. April 7, 1972. Director, Nona Faso; lighting, Spencer Mosse; costumes, Susan Tsu. With Bart Braverman, Scotch Byerly, Antony Hoty, Maggie Hyatt, Doris Jamin, Irving Lee, Patti Mariano, Dean Pitchford, Lynn Thigpen, and John-Ann Washington. Produced by Ford's Theater Society, Frankie Hewitt, executive producer, in association with Edgar Lansbury, Stuart Duncan, and Joseph Beruh.

Folger Library Theater Group

LANDSCAPE and SILENCE (24). Program of two one-act plays by Harold Pinter. October 12, 1971. Director, Louis W. Scheeder; scenery, Robert C. Miller; lighting, Michael Lodick; costumes, Cathy Wills. With Peter Vogt.

THE REVENGER'S TRAGEDY (19). By Cyril Tourneur. December 16, 1971. Director, Louis Scheeder; scenery, Paul Hastings; lighting, Michael Lodick; costumes, Anna Garris Hampton. With Peter Vogt, Robert Reilly.

SUBJECT TO FITS (22). A response to Dostoevsky's The Idiot; words and music by Robert Montgomery. February 10, 1972. Director, Paul Schneider; scenery, Emile Douglas; lighting, Michael Lodick; costumes, Anna Garris Hampton. With Randy Kim, Michael Gabel.

ROMEO AND JULIET (28). By William Shakespeare. April 6, 1972. Director, Munson Hicks; scenery, Paul Hastings; lighting, Michael Lodick; costumes, Laura Shultz Hastings. With Peter Vogt and Neil Elliot.

Catholic University: Hartke Theater

PYGMALION (18). By George Bernard Shaw. November 26, 1971. Director, William Graham; scenery and lighting, James D. Waring; costumes, Veronica Gustaff. With Robert Milli, Roni Dengel, Edward McPhillips, Eleanor Phelps.

JUNO AND THE PAYCOCK (18). By Sean O'Casey. January 7, 1972. Director, Leo Brady; scenery and lighting, James D. Waring; costumes, Veronica Gustaff. With Geraldine Fitzgerald, Edward McPhillips, Robert Gerringer, Ruby Holbrook.

WATERFORD, CONN.

Eugene O'Neill Theater Center: Playwrights Conference

AMERICAN TRIPTYCH (2). By Werner Liepolt. July 14, 1971 (world premiere). Director, James Hammerstein; dramaturge, Dale Wasserman

Man 1; Dick; Friend ....Lenny Baker
Man 2; Harry; Frankenstein ...Harold Scott
Man 3; Tom; Leo the Liar ..Keven O'Connor
Nude; Ringleader ....Elaine Aiken

A LITTLE SINGING, A LITTLE DANC-
ING (2). By Robert K. Smith. July 14, 1971
(world premiere). Director, Glenn Jordan;
dramaturge, Edith Oliver.

Willie James Greer ............J.A. Preston
Sidney H. Pollack ....Roy Shuman
    The entire action takes place in an Internal
Revenue Service office in New York City.

BODY AND SOUL (2). By Helen Rathje.
July 16, 1971 (world premiere). Director, J.
Ranelli; dramaturge, Sam Hirsch.

Stage Directions; Ilya ....Stephen McHattie
Count Tolstoy ....Stephen Scott
Countess Tolstoy ....Jacqueline Brookes
Madame Kuzminskaia ....Anita Dangler
Tolstoy's Children:
    Serge ....David Berry
    Tania Lvovna ....Elaine Bromke
    Leon ....Miles Barnes
    Masha ....Marsha Mason
    Sasha ....Gayle Bruno
Shertkov ....David Little
The Grand Duke ....Roy Shuman
Niania ....Elaine Aiken
Fet ....Jess Adkins
Churis; Father Troitsky ......Peter Turgeon
Dr. Behrs ....Bud Tucker
Elizabeth Behrs ....Therese Verhoogen
Miss Hannah ....Geraldine Sherman
Herr Kaufman; Nikolas ....Tom Doran
Aunt Tatenka ....Dee Victor
Martin; Young Man ....Richard Ludgin
Ivan; Man ....Lenny Baker
    The action takes place at the Tolstoy
homestead at Yasnaia Poliana, with the ex-
ception of Act IV, which takes place in the
Countess Tolstoy's house in Moscow. Five
acts, two intermissions.

CAMPION (2). By William Griffin. July 20,
1971 (world premiere). Director, Wallace
Chappell; dramaturge, Edith Oliver.

Sir Owen Hopton ....Kevin O'Connor
Edmund Campion ....James Ray
Robert Dudley ....Stephen Scott
Foggy Nan ....Joan Moignard
William Cecil ....Peter Turgeon
Francis Fox ....J. A. Preston
Elizabeth I ....Anita Dangler
Chief Justice ....Jess Adkins
Clerk of the Court ......Stephen McHattie
Guards ....Miles Barnes, Richard Ludgin
    The action takes place in the palace of
Queen Elizabeth and the dungeon of the
Tower of London in 1581.

RESPECTS (2). By Jerry Spindel. July 22,
1971 (world premiere). Director, Glenn Jordan; dramaturge, Edith Oliver.

Marion ....Marsha Mason
Arnold ....Roy Shuman
Carl ....Harold Scott

Nellie ....Elaine Aiken
Al DeLacy ....Lenny Baker
    Place: the living room of the Schneider
home, evening. Time: the present.

PROJECT OMEGA: LILLIAN (2). By Corinne Jacker. July 22, 1971 (world premiere).
Staged reading. Director, Glenn Jordan;
dramaturge, Edith Oliver; music by Jonathan
Tunick; lyrics by Corinne Jacker.

Stephen ....David Little
Baby ....Lenny Baker
Leon ....Harold Scott
Lillian ....Jacqueline Brookes
Nan, her daughter ....Elaine Bromke
Ken ....Miles Barnes
Dora ....Dee Victor
    The action takes place in one of the chil-
dren's playground areas in Central Park, to-
morrow at noon. There are seven musical
numbers.

AFRICAN STAR (2). By John Jiler. July
23, 1971 (world premiere). Director, Wallace
Chappell; dramaturge, Samuel Hirsch.

Captain ....Peter Turgeon
A ....Stephen McHattie
B ....Kevin O'Connor
Franz ....Stephen Scott
Max ....James Ray
    The action takes place in the lower hold of
the freighter, African Star.

AUTO-DESTRUCT (2). By Jeff Wanshel.
July 27, 1971 (world premiere). Director, J.
Ranelli; dramaturge, Martin Esslin.
    The action takes place in Mexico. Act I:
Bare stage. Act II: A car.

THE COMPLAINT DEPARTMENT CLOSES
AT FIVE (2). By Edward M. Cohen. July 28,
1971 (word premiere). Director, James Hammerstein; dramaturge, Martin Esslin.

Hershey ....Roy Shuman
Estelle ....Anita Dangler
Larry ....Tony Melchior
Matthew Segal ....Lenny Baker
Ben Segal ....Peter Turgeon
Beverly ....Elaine Aiken
    The action takes place in the Hersheys'
apartment in a middle income housing devel-
opment in Queens. Act I: Early Friday eve-
ning. Act II: A few minutes later.

BRUCE (2). By Gerry Carroll. July 30, 1971
(world premiere). Director, Glenn Taylor;
dramaturge, Martin Esslin.

Peasant Woman ....Geraldine Sherman
The English:
    Edward I ....James Ray
    Queen Eleanor ....Elaine Aiken
    Prince Edward ....Rob Christian
    Henry De Bohun ....Harold Scott

Physician .... Bud Tucker
Bohun's Son .... George White Jr.
Captain .... Tom Doran
Soldier .... Link Watkins
The Scots:
Robert Bruce .... Stephen Scott
Elizabeth Bruce .... Jacqueline Brookes
Isobel Buchan .... Gayle Bruno
John Comyn .... J. A. Preston
Andrew Girvan .... Miles Barnes
Marjorie Bruce .... Marsha Mason
Walter Stewart .... Richard Ludgin
William Wallace .... Kevin O'Connor
Neil Bruce .... Stephen McHattie
Ned Bruce .... David Little
James Douglas .... Jess Adkins
Soldier .... Leon Calanquin

THE MORGAN YARD (2). By Kevin
O'Morrison. August 3, 1971 (world pre-
miere). Staged Reading. Director, J. Ranelli;
dramaturge, Edith Oliver.
Carrie .... Dee Victor
Jess .... Lenny Baker
Orpha .... Anita Dangler
Barry B. .... James Ray
Lt. Bonheur .... David Little
Mayor Hesseltine .... Jess Adkins
The action takes place in the Morgan Yard,
a private burial ground in the Missouri Ozark
Mountains, on a day in late summer. Three
acts.

ISHTAR (2). By Robert Ross. August 5,
1971 (world premiere). Staged reading. Direc-
tor, James Hammerstein; dramaturge, Edith
Oliver.
Carolyn .... Jacqueline Brookes
Nugent .... Peter Turgeon
Stat .... Stephen McHattie
Joya .... Marsha Mason
The play takes place in a modest suburban
home outside of New York City. Act I, 3
scenes: Morning, the following day, early
afternoon. Act II, 3 scenes: 2 a.m. the follow-
ing morning, that afternoon, two days later.
Two acts.

LONNIE, JAMES, BERNHARDT AND
ZOOWOLSKI (2). By John E. Sedlak. Au-
gust 6, 1971 (world premiere). Staged read-
ing. Director, Wallace Chappell; dramaturge,
Samuel Hirsch.
James .... Rob Christian
Lonnie .... J. A. Preston
Cop .... Kevin O'Connor
Judge .... Stephen Scott
Tessy Lou Parker .... Lisa Wilkenson
Malcolm .... Harold Scott
Mother; Black Girl ..... Jeanne Heningburg
Porgy-like Man;
Black Man .... K. Michael Talbot
McNaughton .... Lenny Baker
Prosecutor .... Roy Shuman
White Man .... David Little
White Girl .... Elaine Bromke
Sy .... Jess Adkins

Resident designers: scenery, Peter Larkin; lighting, John Gleason; costumes, Fred Voelpel.
Performances are given in three theaters, the Barn (indoors), the Amphitheater and the Instant Theater (outdoors).

WEST SPRINGFIELD, MASS.

Stage/West Theater

THE MIRACLE WORKER (20). By William
Gibson. November 12, 1971. Directors, John
Ulmer and William Guild; scenery and cos-
tumes, Robert Federico; lighting, Anthony
Quintavalla. With Marion Brash, Denise Nick-
erson, Jerry Hardin, Diane Hill.

COUNT DRACULA (20). By Ted Tiller;
based on Bram Stoker's novel Dracula. December 10, 1971. Director, John Ulmer; scenery, Robert Federico; lighting, Erica Lee
Lewis; costumes, Joyce Fessides. With Diane
Hill, John Wardwell, Eric Tavares.

THIS AGONY, THIS TRIUMPH (20). By
Reginald Rose. January 7, 1972 (world pre-
miere). Director, John Ulmer; scenery and
lighting, William F. Matthews; costumes,
Betty Williams and Susan Harvuot.
Newsboy .... Glen Lane

Winthrop Davis .... Bruce Kornbluth
Guards .... Robert Casal, William Waste
Fred Katzmann .... Jerry Hardin
Captain Proctor .... Wallace Androchuck
Jeremiah McAnarney ...... Richmond Hoxie
Paolo Bellini .... Raymond Singer
William Daly .... Michael Dattorre
Martha Kelly .... Laura Byrne
Nicola Sacco .... Jack Gianino
Bartolomeo Vanzetti .... Eric Tavares
Andreas Salsedo .... David Scopp
Walter Ripley .... Hamp Watson
Judge Webster Thayer .... John Wardwell
Chief Crane .... James Caporale
Mary Splaine .... Diane Hill
Lola Andrews .... Hannah Brandon
William G. Thompson .... Edward Fuller
Celestino Madeiros .... Richard Larson
Captain Connors .... Kit Randall
Governor Fuller .... Humphrey Davis

Spectators, Court Reporters,
Extras ......Jeffrey Morgan, Alan Lerner,
Elena Grechko
The action of the play covers the period from April 1920 until August 1927, in and around Boston. Two acts.

SCAPIN (20). By Molière. February 3, 1972. Director, John Ulmer; scenery and lighting, William F. Matthews; costumes, Betty Williams and Susan Harvuot. With Eric Tavares, Hannah Brandon, Humphrey Davis, Jerry Hardin.

SLOW DANCE ON THE KILLING GROUND (20). By William Hanley. March 3, 1972. Director, William Guild; scenery, William F. Matthews; lighting, Peter Glynn, Lisi Oliver, Erica Lewis; costumes, Susan Harvuot. With Humphrey Davis, Ron Glass, Hannah Brandon.

PLAZA SUITE (20). By Neil Simon. March 31, 1972. Director, John Ulmer; scenery, Richard Blair; lighting, Erica Lewis; costumes, Susan Harvuot. With Jerry Hardin, Carole Couche, Raymond Singer, Hamp Watson, Hannah Brandon.

CANADA

HALIFAX

Neptune Theater: Main Stage

THE SERVANT OF TWO MASTERS (15). By Carlo Goldoni; adapted by David Turner. November 18, 1971. Director, Robert Sherrin; designer, Robert Doyle; lighting, Rae Ackerman. With Tony Van Bridge, James Valentine; Nicola Lippman, Susan Hogan.

A DAY IN THE DEATH OF JOE EGG (15). By Peter Nichols. January 20, 1972. Director, Joseph Shaw; designer, Aristides Gazetas. With Colin Fox, Anne Butler, Elizabeth Thomson, Dora Dainton.

I DO! I DO! (21). By Tom Jones and Harvey Schmidt; based on The Fourposter by Jan de Hartog. February 10, 1972. Director, Robert Sherrin; designer, Maurice Strike; lighting,

Rae Ackerman; musical director, Barbara Spence; choreographer, Walter Burgess. With Mark Alden, Evelyne Anderson.

THE PRICE (15). By Arthur Miller. March 9, 1972. Director, Kurt Reis; designer, Aristides Gazetas. With Edward Binns, Ludi Claire, Albert M. Ottenheimer, Laurence Hugo.

THE MATCHMAKER (15). By Thornton Wilder. March 30, 1972. Director, Robert Sherrin; scenery, Aristides Gazetas; costumes, Hilary Corbett. With Sandy Webster, Dean Regan, David Renton, Helene Winston, Brian McKay, Patricia Hamilton.

Neptune Theater: Special Productions

G.K.C. (2). The Wit and Wisdom of Gilbert Keith Chesterton compiled and performed by Tony Van Bridge. November 21 and 28, 1971.

THE DANDY LION (16). December 26, 1971. Children's Christmas show.

Neptune Theater: Second Stage Studio Productions
(new plays project)

CREEPS (25). By David Freeman. February 24, 1972. Director, David Renton; designers, Phil Phelan, Geoff LeBoutelier.
Michael ....Ian Deakin
Pete ....Lionel Simmons
Tom ....Keith Maddock
Sam ....Don Allison
Jim ....David Miller
Miss Saunders ....Flora Montgomery
Thelma; Miss C. P. ....Dianne LeDuc

Shriner ....Ernest Fleet
Shriner ....Brian Crocker
Mr. Carson ....David Renton
Place: A sheltered workshop for cerebral palsy victims. (a "sheltered workshop" is a place where disabled people can go and work at their own pace without the pressure of the competitive outside world. Its aim is not to provide a living wage but rather to occupy idle hours.) One act.

SWEET HOME SWEET (17). By James Nicol. April 12, 1972. Director, Robert Reid; scenery, Phil Phalen and Geoff LeBoutelier; lighting, Jane Boland; costumes, Barbara Joudrey.

Billy Brown	Bruce Wilson
Marcey	Heather Chandler
Ruth Brown	Flo Patterson
Abraham Lincoln Brown	Vernon Cain

About destruction of the basic social unit, the family, by barriers and prejudices erected to protect society as a whole. Two acts.

STONEHENGE (17). By Douglas Bankson. May 10, 1972. Director, Don Allison; scenery, Hugh Jones; lighting, Jane Boland; costumes, Barbara Joudrey.

Helga Helmgrin	Karen Marginson
Chester	Keith Maddock
Dorthy	Nicole Lippman
Wanda Weaver-Cartlidge	Flo Patterson
Dr. Tom Suture	Bob Reid
Gelda Pratt	Joan Orenstein
Frank Pratt	Lionel Simmons

Ancients: Bruce Armstrong, Phyllis Malcolm-Stewart, Joan Stebbings, Flora Montgomery-Moore. About an old man who refuses to stay within society's rules for the aged. Two acts.

MONTREAL

Centaur Theater

TOTAL ECLIPSE (33). By Christopher Hampton. October 20, 1971 (North American Premiere). Director, Elsa Bolam; scenery and lighting, Mousseau; costumes; Doug Robinson.

Mme. de Fleurville;

Eugenie	Monique Mercure
Mathilde Verlaine	Anne Scarfe
Arthur Rimbaud	Percy Harkness
Paul Verlaine	Alan Scarfe
Charles Cros	Richard Donat
M. Mauté de Fleurville	Maurice Podbrey
Etienne Carjat	Peter Elliott
Ernest; Man in II, 6	Brian Stavechny
Jean Aicard	Maurice Podbrey
Isabelle Rimbaud	Dana Ivey
Barman	Griffith Brewer
Maid	Susan Shillingford

Act I, Scenes 1 and 2; The Paris home of M. Mauté Fleurville, Sept. 1871. Scene 3: Charles Cros's apartment, Nov. 1871. Scene 4: Café du Théâtre du Bobino, Dec. 1871. Scene 5: Café du Rat Mort, June 1872. Act II, Scene 1: A hotel room in Brussels, July 1872. Scene 2: 34-5 Howland Street, London, Nov. 1872. Scene 3: 8 Great College Street, London, July 1873. Scene 4: A hotel room in Brussels, July 1873. Scene 5: The Black Forest, near Stuttgart, Feb. 1875. Scene 6: a Cafe in Paris, 1892.

THE MAIDS by Jean Genet, directed by André Brassard and THE EXCEPTION AND THE RULE by Bertolt Brecht, directed by Alan Scarfe (27). November 24, 1971. Scenery, Michael Eagan; lighting, Vladimir Svetlovsky; costumes, Erla Gliserman. With Monique Mercure, Dana Ivey, Mia Anderson, Maurice Podbrey, Griffith Brewer, Peter Elliott, George Dawson.

AT THE HAWK'S WELL, A FULL MOON IN MARCH, THE CAT AND THE MOON (26). By William Butler Yeats. January 5, 1972. Director, James Flannery; scenery and costumes, Maria Kolodziej; lighting, Vladimir Svetlovsky; masks, Felix Mirbt. With Dana Ivey, June Keevil, Rosemary Toombs, Peter Elliott, Brian Stavechny, Richard Donat, Alfred Therien.

SUMMER DAYS (26). By Romain Weingarten; translated by Suzanne Grossman. February 2, 1972. Director, Maurice Podbrey; scenery, Germain; lighting, Vladimir Svetlovsky; costumes, Susan Parkou. With Derek McGrath, Caryne Chapman, Peter Elliott, Alan Scarfe.

THE ENTERTAINER (33). By John Osborne. March 1, 1972. Director, Elsa Bolam; scenery and costumes, Michael Eagan; lighting, Vladimir Svetlovsky. With Dana Ivey, Gerard Parkes, Jennifer Phipps, Adrian Waller.

ELECTRA (26). By Euripides; translated by Phillip Vellacott. April 5, 1972. Director-designer, Alan Barlow; lighting, Vladimir Svetlovsky; costumes, Erla Gliserman; masks, Felix Mirbt. With Dana Ivey, Richard Donat, Jennifer Phipps, Antonio Lo Pilato.

THE BLOOD KNOT (27). By Athol Fugard. May 3, 1972. Director, Alan Scarfe; scenery, Felix Mirbt; lighting, Vladimir Svetlovsky; costumes, Janet Knechtel. With Zakes Mokae, Maurice Podbrey.

STRATFORD, ONT.

Stratford Festival: Festival Theater

MUCH ADO ABOUT NOTHING (37). By William Shakespeare. June 7, 1971. Director, William Hutt; designer, Alan Barlow; lighting, Gil Wechsler. With William Needles, Pamela Brook, Jane Casson, Kenneth Welsh, Mervyn Blake, Eric Donkin.

THE DUCHESS OF MALFI (36). By John Webster. June 8, 1971. Director, Jean Gascon; designer, Desmond Heeley; lighting, Gil Wechsler. With Barry MacGregor, William Needles, Powys Thomas, Roland Hewgill, Pat Galloway.

MACBETH (22). By William Shakespeare. June 9, 1971. Director, Peter Gill; designer, Deirdre Clancy; lighting, Gil Wechsler; fights, Patrick Crean. With Ian Hogg, Pat Galloway, Kenneth Welsh, Karen Ludwig, Mervyn Blake.

VOLPONE (17). By Ben Jonson. July 27, 1971. Director, David William; designer, Annena Stubbs; lighting, Gil Wechsler. With William Hutt, Douglas Rain, Pamela Brook, Ruby Holbrook.

Stratford Festival: Avon Theater

AN ITALIAN STRAW HAT (18). By Eugene Labiche and Marc-Michel; translated by Michael Bawtree. July 2, 1971. Director, Stephen Porter; designer, Lewis Brown; lighting, Gil Wechsler. With Gary Files, Joseph Shaw, Robin Gammell, Tony Van Bridge; Suzanne Grossmann, Mary Savidge, Donald Ewer.

THERE'S ONE IN EVERY MARRIAGE (24). By Georges Feydeau; translated and adapted by Suzanne Grossmann and Paxton Whitehead. August 6, 1971. Director, Jean Gascon; designer, Alan Barlow; lighting, Gil Wechsler. With Martha Henry, Peter Donat, Richard Curnock, Jack Creley, Dinah Christie, Tony Van Bridge, Mary Savidge, Elva Mai Hoover.

Stratford Festival: Third Stage

THE RED CONVERTIBLE (18). By Enrique Buenaventura; translated and adapted by Michael Bawtree and Antony Sampson. July 28, 1971 (continental premiere). Director, Michael Bawtree; designer, Art Penson; lighting and sound recording, Ian Johnson; songs composed by Michael Bawtree; other music, Michael Bawtree, Alan Laing.

1st Jay ....Mari Gorman
2d Jay ....Patricia Grant
1st Man ....Edward Henry
2d Man ....David Schurmann
    The action of the play takes place in and around Piccadilly in a London born out of the imagination of a Latin American. Two acts.

VANCOUVER

The Play House Theater Company: Mainstage

THE CHEMMY CIRCLE (24). By Georges Feydeau; translated and adapted by Suzanne Grossmann. October 8, 1971. Director, Paxton Whitehead; scenery, Brian Jackson; lighting, David Hinks; costumes, Hilary Corbett. With Lee Taylor, Frances Hyland, Bob Roberts, Christopher Newton.

THE SORROWS OF FREDERICK (26). By Romulus Linney. November 12, 1971. Director, Paxton Whitehead; scenery and costumes, Brian Jackson; lighting, David Hinks. With Donald Davis, Derek Ralston, Dorothy Davies, Shirley Broderick.

TREASURE ISLAND (18). By Bernard Miles; adapted from the novel by Robert Louis Stevenson. December 18, 1971. Direc-

tor, Patrick Crean; scenery and costumes, Cameron Porteous; lighting, David Hinks. With John Pozer, Michael Ball, Derek Ralston, Graeme Campbell. Note: this production was also presented in Ottawa for two weeks in January 1972, under the auspices of the National Arts Center.

CRABDANCE (25). By Beverley Simons. January 14, 1972. Director, Frances Hyland; scenery and costumes, Cameron Porteous; lighting, David Hinks. With Jennifer Phipps, Hutchison Shandro, Sandy Webster, Neil Dainard, Ed Willsher.

RELATIVELY SPEAKING (25). By Alan Ayckbourn. February 11, 1972. Director, Tom Kerr; scenery and costumes, Brian Jackson; lighting, Ian Pratt. With Paxton White-head, Gay Rose, Tony Van Bridge, Mary Huggins.

THE NATIVE (25). By Merv Campone. March 10, 1972 (world premiere). Director, Neil Dainard; scenery, costumes and lighting, Cameron Porteous; music, Pat Rose.

The Custodian . . . . Robert Clothier
Joe . . . . Stephen Markle
Palana . . . . Len George

Pal's Sister . . . . Elizabeth Murphy
Natives: David Foster, Pat John, Nick Man-cuso, Joe Sala.

HADRIAN VII (24). By Peter Luke; based on works by Fr. Rolfe (Baron Corvo). April 7, 1972. Director, Alan Scarfe; scenery and costumes, Brian Jackson; lighting, Lynne Hyde. With Robert Casper, Diana Wassman, Patrick Boxill, Stuart Kent.

WINNIPEG

Manitoba Theater Center: Main Stage

WHAT THE BUTLER SAW (18). By Joe Orton. October 25, 1971. Director, John Hirsch; scenery and lighting, William Rit-man; costumes, Doreen Brown. With Biff Mc-Guire, Jeannie Carson, Linda Carlson, Robin Ward, Donald Ewer, Sandy Webster.

ALICE THROUGH THE LOOKING GLASS (23). By Lewis Carroll; adapted by Keith Turnbull. November 29, 1971 (world premiere). Director, Keith Turnbull; scenery and costumes, Maurice Strike; lighting, Gil Wechsler; music composed and directed by Alan Laing.

White Knight . . . . David Dodimead
Alice . . . . Margaret Bard
White Queen . . . . Charles Hudson
White King; Man in the White
    Paper Suit . . . . Dennis Thatcher
Caterpillar; Lion . . . . Michael Mawson
Red Queen . . . . Jack Medley
Fawn, Haigha . . . . Arif Hasnain
Tweedledum . . . . Tibor Feheregyhazi
Tweedledee . . . . George Popovich
Humpty Dumpty . . . . David Sabin
    Gremlins: Abraham Alvarez, Guy Banner-man, P. M. Howard, Alan Jones, Terry Judd, Bob Land, David Stein, David Dexter, Brian Horsfall, Jon Kirk Inman.
    Taped sequences were created by Bill Wil-liams and percussionists Bill Graham and Jim Watts. Played without an intermission.

THE HOMECOMING (18). By Harold Pin-ter. January 10, 1972. Director, Michael Maw-son. Scenery, lighting and costumes, Peter Wingate. With David Dodimead, Christopher Newton, Robert Clothier, Peter Rogan, Jack Davidson, Irena Mayeska.

THE SUN AND THE MOON (18). By James

Reaney. February 7, 1972 (world premiere). Director, Keith Turnbull; scenery and cos-tumes, Peter Wingate; lighting, Robert Rein-holdt.

Tramp . . . . Charles Hudson
Andrew Kingbird . . . . Brian Horsfall
Mrs. Fall . . . . Jean Panton
Ellen Moody . . . . Jean Bergmann
Frank Fall . . . . Terry Judd
Susan Kingbird . . . . Mary Hitch
Rev. Francis Kingbird . . . . . David Dodimead
Edna Moody . . . . Margaret MacLeod
Ralph . . . . Brian McKay
Samuel Moody . . . . Clesson Goodhue
Rev. F. Conybeare . . . . Victor Sutton
Charlotte Shade . . . . Olive Deering
Stephen . . . . Guy Bannerman
Dennis . . . . P.M. Howard
Mrs. Irving . . . . Phyllis West
Mrs. Verge . . . . Naomi Permut
Mrs. McAdams . . . . Margaret Lyndon
Mrs. Tufts . . . . Pat Van Der Tol
Mrs. Walton . . . . Joyce Humeniuk
Amelia Tufts . . . . Margaret Bard
    The play takes place in the Manse, both in-side and outside, Millbank, Ontario, 1935. Three acts.

LADY FREDERICK (18). By W. Somerset Maugham. March 6, 1972. Director, Leslie Lawton; scenery and costumes, Maurice Strike. With Irena Mayeska, Basil Hoskins, Norman Comer, Margaret Macleod.

THE COMEDY OF ERRORS (18). By Wil-liam Shakespeare. April 17, 1972. Director, Keith Turnbull; scenery and costumes, Tiina Lipp; lighting, Robert Reinholdt. With Jeff Jones, Bernard Hopkins, Dean Harris, Peggy Mahon, Irena Mayeska, Robert Haley, Peggy Cosgrave, Clarence Felder.

Manitoba Theater Center: Warehouse Theater

HEAD 'EM OFF AT THE PAS (18). Con-ceived by John Wood; researched by Penny

Burk and Roxy Freedman. January 5, 1972 (world premiere). Director, John Wood; visual designer, Bill Williams. With Abraham Alvarez, Margaret Bard, Jean Bergmann, P.M. Howard, Alan Jones, Robert Land. This play is "a kind of historical documentary of Manitoba Province with song and dance."

Manitoba Theater Center: Children's Theater

ALICE THROUGH THE LOOKING GLASS (10). By Lewis Carroll; adapted by Keith Turnbull. December 20, 1971.

NAMES AND NICKNAMES (10). By James Reaney. March 27, 1972.

THE SEASON IN LONDON

AN ALTERNATIVE BRITISH THEATER

By John Spurling

Author of the plays *Macrune's Guevara* (1969), *In the Heart of the British Museum* (1971) and *Shades of Heathcliff* (1971) and co-author with John Fletcher of *Samuel Beckett: A Study of His Plays* (published 1972 by Eyre Methuen).

OUTSIDE Britain, the British theater, by which is meant the London, or West End theater, is generally agreed to be flourishing. It is certainly true that tourists flock to see it; that as an industry it just continues to pay its successful investors a sufficient profit; that many of its shows enjoy long runs (so much so that there is nowadays usually a string of productions waiting to "come in," like airliners circling a too popular airport, which would suggest that the 34-odd proscenium theaters are too few, not too many); that there has perhaps never been such a varied and talented choice of actors and actresses; that there is even a notable supply of living playwrights for whose new works European directors come shopping as they might for Savile Row or Carnaby Street suits. When my own first play was performed by the National Theater, for example, it was almost immediately translated into eight languages, and its first performance in West Germany was one of 40 first performances of British plays in West Germany in that season alone.

As show business the West End theater is undoubtedly entertaining its audiences and contributing to British dollar-earnings. In the three main companies which receive government subsidies—the National, the Royal Shakespeare and the Royal Court—it is doing more: mounting fine performances of classic plays from Shakespeare to O'Neill, as well as airing forgotten minor classics and even new works by a few living writers. The Royal Shakespeare specializes in Pinter and Albee, the National in Stoppard and Nichols, the Royal Court in Osborne, Bond and Storey. By a curious twist of fate, the Royal Court Theater, famed for its break with the old theatrical values of the commercial West End in the 1950s, has now become one of the West End's most reliable suppliers of commercially successful plays.

But all that glisters is not gold. West End audiences are for the most part elderly and not getting any younger, while the plays they go to see are tinsel gewgaws (musicals, light comedies, personality shows, museum pieces, or

85

what painters would call "academy" pieces—that is to say, new plays which are really only anemic copies of past masters).

The West End theater, then, is alive and apparently hearty, but actually suffering from a bad attack of hardening arteries. The reason for this is perhaps largely financial. When it costs anything from 15 to 30 thousand pounds to put on a straight play with a small cast; when a play has to run for at least three months before it even begins to show a profit; when the audience has to pay sometimes two pounds for a seat, let alone what it costs them to get there and have a meal afterwards, small wonder that everyone plays for safety. The audience will not dare to spend without the strong recommendation of the critics and not always with that if the play sounds "difficult" or lacks a star performer. The management will aim for something as much in the middle of current taste as possible. The playwrights will either write "academy" pieces or be made to rewrite their work to the formulas required by the management. The buildings themselves, custom-built for a particular kind of "picture-frame" play, impose these same well-worn formulas.

Nevertheless, there is an alternative British theater. It is not often seen in London, where there are few buildings suited to it; it is often travelling, in the manner of those old actor-managers' companies of the 19th century, from one provincial center to another; to see it usually costs much less than a pound, often less than 50 new pence; its expenses are measured in tens of pounds instead of thousands; its performers live more like gypsies than like ratepayers and householders; its choice of plays does not depend on the purse strings and therefore the taste of commercial managements; its audiences are mainly young, though not exclusively so, and many of them have probably never seen a picture-frame play on a picture-frame stage in their lives.

Of course, I've put everything the wrong way round. Does it matter how much the thing costs or how old the audience is, so long as the event itself has some artistic value? The point is this: theater works best when it best seizes the imagination of the audience, when it sets that imagination to work as an integral part of the whole experience. The longevity and consequent predictability of the picture-frame plays have increasingly stultified the audience's imagination, reduced it to a quiescent role, impaired its appetite with the packaged goods of mere surface naturalism. A man from one of the big movie companies once tried to explain to me the advantages of writing for the screen rather than for the theater: "You can have a hundred different sets if you want." But on a bare stage, without a stick of furniture, I can have two hundred sets merely by saying the word.

We are back, in other words, behind the days of Restoration Comedy, behind the invention of the dramatic fish-tank. We are discovering that the theatrical conditions suitable for reflecting the late 17th, the 18th, the 19th and half the 20th centuries no longer reflect our world. We need the spaciousness, the flexibility, the simplicity of those empty areas used by the Greeks, the Japanese Noh, the Elizabethans. A few years ago, when I was still struggling to overcome in myself the conventional idea of how a play should be written, I used to dream of being cast away on a desert island with a large party of survivors: it would be so much easier to write plays to be performed in those conditions, by non-actors on a non-stage, without sets or props. Looking back now, it seems extraordinary how long it took me to realize that if Mahomet couldn't go to the desert island, the island could come to him.

But the moment you've disposed of the sofas, the occasional tables, the trays of drinks and the cunningly-painted flats, you also discover that you've disposed of the actors—at least these actors you were used to. That bare space you've cleared is not just a place for speaking lines from, it has got to contain a spectacle. Physical things have got to happen there, otherwise you might as well sit your actors on chairs and have them read your text. So the actors become all-purpose dancers, singers, acrobats, tumblers as well as speakers. And then the playwright ceases to be a person who simply writes an oral form of literature in the privacy of his study and becomes something more like an architect or a dramatic sculptor. His task is to envisage a dramatic event in its completed form, an amalgam of speech, dance, song, acrobatics, mime, gesture, tableau, a whole repertoire for the whole human body; through which he will express, not just illustrate, his theme. He will supply the blueprint for the event as well as one of the building materials (the text), but the actual creation of the finished work will be shared with him by the director and actors. It is no longer, then, a question of a playwright writing a play and sending it round until a management finds a company to perform it, but of a concerted creation on the basis of a preliminary design.

In certain companies, of course, the playwright's role is much more subordinate to the actors' or the director's than I have suggested; some companies even dispense with the writer altogether. But my own experience of working with two quite different "desert island" companies is that the more the playwright can give them to build on, the more they themselves can build: my least successfully envisaged scenes, those where I had perhaps lazily fallen back on old tricks, or not sufficiently developed my initial idea, could not be rescued by the actors; while scenes where I had reached out for something difficult, seemingly impossible, made the actors go well beyond what I had envisaged. Since I was writing both plays at more or less the same time (a scene or two ahead) as they were in rehearsal, the actors' discoveries of what they themselves could do with a scene encouraged me to make bolder demands on them.

But what's in it for the audience? What do they get in exchange for their plush seats, "theater atmosphere," realistic sets, star actors, "character parts," sitting-room or kitchen-sink chronologies? Is it just hard benches, ubiquitous dust, protracted contortions by young and possibly inexperienced performers, unintelligible "experimental" texts? Alas, it sometimes is. What they *should* get, however, is an indispensable part in the event, and by this I don't mean "audience involvement" in the crudely literal sense, which is more often in my experience audience alienation, since performers who confront and even bully members of the audience verbally or physically only succeed in pushing them back into themselves as individuals—"I am Jack Smith and I do not like being treated like this"—people, in other words, who are no longer taking part in the concerted event, but who are for at least as long as the confrontation lasts, and probably for the rest of the evening, damagingly isolated.

No one, so far as I know, has yet satisfactorily explained what exactly happens when audience and performers become successfully integrated in a theatrical experience. As a frequent member of audiences myself I know that when the performance works I am aware all the time of being physically in my seat but at the same time am taking part, both mentally and emotionally, in what is happening on stage; taking part, not just as an observer, but actually affecting, in concert with the rest of the audience, the mental and emotional quality of the performance.

As a playwright, then, what I must aim for is to create a series of effects, using all the verbal and physical means at my disposal, which will arouse the mental and emotional attention of the audience. As this attention is fed back to the stage, so the performers must build on it and pass it back in turn, until what is happening in that theater (or dusty room) is as different in quality from what happened in rehearsal as the rehearsal from the playwright's original design.

It is not necessary—indeed it is perhaps actually an impediment—for the stage effects which bring about this shared experience to be intellectually intelligible at first viewing (any more than the Mona Lisa is) but it is necessary for them to strike directly at the audience's heart, bowels, mind, or wherever it keeps its emotions. They must also keep striking, and in a variety of modes, according to a distinct and satisfying pattern of rising and falling intensity, for the duration of the performance.

I am not suggesting that this has not been achieved in the past or that it is not occasionally still achieved by picture-frame plays with star actors in plush theaters. What I do suggest is that for the true theatrical event this is all that matters. However often the desert-island companies may disappoint one in their results, the means they are using, the ends they are aiming at are the right ones, the only ones, the ones for which audiences sat on hard seats in dusty theaters for days at a time when Aeschylus invented modern drama by the introduction of the second actor. Furthermore, when it only costs a button you can afford to go in defiance of the critics and leave at the interval if you don't like it.

THE SEASON IN THE WEST END

By Ossia Trilling

Critic, lecturer, broadcaster; member of the Council of the Critics' Circle; vice president of the International Theater Critics' Association; European editor of *Best Plays*

THE SEASON GOT OFF TO A SPANKING START on its very first day with Peter Hall's production of Harold Pinter's latest fantasy-drama *Old Times*. This was one of several plays, Peter Brook's *A Midsummer Night's*

Dream being another, that kept the house-full notices permanently in place outside the London home of the Royal Shakespeare Company, the Aldwych Theater, throughout the year and enabled the four-man board of directors to boast that the box office records had reached an all-time high both in London and in Stratford. Just as strong was the demand for seats at R.S.C.'s temporarily leased experimental stage, the Place, where an exceedingly realistic production of *Miss Julie* shocked some members of the audience with a degree of frankness that went far beyond anything even its author had imagined. Another box office draw at the Aldwych, with its subsidy nearly half that given to the National Theater, was Pinter's own production of James Joyce's *Exiles,* earlier given an airing at the Mermaid Theater but now revived with some cast changes and a marked improvement in delivery. No less popular was the appeal of Gorky's *The Enemies,* a forgotten pre-revolutionary drama with unexpected lessons for some of today's hotheads. George Etherege's *The Man of Mode* gave London a chance to renew acquaintance with this little-known Restoration author and to enjoy the sight of Alan Howard taking an on-stage bath in the buff. These productions, so dissimilar from the point of view of their style, confirmed the rightness of the R.S.C.'s diversification policy, introduced more than ten years back by Peter Hall and taken over wholeheartedly by Trevor Nunn and his collaborators. The closing production of Albee's *All Over* was also staged by Peter Hall. Its symbolical decor, like that for *Old Times,* was designed by John Bury. My American friends found its American accents (except Angela Lansbury's) phony and unacceptable, but this is a fault that British theatergoers seem never to worry about. The same criticism, incidentally, was leveled at *Long Day's Journey Into Night,* with the National Theater company.

Like the R.S.C., the National Theater under Laurence Olivier, or Lord Olivier for those who insist on titles, branched out into new pastures by leasing the New Theater in the heart of the West End in an effort to meet the growing demand for tickets that the smaller Old Vic was unable to satisfy. The move proved financially disastrous, largely because of the choice of repertory, but also because inner dissension, resulting in the departure of certain leading players and quarrels among some of the newcomers, were reflected in the uneven work. Christopher Plummer made a brave shot at the title role of Jonathan Miller's evocative, if emasculated, version of Büchner's political masterpiece *Danton's Death,* but did not stay the course; and even Paul Scofield, for all his insinuating graces as the misogynist cuckold of Pirandello's *The Rules of the Game,* left precipitately despite his nomination as Olivier's new assistant director. Eventually the O'Neill revival saved the company's fortunes, both artistically and financially speaking, and for the last three months replaced the alternating repertory planned at the New, vying in public appeal with the offerings at the rival Aldwych Theater. One American visitor, a director by profession, swore to me that one evening she saw Olivier leave the stage in mid-action on an exit line not in the published text or in any known version of *Long Day's Journey Into Night.* He returned some seconds later presumably having steadied himself offstage and said to Ronald Pickup's Edmund

Tyrone "I feel better now." Nobody but my informant seemed ever to have noticed this bit of extemporizing, but I report the story here in good faith as a remarkable example of one great actor's extraordinary presence of mind.

Having turned the National's fortunes, the O'Neill went into cold storage until the following fall, but the ensuing productions at the Old Vic, where it is to be revived, proved that the tide had truly turned. The announcement that the 44-year-old Peter Hall, after much dillying and dallying, had been appointed director-designate to succeed Olivier when the new National Theater building opens in 1974, gave evident satisfaction to all concerned. For the time being Hall retains his connection with the R.S.C. as one of its directors, but whether the nine-year-old rivalry between the two companies will now turn into a spell of closer collaboration time alone can tell. Certainly in the field of foreign visitors the R.S.C. has had it all its own way. The productions invited by Olivier to the Old Vic left little impression, and even the undoubted artistic merits of the season given there by the Belgian National Theater were not enough to fill the seats. By contrast, Peter Daubeny's 9th World Theater Season at the Aldwych broke all box office records, which only goes to show that managing a foreign theater season is not merely a matter of using the telephone and signing a contract, but requires time, application and good judgment as well. Even the Parisian actors under Ariane Mnouchkine, with their collectively mounted drama of the French Revolution entitled *1789,* were unable to pack the Round House. Towards the end of the season the National had two more smash hits to its credit: Tom Stoppard's mock-philosophical thriller *Jumpers,* which introduced, unless I'm much mistaken, full frontal female nudity for the first time on this august stage in the shape of the shapely Diana Rigg; and Jonathan Miller's Hogarthian *The School for Scandal,* which gave its audience a new view of life in 18th century Britain, and not a flattering one at that. Before we leave the National Theater, we must not forget the work of the Young Vic company under the inspired and adventurous Frank Dunlop, who was able during this time to open a studio stage alongside the main stage for smaller-scale productions.

One other modern theater opened its doors in London during the season. This was the Shaw Theater, named after the dramatist and inaugurated by the National Youth Theater under Michael Croft and its new professional wing, the Dolphin Players, with *The Devil's Disciple.* Here, too, Vanessa Redgrave, after a halting attempt at management and even direction when she took over the staging of Robert Shaw's *Cato Street* at the Young Vic, returned to her first Shakespearean role in many years as Viola in *Twelfth Night,* with its palpable echoes of her earlier, adorable and unforgettable Rosalind at Stratford of over ten years ago.

Strictly speaking, the statement about the Shaw being London's only new theater requires qualifying: true as far as it goes, it ignores the mushrooming of a host of lunchtime and cellar theaters, and even a number of "pub theaters," in which out-of-work actors and authors of one-acters can stretch their talents, often for the audience's benefit just as much as for their own. This is a welcome innovation, not unlike Paris's cafe theaters, because it also provides a shop window for theater people who might otherwise have perished in the frustrating rat race of the commercial and subsidized playhouses. I should also mention the re-emergence of Ed Berman's Interaction troupe, and his Almost Free Theater, housed temporarily in a block under sentence of demolition—and so-called because audiences may enter without payment and are free to leave a monetary contribution on departing, if they are so minded.

Lest I be accused of irresponsibility when I say that the only newsworthy event at the Mermaid was a topless Desdemona, let me also recall Pinter's *The Caretaker,* revived by Christopher Morahan; Michael Redgrave's return to the live theater after a nine years' absence in a curious drama, William Trevor's *The Old Boys,* in which he appeared yet again as a seedy schoolmaster; Shaw's *Geneva,* which appears even more senile with its new, hitherto unperformed last act than it did in 1938; and a failed, if brave, attempt to give Camus his theatrical due in a version of *Les Justes* called *The Price of Justice.* At the Royal Court the policy, unannounced but assiduously followed, of providing the commercal theater with some of its most notable transfers was kept going in the case of John Osborne's *West of Suez,* E.A. Whitehead's *Alpha Beta* and David Storey's *The Changing Room,* but not in the case of a play far more deserving than any of these, Edward Bond's *Lear,* nor even in that of Charles Wood's *Veterans,* a *jeu d'esprit* in which John Gielgud not only played himself but did so surpassingly well. At the Royal Court's junior stage, the Theater Upstairs, an unusually large number of noteworthy plays included the prizewinning *As Time Goes By* by a Trinidadian author, Mustapha Matura, and Athol Fugard's own production of the British premiere of *Boesman and Lena.* The T.U. seems willy-nilly to have inherited the Royal Court's old role.

Outlying theaters in London had their significant contributions to make. Among them might be noted Joan Littlewood's long-delayed return to the theater at her East London home with a musical rehash of *Sparrers Can't Sing,* entitled *The Londoners,* and a revival of Brendan Behan's *The Hostage* with most of the original 14-year-old company. At Charles Marowitz's Open Space a second politically-oriented play by Trevor Griffiths called *Sam Sam* was preceeded by a delightful if not wholly successful attempt to turn Roland Penrose's English translation of Picasso's 25-year-old poetic fantasy *The Four Little Girls* into a viable stage vehicle for the first time. If it is remembered at all, it may well be for the four naked little actresses who contrived to look like ten-year-old Lolitas while qualifying for Equity contracts as adults.

London had its usual invasion of American imports, from failures like *Ambassador,* adapted from Henry James's *The Ambassadors* and starring Danielle Darrieux, to smash hits like *Company.* A revival of *Show Boat* revealed the business acumen of impresario Harold Fielding, as did the world premiere—also produced by him—of the Harold Rome musical version of *Gone With the Wind* which, for all its attractive staging and lighting and the talented June Ritchie in the Vivien Leigh part, must surely go down in history as one of the few London stage shows in this century in which a real horse was brought on and disgraced itself shamefully at the most inopportune moment in the plot (or else openly expressed its candid opinion of the quality of the entertainment in the only way it knew how).

This leads me to bring this report to a close with only a superficial reference to what is misleadingly known as the commercial theater, either because it stages long-running smash hits which reimburse its backers handsomely, or else because it puts on flops and causes gnashing of teeth in managerial offices. Well, we have had the usual run of hits for other people's money, and this year as usual I find it hard to tell one from another. Often I suspect the titles might be interchangeable, without anyone's being the wiser. Take for instance the following: *Move Over Mrs. Markham; Don't Just Lie There, Say Something; No Sex Please, We're British.* I have a feeling I've seen all these plays, but somehow they merge into one single blurred image. No doubt the fault is entirely mine. I do remember the details of Simon Gray's *Butley,* not only because Pinter directed it, but also because of Alan Bates's moving performance as a homosexual university professor with an unhappy marriage to make things even worse for him. This play belongs to a category all its own. And, of course, I remember *Dear Antoine* because it shows up Anouilh as the shallowest of stage philosophers, and *The Threepenny Opera* because this piece of Brechtian class-war propaganda came in the midst of a strike and power cuts and seemed somehow to be pointing a finger of scorn at the class war raging in the street outside. And there was Frank Marcus's latest tragicomedy of marital relations in Pirandellian garb called *Notes on a Love Affair,* starring Irene Worth, the only American who can credibly pass for an Englishwoman in a realistic play, which this, incidentally, was far from being. And a lot more besides. Truly, the London theater is one in which one can easily suffocate from a surfeit of theatrical fare if one is not very, very careful and choosy.

Highlights of the London Season

Selected and compiled by Ossia Trilling

OUTSTANDING PERFORMANCES

COLIN BLAKELEY as Deeley in *Old Times*	PAUL SCOFIELD as Leone Gala in *The Rules of the Game*	PEGGY ASHCROFT as Claire Lannes in *The Lovers of Viorne*
ALAN BATES as Butley in *Butley*	YVONNE BRYCELAND as Lena in *Boesman and Lena*	ALEC GUINNESS as Father in *A Voyage Round My Father*
ALAN HOWARD as Mr. Dorimant in *The Man of Mode*	BRENDA BRUCE as Mme Irma in *The Balcony*	LAURENCE OLIVIER as James Tyrone in *Long Day's Journey Into Night*
MARGARET LEIGHTON as Elena in *Reunion in Vienna*	DAVID WARNER as Hammett in *The Great Exhibition*	JOHN GIELGUD as Sir Geoffrey Kendle in *Veterans*
VANESSA REDGRAVE as Polly in *The Threepenny Opera*	MICHAEL HORDERN as George in *Jumpers*	JUNE RITCHIE as Scarlet O'Hara in *Gone With the Wind*

OUTSTANDING DIRECTORS

PETER BROOK
A Midsummer Night's Dream

TERRY HANDS
The Balcony

JONATHAN MILLER
The School for Scandal

OUTSTANDING DESIGNERS

PATRICK ROBERTSON
Danton's Death

DAVID HAYS
and TIM GOODCHILD
Gone With the Wind

FARRAH
The Balcony

OUTSTANDING NEW BRITISH PLAYS

(D)—Playwright's London debut. Figure in parentheses is number of performances; plus sign (+) indicates play was still running on June 1, 1972

OLD TIMES by Harold Pinter. Triangular recollection of times past. With Vivien Merchant, Colin Blakeley, Dorothy Tutin. (70 in repertory)

TYGER by Adrian Mitchell. National Theater's production of "a celebration of the life and works of William Blake." With Gerald James, Jane Wenham. (57 in repertory)

WEST OF SUEZ by John Osborne. The death of British upper-middle-class "colonialism." With Ralph Richardson, Jill Bennett. (206)

AS TIME GOES BY by Mustapha Matura (D). Edinburgh Traverse Theater's production by a Trinidadian-born author about immigrants' problems in the U.K. With Stephen Kalipha, Carole Hayman. (17)

LEAR by Edward Bond. New, horrific version of the old legend of uncontrolled and willful power. With Harry Andrews, Mark McManus, Rosemary McHale, Carmel McSharry. (33)

OCCUPATIONS by Trevor Griffiths. Revival of 1970 Manchester Stables Theater production about a revolutionary dilemma in pre-

Fascist Italy, in the R.S.C.'s new experimental season. With Estelle Kohler, Philip Locke, Clement McCallin. (19)

THE CHANGING ROOM by David Storey. The world seen through the eyes of a 13-man football team. With Edward Judd, Bill Owen, Warren Clarke, Mark McManus. (108)

ALPHA BETA by E.A. Whitehead. How marriage treats two of its victims. With Rachel Roberts, Albert Finney. (107+)

JUMPERS by Tom Stoppard. Philosophical anti-thriller comedy. With Michael Hordern, Diana Rigg (51+ in repertory)

THE GREAT EXHIBITION by David Hare. Labor M.P. exposes himself. With David Warner, Caroline Seymour, Penelope Wilson. (27)

VETERANS by Charles Wood. Strange events while shooting a film in Turkey. With John Gielgud, John Mills, Ann Bell. (40)

NOTES ON A LOVE AFFAIR by Frank Marcus. Pirandellian view of the eternal triangle. With Irene Worth, Julia Foster, Nigel Davenport. (71+)

LIMITED RUNS OF INTERESTING NEW BRITISH PLAYS

AMARYLLIS by David McNiven. The rhythm of birth and death. With the Edinburgh Traverse Theater Workshop Company. (4)

ALBERT AND VIRGINIA by Richard Harris. Double bill of marital situation comedies. With Virginia Stride, Paul Hampoletz, David Jason. (12)

SWEET ALICE by Stanley Eveling. Morality on current fashion. With the Edinburgh Traverse Theater Workshop Company. (6)

BOY IN DARKNESS by Paul Alexander. Adapted from a short story by Mervyn Peake.

With Raymond Platt, Bernard Hopkins, Peter Dennis, Candida Fawsitt. (12)

MAYBE THAT'S YOUR PROBLEM lyrics by Don Black (British), music by Walter Scharf (American), story by Lionel Chetwynd (Canadian). World premiere of Anglo-American-Canadian musical. With Douglas Lambert, Harold Kasket, Andee Silver, Al Mancini. (16)

OUR SUNDAY TIMES by Stanley Eveling. What made the yachtsman Donald Crowhurst go mad. With the Edinburgh Traverse Theater Workshop Company. (15)

THE LAST EMPERORS by David Shellan (D). The fall of Constantinople. With the Questors Theater Company. (4)

JOHN by David Mowat. The relationship between four people and the mute, catatonic drop-out John. With the Questors Theater Company. (4)

JOE LIVES by Alex Glasgow (D). Portrait of the Tyneside bard of the 1850s, Joe Wilson. With John Woodvine, John Gould. (6)

POOR DUMB ANIMALS by James Hepburn. Surrealist view of life through animals' eyes, based on stanzas by Wallace Stevens. With the Questors Theater Company. (4)

PACKAGE DEAL by Peter Robert Scott (D). Three two-character pieces about the varying doings of three couples. With Christine Edmonds, the author. (11)

THE WHAT ON THE LANDING by Alan Plater. Solitary man's imagined bugbears and bogeys. With Brian Poyser, Barry McGinn. (6)

APRICOTS by Trevor Griffiths. Sex-starved couple's frustrations. With the Edinburgh Festival 7:84 Theater Company. (12)

ROYAL TUMBLE by William Hobbs. Mixed bill of tumbling, clowning and swordplay. With the Music and Motion Theater Company. (19)

LADIES' NIGHT double bill of LADY by David Cockshott, about a pub bore, with Alexandra Berlin; and THE GIRL WHO DIDN'T LIKE ANSWERS by David Halliwell, TV play about two men's attempts to win over a reluctant female, with Elizabeth Hughes, Noel Collins, Malcolm Ingram. (12)

BACK ON YOUR HANDS by Walter Hall. Kafkaesque exercise in torture, fear and despair. With Anthony Hall, John Hartley, Peter Pacey. (12)

A RANCID PONG by Mike Leigh (D). One-acter about the illusions of sex. With Reginald Stewart, Joolia Cappleman. (12)

PROVISIONS by David Campton, tackling cannibalism as a sick joke, with Alan Bryce, Bernard Stirlin; and CADMIUM FIRTY by Peter Terson, about the effects of an atomically active substance on two thieves, with Michael Carter, Roger Steel; and THE COMMUTERS by Beryl Beace, about two city men's post-retirement dreams, with Ian Calder, Stephen Parkins. (18)

I WAS HITLER'S MAID by Christopher Wilkinson. Transfer to King's Head Theater of Sheffield Playhouse production. With Maev Alexander, Alun Armstrong. (23)

THE LEDGE by Bryan Henry. The unbalanced mind of a would-be suicide. With David Ritchie. (8)

FACES IN THE WALL by Peter Uys (D). The plight of two sad homosexuals. With Ian Lowe, the author. (6)

OH! STARLINGS by Stanley Eveling. Unexpected sequel to a recluse's self-immurement. With Tony Haygarth, David Henderson. (12)

PLAYS FOR RUBBER GO-GO GIRLS by Christopher Wilkinson. Four melodramatic fantasies on the American dream. With Portable Theater Company. (6)

PLUGGED INTO HISTORY by John McGrath and COLLIER'S WOOD by Charles Wood. Transfer of two one-acters about illusion and reality from the Liverpool Everyman. With Gavin Richards, Lisa Daniely. (12)

THE PIRATE KING by Richard Gill (D). A children's play about swashbucklers. With the Polka Puppets and Actors Company. (16)

MEET THE SCRIBBLE KIDS and THE DRAGON WHO LOVED MUSIC by Jane Phillips (D). Two playlets for the very young. With the Caricature Theater Company. (4)

THE PEOPLE SHOW (39th edition) by and with Mark Long, Jose Nava, Laura Gilbert. (12)

DO IT by Pip Simmons. Scenario for the revolution adapted from Jerry Rubin's book. With the Pip Simmons Theater Company. (14)

. . . AND THE CANDLESTICK-MAKER by Douglas Blake (D), CAESAR'S WIFE by Cyril Bolton (D) and THING-THONG by Leon Rosselson (D). Triple-bill one-act plays about an errant, a frightened and a puzzled wife. With Barbara Angell, Carmen du Sautoy, Rita Godfrey, Tom Browne. (11)

I GOT TO DO EVERYTHING MYSELF by Denneth Hill (D). One-acter about youth replacing age. With Simon Chater, Patrick Murphy. (8)

MUDDLETOWN by Bernard Goss. Exeter Northcott Youth Theater's London visit. With Young People's Department Company. (11)

THE OLD SOLDIER by Charles Gray (D). One-acter about a stale marriage. With Julie Martin (later Jill Bridges), Teddy Gray. (18)

LOVERS by Carey Harrison. Transfer of 1969 Manchester Stables production about a sexual joust. With David Shaw, Jennifer Armitage. (12)

LAST DANCE OF THE CORMORANTS by Raoul Alkazzi. Nightmare drama of drugs and death. With Peter Lindsay, Shelly Lambert, Phyllis Lerguson. (18)

TRIP TO MALU by Rikki Logan. Musical one-acter in an Anglo-Spanish setting. With Peter Bert-Jones, Karin Dominic. (5)

WHAT A WAY TO RUN A REVOLUTION by David Benedictus. Musical about the 1926 General Strike, originally conceived for the R.S.C. With the Cockpit Theater Company. (12)

MEETING AT DUSK, THE SWAP and HARRY TOMORROW by Tony Parkin. Three playlets on identity. With Peter Bert-Jones, the author. (6)

THE LAUGHING CAVALIER by Stanley Eveling. A strange meeting in bed. With Neil Seiler, Patricia Doyle. (12)

SEAN, THE FOOL, THE DEVIL AND THE CATS and BEAUTY AND THE BEAST by Ted Hughes and ERNIE'S INCREDIBLE ILLUCINATIONS by Alan Ayckbourn. For the 7-14 age group. With Laurence Keane. (16)

ONE FOR THE ROAD by the Company and Ray Herman. Show based on four Decameron tales. With the Scarborough Theater in the Round Company. (5)

THE SAMARITAN by Peter Terson. National Youth Theater production about a present-day do-gooder. With Timothy Dalton, David Cooke, Richard Moore. (19)

ALICE IN WONDERLAND a new version by and with the Pip Simmons Theater Group. (15)

THE DEED by Philip Martin. The problems of joint houseownership. With Douglas Ridley, Mary Gillingham, Kenneth Oxtoby. (12)

ROMANCE by John Spurling and Charles Ross. Transfer of Leeds Playhouse production of musical satire on musicals. With Bill Simpson, Jess Conrad, Roberta d'Este. (5)

YOUR HUMBLE SERVANT about the Scots poet William McGonagall. One-man show with Robert Robertson. (14)

OSCAR X by Tudor Gates (D). Black-skinned Londoner is victimized by a crazy cop. With Norman Wooland, Derek Griffiths. (6)

THE CLINIC by Peter Crichton-Williams (D). The dangers of V.D. With Roland Oliver; in a double bill with a revival of NIGHT by Harold Pinter. A conversational two-hander. With Dudley Sutton, Tamara Hinchco. (6)

THE NATIONAL INTEREST by David Edgar (D). Anti-Tory satire. With the Bradford University Group. (5)

AUTUMN IN BRAUNSTONE by Claude Durnstone (D). A French schoolmaster reviews his past life. With Mavis Villiers, André Smejkal. (12)

WHITE KNIGHTS by Harvey Webb. Adapted from the Dostoevsky story. With the Attic company. (3)

AS IS PROPER by Tom Mallin. Tragic new view of the marital tussle. With Sheila Allen, Edward Phillips. (14)

BLOOD ON THE TABLE by David Mercer, about sexual frustration, with Barry Lineham; and A WINDOW IN THE ROOF OF THE SKY by Philip Martin, a multi-viewpoint drama, with Yvonne Antrobus. (12)

DEATH IN LEICESTER by Roy Minton. Two city clerks, parading as tramps, wait in vain for salvation. With Philip Stone, Howard Goorney. (23)

ENGLAND EXPECTS by Terence Lewis. Black comic satire on the corrupting ecology. With Gillian Brown, Phillip Ross. (10)

GEORGE AND MOIRA ENTERTAIN A MEMBER OF THE OPPOSITE SEX TO DINNER by John Grillo. Absurdist view of sex and marriage. With David King, Donna Reading. (12)

A LETTER TO MY DEAD WIFE by George Harvey Webb. Dramatic monologue. With the Attic company. (3)

RETURN THE RAIN by Robin McGee. A multimedia musical about the atom bomb. With Center Theater Company. (11)

ROBERT OWEN by James R. Gregson. Documentary of the early socialist and his life. With Ron Bevan, Colin Semel. (18)

CAPTAIN FANTASTIC MEETS THE ECTOMORPH by Barry Pritchard. Suicide of a pop-culture hero. With David Baron, Clive Endersby. (12)

THE ANT AND THE GRASSHOPPER by Keith Darvell. Based on the writings of Scott and Zelda Fitzgerald. With Christopher Guinee, Veronica Lang. (6)

THEATER OF DEATH by Philip Martin. Multi-fantasy play. With David Dixon, Heather Kidd. (10)

PETA, PAM AND WENDY by Julia Barry. Female *Boys in the Band*. With Chili Bouchier, Mareka Mann. (9)

FIREWORKS comprising six commissioned and professionally directed playlets: PROLOGUE by John Grillo and BUM by John Halle, Philosophical soliloquies; MEATBALL by Michael McClure, a crazy view of life; WILL THE KING LEAVE HIS TEAPOT by John Grillo, Hamlet-inspired revolutionary satire; THE COMMITTEE by Olwen Wymark, triangular exchange of identities; UNDER THE HILL by Aubrey Beardsley, adapted by Jack Shepherd, eccentric view of life on Venusberg. With Central London Polytechnic Student Players. (5)

SWAG by John Boland. How to share the proceeds of a robbery. With the Unicorn Company. (18)

BLOW JOB by Snoo Wilson. Surrealist farce linking sex and crime. With the Portable Theater Company. (12)

A LIBERATED WOMAN by Barry Reckord. Re-write of *Don't Gas the Blacks* about female lib. With Linda Marlowe, the author. (18)

THE PROBLEM, with Geoff Hoyle; IF YOU DON'T LAUGH, YOU CRY, with Patrick Barlow; THE DAFFODIL, with Margaret Jones and SENTIMENTAL VALUE with Katya Benjamin. Four whimsical absurdities by David Cregan. (6)

THE TECHNICIANS by Olwen Wymark. Guignolesque variant on the eternal triangle. With Philip Lowrie, Ruth Goring. (13)

OPUS by James Saunders. Science fiction view of man's future. With E15 Acting school students. (5)

THE PONGO PLAYERS by Henry Livings: BEEWINE, THE RIFLE VOLUNTEER and CONCILIATION. Three one-acters based on Lancashire folk tales, set in late Victorian times. With Marilyn Finlay, Patrick Needle. (18)

HOT PANTS by Andrew Carr. A decadent view of sex. With Maggie Maxwell, Stephen Berkoff. (6)

CATO STREET by Robert Shaw. The 1819 Peterloo massacre and the trial of the champions of parliamentary reform. With Vanessa Redgrave. (24)

THE MAN WHO ALMOST KNEW EAMONN ANDREWS by John Heilpern. TV satire. With Andrew Robertson. (4)

HOUSE IN A LONDON SQUARE by Buz Francis and Angela Crow. Study in claustrophobia. With Jonathan Burn, Roger Lloyd-Pack. (10)

A SKY-BLUE LIFE by Howard Brenton. The life of Maxim Gorky. With Stephen Moore, Diana Quick. (15)

SONNY BOY by Paddy Fletcher. The strange story of an even stranger schoolboy. With Incubus Theater Company. (2)

ST. SYLVESTER AND THE DRAGON adapted by Roland Joffe and the cast, from a Cornish medieval play. With the young Vic Theater Company (10)

THE OZ TRIAL by David Illingworth. R.S.C.'s reading of the trial court transcript. (5)

MOTHER ADAM by Charles Dyer. The humor and humors of two lonely people. With Roy Dotrice, Beatrix Lehmann. (12)

THE LOVE SONGS OF MARTHA CANARY by Iain Blair. Three one-acters about a relationship gone sour. With Heather Sears, Boyd Mackenzie, the author. (21)

JUST KEEP LISTENING by John Kendrick. Disillusion of a boxer. With the Pool Lunch Hour Company. (3)

PINOCCHIO by Brian Way. Christmastime revival of established favorite. With the Theater Center Company. (12)

THE ACHIEVEMENTS OF MAN AS RECORDED IN THE GUINNESS BOOK OF RECORDS by Peter Crichton-Williams. With Chris Discoll, Judy Nunn. (12)

THE EXTRAORDINARY CASE OF THE KIPPER AND THE CAFE by Gregory Marshall. Eccentric spy thriller. With the Unicorn Company. (16)

ESKIMO MAGIC by Richard Gill. Children's play of the far North. With the Polka Puppets and Actors Company. (9)

GENESIS by Roy Kift. A mime drama about the Bible story. With the Freehold Company. (8)

AN ARMOUR and A FEAST by David Halliwell. Two one-acters about sex relationships. With Carol Boyd, J.B. Lesley. (10)

IN THE HEART OF THE BRITISH MU-SEUM by John Spurling. An Olympian view of man through the ages. With the Edinburgh Traverse Workshop Company. (11)

EBONY by Ebony White. Black artist's one-woman show. With the author. (14)

ANGELS by Geoff Moore. Based on *Paradise Lost* and Michael McClure's *Poisoned Wheat*. With the Moving Being Company. (2)

THE MEANING OF THE STATUE and WRITING ON STONE by Roger Howard. Two one-acters about people carved from stone. With Mark Penfold, Candida Fawsitt. (2)

LOVE . . . LOVE . . . LOVE by and with Barry Ingham. London premiere of one-man show. (12)

HOW THOR GOT HIS HAMMER and THE WILLOW PATTERN STORY by and with the Argyle Theater of Youth Company. (1)

THE FALL AND RISE OF DEBBIS THE MENACE a children's participatory play by and with Interaction's Dogg's Human Flee Circus. (6)

P.C. PLOD by and with the Scaffold company, based on Roger McGough's poems. (4)

FAMILY by Neil Johnstone. Family situation around a stolen baby. With the Oval Theater Group. (7)

DIZZY'S FAERY by and with the Oxford Playhouse Theater for Youth company. About Queen Victoria and Disraeli. (1)

BUT DAD I WANT TO BE A GOLFER adapted from John Lennon's *In His Own Write* by Fabian Worsfield. With Center Stage company. (2)

TWO FOR THE ANGEL comprising OR-DERS FROM THE 14TH DICTATOR by Richard Bronerer (D) and JOHNNY ROYAL by Bob Graham (D) about a courtship that failed and the death of a Vietnam G.I. With Karin Dommie, Donald Cox, Harry Ditson. (11)

R.M. RENFIELD AGE 29. Study of lunacy. With the London La Mama Troupe. (2)

SWEET MR. SHAKESPEARE by Richard Digby Day. The story of the Shakespeare myth. With the Young Vic Theater Company. (4)

BYRON by Misha Williams and Nicholas Petrides (D). Dramatic mosaic about the

poet, for a solo actor. With John Stuart Anderson. (7)

JOURNEY INTO AUTUMN by Brian Fogarty. Dying man finds a new world. With the Intimate Theater company. (2)

NEITHER UP NOR DOWN by Peter Nichols, sex with the kids to look after; and FROM THE 1ST DAY OUT by Chris Bailey, seaside triangular drama. With Paola Dionisotti, Stephen Whittacker, Will Knightly. (12)

THE THOMSON REPORT by Peter Ransley. Documentary on Ulster. With André van Gyseghen, Hugh Manning, Allen Cullen. (12)

HANDY FOR THE HEATH by and with Rogers and Starr. Transvestite show. (4)

JOHN GOULD'S one-man show, with new items. (11)

WAIT FOR THE BELL by Rony Robinson. Mass-media view of school life from Sheffield Crucible Theater. With the Vanguard Theater Company. (3)

SHADES OF HEATHCLIFF by John Spurling. Dramatic view of Emily Brontë's Wuthering Heights. With the Sheffield Crucible Theater's Vanguard Theater Company. (9)

THE 100 WATT BULB by George Frederick Thatcher (D). Inmate's view of prison life. With Anthony May, Robert Booth. (12)

PLAYBACK 42 by George Foa. Aftermath of an air raid. With Wanda Moore, Tim Hardy. (12)

PLEASE DON'T PLAY ELEPHANT GAMES ON THE GRASS by Leon Rosselson. Two-handed battle of wits. With Alan Helm, Roger Mortimer.

SIEGE by David Ambrose. Two P.M.'s in clubland. With Alastair Sim, Michael Bryant, Stanley Holloway. (20)

ACHILLES by Charles Napier. Achilles's withdrawal from the fighting. With Brandon Hawkins. (4)

ONE LONG HUNT OR HOW WOULD YOU LIKE IT by Philip Martin. Two-hander about an out-of-work victim. With Hugh Armstrong, Jan Edwards. (12)

FACE ACHE by Howard Barker. Triangular tussle of wills. With Recreation Ground Company. (12)

THE BEHEADING by Thomas Muschamp. A political upheaval in a developing Mediterranean country sometime in the future. With

John Moffatt, Virginia McKenna, Robert Lang. (20)

TYRANTS and PANTS. Dynastic family seeks power, and the abysmal day in the life of a housewife. By and with Action Theater. (5)

THE DAMNATION OF FAUST by Steven Rumbelow. Adapted from Goethe and Marlowe. With Nigel Watson, Bronson Shaw, the author. (3)

THE DEFORMED TRANSFORMED by Lord Byron. World premiere of unfinished drama adapted by Steven Rumbelow. With Teresa d'Abrua, Paul O'Connor, Bronson Shaw. (9)

MARY MARY by Roy Kift. The mind of a disturbed child. With the Freehold Company. (13)

JIBES comprising three plays: PAPER TIGER by Michael Almaz, emasculation of a British male; SCREAM by Kate Quillan, British-American encounter; GAME FOR THREE PLAYERS by Frank Wyman, a writer loses his innocence. With Donald Cox, Robert Mill, Chris Discoll. (11)

THE ADVENTURE OF SPACEMAN JACK by Malcolm McKay. Children's play with the Argyle Theater for Youth Company. (1)

THE LAST OF THE FEINSTEINS by Tony Connor. Nazi camp murderer meets her deserts. With Jack Shepherd, Bridget Turner. (12)

TRIAL OF SAINT GEORGE by Colin Spencer. Husband's self-exposure to his wife. With Carole Boyd, Nigel Hawthorne. (16)

EVELYN by Rhys Adrian (D). A mother and her many suitors. With Shirley Dixon, Jon Rollason, Peter Pacey. (10)

HAVE YOU SEEN OUR RABBIT? by Michael Stevens. The stresses dividing a mother from her son. With Brenda Saunders, Roger Tolliday. (20)

HITLER DANCES by Howard Brenton. A modern morality. With the Edinburgh Traverse Theater Workshop company. (4)

THE PACKING CASE by Timothy Kidd. Two nuclear war survivors destroy each other. THERE'S NO BUSINESS . . . by Frank Long. Two vaudeville old-timers destroy one another. THE SWAP by Tony Parkin. A strange master-servant exchange. With David Taylor, Hugo Myatt, Gillie Graham, Jon C.P. Mattocks. (12)

THE CENTAUR by John Hales. Dilemma of an elderly poet, modeled on Ezra Pound. With Alfred Burke, Isabel Dean. (1)

THE RAGPICKERS by Norman Smythe. Inner loneliness in a Dublin sweat-shop. With Ritchie Stewart, Donal Cox, Rio Fanning. (12)

QUETZALCOATL by Berta Dominguez (D). Dramatic history of Mexico. With Michael Mackenzie, Oliver Cotton, Geoffrey Larder. (20)

THE FANTASTIC FAIRGROUND by Bernard Goss. Children's entertainment. With Cleo Sylvestre, Trevor Peacock. (31)

OUT OF SIGHT by John McGrath. A hippie's adventures. With Anthony Haygarth, Selina Lucas. (10)

GOTTLE by John Boland. Children's play about a travelling circus. With the Unicorn company. (15)

EXIT SLATTERLY ON TIPTOE by Peter King. Fulminating husband's battle with his wife. With George Innes, James Cocker. (12)

2 PLUS FLOWER = CHRISTMAS by Amos Mokadi. Children's show. With Gilbert Wynne, Tricia Hawkins. (10)

SHIPS AND SEALING WAX by Paddy Campbell; and WITCH GRUMPUS adapted from Madeline Sotheby's story. A show for the little ones. With the Unicorn Company. (7)

LYING FIGURES by Francis Warner (D). 1971 Edinburgh Festival play about birth, copulation and death. With Evie Garnett, Terrence Hardiman, Jenny Earl. (18)

WHO KILLED WHO IN TIMBUKTU by Terence Lewis. The ease with which man is manipulated. With Michael Edgar, Susan Glanville. (12)

BAKERLOO LINE by Mustapha Matura. Black and white meet in London. With Stephan Khalifa, Ann Lynn. (12)

MAQUETTES by Francis Warner. Trilogy of plays from 1970 Edinburgh Festival about the human condition. With Nova Llewellyn, Richard Stroud. (6)

HAM-OMLET an improvised divertissement created by the Marowitz Hamlet cast of the Open Space Company. (7)

CANNED HUMANS by Rodney Cardiff. The penance of admass man. With Brian Davey, the author. (3)

HOPP SCOTCH by Brad Ho Riley. Dream-like conflict between spiritual and mundane preoccupations. With the Kindred Center Company. (20)

DING THE DASTARD DOWN by Alun Armstrong. Wakefield Mystery play adaptation. With John Ording, Alison Groves, John Price. (10)

THE FLIES REVUE by various authors. A skit on TV. With John Collis, Peter Wear, Peter Till, Don Partridge. (8)

THE DREAM OF GIERONIMOUS BOSCH by Tudor Gates. A great nephew relives the life of his dying relative. With Dennis Blanch, John Fahey. (12)

THE KING by Stewart Conn. Ritual slaughter in a modern milieu. With John Yule, Alan Bennion, Isobel Nisbett. (10)

THE TREMENDOUS GHOST by Patrick Garland. Collage for the Southwark Shakespeare Festival. With Max Adrian, Janet Suzman. (1)

YOU'LL NEVER BE MICHAEL ANGELO by Roger Milner. An artist's dilemma. With Gary Soper, Leonard Fenton. (1)

AND OR POLYMORPH AND POLY-DWARF by R.H. Bowden. Semantics gone mad. With the Questors Theater Company. (1)

CUCKOLDS by Catherine Itzin. Extramarital relations. With Paul Arlington, Gary Waldhorn. (10)

IIOW BEAUTIFUL WITH BADGES by Howard Brenton. Hell's Angels and the contemporary society. With Anthony Milner, Malcolm Storry, David Schofield. (15)

WHO THOUGHT IT by Colin Burnett and Alex Durant. One-man show with Edward Petherbridge. (8)

BURLESQUE by Raymond Cross. The story of American vaudeville. With Marilyn Marco, John Sankovich. (18)

THE BLITZ SHOW by and with London's only travelling outfit, the Bubble Theater. Story of the wartime Blitz. (18+)

FREE FESTIVAL with the Tokyo Kid Brothers, Soho Theater, Pip Simmons Theater Group, the People Show, Quipu Theater Company, Theater Machine, Incubus, Friends, Portable Theater, Interaction Dogg's Troupe, Bath Natural Theater, York Shoestring Theater, Leeds Everyday Occurrences, The Gentle Fire. (10)

EDGAR ALLAN POE, one-man show by and with Tony Parkin. (4)

BETWEEN THE BARS by Donald Swann. Musical of Swann's novel of that name. With Richard Day-Lewis, Heather Kay, the author. (13)

PICK A CANDY by various authors. Lunchtime variety show. With Adam Daye, Graham Jolley. (12)

THE TENANT by Richard Crane (D). A look at London's multi-racial society. With Frank Cousins, John Pullen. (11)

THE WHEEL by Bettina Jonic and Charles Robinson. Philosophical multimedia show. With Pauline Munro, Eric Allen, the author. (15)

I AM REAL SO ARE YOU by Tony Connor. An interview; part 1 of a three-part play trilogy. With Caroline Burt, Ian Price. (10)

THE BED by Timothy Kidd, a reversal of roles, with Sally Faulkner, Roger Oakley, Chris Bradwell; and WATCH WHAT YOU THINK by Peter Brett, metaphysical holiday slide-show, with John Rainer, Susan Sheers. (8)

SHOW ME THE WAY TO GO HOME by and with Phil Woods and the Company. The problem of London's housing. (18+)

SITTING PRETTY by Tim Dartington. An old lady faces eviction. With Betty Hardy, Amanda Murray. (10)

THE SWEET MISERY OF LIFE and THE TRAVELS OF LANCELOT QUAIL by and with the Leeds Welfare State company. Two kaleidoscopic variety shows. (10)

MASQUERADE devised by Pat Keysell. Mixed program for both normal and deaf spectators. With the National Theater of the Deaf Company. (4)

DOUBLE ACT comprising JANET AND JOHN and CHELSEA HATE WHORES by Frederick Proud, about results of inadequate education. SOCIAL CIRCUS comprising JOSEPH ARCH by Paul Thomson (D), about the Agricultural Workers' Union; SUPERSCUM by Mary O'Malley (D), uses and abuses of Social Security; and TEN MINUTE PROBLEM by Tom Hedge (D), a schoolmaster's indifference. With Margaret Brady, James Marcus, Peter Attard. (10)

THE RELIEF OF MARTHA KING by David Parker. Trans-sexualist drama. With Brian McDermott, Meg Clancy. (3)

PRAGUE 68 by Leslie Blair. Improvisation on the Russian invasion. With George Costigan, Eve Willingham. (9+)

THE LITTLE MAN IS OFF ON HIS OWN by Ronald Groom (D). An idealistic schoolteacher destroyed by TV. With the Tower Theater Company. (4+)

THE ONLY GOOD INJUN IS A DEAD INJUN by Misha Williams. What they did to the Indians after opening up the West. With the Young Vic Theater Company. (4+ in repertory)

A VISIT FROM THE FAMILY by Tony Connor. The interviewee remarried; part 2 of three-part play trilogy. With Ian Price, Sally Faulkner. (3+)

TWO OF THEM by Raymond Bantock. Lifestyle of two whores. With Jean Ferguson, Gillie Gratham. (4+)

LOU by Hilton Root (D), preoccupations of the American dream; and LIFELINE by Frank Wyman, comedy of man's moods. With Jacquie Dubin, Tim Craven, Donald Cox. (2+)

STILL WATERS devised by Mike Lucas. Musical documentary about the canals. With Danny Schiller, Roger Oakley, Peter Denan, Carinthia West, Kerena Mond. (2+)

POMP AND CIRCUMSTANTIAL EVIDENCE by Norman Clare (D), farcical view of a divorce trial; and THE OLD TUNE by Robert Pinget, adapted by Samuel Beckett. With Roger Hume, Roger Kemp. (2+)

POPULAR ATTRACTIONS

INTERACTION DOGG'S TROUPE gave street events, game plays, participatory plays by and with the company, or by various authors, including Tom Stoppard, Henry Livings, Chris Bailey and Ed Berman; and THERE'S NO BUSSINESS LIKE SHOW BUSSINESS by Leon Rosselson for the Interaction mobile Fun Art Bus. (250+)

NIGHT SCHOOL by Harold Pinter. Stage premiere of radio and TV drama. With Shelagh Fraser, Rosamund Greennod. (18)

OLDENBERG by Barry Bermange. Revival of popular lower middle class prejudice drama. With David Allister, Sue Glanville, Peter Brenner. (20)

HAPPY DAYS by Samuel Beckett. With Denise Coffey, Andrew Robertson. (15+ in repertory).

ROMEO AND JULIET by William Shakespeare. Richard Digby Day's Open Air Theater production. With Hugh Ross, Marilyn Tylerson. (49)

RITUAL FOR DOLLS by George MacEwen Green (D). Drama of colonial power. With Nicholas Simmonds, Madeline Cannon. (20)

NO SEX PLEASE, WE'RE BRITISH by Anthony Marriott and Alistair Foot. Lubricious farce behind a mask of seeming Puritanism. With Michael Crawford, Linda Thorsen, Anthony Valentine, Evelyn Laye. (424+)

BEDTIME AND BUTTER by Douglas Livingstone. Two-hander about incompatibility in marriage. With Prunella Scales, Peter Jeffrey. (28)

THANK YOU LADIES by Sandy Wilson. A tribute to the great theatrical ladies the author has worked with. With the author. (15)

A MIDSUMMER NIGHT'S DREAM by William Shakespeare. Peter Brook's Stratford production transferred. With David Waller, Sara Kestelman, John Kane, Alan Howard. (91 in repertory)

THE PATRICK PEARSE MOTEL by Hugh Leonard. Feydeau-type farce at the expense of the Irish. With Norman Rodway, Moira Redmond, Godfrey Quigley. (84)

THE DISAPPEARING SPELL by Christopher Brock (D). The adventures of two spellmakers. With the Unicorn Company. (25)

SKYVERS by Barry Reckord. Revival of West Indian's indictment of school system. With Jo Blatchley, Leonard Fenton. (44)

DYNAMO by Chris Wilkinson. Mock-up strip show. With Linda Marlowe. (24)

THE DEVIL'S DISCIPLE by George Bernard Shaw. Inaugural production of National Youth Theater's professional company, the Dolphin Players. With Tom Bell, Jennie Linden, Ray McNally, Ronald Hines. (44)

ENTERTAINING MR. SLOANE by Joe Orton. Revival of Orton's black farce. With Pamela Strong, Tony Bateman, Anthony May, Alan Helm. (34)

A HEARTS AND MINDS JOB by Don Haworth (D). Black farcical comedy pokes fun at beaurocracy, revivalism and much else besides. With John Livesey, Colin Gordon, Robert Edison, Madge Ryan. (27)

TITUS ANDRONICUS by William Shakespeare. Keith Hack's astringent adaptation transformed from Glasgow Citizen's Theater and Wiesbaden Festival. With Trevor Peacock, Ann Mitchell. (13)

BUTLEY by Simon Gray. University lecturer is abandoned by wife, boy friend and academic success. With Alan Bates, Mary Wimbush. (223+)

EL COCA COLA GRANDE by and with the Low Moan Spectacular. Send-up of Spanish tradition. (18)

A MIDSUMMER NIGHT'S DREAM by William Shakespeare. Richard Digby Day's Open Air Theater production. With Gary Raymond, Delena Kidd. (50)

LOOK, NO HANDS by Lesley Storm. Should the offspring of a mixed marriage be told the facts of life? With Harry Towb, Janet Munro, Gerald Flood. (40)

THE OLD BOYS by William Trevor (D). Author's adaptation of his novel about the obsessions of old age. With Sylvia Coleridge, Michael Redgrave, Peter Copley. (53)

SLEUTH by Anthony Shaffer. Carryover from 1970/71. With Marius Goring and John Fraser taking over roles of Wyke and Milo from Paul Rogers and Donal Donnelly. (427+)

THE AVENGERS by Brian Clemens and Terence Feeley. Stage version of famous TV thriller series. With Simon Oates, Sue Lloyd, Kate O'Mara. (24)

A VOYAGE ROUND MY FATHER by John Mortimer. Transfer of Greenwich Theater production. With Jeremy Brett, Alec Guinness (later Michael Redgrave), Leueen McGrath. (342+)

HAMLET by William Shakespeare. Provincial and European tour production by Prospect productions. With Ian McKellen, Faith Brook, Susan Fleetwood, John Woodvine, James Cairncross. (63)

GOOD LADS AT HEART by Peter Terson. Educating delinquents in an approved school. With the National Youth Theater Company. (22)

ANNA LUSE and THE DIABOLIST by David Mowat. Revivals of gifted author's absurdist dramas. With Susan Carpenter, Pamela Fairbrother, Alison Percy, David Stockton. (23)

MUCK FROM THREE ANGELS by David Halliwell. Revival of Quipu Theater multi-viewpoint production. With Shirley Dynevor, Jean Marlow, Mahael Francis. (12)

THE MAN OF MODE by Sir George Etheredge. New Royal Shakespeare Company production of 18th century comedy. With Frances de la Tour, Brenda Bruce, Alan Howard, Vivien Merchant, Helen Mirren, David Waller. (30 in repertory)

THE BIG BAD MOUSE by Philip King and Falkland Carry. Popular hit returns to West End. With Jimmy Edwards, Eric Sykes. (157)

DON'T JUST LIE THERE, SAY SOMETHING! by Michael Pertwee. Brian Rix's Garrick Theater farce of sexual innuendo. With Alfred Marks, Joanna Lumley, Leo Franklyn, Brian Rix. (293+)

OTHELLO by William Shakespeare. Mermaid Theater production featuring nude Desdemona. With Bruce Purchase, Kay Barlow, Bernard Miles. (53)

THE SANDBOY by Michael Frayn. The surprising contradictions in the private life of a celebrated ecologist. With Patrick Allen, Eleanor Bron, Joe Melia, Avril Elgar. (25)

GORM, THE FANTASTIC ADVENTURES OF MOG AND IZZY IN THE MYSTERIOUS LAND OF THE GIANT GORM by Victoria Ireland. With the Unicorn Company. (13)

LAY-BY by Howard Brenton, Brian Clark, Trevor Griffiths, David Hare, Steven Poliakoff, Hugh Stoddart. Transfer of Edinburgh Festival documentary about a rape. With Portable and Traverse Theater Club companies. (26)

LIGHTS UP! devised by Josephine Wilson. New version of 1968 children's show. With the Molecule Company. (19)

SUDDENLY AT HOME by Francis Durbridge (D). Stage thriller by famous TV author, about a wife-murder. With Gerald Harper, Terence Longdon, Veronica Strong. (277+)

EXILES by James Joyce. R.S.C. revival of Harold Pinter's Mermaid Theater production. With Vivien Merchant, John Wood, Estelle Kohler, T.P. McKenna. (26 in repertory)

AC/DC by Heathcote Williams. Revival of popular avant-garde drama. With John Grillo, Henry Woolf, Claudette Houchen. (21)

SLIP ROAD WEDDING by Peter Terson. Newcastle Festival production of North Country variant on Lorca's Blood Wedding. With Avis Bunnage, Joseph O'Conor, Tamara Ustinov, Eileen Way. (26)

TALKING ABOUT YEATS by and with Micheal MacLiammoir. One-man show about the Irish poet. (19)

GETTING ON by Alan Bennett. Middle-aged labor politician faces reality. With Kenneth More, Gemma Jones, Mona Washbourne. (227)

THE NOVELIST by Tom Mallin. London premiere of Edinburgh Festival Traverse Theater play about the creative and sexual responses of a middle-aged writer. With Gillian Martell, Trevor Peacock, Tom Baker. (27)

GENEVA by George Bernard Shaw. Revival of political extravaganza with its new final act. With Christopher Hancock, Bernard Bresslaw, Edward Atienza, Ernest Clarke, Barbara Ferris, George Benson. (39)

THE DOUGLAS CAUSE by William Douglas Home. Strange fruit on the author's own family tree. With Andrew Cruikshank, Sophie Stewart, Duncan Lamont. (36)

EVOLUTION OF THE BLUES by Jon Hendrix. The story of the Blues. With the Hendrix family. (45)

THE LONG AND THE SHORT AND THE TALL by Willis Hall. Dolphin Company's revival of famous Royal Court all-male wartime drama. With Barrie Rutter, Richard Moore. (36)

PLASTIC BIRTHDAY by John Kane (D). One way of handling an unwanted pregnancy. With Peter Dennis, Illona Linthwaite. (20)

ROMEO AND JULIET by William Shakespeare. New Young Vic Theater Company production. With Richard Kay, Louise Purnell. (42 in repertory).

CHARLEY'S AUNT by Brandon Thomas. London transfer of Manchester Theater 69 production. With Tom Courtenay, Dilys Hamlett, Wolfe Morris. (71)

THE OWL AND THE PUSSYCAT by David Wood and Sheila Ruskin. First West End production of popular Edward Lear adaptation. With Ray Davis, Joyce Raye. (66)

THE GOOD-NATURED MAN by Oliver Goldsmith. New National Theater Company production. With Jim Dale, Sarah Atkinson. (37 in repertory)

DOGG'S OUR PET by Tom Stoppard, an opening ceremony, with Interaction Dogg's Troupe (30); and COMPANION PIECE, a river-bank duologue by Michael Stevens. With Corin Redgrave, Simon Rouse. (11)

GAMES AFTER LIVERPOOL by James Saunders. Revival of twin bill from Edinburgh. With Judy Monahan, Jane Bond, Andrew Norton, Robert Walker. (38)

DICK TURPIN by Anthony Loynes and Ron Pember. Revival of Mermaid Theater Christmas show. With Gary Raymond. (64)

MUCH ADO ABOUT NOTHING by William Shakespeare. Short-run transfer of Ronald Eyre's Stratford production. With Derek Godfrey, Elizabeth Spriggs. (9)

THE PLOTTERS OF CABBAGE PATCH CORNER by David Wood. The revolt of the garden insects. With Timothy Davis, Ben Aris, Bridget Turner. (50)

STRAIGHT UP by Syd Cheatle. Black farce of sexual misunderstanding. With James Grout, Antonia Pemberton, Marty Cruikshank. (36)

JACK AND THE BEANSTALK by Alan Vaughan Williams. Greenwich Theater's Christmas show. With Ian Lavender. (39)

HIS MONKEY WIFE by Sandy Wilson. Musical version of John Collier's novel about a chimpanzee wife. With June Ritchie, Robert Swann. (34)

SLEEP FAST THEY'VE LANDED by Christopher Langham and Stuart Olesker. Bristol University revue. With Christopher Langham, Thirzie Robinson. (21)

BETTY'S WONDERFUL CHRISTMAS by Pam Gems. The picaresque adventures of a runaway. With Yvonne Antrobus, Charles Hyatt. (17)

PETER PAN by James Bridie. Robert Helpmann's new production at the Coliseum. With Dorothy Tutin, Eric Porter. (25)

SYLVESTE by and with the Ken Campbell Roadshow Company. (24)

UPPER STREET SUPPER TREAT by Neville Phillips and Paul Horner. A local revue. With Barbara Argyll, Hugh Walters. (29)

RIDE A COCK HORSE by David Mercer. Hampstead Theater Club revival of prize-winning drama of 1965. With John Hurt, Sylvia Kay, Sarah Leyton, Angela Richards. (26)

OK FOR SOUND devised by Gerald Frow and Powell Jones. New script of 1968 children's show. With the Molecule Company. (19)

LIVE LIKE PIGS by John Arden. New production of 12-year-old play. With Queenie

Watts, Len Fenton, Michael Crofts, Godfrey James, Mary Healey. (23)

ROMEO AND JULIET by William Shakespeare. Michael Croft's National Youth Theater's Dolphin company production at Shaw Theater. With Simon Ward, Sinead Cusack, Joseph O'Conor. (55)

SHE STOOPS TO CONQUER by Oliver Goldsmith. Young Vic Theater Company revival. With Denise Coffey, Nicky Henson, Gavin Reed, Kathleen Harrison. (28 in repertory)

TWO WEELER by Ed.B. Solo performance on stage and screen by American-born London playwright. With Geoff Hoyle. (30)

SAM SAM by Trevor Griffiths. A provincial misfit becomes a Trades Union leader. With Nicholas Simmonds, Vanda Godsell. (34)

THE FEYDEAU FARCE FESTIVAL OF NINETEEN NINE by Bamber Gascoigne. Feydeau the farceur turns up in Brazil. With Gaye Brown, Andrew Ray, Bill Wallis, Anna Dawson. (25)

THE DAY AFTER YESTERDAY by Micheline Victor (D). Variations on the eternal quadrangle. With Frank Dux, Pamela Coveney. (21)

TAM AND CAM by Kate Hounsel-Robert, Vietnam folktale dramatized for Unicorn Theater; and SURPRISE II by Paddy Campbell, space-ship adventure. With Unicorn Company. (22)

EDWARD—THE FINAL DAYS by Howard Barker. Undisguised satire on an eminent P.M.'s career. With John Rainier, Hugh Ross. (20)

THE BLACK MACBETH by William Shakespeare. Peter Coe's all-black adaptation. With Oscar James, Mona Hammond. (26)

GOING HOME by William Trevor. Odd encounter between a schoolboy and his matron. With Doreen Mantle, Carlo Cura. (48)

HANDY FOR THE HEATH NO. 2 by and with Rogers and Starr. Second transvestite show. (15)

THE CARETAKER by Harold Pinter. New production of Pinter's best-known play. With Leonard Rossiter, John Hurt, Jeremy Kemp. (85)

MR. BICKERSTAFF'S ESTABLISHMENT by John Grillo. A wife-murderer opens a brothel. With Leonard Fenton, Peter Baldwin, the author. (27)

THE PERFORMING HUSBAND by Donald Churchill (D). Comic view of adultery. With Jane Downs, Pauline Yates, James Beck, Ronald Hines. (25)

JULIUS CAESAR by William Shakespeare. Jonathan Miller's O.U.D.S. production. With the O.U.D.S. Company (16)

SYLVESTE AGAIN: YET ANOTHER EVENING WITH SYLVESTE MCCOY (HUMAN BOMB) by and with the Ken Campbell Roadshow Company. (18)

THE LONDONERS by Stephen Lewis and Lionel Bart. Musical version, staged by Joan Littlewood, of Sparrers Can't Sing. With Brian Murphy, Bob Grant, Valerie Walsh, the author. (64)

RICHARD II by William Shakespeare. David William's sober debut as director of a National Theater production. With Ronald Pickup, Michael Hordern, Anna Carteret. (29+ in repertory)

LORD ARTHUR SAVILE'S CRIME by Constance Cox. Adapted from Oscar Wilde's novel. With Jack Hulbert, Elsie Randolph, Mervyn Johns. (16)

LONDON ASSURANCE by Dion Boucicault. Transfer of Ronald Eyre's R.S.C. production. With Judi Dench, Donald Sinden (64+)

COME WHEN YOU LIKE by Joyce Rayburn. Father-fixated spinster's battle with the inevitable. With Raymond Francis, Amanda Barrie. (20)

THE COLLECTOR by John Fowles. Revival of popular thriller, at London's newest pub-theater, the Bush. With Brian McDermott, Annette André, alternating with Robin Chadwick, Yvonne Quenel. (48)

THE LITTLE GIANT by John Pudney. Musical documentary about Brunel's great railroad. With Freda Dowie, David Ashton, Eliza Ward, Antony Webb. (32)

WITHIN TWO SHADOWS by Wilson John Haire. Religious infighting in a Northern Irish home. With Peggy Marshall, Frances Tomelty. (23)

THE MAROWITZ HAMLET, revival of reworked version. With David Schofield, Candida Fawsitt. (27)

THE DRESSING-ROOM, program of three one-acters by Barrie Stacey: WHERE HAVE I SEEN YOU BEFORE?, THAT'S SHOW BUSINESS and I HAD THE CRAZIEST DREAM. Backstage in-dramas for theatricals. With Joe Cook, Jo Beadle. (24)

UNDER MILK WOOD by Dylan Thomas. Revival of London Theater Company's production. (8)

THE MAID OF THE MOUNTAINS by Frederick Lonsdale and Emile Littler. New revised version of Harold Fraser-Simpson operetta. With Lyn Kennington, Jimmy Edwards, Gordon Clyde, Jimmy Thompson. (36+)

THE RIVALS by Richard Brinsley Sheridan. London Theater Company's revival at Sadler's Wells. With Maxine Audley, Anthony sharp, Philip Bard. (16)

TOC: THE BUS HI-JACK MYSTERY by Neil Hornick; FUN ARTING ABOUT by James Saunders; SHURRUP by Henry Livings; WE'RE ALL GOING TO SOUTHAMPTON by Michael Stevens. Mobile theater-cinema event mounted on a bus. With The Other Company. (40+)

THE TAMING OF THE SHREW by William Shakespeare. Frank Dunlop's Young Vic production revived, with new cast. With Trevor Peacock, Joanna Wake. (22+ in repertory)

TOM BROWN'S SCHOOLDAYS by Joan and John Maitland. Musical version of the Thomas Hughes classic. With Roy Dotrice, Christopher Guard, Adam Walton, Judith Bruce. (27+)

THE SCHOOL FOR SCANDAL by Richard Brinsley Sheridan. Jonathan Miller's National Theater revival. With Sheila Burrell, Paul Curran, Ronald Pickup, Louise Purnell. (12+ in repertory)

DRAGON LESS by Brian Hayles. A modern fable about dragons, mediaeval gangsters and loot. With the Unicorn Company. (5+)

JOURNEY'S END by R.C. Sherriff. Manchester Theater 69 revival of famous World War I play. With Peter Egan, James Maxwell, Harry Landis. (17+)

TWELFTH NIGHT by William Shakespeare. Michael Bakewell's revival for Dolphin Theater Company. With Vanessa Redgrave, Nyree Dawn Porter, Ann Beach, Oscar Quitak. (14+)

THE ALCHEMIST by Ben Jonson. Young Vic Theater production. With Ian Trigger, Denise Coffeey. (3+ in repertory)

CRETE AND SERGEANT PEPPER by John Antrobus. Drama of a 1941 P.O.W. camp. With Bill Maynard, Bernard Gallagher, Raymond Francis. (8+)

WILL WAT? IF NOT, WHAT WILL? by Steve Gooch and the Half Moon. Wat Tyler's peasant uprising of 1381. With The Half Moon Company. (5+)

THE TEMPEST by William Shakespeare. Open Air Theater production. With Michael Denison, Celia Bannerman, Wayne Sleep. (3+)

THE HOSTAGE by Brendan Behan. Joan Littlewood Theater Workshop revival of 14-year-old Irish comedy drama. With James Booth, Brian Murphy, Celia Salkeld, Dudley Sutton, Philip Davis. (3+)

WE'RE ALL NIGGERS UNDER THE SKIN by Robert Ray (D). Black power drama based on Gale Benson's murder and talks with Hakim Jamal. With Mona Hammond, Sean Hewitt, Jimmy Owens. (1+)

SOME AMERICAN PLAYS PRODUCED IN LONDON

MOONEY'S KID DON'T CRY by Tennessee Williams. With Howard Bembrook, Joyce Timson. (6)

BLEACH by Arnold Meyer (D). World premiere of short play about the American dilemma, by an American Londoner. With the Questors Theater Company. (4)

PROMETHEUS BOUND by Robert Lowell. With Kenneth Haigh, Angela Thorne. (31)

CALLEY AND MANSON by Andrew Dallmeyer. The twin symbols of U.S.A. violence in the same cell. With Paul Moriarty, Peter Marinker. (12)

IT'S CALLED THE SUGAR PLUM by Israel Horovitz. With Blain Fairman, Liza Ross. (12)

NEXT and SWEET EROS by Terrence McNally. With David Healey, Andonia Katsaros, Peter Marinker, Jane Cardow. (20)

KISS ME KATE by Sam and Bella Spewack and Cole Porter. With Emile Belcourt, Ann Hood. (22)

THE WING an improvisation by and with the San Francisco Wing Company. (5)

THE MAGICIAN one-acter adapted by Helena Kant-Howson from Thomas Mann's novella. With Heinz Bernard, Raymond Cross. (12)

SHOW BOAT by Jerome Kern and Oscar Hammerstein II. Revival of famous musical play. With André Jobin, Lorna Dallas, Thomas Carey, Cleo Laine. (348+)

PORK by Andy Warhol. Sex obsessions dramatized, from off-Broadway preview. With Julia Breck, Suzanne Smith, Michael Mundell. (32)

JUMP by Larry Gelbart. World premiere of American-Jewish farce of a couple with two difficult offspring. With Warren Mitchell, Sheil Steafel. (52)

SARAH AND THE SAX by Lewis John Carlino. With Mary Henry, Ken Gajadhar. (10)

THE LAST SWEET DAYS OF ISAAC by Gretchen Cryer and Nancy Ford. Theater Royal, York, production of U.S. rock musical at Old Vic. With Bob Sherman, Julia McKenzie. (8)

THE CHINESE MACHINE by Frank Dux (D). World premiere of new play about race relations and human identity by an American Londoner. With Howard Johnson, Connie Booth, Myrna Stephens, the author. (18)

IPHIGENIA by Euripides. World premiere of Doug Dyer's rock musical adaptation of Iphigenia in Aulis. With New York Shakespeare Festival Public Theater company. (17)

DISASTER STRIKES THE HOME by Charles Dizenzo. With the Edinburgh Traverse Theater Company. (5)

AWAKE AND SING by Clifford Odets. With Harold Kasket, George Pravda, Cyd Hayman. (27)

I RISE IN FLAME CRIED THE PHOENIX by Tennessee Williams. With Graham Lines, Yvonne Bonnamy. (12)

A DAY FOR SURPRISES by John Guare. With Connie Berry. (5)

AMBASSADOR by Don Ettlinger and Hal Hackady, music by Don Gohman. World premiere of U.S. musical based on Henry James's novel The Ambassadors, about the dangers of Paris. With Howard Keel, Danielle Darrieux. (86)

SUBJECT TO FITS by Robert Montgomery. With Isla Blair, John Kane, Sara Kestelman. (22)

THE SECRET and VERNON HOFFMAN by Herb Greer. Two absurdist sketches by an American Londoner. With the Doggs' Troupe Company. (6)

HOT DAMN HIGH IN VIETNAM by Bernard Pomerance. Anti-establishment broadside by an American Londoner. With Interaction's Ambiance Company including Susan Drury, Glenn Beck. (23)

McNECKEL'S COMMUNE a group production by itinerant U.S.A.-born Theater of All Possibilities Company. (8)

BLUEBEARD by Charles Ludlam. With The Ridiculous Theatrical Company of New York. (11)

GODSPELL by John-Michael Tebelak and Stephen Schwartz. With David Essex, Julie Covington, Marti Webb. (211+)

DANDELION by Judith Martin. With the New York Paper Bag Players. (22)

LONG DAY'S JOURNEY INTO NIGHT by Eugene O'Neill. With Laurence Olivier, Ronald Pickup, Denis Quilley, Constance Cummings. (61+ in repertory)

PINS AND NEEDLES by Harold Rome and others, adapted by Bernard Sarron. With Unity Theater Company including Ulysses Windon St. John, Percy Kaye. (28)

COMPANY by Stephen Sondheim and George Furth. With Larry Kert, Elaine Stritch. (161+)

ALL OVER by Edward Albee. With Peggy Ashcroft, Sheila Hancock, Angela Lansbury, Patience Collier. (26 in repertory)

BIRDBATH and LUNCHTIME by Leonard Melfi. With Jeffrey Haynes, Jill Voight. (9)

THE UNEXPECTED MEMOIRS OF BERNARD MERGENDEILER by Jules Feiffer. With Shirley Anne Field, Robert Bernal. (10)

REUNION IN VIENNA by Robert Emmet Sherwood. With Margaret Leighton, Nigel Patrick, Beatrix Lehmann. (20)

WAITING FOR LEFTY by Clifford Odets. With the Unity Theater company. (18)

CHILDHOOD and INFANCY by Thornton Wilder. With Carole Allen, Paul Maxwell, Jill Voight. (13)

SPLENDOR HARMONIES RETURNING by Dalt Wonk. With the New York Bird in Hand Theater Company. (7)

DR. GALLEY by Conrad Bromberg. World premiere of an American Londoner's one-acter about a psychology professor's revelations. With Henry Woolf. (10)

ROOMING HOUSE by Conrad Bromberg. World premiere of one-acter about a curious sexual encounter. With Liza Ross, Rick Parmentier. (5)

ALL MY SONS by Arthur Miller. With Maxine Audley, Ken Wayne. (16)

HIGH TIME by Alan Rossett. World premiere of U.S. play about the pot syndrome. With Miriam Karlin, Frances de la Tour, Paul Seed. (26)

THE PANSY by Michael McClure, and THE HERO by Arthur Kopit. With Frederick Proud, Emily Richard, Jean Hewitt. (13)

HEIMSKRINGLA! OR THE STONED ANGELS by Paul Foster. With the Stanhope Theater Company. (1)

ONE FLEW OVER THE CUCKOO'S NEST by Dale Wasserman. With the Oxford University Players and Wadham Dramatic Society. (1)

GONE WITH THE WIND by Horton Foote and Harold Rome. World premiere of spectacular musical of Margaret Mitchell's best seller. With June Ritchie, Harve Presnell, Patricia Michael, Robert Swann. (32+)

THE WIVES by Jack Matcha. World premiere of American play about the revelations of an unplanned meeting. With Alexandre Dané, Margaret Robertson. (24)

CARTOONS by Bob Graham. World premiere of drama of life in strip-cartoon by an American Londoner. With Michael Jeffries, Miranda Bell. (15)

THE SLAVE by LeRoi Jones, with Frank Cousins, Jean Alcorn, John Pullen; and THE TENANT by Richard Crane (D), a look at London's multi-racial society, with John Pullen. (11)

THE LOTTERY by Patricia Welles (D). World premiere of American novelist's first play, about a trio bound together by greed. With Lisa Daniely, Mary Eden, Philip Lowrie. (8+)

NOBODY LOVES WEDNESDAY by Allan Weiss (D). World premiere of Hollywood script writer's drama on burning topics of the day. With Mel Taylor, Liza Ross. (1+)

BAD BAD JO JO by James Leo Herlihy. With David Hedison, Tim Preece, Richard Harbord. (15+)

SOME FOREIGN PLAYS PRODUCED IN LONDON

LIEUTENAT GUSTL by Arthur Schnitzler. With Christopher Guinee. (9)

PARDON ME HELEN by Pierre Rondy. Adapted from his novel La Florisane by the author. With David Barclay, Sandra Frieze. (6)

MISS JULIE by August Strindberg. With Jill Spurrier, Liam Clancy. (6)

BURKE'S COMPANY by Bill Reed. British premiere of Australian play about the first cross-continent expedition. With the Tower Theater company. (7)

THE RULES OF THE GAME by Luigi Pirandello. With Joan Plowright, Paul Scofield. (56 in repertory)

AMPHITRYON 38 by Jean Giraudoux. With Geraldine McEwen, Christopher Plummer, Constance Cummings. (46 in repertory)

FISH OUT OF WATER (La Main Passe) by Georges Feydeau, adapted by Caryl Brahms and Ned Sherrin. With Gerald Harper, Fenella Fielding. (25)

THE LOVERS OF VIORNE (L'Amante Anglaise) by Marguerite Duras, adapted by Barbara Bray. With Peggy Ashcroft, Maurice Denham, Gordon Jackson. (34)

BOESMAN AND LENA by Athol Fugard. British premiere of South African drama, first done off Broadway. With Zakes Mokae, Yvonne Bryceland, Bloke Modisane. (36)

OUR CIRCUS a spectacular entertainment for all ages between 7 and 70. With the company of the Leningrad Theater of the Young Spectator. (10)

ENEMIES by Maxim Gorky. With Brenda Bruce, Alan Howard, Helen Mirren, David Waller, Sara Kestelman. (29 in repertory)

DANTON'S DEATH by Georg Büchner, adapted by John Wells. With Christopher Plummer, Charles Kay, Ronald Pickup. (51 in repertory)

THE CITY by Loula Anagnostaki. With Neale Goodrum, Caroline Hutchinson (6); with Pauline Munro, Robert Lloyd (13).

THE FATHER by August Strindberg. Old Vic preview of Bolton Octagon Theater production. With Jenny Laird, Wilfrid Harrison, Lorraine Peters. (7)

ARCHITRUC by Robert Pinget. With Alistair Cameron, David Shaw. (6)

PANTAGLEIZE by Michel de Ghelderode. Frank Dunlop's Belgian National Theater

Production at the Old Vic. With the Belgian National Theater Company. (6)

THE SEVENTH COMMANDMENT OR STEAL A LITTLE LESS! by Dario Fo. Second Belgian National Theater guest play at the Old Vic. With the Belgian National Theater company. (6)

MY FOOT, MY TUTOR by Peter Handke, and HOME FRONT by Martin Walser. With Mary Yeoman, Garfield Morgan. (18)

STEINWAY GRAND by Ferenc Karinthy. With David Allister, Una Brandon-Jones. (10)

THE FRONT ROOM BOYS by Alexander Buzo. Sunday night production of new Australian play about clerks in the city jungle of a giant corporation. With Kevin Brennan, John Gregg. (2)

1789 by and with Ariane Mnouchkine's Théâtre du Soleil Company from Paris. (17)

LES FOURBERIES DE SCAPIN by Molière. With the Théâtre de Bourgogne company. (6)

IMPOSSIBLE LOVES by Fernando Arrabal (with *A Day for Surprises* by John Guare). With Connie Berry. (5)

ANTIGONE by Sophocles, newly translated by Leo Aylen. With Freda Dowie, Freddie Jones. (12)

OEDIPUS by Sophocles. With Desmond Macnamara, Jane Wenham. (7)

MISS JULIE by August Strindberg. With Helen Mirren, Donal McCann. (13)

ELECTRA by Sophocles. With Freda Dowie, Yvonne Mitchell, Derek Jacobi. (31)

SELF-ACCUSATION by Peter Handke. With Judy Monahan, Robert Walker. (5)

VICTIMS OF DUTY by Eugène Ionesco. With Patricia Neale, Alex McAvoy. (8)

DEAR ANTOINE by Jean Anouilh. London transfer of Chichester Festival production. With John Clements, Isabel Jeans, Joyce Redman, James Faulkner, Peter Copley. (45)

THE TRIAL by Franz Kafka, adapted by and with Steven Berkoff. (11)

THE PAINTERS by Heinrich Henkel. With Sam Kelly, Seymour Matthews. (17)

FAUST I adapted from Goethe, by and with the itinerant U.S.A.-born Theater of All Possibilities Company. (6)

HOW I OVERCAME MY FEAR etc. one-man show by and with Justin Thomas, a Canadian, in aid of Mental Health campaign. (3)

FRIDAY by Hugo Claus. With Diana Coupland, Tony Selby, John Shaw. (24)

GODOT HAS COME by Miodrag Bulatovic. With the Edinburgh Festival Cambridge University Company. (5)

THE BALCONY by Jean Genet. With Brenda Bruce, Estelle Kohler, Clement McCallin, Alan Howard, Philip Locke, Helen Mirren, (24 in repertory)

A FEW FALSE SLAPS by Paul Everac, WEEKEND by Iosif Naghiu and STRIP-TEASE by Slawomir Mrozek. With Questors Theater Company. (6)

CUT by Michael Almaz. About the fall of a film director. With the Pool Lunch Hour company. With Shirley Ann Field, Robert Bernal. (13)

THE STORY OF THE LITTLE BULL and EAST-WEST by Andrei Amalrik. World premieres of Soviet satirical comedies. With Lisa Hughes, Stephen Turner. (12)

THE FOUR LITTLE GIRLS by Pablo Picasso. World premiere of Roland Penrose's translation of the artist's poetic fantasy. With Suzannah Williams, Ann Holloway, Susan Penhaligon, Mia Martin. (40)

DING DONG! (Le Dindon) by Georges Feydeau. With Questors Theater Company. (12)

SINCLAIR by John McGahern (D). Award-winning Irish author's first play of terror and incomprehension. With Maurice Brooks, Bill Mitchell. (12)

SWANWHITE by August Strindberg. With Sara van Beers, Katina Noble. (2)

OFFENDING THE AUDIENCE by Peter Handke. With Jane Bond, Judy Monahan, Andrew Norton, Robert Walker. (24)

ISLAND OF SLAVES by Marivaux. With Paul Neunie, Barrie Shore. (17)

THE PRICE OF JUSTICE by Albert Camus. With Kate Coleridge, Gary Raymond, Leigh Lawson. (27)

IN THE JUNGLE OF CITIES by Bertolt Brecht. With Michael Irving, Peter Gordon. (21)

NEVER THE TWAIN by John Willett. Brecht-Kipling collage. With John Dalby, Eliza Ward. (19)

PRE-PARADISE SORRY NOW by Rainer Werner Fassbinder. With Stephen Bill, Sheila Kelly. (7)

PEOPLE ARE LIVING THERE by Athol Fugard. With Maureen Prior, Roger Gartland. (29)

DEATH IN INSTALMENTS by Janusz Krasinski and THE WITNESSES by Tadeusz Rozewicz. With Richardson Morgan, Donald Sumpter. (8)

THE THREEPENNY OPERA by Bertolt Brecht and Kurt Weill, newly translated by Hugh MacDiarmid. With Vanessa Redgrave (later Helen Cotterill), Joe Melia, Barbara Windsor. (127+)

A DREAM, BUT PERHAPS IT ISN'T by Luigi Pirandello. With Ian Frost, Dalphne Rogers. (21)

THE CHAIRS by Eugène Ionesco. With Gavin Reed, Denise Coffey. (13+ in repertory)

SELF-ACCUSATION and PROPHECY by Peter Handke. With The Other Company. (27)

THE BRIDE AND THE BUTTERFLY HUNTER by Nissim Aloni. With Robert Rietty, Jacqueline Ellis. (1)

WIDE OPEN SPACES by René de Obaldia. With James Woolley, Vivien Berry. (12)

THE MAIDS and DEATHWATCH by Jean Genet. With Nicky Henson, Andrew Robertson, Richard Kane. (17+ in repertory)

THE CENCI by Antonin Artaud. With Guildhall School of Music and Drama students. (1)

KATAKI by Shimon Wincelberg. With Rex Wei, Chris Muncke. (13)

IMPROMPTUS FOR LEISURE by René de Obaldia (comprising THE LATE, THE TWINKLING TWINS and NITROGEN). With Selina Lucas, Lisa Hughes, Jonathan Turner. (18)

EASTER by August Strindberg and THE HOUSE OF BERNARDA ALBA by Federico Garcia Lorca. With the Drama Studio Players. (3)

THE CELL by H.B. Kimmel. South African apartheid drama. With Robert Booth, Peter Sproule. (10)

MOLIÈRE—THE LEAGUE OF HYPOCRITES by Mikhail Bulgakov. With the Rose Bruford Theater School Company. (4)

CREDITORS by August Strindberg. With Gemma Jones, Brian Cox, Sebastian Graham-Jones. (19)

WORLD THEATER SEASON comprised Natal Theater Workshop Company from Durban in UMABATHA (in Zulu) (16); the Nuria Espert Company, Madrid, in YERMA (8); the National Theater of Athens in THE ORESTEIA (15); Eduardo De Filippo's Company from Naples in NAPOLI MILIONARIA (8); the Kathakali Drama Company, Kerala, in THE RAMAYANA and THE MAHABHARATA (8); and the Cracow Stary Theater company in THE POSSESSED (8).

OUT AT SEA by Slawomir Mrozek. With David Foxxe, Philip Jackson. (18)

DIVORCE COURT JUDGES by Miguel de Cervantes and THE BEAR by Anton Chekhov. With the Cervantes Players. (16)

ALKESTIS by Euripides. With Drewe Henley. (15)

JOHN BROWN OF KANSAS by Charles Taylor (D). World premiere of Canadian writer's historical drama. With J.M. Bay, Caroline John. (5)

THE MOON IS EAST, THE SUN IS WEST by and with the Tokyo Kid Brothers Company. (8)

BIG WOLF by Harald Mueller. With Michael Grady, Nigel Terry. (28)

THE GRAND CEREMONIAL by Fernando Arrabal. With Sheila Scott-Wilkinson, Donald Sumpter. (22)

MEDIOCRE VICTIMS by Jean Cocteau. Triple bill comprising DUET FOR ONE VOICE, THE HUMAN VOICE, THE PHANTOM OF MARSEILLES. With Jane Hilary. (15+)

THE SOLDIER'S TALE by Charles Ramuz and Igor Stravinsky. With the Théâtre de la Tempête Company. (3)

LADYBIRD by Monique Wittig. With Patricia Leventon, Jean Gilpin. (18)

MR JOYCE IS LEAVING PARIS by Tom Gallagher. With Robert Bernal. (20+)

UNDESIGNATED by Kuldip Sondhi and THE SONG OF LAWINO by Okot p'Bitek. With the Los Angeles Center for the Performing Arts Company. (2)

THE RIDE ACROSS LAKE CONSTANCE by Peter Handke. With the Frankfurt TAT company. (2)

THE OLD TUNE by Robert Pinget, adapted by Samuel Beckett. With Roger Hume, Roger Kemp. (2+)

O
O
O

THE SEASON ELSEWHERE
IN EUROPE

O   *By Ossia Trilling*
O
O

ACCUSTOMED AS MY READERS MUST BY NOW BE to my annual German gambit, they will not be let down this year. Germany, Austria and Switzerland remained the Continent's key centers of theatrical activity and innovation. All kinds of changes took place or threatened to do so. The arrival of Ivan Nagel, in Hamburg, to take over the fortunes of the State Schauspielhaus deepened the long-standing rivalry between it and the municipally-owned Thalia Theater, under Boy Gobert. This was in the main a healthy portent, except that each theater found itself competing for more public funds to underwrite its growing activities, and this led to unhappy recriminations. Gobert developed his penchant for British drama and British methods by having William Gaskill over to stage Farquhar's *The Beaux' Stratagem* (just as Rolf Liebermann was discovering how useful John Dexter was proving to him as a director of opera at the State Opera House down the road), though the designer was the same Frenchman, René Allio, who had worked with Gaskill in London. He also enrolled Germany's leading designer, Wilfried Minks, as a director. Minks came along from Bremen to make his debut in this role with Schiller's *Maria Stuart,* choosing to make his characters larger than life, literally, the whole scene dominated by an outsize figure of Christ. As a token of his impartiality, Minks then went over to the rival theater to stage an even more non-naturalistic production, this time of Molière's *The Miser.* The inauguration of a small studio-stage in the paint shop (the Malersaal) with a series of plays by the British writer, Howard Brenton, resulted in its being nicknamed the Brenton Hall. It was here, too, that Nagel produced the latest drama by the Marxist writer Hartmut Lange, called *Trotsky in Coyoacan,* starring Karl Maria Schley as an overly idealistic revolutionary whose main error had been his failure to stand up to and destroy Stalin.

Imminent changes in Dusseldorf—the replacement of Karl Heinz Stroux by Ulrich Brecht—did not prevent Stroux from mounting a spectacular season culminating in his swan song production of *Richard III,* with the veteran Elisabeth Flickenschildt as the censorious old Queen Mother. Two highlights had been the world premiere, directed by Peter Arens, of Slawomir Mrozek's ironic parable *A Happy Event,* in which a monstrous new-born babe, symbolizing the authoritarianism the author sought to evade, strangles its parents; and the return of Kazimierz Dejmek, another Polish guest, to stage the European premiere of Daniel Berrigan's *The Trial of the Catonsville Nine*. Dejmek also visited neighboring Essen again to direct, much in the style of his own well-known experiments in the field, *A Resurrection Play* by the City Theater's "dramaturg," the Polish-born Ilka Boll. The stadium in Essen, incidentally, was the scene of the final collapse, after a week's try-out in Munster, of Lars Schmidt's German-language production of *Jesus Christ Superstar*, on which so many hopes had been set. In nearby Wuppertal the main novelty was Arno Wüstenhofer's production of *Wetterstein Castle* by Frank Wedekind, designed by the ubiquitous Minks. Although first performed in 1918 after the abolition of the Kaiser's censorship, this anti-bourgeois satire was after eight performances too much even for the nascent Weimar authorities. Its revival 54 years later goes some way toward explaining how and why its author got to know a good deal about the jails of Wilhelminian Germany from the inside. Splendidly staged, it was acclaimed as the best contribution to the 1972 Theater Review in Berlin. The choice of Munich's entry puzzled Berlin audiences, however, though many admired Grete Mosheim as the sinned against wife, in the Kammerspiele version of Edward Albee's *All Over*, staged no more than competently by August Everding. Other of this company's work was thought to have been more representative, e.g. the latest, outspoken, though admittedly offensive, plays by Peter Turrini and Franz Xaver Kroetz (Martin Sperr's successor as Bavaria's most uninhibited playwright) or even the world premiere of Odön von Horvath's *Sladek, or the Black Army,* a prophetic foretaste of Nazism, written in 1923.

Before leaving Stuttgart for Frankfurt, Peter Palitzsch recorded an outstanding year that included Hans Neuenfels's new view of Ibsen's *A Doll's House* as a plea for Women's Lib, and his own staging of Peter Weiss's *Hölderlin,* a world premiere, to say nothing of yet another successful visit to the Berlin annual review, this time with his highly praised *Waiting for Godot* from the preceding season. *Hölderlin,* which was also staged within the same week though in vastly different fashion by Claus Paymann in Hamburg and Hans Hollmann in Berlin, purported to mirror the German poet Friedrich Hölderlin's dilemma at a time when revolutionary fires were flickering or even doused; but it also contained strong autobiographical traits, implying an ambivalent faith in Marxist doctrine and attributing to Hölderlin Marx's philosophy of life well before its time. In Cologne, Hansgünther Heyme provoked a major theatrical scandal by staging Dieter Forte's anti-Luther drama "in a rectangle" suggestive of the inside of a church and having Luther's friend Münzer crucified naked in the audience's full view. This did not deter his management from extending his contract and even introducing a new formula, in which he would be joined in a new three-man directorial team by Geoffrey Reeves from England and Robert Ciulli-Centrens from Italy. Centrens has already made a stir with his use of Japanese theatrical convention in Gottingen in Machiavelli's semi-autobiographical comedy on the empty aspirations of old age, entitled *Clizia*. Gottingen is typical of the small towns where first-rate work is often to be seen. Others are Darmstadt and Heidelberg and Tubingen, where George Tabori himself staged the world premiere of his latest satire on Americans, *Clowns,* on a trampoline. Bremen, which holds a position between the two, saw its inspired management, led by Kurt Hübner, come under critical fire from the ungrateful authorities, despite its undoubted artistic achievements. Hubner, his contract not renewed, has been tipped as Hansjörg Utzerath's successor next year at the Berlin Free People's Theater. Meantime the popular success of his theater's entry for the Berlin review, Rainer Werner Fassbinder's *Bremen Freedom,* a didactic verse-play about a real life Bremen murderess (of 1831), set by Minks (yes, again!) in a symbolical setting of congealed blood and staged centrally by the author, was also the occasion for the inauguration of a third stage for the City Theater in a converted movie-house. This alone should have shown up the error of the authorities' short-sighted negative attitude towards Hübner.

West Berlin

Nothing seen in Berlin has compared with the popular appeal or artistic invention of Peter Stein's marathon *Peer Gynt,* held over from the previous season and entered for the current Theater Review, after transferring from the smallish Schaubuhne am Halleschen Ufer to the vast spaces of the Berlin Exhibition Stadium. It's been abroad, played under canvas in Zurich, and only its size and costliness have prevented its producers from accepting numerous other invitations to various parts of the world. Otway's *Venice Preserved* in Hugo von Hofmannsthal's version was entrusted by Stein and his five-man directorium to two disciples, Frank-Patrick Steckel, who has since joined the board, and Jan Kauenhowen. It, too, was set in a sunken arena, the audience eavesdropping, as it were, on the goings-on below. Stein himself aroused some local antagonism, both political and esthetic, by staging, in a manner even more unorthodox, with the audience occupying an L-shaped rostrum, Vishnevsky's revolutionary drama of the Red Navy, *An Optimistic Tragedy,* once a favorite of the Berliner Ensemble on the other side of the Brandenburg Gate. At the Free People's Theater, Utzerath's dying regime began to grind to a halt, though not without a couple of compensations, among them his own soberly thought-out and faithfully Strindbergian version of *The Father,* and Leopold Lindtberg's first Berlin guest production, of Hans Weigel's new translation of Molière's *L'Étourdi.* An altercation on interpretation and artistic method between Boleslaw Barlog, retired manager (after 25 years) of the Schiller Theater, and the Italian guest director of an experimental drama at the Studio Stage, resulted in the breaking off of rehearsals, indefinite postponement of the play, and the suicide of the guest, a final tragedy that Barlog's enlightened regime could have been spared. The final year's productions, many of them by Barlog himself, were conspicuously lacking in distinction, with the possible exception of the *Hölderlin.* Even Ernst Schröder's way with Gombrowicz's third play *Operette* proved uninspired, Josef Svoboda's intriguing mirrored setting notwithstanding. Samuel Beckett directed his own

Happy Days in a heavy-handed manner at the Studio Theater, and only Rudolf Noelte's one-night condensation of Strindberg's *The Dance of Death,* entered for the Review by the Schlosspark, the Schiller's second substage, was able to stand comparison with the rest; I myself found it too emasculated and willfully portentous for any convincing idea of Strindberg's own tragic emotional involvement to emerge.

The dominance of the established subsidized theaters often makes one overlook the private theaters that exist to satisfy theatergoers' varied needs. One example of a commercial hit this year was O'Neill's *More Stately Mansions,* produced by Professor Kurt Raeck, for 25 years manager of the Renaissance Theater, and directed by Karl Heinz Stroux. It featured the agelessly enchanting Elisabeth Bergner in the role of the unforgiving Deborah Hartford. Another, at the Hebbel Theater, was a comedy hit called *Please Do Not Disturb.* This was none other than our old friend *Norman, Is That You?* by Ron Clark and Sam Bobrick. Having flopped on Broadway, it was resuscitated by Arthur Lesser and produced in Paris in Jean Cau's adaptation as *Poor France.* The Berlin success is a German equivalent based on the Cau text. There should be a lesson for Broadway producers in there somewhere.

East Berlin

Since the appointment of Ruth Berghaus as the new head of the Berliner Ensemble, the world is still waiting for something new and stimulating to make its appearance there. A revival, faithfully re-staged by Fritz Bennewitz, of Brecht's *The Life of Galileo* had nothing new to offer except to audiences unfamiliar with this production, though Wolfgang Heinz's performance in Ernst Busch's old role was never less than compelling. Heinz's departure from the Deutches Theater two years back to make room for Hanns Anselm Perten left many persons sad, both inside the theater and outside. Now that Perten has been removed, with no successor named as of this writing (though Horst Schönemann and Gerd Wolfram, from Halle, may well be occupying the manager's office by the time these lines appear in print), the atmosphere backstage at the Deutsches has much improved. It remains to be seen whether artistic standards will follow suit. Already two outstanding new productions have been staged, though both were in fact begun or mounted during Perten's period in office: *Richard III* staged with superlative imagination by Manfred Wekwerth, as guest, starring Hilmar Thate as a clownish assassin and with Wekwerth's wife, Renate Richter, also a guest-artist, as the pitiable Lady Anne; and Heinz's sensitive *Uncle Vanya,* which comes nearer to attaining a truly Russian ambiance than any previous German Chekhov production I have seen.

The finest work is still that being done by Benno Besson and his team at the People's Theater. Before describing that, I must, however, correct an unfortunate error that crept into my last year's report, when I wrote of the two remarkable examples of music-theater to be seen at Walter Felsenstein's Komische Oper. If you refer to that report, you will read a line about "two stunning productions" which then goes on to mention *Porgy and Bess* but omits any mention of a second title. How many of my readers guessed, I wonder, from the ensuing description of the production designed by the two Muscovite Jews, that this and all the subsequent comments about anti-semitism and the rest referred not to the Gershwin opera with its setting in black America, but to Felsenstein's own production of *Fiddler on the Roof* and its setting in Tsarist Russia? Both productions are still playing to packed houses at his theater. Besson's third revision of *The Good Woman of Setzuan* has now been seen by many audiences outside East Germany, including Italy and Finland, where it got exceptionally appreciative notices. Ursula Karusseit, the Shen-Te, displayed her versatility in two further productions: in Heiner Müller's *Women's Comedy,* which was no adaptation from Aristophanes but, using a somewhat kindred theme, dealt with Women's Lib in the new socialist society of the German Democratic Republic; and in Besson's witty rendering of Gozzi's *King Stag,* a delightful theatrical experience, full of color and magical effects, to charm the hearts of children of all ages and of all political persuasions. For part of the season Besson's theater has been closed awaiting the builders, who have converted the awkward old three-tier hanger-like auditorium with its poor acoustics and bad sight-lines into a single-tier amphitheater more adequately shaped and suited to present-day needs.

Switzerland and Austria

The news that Friedrich Duerrenmatt had agreed to take over the management of the Zurich Schauspielhaus on Harry Buckwitz's retirement next season was gladly received until it was followed almost immediately after by the dramatist's second thoughts. Several of his own essays into the field of direction had clearly misled him about his real strength, which, to judge from his dramaturgical adaptation of Büchner's *Woyzeck,* was firmly rooted in writing. The season had begun with Karl Heinz Stroux's one-night guest production of *Mourning Becomes Electra,* faithfully echoing O'Neill's preoccupations, despite the heavy cuts, and it reached a climax with Buckwitz's own revival of *The Life of Galileo,* starring Hans-Dieter Zeidler and set within a reflecting mirror-setting by the new resident designer, John Gunter, from England; and the world premiere, staged simultaneously with three German theaters, of Rolf Hochhuth's *The Midwife.* Written as a comedy this time, Hochhuth's latest polemical drama affected to satirize injustice and municipal corruption in West Germany, the titular character (like the hero of *Guerrillas*) being a wily councillor who breaks the law for a great cause. The Zurich version, featuring Heidemarie Hatheyer, was only moderately amusing, but Maria Becker in Munich had her audience in stitches. The new regime at the Neumarkt Theater, under Horst Zankl, began impressively with Zankl's highly stylized rendering of Handke's *The Ride Across Lake Constance,* which was one of the competitors at the Berlin Review.

The other Swiss guest at the Review was the Basel production of *The Seagull,* newly translated by Peter Urban and staged in anything but a conventional manner by Jan Kacer, from Prague. Under Werner Düggelin's management, Basel has increasingly overshadowed Zurich, what with a new *Macbeth,* staged by Hans Hollmann and adapted by the East German Heiner Müller, which depicts Macbeth as a brutal sadist and stylizes his unspeakable atrocities against his rivals and the heroic Scottish peasantry. Basel also offered Heinrich Heinkel's latest socio-critical drama *Money Games* and Dieter Forte's adaptation of Webster's Jacobean tragedy as *White Devils.*

When the Volkstheater in Vienna finally came to staging Wolfgang Bauer's *New Year's Eve,* it proved a fiasco, but Bernd Fisherauer's witty production of Peter Barnes's *The Ruling Class,* adapted by Martin Esslin to an Austrian milieu, worked rather better. Alongside Walter Lieblein's adaptation of Dostoevsky's *The Eternal Husband* at the Josefstadt, Reinhardt's old theater presented one of the best of Europe's countless productions of David Storey's *Home.* At the rival Akademie, the Burgtheater's substage, his *Celebration* was impressively staged by Dieter Dorn, with Werner Hinz and Alma Seidler as the parents, while on the main stage the year's undisputed highlight was Hans Schweikart's guest production of *The Captain of Koepenick* with Hinz again in the lead, in a performance that ranked in importance with that of Christoph Bantzer, a newcomer to the Burg, in the title role of Hugh Leonard's Joycean dramatization of *Stephen D.*

France

The convulsions that shook the French theater both before and during the season under review have proved palpably beneficial. The new regime at the Comédie Française has justified itself several times over, both on the main stage, the Salle Richelieu and at the two substages at the newly re-named Théâtre National de l'Odéon. Here the program of new works began with Jean-Claude Grumberg's wordy but nonetheless memorable anti-fascist satire of *Amorphe of Ottenburg* and showed the newly-recruited Young National Theater company at their best in Suassuna's hilariously iconoclastic South American romp of *The Dog's Will,* unusual, as far as Paris goes, because the role of Jesus Christ was given to a black actor. Among visiting companies was the Tourcoing ensemble with Vitrac's surrealist *The Stroke at Trafalgar,* staged with delicate drollery by Planchon's onetime partner, Jacques Rosner. Jacques Charon, outrageously costumed by Germinal Cassado, shone in *Volpone* no less than he did, with a difference, on the main stage in *The Imaginary Invalid,* or later, alongside Robert Hirsch's cajoling Duke of Gloucester, as Buckingham in Terry Hands's eye-catching production of *Richard III,* the first truly Elizabethan Shakespeare to be seen on this stage, at least in French. Exciting, modern productions of Molière, Corneille, Anouilh, and Labiche contributed first-class fare to the year's repertory and helped to account for the full houses.

Sad to relate, audiences at the T.N.P. began to fall off as never before, despite the worthiness of such items as Bond's *Saved,* Wesker's *Chips With Everything,* Brecht's *Turandot,* and a real dramatic find in the case of the satirically scurrilous first play of the half-Russian, half-Iranian playwright Rezvani, author of *The Sucking-Fish,* that was later performed with great skill by the Comédie Française actors at the Petit Odéon, or Jorge Lavelli's revolutionary breathtaking production of Arrabal's anti-establishment musical *Bella Ciao.* Not surprisingly, then, Georges Wilson's contract was not renewed, and the government wound up the T.N.P. as a Parisian popular theater, transferring it to Lyons and handing over its management to the three-man team of Planchon, Robert Gilbert, and the newly-recruited Patrice Chéreau. Chéreau's directorial debut here began auspiciously with a fabulously inventive staging of Marlowe's little-known horror-drama *The Massacre at Paris,* featuring Planchon as the Duc de Guise, Alida Valli as Catherine de Medici— and Richard Peduzzi as the star of the show for designing a setting consisting of an acting area shallowly covered with water. It was meant symbolically to represent the River Seine as the scene both of the historical St. Bartholomew Night killings and of more recent well-authenticated atrocities. It achieved strong dramatic effects without precedent in an indoor auditorium.

The principal attractions at the Théâtre de la Ville included the Dario Fo farce about Christopher Columbus that the troupe had tried out at the Avignon Festival and Camus's *The Possessed,* impressively staged by Jean Mercure. Those at the Théâtre de l'Est Parisien, formally elevated to the status of National Theater, were Guy Retoré's two popular hits *The Merchant of Venice* and *Saint Joan of the Stockyards,* the last-named physically involving the audience by extending the acting area outward on both sides. The Strasbourg National Theater, also newly so promoted, was seen at the T.E.P. in a Marxistic variant of Labiche's bourgeois comedy *The Kitty,* which drew the scorn of the orthodox critics but successfully toured other parts not only of France but also of Europe. At the Cartoucherie de Vincennes, Ariane Mnouchkine and her Théâtre du Soleil unveiled their collectively mounted sequel to the French Revolution drama, *1789,* under the title *1793,* the year of momentous if bloody events; and, just opposite in another disused hangar vacated by the government, the Théâtre de la Tempête under Jean-Marie Serreau took up its residence, and offered a temporary home to a new festival chiefly for young, experimental companies. At the other major venue for avant-garde drama, the Cité Internationale of the University of Paris, long-running entertainments were, first, Copi's satire on transvestitism staged by his Argentinian countryman, Lavelli, and, second, the latest anti-heroic non-sense-show conceived for children of all ages and presented by the Grand Magic Circus company under the management of that other Argentinian-born theatrical ringmaster, Jérôme Savary.

The commercial theater continued undisturbed, providing a staple diet of light entertainment mixed with some more serious stuff. To the latter category belong an autobiographical comedy by Bernard Kops, *David It Is Getting Dark,* not yet seen in his native England, Pinter's *Old Times,* imaginatively handled by Lavelli and starring Delphine Seyrig and Françoise Fabian in the roles created in London by Dorothy Tutin and Vivien Merchant, and Ionesco's absurdist adaptation of Shakespeare's *Macbeth* (rechristened *Macbett* "to avoid confusion"), alongside a preponderance of other British dramas by Orton, Coward, Spurling, Nichols, Jellicoe and Whitehead. Though Curd Jurgens's venture into management at the Hébertot, launched with Marasco's *Child's Play*, failed, Pierre Cardin's at the Ambassadeurs continued to flourish by providing a home for Robert Wilson's experiments, for the French premiere of *Incident at Vichy*, and much else besides. In the same way, Barrault's Théâtre Récamier became the new headquarters of a reformed Theater of the Nations, its activities extended from a limited seasonal festival to a series of wide-ranging experimental productions the whole year round.

Italy

The big news from Italy as the season drew to a close was of Strehler's return to the Milan Piccolo, now that his partner Paolo Grassi had finally left to take over the administration of the La Scala opera house. At the Piccolo a number of guest directors worked with varying results. They included Eduardo de Filippo and his review of the 1930's, *Every Year, Stop and Begin All Over Again,* though this nostalgic show had nothing to compare with the heartfelt humanity of his 25-year-old *Napoli Milionaria*, which he revived with his Neapolitan troupe especially for the World Theater Season in London and for which he got deservedly rave notices from the British critics; Kazimierz Dejmek, from Poland, with a new *Passion Play* featuring Franco Graziosi as Judas, probably the most likable character in the cast; Franco Parenti, who directed, designed and acted the lead in Mayakovski's *The Bathhouse;* and Patrice Chéreau, responsible for an anti-traditional version of Marivaux's *The False Servant,* previewed at the Spoleto Festival, and subsequently toured in France, and for Kadidja Wedekind's adaptation of Frank Wedekind's dramatic twosome *Lulu,* updated into pre-Nazi Germany and starring Valentina Cortese in the title role and Alida Valli as her Lesbian protectress.

Elsewhere the most durable impressions were made by the rejuvenated "I Giovani" touring company. Their original foursome was joined by Rina Morelli and Paolo Stoppa to enable Giorgio Du Lullo to put on Pirandello's *Right You Are If You Think You Are* at the Valle, in Rome, after they had previously been seen in Diego Fabbri's third version of *The Girl Who Tells Lies,* which satirizes present-day Roman mores and has the gorgeous Rossella Falk playing one scene in a topless creation. At the Genoese City Theater Luigi Squarzina staged the third member of Pirandello's backstage trilogy *Tonight We Improvise* with Eros Pagni as the fictional central European producer Dr. Hinkfuss, whom the Sicilian author based on an amalgam of Max Reinhardt and Erwin Piscator. Besides directing Alberto Lionello in *Hadrian VII,* a courageous enterprise when within Papal jurisdiction, Giorgio Albertazzi also joined forces again with Anna Proclemer to appear in D'Annuzio's *La Gioconda.* Turi Ferro (remembered with warmth for his *Liolà* at the 1970 World Theater Season) returned to a similar theme in Catania with Pirandello's *Cap and Bells,* while in Turin Franco Enriquez staged *Macbeth* with Glauco Mauri and Valeria Moriconi, and himself wrote (jointly with Vito Pandolfi) and directed *Isabella, Jealous Comedienne,* with Miss Moriconi as the 16th century actress Isabella Andreini. Curiously, this was the year for a revival of interest in the Communist leader and theater critic Antonio Gramsci. Not only had the Royal Shakespeare Company staged Trevor Griffiths's play about Gramsci in London, but no less than three plays about him were seen in Italy. Of these *Comrade Gramsci,* by Maricia Boggio and Franco Cuomo, produced by the Teatro Insieme, opened with the protagonist commenting professionally on the play at the first night of Pirandello's *Six Characters.* Finally Dario Fo was represented by his newly formed "Collettivo Teatrale La Comune" in Milan by a satire against the extreme right entitled *Death and Resurrection of a Puppet,* and by another against the left, an extension of an early one-acter and entitled, *Order! By Goo,ooo,ooo,-ooood!*

Spain

The outstanding events in the Madrid theater this year were the revivals of two plays proscribed for years by the fascist regime by writers long since dead. Lorca's *Yerma,* about the emotional frustrations of a barren woman who slays her husband rather than sin even in her mind, was performed at the Comedia by the Nuria Espert troupe in an unorthodox production by Victor Garcia that discarded any pretense at naturalism and set the action partly on an annular walkway and partly on a flexible trampoline capable of assuming a variety of symbolical shapes, angles and positions. *Yerma* was brought by Peter Daubeny to the 9th World Theater Season, to become the sensation of the year. At the Bellas Artes José Tamayo put on Ramon de Valle Inclàn's 52-year-old socio-critical drama *The Lights of Bohemia,* in which the display of public corruption and police brutality assumed an uncanny and ironic topicality. *The Arrival of the Gods,* the latest play by Antonio Buero Vallejo at the Lara, reminds one that this contemporary dramatist has been too long and quite unjustly neglected abroad, and there is welcome news that Oleg Yefremov is to stage a play of his at the Moscow Art Theater.

Belgium and Holland

The Belgian National Theater celebrated its first visit to play at the Old Vic in London 25 years ago with a return visit, bringing with them a delightful version of Dario Fo's *Seventh Commandment* and Frank Dunlop's guest production of Michel de Ghelderode's baroque comedy *Pantagleize.* This was capped by Dunlop's return to Brussels to stage *Antony and Cleopatra* there, where a curious novelty was the Argentinian marital comedy *Phlegm,* by Ricardo Talesnik, neatly adapted to Belgian conditions. At the Netherlands Playhouse in Antwerp an acceptable production by Walter Tillemans of Brecht's *Puntila* served to remind the audience that it was high time that its aging 126-year-old theater was modernized, if not replaced by one entirely new.

In the Dutch capital, the veteran Paul Steenbergen was feted for his performance in Karl Guttman's guest production of *Home,* while the death of Albert van Dalsum was mourned by all and sundry. Guttmann was invited by the Rotterdam city authorities to take over the running of the playhouse there in an effort to renew its forces after a disastrous decline under the previous director. In Amsterdam, Jan Grossman, former head of the Prague Balustrade Theater, staged a popular version of *The Good Soldier Schweik* for the so-called "Teater" ensemble, while Holland's best-known dramatist, the Belgian-born Hugo Claus, turned in his most recent controversial drama, entitled *Interior,* about the traumatic encounter between a well-meaning Catholic priest and a former young homosexual.

Scandinavia

The practise of having foreign guests was well kept up in several northern theaters. Casper Wrede (director of the film *A Day in the Life of Ivan Denisovich*) and John Fernald, from London, went respectively to the National Theater in Bergen, in Norway, and to that in Rejkjavik, in Iceland, to put on *Macbeth* with Espen Skjönberg and Mona Hofland in the former, and *Othello* in the latter. Jan Kacer, from Prague, staged *The Cherry Orchard* at the National Theater in Oslo, while Georgi Tovstonogov, from Leningrad, reproduced his famous modern version of *Three Sisters* in Helsinki. Adam Hanuszkewicz, from Warsaw, commuted to and fro to put on several Polish dramas in various parts of Finland. At the Swedish National Theater in Finland May Pihlgren gave an outstanding performance as the possessive mother in *Days in the Trees,* rivaled in popular appeal only by Erik Lindström in Strindberg's *The Father,* or, at the Finnish National Theater, by Jack Witikka's strikingly staged *Endgame.* Lars Holmberg left the Helsinki City Theater for Turku, where he and Ralf Langbacka took over joint control of the City Theater there, opening with *King Lear.* Tampere's 70-year-old Workers' Theater celebrated the centenary of the Finnish Theater with Vili Auvinen's colorful revival of the 70-year-old folk-comedy *The Log-Rollers,* by Teuvo Pakkala. In Denmark a dance-drama inspired by Ionesco's *Death Games* was staged at the Royal Theater as *The Triumph of Death* by Flemming Flindt with several members of the ancient and august Royal Danish Ballet, including himself, performing in the nude.

In Sweden, pride of place at Stockholm's Royal Dramatic Theater was taken by Ingmar Bergman's attempt to throw new light on Ibsen's *The Wild Duck* (featuring Lena Nyman as Hedwig and Max von Sydow as Gregers Werle) by having most of the otherwise unseen off-stage business enacted on an apron in full view of the audience. Alf Sjöberg's main offering here was Witkiewicz's *The Mother,* with Margareta Krook (Bergman's remarkable Gina Ekdal) in the title role, while Michael Meschke's original presentation of *Danton's Death* broke all precedent by being mounted within the debating hall of the Old Parliament House. The new debating chamber is situated in Stockholm's new Cultural Center which it shares with the City Theater's new dependency, the Klara Theater. Here Vivica Bandler produces shows for children and young people round the clock, as well as manages the home-base theater with its two stages. The main events at the latter were a new play that queried the official line on John F. Kennedy, and Johan Bergenstrahle's novel attempt, with Lena Granhagen in the lead, to give a valid new dimension to *The Good Woman of Setzuan*.

Eastern Europe

Most of the new plays staged in Russia conform to Cultural Minister Ekaterina Furtseva's formula of the edifying and humanist purpose of socialist art, a definition that permits her to malign the work of a non-person like Solzhenitsin. Examples are Boris Shchedrin's new version of Alexander Tvardovsky's poem about a Soviet soldier entitled *Vasili Tyorkin* at the Mossoviet Theater. In it, the hero, like that of Peter Stein's *Peer Gynt* in Berlin, is played by seven separate actors, each exemplifying a different facet of this very Russian type. Two news plays at Anatoli Efros's Malaya Bronnaya Theater were Andrei Makayonok's *The Tribunal,* about an alleged collaborator who successfully clears his name, and *The Man from Outside,* based on Ignati Dvoritsky's *The Country Lad,* in which an engineer carries on a running fight with conservative prejudice. A third play, by Viktor Rosov, *Brother Alyosha,* depicts the younger Karamazov brother's war on public apathy and cruelty. Aleksei Arbusov was represented at the Vakhtangov by *The Choice,* built on a moral dilemma; and there, *Antony and Cleopatra,* starring Yulia Borisova, became the season's hit. Oleg Yefremov began to revive the Moscow Art's fortunes with a strikingly modern version of Gorky's *The Last Ones,* followed by Aleksander Volodin's sequel to the Don Quixote story called *Dulcinea of Toboso,* with Tatyana Doronina in the title role. At Yefremov's former Contemporary Theater, Mikhail Roshchin's *Valentine and Valentina* turned out to be a lyrically conceived drama of first love, while the *pièce de résistance* at Yuri Liubimov's Taganka was the guitar-playing Hamlet of Vladimir Vysotsky in a production of Shakespeare's tragedy in which the grave-diggers ply their trade throughout the action, which unfolds against earth-gray woollen tabs designed by David Borovsky. One curiosity in the Soviet theater was *Fiddler on the Roof,* translated back into Yiddish and acted on the stage of the 15-year-old Jewish People's Theater in Vilna.

Elsewhere in the East, the story is shrouded in gloom. In Romania, state cultural policy has been acting as a brake on modernity, though ironically its second visit to the West seems to have given a new breath of life to Liviu Ciulei's highly theatricalized version of Büchner's *Leonce and Lena,* denounced as being contrary to party artistic dogma a year ago. George Teodorescu's spectacular production of Paul Anghel's *Passion Week,* about the struggle of Prince Stephen the Great against the Turks at the Battle of Valea Alba in 1476, at the National Theater, met with general approval. The Warsaw Theater Festival confirmed the claim that there was no real "provincial theater" in Poland, witness Andrej Wajda's original semi-filmic treatment of Dostoevsky's *The Possessed,* which went on to be one of the artistic mainstays of London's World Theater Season; Jerzy Jarocki's of Witkiewicz's prophetic *The Shoemakers,* both with the Cracow Stary Theater company; and Helmut Kajsar's self-revealing drama from Wroclaw of a young man's split personality, entitled *Paternoster.* Warsaw Theater highlights included Josef Szajna's *Faust* collage, by the designer who created the decor for Grotowski's *Akropolis,* and Chekhov's *Three Sisters,* staged as an absurdist farce by Hanuszkewicz at the National. The replacement of Otomar Krejca by Ladislav Bohac as head of the Gate Theater in Prague could not save it from being eventually axed out of existence by the authorities, determined to quell Krejca's non-conformism, though not before he had put on his third, much revised, version of *The Seagull,* that opens with an excerpt from Act IV and flashes back and to and fro along a newly invented time scale. Another avant-garde theater to disappear following official disapproval was the Corso in the Slovakian capital of Bratislava. The Cinoherni Klub avoided official displeasure and Jan Kacer not only travelled abroad but also staged two notable productions, of *The Lower Depths,* at the Cinoherni, and of *Mother Courage,* in Svoboda's symbolist decors, starring Dana Medricka, at the National. The two salient features of the Budapest season were the premiere of Istvan Orkeny's comic dialogue *Cat's Games* at the Pesti Theater and the opening of the experimental "25th Theater" with its flexible 150-seat auditorium and its "modular stage."

Highlights of the Paris Season

Selected and compiled by Ossia Trilling

OUTSTANDING PERFORMANCES

ANNIE DUPEREY
as Isabella in
*Isabella, Three Caravelles
and a Big Mouth*

JACQUES ALRIC
as Shylock in
The Merchant of Venice

JACQUELINE MAILLAN
as Amanda in
Crazy Amanda

DELPHINE SEYRIG
as Anna in
Old Times

JACQUELINE GAUTHIER
in several roles in
Plaza Suite

EDWIGE FEUILLÈRE
as the Princess in
Sweet Bird of Youth

LOUIS DE FUNÈS
as Oscar in
Oscar

JEAN-PAUL ROUSSILLON
as Amorphe in
Amorphe of Ottenburg

BERNARD BLIER
as Jose Galapagos in
Galapagos

PIERRE DUX
as Ulysses in
The Day He Came Back

JACQUES MAUCLAIR
as Macbett in
Macbett

JUDITH MAGRE
as Princess Turandot in
*Turandot or the Whitewashers'
Congress*

ANNE DOAT
as Joan Dark in
Saint Joan of the Stockyards

LAURENT TERZIEFF
as David in
David, It Is Getting Dark

ROBERT HIRSCH
as the Duke of Gloucester in
Richard III

OUTSTANDING DIRECTORS

JEAN-LAURENT COCHET
The Imaginary Invalid

JEAN-PIERRE VINCENT
Captain Schelle, Captain Eçço

TERRY HANDS
Richard III

OUTSTANDING DESIGNERS

ANDRÉ ACQUART
St. Joan of the Stockyards

ABDEL FARRAH
Richard III

HUBERT MONLOUP
The Stroke at Trafalgar

OUTSTANDING NEW FRENCH PLAYS

(D)—Playwright's Paris Debut

ICI, MAINTENANT (Here and Now) by Claude Mauriac. The relativity of human illusions in a barroom. With Laurent Terzieff, Yvette Étiévant, Pascale de Boysson.

JE . . . FRANÇOIS VILLON (I . . . François Villon) by Frédéric Cambre (D). Biographical drama, collectively mounted by the author and the Paris La Mama company. With the Paris La Mama Company.

AMORPHE D'OTTENBURG (Amorphe of Ottenburg) by Jean-Claude Grumberg. Fictional monarch becomes a genocidal tyrant. With Francis Huster, Rosy Varte, Georges Aminel, Jean-Paul Roussillon, Jean-Francois Rémi.

LE PIANO DE LUNE (The Moon Piano) by Pierre-Jacques Arrèse (D). A minister accidentally sets off a giant bomb. With Georges Bruce, Dominique Le Cam.

CAPITAINE SCHELLE, CAPITAINE EÇÇO (Captain Schelle, Captain Eçço) by Rezvani (D). Iranian writer's dramatic debut with a scurrilous satire on oil-kings and their nefarious habits. With Maurice Bénichou, Emmanuelle Stochl, Philippe Clévenot, Gérard Desarthe, Hélène Vincent.

POLLUFISSION 2000 by Eric Westphal. Horror fiction of a polluted and atomized earth. With André Reybaz, Paule Noëlle, Georges Chamarat.

L'HOMOSEXUEL OU LA DIFFICULTÉ DE S'EXPRIMER (The Homosexual or the Trouble With Expressing Oneself) by Copi. Futile search for identity. With Raymond Jourdan, Marian Eggerickx, the author.

LE REMORA (The Sucking-Fish) by Rezvani. A parasite destroys a happy home. With Dolorès Gonzalès, Yves Fabrice.

MACBETT by Eugène Ionesco. An absurdist rewrite of *Macbeth*. With Jacques Mauclair, Brigitte Fossey, Geneviève Fontanel, Alain Mottet.

EUGÉNIE KOPRONIME by René Ehni. The elitist survivors of a total war are banished by the Chinese conquerors to a remote island, only to fall out among themselves. With Judith Magre, Jean-Pierre Gernez, Jean-Claude Houdinière, Guy Michel.

MARCHANDS DE VILLE (City Salesmen) by Jacques Nichet and the Théâtre de l'Aquarium. A collectively mounted agit-prop show on the housing problem. With Thierry Bosc, René Lévy, Karen Rencurel.

BELLA CIAO, LA GUERRE DE 100 ANS (Bella Ciao, the 100 Years' War) by Fernando Arrabal. A mixed media protest against the class-war. With Karen Mesavage, Gilles Guillot.

POPULAR ATTRACTIONS

LES FEMMES ET LA MER (Women and the Sea) by Robert Rocca, Remo Forlani, René de Obaldia. Songs and sketches. With Colette Renard, Noëlle Musard.

LA DOUBLE INCONSTANCE (Double Inconstancy) by Marivaux. Roger Mollien's 1971 Marais Festival production. With Pascale Audret, Roland Blanche, Jean-Claude Jay, Laurent Benoit.

UN MOT POUR UN AUTRE (One Word for Another) and CONVERSATION SINFONIETTA by Jean Tardieu, and LES PAR-

ENTS (The Parents) by Jacques Audiberti. Three absurdist playlets revived. With Henri Labussière, Catherine Arditi.

L'HISTOIRE DU SOLDAT (The Soldier's Tale) by Charles Ramuz and Igor Stravinsky. Revival of famous music-drama-ballet with the Théâtre de la Tempête company.

DEUX IMBÉCILES HEUREUX (Two Happy Idiots) by Michel André. A mystery girl disrupts the life of two friends. With Robert Murzeau, Christian Alers, Anne Berry.

RUY BLAS by Victor Hugo. Spectacular Comédie Française revival. With Jean Piat, François Beaulieu, Claude Winter.

PUCELLE (Maid) by Jacques Audiberti. Marais Festival revival of 20-year-old baroque drama about St. Joan. With Sylvia Montfort, France Beucker.

AMÉDÉE OU COMMENT S'EN DEBAR-RASSER (Amédée or How to Get Rid of It) by Eugène Ionesco. Jean-Marie Serreau's new pocket theater production. With Étienne Bierry, Renée Delmas.

LA SOUPIÈRE (The Soup-Tureen) by Robert Lamoureux. Cornered industrialist solves his financial problems. With Françoise Rosay, Dora Doll, Magali de Vendeuil, Jean-Pierre Moulin, the author.

CHEZ MADAME SINTÈS (At Madame Sintès's) by Geneviève Bailac and Anne Berger. Latest adventures of the Hernandez family. With Lydia Lévy, Gaston André, Renée Cotto.

ET ALORS (And Then) Satirical smash-hit one-man show by and with Bernard Haller.

FOLLE AMANDA (Crazy Amanda) by Pierre Barillet and Jean-Pierre Grédy. 1950s star and her revelations. With Jacqueline Maillan, Daniel Ceccaldi, Jacques Jouanneau.

LE PARTAGE DE MIDI (Break of Noon) by Paul Claudel. Boulevard revival of erotico-religious drama. With André Oumansky, Denis Manuel, Maryvonne Schiltz, Yan Brian.

LA MAISON DE ZAZA (Zaza's House) by Gaby Bruyère (D). Cavalry general's single-minded widow is taken for a ride. With Mary Marquet, Robert Manuel, Jacqueline Jefford.

CALIGULA by Albert Camus. Georges Vitaly's new production of existentialist drama. With Jean-Pierre Leroux, Julia Dancourt, Benoît Allemane.

LE MAIN PASSE (Fish Out of Water) by Georges Feydeau. Wife-swapping in the Belle Époque. With Sophie Desmarets, Pierre Doris, Pierre Mondy, Jean-Pierre Darrès, Alfred Adam.

GALAPAGOS by Jean Châtenet (D). Political thriller set in South America. With Bernard Blier, Gérard Depardieu, Nathalie Baye.

BECKET OU L'HONNEUR DE DIEU (Becket, or The Honor of God) by Jean Anouilh. Anouilh's debut at Comédie Française. With Jacques Charon, Robert Hirsch, Georges Descrières.

LES CHAISES (The Chairs) by Eugène Ionesco. Revival of Jacques Mauclair's long-running production. With Tsilla Chelton, the director.

LE PERSONNAGE COMBATTANT (The Protagonist) by Jean Vauthier. A soliloquy of philosophical outpourings. With Jean-Louis Barrault, Michel Robin.

SPECTACLE SADE compiled by Nicolas Bataille. An introduction to the Marquis de Sade. With Gaby Sylvia, Jean-Pierre Cisife.

LE VOYAGE D'ORPHÉE (Orpheus' Journey) by Jean Menaud. Biographical drama about Jean Cocteau and his works. With Claude Darny, Louise Besançon, the author.

LIBRE PARCOURS (Free Run) by Ève Grilliquez. A free-wheeling variety show. With Yvan Dautin, Annie Colette, Jack Treese, Alfred Street.

FLASH by Marc Cat and Claude Dufresne. Would-be seducer assumes detective's disguise. With Roger Nicolas, Patricia Karim.

LES BANCS (The Benches) by Georges Michel. A man shivers nostalgically on a park bench. With Jean-Michel Molé, Huguette Cléry. FOLLEMENT (Madly) by Christian Colin. A boy shivers nostalgically on a school bench. With Serge and Lionel Ruest, the author.

LA BELLE AUVERGNATE (The Lovely Auvergnate) by Raymond Lavigne. Operetta about a country girl. With Raymond Souplex, Denise Benoît.

LES SINCÈRES (Honest Folk) by Marivaux. With Michel Duchaussoy, Claude Winter. LE MALADE IMAGINAIRE (The Imaginary Invalid) by Molière. With Jacques Charon, Françoise Seigner. Double-bill of new Comédie Française productions.

SQUARE X by Michel Le Bihan (D). A tramp's dream. With Renée Faure, Louis Arbessier, Julien Bertheau.

LE TOMBEAU DE MALLARMÉ (Mallarmé's Tomb) compiled by Jean-Marie Patte. Mallarmé, the man and his works. With Dominique Dullin, the author.

LA GUERRE DE TROIE N'AURA PAS LIEU (Tiger at the Gates) by Jean Giraudoux. Théâtre de la Ville revival. With Michel de Ré, Louise Conte, Anne Doat, Annie Duperey, Jean Mercure.

UN PETIT NID D'AMOUR (A Little Love-nest) by Georges Michel. Love takes refuge from the bomb. With Coline Serreau, Albert Delpy.

DOUBLE V by François Dusolier. Space-age musical about the hopes of the young. With a multi-racial cast of youngsters.

MOI ET MOI (Me and Myself) by Alex Metayer (D). Two-handed view of one man. With France Dary, the author.

DEUX FEMMES ET UN FANTÔME (Two Women and a Ghost) by René de Obaldia. Wife and mistress fight over a dead man. LA BABYSITTER by René de Obaldia. A married couple get a shock. With Maria Mauban, Henri Garcin, Micheline Luccioni.

AFTER SHOW by Roland Dubillard. Late-night entertainment. With Jacques Seiler, Marc Dudicourt.

BARBE-BLEUE (Bluebeard) by Henri Meilhac and Ludovic Halévy. Maurice Lehmann's revival of Offenbach's comic opera. With Jean Le Poulain, Arlette Didier, Michel Caron.

ALLÔ, C'EST TOI PIERROT? (Hello, Is That You, Pierrot?) by Pierre Louki (D). The adventures of a modern Pierrot. With Michel Piccoli, Hélène Gauthier, Michèle Moretti.

HUIT FEMMES (Eight Women) by Robert Thomas. Revival of long-running thriller. With Claude Génia, Mony Dalmès.

OSCAR by Claude Magnier. Revival of 1950s smash-hit comedy. With Louis de Funès, Maria Pacôme, Gérard Lartigau.

LES FEMMES SAVANTES (The Learned Ladies) and LES PRÉCIEUSES RIDICULES (The Affected Ladies) by Molière. Double bill of new Comédie Française productions. With Yvonne Gaudeau, Michel Aumont, Pierre Dux, Virginie Pradel, Jean-Luc Moreau.

AQUARIUS DREAM by Jean-Marie Florensa. Magic flight into a nudist future. With Chantal Bataille, Thierry Lauret.

HORACE by Corneille. New Comédie Française production. With François Beaulieu, Simon Eine, Claude Winter, Ludmila Mikaël.

LE CROCODILE by François Campaux. What happens when a white politician's son marries a black girl. With Robert Murzeau, Nelly Vignon.

MONSIEUR POMPADOUR by Françoise Dorin. Operetta about a present-day male Pompadour. With Jean Richard, Georges Guétary, Micheline Dax.

FEMMES + FEMMES = FEMMES (Women + Women = Women) by André Halimi. Highly revealing feminine dialogue. With Gaby Sylvia, Isabelle Ehni.

LES IMMORTELLES (The Immortal Women) by Dominique Serreau. Based on Pierre Bourgade's novel of erotic fantasies. With Christine Drangy, Michèle Eichler.

LE GOÛTER (The Tea-Party) by Janine Worms. Two-handed female tea-time gossip. TOUT-À-L'HEURE (Later) by Janine Worms. Six-handed debate on life. With Luce Garcia-Ville, Marc Dudicourt, Henri Labussière, Dominique Blanchar.

ANGEL by Jean-Michel Sénécal and Yves Jacquesmard. Frankly erotic show for gay folk. With Jean-Claude Bois, the authors.

LES POSSÉDÉS (The Possessed) by Albert Camus. Théâtre de la Ville revival of adaptation of Dostoevsky novel. With José-Maria Flotats, Pierre Vernier, Jean Mercure, Jacqueline Danno.

TU ÉTAIS SI GENTIL QUAND TU ÉTAIS PETIT (You Were So Nice When You Were Little) by Jean Anouilh. Pirandellian variant on the Orestes fable in a present-day playhouse. With Francine Bergé, Harvé Bellon, Odile Mallet, Danièle Lebrun.

L'ALBUM DE ZOUC (Zouc's Album) One-woman show by the brilliant 24-year-old Swiss diseuse Zouc.

LE JOUR DU RETOUR (The Day He Came Back) by André Obey. Comédie Française world premiere of variant on the return of Ulysses legend. With Pierre Dux, Annie Ducaux. LE OUALLOU (The Cell) by Jacques Audiberti. The difficulty of adapting oneself. With Catherine Hiegel, René Camoin.

LE MILLION by Georges Berr and Marcel Guillemaud (D). Based on the famous René Clair film. With Franck Fernandel, Corinne Lahaye, Patrick Préjean.

LES DERNIERS JOURS DE SOLITUDE DE ROBINSON CRUSOË (Robinson Crusoe's Last Days of Loneliness) by Jérome Savary. Hilarious pretext for burlesquing and parodying countless theatrical genres. With the Grand Magic Circus company.

AMOUR EN DIRECT (Live Love) by Pierre-Jacques Arrèse. Send-up of several theatrical genres. With Nathalie Courvel, the author.

TRIO POUR DEUZ GRUES MADRI-LÈNES (Trio for Two Madrid Whores) by

Bernard da Costa. Two ladies of easy virtue reveal their natures. With Michèle Baron, Monique Mauclair.

LE DIABLE and MOI QUI DIRAIS TOUT (The Devil and I'd Tell All) by Rita Renoir and Jean-Pierre George. Women's Lib masquerades as erotic provocation. With Rita Renoir.

GIPSY by Francis Lopez. Spectacular gypsy operetta. With José Todaro, Maurice Baquet, Jeanine Roux.

BAJAZET by Racine. Parodistic production of classical drama. With Anne Bellec, Jacques Seiler.

LA BONNE ADDRESSE (The Right Address) by Marc Camoletti. Four classified ads and what ensues. With Denise Grey, Christian Alers.

LE MOTIF (The Design) and L'ANNONCE MATRIMONIALE (The Lonely Hearts Ad) by Guy Foissy. Double bill of matrimonial sketches. With Michèle Delanty, Amélie Prévost, Maurice Travail.

FOLIE DOUCE (Sweet Madness) by Jean-Jacques Bricaire and Maurice Lasayques. Tangled web of marital deception. With Danielle Darrieux, Dany Carrel, Michel Roux, Jean-Pierre Daney.

GISELLE TO-MORROW by Graziella Martinez (D). Show business parody from *Giselle* to strip-tease. With Jacot Leleveur, the author.

JE SUIS UN STEAK (I'm a Steak) by Jean-Michel Ribes. Satirical revue of man's inadequacy in the modern world. With Florence Beday, the author.

CORRIDA (Bullfight) by Fernando Arrabal. The poet impotently at grips with a hostile world. With Jean Lefèvre, Viviane Lucas, François Pétriat.

IL FAUT TOUT REPENSER, PAPA (Make It Over, Dad) by Gérard Louault. How to stage a non-violent revolution. With Chantal Touzet, Hélène Lestrade, the author.

LA POIGNE (The Grasp) and HOMO-C.V. by Guy Foissy. Two comic sketches about gender. With Bruno Balp, Christian Duroc, Pierre Eymaux.

OVE STORY by Mitzi. Nudist pop musical. With Claudine Vattier, Jacques Civel, the author.

NUS ET BLEU (Stripped and Rare) by Jean-Loup Philippe. A surrealist view of the human body. With Laurence Imbert, the author.

LE COUP DE TRAFALGAR (The Stroke at Trafalgar) by Roger Vitrac. Jacques Rosner's production, with the Tourcoing Théâtre du Lambrequin company, of surrealist comedy on World War I and after. With Catherine Hubeau, Monique Mélinaud, François Guérin, Jacques Boyer.

LE SOIR DES DIPLOMATES (The Diplomatic Evening) by Romain Bouteille. A spy in diplomatist's clothing. With Coline Serreau, Patrick Dewaere, Stéphane Meldegg, the author.

NOIR EDEN (Black Eden) by Pierre Lose. Dying poet revives his erotic fantasies. With Dominique Mareas, Emmanuèle Clove, Kim Frossard.

LA CAGNOTTE (The Kitty) by Eugène Labiche. Pierre Vincent's Marxist production of popular old comedy. With the Strasbourg National Theater Company.

METS TON ECHARPE, ISADORA, LE TEMPS SE GÂTE (Put on Your Scarf, Isadora, the Weather's Getting Bad) by Jean-Pierre Tribout (D). Musical documentary of the years 1870-1914. With Christine Casanova, Étienne Diraud, Bernard Valdeneige.

LA STATION CHAMPBAUDET (Champbaudet Station) by Eugène Labiche, with new couplets by Françoise Dorin. Comédie Française's new "musical" version of old comedy. With Francis Hunter, Paule Noëlle, Michel Duchaussoy, Yvonne Gaudeau, Georges Chamarat. And LA FILLE BIEN GARDÉE (The Girl Was Well Looked After) by Eugène Labiche and Marc-Michel. One-act curtain-raiser to the above, about a pair of lucky baby-sitters. With Helene Perdrière, Virginie Pradel, Jean-Paul Roussillon.

L'AZONE (Nitrogen) by René de Obaldia. Daydreams of a mother, her son and his fiancee. With Diane and Philippe Poliac.

1793. A revolutionary entertainment, sequel to *1789*. By and with the Théâtre du Soleil company.

PATINS-COUFFINS ET TALONS ROUGES (Straw Slippers and Red Heels), a double bill comprising *Chez Madame Sintès* and *Hommage à Molière* by Geneviève Bailac and Anne Berger. With Renée Cotto, Anne Berger, Jean Magnan.

JE M'APPELLE PIED (Call Me Foot) devised by Jean-François Prévand. Collage of Jean Richepin's writings. With Gérard Louault, Stéphane Bouy, the author.

SOME AMERICAN PLAYS PRODUCED IN PARIS

COCKSTRONG by John Vaccaro. By and with the New York Playhouse of the Ridiculous company.

HEAVEN GRAND IN AMBER ORBIT by Jack Curtis. With the New York Playhouse of the Ridiculous company.

TOGETHER by George Knowles and THE FIRST by William Holt. With Diane de Segonzac, Jacques Lecarpentier.

PLAZA SUITE by Neil Simon. With Pierre Mondy, Jacqueline Gauthier.

SWEET BIRD OF YOUTH by Tennessee Williams. With Edwige Feuillère, Bernard Fresson.

CHILD'S PLAY by Robert Marasco. With Curd Jurgens, Jean Servais, Raymond Gérome.

SAMMY by Ken Hughes. With Claude Mercutio, André Génin, Jean Barrier.

INCIDENT AT VICHY by Arthur Miller. With Sacha Pitoëff, Gabriel Cattand, Jean-Pierre Granval.

NEXT and BOTTICELLI by Terrence McNally. With Jacqueline Stoup, Max Vialle, Jean Larroquette.

EVERYTHING IN THE GARDEN by Edward Albee. With Jean Dessailly, Simone Valère.

GODSPELL by John-Michael Tebelak and Stephen Schwartz. With Bernard Callais, Nicole Vassel.

THE ME NOBODY KNOWS by Bob Livingston, Gary William Friedman and Will Holt. With a mixed group of young players.

THE LAST OF THE RED HOT LOVERS by Neil Simon. With Michel Serrault, Monique Tarbès.

THE SERPENT by Jean-Claude van Itallie. With the Experimental Theater company.

THE LIQUID THEATER from Los Angeles.

DOS PASOS U.S.A. Documentary at the American Cultural Center. With Jean Sincire, Gordon Heath, Lee Payant.

SOME OTHER FOREIGN PLAYS PRODUCED IN PARIS

THEATER OF THE NATIONS season included New York Manhattan Project's *Alice in Wonderland;* Patrice Chéreau's Italian production from Spoleto and Milan of Marivaux's *La Finta Serva;* Los Mascarones from Mexico; Los Camesinos from Los Angeles; La Cuadra from Seville; *Le Babar* by Jean de Brunhoff with the Toronto Dance Theater; and excerpts from Peter Handke's *Kaspar* with Pete Brook's International Theater Research Center company.

THE LUSITANIAN BOGEY by Peter Weiss. With the Calvi Experimental Theater company from Colombia.

JAPANESE NO THEATER with the Japanese KBS Society, Tokyo.

THE EXCEPTION AND THE RULE by Bertolt Brecht. With the Théâtre de Gennevilliers company.

VOLODIA adapted by Fabienne Mai from a Chekhov short story. With Catherine Seneur, Jean-Louis Faure. And THE LADY WITH THE DOG adapted by Fabienne Mai from a Chekhov story. With Gabriel Cinque, Fabienne Mai.

AMOUR SANS TÊTE (Headless Love) by Miguel Angel Asturias. World premiere of

Nobel prizewinning author's drama for two mimes and recorded tapes. With Marc Olivier Cayre, Michèle Delanty.

THE MARQUIS OF MONTEFOSCO by Carlo Goldoni. With the Grenier de Toulouse company.

STRIP-TEASE by Slawomir Mrozek. With Bernard Caro, Gabriel Chevalier. Also in English, with Ron East, Lisbeth Heuble.

TWELFTH NIGHT by William Shakespeare. With Jean-Jacques Moreau, Patrick Chesnais, Jany Gastaldi.

OLD TIMES by Harold Pinter. With Delphine Seyrig, Françoise Fabian, Jean Rochefort.

ENTERTAINING MR. SLOANE by Joe Orton. With Madeleine Robinson, Daniel Colas, Harry Max.

NAKED by Luigi Pirandello. With Emmanuèle Riva, Claude Dauphin, Rene Dupuy.

MR DUCOMMUN IS AFRAID OF WOMEN by Alain Kapp and Philippe Adrien. With the Lausanne Théâtre Création company.

DON JUAN OR THE LOVE OF GEOMETRY by Max Frisch. With Henry Courseaux, Josiane Lévèque, Catherine Monnot.

RUZANTE'S ADDRESS ON RETURNING FROM THE WARS by Ruzante, alias Angelo Beolco. With the 2+2 Theater company.

ISABELLA, THREE CARAVELLES, AND A BIG MOUTH by Dario Fo. Avignon Festival production. With Maurice Chevit, Annie Duperey, Christian Marin.

THE MEMORANDUM by Vaclav Havel. With Bernard Lavalette, Olivier Hussenot, Nana Fischerova.

THE MERCHANT OF VENICE by William Shakespeare, adapted by Jean Cosmos. With Victor Garrivier, Evelyne Dandry, Jacques Alric.

LORD KURT by Alberto Moravia. With Claude Génia, Jacques François, Pierre Michael.

CASIMIR AND CAROLINE by Odön von Horvath. With the J.P. Dougnac company.

MACRUNE'S GUEVARA by John Spurling, adapted by Pol Quentin. With Claudine Coster, Gilbert Beugnoit.

REAL RÉEL by Frédéric Baal. With the Bruxelles Théâtre du Laboratoire Vicinal company.

AUGUST, AUGUST, AUGUST by Pavel Kohout. With Rufus, Guyette Liv, Armand Meffre.

HANAFUDA by Shuji Terayama. With Nicolas Bataille, Catherine Hubeau.

TURANDOT OR THE WHITEWASHERS' CONGRESS by Bertolt Brecht. With Georges Wilson, Judith Magre, Pascal Mazzotti, Georges Riquier.

THE HUNTING OF THE SNARK by Lewis Carroll. With Catherine Dasté's Théâtre de la Pomme Verte company.

THE SEVENTH COMMANDMENT by Dario Fo. With Magali Noël, Georges Audoubert, Nita Klein.

THE TUTOR by Reinhold Lenz, adapted by Bertolt Brecht. With Pierre Lefont, Gérard Dourmel, Jacques Debarry.

THE THREEPENNY OPERA by Bertolt Brecht. With Jacques Alric, Michèle Amado.

FORTUNE AND MEN'S EYES by John Herbert. With Georges Faget-Bernard, Roland Blanche, Christian Risi, Georges Staquet.

THE POLICE by Slawomir Mrozek. With Roger Lumont, Gabriel Blondé.

THE PELICAN by August Strindberg. With Tatiana Moukhine, Paul Annen.

NUDE WITH VIOLIN by Noel Coward. With Jacques François, France Delahalle.

THE DOG'S WILL by Ariano Suassuna. With the Young National Theater Company.

SAVED by Edward Bond. With Elisabeth Wiener, Gérard Depardieu, Hugues Quester.

CHIPS WITH EVERYTHING by Arnold Wesker. With Gérard Giroudon, Claude Brosset, Georges Riquier.

VOLPONE by Ben Jonson, adapted by Jules Romains and Stefan Zweig. With Jacques Charon, Francis Huster.

FORGET-ME-NOT-LANE by Peter Nichols. With Daniel Gélin, Nelly Vignon, Yvonne Clech, Guy Tréjean.

ODYSSEUS adapted from Homer by and with the Jacques Buillon company.

THE MAN WITH THE FLOWER IN HIS MOUTH by Luigi Pirandello and THE EVILS OF TOBACCO by Anton Chekhov. With Roger Coggio, Jean-Marie Richier.

THE CURVE by Tankred Dorst. With Stephan Meldegg, François Gamard.

SAINT JOAN OF THE STOCKYARDS by Bertolt Brecht. With Anne Doat, Jacques Alric.

MOHAMED TAKE YOUR BAG by Kateb Yacine. World premiere of anti-colonialist thesis-drama about foreign labourers. With the Algiers Théâtre de la Mer company.

MASQUES OSTENDAIS by Michael de Ghelderode. With Georges Sauvion, Arièle Semenoff. And THE CAT ON THE RAILS by Josef Topol. With Bernard Verlay, Éliane Borras.

NON-STOP by Maciej-Zenon Bordowicz. With Tania Balachova, Annie Cariel.

EUX OU LA PRISE DU POUVOIR (They or the Seizure of Power) by Eduardo Manet. World premiere of Cuban play about a couple's varied attempts at communicating. With Michel Duchaussoy, Catherine Samie.

COUNT ODERLAND by Max Frisch. With Michel Aumont, Nicole Calfan, Georges Aminel.

DAVID, IT'S GETTING DARK by Bernard Kops. World première of English play about a failed writer. With Laurent Terzieff, Françoise Brion.

THE NIGHT I CHASED A WOMAN WITH AN EEL by William Payne. With Christiane Minnazzoli, Jany Holt, Jean-Paul Zehnacker.

KEFKA AND THE GIFT by Milan Sladek. World premiere of a Czech exile's mixed-media show. With Edouard Sladek, Uta Behrens, the author.

NASTENKA'S STORY adapted from Fyodor Dostoevsky, THE GAMEKEEPER by Anton Chekhov and THE STRONGER by August Strindberg. With Sylvia Morrisson, Lydia Pruvost.

LE MYTHOPHAGE (The Eater of Myths) collective adaptation of Georg Kaiser's *From Morn to Midnight*. With Brigitte Ariel, Henri Nicol.

THE KNACK by Ann Jellicoe. With Xavier Gélin, Marie-Hélène Breillat.

RICHARD III by William Shakespeare. With Robert Hirsch, Jacques Charon, Denise Gence, Ludmila Mikaël.

LES ROIS DU JOUR ET DE LA NUIT (Kings of Day and Night) Shakespearean panorama compiled by Jean Paris, Michel Bernardy. With François Beaulieu, Christine Fersen, Michel Bernardy.

LES CONCIÈRGES (The Housekeepers) by Rouiched. Popular farce of workers' lives by Algerian dramatist, in Arabic. With the Algerian National Theater company.

ALPHA BETA by E. A. Whitehead. With Bruno Cremer, Héléna Bossis.

LES AVEUGLES (The Blind Ones) by Maurice Maeterlinck. With the Belgian Théâtre Oblique company.

THRILLER COMEDY by Javier Arroyuelo

and Rafael Lopez Sanchez. World premiere of Alfredo Rodriguez Arias's Théâtre National Populaire production about the origins of a theatrical genre with the TSE Group from Buenos Aires. With Facunda Bo, Marucha Bo, Zobeida Jaua.

JESUS CHRIST SUPERSTAR by Tim Rice and Andrew Lloyd Webber. With Daniel Beretta, Anne-Marie Danicl, Farid Dali.

THE CONVALESCENT by José Vicente, adapted by René Ehni. With Anne Bellec, Dominique Maurin.

MOVE OVER MRS. MARKHAM by Ray Cooney and John Chapman, adapted by Marcel Mithois. With Micheline Boudet, Guy Tréjean, Jean-Jacques, Tsilla Chelton.

INSULTING THE AUDIENCE by Peter Handke. With Catherine Sellers, Pierre Tabard, Jean-Pierre Sentier, Florence Giorgetti.

PAUVRE RUZANTE, OU LA FAIM, L'AMOUR ET LA GUERRE (Poor Ruzante, or Hunger, Love and War) by Ruzante, alias Angelo Beolco, adapted by Michel Arnaud. With the Tréteaux du Sud Parisien company.

RICHARD III by William Shakespeare, adapted by André-Louis Perinetti. With Daniel Volle, Sylvie Fabre, Dominique Dullin.

PEER GYNT by Henrik Ibsen, adapted by Michel Hermon and Pierre Ribié. With Pierre Maxence, Christiane Barry, Edith Scob, Marie Pillet.

ANTIGONE by Bertolt Brecht. With the "Non!" Theater Group.

THE DUTCHMAN by August Strindberg. With the Bernard Loyal Studio company.

LIMITED RUNS OF INTERESTING NEW FRENCH PLAYS

ADOLPHE by Michèle Lahaye. Adaptation of Constant's novel of wounded romance. With Jean-Pierre Malo, Rachel Boulanger.

LA COMMUNE, SON CRI, SES ÉCRITS (The Commune, Its Cry, Its Writings) by Bernard Wentzel and Luc Ritz. Dramatized history of the Paris Commune. With Danielle Devillers, the authors.

ODYSSÉE (Odysseus) and TOUT HOMME (Everyman). Collective productions by and with the Toulouse Théâtre de l'Acte company.

AURORA by and with the Théâtre du Chêne Noir from Avignon. Fairy tale about mother earth.

NE M'ATTENDEZ PAS CE SOIR (Don't Expect Me Tonight) by François Billetdoux. The daydream of a man no longer young. With Virginie Duvernoy, the author.

L'APOLOGUE (The Fable) by the Phénoménal Théâtre. Prizewinning 1971 Biennale de Paris collective didactic drama. With Jacqueline Sandra, Frédérique Zulmira.

L'EXEMPLAIRE HISTOIRE DE LA CONDAMNATION, DE LA GRÂCE, PUIS DE L'ÉLÉCTION DU LIEUTENANT WILLIAM CALLEY, MARCHAND D'ARMES ET CHAMPION DE L'ORDRE NOUVEAU (The Exemplary History of the Sentence and Pardon and Subsequent Election of Lieutenant William Calley, Arms Trafficker and Champion of the New Order) by Jean-Pierre Bisson and Ali Raffi. Documentary on the Mylai episode. With the Matin Rouge company.

QUE LA PAIX FUT JOLIE! (Oh What a Lovely Peace!) by Catherine Brieux (D). The Belle Époque in retrospect. With Christian Laurent, the author.

MADAME DE . . . by Louise de Vilmorin, adapted by Jean Anouilh. Paris premiere of dramatized short story of marital misunderstanding. With Ariel Daunizeau, Claude Cales.

ITINÉRAIRE DU TEMPS PERDU (Itinerary of Time Lost) by Jean Nazet (D). Based on Marcel Proust's novels. With Bernard Goupil, the Centre Théâtral company.

VOUS AVEZ LE BONJOUR DE . . . ROBERT DESNOS (Good Day to You From . . . Robert Desnos) Anthology of Desnos's poems and lyrics. With Jacques Doyen, the author.

L'AVARE AND CO. (The Miser and Co.) after Molière. A modern view of an old tale. By and with Jacques Livchine's Théâtre de l'Unité company.

LE CHANT DU MANAR, OU SCHIZO-FREE (The Manar's Song, or Schizofree) by Louis Berthommé. A neurotic's nightmare. With Gabriel Blondé, the author.

DANSES ET CONTREDANSES by Julien Carnet. A rich taxpayer and his tax problems. With André Nader, Denise Dax, Frank David.

CATHERINE, OU LE SOIR DE LA TOUS-SAINT (Catherine, or All Saints' Evening) by Aristide-Christian Charpentier (D). Poetic tragedy of three lonely farmers. With Guy Kerner, Jean-Edmond Pierre Romans.

LES PERLES DE CULTURE (Cultured Pearls) by Jacques Laurent and Claude Martine. Program of critical reviews and sketches in the manner of famous critics and playwrights. With Evelyne Buyle, Claude Rollet, Francis Lax, Henry Courseaux, Georges Faget-Bénard.

L'ECLIPSE DE L'INDIEN (The Indian Eclipsed) by Gérard Gélas. The corpse walks again. With Théâtre du Chêne Noir company from Avignon.

SI L'ÉTÉ REVENAIT (If Summer Returned) by Arthur Adamov. World premiere of posthumous Strindbergian fantasy of a man and his longings. With Anne Wiazemsky, Corinne Gasset, Denise Bonal, Jacques Spiesser.

OPHÉLIE N'EST PAS MORTE (Ophelia's Not Dead) by Nabyl Lahlou (D). Moroccan author's symbolical anti-colonialist drama. With Michel Demaulne, the author.

DEMAIN LA FÊTE (Tomorrow the Party) by Guy Foissy. A futurist fun-view of the world. With the Jean-Marie Cornille Studio company.

LES DERNIERS JUGALEURS (The last of the Jugalors) by Eric Cyrille (D). A vicious talking circle. With Anne-Marie Lazarini, the author.

À DÉFAUT DE SILENCE (Failing Silence) by Jean Maisonnave (D). Strange assortment of celebrities from all ages get together. With the Grenier de Bourgogne company.

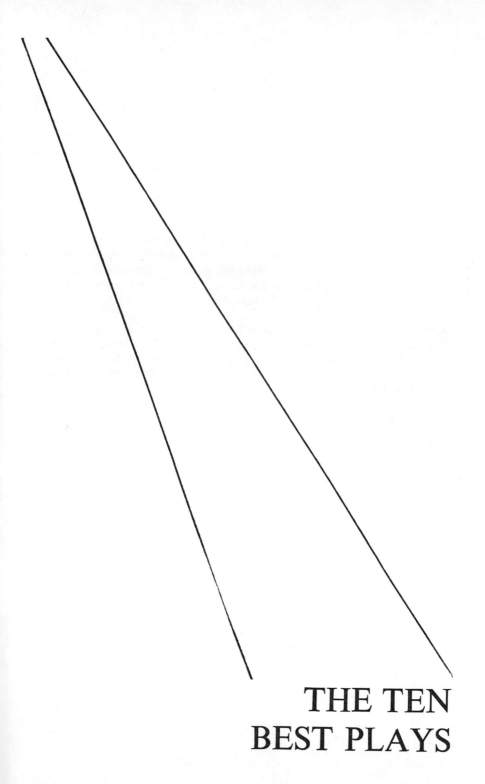

THE TEN
BEST PLAYS

Here are the synopses of 1971-72's ten Best Plays, one of them in photos. By permission of the publishing companies which own the exclusive rights to publish these scripts in full in the United States, our continuities include many substantial quotations from crucial/pivotal scenes in order to provide a handy permanent reference to the actual literary quality of each play as well as to its theme and structure.

Scenes and lines of dialogue, stage directions and description quoted in the synopses appear *exactly* as in the stage version unless (in a very few instances, for technical reasons) an abridgement is indicated by five dots (. . . . .). The appearance of three dots (. . .) is the script's own punctuation to denote the timing of a spoken line.

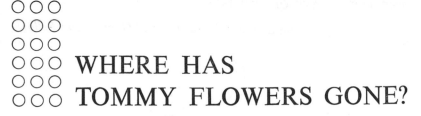

WHERE HAS TOMMY FLOWERS GONE?

A Play in Two Acts

BY TERRENCE McNALLY

Cast and credits appears on page 355

TERRENCE McNALLY was born and grew up in Corpus Christi, Texas. He received his B.A. in English at Columbia, where in his senior year he wrote the varsity show. After graduation he was awarded the Harry Evans Travelling Fellowship in creative writing. He made his professional stage debut with The Lady of the Camellias, *an adaptation of the Dumas story which was produced on Broadway in 1963. His first original full-length play,* And Things That Go Bump in the Night, *was also produced on Broadway, in 1965, following a production at the Tyrone Guthrie Theater in Minneapolis.*

McNally's short play Tour *was produced off Broadway in 1968 as part of the* Collision Course *program. In the next season, 1968-69, his one-acters were produced all over town:* Cuba Si *was staged off off Broadway in the ANTA Matinee Series, and* Noon *formed part of the Broadway program* Morning, Noon and Night; *off Broadway an all-McNally program of one acters—*Sweet Eros *and* Witness—*appeared in November and in February his one-acter* Next *opened with Elaine May's* Adaptation *on a bill which was named a Best Play of its season.*

McNally's second Best Play, Where Has Tommy Flowers Gone?, *had its world premiere at the Yale Repertory Theater before coming to New York, and his works have been staged in many regional theaters as well as in South America and Europe. Two programs of McNally plays,* Apple Pie *and* Last Gasps, *have been produced on TV, and he has recently completed screen plays of his own* Sweet Eros *and* Noon. *McNally is a member of the Actors*

Studio and the Playwrights Unit and was the recipient of Guggenheim Fellow-
ships in 1966 and 1969.

Time: Now

Place: New York City; here, there and everywhere

ACT I

SYNOPSIS: Tommy Flowers—a cheerful, pleasant-looking but undistinguished
young man of today—comes forward to speak to the audience.

TOMMY: I would like to thank the following people for making me what I
am today: Mom and Dad; my big brother Harry; my wonderful Nana; my
beloved Grandpa; Walt Disney; The Little Engine That Could; Golden Books;
American nuns; Batman and Robin and all the gang over at Dell Comics;
Little Lulu; Wonder Woman; Betty and Jughead; Rossini, the Lone Ranger
and Tonto, too; Cream of Wheat for Let's Pretend; all MGM musicals but
especially the one with Abba Dabba Honeymoon; Ringling Brothers, Barnum
and Bailey; Francis the Talking Mule; Ma and Pa Kettle and their farm;
B.O. Plenty and Sparkle; Henry Aldrich in the Haunted House; Abbott and
Costello; the Wolf Man; Kukla, Fran and Ollie; Uncle Miltie and my real
Uncle Fred; Harry S. Truman; Margaret S. Truman; Gene Autry and his
girdle (if he ever really wore one); Roy Rogers and Dale Evans; Johnny
Weissmuller; Johnny Sheffield; Sabu; Esther Williams; Joe DiMaggio; PeeWee
Reese; Jackie Robinson; Ralph Bunche; Trygve Lie; Miss America; Mr.
America; the Weavers; Patty Page; Babe Diedrickson Zaharias; Mme. Chiang
Kai-Chek; Chuck Berry; the Coasters; Candy Barr; Lily St. Cyr; all strippers
who worked with animals but especially snakes; Ava Gardner; Hal Wallis;
Corinne Calvet; Jerry Lee and plain Jerry Lewis; Johnny Mathis; Terry
Moore; ol' Marilyn up there, of course; James Dean; Elvis Presley; John F.
Kennedy; Rose F. Kennedy; Fidel Castro; Bernadette Castro (hell, why not?);
Che Guevara; Bob Dylan; Ho Chi Minh; the Beatles; Miss Teenage America;
Mme. Nhu; Lady Bird Johnson; Lyndon Bird Johnson; Lynda Bird Johnson
Robb; Luci Bird Johnson Nugent; the Rolling Stones; Janis Joplin; the Man
From Glad; Richard M. Nixon; the last girl I balled and all the sisters of
mercy to come *and* . . . whew! . . . we really do get by with a little help from
our friends . . . Mr. Thomas Jefferson, who said something about God forbid
we should ever be twenty years without a rebellion! To all of them I dedicate
this act. Oh yeah, I'm Tommy Flowers. Hi.

Free Flight
   Tommy is on an airplane in flight from Miami to New York, riding first
class, drinking champagne. He tries without success to get the stewardess to

sit and talk with him. He was on his way home to St. Petersburg, Florida, but changed his mind and decided to go to New York, though he has no place to stay or sleep there.

Looking down at the twinkling lights of America from 33,000 feet puts him in a philosophical mood. After a change of lights, Tommy is suddenly dressed in a red baseball cap, idly skimming stones . . .

Summer of '52

. . . When they asked young Tommy in Civics class "Who are the ten most admired men today in America and why?" he simply wrote down "Holden Caulfield" ten times, and his reason: "Because he's not a phony." Tommy always imagined he'd be walking along a beach some day and meet this other fellow in a red baseball cap skimming stones, and they would recognize each other and understand their kinship at once, without any formalities.

But Tommy was given an F for this answer, and his parents and teachers worried about his antisocial behavior. When they allowed him to take the test again he answered it sensibly—Eisenhower, Truman, Acheson, etc.—but considered himself a phony for doing so.

When Tommy's older brother went off to the Korean War, Tommy said goodbye to him in the only non-phony way he could think of: "Just don't get killed over there." This upset his mother so much that Tommy left home for a while; but he did not find Holden Caulfield, not even at Seventh Avenue and 42d Street, the Crossroads of the World.

Now several years later he is on an airplane bantering with the stewardess, whose name is Greta Prince. Tommy is determined to meet her again once they get to New York.

Tommy's Mother, or I Am the Walrus

Tommy's mother reassures Tommy in monologue, as though writing him a letter, that she'd rather hear from him even by collect phone call than not at all. She worries about him. She tells Tommy of her aches and pains, and his father's, and something of their life in St. Petersburg: ". . . . . The good TV is on the blink so we're back to watching all the shows in black and white. It's like the Middle Ages. Well, I don't want to depress you with all our little problems and travails, so I'll sign off. I just missed you tonight. Say hello to Manhattan for me and have one on me while you're at it. Love you, Mom."

Back in the Big Apple

In New York, Tommy has indeed pursued Greta successfully, and Greta is undressing, getting ready to make love.

TOMMY: . . . . . I'm thirty years old which is neither as young as I was nor as old as I'm going to be but still kind of late in the ball game. You know what I mean. I'm just a child of the fifties, a little seedy and the worse for wear, but who isn't lately?

GRETA: It's true what they say about stewardesses!

TOMMY: I'm finding out!

GRETA: Then hurry up!

TOMMY: What else should you know about me? I've got a summa cum something from somewhere in my head, no prospects in mind and lots of bridges burned behind me, an honorable discharge from Uncle Sam, and a three-dollar bill in my wallet, call it lead in my pencil or love in my heart, Greta Prince in the next room lusting for my perfect body, no place to live, and a terrific dog named Arnold who's staying with a terrific girl who just kicked me out, which wasn't so terrific of her but she knows how much Arnold hates to fly.

GRETA: Tommy!

TOMMY: I'm coming! I'm coming!

GRETA: Well hurry up!

TOMMY: I don't always think about girls. I don't want you to get the wrong impression. I also think about blowing this country up so we can start all over again. I sort of dig this country, see? That's why I think about blowing it up so we can start all over again. Now we can blow it up nice or we can blow it up tough. What I'm doing now is nice. What some of my friends are doing is tough. I'd prefer nice. Wouldn't you?

GRETA: Tommy!

TOMMY: She really does have nice legs all the way up.

GRETA: Tommy!!

TOMMY: A little weak in the chest department but her heart's in the right place. Okay, Greta, here I come!

Tommy's Nephew Speaks His Piece

Tommy's young nephew addresses his uncle in monologue, as though writing a letter. He speaks in the language and adopts the attitudes of a radicalized revolutionary: "Power to the people! Off the pigs! Right on! Peace . . . . . Right now they're pissed off at me because they caught me with a little grass again. Big deal! . . . . ." The nephew admires Tommy and is planning to run away from home. He is thinking about joining Tommy in New York, or maybe taking off for Mexico or Peru. He signs off as "Your loving, spaced out, increasingly radicalized, funky, freaky nephew, Charles Flowers the First."

Travel Light

After two wonderful weeks with Greta, Tommy Flowers is back on the street, adrift, accompanied only by his dog Arnold. Tommy thinks a lot of Arnold.

TOMMY: . . . . . I'm going to tie-dye him, too, one day. I've even bought the colors. In my book, he's right up there with Lassie and Rin Tin Tin among your all-time major dog stars . . . Hello.

MAN: No.

TOMMY: No what, man?

MAN: Just no.

TOMMY: I didn't ask for anything

MAN: I don't have any.

TOMMY: I said hello.

MAN: The answer is no.

TOMMY: Thank you. Thank you very much (*To us.*) Travel light. That's my first piece of advice. Yes sir, travel light. Everything I own is right in here. A toothbrush, a change of shorts, my autographed picture of James Dean, my nun's habit. This is a true play and already you don't believe me. That's about it from the permanent collection. Everything else is temporary, disposable and eminently replaceable. Everything breaks, nothing works any more anyhow. Hot enough for you?

MAN: Get a job.

The only clutter he allows himself to carry with him, Tommy adds, is the clutter of apparently useless facts in his mind. Finally he asks the Man for spare change, and the Man gives him the time of day instead.

An older panhandler named Ben tries to move onto Tommy's corner, but Tommy stops him. Ben admits that money is tight these days and Tommy agrees; and what makes it worse is the competition from all the fake Buddhist monks.

Ben notices Arnold and declares his dislike for dogs, ever since he had one that committed suicide by jumping out of the window during an Ed Sullivan TV program. A woman passerby gives Tommy a coin, but it turns out to be a subway token; Ben doesn't want it either.

Ben finds a movie magazine in Tommy's bag and borrows it. A passerby hails Tommy.

MAN: Hi there.

TOMMY: You got any spare change, brother? I'm strapped, really and truly strapped.

MAN: That depends.

TOMMY: Can I guess what it depends on?

MAN: You're a big boy, you should be able to.

TOMMY: You're the best offer I've had all day. Thanks, but no thanks.

MAN: Hostile bitch.

TOMMY: I love talking to people. I majored in conversation in college.

BEN: "Lucille Ball's Night of Terror."

TOMMY: It's a terrific story.

BEN: "Bob Hope's Biggest Fear."

TOMMY: The whole issue's great.

BEN: "Mia Farrow's Cry for Help."

TOMMY: It's heartbreaking.

BEN: "Marlon Brando's Night of Terror."

TOMMY: Yeah, they're all scared shitless on the West Coast, too.

Speaking of movie stars, Ben claims to have known Franchot Tone (they rather disliked each other). Tommy elaborates on his view that only in

America do people have strange tales to tell of their lives, and strange things happen. For example, his high school English teacher was "hit by a bolt of lightning while making a deposit at a drive-in bank. Her, the car, the money. Rumble! Zing! Pfft! Zap! Really. Only in America could your high school English teacher die like that. I mean, it just wouldn't happen to a Laplander . . . . ."

While Tommy is talking, a pedestrian passes and gets away without being asked for money, and this makes Tommy realize that he must stop rambling on and concentrate on business. Tommy gets his movie magazine back while Ben tells him contemptuously that the legitimate theater is the important medium. Ben claims to have been in *Kismet* with Otis Skinner—"lots of feathers in that one." His stage name was Ben Delight (his real name was Jack Wonder, but he changed it) and he once was a professional rival of Paul Muni.

Tommy panhandles a lady passerby, drawing her into conversation about her favorite movie star, who it turns out is Charlton Heston; but she gives him nothing. Tommy was an actor once himself and didn't like it. He was once a lot of things, he explains to nobody in particular, and "What I am now, you see, is free."

Ben finds James Dean's picture in Tommy's bag but doesn't recognize him; he has never heard of this star of two plays and three movies who died young. Tommy addresses the audience: "How can anybody not have heard of James Dean? And how do you tell somebody who hasn't what he was like? He was just like you, only he was your big brother, too. I know this for a fact: James Dean, the movie star, liked me, Thomas P. for Prospers Flowers, a high school kid with pimples."

Jimmy

The Warner Brothers emblem appears to the tune of *East of Eden* theme music. The scene is a bar; Tommy Flowers is James Dean and he has befriended little Tommy Flowers. After a few moments, "James Dean" tells little Tommy he has to be going.

TOMMY: You see the Porsche Spider out there? They told me it'll do 160. I'm gonna find out.
YOUNG TOMMY: That's too fast, Jimmy.
TOMMY: I've got to.
YOUNG TOMMY: Okay, Jimmy.
TOMMY: Hey, and listen, Tom. Your father likes you. He just don't know how to say it. Just try talking to him, man to man. He's . . . unh . . . shy, Tom. It's hard for him to tell you he loves you. Try making it easy for him, what do you say?
YOUNG TOMMY: Thanks, Jimmy.

"James Dean" reassures the lad that his girl likes him, too. Young Tommy offers to go along in the Porsche, but "James Dean" must make the trip solo.

There is the sound of a rending automobile crash, and the scene returns to the reality of the street corner and Ben.

Ben now recognizes Tommy Flowers as a minor actor he once saw in a play called *Kumquats* at the Belasco. Tommy only had ten lines, he was made up with green stripes and the play only lasted one night, but Ben remembers: "One of your all-time super-flops, that one." Ben hated the play and Tommy's performance in it: "All nerves, no style."

Tommy reacts in deep anger. Ben is typical of old people, he says, everything about him is old and he resents anything young. Then suddenly, Tommy is ashamed of himself for insulting the old man. Tommy goes to the other extreme, hugging him, offering to take him to Bloomingdale's and outfit him with a new fall wardrobe. Ben somewhat resembles Tommy's beloved grandfather who once gave him a valuable tip on getting into the movies without paying: "Walk in backwards and they'll think you're coming out," a true and tested statement.

Tommy hails a taxi, and the two men get in with Arnold and head for Bloomingdale's. The driver accepts Tommy's invitation to leave the meter off. The driver is one of those philosophers who treats his passengers to a running commentary (he takes life as it comes, picks up anybody, has been mugged 16 times in the last three years but has been driving for 20 years and figures this averages out to less than one mugging per year). The driver bets his passengers a dollar they can't guess his age, and they don't even come close; they guess 40s, he is 63. When they arrive at Bloomingdale's Tommy pays the bet with loose change and the subway token. He thanks the driver for the "lift," and when the astonished hackie demands payment for the ride, Tommy threatens to have him arrested for running without the meter.

The driver flees. Tommy enters Bloomingdale's while Ben waits outside with Arnold. The lights fade to black.

Love Is Where You Find It

The lights come up on a row of toilet stalls in a ladies' room at Bloomingdale's. Tommy Flowers is behind one of the doors singing "Shenandoah." A young woman in another stall, Nedda Lemon, is astonished to find a man in the ladies' room. She is carrying a cello case. She threatens to have Tommy arrested, but Tommy tells her it's not against the law for him to be here, and he recognizes her for a fellow-conspirator—a shoplifter like himself whose cello case is full of valuable items with the price tags still attached. Tommy suggests a truce, and Nedda agrees. She has almost decided to take everything back anyhow. This is her first attempt at shoplifting and she didn't realize she'd feel so guilty.

Tommy thinks of Bloomingdale's as a "terrific free store" and shows her some of his own loot collected from its counters. He has a Japanese import radio because there was no Zenith (Nedda admits she took the last Zenith).

Nedda and Tommy hide as a woman comes into the room. Tommy starts talking baseball in a loud voice and the intruder, thinking she is in the wrong place, runs out.

NEDDA: What am I going to do now?

TOMMY: You can come out of there for openers. Hello again.

NEDDA: What do I do with all this?

TOMMY: Pack up your Stradivarius and wait till the coast clears. You're better off in here with me. You like rock or classical?

NEDDA: Hunh?

TOMMY: A little music will calm you. Rock or classical?

NEDDA: Classical.

TOMMY: Classical? Fancy! Classical it is.

> *He turns on the radio.*

Listen to that resonance. Must be all the tile. Hey, this is nice.

NEDDA: Are you sure it's not against the law for you to be in here?

TOMMY: Unh-hunh.

NEDDA: I can't believe it.

TOMMY: You'd be surprised how many laws against things they haven't gotten around to thinking of yet. Did you know you can have a complete Chicken Delight dinner delivered to your seat in a movie theater? They don't like it, they discourage it, in fact, but it's not against the law. And you know those tags on mattresses that say "Do Not Remove Under Penalty of Law?" There's no such law. Rip 'em off, rip 'em off. It's your fucking mattress and you can do anything you want with it. And you can, too, return a bathing suit. They just say the Board of Health says you can't so they don't have to be bothered. I pee in them first and then I return them, that's how un-against the law returning a bathing suit is.

Nedda is grateful to Tommy for not turning her in, and Tommy urges her to stay and talk. Nedda is still frightened at what she has done, and Tommy shares a marijuana cigarette with her as an act of reassurance. Nedda hates the city for making a shoplifter out of her in only the three short months she has been here. Tommy draws her into telling him something about herself: she is a cellist and "With a lot of practise and a little luck, I may one day be asked to play the Lord's Prayer at somebody's bar mitzvah in Brooklyn."

New York makes Nedda feel very small, but going home would be worse. She confides in Tommy: "My father wants me to go back home and marry this creep lawyer and be a creep music teacher until we start having creep babies and then I can become a creep housewife and maybe he's right, only I don't want to and I just broke up with this creep oboist who all he did was suck on his reeds and now I'm a criminal . . . . ."

Tommy finally makes a pitch: Nedda has a place in the Village, and Tommy (and Arnold and also Ben) needs a place to stay. He reassures Nedda that they won't make love unless Nedda wants to; as for Tommy, he wants to all the time.

POLICEMAN (*off*): All right, buddy, come out with your hands up!

TOMMY: Kill the joint!

> *Tommy hides in a booth.*

POLICEMAN (*off*): I know you're in there! Now are you coming out or am I coming in there after you? One, two, three. I'm coming in.

Policeman enters with Woman. Nedda nonchalantly combs her hair.

NEDDA: I beg your pardon?

POLICEMAN: Step aside, miss, there's a man in there.

NEDDA: There's no one in here. You're the only man in here.

POLICEMAN: Now ssh!

NEDDA: This is a ladies' room!

POLICEMAN: And I'm going to keep it that way! All right, buddy, I know you're in there. Now come out of there. Come out I say. Now open up or I'll shoot. (*To Woman.*) There better be a man in there.

NEDDA: If there is a man in there, I don't think you have to shoot him.

POLICEMAN: One.

NEDDA: You must be crazy.

POLICEMAN: Two.

NEDDA: He's got a gun!

POLICEMAN: Three!

NEDDA: No!

The door swings open to reveal Tommy disguised in the habit of an Ursuline nun.

Tommy blesses the embarrassed policeman and exits with Nedda on his arm, pretending that she is a nun who has run away from the convent. The Policeman goes out, and the Woman enters one of the booths. There is the sound of the Store Announcer telling the customers storewide that Bloomingdale's will remain open until 9. The Announcer is suddenly interrupted. The voice of Tommy Flowers comes on to the public address system, announcing that Bloomingdale's is going to be bombed, and the customers have exactly three minutes to grab what they can and run.

. . . . . *Lights up on Tommy taking off his improvised nun's habit.*

TOMMY: I haven't really put a bomb in Bloomingdale's but don't think it hasn't crossed my mind. A lot of things have crossed my mind . . . but so far I'm still playing it nice. Well why not? Somebody might get hurt. Besides, so far nice is fun. Try it some time. Try the ladies' room, try the men's room. You might be pleasantly surprised. You've got fifteen minutes. That's a lot.

Curtain.

ACT II

Comrade Marilyn

After a 20th Century-Fox fanfare, the face of Marilyn Monroe appears. A voice begins asking interview questions, which Tommy Flowers answers on behalf of Marilyn. The interview imagines that on the other plane of existence to which Marilyn has progressed, her new love interest would be Che Guevara (she calls him "Kay").

When the interview voice tells Marilyn she is dead, she becomes angry. The voice reassures her that everyone misses her, everyone still loves her, so in that sense she is still very much alive.

Marilyn boasts of having been billed above Jack Lemmon and Tony Curtis in *Some Like It Hot*. Asked to comment on what is going on in the world, she answers that from where she sits all the bombs look "very pretty," but "I just think people should be nicer to one another."

The Great Atlantic & Pacific Tea Party

Tommy is wheeling a shopping cart and eating yoghurt. Life has been good to him lately; he and Arnold have a home with Nedda. Nedda comes in with a shopping cart. She looks very pregnant, but is not. They are shoplifting the A & P, and Nedda's midriff bulge is part of the loot.

NEDDA (*through clenched teeth*): As soon as we get out of here, *you* take the turkey. It's leaking. Now what do I do with these?

TOMMY: Find some thirty-nine cent tops to fit the ninety-six cent jars and play it cool at the checkout.

NEDDA: Anything else, maestro?

TOMMY: How are we fixed for fruit?

NEDDA (*nodding to her bosom*): Apples, oranges . . . take your pick.

TOMMY: You're catching on.

NEDDA: I've got a good teacher.

Ben enters walking rather stiffly.

BEN: I've got six eggs in my drawers.

TOMMY: I think maybe five now.

BEN: I was afraid I felt something.

TOMMY: Put the lamb chops *under* the potatoes, not on top. They'll over-charge us. You're a novice in crime, Ben.

BEN: I can't seem to get the swing of it, Tom.

TOMMY: Hang in there, you will. And walk tall!

A egg rolls out of Ben's pants as he walks off. Tommy takes out a can-opener and helps himself to some food. Also, a straw for the twist-open bottle.

Bourgeois, vous n'avez rien compris. Bourgeois, you have understood nothing. French rebellion poster. But I look at it this way: America's a rich country. It can afford me. Of course if I really had balls I'd light a can of Sterno and rustle me up a Spanish omelette right here in aisle D. This is delicious!

Tommy's Old Flame

Tommy's old girl friend back in St. Petersburg is awake while her husband snores. She is remembering the old days with Tommy in a pink and white Ford Fairlane: "We were just terrible together, Tommy!" Perhaps it's just as well that she never trapped him into marriage by deliberately neglecting to use a contraceptive, perhaps they both have what they really want (she has someone called Norman), but still and all she would like to see Tommy again some day.

A Quiet Evening at Home

At Nedda's, Tommy lies on the floor listening to Nedda play the cello. Ben is reading *Variety,* Arnold beside him. Ben confides to the audience that he likes Tommy, but "What I can't always figure is why the kid likes *me*. I knew Eugene O'Neill. Tommy can't get over it. Hell, I toured *The Count of Monte Cristo* five straight seasons with his father! Hick towns then like Waco, Texas, or Topeka, Kansas, real flea bags, and he's impressed. I've been everywhere and seen everything and there's nothing new under the sun. But try telling Tommy that. I checked up on that Mr. James Dean of his. Seems he was pretty good. But as Tommy says, he died young. Poor sonofabitch. Me, I want to live forever and I nearly have . . . . ."

Nedda is dreaming her own dream as she plays the cello: "I'd like to ask Tommy if he loves me." Tommy is like her music, a pleasant surprise in her life. She is determined to practise until she becomes a very good cellist.

NEDDA: . . . . . I don't know what Tommy wants, so I have to play it by ear with him. That's hard for me and I'm pretty smart about men. It's not like practising my music; Tommy has to help, too. And which is real or which is realer? All these little, wonderful, difficult notes some man wrote once upon a time somewhere, or me, right now, in a whole other place, trying to play them and wanting to ask Tommy Flowers if he loves me and wanting him to answer, "I love you, Nedda Lemon"? They're both real. I don't want to change the world. I just want to be in it with someone. For someone with such a sour name, I could be a very happy girl. (*Nedda stops playing.*)

TOMMY: You stopped.

NEDDA: Do you love me?

TOMMY: I love you, Nedda Lemon. I'm here. You're there. We're together and it's nice.

NEDDA: I know . . . . .

The phone rings and Tommy answers it. It is Nedda's father, and Tommy tries to explain away his presence in the apartment with a joke. Nedda takes the phone into the other room, and Ben and Arnold drift off to bed.

When the coast is clear, Tommy brings out from a hiding place the makings of a home-made bomb and an instruction manual and explains: "A cigar box. A dry cell battery. Some wire. An alarm clock. And dynamite. I know it doesn't look like much but according to this pamphlet it packs some little wallop. *The Civilian Guide to Explosives.* It's free from the United States Army Corps of Engineers. All this talk about bombs . . . even the government wants to get in on the act. I'm up to lesson four. (*He turns on the television and settles back to work.*) Maybe there's a good revolution on."

After a couple of fatuous news notes, the TV announces, "The First Lady was in town today to officially open the Carmen Hernandez Center for Blind

Child Study. The muli-million-dollar center is named for the nine-year-old girl who got her wish to meet the President a few short weeks before she succumbed to leukemia. Blind at birth, Carmen was also mentally retarded. 'She was the bravest little girl who ever lived,' said her father, Hector Hernandez. Carmen had her big day in Washington and now there's a center named for her but her parents are still on relief . . . . ."

Instant Replay

. . . . . The above scene is acted out as the First Lady and an Interviewer appear. The First Lady opens the center, and the interview proceeds in cliches of enthusiasm and sympathy. The whole scene becomes a burlesque of official charitable functions. The First Lady tells the Interviewer, whose name she cannot remember, "I genuinely like poor people and minority groups and the physically handicapped. Yes, I do. I've been lucky to be able to sit down and have a real heart-to-heart with people less fortunate than myself. I'm very convinced we all should. I'm sorry more people haven't. It's such an enriching experience . . . . . There are no poor people . . . no, not really! . . . only poor hearts."

The First Lady expresses her feelings for young people: "Pretty darn wonderful." Tommy Flowers comes onstage in the role of Rachel Gonzales, a 10-year-old Puerto Rican child in a pink satin party dress and a rose in her hair, carrying flowers for the First Lady. She is the poster girl of the year—blind, retarded, leukemia-stricken. Rachel blows kisses to the crowd and warns them "You better donate!" The First Lady and the Interviewer try to be kind to Rachel, but the child reacts as though she were afraid someone was going to hit her.

Rachel is pawing the First Lady, trying to feel what she looks like, while chattering about her home life—stabbing a man who tried to seduce her, fighting off rats, hunger. The First Lady promises to buy Rachel a huge cheeseburger after the ceremony. Rachel responds by offering to sing and dance for the First Lady.

RACHEL: You're a nice lady. That's too bad. (*She comes downstage.*) Hit it, chicos!

> *Rachel goes into her number like a hard-driving little professional. All traces of the shy little girl vanish when she entertains. The full stage lights come up fast, as Rachel socks into her grand finale. Ovation.*

Goodbye, goodbye, everyone! I love you!

> *Blowing kisses, she is on her way out, stumbling, tripping, groping. She suddenly whirls around to face us and makes the clenched fist salute.*

Venceremos!

> *And Rachel/Tommy is gone.*

FIRST LADY (*smiles, sighs*): So afflicted and yet so full of life!

INTERVIEWER: If that isn't the cutest little Puerto Rican child I've ever seen I'll eat my hat.

FIRST LADY: She forgot all about her cheeseburger! No, a sight like Rachel Gonzalez really tears the heart out of you. If only she were more retarded, then maybe it wouldn't occur to her that she was blind. As our President is so fond of saying, "What they don't know won't hurt them."

INTERVIEWER: This is in reference to Rachel?

FIRST LADY: No. I think it's in reference to just about everyone.

Explosion. The bouqet of flowers Rachel has given her blows up in her face. The First Lady and the Interviewer are gone.

The Last of the Big Spenders

At Howard Johnson's, Nedda and Tommy are finishing dinner. They are celebrating Nedda's first job, at a Newark wedding. Tommy tells Nedda he earned the money for this dinner by selling his body to a faded movie star, he can't remember which sex. Nedda's only response is to tell Tommy she loves him.

They collect the salt and catsup and some of the silverware, almost out of habit more than cupidity, just before the waitress brings the check. Also as a sort of reflex, Tommy engages the waitress in conversation about her job and her pay, $1.30 an hour plus tips. The check is for $8.68. Although Tommy denies Nedda's accusation that he is going to try to beat the check instead of graciously paying it, that is exactly what he is going to do.

First, Tommy pretends it's Nedda's birthday, and the Greek manager of the restaurant comes over with a cupcake and candle, the price of which is added to the check total: "In Howard Johnson's nothing is on the house." Tommy complains about roaches and "finds" one in his plate, but the manager recognizes the insect as a novelty shop item, three for a dollar. Tommy then reveals that Nedda is in reality the food editor of a gourmet magazine, covering this restaurant incognito, but the manager won't fall for this either and returns to his cash register. Tommy clearly enjoyed this battle of wits, but Nedda doesn't find it amusing.

NEDDA: Just once I wanted to enjoy my meal, pay the check and walk out like a normal person.

TOMMY: Go ahead, I'll wait for you. Play that gig in Newark, come back tomorrow with the bread and bail me out.

NEDDA: I'm thinking of it.

TOMMY: You want to call your father?

NEDDA: I'm thinking of that, too. I'm tired, Tommy. People can't live like this.

TOMMY: Like what?

NEDDA: Like we are!

TOMMY: We could always blow this place up.

NEDDA: I'm being serious!

TOMMY: So am I. Now hang on.
> *He suddenly stands up and begins shouting.*
I've had it with you, Fred. I'm fed up to here with you!
NEDDA: People are looking.
TOMMY: Of course, people are looking, Fred! I don't blame them, Fred!
They can look all they want! The analyst told us he was over all this. Maybe
you can fool these people, Fred, but you can't fool me. I wanted to be proud
of you, Fred, but you're a disgrace. Pay for your own dinner. I don't take that
shit from any man. Hell, you can earn it right here.
> *He violently overturns the table.*
Do a little floor show for them, you . . . tatty transvestite. Out of my way,
please, out of my way. I can't bear it.
> *He storms out, leaving Nedda, overwhelmed to say the least, sitting
> alone at the table.*
The ability to improvise in my line of work can't be overemphasized. That's
called the Tommy Flowers Foolproof Free Eats Plan, emergency phase three.
I just thought of it. You loved that one, right, Grandpa? Let's see if Nedda did.
> *The manager has escorted Nedda out of the restaurant and onto
> the street. She stands there now, thoroughly and totally wretched.
> Tommy watches her, and then speaks to us.*
I didn't want this. Honest. (*Calling for her.*) Psst!
NEDDA: What?
TOMMY: Get over here.
NEDDA: I don't want ever to see you again.
TOMMY: You can take off that wig now, Fred. I beat the check, didn't I?

Nedda tells Tommy how unhappy he has made her feel, even though she
has soon slipped into his arms. Still she continues to reproach him with
"You're not even that good in bed" and "I want a nice doctor with a good
practise who smokes a pipe."

TOMMY: Look, I'm not a doctor and I hate pipes. I like who I am and where
I am. I like you.
NEDDA: Why does everything have to be guerrilla warfare with you?
TOMMY: You're not the enemy.
NEDDA: I don't see the point.
TOMMY: The point is, get it while you can.
NEDDA: I don't see any future in it.
TOMMY: Future? The whole thing's gonna collapse.
NEDDA: What do you want?
TOMMY: I don't know.
NEDDA: That's childish.
TOMMY: It's honest.
NEDDA: What do you want from me?
TOMMY: I want to go home and make love to you.

Tommy finally decides "I think maybe I want everything," and he has no intention of paying for any of it. Nedda decides to go back in to Howard Johnson's to pay the bill, as Tommy goes off to buy a paper. When he comes back Nedda has vanished. It turns out that she has been put under arrest and taken to the Women's House of Detention, and Tommy and Arnold set out to visit her there.

Nedda Incarcerated

Tommy is out on the street outside the Women's House of Detention, calling to Nedda who is imprisoned on an upper floor but can talk to Tommy out of the window. When Nedda went back into the restaurant to pay the bill, the manager wouldn't speak to her but simply called the police.

Nedda asks after Arnold and Ben. Tommy reports them both "fine" but turns to tell the audience the truth.

TOMMY: . . . . . We were just sitting in the Automat the other night, Ben and me, having a cup of coffee, when this awful rattle sound started coming out of him. It was awful trying to get him out of there or anyone to help us. Don't ever be old and sick and poor in this town. Just don't you ever.

The lights have come up on Ben.

BEN: They don't like that.

TOMMY: He was just sick, ol' Ben was, you know? And they were asking for deposits, like.

BEN: Admittance fees, they're called admittance fees.

TOMMY: Jesus Christ, Jesus Christ, Jesus Christ.

BEN: Finally they got me into Bellevue.

TOMMY: After I told the nurse on admission I'd personally take that stethoscope and ram it down her fat dumb throat if she didn't let Ben in.

BEN: He meant it, too, and she knew he did.

TOMMY: He's been there ever since on the critical list. They put him in a ward with ten other old men on the critical list. Nice. I'll come again tomorrow.

BEN: That's okay.

TOMMY: You can count on it. I still want to hear about you and Paul Muni.

Ben confesses to Tommy that he never really knew Paul Muni or any of the other people he's talked about. He was only a vagabond actor, a barnstormer.

Ben died peacefully the morning after he was admitted to the hospital (Tommy confides to the audience). But still Tommy pretends to Nedda that Ben is fine. He reassures Nedda that he will get her out if he has to blow the place up, but Nedda has already phoned her father, who is coming to get her.

Nedda asks Tommy to take his things out of her apartment "for awhile." Once again, Tommy and Arnold are homeless.

Tommy's Big Brother

Tommy's brother speaks in a monologue, as though talking to Tommy, about his marriage; his unfaithful wife and inconvenient child. He envies Tommy's freedom. He is tied down to a marriage in which his wife rejects him as a lover.

Tommy calls collect to his brother from New York. The brother, guessing it is Tommy calling, is only too eager to accept the charges and talk to Tommy, who identifies himself to the operator as "no one." But when his big brother greets Tommy on the phone with "Hey, Tommy, old man! What's this 'no one' business?" Tommy merely hangs up on him.

California Dreamin'

Tommy happens to meet a talkative creature named Bunny Barnum from Tarzana, California, visiting New York with her high school class, all of whom have gone on a boat ride around Manhattan. Bunny doesn't believe Tommy when he tells her he is only 25—30 would be more like it, she guesses, but maybe Tommy has been ravaged by drugs, of which Bunny thoroughly disapproves. She likes surfing, and she is astonished that Tommy has never heard of her friend Randy Nelson.

BUNNY: . . . . . He's the world's champion seventeen-year-old surfer. He's got fantastic knobs on both knees. I'm supposed to be going with him. He may even need surgery.

TOMMY: From going with you?

BUNNY: For his knobs! From surfing, dolt! It's true, people don't listen to one another.

TOMMY: I'm listening to you, all right, it's following you I'm having trouble.

BUNNY: Drugs again, hunh? Boy, I'd like to take a look at your chromosomes under a microscope. I bet they're really bent.

TOMMY: That's the most erotic thing anybody's ever said to me.

BUNNY: Erotic! Don't get me started on that! I'll talk your ear off. There was a man in Tarzana they found out was a pervert. Trevor Sloane his name was. He used a cigarette holder and wore Capezio ballet slippers to work.

TOMMY: Let me guess: citizen's arrest.

BUNNY: They burned his house down. Twenty-five years old! I can't believe it! You're too pale and you don't look happy. You ought to come to California.

TOMMY: It's my fondest dream.

BUNNY: Too poor, hunh?

TOMMY: Too poor, right.

BUNNY: I'd hate to be poor. I couldn't stand it. I'd probably have another nervous breakdown.

TOMMY: How many have you had?

BUNNY: Just one! How many does it look like?

TOMMY: Oh, no more than that certainly.

BUNNY: I was president of the Hi-Y's, Student Council recording secretary, head cheerleader and going steady with Rusty Winkler all in one semester! No wonder I flipped . . . . .

Tommy tells Bunny something of his trouble with Nedda. Bunny is sympathetic, and she would even like to console Tommy, but she notices Arnold and informs him that she is intensely allergic to dogs or anyone who has been near a dog. She is plain spoken about sex: "I hate bad words. They sicken me. I actually vomit. But I also think the word 'love' is the most overworked word in the English language. Everything is love nowadays, I can't stand that. Fuck is something else. . . ."

They decide to continue this conversation in Bunny's hotel room (she can tell the chaperone Tommy is her cousin if anyone sees them). They go off, Tommy carrying his bag with the bomb in it, leaving Arnold tied up by his leash.

Arnold's Speech

ARNOLD: I didn't always have Tommy Flowers and I'm not at all sure I always will. I got him when I was given back to him by a friend of his who didn't want me after Tommy had given me to him in the first place. It's complicated, I know. This friend was a very lonely sort of person and Tommy decided that he should have a dog. Only he didn't want a dog. But when he saw me something inside of him must have snapped because his eyes kind of filled up like he was going to cry, and he held me very close. I was this big then! And he didn't say anything and he walked a few feet away from everyone and stood with his back to then and just held me like a little baby. No one had to ask if he wanted me. You could just tell. I was so happy. But the next morning he didn't want me at all. There I was, just kind of slumped in my box, all droopy-eyed and warm-nosed and not looking at all too hot. Puppy chill is all it was. Tommy said they'd just take me to the vet but the friend didn't want a sick dog. He didn't want any dog. And you know what his reason was? They die on you. That's what he said. They die on you. We do, you know. Everything does. But is that a reason? How could anyone not want me? Oh, don't get any ideas. I'm not a talking dog. I'm a thinking one. There's a difference!

Last Scene

It is night, cold, raining, and Tommy has been thrown out of the hotel by Bunny's chaperone. He has a bone as a peace offering for Arnold and a job for Nedda playing *H.M.S. Pinafore* at Columbia.

Back at the House of Detention, Tommy shouts for Nedda but can't make contact with her. Arnold has disappeared, too, leash and all. The passersby and then a policeman have seen no sign of a stray dog. The policeman warns him about loitering. Tommy is worried about Arnold, afraid something may have happened to him.

Tommy dreams of perhaps taking Nedda and Arnold home to Florida to enjoy the sun, but when he calls for Nedda again the voices from the House of Detention crudely reject him. The policeman returns and orders Tommy to move on. Tommy tries to joke with the policeman, but he is adamant. Tommy tries to explain that he must stay here looking for Nedda and Arnold, he has nowhere else to go. Finally, to avoid being forcibly removed, Tommy jumps into a phone booth and closes the door. The cop beats on the phone booth door with his stick.

TOMMY: I'm trying to tell you something! You and me, we're the same age practically! We could be friends!
> *Cop pulls his gun; Tommy freezes, puts his hands up. Cop kicks the door open, grabs Tommy out of the booth, stands him against the wall and frisks him. Tommy's red shopping bag is still in the phone booth.*

(*While the Cop frisks him.*) Hey, man, I got friends. You don't know who you're messing with, JFK, RFK, the Beatles, Thomas Jefferson, Jimi Hendrix, Frank Sinatra, Chairman Mao, Tricia Nixon, Marilyn, General MacArthur, Superman, Walter Cronkite, Angela Davis, John Lindsay—

COP (*finished with him*): Now move.

TOMMY: They're not going to like what you're doing to me, they're not going to like it at all.

COP: Move!

TOMMY: Sure thing, officer. See you around. And thanks.
> *Tommy goes. Cop stands there a moment. We see Tommy sneaking back in already. As soon as the Cop is gone, Tommy goes to phone booth and retrieves his red shopping bag.*

TOMMY: Move! Move! I'm not moving anywhere!
> *He sits, takes out the bomb.*

Lesson five. The last. (*As he works on the bomb.*) Did you see the paper today? That projected profile of a revolutionary? A lot of psychological garbage about how screwed up his childhood was—why, we had wonderful childhoods: Saturday afternoons at the movies, lots of girls to kiss, Schwinn bicycle and pictures of Yogi Berra—and how rotten his parents were, them, those two sainted angels, and how he had feelings of inferiority that were now manifesting themselves in anti-social aggression. Anti-social aggression! Why we love the world! And his politics, it said, were probably influenced by a left-wing professor under whose tutelage his impressionable mind was easily swayed. Tutelage. That's a New York *Times word* if ever I heard one. Tutelage your own horn, Mr. Sulzberger. My politics. I have no politics. I am my politics.
> *The bomb is finished. He holds it up to us.*

What did you expect me to do? Run for President? Who'd vote for me? Play ball with the Man? I can't even get a library card. I do know what I want. I want everything. I want everything. I want everything.
> *The Cop is seen returning. Tommy sets the bomb. Next, he takes a green grease pencil out of bag, puts stripes on his face and feathers in his hair.*

Warpaint!
> *Cop sees him, pulls his gun.*

COP: Hey, now move along.

TOMMY (*springing up, leaving the bomb behind*): I'm moving. Don't worry. I'm moving. Everybody's moving. I've got a date with Elizabeth Taylor. We're going to an after-hours club in Port Aransas, Texas. We'll shoot craps in the back room and drink tequila like the Mexicans: straight, with a piece of lime and a little salt. She'll like that, Liz. And there's a girl I know in San Francisco I'm gonna see again. She'll drive up to Tiburon in her Mustang and we'll sit on the dock eating abalones. Sure we will. And then I'm going to play touch football on the beach at Hyannisport with the surviving Kennedys and we'll all go out in sailboats singing songs of the day. Sound good to you, officer? You are so fucking handsome when you smile like that. Excuse me for saying this but just talking to you I feel like some fucking handsome ten-foot-tall prince myself. And if anybody wants me now they're never gonna find me because I'm never gonna stay. Tell them I had green stripes, a dog named Arnold, and I walked backwards until they thought I was coming out. Tell them my name was Tommy Flowers. Tell them I was a prince. (*To us.*) Bet he can't count to ten without smiling.

> *He goes. The Cop stands there, staring straight ahead, smacking his night stick into the palm of his hand. Ticking sounds. The lights have faded to a pin spot on the Cop. It, too, begins to fade as the ticking sounds grow louder. The stage is dark. The ticking is very loud.*
>
> *And at once: an enormously loud explosion. When the lights come up the stage is bare. The play is over.*

THE SCREENS

A Play in 17 Scenes

BY JEAN GENET

Translated by Minos Volanakis

Cast and credits appear on page 368

*JEAN GENET is the celebrated French author who has spent 28 of his 52 years in various reformatories, jails and prisons. Born in France in 1910, he got into trouble with the law before reaching adolescence and has paid more than half of his life behind bars for theft, narcotics and prostitution violations. In the early 1940s, in prison, he began to write, and he attracted the attention of the French literary world with two novels—*Our Lady of the Flowers *and* Miracle of the Rose*—and an autobiographical work entitled* The Thief's Journal. *His first two plays,* The Maids *(produced off Broadway in 1963 for 62 performances) and* Deathwatch *(produced off Broadway in 1951, 1959 and 1962) were written while he was still in prison. In 1948, through the efforts of Sartre, Gide, Cocteau and others, he was pardoned and released from a sentence of life imprisonment as an habitual offender.*

The next Genet play, The Balcony, *was written in 1957, translated into English in 1960 and produced off Broadway for 672 performances. His next,* The Blacks, *was written in 1959, translated in 1960 and produced off Broadway in the 1960-61 season and became the longest-running straight play in off-Broadway history with 1,408 performances.*

The Screens *was written in 1959, but so sensitive was the subject of Algeria*

150

in France at that time that it wasn't published until 1961. Abbreviated versions of it were staged in various theater capitals, but it wasn't produced in its entirety until Jean-Louis Barrault put it on in Paris in 1966. This 1972 production by the Chelsea Theater Center in the Minos Volanakis translation is the first full production in English and has won the New York Drama Critics Circle Award for the best foreign play of 1971-72, as well as Genet's first Best Play citation.

MINOS VOLANAKIS (translator) was born in Athens and entered the theater as an actor. He soon branched out into directing and translating many plays for performances in modern Greece and seven ancient Greek plays for performances in English-speaking countries (including The Oresteia *for the Old Vic and* The Bacchae *for the Oxford Playhouse. He has served as visiting professor at the Carnegie Institute, and his adaptation of* Iphigenia in Aulis *was produced off Broadway under Michael Cacoyannis's direction in 1968, for 232 performances. He directed his own translation in this 1972 Chelsea production of Genet's* The Screens.

Volanakis served as artistic director of the National Theater of Northern Greece in Thessalonika until the political coup of 1967, when he left his native country. He now lives in London, where his credits have included directing Lysistrata *and* Hedda Gabler *in the West End,* The Oresteia *and* Julius Caesar *at the Old Vic and Genet's* The Blacks *and* The Maids, *Brecht's* The Exception *and the Rule and his own translation of Aristophanes's* Parliament of Women *at the Oxford Playhouse, where he is a frequent guest director.*

Because of the absurdist narrative concept and style and episodic construction of The Screens, *we depart from our usual mode of presentation of a Best Play in these volumes in the form of a synopsis or precis. No useful purpose would be served by tracing the event-by-event development of a work of this sort. It develops, not in a flow of events, but in the mounting pressure of its symbolism in a sort of epic poem about mankind in the negative circumstances of colonialism and oppression, with all the events, characters, props and lines of dialogue existing as symbolical projections.*

Therefore we present The Screens *in these pages, not as a detailed outline of the play itself, but as a scene-by-scene review of its intents and thrusts. As always, we include quotations from the script in this* Best Plays *record as a sample of the playwright's art in its original state. In the special case of* The Screens, *however, we use, not separated excerpts, but three full episodes almost in their entirety and running consecutively—Scenes 10, 11 and 12—as the script's clearest representation of its three major human elements: the Colonists, the Army and the Rebels.*

Scene 1: On the road

Genet's play derives its title from the paneled screens which are used singly and in multiples to represent the many different locales of the action. For example, in this first scene a four-paneled screen shows a painted palm tree and an Arab grave, as background for a roadside scene which also uses as solid props a heap of stones and a milestone.

The opening scene introduces a 20-year-old Arab, Said, and his mother, who are on their way to a nearby village for Said's marriage to the ugliest girl in the district. They are underdogs, totally non-privileged, garbage-pickers, having nothing (the Mother's suitcase full of "gifts" for the ugly bride will turn out to be empty) and en route to nothing. Their only palpable posession is the enjoyment, almost the relishing, of their own misery. The Mother enjoys walking barefoot to save her shoes, which she found long ago on a garbage dump. Said enjoys thinking of himself as one of life's human "left-overs" on his way to marry a left-over girl whom nobody else wants.

Scene 2: The brothel

Genet's whores, Warda and Malika, have long since been driven to extremes—extremes of rotting inside, with even the teeth decaying, extremes of gilding and painting outside. Additionally, they are objects of discrimination, since the French Legionnaires patronize them but resent the Arabs' patronizing the French whores. But the fire that burns in Malika, as well as the fire that burns in the groins of her Arab patrons, is not sexual passion but a deep and abiding hatred for the French, so that the sex act becomes a kind of release of anger. Only Said's needs remain physical; he's been patronizing Warda since the eve of his wedding.

Scene 3: At home

Said's new wife Leila represents an intrusion of hope into a family dedicated to despair; though she wears a black cloth over her head to hide her celebrated ugliness, she still hopes and dreams for a better life than she has known. Said and his mother, on the other hand, hope only for an apocalypse which, perversely, would release them into an ultimate paroxysm of joy and laughter.

Scene 4: Sir Harold's field

Here is where Genet introduces his cartoon of a colonist oppressor and also indicates the presence of secret pressures building against the foreigners. His colonist, Sir Harold, has all the cliche attributes and paraphernalia: he is bossy, with bushy red hair, cork helmet, boots, riding crop. He bullies Said and Habib who work for him; he even goes so far as to ridicule Said's domestic situation with a wife so ugly that he must spend all his money on whores (Said thinks maybe he will save up some more money, buy another wife and take her to Paris).

Leaving his Arab underlings to their work, Sir Harold places one of his pigskin gloves, stuffed to look like a fist, to keep watch over the workers after he departs. Habib hints that plans of rebellious reaction are in the making, and he voices one of Genet's key concepts: "We shiver because leather gloves and bosses no longer make us shiver." And Habib, a devoted patriot, suspects that Said is capable of betraying the rebel cause for the money he says he wants.

Scene 5: The prison gate

Taking another step along his deliberately nihilistic, antiheroic path, Said has stolen another man's jacket so that he can be sent to prison—a refuge exalted not by accident on a hill looking down on the rest of the town. Leila, trying to be loyal to Said, trying to adapt to his values, follows him to prison. There is no joy in Said's heart—or gratitude to Leila—when he is released.

Scene 6: The square of an Arab village

A local rebel hero, Si Slimane, has died and the women have gathered to mourn him in the fly-infested open air. The Mother tries to join them but she is ostracized because her son and daughter-in-law are thieves. Genet uses animal imagery and causes his characters to emit the sounds of cows and dogs in order to project the kind of society they represent.

Scene 7: In court

In Genet's caricature of justice, the local authority is the Cadi who considers his authority heaven-sent and believes that God enters into him to dispense just decisions. His first defendant, a flute-player accused of playing his instrument with his nose, is pardoned after the man pleads: "For the first time in this world, the dirty breath out of two snotty nostrils can modulate a hymn, a song, imitate the rippling of a stream, the wind sighing in the branches!"

Said comes before the Cadi for continuing to steal jackets. In Genet's words, Said is a nail to be driven deeper and deeper, and he longs to be punished. But in the Cadi's reaction Genet casts doubt on the function of the hammer. The Cadi doubts that he can be of any use in this matter. Either God will judge Said through the Cadi's decision, or there is no God and no good, and therefore the only qualified judge of Said's actions would be Said himself. Genet's point is that in either case, the Cadi—representing the judge and justice—is useless.

Scene 8: The cemetery

Ostracized by the living, the Mother goes to keep company with the dead, Si Slimane, speaking to him at graveside through a "mouth," a medium. But she gets no comfort from the dead hero, as this scene plays upon an image of life and death as a single unit of experience, with no important difference between them, both being states of decay.

Scene 9: At home

Leila draws from under her skirt, as though giving birth, a clock she has stolen from a home in the village (she isn't in possession of a three-dimensional object, she draws a sketch of her "loot" on the screen as though setting it down on a painted stool). A very broad caricature of a gendarme—who specializes in dressing up in women's clothes to find out how women are apt to behave—comes to arrest Leila, but she escapes.

Scene 10: Sir Harold's orange grove

The stage is set with three screens of five panels each, with the painted orange trees silhouetted against a dark painted sky. Sir Harold is still in his riding clothes and stands watching a trio of Arabs—Abdil, Malik and Nasser—hoeing the ground, wearing loud-colored European suits.

With Sir Harold is Mr. Blankensee in *"black and yellow striped trousers, violet dress coat, wing collar or stand-up collar, but very high. He has a big belly and a big behind (we shall soon know why). He has red sideburns and a red moustache."*

MR. BLANKENSEE: My roses before anything. My greatest pride! My dear friend, I suppose I have one of the loveliest rose gardens in Africa . . .
    Sir Harold makes a gesture.
No, no, simply for my personal pleasure, my roses are ruining me! My roses are my dancing girls. *(Laughs.)* You wouldn't believe it, but I get up at night to smell them.
    SIR HAROLD *(glares at Arabs who stopped hoeing)*: At night? Can you find your way about?
    MR. BLANKENSEE *(mischievous)*: Ah, there's a cunning little trick: I've attached to each rosebush a bell with a different note. So at night I recognize them by their fragrance *and* their voice. My roses! *(Lyrical.)* With their strong, hard, triangular thorns, stern as guardsmen. Ah, it's like being on a parade ground!
    SIR HAROLD: And on windy nights, like being with a herd of cows in Switzerland. *(Curtly, in the same tone, but now to Abdil.)* When you're on my land, forget your quarrels! An Arab's an Arab! If Said is a thief, you should have told me in time to engage another man.
    MALIK: I know an Arab's not much good, Sir Harold. But one who steals from his fellow-workers! And do you think it's nice for us to work with a thief? We bend over the soil at the same time as Said, in the same way as Said —who knows, thievery might creep into our bodies from the same backache as Said's?
    SIR HAROLD: Did anyone bother to warn me? Now that I've taken him on, I keep him.
    A silence.
    ABDIL: What if we get rid of him by ourselves?
    SIR HAROLD *(incensed)*: Yourselves! Am I no longer the boss here?

MALIK: Oh, yes, Sir Harold! You're our father. Too bad we're not your children.

SIR HAROLD (*looking into the distance*): Where is he?

MALIK: Messing around down the lemon grove. That red down there, that's his jacket.

SIR HAROLD (*furious*): Ostracized! You've ostracized him! . . . Without telling me!

NASSER (*sharply*): He only takes a job to be near our jackets, hanging from the branches or lying on the grass. When it comes to work—he just messes around. He's a slob and a stinker. And I'm not talking about his body-stink. If he gets within a yard, you go limp. The whole farm is contaminated.

SIR HAROLD: You've ostracized him! Without orders from me! I want him back. (*He yells.*) Said! (*To the others.*) He's never taken anything from *me*. And he'd better not try! So whether he robs you or not, whether you like him or not, he's an Arab like the others. He's on the payroll, so are you; you must cooperate. And no quarrels. At home you can have all the sensitivities and— why not? You're entitled to them—all the moral refinements you like. Is that clear?

> *Pause.*

All right, it's getting dark. Go home. Good night.

> *The three Arabs line up with their hoes on their shoulders and leave.*

Abdil . . . Nasser . . . Said . . . Malik! Tomorrow on the job. At four o'clock, while the ground's still damp. (*To Mr. Blankensee.*) Not bad, eh? Never forget to call them by their names: Abdil . . . Said . . . Malik . . . Nasser . . .

MR. BLANKENSEE: Quite the right tone. Both firm and familiar. But stay on your guard. One day they'll lift their heads and answer back . . .

SIR HAROLD: That's the danger. Once they get into the habit of answering, they'll get into the habit of thinking. But I use three hundred and fifty of them. I can no longer lead them with a whip. (*He looks about him.*) That Said . . . he's really light-fingered.

> *They walk up and down, turning their backs slightly to the screens. Darkness comes on gradually.*

MR. BLANKENSEE: You're armed, of course.

> *Sir Harold slaps his holster.*

What about your European foremen? You have armed them as well?

SIR HAROLD: All of them. Not that I always trust them. You know, Italians, Spanish, Maltese . . . even a Greek from Corfu . . . and Communism in the air.

> *While they speak, an Arab enters, bending forward. At the foot of the orange tree he draws a yellow flame with chalk, then he leaves.*

MR. BLANKENSEE: I import all my foremen from the banks of the Rhine. Germans—discipline . . . honesty . . . it's the farmhands that worry me.

SIR HAROLD: You, yourself—you are?

MR. BLANKENSEE (*snapping to attention*): Dutch. My great-great-grandpa. More recently on my wife's side. Her father was an official. Post Office Department. (*Pause.*) One can say that it's men like us that made this country.

SIR HAROLD: You grow cork oaks?

MR. BLANKENSEE: One-hundred-and-five-thousand,   two-hundred-and-twelve trunks!

> *Sir Harold makes a gesture of admiration. Another Arab has entered and, in the same way as the first, draws flames at the foot of the orange trees of the second screen.*

But the essential is my rose garden. And my pad.

> *Smiling, he opens his trouser belt, showing his whole orthopedic outfit.*

SIR HAROLD (*interested*): Ah ha, you wear a pad. On your backside too, no doubt.

MR. BLANKENSEE: To balance the front. A man of my age who doesn't have a belly and an ass hasn't much prestige. So one has to help nature a little. (*A slight silence.*) In the old days, wigs you know . . . It's well adjusted.

> *He shows it again.*

SIR HAROLD: But the maid? She is an Arab?

MR. BLANKENSEE: Oh, doesn't know about it. I'm discreet . . . It's as delicate a matter as my dentures or my glass eye in a glass of water. Personal secrets. (*A sigh.*) Yes, it's a bit of an imposition but it's imposing. Ha! Ha! I've come to ask your help. We are working out a defense plan . . .

SIR HAROLD: As I was saying before, one of the ringleaders, Si Slimane, has been killed. But the whole region's beginning to effervesce.

> *Offering his cigarette case.*

Cigarette? . . . a light?

> *A third Arab has entered and draws flames at the foot of the third screen trees.*

You know that at least ten or twenty telegraph poles are cut down every night? Next, they'll chop down olive trees . . . millenial trees! Then it'll be the orange trees, the . . .

MR. BLANKENSEE (*carrying on*): . . . Cork oaks, I love my cork oaks. Nothing more beautiful. People laugh at our love of this country, but you . . . (*He is moved.*) . . . you know that it's we who made it, not they! Find a single native who can talk about it as we do! For instance, about the thorns of my roses.

SIR HAROLD: Say a word about them.

MR. BLANKENSEE (*as if he were reciting Mallarmé*): The stem straight and stiff. The green foliage, sound and glossy, and on the stem, the thorns. You can't play about with the rose as if it were the dahlia. Thorns! Sentinels watching over the delicate *IT*. Warriors! We're the lords of language. To tamper with roses is to tamper with language.

> *Sir Harold applauds delicately. An Arab comes crawling in. He blows on the fire at the foot of the orange trees. The men do not see him.*

In a German operetta, I forget which, the conclusion is that "Things belong to those who know how to improve them" . . . Who has improved this country with your orange groves and my roses? My rose-bushes are my life-blood. For a moment I had hoped that our troops . . .

A second Arab crawls in. Like the first, he stirs up the fire.

SIR HAROLD: Don't be naive. The army's playing with itself, like a horny lad behind a fence. (*Bitterly.*) It prefers . . . its own company.

MR. BLANKENSEE: Think we ought to clear out?

SIR HAROLD (*proudly*): I have a son. To save my son's patrimony, I'd sacrifice even my son.

A third Arab crawls in. He too blows on the fire at the foot of the orange trees. He stirs with his hand. Sir Harold and Mr. Blankensee leave. Five or six more Arabs dressed like the others come crawling in. They draw flames and blow on them. Said is not amongst them. A loud crackling of burning trees offstage in the wings. Sir Harold and Mr. Blankensee reappear. They seem very animated by their discussion and do not see the cataclysm. The Arabs disappear behind the screen.

(*Playing with his switch.*) How could *we*, even if we wanted to, make the subtle distinction between an Arab who's a thief and an Arab who is not? How do they manage it themselves? If a Frenchman robs me, that Frenchman's a thief, but if an Arab robs me, he hasn't changed. He's an Arab who has robbed me, that's all. Isn't that the way you see it? (*More and more animated.*) There's no proprietorship in immorality—pornographic writers are aware of the fact. They can never sue another pornographer for robbing them of a . . . a disgusting situation . . .

Mr. Blankensee laughs heartily.

(*Sniffing the fire.*) Smells like marmalade. I don't mean, mind you, that Arabs have no code of ethics. What I say is that in no case can their ethics be modeled on ours. And they probably guess as much; ah, that Said, his reputation keeps spreading! I ought to . . .

They go behind the screens. Ten or twelve Arabs, dressed like the others, crawl in. They blow on the flames and draw them so big that all the orange trees are aglow. By the time that Sir Harold and Mr. Blankensee re-enter, the Arabs have disappeared.

MR. BLANKENSEE: . . . of a well thought out policy. But the army isn't interested in policies. It seeks out the enemy the way a dog seeks out game. The army doesn't give a damn about my roses and your oranges. They'd rather see everything go up in flames, if that would give them the pretext to have a wilder time.

SIR HAROLD (*as if preoccupied*): I should have . . .

MR. BLANKENSEE: What, my dear fellow?

SIR HAROLD: . . . suspected it. (*A pause.*) for some time they've stopped believing in the virtue of my pigskin glove. (*Even more anxiously.*) Furthermore, my glove itself no longer keeps me informed! Now we'll have to keep watch on them ourselves!

MR. BLANKENSEE: Those worms will end up making *us* intelligent.

Scene 11: The night of the revolution

Two screens at floor level represent the prison, where Said and Leila are watched by a guard. On a level above is a screen representing the Blankensees' window and balcony. Above that is a sky blue screen which slides in on cue, as a voice sounds a bugle call. On this level, a Lieutenant is giving orders to five Legionnaires. He dismisses a chaplain with his altar and ceremonies, then calls for his best white gloves.

LIEUTENANT (*putting on his gloves very carefully*): Rarin' to go. Rarin' and erect! Hard, dammit! For the battle! The bed of love for you is the battlefield! Make war *and* love! In full array, gentlemen.
> *He stares at the audience.*

. . . I want the army to send your families, your watches and your belongings caked in your blood and your spunk! Preston! . . . My revolver! . . . I want the peaks of your kepis shinier than my boots, more polished than my nails . . .
> *Preston, another Legionnaire, hands the officer the holster and leaves. The Lieutenant hooks it to his belt.*

. . . your buttons, buckles, clips, hooks, like my spurs: sparkling! Fighting, fucking, it's all one! I want pictures sewn into your linings, both naked pin-ups *and* the Holy Virgin! Your identity is your golden bracelet, your army number is your pearls! Brilliantine on your hair, ribbons in the hair on your ass—for those who have, but God dammit, a soldier should be hairy—and handsome . . . Preston! Binoculars!
> *Lieutenant carefully puts the strap around his neck and then opens the case and surveys the landscape. Then he puts the glasses away . . . in short, he is acting.*

Hairy and handsome! Make no mistake, good warriors, brave warriors, of course, but above all, handsome warriors! Therefore, shoulders perfect! Rectified by artifice if necessary. Necks massive and muscled! Work on your necks . . . by torsion, tension, contraction, distortion, suspension, compression, flexion, friction, fluction . . . Hard, massive thighs. Or to look so. Knee-high, beneath, your pants . . . Preston, my boots!
> *Enter Preston, who kneels in front of the officer and rubs his boots with a rag.*

. . . Beneath your pants sandbags to swell your thighs, but look like gods! Your guns . . .

A VOICE: Christ! Did you get that, boys? Upholstered gods!
> *The Sergeant appears and salutes the Lieutenant. His fatigue jacket is unbuttoned, and he doesn't care. His fly, too, is open.*

LIEUTENANT: Your gun waxed, polished, scrubbed, supreme adornment the bayonet, crown jewel, lily of the oriflamme, the bayonet, its steel more pitiless than the eye of the Sergeant . . .

SERGEANT (*at attention*): Sir!

LIEUTENANT: At ease. And your eyes like bayonets. Fighting is fucking.

Get me: war's a roaring gang-bang. Make my boots shine! You're the monstrous prick of France who dreams she's fucking. My boots brilliant, Preston! I want fighting and fucking in the sun! And guts oozing in the sun. Right?

SERGEANT: Right!

LIEUTENANT: Clear?

ALL (*behind the screen*): Clear!

LIEUTENANT: We'll approach them under cover of darkness, but we shall not enter until dawn, when the sun blazes! There'll be blood . . . yours or the other's, it doesn't matter. You'll respond to liquid, whatever the source . . . Walter? You!

The following speeches at breakneck speed.

VOICE OF WALTER: If both my hands are cut off, if both my feet are chopped off, let my blood spurt in four jets, let it stream back down into my open mouth!

During this time, light snoring of Leila, Said and Guard.

LIEUTENANT: Good! Hernandez?

VOICE OF HERNANDEZ: No. Blood will spring not from *my* guts but from the one I gut.

LIEUTENANT: Brandineschi?

VOICE OF BRANDINESCHI: Blood, sir, mine, yours, the enemy's! But blood!

After his lines, each soldier collapses into an attitude of boredom.

LIEUTENANT: Ready?

ALL: Ready!

LIEUTENANT: Language? So long as we are on foreign soil, let the alien hills echo with your most savage oaths. Sergeant! Your men are brushing up their Foreign Legion oaths, I hope? I want my men to sound lyrical, earthy, and in heat! (*Suddenly calmer, almost gentle.*) Gentlemen, beyond those hills it's men you'll have to gut, not rats. I know the natives are rats. But for a split second, in the hand-to-hand fighting, take a good look—if they give you time—and discover-but-quick the humanity in them. Otherwise, you'd be killing rats, and you'd have made war and love only with rats. (*He looks sad, almost discouraged.*) Get it?

The Sergeant takes out a pack of cigarettes. He drops one. The Lieutenant picks it up and hands it to him. Without a word the Sergeant puts it in his mouth.

SERGEANT: Got it.

LIEUTENANT (*same discouragement*): Right?

While Preston shines his boots, he examines the auditorium with field glasses.

SERGEANT (*unhurried, buttoning his trousers and fatigue jacket*): Right!

Leila and Said awaken and reproach each other for lack of skill and commitment; Said likens Leila to his shame which, "like my shadow, walks behind me." The guard reproaches them for talking, then dozes back to sleep. Said resumes railing at Leila.

SAID: It's dark in my cell too. My only light comes from your decaying teeth, your dirty eyes, your dull skin. Your lazy eyes, your hazy eyes, one looking into the bottom of a cup; and the other to Rio de Janeiro, that's you! And your stale skin, like an old scarf around the neck of a school teacher: that's you. I can't take my eyes away from you!

LEILA: Like the time you examined me piece by piece to beat my father's price. Every detail cheered you up—you didn't have a penny. You had me as cheap as a potato peeling!

SAID (*sad*): Your father and I soon made a bargain. The lowest price. Is there anything in you one could still respect? A spot one could bow to?

LEILA: There must be, but the one who bows to it—wow!—must have a strong stomach.

A pause.
You've never beaten me, Said.

SAID: I spend all my nights training. As soon as I get out, you'll get it in the puss.

A silence. A Voice is heard.

VOICE (*very manly and decided*): No, if I were to do it again, I wouldn't come up behind her with a sickle. I would face her smiling. I would offer her an artificial flower, the kind she liked. A violet iris, a satin rose. She would say thank you—

LEILA (*admiringly*): Who's that?

GUARD (*grumbling*): The condemned man. He killed his mother.

VOICE: . . . when my speech was finished, when she had smelled the rose and stuck it in her gray hair, I'd have . . . (*Becomes exultant at the end, intones and sings.*) . . . opened her belly delicately. I'd have lifted up the curtain of her skirt to watch her guts flow. I'd have toyed with them as fingers play with jewels. And the joy in my eyes would have lit the darkening eyes of my mother!

A silence.

SAID (*sadly*): He's reached the point where he can sing.

GUARD (*roughly*): Where he *must* sing. And you beginners, shut up!

The light changes to focus attention on the Blankensees in their bedroom. They can hear the rose bushes tinkle with the sound of intruders, and they know that the Arabs are astir. Mrs. Blankensee is holding a pistol, while Mr. Blankensee gropes around for his padding; he refuses to permit the rebels to see him without it. Mrs. Blankensee is excited by the prospect of danger, Mr. Blankensee senses that some original sin is at the bottom of all their trouble. Mrs. Blankensee fires her pistol into the darkness.

Said and Leila continue quarreling, and the condemned man contemplates his crime and the forthcoming execution by hanging. The soldiers are getting ready for action. The Sergeant is still fussing with his buttons.

LIEUTENANT: In a little while we'll brush shoulders with death . . . they're waiting for us behind the casbah . . .

SERGEANT (*limp voice*): I'm ready.

LIEUTENANT (*staring at him*): I don't doubt it. You have the transparent eyes of the tall, red-haired Scotsmen. The Saxon eye, icier than the German . . . and so sad sometimes . . .

SERGEANT: Do you often look at my eyes?

LIEUTENANT: I'm a leader. I observe the eyes of my men . . . when your peak is not too far down.

> *With his own handkerchief he wipes the Sergeant's belt. The Sergeant does not stir.*

SERGEANT (*continuing to button up*): I'd like to weave myself a crown of cornflowers . . . Sit by the river patching up my buttons . . . to snuggle all naked into white sheets . . . (*A pause.*) A big girl who's just hung out her washing . . .

LIEUTENANT (*sternly*): Your eyes are icy; you're a born warrior. In a little while we'll brush shoulders with death. We must try to corner them between the casbah and the cemetery. Born warrior. The proof is that the peak of your kepi is always a little too far down over your eyes . . . which it shadows . . .

Scene 12: The day of the revolution

A crowd of ten Arabs, some in European and some in Oriental dress, is gathered before screens whose panels represented *"a high, white crenelated rampart."*

DIGNITARY (*wearing a fez and a blue, Western-style suit with many decorations*): Quiet. Everyone must be dignified. No children here. Nor women.

KADIDJA: Without women, what would you be? A spot of sperm on your father's pants. Three flies would have drunk you up!

DIGNITARY: Go away, Kadidja. This isn't the day.

KADIDJA (*furiously*): This is the day! They accuse us, they threaten us, and you want us to be dignified! And prudent. And humble. And submissive. And ladylike. And honey-tongued. And white bread! And pale cigarette! And gentle dust on their red slippers and their boots!

DIGNITARY: Kadidja, it's a matter of safety for all. Go away.

KADIDJA: I won't! (*She stamps her heel.*) This is *my* town. My bed is here. I was fucked fourteen times here and gave birth to fourteen Arabs. I won't go.

DIGNITARY: Either she goes, or she is gagged!

> *A Chief has come up. Silently, veiled in silk and gold cloth, he bows to the crenelated screen. As Kadidja is taken away, the first chord of the "Marseillaise" is struck up. Kadidja tries to scream, facing the audience. A man puts a fist into her mouth; she keeps it there. The Arabs remain motionless. Silence. Clusters of French flags rise to the top of the screens. Continue silence.*
>
> *Then, at the top of the screens, visible from the waist up, appear: the Academician, the Soldier, the Vamp with her cigarette holder,*

*a News Photographer, a Widow (Mrs. Blankensee), the Judge, the
Banker, the Little Girl wearing a Communion dress, and the General. They are all in costumes of the 1840s; the Soldier in the uniform of the period, the Vamp with lace umbrella, the Banker with
sideburns and top hat, etc, resting their elbows as on a parapet or
looking off into space. They speak among themselves. The Arabs
are silent. The following speeches are spoken at very great speed.*

PHOTOGRAPHER (*to the Vamp*): You should be in evening gown. On the
ramparts. It would look marvelous.

*The Vamp elegantly throws back her fur piece and exhales a
mouthful of smoke. Yes, the 1840 Vamp may smoke.*

VAMP (*laughing*): They keep saying it's too hot in the desert . . . I'm shiv-
ering—but not with fear, don't worry!

ACADEMICIAN: Place your pretty little finger on the book of History. It will
burn, for the word France is written in letters of fire . . .

VAMP (*laughing*): And where are your savages? One doesn't see much of
a rebellion . . . where are all these uprisings?

SOLDIER: In my trousers, Mademoiselle . . .

PHOTOGRAPHER: And no sound, except the beating of the drums!

ACADEMICIAN (*to the Soldier*): Romans. You are the Romans of our times.
Although history never repeats itself. My dear General? . . .

GENERAL: We're doing what we can to win the masses. One of them is
friendly to us. The other mass is hostile and we have to keep watch on two
fronts.

VAMP: And why do they write . . . "the revolution rumbling underground"?
It's all too silent . . .

SOLDIER (*forcefully*): The fact remains that manly beauty means *us* soldiers. I've read it. The desert would be limp without the rebel and the soldier.
There's flab around here, no question about it; there's still flabby flesh around
here. Let's have some muscle and some bones, and some muscle hard as
bones!

VAMP: Oh, yes!

GENERAL (*with outstretched arms*): Bear our conquests, our fame, ever
southward. We, people of the North! And our Sahara territories even further
south; some day they'll be our new Picardie!

ACADEMICIAN: With a cathedral pointing the way to heaven! Stained glass
windows gleaming in the desert! And pilgrims! Thousands of Moslem boys
reciting Claudel in the original! Ah, General, the Arab boy between fourteen
and seventeen! (*He smacks his tongue knowingly.*)

SOLDIER (*looking into the General's eyes*): Watch out, sir! It begins with
a taste for Arab boys. Three months hence—you understand them. Next, you
support one of their demands—and next you are a traitor to your race. That's
how it all begins.

*Embarrassed pause. They seem to whisper to each other and burst
out laughing.*

PHOTOGRAPHER: Sensational! A sensational photo! The flies! The famous flies of the Orient, huge, disquieting—all over his corpse and on the kid's eyes. The photo was buzzing.

VAMP: Don't! You make me puke!

BANKER: Don't be shy, my dear. Vomit to your heart's content! It won't be lost on everyone.

Indicating Arabs below. Laughter on the ramparts.

SOLDIER: Our soldiers hold the ground for us. They're buried everywhere—in the sand, their weatherbeaten masks, eyes looking one way and mouth the other. In the sand!

BANKER: Every one of us must hold his position.

GENERAL: The army will do its duty. The communiques are excellent. Flawless French: terse, firm, sound, reassuring . . .

BANKER: Full of interesting tips . . .

A silence.

LITTLE GIRL: I, too, would like to say a word. I've kept a piece of Holy Communion Bread. I'll crumble it for the little birds of the desert. Poor poppets.

Suddenly a shot. The Little Girl falls backwards. The characters at the top of the screen look at each other in consternation, then disappear. Below, the Arab removes his fist from Kadidja's mouth . . . . .

On a platform above there appears a gilded screen and a "very tall dummy" covered from head to foot with decorations. A woman and an old gentleman are busy pinning even more decorations on the dummy, though there is hardly any empty space on the tall figure to pin them.

The two are admiring their work, when the Arabs return. So does Sir Harold, leaning on the shoulder of his son, who is about 16 or 17. He speaks to the Arabs.

SIR HAROLD: In the famous and immortal phrase: you're stinking desert jackals!

Kadidja takes the Arab's fist and imperiously stuffs it in her mouth. The Arab withdraws it.

KADIDJA (*trembling*): Leave your fist in my mouth or I shall yell.

The Arab quickly stuffs his fist back.

SIR HAROLD (*to his son*): My son, I've worked all my life to hand this estate down to you. Now all that remains is ashes . . .

The flags disappear from the top of the screens, so do the characters.

Ashes, desolation, silence. The very day of her First Communion with God, your sister was assassinated, murdered! My son, protect roses and orange trees! If their roots must be watered with sweat, blood and tears of thousands of men, do not hesitate. A handsome tree is worth more than a fine man, and even a handsome one. You are armed?

His son takes out a revolver.

Good. Beyond—there! will always be France . . .

KADIDJA (*screaming*): . . . and I say your violence is no match against our hatred . . .

> *The Arab rushes on stage and puts his fist back.*

ARAB: Don't listen to her. She's crazy . . .

KADIDJA: Yes! Ashes, desolation, and your little sister . . .

> *A shot. She falls, supported by the Arab. The shot was fired by Sir Harold's son, who calmly puts his revolver back in its holster. The two men walk offstage backwards, in silence.*

ARAB (*to the audience*): She's dead.

> *Darkness for a few seconds. The light returns, but very weak. Kadidja, alone, is holding a lighted candle and standing against the screen at right.*

KADIDJA (*in a very severe tone*): So I'm dead? Well, not yet! I haven't finished my job. Death, let's fight it out! Said, Leila, I loved you! You, too would sit together in the evening, relating the day's evil to each other. You know that evil is the only hope! Evil, wonderful, evil, you who stay with us when everything else is gone to hell, miraculous evil, help us! I beg you, stand up, and beg you, impregnate my people! And don't let them be idle! (*She calls out with authority.*) Kaddur!

> *An Arab appears.*

What have you done to help evil?

> *Dialogue and gestures will be very rapid, characters rushing each other.*

KADDUR (*in a voice muffled but proud*): The muzzles are still hot—put your hand on them—look, I stole two revolvers.

KADIDJA (*curtly*): Set them down . . . the muzzles smoking . . .

> *Kaddur very quickly draws the revolvers on the screen with a piece of charcoal. The drawings are monstrously enlarged. Kadidja will speak throughout in the same severe tone.*

M'Barek!

> *Enter M'Barek.*

What did you do?

M'BAREK: At the stroke of noon, disemboweled three of their cows. One with calf. Here are the horns.

> *He draws the horns and goes.*

KADIDJA: And do everything silently. They're listening. Salem!

> *Salem enters. Like the others, his voice is muted but violent.*

SALEM: Under the orange trees, one of their girls. Raped. I bring you the bloodstain.

> *He draws the bloodstain in red on the screen. The Arabs now enter at a more rapid rate. They wait at the right, eager to appear.*

KADIDJA (*severely*): That was your pleasure. And hers. But where is the crime that serves *us*?

SALEM (*loudly*): The one who fucks her next will never see her eyes! Those eyes that looked up at the color of the oranges in the sky.

KADIDJA (*laughing*): Button your fly, boy.

Kadidja calls the names of others who have torn out the hearts of their enemies or vengefully disemboweled them, drawing their deeds on the screens. Ali comes in and draws the severed head of a Captain, still wearing his kepi. Kuider comes in—he ran away, so he must draw his fear. Amer has robbed a bank, and in his turn he draws a pile of bank notes on the screen.

KADIDJA: Attrache!
    Enter Attrache.
And you?
  ATTRACHE: Blew up lemon trees.
  KADIDJA: Set them down.
    Attrache draws a lemon branch and goes.
Azuz!
    Enter Azuz.
And you?
  AZUZ: The sun—the sun of a fireman's helmet—the setting sun—too bright, blinded me. I felt sad—
  KADIDJA (*smiling*): Speed up your song and dance . . .
  AZUZ: I didn't know the smoke would be so heavy when I struck my match.
  KADIDJA: Show the embers. Or the ash! Or the flames. Or the smoke. Let it enter me through the nose and fill my lungs! Let me hear the crackling of the fire.
    Azuz draws a house in flames, imitates the sound of a crackling fire, then goes.
Abdesselem!
    Enter Abdesselem.
And you?
  ABDESSELEM: Cut off feet!
  KADIDJA: Set the trotters down!
    Abdesselem draws four feet very quickly.
What about the smell? Let me see the smell . . .
    He draws a spiral of smoke.
Strong! (*Calls into the wings.*) You all! Come along, let it go! Come on. Each must know what the others've done! And put in some color!
    The Arabs crowd around and draw on the screen, all at the same time, heads, hands, guns, bloodstains.
Don't be ashamed, my sons! Be worthy of the whole world's contempt! Cut throats, my sons . . .
    They continue drawing in silence . . .
  ARAB: There's no more room.
  KADIDJA: Bring a new rampart!

Another screen representing a crenelated rampart with flags is brought in for the Arabs to draw on. Meanwhile, on the other level, the two old people are pinning more and more medals on their tall dummy, admiring it as they do so.

Kadidja calls upon God to send her more cruelties, more crimes. Finally the Arabs drift offstage, as the Cadi enters.

KADIDJA: You are late. What have you done?

CADI: I only learned something. The world is divided. I cannot judge. Now I have to take sides.

KADIDJA: You only found out today? Where the hell have you been?

CADI: Asleep . . . or wandering. That was the time of the caterpillars. Now comes the butterfly. My metamorphosis!

KADIDJA: Paint it there!

CADI: It would take up all the space.

KADIDJA: Then get lost!

    Exit Cadi.

(*To herself.*) True, we'll need more space . . . You, females!

    A woman enters right, carrying a child.

Is that you, Srira? Bring in your vermin . . . show him the ramparts . . . let him fill his eyes, his lovely black eyes, with all the beauties of the land.

    Four or five women enter, each carrying a baby, but they remain
    near the wings. Suddenly everybody is silent. Enter Said's mother.

Well, well, we had all forgotten you.

MOTHER (*shrugging*): And you—still here? It's written that I'm to spend my nights face to face with the dead. Not dead for long, either. All that rage is still fresh, your blood hasn't stopped flowing.

KADIDJA: What have you done for us?

MOTHER: While your men were piling up heads and hearts, I kept watch, for Leila to steal your dresses and your coffee grinders. Said helped her.

    All the Arabs show contempt for her, but Kadidja stops them.

KADIDJA: Go on! Do well what you have to do!

MOTHER: I give advice. I don't take it. I sow my seed where I like.

KADIDJA: I know you're intimate with what no longer has a name on earth, but you've got to . . .

MOTHER (*interrupting her and leaving*): Don't *you* tell me what I got to do. I sang that song before my time.

    The Arabs drive the Mother away.

KADIDJA (*taken aback; to the Arabs that remain*): Get the hell out. Don't let her return to the village. Let her destroy; let her ravage!

    The Arabs leave. A long pause. Kadidja is alone. Then five or six
    women enter.

Come near; you have what's needed! . . . . .

HABIBA: I have a sponge and vinegar.

LALLA: Where are you going? Not to die?

KADIDJA: To die. To go to sleep as after a good meal, and belch it for all eternity.

NEDJMA: I've got the Turkish towels. And my gentleness. To help me close your eyes.

KADIDJA: It's strength in your wrist you are going to need to close my eyes. Lay me out and wash me well. No silly chatter. No, don't chase the flies away. I want to know them all by name.

The women begin to bury Kadidja.

Don't forget to bind my jaw and stuff cotton in my ears and nostrils; and up my ass . . . I've already been among the dead three minutes. I'll see how I can help you . . . I'm carrying tons of hatred here. Above all . . . wash my feet properly . . . It's the second time in three years . . .

Scene 13: On the road

To Leila's ugliness has now been added a limp; and like Said she now wishes to march only in the direction of blacker and blacker evil, feeling only hate. She has become the perfect companion for Said on the long downward path.

Several of the characters drift in and out of this scene, making position statements, as it were. Sir Harold's son, now representing the colonists, is determined to wipe out the last Arab. The Mother sees herself as kin to the nettles and hopes for her son Said that he will go to the limit of evil. The Lieutenant spruces up his men in readiness for an attack. Their mission as he sees it is not to conquer (what is there worth conquering here?) but to return to France war-damaged, mutilated, rotting, so that in the mirror of their condition the country can see itself rotting.

Almost accidentally, the Mother manages to strangle one of the Legionnaires while helping him on with his pack. Said has turned traitor and helped the soldiers. The Sergeant has turned out to be the most "beautiful," that is to say the most brutal, of the military group, somewhat to the Lieutenant's envy. The General is killed by a burst of machine-gun fire.

Scene 14: The village square

In the brothel, the activity is even more joyless than ever, the customers mostly Arab soldiers carrying machine guns. Any trace of beauty has disappeared from the rebels' lives—beauty is now a monopoly of the oppressor. The whores and Arab soldiers have no alternative but to live the dregs and degradation that are left to them, to pursue evil as far as it leads. They go to the extreme of poisoning their own wells with arsenic in order to deny the enemy water.

Said has committed the ultimate offense against his clan by betraying the Arab soldiers' position to an enemy Admiral; an ineffectual betrayal because of course the Admiral cannot bring his ships into the mountains to cut off the rebel forces. Said invokes Leila, who is absent: "I'm free, Leila. With my thumbs in my belt and my hands flat on my thighs, the way they walk in America . . . . . I've gone all the way."

Scene 15: Among the dead

The dead, even the hero Si Slimane, care little for the passionate concerns of the living. Kadidja has a lingering interest in the revolt, but Slimane advises her that she must cultivate indifference, die more and more, spit out the last traces of finite time. The Mother drops her dead soldier among the dead; soon after, she herself is dead and joins the others. Kadidja, striving, finally learns and can recite the names of the flies.

In the world of the living the Lieutenant is shot and soon dies breathing the air of his native land provided by his men who one after the other break wind in his face.

Things have sunk to a level of rot and disaster at which the Mother can begin to enjoy the apocalyptic laughter for which she had so earnestly hoped and worked, the laughter of total defeat and decline.

The scene ends with Leila, one eye put out by Said, wandering about and looking for death, which she is soon to find.

Scene 16: Warda's murder

The Lieutenant, the General, the Sergeant and many French and Arab soldiers join the company of the dead, each in his turn amazed at how easy the process of dying turned out to be.

Warda is stabbed to death with knitting needless by women jealous of her attractions and joins the dead. In the conversation of the Sergeant and Warda, Genet draws a parallel between the act of defecating and the act of dying.

Scene 17: After the revolution

The nihilistic spell is now wound up. Said is pursued by the armed villagers and shot dead in his running tracks. All individuals, even the representatives of the future such as the colonist's son, have joined the dead; death is the fruit of both victory and defeat, the destiny and destination of human life.

THAT CHAMPIONSHIP SEASON

A Play in Three Acts

BY JASON MILLER

Cast and credits appear on page 362

JASON MILLER was born in Scranton, Pa. in 1940. He studied at Catholic University and entered the theater as an actor, playing Shakespearean roles at the Champlain and Cincinnati Festivals. He created the role of Rogozhin in Subject to Fits *last season at the Public Theater.*

As a playwright, Miller is the author of a program of one-act plays entitled The Circus Theater *and of* Nobody Hears a Broken Drum, *about the Molly Maguires in Pennsylvania in the Civil War era, which played 6 performances off Broadway in March 1970. That same month his* Lou Gehrig Did Not Die of Cancer *was produced for three performances as an Equity Theater Informal. With his second off-Broadway script,* That Championship Season, *he has won the New York Drama Critics Circle Award for the best of all the plays of 1971-72 as well as a Best Play citation—and also added still another acting credit, since he served as an understudy for the Public Theater production. He is married, with three children.*

As of this volume's press time, it had been announced that That Championship Season *was to be transferred to Broadway early in the fall of 1972 for a continued run.*

That Championship Season peers into the shadows of the American Dream, searching out the signs of excess which so often accompany success, dramatizing the fatal flaw in the competitive, must-win lifestyle and its traumatic consequences to individuals. Because of special provisions in the publishing contracts for Miller's script, we cannot arrange to present it in a formal precis with extensive quotes as we do with most Best Plays in these volumes. But the review and resume of *That Championship Season* hereinunder describes most of the play's events and thrusts.

The single setting represents the living room, downstairs hall and staircase

169

of the Coach's house somewhere in the Lackawanna Valley in Pennsylvania, in the present time. The Coach is a bachelor who has lived much of his life in this house, which has a nostalgic atmosphere. A colored glass transom over the front door upstage center echoes a Tiffany lampshade on a table at right. Featured in the room are a gun rack and a Stromberg-Carlson radio console. Framed pictures of distinguished Americans are part of the room's nostalgia: Theodore Roosevelt, John F. Kennedy—and Sen. Joseph McCarthy. The kitchen door is at left and the stairs lead upward to the bathroom door. At right, in an alcove with bay window, is a table bearing a large silver trophy.

The room is all ready for the annual reunion at the Coach's house of his 1952 high school basketball team which won the state championship—and the highly visible trophy. One of the members of the team, Tom Daley—a well dressed but rather unprepossessing man in now his middle 30s—takes down a gun from the Coach's rack while George Sikowski (the mayor of the town, overweight, hypersensitive) comes in with drinks. The Coach is briefly absent—he has gone out to get some fried chicken for the party. Tom returns the gun to the rack after ascertaining that it is loaded and on hair trigger. The two men remind each other what great basketball players they once were, but Tom's remarks come out flat and insincere compared to George's.

George is under pressure these days. He's coming up for re-election, and his opponent is one of their former classmates, though not a member of the old team: Sharmen, a Jew who has changed his name from Sharmawitz. George reminds Tom—who asks for another drink perhaps a mite too quickly —how much the Coach contributed to his career, persuading him to run for mayor, pulling him through a close contest which he won by a mere 32 votes. The Coach has been ill recently, and required an operation for a case of ulcers.

George cautions Tom about his drinking, and Tom cynically admits his love for booze. He needles George by reminding him how they once seduced an unfortunate girl in George's garage. George winces and changes the subject to Phil Romano, another member of their old basketball team. George counts on Phil to pay his campaign expenses, and in exchange Phil can keep the strip land he's leased from the city. But it seems to George that Phil is showing signs of holding back, even though his opponent Sharmen favors an ecology program which runs counter to Phil's interests.

Phil—dark, heavy set, expensively dressed—comes in with James Daley. James is Tom's brother, a balding academic type who is George's campaign manager and will be given the post of superintendant of schools if George is re-elected. James is carrying beer and Phil is carrying the chicken (the Coach is outside parking Phil's Cadillac, which he loves to drive). Phil and George go into the kitchen to put the chicken in the oven, leaving the two Daley brothers alone for a few moments. James orders Tom to stay sober this evening; James has a plan and may need his help.

As George and Phil come back from the kitchen, a loud whistle is heard from the direction of the front porch. The Coach enters; he is powerfully built, dressed in an old but neat brown suit, white shirt and tie. A gold watch chain is part of his imposing presence. He barks orders to his middle-aged "boys" in a loud voice, facetiously, trying to recreate the old basketball-court relationships, slapping them on the back, loving every minute of this reunion and all that it brings to mind of past glories. The Coach demonstrates his continuing fitness by doing ten pushups in spite of his recent operation (he shows the others his scar). The Coach raises a toast to his team, the 1952 Pennsylvania state champs, an aggregation which he likens to a fine, smooth-running watch.

They all adopt the Coach's mood, kidding each other affectionately; all that is except James whose responses are a little too serious. He has just had all his teeth pulled and is sleeping badly. He is tense, irritable, with a fire burning in him somewhere.

They relive the last ten seconds of the final championship game. One point behind, they funneled the ball to Martin (the fifth member of the team who is absent and who, it seems, never attends these reunions, but was probably the best player of them all). Martin scored the winning two-point basket in the last second of play, winning the championship from their opponents, who were led by a huge black man playing center. They experience a moment of sadness when they remember that Martin hasn't tried to get in touch with any of them for 20 years. They pray that he is safe and well, wherever he is.

George brings up the subject of his re-election, reminding Phil that Sharmen has attacked Phil for the destructive effects of his strip-mining operation. George himself is especially sensitive to ridicule in the press.

The Coach assures them that they were all born to be winners. But in this era of disrespect (George comments) the high school paper ran a pig's picture with Phil's name on it, attacking him for polluting the environment.

Tom makes a sarcastic observation and heads upstairs for the lavatory. Tom is planning to leave town soon, James tells the others. James is the responsible one in the family, who took care of his father during a long terminal illness and has been supporting his brother. George wishes Tom would stay around; he could use Tom's help as a speech writer in the coming election.

Phil agrees that they are going to need all the help they can get to defeat Sharmen. He enumerates George's mistakes as mayor: permitting higher taxes, loss of jobs in the area, an unpleasant garbage strike. George defends his record and James backs him up against Phil's accusations. But Sharmen has IBM ready to move into town—Phil reminds George—and besides, there was the incident of the elephant. George acquired an elephant for the zoo, but it died, and he wasn't able to have it buried for ten days. It was a highly conspicuous failure.

Tom comes downstairs, as the argument continues. The Coach is disturbed by dissension among his "boys". The Coach warns them that dissent is ruining the country and has inspired the murders of its great men like President Kennedy. The insidious machinations of such as Jews and Communists (the Coach insists) destroyed true patriots like Joseph McCarthy and Father Coughlin. All right-thinking people must stick together to save the country.

The Coach grabs George and dances around in anticipation of the joy that winning the election will bring them. But suddenly the Coach is in pain. He has overdone it; the adhesions from his operation are troubling him. George helps the Coach upstairs to get his therapeutic girdle.

In George's absence, Phil confides to James that their mayor is a loser who doesn't stand a chance of getting re-elected. James accuses Phil of putting George down because Phil is having an affair with George's wife. Phil admits that the charge is true. George's wife Marion was one of the more promiscuous members of their group in high school, and apparently she never got over her yen for Phil.

James reminds Phil that he needs George's protection for some of his more questionable activities. But Phil hints that he might dump George and make his campaign contribution instead to Sharmen. James sees which way the wind is blowing, and he too deserts George. James offers himself to Phil as a candidate for mayor in place of both George and Sharmen. James sees himself as first and foremost a career politician who up to now has been working in the field of education but had always planned to look higher. Phil rejects James's proposed candidacy, coming close to ridiculing him in the process.

George comes in with a basketball and they start to throw it to each other but can't seem to get any sort of rhythm going without Martin.

George wants to talk about plans for his campaign, but James gives him the disquieting news that their chief backer, Phil, has serious doubts about their chances. George has an ace up his sleeve, he tells Phil. He and the Coach have done some digging and have discovered that Sharmen's uncle was a Communist, a blacklisted Hollywood writer who took the Fifth Amendment in 1952. Phil ridicules this piece of information as being out of date and virtually worthless.

Phil's attitude angers James, who points to the unfair difference in their circumstances: Phil with his tailor-made silk suits and new Cadillac every year, James reduced to virtual anonymity and left to support five children and an alcoholic brother. James insists that his talent played a large part in getting George elected, and he wants his share of the spoils and recognition.

Phil accuses George and James of having mishandled their careers, calls James a nobody. James, furious, reveals to George that his friend Phil is having an affair with George's wife. George is thunderstruck, at first paralyzed by the revelation, then becoming angry at Phil, calling him names. George grabs a loaded, hair-triggered gun from the rack just as the Coach comes back into the room. Tom exacerbates the situation by informing George that the safety catch is on. George flicks off the safety as the curtain falls, ending the first act.

As the second act of *That Championship Season* begins, the men are in the same positions with George pointing the loaded gun menacingly at Phil. George can't quite bring himself to pull the trigger, however, and gradually the others calm him down and get the weapon away from him.

George tells the Coach what is happening between Phil and his wife, and the Coach is greatly distressed because he sees his "team" coming apart before his eyes. He wants to know how such a thing could happen, and Phil explains (in between Tom's sarcastic comments) that Marion came to his office one day to solicit campaign funds, and it happened. They had a couple of drinks, and it just happened.

The Coach warns them all that sticking together for survival is the name of the game in the 20th century. The fact that his boys stayed near him helped him to survive his illness in the hospital. But George is too angry at Phil to be easily soothed. He feels betrayed, he feels that Phil took advantage of his wife, who has never been quite herself since bearing a child that had to be taken away immediately and institutionalized.

The Coach harks back to his own experiences with women. His mother was very important in his life, and somehow he remained a bachelor, he put off getting married until it was too late. He wasn't always lonely, though; Mrs. Morriss the music teacher would come over and spend Saturday afternoons at the Coach's house, where they would read poetry, bake honey biscuits and make love. As for the rest of it, the Coach has devoted his life to excellence. His vocation was excelling, winning, and his boys are his trophies. Tom, who is getting drunk, ridicules them all by characterizing them as a team of gentiles organizing to beat one Jew. The others hush him up, half annoyed at him, half concerned about his condition.

Phil tells the Coach flatly he can't support George for mayor this time around. The Coach turns to George and warns him that if he wants to win he must pay the price in pain and endurance. This translates that if George wants to be re-elected mayor he needs Phil's support and so must overlook Phil's adventure with his wife.

On his part, Phil has decided adamantly that George is bound to lose. Phil doesn't believe any dirt about Sharmen's uncle being a Communist is going to help George win.

George goes upstairs to the bathroom, half-fearing to leave the room while the conversation is taking this turn. In his absence, the Coach tries to persuade Phil that Communists are as much hated today as they were years ago, in the darkest Depression, when one of them tried to organize in the area and was thrown out of town after having his legs broken with a two-by-four. A Communist relative, the Coach insists, is still an exploitable weakness, and exploiting an opponent's weakness is the strategy the Coach has drummed into his boys from the beginning.

Tom objects to their using smear tactics and stumbles upstairs to the bathroom as George comes back into the room. James challenges Phil to phone Sharmen right now in front of them all, and offer Sharmen his support in the campaign. James is of course insinuating that Phil really has no choice other than to back George, that Sharmen wouldn't accept Phil's backing even if he offered it.

Phil takes up the challenge and dials Sharmen. He calls Sharmen by his first name, Norman, and makes a joke about pollution, hoping to laugh off his problems at the same time as he buys them off, hoping to establish himself with Sharmen as a high school crony. He flatters Sharmen, hints at forthcoming campaign contributions. From Phil's side of the conversation it is obvious that Sharmen is turning Phil down hard, and Phil becomes angry, making a racial slur and mentioning Sharmen's Communist relative. This only makes Sharmen laugh at him, and Phil slams down the receiver.

Phil is angry at James for goading him into making a fool of himself by phoning Sharmen; he sees himself as a man who might have been friendless in high school and would be friendless now if it weren't for his money—they all love his money, not him. The Coach reassures Phil that no outsider is going to beat them, they are still crowd-pleasers, famous. A policeman even tore up a ticket this evening when he recognized the Coach at the wheel of Phil's car.

James observes fatuously that perhaps they should soft-pedal the Jewish angle, they might be accused of anti-Semitism. The Coach is indignant; he's not anti-Semitic, he's all for Israel and the tough guy with the eye patch.

Tom interrupts the conversation by falling downstairs, drunkenly, all the way from the top to the bottom. He's not hurt. The Coach is somewhat nettled because his boys seem unable to hold their liquor.

The Coach takes Phil outside onto the porch for a private talk. Tom goads George about his wife, and George warns him that he is capable of deep rage and understands the impulse to grab a gun and start firing at everybody, indiscriminately. Suddenly George remembers how his deformed baby looked in the hospital. On the Coach's advice he and his wife gave up the unfortunate infant, institutionalized it without even pausing to name it.

James wants to talk practical politics with George. Will he accept Phil's backing if it's offered and let bygones be bygones? Tom taunts James: would *he* accept Phil's backing if it was a question of James's wife, Helen? Both Tom and George demand an answer from James, who finally declares angrily, yes, he'd accept Phil's money in any case.

James resents his brother Tom's mocking attitude. James saved Tom's life and has carried him financially as he has always carried everybody until now at 38 years of age he's exhausted. Still Tom taunts his brother: James has never been motivated by love, a word which actually embarrasses him. James is merely dutiful, compulsively and reflexively obedient.

Both George and James are sorry for themselves. George sees his life slipping away from him, as though he existed only in the past. (James tries to make George feel a little better by arguing that maybe his wife Marion slept with Phil because she loves her husband and wanted to obtain money for his campaign.) James sees himself as having fallen ten years behind everybody else because he was saddled with his dying father's care and medical bills. Pitying himself as he does, James nevertheless will refuse to permit his son to look upon his father as one of life's mediocrities. James has decided to step up the pace of his career in politics, with Congress as his distant goal.

Phil comes in and sends George out to the porch to talk to the Coach in his turn. James informs Phil that George is willing to overlook the affair with his wife and accept a donation, but Phil hardly seems to care. He is restless and bored with this town, tired of all the familiar faces. His only release is to run away in his car on the turnpike to some far and unknown place, pick up a faceless girl to sit next to him in a bar while he replays all the old basketball games in his head. The events of that championship season are still the strongest and maybe the only thing that Phil is still able to feel. Otherwise, he gets his kicks out of driving his Porche wide open at 140 miles an hour while dead drunk, laughing at the certain knowledge that some day he will come to a sudden, inexpressibly violent end.

Phil confides to James that he prefers married women because there's no involvement with them afterward. Phil made love to Marion because he was curious to see if he could straighten out some of the mess George had made of her since high school (he couldn't, it was no use). He warns James to take good care of his own wife, Helen, but James has no fears. Helen is devoted to chastity and happy only when she's pregnant. Phil remembers Helen rather fondly as someone who didn't laugh at him when he made a mistake in art class.

With George's wife Marion it's something else again; she's been playing around for a long time. It was she who persuaded George to give up their baby, Phil tells the others. George wanted to keep the child until Marion and the Coach talked him out of it.

Phil looks at Tom and for an instant sees him clearly as a loser, abandoned to alcohol. This insight upsets Phil, who reacts in the only way he knows. He offers Tom money, but of course Tom refuses to accept it.

Phil explains to the brothers that he is a modern man with a modern arrangement with his own wife Claire. George, in contrast, is not a modern man. Phil and his wife live and let each other live, and Phil plans to get a vasectomy soon because he's very active sexually and has found that abortions can be expensive.

George comes back, and James in his turn goes outside for a brief consultation with the Coach; then they both come back into the room. The Coach has explained to James that George won't need his services as campaign manager. They are going to hire a Philadelphia advertising agency, they need professional help.

James is furious. He accuses his friends of dumping him, of ruining his planned political career. George assures James that he'll still endorse him for superintendent of schools, but James is not satisfied, he is hurt and angry. Phil warns James that he can't put thousands of dollars of campaign contributions in the hands of an amateur, and James calls him an ignoramus. Phil slaps James across the mouth, knocking out his dental plate, sending James to his knees searching for it in a state of helpless rage. Tom finds the plate— it isn't broken—but James's feelings are almost irreparably damaged. He threatens to make a public fool of George, ruin his chances in the campaign, by telling the story of Phil and Marion all over town and by exposing the petty secrets and favoritisms of George's administration.

George sees clearly that James intends to ruin him, just as they all intend to ruin James by depriving him of his campaign responsibilities. George feels sick at this knowledge; nausea overwhelms him. He lunges toward the trophy on its table at right as the curtain falls ending the second act.

As the third act of *That Championship Season* begins, George has vomited into the trophy and is being taken upstairs by the Coach, who also sends James out to the kitchen to wash out their precious prize.

Phil is still in a state of self-pity. Everybody wants a piece of him, he feels. He just paid a $4,000 dentistry bill for his wife, and even Marion began to talk about money, about possible campaign contributions, after the third time they had been together. Phil finally decides that the only woman he ever really loved was his mother.

James comes in, still feeling his betrayal keenly. He has made his sacrifices, and now he demands success as his right. He's ashamed that he once had to borrow money from Phil for his father's burial expenses. Phil is proud of his money, proud of owning two of everything, grateful that he doesn't have to live a slavish, faceless existence devoted to building up a business, as his own father did.

The Coach comes back and reports that George is cleaned up and is now phoning his wife. When the Coach expresses his surprise that his boys would turn on each other, Tom comments that perhaps they are all just myths anyway. The Coach points to the hard, realistic silver trophy upon which all their names have been carved to last forever, and once more he urges them all to keep their mutual faith.

James is still preoccupied, morosely, with his own insignificant status as a mere junior high school principal and not a very authoritative one at that. The Coach admits that taking care of his father may have slowed James's career a little. James recalls how he used to wash and feed his dying father and complains that he never felt love from him in return; in fact, he never even felt that his father respected him.

The Coach accuses James of whining. The Coach himself felt a lack of respect when after 30 years as a coach and teacher devoted to excellence he was forced into retirement simply because he hit a student who made an obscene gesture. They gave him a gold watch and put him out onto the streets at 8 a.m. every morning with nowhere to go, nothing to do but listen to the radio or watch TV. You cannot expect respect, the Coach decides, you have to demand it.

George comes back. He has phoned his wife, and he has chosen to believe her reassurance that she only made love to Phil to help her beloved husband's campaign for mayor. The Coach advises George to punish her severely. When George shrinks from this suggestion, the Coach sees him as having gone soft. All of his boys seem to have lost their precious winning spirit, their idealism of the classic Greek athlete.

The Coach tries to whip up their morale against Sharmen. But James hangs back; he won't play his assigned position in their game until his share of the prize is settled. The Coach calls James's bluff. He ignores him and orders the others to get in touch with the Philadelphia ad agency at once. James makes a last-ditch complaint and threat, but finally he backs down; he will go along; he is beaten.

Having brought James back into line by the force of his will, the Coach turns on Tom who has done nothing all evening but sneer, who is obviously a quitter. Replying to the Coach, Tom brings up the subject of Martin—why has Martin abandoned them, why does he never come to these reunions? The Coach knows perfectly well why, Tom continues. Martin, the best player of them all, washed his hands of the whole championship business because it was dirty. In the third quarter, when they were losing, the Coach ordered Martin to get tough with the tall black man playing center for the opposing team so effectively. Martin went out and broke the man's ribs, putting him out of the game. (The Coach agrees that winning is everything, that he inspired his boys to hate and fight their opponents in order to win, but he denies ordering anybody's ribs broken).

Martin came to the Coach afterwards and urged the Coach to refuse the trophy and the championship publicly. When the Coach wouldn't do it, Martin would have no more to do with any of them or their championship, which, Tom agrees, they stole. Tom urges the Coach to admit out loud that the "championship season" was a lie. The Coach cites the physical presence of the trophy in this house as concrete evidence of truth, but Tom has stopped believing in any trophy but whiskey. The Coach slaps Tom and orders him out of the house.

George, Phil and James close ranks around the Coach, deprecating Martin and his strange ideas. Their loyalty and his memory of their accomplishment sets the Coach to dreaming about the idyllic days of his youth with picnics by the clear water of the lake, silver pails of beer, pitching horseshoes. The Coach's father ran the only bank in town until the sudden Depression ruined and gradually killed him. He warned the Coach before dying never to forget that Marx was a Jew.

The Coach feels a deep-seated, instinctive need for lost leaders like Joseph McCarthy, John F. Kennedy, George Patton. What the country needs most is winners (the Coach assures his boys), and he means to make them winners and keep them winners even if he has to beat and drive them to it.

The Coach plays the recorded radio narration of the last moments of their championship game (playing this record is an important ritual of their annual reunions). With ten seconds to go they are behind 70-71, but they have the ball. George Sikowski throws the ball out to Tom Daley, who passes it to his brother James Daley, who fires it across the court to Phil Romano. With five seconds left, the ball is passed to Martin Roads at the foul line. With two seconds left, Martin jumps and shoots the ball into the basket. The Coach's team—Fillmore High School—wins the Pennsylvania state championship 72-71.

There is a loud crowd noise, then the recording ends. It has exorcised all their demons, wiped out the hostilities of the evening with the strong evocation of their common past; they are as they were when the reunion began, as they were on that basketball court: a team led by the Coach. Tom comes back into the house and takes his place with the others, who sing a chorus of the Fillmore school song. Overcome with emotion, Phil apologizes to George. James reaffirms his loyalty to George, who loves James like a brother. They will all meet Monday at the mayor's office at noon to start mapping out George's campaign, and James and Tom will have a speech ready for George's appearance at the K of C next week. (Even so, Tom cannot help thinking of them all, himself included, as whooping cranes en route to extinction.)

Now it is time for their annual ritual photos. They put their coats on and gather around the trophy for the Coach to take a snapshot. Then the four team members insist over the Coach's objections that they want one of him alone with the trophy. He holds the silver prize in his arms and poses dutifully. While James is getting ready to take the picture, Phil invites the Coach to come over to his house the next day and watch a basketball game in color, but the Coach turns Phil down. The Coach no longer watches basketball, the game has changed so much. It has become a tall black athlete's game, the Coach insists, the white athlete is extinct in it, and so the Coach no longer takes an interest.

There is a flash from the camera as James snaps the Coach's picture holding the trophy and the lights fade as the curtain falls.

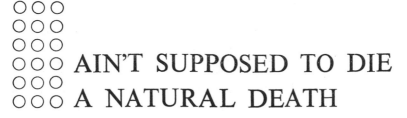

AIN'T SUPPOSED TO DIE
A NATURAL DEATH

(Tunes From Blackness)

A Musical in Two Acts

BOOK, WORDS AND MUSIC

BY MELVIN VAN PEEBLES

Cast and credits appear on page 316

MELVIN VAN PEEBLES was born Aug. 21, 1932 in Chicago. Twenty-five years later, in 1957, his first published work appeared, The Big Heart, *a photographic essay on San Francisco's cable cars. In between those two events occurred what Van Peebles calls "the overwhelming statistic" of his early life, which was being a black and growing up in America; a fact so overwhelmingly important in his frame of reference that he will neither acknowledge nor discuss any other detail of his youth and education.*

From 1957 on, however, Van Peebles's career is a matter of record, the record of an outstandingly gifted and incredibly versatile creative artist. In 1957 he started to make movies because, he says, "I got disgusted looking at crap." Between 1957 and 1966 he made ten short films—and in the case of Van Peebles "made" means wrote, produced, directed and edited. Meanwhile, back at the writing desk, Van Peebles wrote five novels for publication in France between 1960 and 1968, the first in English which he translated into French, and the last four directly in French (one of them, A Bear for the FBI, *was translated into English and published in 1968 in the United States).*

In 1967 in France Van Peebles wrote and directed his first feature-length movie, La Permission *(English title,* The Story of a Three-Day Pass*). When Van Peebles showed up with his film as the French delegate to the 1967 San Francisco film festival, he found his colleagues "totally unprepared" for the fact of his blackness, since for almost two generations no black had directed a feature film for commercial presentation. He was besieged with offers and directed* Watermelon *for Columbia in 1969. In 1971 Van Peebles "made" the popular film* Sweet Sweetback's Baadasssss Song—*that is, he wrote, produced, directed, scored, edited and starred in it; to him, "It all seems part of the same process."*

Meanwhile, back at the writing desk Van Peebles was expressing himself by writing and recording songs. It seems he cannot sing professionally, and so when he recorded his songs he merely spoke the words to the musical accompaniment in the recorded collections Brer Soul *in 1968 and* Ain't Supposed to Die a Natural Death *in 1969. Someone suggested that these musical impressions of life and death in the big city would make good theater, and so Van Peebles made his debut as a Broadway author Oct. 20, 1971 with* Ain't Supposed to Die a Natural Death, *a Best Play and a Tony nominee. He did not direct it or star in it himself, but he carried over the records' technique as well as title to Broadway; the lyrics are spoken, not sung, so that the audience can absorb the ideas undistracted by melody. Like a long distance runner who finds himself loaded with energy after a long race and does a few more laps just for the exhilaration of it, Van Peebles provided Broadway with a second musical this season,* Don't Play Us Cheap!, *a book show which he directed himself.*

Our method of representing Ain't Supposed to Die a Natural Death *in these pages differs from that used for the other Best Plays. The Van Peebles musical, subtitled* Tunes From Blackness, *appears here as excerpts from the words of nine of the show's 19 numbers, each illustrated with photos to record the total "look" of a Broadway show in 1971-72.*

The photographs depict scenes as produced by Eugene V. Wolsk, Charles Blackwell, Emanuel Azenberg and Robert Malina and directed by Gilbert Moses, as of the opening October 20, 1971 at the Ethel Barrymore Theater, with scenery by Kert Lundell, costumes by Bernard Johnson and lighting by Martin Aronstein. Our special thanks are enthusiastically tendered to the author, the publisher of the original albums (A & M Records), the producers and their press representatives—Merle Debuskey and Faith Geer—for their help in obtaining this material including the excellent photographs by Bert Andrews.

Time: Now
Place: Here

ACT I

Arthur French in
"Just Don't Make No Sense"

"Just Don't Make No Sense"

Just don't make no sense
The way my corns are hurting me
When the man runs his game
Lord knows he sure runs it mean
Four busses gone by for them
And not one gone by for me . . . .
When you black
                even waitin ain't easy
Stand here I'm loitering
If I walk, I'm prowling
And if I run, I'm escaping
No, just don't make no sense

The way my corns are hurting me
If I sit I'm shiftless
But Lord knows there'd be hell to pay
If I look like I even look like I
         was even getting ready to get
               on my feet someday
Everybody be getting in the race to
             keep me in my place
Brothers be rushing in there
              to fat mouth me down
And the man to shoot me down
And it just don't make no sense . . . . .

Right, Clebert Ford, Sati Jamal and Toney Brealond in "Catch That on the Corner"

Below, Dick Williams and Gloria Edwards in "The Coolest Place in Town"

"The Coolest Place in Town"

. . . . . Take your hands off me Mother
If I didn't leap when Medgar
                         got your message
Or Malcolm, or Martin Luther King
Take your hands off me Jim
You know I ain't gonna do it now
Take your hands off me buddy
If I go you'll know it
I'm taking one or two like you
Along with me . . . . .
Take your hands off me baby
I'm just leaning out to catch a little
Breeze and see
The tail light gliding to eternity
Don't poke out you mouth mister
Your folks foreclosed on my air conditioner
Take your hands off me mister
I ain't leaping I'm leaning

"Catch That on the Corner"

. . . . . Catch that on the corner
She passed this way a moment ago
She's probably tall and wearing
Something cool maybe green
Do you see her
Rap to me . . . . .
Start from the top and go to the toe
Natural or comb or conkaleen
What's on the corner . . . . .

. . . . . Voices are my thing
Offered her a pencil once
             and chewing gum
Shoulda heard her say no thank you
Low and warm like alaga syrup
Molasses to a country boy like you
Come on Baby rap to me
Are you hip to what you see
             on the corner . . . . .

Toney Brealond and Madge Wells in
"Funky Girl on Motherless Broadway"

"Funky Girl
On Motherless Broadway"

. . . . . She don't have a lease
On this sidewalk officer
She creates the havoc officer
I'm a girl of peace officer . . . . .
All that beg don't get none
Them that don't ask don't want none
Love for sale
           better spread than dead sugar
Motherless old Broadway . . . . .
Just a little old funky me
The world is all scabs
           and broken needles
Unless someone cares for you anyway
We only live once anyway
You know what balling is
It's a poot in old deaths face
Isn't that a giggle
I do like you a lot anyway
You're terrible take my hand
Come let's go to my place
And sit in old deaths face
Just a funky girl
You're crazy but ok
If you want

Ok I'll race you there
You take a lead
I could beat you with heels on anyway
This old motherless Broadway
Here I come
Motherless old Broadway

ACT II

"Heh, Heh (Chuckle)
Good Mornin' Sunshine"

. . . . . Good mornin' sunshine
Take a good squint at me
I ain't the man I used to be
I ain't the cat you saw yesterday
At least I mean by tomorrow
      I mean I won't be anyway . . . . .
My Aunt Emma came to me
The one who drowned off
      the boat ride on that Labor Day
She had a big wide yellow hat
It was all yella again
      and brand new . . . . .
Aunt Emma always was the practical
      one in the family anyway
Then she reach in her bosom
      and handed me the number
      that was gonna hit today
(Chuckle) good mornin' sunshine
Take a good squint at me . . . . .

*Albert Hall in
"Three Boxes of Longs Please"*

"Three Boxes of Longs Please"

Green ain't only bread you know
It's silence and things that grow
      and country
Greens the big color isn't it
Goes all the way round in a circle
      is what I mean
All starts and finishes with green
Like a dog chasing his tail
Here ain't no way a weed could grow
That a weed could make it
Green is the big color these days
Always has been face it
Money, rich folks graves, green berets
And a tree with the leaves
      hanging heavy
But the leaves keep turning brown
      and its me
The flag shoulda been green too
      you know
Green and red anyway
Three boxes of longs please . . . . .
Green is in the life bag
But it can lead to a death bag too
Green and red anyway
They just pushed it too strong
Too many ocean cruises and pot guts
      and lawns and third cars
Three boxes of longs please

*Arthur French in "Heh, Heh
(Chuckle) Good Mornin' Sunshine"*

"Salamaggi's Birthday"

I know you didn't cut that ofay
It happened last month anyway
Just an excuse you too new
Here's the deal
I've had my eyes on you
You just been walkin' a week or two
Smile brown sugar
It's Salamaggi's Birthday . . . . .
So I'm takin' you in
So to speak for a little questionin'
Collectin' a little dues
So to speak police dues
Smile brown sugar
It's Salamaggi's Birthday
Smile and the world smiles with you
Ain't gonna pull no train on you
No freight train anyway
Maybe one or two after the surprise
He's first cause it's his party
First as far as they'll know anyway

Smile brown sugar . . . . .
Soon as you finish straightenin' me
You got peace on my beat
What they don't know don't hurt me
Smile brown sugar
It's Salamaggi's Birthday
Smile if you know what's good for you
All right now brown sugar
I'm changing places with Dave
Now just don't get impatient
Just one more little detour
Before we see the station . . . . .
Us bloods gotta stick together
So here's a tip for you
Always get questioned by young guys
Old ones can turn mean
Specially if they can't and try . . . . .
Smile if you know what's good for you
          smile . . . smile . . . smile
Smile brown sugar smile

Gloria Edwards, Joe Fields and Dick Williams (foreground) in "Salamaggi's Birthday"

Dick Williams (at top) and Sati Jamal
in "Come on Feet Do Your Thing"

"Come on Feet
Do Your Thing"

Come on feet
Cruise for me
Trouble
Ain't no place to be
Come on feet
Do your thing . . . . .
You're on
To old whitey's game
Come on legs
Come on run . . . . .
Guilty's
What he say you done
Come on knees
Don't be mean
Ain't first red
You ever seen
Come on feet
Do your thing
Come on baby
Don't cop out on me
Come on baby
Don't give in on me
Cruise for me
Come on legs
Come on run
Come on feet
Do your thing
Who put the bad mouth on me

Anyway the way
I pick 'em up
And put 'em down
Even if it got my name on it
Won't catch me now
Come on feet
Cruise for me
Come on legs
Come on run

(continued on the next page)

Come on feet
Do your thing
Lord
Feet we sure do get around
Never put us in
Some cold ass ground
Sure is dark
Never been out this way
Mama—Anyway
I'm safe and sound
Bet we broke the olympic two twenty
Or cross country
Or something
Sure is lonely
Sure most quietest turf I ever seen
Whatever happened to the sun

Sure gone away
Sure blacker than a landlords soul
Musta run all day
Sure yeah
Yeah baby
Come on feet
Cruise for me
Come on feet
Come on run
Come on legs
Come on run
Come on feet
Do your thing
Come on feet
Do your thing

Minnie Gentry and the company in the finale "Put a Curse on You"

"Put a Curse on You"

Put a curse on you
May all your children
                    end up junkies too
Yo mammy trick by the pound
                    to buy that ounce
Yo young daughters
Give rich old dudes head
                    in limousines too
Put a curse on you
Put a curse on you
Your warriors maimed
Or on the run
Your sons lag for pennies
All night long in the bus depot
Cause they ain't got no place to go
And lose too
Put a curse on you
Put a curse on you
Closest to heaven you go
Rum and coke and cocaine
And a jive pusher
Come cuttin' your stuff with talcum too
Put my curse on you . . . . .

May the block gobble up
                    your futures too
And them rats come slippin'
                    out your trash
And slidin' into
                    your children's cribs too
Put my curse on you
Put my curse on you
Gonna fix it so yo menfolk
Can't see no beauty
                    in yo womenfolk too
So you menfolks be boys
To the man
And to your womenfolk too
I'm putting a curse on you . . . .
May the man feast on your goose too
Police chomp on your children's
                    head too
And cackle at their moans too
And the mafia get to work the carcass
And suck your bones too
Put a curse on you

STICKS AND BONES

A Play in Two Acts

BY DAVID RABE

Cast and credits appear on pages 334 and 360

DAVID RABE was born in 1940 in Dubuque, Iowa, the son of a school teacher. He was educated at Loras Academy and Loras College, both in Dubuque, and served in the Army from January 1965 to January 1967 as a Specialist 4th Class, the final 11 months in Vietnam.

Rabe studied writing with Raymond Roseliep, Dick Duprey and George Herman, and in 1967 and 1968 at Villanova (under a program partly supported by the Rockefeller Foundation) he wrote the first drafts of two plays about the Vietnam war: The Basic Training of Pavlo Hummel *and* Sticks and Bones. *He went from Villanova to the New Haven* Register, *where he won the Associated Press Award as a newspaper feature writer.*

Last season Rabe's professional stage debut took place on May 20 when the New York Shakespeare Festival presented Pavlo Hummel *at its Estelle R. Newman Theater. The play ran 363 performances through April 1, 1972 (the Shakespeare Festival's longest run) and won its author a citation as "most promising playwright" in* Variety's *poll of drama critics and in the Drama Desk voting, an Obie Award and the Hull-Warriner Award voted by the Dramatists Guild Council as the season's best play on a controversial subject.* Sticks and Bones, *which had been staged at Villanova in 1969, opened at the Shakespeare festival Nov. 7 while* Pavlo Hummel *was still running there, played 121 performances and was selected as a Best Play on the basis of this off-Broadway production, then was moved to Broadway March 1 for a continuing run. It received a Tony Award as best play.*

Rabe is married and lives in Pennsylvania, where he teaches in Villanova's theater department. He sometimes signs himself David W. Rabe but does not use the middle initial in the authorship credits of his New York theater programs.

Time: Autumn 1968

Place: The family home

ACT I

SYNOPSIS: Two screens on either side of the dark stage are lighted with typical family-album photographs: grandpa's father, grandpa as he looked when he was a little boy, a brother who died young, "somebody sick," etc. Amplified voices are heard identifying the various photos. Finally there is a slide showing Ozzie and Harriet—a middle aged, middle class married couple—in their home with Ozzie on the phone and Harriet sitting on the sofa knitting. *"There is a bright flash and the stage is immediately illuminated. The set is an American home, the present, very modern, a quality of brightness as if it were an advertisement, a photo of a home. Yet there is a naturalness."*

The front door is upstage right. The living area is down center, with sofa, chairs, desk and TV set. The stairs are at left, and on a split level up left is a bedroom and a hall leading off to the rest of the upstairs including the attic.

Ozzie and Harriet are posed in their living room exactly as in the last slide. There is a tension in the room as Ozzie puts down the phone and informs Harriet that this was an official call from the Army. Their son David is to be discharged soon. He has been in Vietnam, he has survived, and soon he will be coming home.

> *The door opens and Rick comes in. He is young, 17, and the door slams. His hair is long and neat, sideburns, tapered trousers, striped Western shirt. He carries a guitar on his shoulder.*

RICK: Hi, Mom, hi, Dad.

HARRIET: Hi, Rick.

OZZIE: Hi, Rick.

HARRIET: Ohhh, Ricky, Ricky, your brother's on his way home. David's coming home!

OZZIE: We just got a call.

RICK: Ohhh, boy! Ohhh, wow! Boy!

HARRIET: Isn't that wonderful? Isn't it?

RICK: Did anybody talk to him?

HARRIET: Your father; oh, I bet you're starving, sit, sit.

OZZIE: I talked to *somebody*, Rick. Not Dave.

HARRIET: There's fudge and ice cream in the fridge, would you like that?

RICK: Oh, yeah, and could I have some soda?

Harriet is on her way to the kitchen, nodding. She exits.

Wow, that sure is good news, huh, Dad? I'm awful hungry.

OZZIE: Never had a doubt. A boy like that—if he leaves, he comes back.

RICK: How about me? What if I left?

He picks up a comic book.

OZZIE: Absolutely. Absolutely.

Silence. Rick reads the comic.

I built jeeps . . . tanks, trucks.

RICK: What?

OZZIE: In the other war, I mean. Number Two. I worked on vehicles. Vehicles were needed and I worked to build them. Sometimes I put on wheels, tightened 'em up. I never . . . served . . . is what I mean.

Slight pause.

They got all those people—soldiers, Rick—you see what I mean? They get 'em across the ocean, they don't have any jeeps or tanks or trucks, what are they gonna do, stand around? Wait for a bus on the beachhead? Call a cab?

RICK: No public transportation in a war, huh, Dad.

OZZIE: That's right, that's right.

Harriet comes in with the fudge and ice cream, breaking into this fatuous family conversation with equally fatuous reminiscences of incidents involving her soldier son David as a small boy, locking himself in an ice box, falling from a tree, etc. As Rick goes to the kitchen to get soda, Ozzie and Harriet remember a happy family picnic. Ozzie won a footrace against a friend named Hank Grenweller. (Harriet claims that Hank let Ozzie win to make him feel good). Harriet climbs the stairs to the bedroom for a nap, while recalling the winter day they said goodbye to David and prayed he would come home safe from the war.

Rick turns off the TV, which has been flashing and muttering behind the previous scenes. Ozzie goes on boasting about his trucks, then restlessly remembers something more to the point: "I . . . seen him do some awful . . . awful things . . . ole Dave. He was a mean . . . foul-tempered little baby. I'm only glad I was *here* when they sent him off to do his killing."

There is a knock at the door. Ozzie is reluctant to answer it but drags himself over and opens the door a crack. Outside are two men dressed in uniform. One of them is a Sergeant Major who identifies himself as the man who spoke on the phone. He verifies the address; he has brought David home. He leads David into the house and guides him to a seat. David has been wounded. He is now totally blind and feels about him with a cane.

Rick greets his brother with his noncommittal "Hi, Dave," and Ozzie tries to recover from the shock of David's handicap. The atmosphere in this room doesn't feel like home to David—he insists that he touch his family's faces to reassure himself as to who they are. The Sergeant Major warns Ozzie that it will take David time to adjust. Rick grabs his camera to record the home-coming.

HARRIET (*she is on the stairs, looking*): David ...
            *Silence in which David doesn't move, his hands on Ozzie's face as
            Rick, moving near, snaps a picture of them; then of her.*
OZZIE: Harriet ... don't be upset ... they say ... Harriet, Harriet ... he
can't see ... ! Harriet ... they say—he—can't ... see. That man.
HARRIET (*as she is descending the stairs*): Can't see? What do you mean?
SGT. MAJOR: He's blind.
HARRIET: No. Who says? No, no ...
OZZIE: Look at him; he doesn't look well at all. He looks so old.
SGT. MAJOR: I hope you people understand.
OZZIE: He looks so worn. So old. Look at him; look.
HARRIET (*touching him*): Ohhh, David; David ... !

The Sergeant Major is carrying a large sheet of paper which someone must sign, accepting delivery of David. Ozzie offers him refreshment, but the Sergeant Major is in a hurry; he must be on his way; he has other deliveries to make.

SGT. MAJOR: . . . . . I've got trucks out there backed up for blocks. Other boys, I got to get on to Chicago and some of them to Denver and Cleveland, Reno, New Orleans, Boston, Trenton, Watts, Atlanta. And when I get back they'll be layin' all over the grass; layin' there in pieces all over the grass, their backs been broken, their brains jellied, their insides turned into garbage. No-legged boys and one-legged boys; boys with no hands and no feet. I'm due in Harlem; I got to get to the Bronx and Queens, Cincinnati, St. Louis, Reading. I don't have time for coffee. I got deliveries to make all across this country.
DAVID: Nooooooo ...
            With Harriet, his hands on her face, a kind of realization.
Sergeant ... noo; there's something wrong; it all feels wrong. Where are you? Are you here? I don't know these people!
SGT. MAJOR: That's natural, soldier; it's natural you feel that way.
DAVID: Nooooo.
HARRIET (*he has risen; she is attempting to guide him back to a chair*): David; just sit, be still.
DAVID: Don't you hear me?
OZZIE: Harriet, calm him.
DAVID: The air is wrong; the smells and sounds, the wind.
HARRIET: David ... please ... please. What is it? Be still ... Please ...
DAVID: GODDAMN YOU, SERGEANT, I AM LONELY HERE! I AM LONELY!
SGT. MAJOR: I got to go.
DAVID (*following the Sergeant Major*): Sergeant ... !

SGT. MAJOR: You shut up. You piss-ass soldier, you shut the fuck up!

Ozzie escorts the Sergeant Major out of the door. Rick looks out the window, comments on the long line of trucks, then runs up the stairs to his bedroom, leaving his mother and father (who comes back in) to cope with David. There is a sound of distant thunder, as Harriet gropes in her memory looking for what went wrong, telling Ozzie, "You thought you knew what was right, all those years, teaching him sports and fighting. Do you understand what I'm trying to say? A mother knows *things* . . . a father cannot ever know them. . . . . Never have you come upon him in the night as he lay awake and staring . . . praying." What Ozzie remembers is, "I saw him put a knife through the skin of a cat. I saw him cut the belly open."

His parents try to reach David, but David has only one thought in mind: he wants to get away. He stumbles around trying to find the way out but cannot and finally falls into a chair. Harriet sends Ozzie upstairs to find David a sedative.

> *Silence. Then rain and lightning, distant thunder. David sits, bowed.*

HARRIET: . . . . . You're our child and you're home. Our good . . . beautiful boy.

> *And the door swings open to the outside and there is a small Asian Girl there. She wears the Vietnamese ao dai, white and black. Her hair is long, black. She stands very still. She carries a tiny cardboard suitcase. Harriet hurries to the door.*

What an awful . . . wind.

> *She shuts the door. Blackout.*

When the lights come up again the Asian Girl is standing watching, unmoving, inside the house but as invisible to its occupants as a shred of memory. Ozzie is dozing in the armchair, trying to remember the night David was conceived, believing it would help in some way to remember how it was.

Ozzie goes out the door, still puzzling, while Harriet goes up to David's room carrying a lighted candle. David is lying on the bed. In the meantime, the Asian Girl *"wearily settles into a corner on the landing, where she will remain, watching, sleeping, sometimes eating"* but of course unseen. She is an aura, a memory figure from another continent, another life.

Harriet is trying to soothe David, who wants to be left alone to sleep. In some way Harriet guesses that there is a girl David left behind him, and better so, she tells him—their skins are yellow and they eat the flesh of dogs, she has heard.

Harriet is trying to reassure her son, but it is really she who needs reassurance that now he is home and they are a family all together once more and all will be as it was. David does not respond to his mother, and finally she blows out her candle and leaves.

The Asian Girl moves to David's room.

DAVID (*in moonlight, turning onto his side, his back to the door; he tenses, half-turned toward the door*): Chaco, Zung.

> *He has turned now, his cane extended into the air. He flees up-stairs and off.*

Cho co, Zung. Cho co, Zung.

> *The Asian Girl follows. Blackout.*

It is Sunday and Ozzie is all set to watch a football game on TV—but the sound is out of order. Ozzie makes a move to phone the TV repairman; Harriet insists on talking to him about David. There is something wrong with David; he is unhappy, he refuses to eat. He has not made physical contact with either of his parents since his return, not even to shake hands. David just stays in his bedroom reciting strange-sounding words and phrases. Harriet even hates the way David looks with the tinted glasses he always wears now.

Selfishly, Ozzie insists that Harriet bring him some juice, which she does—and Ozzie wonders, "What do you give me when you give me this?"

David comes downstairs in bathrobe and pajamas. He has heard them talking about their old friend Hank Grenweller, and David remembers him well.

DAVID: You felt when he was with you he filled the room.

OZZIE: It was the way he talked that did that. He boomed. His voice just boomed.

DAVID: He was here once and you wanted me to sit on his lap, isn't that right? It was after dinner. He was in a chair in the corner.

HARRIET: That's right.

DAVID: His hand was gone—the bone showed in the skin.

OZZIE: My God, what a memory—did you hear that, Harriet?—you were only four or five. He'd just had this terrible awful auto accident—his hand was hurt, not gone.

DAVID: No. It was congenital.

OZZIE: What?

DAVID: That hand. The sickness in it.

OZZIE: Congenital?

DAVID: Yes.

OZZIE: What do you mean? What do you think you mean?

DAVID: I'd like some coffee.

OZZIE: Hank's parents were good fine people, David.

DAVID: I know.

OZZIE: Well, what are you saying then?

DAVID: I'd like that coffee.

The request for coffee is something to which Harriet can respond, and she hurries to get him a huge breakfast which he doesn't want.

Ozzie is still worrying the thought about Hank Grenweller. David knows what he is talking about because he ran into Hank in California just before shipping out. He shocks Ozzie with the information that Hank died of this disease—which he himself told David was congenital—after it spread to other parts of his body.

Harriet comes back in with the coffee, insisting that David admit he finds it wonderful to be home but still has "terrible awful ugly dreams." This she could understand and accept, and so could Ozzie. As parents, they claim the right also to see behind David's glasses, to take a look at his mutilated eyes, but David refuses to allow this.

Harriet insists that David has bad dreams during which he speaks out loud—she has waited outside his door and listened. The parents offer their help to work out whatever is wrong, so David confides in them that he wasn't talking in his sleep at all. He was awake, he could sense some presence in his room, and he spoke to it.

In his effort to understand his son, Ozzie grabs for acceptable cliche. David must be suffering from the loss of those close comradely friendships which grow up among men in war. But David denies this: "Dad, you're wrong. I had fear of all the kinds of dying that there are when I went from here. And then there was this girl with hands and hair like wings. There were candles, above the net of gauze, under which we lay. Cannon could be heard . . . I cannot explain a girl . . . to weigh no more than . . . dust . . ."

This is something that Harriet can understand—if it was a nurse or Red Cross girl, white—and Ozzie can understand—if it was a purely physical need brutishly satisfied by a professional. Perhaps they could accept their son's sexual experiences on this level, but David rejects such explanations with contemptuous silence, rising, and making a move to leave.

This silent rejection of Ozzie's men-will-be-men cliche drives Ozzie to hysterical criticism of his son for having had relations with a girl of another race.

OZZIE: . . . . . You screwed some yellow fucking whore!
> *He has chased David in this as David has moved away from him, bumping against Harriet who has turned her back on them.*

HARRIET: That's right . . . that's right. You were lonely . . . and young and away from home for the very first time in your life, no white girls around—

DAVID: NOOOOO!
> *Harriet cries, a high thin hum in her throat, her hands at her mouth.*

They are the color of the earth . . . ! And only *winter* is white and the earth under it like a suicide.
> *Harriet vomits. There is silence. They stand. Ozzie starts toward her, falters, starts, reaches, stops.*

OZZIE: Why—don't . . . you ask her to cook something for you, David, will you? Make her feel better . . . okay . . .

DAVID: I think . . . some eggs . . . might be good, Mom.

The request for food calms Harriet, and she goes to prepare it. Ozzie lights a cigarette for David and extols the virtues of its cornhusk filter. Harriet returns stirring eggs in a bowl and proposes a family visit to church. But David turns his back on his family and slowly disappears to his bedroom. Harriet goes to the phone to call her priest, Father Donald, and ask his help.

Rick comes in with his cheery "Hi, Mom; hi, Dad," and his parents echo his cheerful pretenses. Rick feels that David is too serious, hopes that he will soon be himself again, and he is busy with his camera taking pictures of Harriet on the telephone as she begs Father Donald to come to the house and talk to her deeply troubled son. Ozzie tries to express his own misgivings: ". . . . . how . . . is it that . . . he . . . is . . . my son? I mean, they say something of you joined to something of me and . . . became . . . him . . . but what does that mean . . . ? One mystery replacing another . . . ? Mystery does not explain mystery . . ."

Rick breaks into Ozzie's thoughts by asking for fudge, but Ozzie refuses to be distracted. He frightens himself with the thought that perhaps David came into contact with a strange disease. Harriet runs to get fudge and milk, even bringing in some for Ozzie and forcing it on him.

Harriet leaves the house on an errand with Rick to drive her, as Ozzie toys with the idea of throwing his wife down on the floor and creating another child. Ozzie shouts after her, "You think you know me and you know nothing. You don't know how I feel . . . How I'd like to beat Ricky with my fists till his face is ugly! How I'd like to banish David to the streets . . . How I'd like to cut your tongue from your mouth!"

Ozzie sinks into a chair. As he hears David moving upstairs he begins to regale his son with a memory or a fantasy of his youth in a town where—Ozzie insists—he had no onerous responsibilities of husband and father but was widely admired as a champion runner.

OZZIE: . . . . . Summer . . . I would sit out on this old wood porch on the front of our house and my strength was in me and quiet and mine and then around the corner would come some old Model T Ford and scampering up the walk this ancient bone-stiff bucktoothed farmer raw as winter and cawing at me like a crow: they had one for me. Out at the edge of town. A runner from another county. My shoes are in a brown paper bag at my feet and I snatch it up and set out into the dusk, easy as breathing. There's an old white fence and we run for the sun . . . For a hundred yards or a thousand yards or a thousand thousand. It doesn't matter. Whatever they want. We run the race they think their specialty and I beat them. They sweat and struggle, I simply glide on one step beyond . . . no matter what their effort and the sun bleeds before me . . . We cross rivers and deserts: we clamber over mountains. I run the races the farmers arrange and win the bets they make; and then a few days after the race money comes to me anonymously in the mail; but it's not for the money that I run. In the fields and factories, they speak my name when they sit down to their lunches. If there's a prize to be run for, it's me they send for. It's to be the-one-sent-for that I run.

DAVID (*now at the top of the stairs*): And . . . then . . . you left.
OZZIE: What?
DAVID: I said . . . "And . . . then you left." That town.
OZZIE: Left?
DAVID: Yes. Went away; traveled.
OZZIE: No. What do you mean?
DAVID: I mean, you're no longer there; you're here . . . now.
   He is descending the stairs.
OZZIE: But I didn't really *leave* it. I mean, not *leave*. Not really.
DAVID: Of course you did. Where are you?
OZZIE: That's not the point, Dave. Where I am isn't the point at all.
   Turning away, going to clothing tree by the door, taking a jacket.
DAVID: But it is. It's everything; all that other is gone. Where are you going?
OZZIE: Groceries. Gotta go get groceries. You want anything at the grocery store? (*He looks at his watch.*) It's late. I gotta get busy.
DAVID (*as Ozzie exits*): That's all right, Dad. That's fine.

The lights fade and then come up on Rick, Harriet and Ozzie preparing for a family evening at home, with David planning to show them some 8 mm film for which they have mounted the projector. Ozzie is worrying over David's remark about the congenitality of his friend Hank Grenweller's disease. When David appears at the top of the stairs Ozzie goes over as though to guide him down, cheerfully commenting, "I think we can figure we're over the hump now and it's all down hill and good from here on in. I mean, we've talked things over, Dave, what do you say?—The air's been cleared, that's what I mean—the wounds acknowledged, the healing begun."

A warm family evening is in the offing with cake, soda pop, potato chips and maybe a singalong with Rick at the guitar. Rick favors them with "Baby When I Find You," a love song to guitar accompaniment, and Ozzie applauds him admiringly. Harriet compliments him, and Rick gives his mother a kiss.

David decides he'd like to sing a song, too, and suddenly there is tension. Rick draws away, protecting his guitar as David reaches for it. Ozzie tries to kid David out of his sudden whim.

OZZIE: C'mon, you couldn't carry a tune in a bucket and you know it.
DAVID: You're so selfish, Rick; your hair is black; it glistens. You smile. You sing. People think you are the songs you sing. They never . . . see . . . you. Give me the guitar . . .
   He is touching Rick with his cane.
RICK: Mom, what's wrong with Dave?
DAVID (*reaching out for the guitar*): Give me.
RICK: Listen, you eat your cake and drink your drink and if you still wanna, I'll let you.
DAVID: Now.
HARRIET: Ozzie, make David behave.

OZZIE: Don't you play too roughly . . .

DAVID: Ricky . . .

RICK: I don't think he's playing, Dad.

> *David, following Rick, bumps into the edge of something. Rick moves warily back.*

OZZIE: You watch out what you're doing . . .

RICK: You got cake all over your fingers, you'll get it all sticky, the strings all sticky—

> *They struggle over the guitar.*

Just tell me what you want to hear, I'll do it for you!

HARRIET: What is it? What's wrong?

DAVID: GIVE ME! (*As there is great tension in him.*) GIVE ME!

OZZIE: David!

> *David gains control of the guitar. Rick goes sprawling.*

HARRIET: Ohhhh, no, no, you're ruining everything. What's wrong with you?

OZZIE: I thought we were gonna have a nice party—

DAVID: I'm singing! We are!

OZZIE: No, no, I mean a *nice* party—one where everybody's happy!

DAVID: I'm happy. I'm singing. Don't you see them? Don't you see them and the soldiers—the hillside, the jungle.

David's mood changes abruptly, puzzling Ozzie and Harriet even more. He forgets about singing, he wants to show them some movies. The family is only too glad to accommodate David. They switch on the projector. But his film is blank; there are no pictures of any kind exposed on it.

As the blank film flashes on the screen David "narrates" it, telling his family what he sees and they should be seeing: a middle aged man and a pregnant woman wired to a tree and hanging by half-severed wrists, the woman dying even as David watches, the man with half of his head blown off, the unborn baby killed by a deliberately savage act of mutilation.

DAVID: . . . . . they ended each buried in a separate place; the husband by chance alone was returned to their village while the wife was dumped into an alien nearby plot of dirt, while the child, too small a piece of meat, was burned. Put into fire . . . as the shattered legs and arms cut off of men are burned. There's an oven. It is no ceremony. It is the disposal of garbage . . . !

> *Silence.*

HARRIET: David . . . David, yellow people did it. Didn't they? Yellow people hanging yellow people. Isn't that right? Oh, Ozzie, I told you—animals—Christ, burn them. Ohhh, David, don't let it hurt you. All the things you saw. People aren't themselves in war. I mean like that sticking that gun into that poor woman and then shooting that poor little baby, that's not human. You know that's not human. That's inhuman. It's inhuman, barbaric and uncivilized and inhuman.

Silence. She explains by cliche in order to insulate herself from real comprehension or feeling; she is not hurt.

DAVID: I'm thirsty.

HARRIET: For what? Tell me. Water? Or would you like some milk? How about some milk?

DAVID (*shaking his head*): No.

HARRIET: Or would you like some orange juice? All golden and little bits of ice.

OZZIE: Just all those words and that film with no picture and these poor people hanging somewhere—so you can bring them home like this house is a meat house—

Harriet murmurs protectively over David, who has noticed their refusal to relate directly to his story. Rick escapes upstairs. Obliquely but bitterly, David informs them that he cannot be expected to witness atrocities and then come home to "drive cars and sing" in a world of "water from faucets, light from wires." David, apparently exhausted from the futile effort to communicate, goes upstairs to bed.

Harriet tries to cover the awkward silence left by David's departure by a comment that she feels hungry, then sleepy. But Ozzie has been reached in some way by David's despair and cannot return so easily to light household chitchat. He tells Harriet: "When he pointed that cane at me . . . I couldn't breathe. I felt . . . for an instant I . . . might . . . die . . ."

Harriet shouts at Ozzie "What do you want!?" warning him that it is dangerous to face the problem of David head-on, signaling Ozzie to lapse back into safe conversation about the whereabouts and efficacy of the family aspirin. But even this subject turns out to contain some peril, leading Harriet to talk of blood, and suddenly she takes a raincoat and goes out the door.

Rick comes downstairs also on his way out, but Ozzie stops him. He demands that Rick drop everything else he may be doing and teach him to play the guitar, right now. Ozzie feels that there is some wonderful mystery in it, some secret he's never been told that could open the door to adulation and applause. Rick starts to tell his father about how to place the fingers for the basic C chord. Impatiently, Ozzie tells him: "You don't do that. I know you don't, you just pick it up and play it." Rick manages to make good his escape from his father, slipping out the front door.

Ozzie is left alone with his thoughts of how he grew up too soon; he didn't mean to "leave" his home town, he thought he would just go away and come back (he pounds on David's door insisting that he did not "leave"). He tells his story to David through the half-open bedroom door: he went to the city, could find no work, became a hobo. His friend Hank was a brakeman on a train Ozzie hopped—that's how they met, when Hank threw Ozzie off the train. Ozzie's story seems to be a kind of fantasy: "We become friends, Hank and me, have good times even though things are rough. He likes to point young girls out on the street and tell me how good it feels to touch them. I start thinking of their bodies, having dreams of horses, breasts and crotches.

And then one day the feeling is in me that I must see a train go by and I'll get on it or I won't, something will happen, but halfway down to where I was thrown off, I see how the grass in among the ties is tall, the rails rusted . . . Grass grows in abundance. No trains any longer come that way; they all go some other way . . . and far behind me Hank is calling, and I turn to see him coming, Harriet young and lovely in his hand, weaving among the weeds. I feel the wonder of her body moving toward me. She's the thing I'll enter to find my future . . . 'Hank,' I yell, 'You sonafabitch! Bring her here . . . C'mon . . . bring her on.' Swollen with pride, screaming and yelling, I stand there, I stand: 'I'm ready. I'm ready . . . I'm ready.' "

During the last part of this speech Ozzie crawls onto the sofa. Ozzie goes to sleep as the lights change, indicating the passage of time.

When the lights come up, Harriet is looking for her crossword puzzle book; Ozzie sleeps; the Asian Girl is sitting on David's bed; Rick goes to get camera and film to take pictures of David, who is left alone with his father momentarily. David bends over and talks to the sleeping figure of Ozzie.

DAVID: I think you should know how I've begun to hate you, Ozzie, yet I feel the wound of you. You cannot tell me, Dad. I must tell you. If I had been an orphan with no one to count on me, I would have stayed there . . . and yet it frightens me, talking to you when you're sleeping. You think us good and we steal all you have.

OZZIE: Good ole . . . Hank . . .

DAVID: No, no, I think he hated us, always sick with rot . . .

OZZIE: Nooo . . . Nooo . . .

DAVID: She would tell me you would not like her ever, she would touch her fingers to her eyes, nose; she knew.

OZZIE: Don't care . . . oh, nooo . . .

DAVID: You must hear me. It is not innocence I have lost, some other more simple virtue. I feel I am constructed of deceptions.

OZZIE: Sleeping . . . Dave . . . Sleeping . . . oh . . . oh . . .

DAVID: Do you see her? Do you hear me in your sleep?

OZZIE: Oh, oh . . .

As Rick is descending the stairs, David is straightening.

RICK: I meant to get some good shots at the party but I never got a chance the way things turned out. You can stay right there, okay?

DAVID (moving to a chair): I'll sit, all right?

RICK: Sure. How you feelin', anyway, Dave? I mean, honest ta God, I'm hopin' you get better. Everybody is. I mean . . .

He takes a picture, moves for a new angle.

. . . you're not gonna go talkin' anymore crazy like about that guitar and all that, are you? You know what I mean. Not to Mom and Dad anyway. It scares 'em and then I get scared and I don't like it, okay?

DAVID: Sure. That guitar business wasn't serious, anyway, Rick. None of that. It was all just a little joke I felt like playing, a kind of little game. I was only trying to show you how I hate you; that's all.

RICK (*startled, looking*): Huh?
DAVID: To see you die is why I live, Rick.
RICK: Oh.

Harriet enters cheerily, having found her puzzle book. Ozzie wakes up exclaiming about his dream, his foot asleep. He had dreamed that David was standing over him, frightening him.

Rick tries to talk about baseball; Harriet does her puzzle. But Ozzie, living dangerously, refuses to take refuge behind these symbols of order and tranquility. He is looking inside himself for answers, he is baffled, upset. He even shouts at Rick to shut up when Rick tries to divert him by suggesting maybe he wants something to eat.

Ozzie turns on David and cries at him that he wants to hear no more about the yellow girl or any of the ex-soldier's other "crybaby stories." He turns on Harriet, suggesting that her internal organs are "backing up some kind of rot into the world. I MEAN, I JUST CAN'T STOP THINKING ABOUT IT. LITTLE BITTY CHINKY KIDS HE WANTED TO HAVE! LITTLE BITTY CHINKY YELLOW KIDS! DIDN'T YOU! FOR OUR GRANDCHILDREN."

Ozzie slaps David twice. David moves away, up the stairs, talking as though to the Asian Girl, who moves to the landing to meet him. He tells her that he will buy her clothes and bring her home with him and pursue their affection in total understanding and delight . . . . .

The lights change to bridge the passage of time. In the twilight, Ozzie is worrying that David hates him; Rick is snapping pictures. "*And Ozzie tries to look and smile for the picture which is taken with a flash and there is a slide of Ozzie's contorted face as the lights are dimming and there are notes from a guitar, odd, faint. The slide in the dark blinks out. Curtain.*"

ACT II

In the darkness, a slide shows a "*close-up of a man, ruddy, smiling round face.*" It is Father Donald, and as the lights come up he is seated with Ozzie and Harriet explaining how he hopes to talk to David and help him. David is up in his room, lying on his bed. The Asian Girl is sleeping at the far end of the room.

Harriet feels that David is troubled because he broke the Sixth Commandment. But Father Donald's approach to the problem is non-dogmatic, tolerant, scientific. Rick comes in with his "Hi Mom, hi Dad" and, seeing the priest, makes straight for the kitchen.

Father Donald is directed upstairs to David's room (but he disappears to visit the bathroom first). Ozzie noted how uncomfortable the priest seemed and he begins to question the quality of the furniture—the armchair, the sofa.

Ozzie tries to disappear, but Harriet detains him; she has something to tell him. The police were here earlier in the day, two of them. It seems that someone from this house had called them in a disguised voice and asked them to come over and search David's luggage. Harriet calls Rick in and asks him point-blank if he called the police. Rick says no and goes out. Ozzie moves off, as Father Donald appears in the hallway and knocks on David's bedroom door, then enters. David makes no effort to greet the priest, who nevertheless approaches David cheerfully.

FATHER DONALD: . . . . . Gollee, I just don't know how to tell you how glad I am to see you in such high fine spirits. Would you like my blessing? Let me just give you my blessing and then we'll talk things over a little and I'll—

> David's cane, slashing through the air, strikes into the hand moving into the position to bless.

Ohhhhhhhhhhhhhh! (*Holding his arm.*) Oh, Dave; oh, watch out what you're doing!

DAVID: I know.

FATHER DONALD: No, no, I mean, you swung it in the air, you—hit me.

DAVID: Yes.

FATHER DONALD: No, no, you don't understand, you—

DAVID: I was trying to hit you, Father.

> *Silence.*

FATHER DONALD: What?

DAVID: I didn't send for you.

FATHER DONALD: I know, I know, your poor mother—your poor mother—

DAVID: I don't want you here, Father, get out!

FATHER DONALD: David!

DAVID: Get out, I'm sick of you. You've been in one Goddamn corner or another of this room all my life making signs at me, whispering, wanting to splash me with water or mark me with oil—some Goddamn hocus-pocus. I feel reverence for the air and the air is empty, Father. Now get the fuck out of here.

FATHER DONALD: No, no, no, no, David. No, no. I can't give that to you. You'll have to get that from somewhere else.

DAVID: I don't want anything from you!

FATHER DONALD: I'm supposed to react now in some foolish way—I see— some foolish, foolish way that will discredit me—isn't that right? Oh, of course it is. It's an excuse to dismiss my voice that you're seeking, an excuse for the self-destruction your anger has made you think you want, and I'm supposed to give it. I'm supposed to find all this you're doing obscene and sacrilegious instead of seeing it as the gesture of true despair that it is. You're trying to make me disappear, but it's not going to happen. No, no. No such luck, David. I understand you, you see. Everything about you.

Father Donald tells David he has read scientific psychiatric data on cases like David's, and it says that men who need to establish relationships with prostitutes of an alien race are demonstrating that they are weaker, more dependent than their fellow soldiers. Again and again Father Donald raises his hand to bless David, but again and again David strikes out with his cane.

Father Donald warns David that when he is *in extremis,* with the pain of death upon him, he will call for religious help. David admits this possibility, then challenges Father Donald to tell his parents that David struck him. Father Donald refuses, telling David "They've pain enough already," then exits in the direction of the bathroom to nurse his wounds.

Harriet suggests to Ozzie it might help to find David a nice girl. Rick promises to look for one, then slips away. Wondering where Father Donald can be, Ozzie calls upstairs and David answers—but the last thing Ozzie wants is to attract David's attention. Father Donald appears on the stairs. He manages to make his way out of the house without talking about David to the parents, blessing them painfully with his injured arm as he goes.

The lights go to black and then come up again with Ozzie knocking on David's door, entering the room and doing his best to begin a heart-to-heart talk with his son. He apologizes for striking David, wishes David and Rick thought more about being extensions or expressions of their father. Ozzie's talk becomes a kind of confidential appeal: "There's no evidence in the world of me . . . no sign or trace, as if everything I've ever done were no more than smoke. My life has closed behind me like water. But I must not care about it. I must not. Though I have inside me a kind of grandeur I can't realize, many things and memories of a darker time when we were very different— harder—nearer to the air and we thought of nothing as a gift. But I can't make you see that. There's no way. It's what I am, but it's not what you are. Even if I had the guitar, I would only stand here telling my fingers what to do, but they would do nothing. You would not see . . . I can't get beyond these hands . . . not ever. I jamb in the fingers, the joints . . . between them where there is no light. I break on the bone I am inside. Locked. I sweat. I stink. I am . . . lonely . . ."

Abruptly Ozzie changes the subject, drawing David's overseas cap from his pocket. He was looking through David's belongings and cut himself on the cap. David explains that razors are sewn into it so that it can be snapped in people's faces to cut them. Once holding their mutilated faces in pain, they are at your mercy.

David tells Ozzie that Hank Grenweller did him a bad turn by persuading Ozzie to buy this house, which David likens to a coffin. David mentions the horrors of Vietnam.

DAVID: . . . . . And now sometimes I miss them, all those screaming people. I wish they were here with us, you and Mom and Rick and Zung and me.

OZZIE: Mom and Rick and who and you, Dave?

DAVID: Zung.

The Asian Girl is moving nearer to them now.

OZZIE: Zung, Dave?

DAVID: She's here. They were all just hunks of meat that had no mind to know of me, until I cared for her. It was simple. We lived in a house. She didn't want to come back here, Dad, she wanted me to stay there. And in all the time I knew her, she cost me six dollars that I had to sneak into her purse. Surprised? In time I'll show you some things. You'll see them. I will be your father.

OZZIE: Pardon, Dave?

DAVID: What's wrong? You sound like something's terribly wrong?

OZZIE: No. No, no, I'm fine. Your poor mother—she's why I'm here. Your poor mother, sick with grief. She's mine to care for, you know. It's me you're after, yet you torment her. No more. No more. That's why I came to tell you.

DAVID (*as Ozzie has moved to the door to leave David's room*): Of course.

OZZIE (*exiting*): I . . . want . . . her happy.

Harriet is downstairs knitting. Ozzie shows her David's cap with the razors, suggests it might be wise to check on whatever other dangerous objects he may have brought home. For an instant, Ozzie even thinks it might be wise to have dental x-rays checked to make sure the returned soldier is really David.

Intuitively, Harriet understands that it is Ozzie who called the police and asked to have David's belongings searched. Ozzie denies it at first then admits it, becoming almost hysterical: "I have a little problem of ambivalence, that's all; a minor problem of ambiguity and now you're exaggerating everything all out of proportion. You're distorting everything. All of you! If I have to lie to live, I will! I'll lie!"

He escapes to the kitchen as the lights go to black. When they come up again Rick has come home and Harriet is doing the dusting, complaining that she can't get Father Donald on the phone: "He's starting to act like Jesus. You never hear from him. Isn't that funny."

Rick drifts upstairs to do his homework, scarcely pausing to say hello at David's door as he passes. Harriet goes back to her dusting. Ozzie comes in the front door, shaken by an experience he has just had on the street. Someone hit him with an egg thrown from a car. The more he thinks about it, the angrier he gets, that someone should demean him in this way, hitting him with an egg. Ozzie calls to Rick, who comes downstairs to hear about the incident. Harriet takes off Ozzie's jacket to clean the egg off it, as Ozzie goes to David's room to tell him about it too.

Rick takes a picture of Ozzie and David coming downstairs, Ozzie explaining about the egg and the car, calling for beer for himself and his sons because in some way the event brings them closer together, gives them a common identity as egg-thrower-resenters, good guys as opposed to bad guys. Ozzie tells them of a childhood friend, Fat Kramer, a good fighter—if he were here today they'd kill the egg-throwers, cut their hearts out.

RICK (*suddenly coughing and coughing and getting to his feet*): Excuse me, Dad; excuse me. Listen, I've got to get going. You don't mind, do you. Got places to go; you're just talking nonsense anyway. (*He moves for the door.*)

HARRIET: Have a good time, Rick.

RICK: I'm too pretty not to, Mom! Bye!
>He is gone, slamming the door behind him.
OZZIE (*startled, staring*): Where is . . . he . . . going? Where does he always go? Why does he always go and have some place to go? Always . . . !
HARRIET (*as she goes*): Just no never mind Ozzie. He's young and you're not. I'm going to do the dishes, but you just go right ahead with your little story . . . and I'll listen from the kitchen.
OZZIE (*quietly, staring off*): I . . . outran a bowling ball . . . They bet I couldn't. (*He starts as if at a sound, turns toward David.*) What are you . . . looking . . . at? What do you think you're seeing?
DAVID: I'm . . . not . . . looking.
OZZIE: I feel watched; looked at.
DAVID: No.
OZZIE: Observed.
DAVID: I'm blind.
OZZIE: Did you do it? Had you anything to do with it?
DAVID: What?
OZZIE: That egg.
DAVID: I can't see.
OZZIE: I think you did. You did it to me.
DAVID: I don't have a car. I can't drive. How could I?
HARRIET (*entering*): Ohh, it's so good to hear men's voices in the house again . . . my two favorite men in all the world, it's what I live for really. Would you like some coffee? Oh, of course you would. Let me put some on. Your humble servant at your command, I do your bidding, bid me be gone.
>And she is gone back into the kitchen, leaving Ozzie further into bewilderment, staring after her.

Ozzie expresses his fears; he fears David, Harriet, Rick (who often walks out on him in the middle of sentences), he wishes he could recapture some of the sense of friendship and achievement of his youth. When Harriet comes back with the coffee, Ozzie accuses her of beguiling him when he was a young, strong youth into a form of surrender and ultimate death. David encourages his father to continue thinking along these lines: "You're going to get rid of all this shit around you and be yourself again, you and me. Dad and Dave. We'll be runners."

But Ozzie lapses back into his mood of acceptance, and David goes to his room, leaving Ozzie and Harriet alone. Harriet notices that Ozzie is trembling as he tells her how once he wanted to leave them all, but Hank Grenweller persuaded him to stay for the children's sakes. He begs Harriet to move away from him, if only for a few minutes. Harriet in her turn reproaches him for self-love, reminds him that they can at least be thankful David didn't marry the Vietnamese girl or bring her home, tells him "You've got to straighten out your thinking." She tells him they are nothing, the children everything. She pretends Ozzie didn't mean the things he said—but he did.

Rick comes in with his customary cheery greeting, offers Ozzie some fudge which Ozzie refuses. He has been thinking about building a wall (Ozzie tells Rick), looking at plans. Rick sinks into a chair and announces to his father: "Whoooooeeeee—boy, oh, boy, I had the greatest piece a ass tonight, Dad; I really did. What a beautiful Goddamn piece of ass."

Ozzie's only reaction is to hope that Rick was careful and to reassure himself that she wasn't any "decent" girl. Rick assures him she wasn't.

The lights black out, and when they come up again Harriet is entering David's bedroom with towel, soap and a basin of water. She urges her son to take off his shirt, cool himself off with a sponge bath. She tells him all she and Ozzie ever wanted was the "good, sweet things" for their children. David replies by telling his mother how Vietnamese beat their children for punishment, murder out of pique, sleep all together in a bed and submit to sexual degradation by the soldiery.

Harriet tries to shut these thoughts out by reassuring David that he did nothing out of the ordinary; he shouldn't continue to remember the experience with such morbidity. Harriet could not bear the thought of grandchildren with Oriental faces, even if the Asian Girl were as nice as David remembers she was. In intermarriage, Harriet tells her son, "It is we who disappear, David. They don't change and we are gone. It is our triumph, our whiteness. We disappear."

David replies by thrusting his cane under his mother's skirt. She pushes it away—and now she too is afraid of him and she backs away and then flees. David stations himself by the front door. When his mother comes running downstairs with a raincoat on, she sees him standing there blocking her passage and cries out in fear, backing away.

DAVID: I want to have a conversation about old times and new times.

HARRIET: You want only to hurt us, don't you. That's all you want. Only to give us unhappiness. You cheat her, David. That lovely, lovely little girl you spoke of. She merits more to be done in her memory than cruelty.

Now she is sitting on the couch as if everything is normal.

DAVID: Do you remember—? It was a Sunday, when we had all gone to church and there was a young man there with his yellow wife and child. You spoke to us . . . Dad and Rick and me as if we were conspirators. "I feel so sorry for that poor man—the baby looks like *her*," you said and your mouth twisted as if you had been forced to swallow someone else's spit.

HARRIET: No, no, no, no. You don't know how badly I feel. I've got a fever, the start of a cold or flu. (*Moving away from him, up the stairs.*) Let me be. I can't hardly move . . . or stand up. I just want to flop somewhere and not have to move. I'm so weak . . . don't hurt me anymore. Don't hurt me— no more—I've got fever, please, fever, don't hurt me.

DAVID: But I have so much to show you.

HARRIET (*on the stairs, stopped to stare down at him*): Who are you? I don't know who you are.

DAVID: David.

HARRIET: Noooo.

DAVID: But I am.

HARRIET: No, no, no.

She moves now to slowly climb the stairs while the Asian Girl comes forward in David's room to look down at him.

DAVID: But it's what you want, don't you see? You can see it. I've seen it. Her wrists are bound in coils of flowers; flowers are strung in her hair and she is beaten. She hangs from the wind; men strike and kick her. They are blind so that they may not see her, yet they howl, wanting not to hurt her but only as I do, to touch and hold her . . . they howl . . . I'm home. (*Now beginning to move about the living room and up the stairs after her.*) Little David . . . David . . . of all the toys and tops and sailor suits, the plastic cards. Drum player, bed-wetter, home-run-hitter, I'm home . . . now . . . and I . . . want to drink . . . from the toilet . . . wash there. Sleep . . . on the floor. You will join me. You will join me.

Ozzie enters from the outside carrying a cardboard box, watched by the Asian Girl who is now sitting on the stairs. He places pieces of paper from the box on the chairs around the living room and pretends that he is a sort of chairman addressing a meeting of members of his family. He tells them he has decided to fight against his overwhelming sense of despair: "At first . . . at first . . . I thought the thing to do would be to learn the guitar . . . But *that* I realized in just the nick of time was a folly that would have taken me into the very agony of frustration I was seeking to avoid. The skill to play like Ricky does is a great gift and only Ricky has it. He has no acids rotting his heart. He is all lies and music, his brain small and scaly, the brain of a snake forever innocent of the fact that it crawls. . . . ."

Ozzie wants to recapture his sense of pride in his identity (he tells the non-existent meeting), and he has made an inventory of everything he owns, everything he is. He has made copies so that the members of his family can pass them out to their friends, to establish who Ozzie is.

The Asian Girl drifts downstairs, and Harriet comes down looking for aspirin, telling Ozzie of her dreadful conversation with David. But Ozzie doesn't want to deal with David, he wants to hide from him, forget that he ever existed. Harriet persuades Ozzie to kneel with her and pray. As they are doing so, Rick comes in the front door.

RICK: Hi, Mom; hi, Dad.

Ozzie and Harriet continue to pray. Rick stops, stares.

Hi . . . Mom; hi, Dad . . . (*Pause.*) Hi . . . Mom . . . hi . . . Dad . . . (*Silence. Then, in realization.*) David.

He goes running up to look in David's room, but the room is empty, and then David, in ragged combat fatigues, appears on the top of the stairs and Rick, frightened, backs away. They come down into the living room where Ozzie and Harriet sit staring dazedly. All this occurs while Rick speaks.

Dave . . . what have you got to say for yourself? What can you? Honest ta

God, I've had it. I really have. I can't help it, even if you are sick, and I hate to complain, but you're getting them so mixed up they're not themselves any more. Just a minute ago—one minute—they were on their knees, do you know that? Just a minute ago—right here on the living room floor, now what's the point of that? They're my mom and dad too.

DAVID: He doesn't know, does he Dad? Did you hear him?

RICK: Let Dad alone.

DAVID: He doesn't know . . . how when you finally see yourself, there's nothing really there to see . . . isn't that right? Mom . . . ?

Rick warns David to let his parents alone, but David goes on in his usual vein. He reminds them all that every once in a while the farmers bring in a dog run wild in the forest to put with their own tame animals, to remind them of their lupine past. There is a rumbling sound, and David tells his family it is the trucks bringing the men back from war all over town, not just the blind ones any more, but the dead ones wrapped in blue plastic bags.

There is a knocking at the front door, as though the dead were trying to get in, and David suggests that they admit all the dead to this room, stack them around the walls. Rick can play the guitar to entertain them. Ozzie resists this morbid suggestion, and the scene becomes a metaphor as David forces the Asian Girl on his resisting father. He insists that his father will love her. Ozzie insists he would rather be blind himself, he would rather disappear.

Resisting this metaphor of Vietnamese death brought into his house, Ozzie pushes David away from him. Rick hits his brother with the guitar.

RICK: Let Dad alone. Let him alone. He's sick of you. What the hell's a matter with you? He doesn't wanna talk anymore about all the stupid stuff you talk. He wants to talk about cake and cookies and cars and coffee. He's sick a you and he wants you to shut up . . . We hate you, Goddamn you.

Now the Asian Girl speaks, a distinct ten words in her language.

OZZIE (*turning to face her and move to her*): Oh, what is it that you want? I'm tired, so tired. I mean it. Forgive me. I'm sick of the sight of you, squatting all the time. In filth like animals, talking gibberish, your breath sick with rot . . . And yet you look at me with those sad pleading eyes as if there is some real thing that can come between us when you're not even here. You are deceit.

Having moved to her, he begins to strangle her.

The sight of you sickens me. The sight of her sickens me, YOU HEAR ME DAVID? Believe me. I am speaking my honest true feelings. I spit on you, the both of you, I piss on you and your eyes and pain. Flesh is lies. You are garbage and filth. You are darkness. I cast you down. Deceit. Animal. Dirty animal.

Ozzie tries to attack the Asian Girl sexually, but Rick pulls him away and Harriet covers the girl with a rug as though blotting her out of reality. Rick tries to bring the mood back to normal by discussing a funny movie he saw; Harriet suggests that someone go for groceries. Ozzie and Harriet and Rick reassure each other that they are fine, then Rick makes a suggestion to David: "I'd kill myself if I were you, Dave. You're in too much misery. I'd cut my wrists. Honestly speaking, brother to brother, you should have done it long ago."

David looks around him seeking support, but Rick reminds him that the Asian Girl is not there, she has never been there: "You decided not to bring her, Dave, remember? You decided, all things considered, that you preferred to come back without her. Too much risk and inconvenience . . . you decided."

Rick offers David his razor, and Harriet urges her son to go ahead and do it. Ozzie agrees, it would be the best thing for David. Rick taunts David for taking human beings too seriously, for never having any fun like a buddy of his who amused himself killing Vietnamese villagers, especially the children, by dropping sacks of cement on them from a truck.

Rick helps David to cut his wrists with the razor. Bleeding, he confesses to his family that what he really wanted was to kill them all.

DAVID: I wanted . . . for you to need what I had and I wouldn't give it . . .

HARRIET: That's not possible.

OZZIE: Nooooo.

DAVID: I wanted to get you. Like poor bug eyed fish flung up from the brief water to the lasting dirt, I would gut you.

HARRIET: David, no. You don't kill us.

OZZIE: No, no.

RICK: I don't even know why you'd want to.

OZZIE: We kill you.

RICK: That's right.

OZZIE: And then, of course, we die, too . . . Later on, I mean. And nothing stops it. Not words . . . or walls . . . or even guitars . . .

RICK: Sure.

OZZIE: That's what happens.

HARRIET: It isn't too bad, is it?

RICK: How bad is it?

OZZIE: He's getting weaker. (*Turns, moves toward the living room where he will sit in a chair.*)

HARRIET: And in a little, it'll all be over. You'll feel so grand . . . ! No more funny talk.

RICK: You can shower; put on clean clothes. I've got deodorant you can borrow. "After Roses," Dave. The scent of a thousand roses.

> *He is preparing to take a picture now; crouching beside the table eventually.*

HARRIET: Take off your glasses, David.

OZZIE: Do as you're told.

> *David's hands are rising toward the glasses to remove them and Rick prepares to take a picture of David.*

RICK: I bet when you were away there was only plain water to wash in, huh?

> *Rick takes the picture. Slide comes on, huge closeup of David's face, nothing visible but the face. It is the slide that, when it appeared at the very start of the play, was referred to as "somebody sick."*

You probably hadda wash in the rain. I like Dave like this, Mom. Too bad he's gonna die.

HARRIET: No, no.

OZZIE: He's not gonna die, Rick. He's only gonna nearly die.

HARRIET: Mmmmmmmmm.

RICK: Oh.

> *Rick, sitting, begins to play his guitar and the music is alive and fast. It has a rhythm, a drive, a happiness that is contagious. As the lights are dimming, the slide blinks out. Curtain.*

○○○
○○○
○○○
○○○
○○○ THE PRISONER
○○○
○○○ OF SECOND AVENUE

A Comedy in Two Acts

BY NEIL SIMON

Cast and credits appear on page 321

NEIL SIMON was born in the Bronx, N.Y. on July 4, 1927. He attended New York University and the University of Denver. His first theatrical work consisted of sketches for camp shows at Tamiment, Pa., in collaboration with his brother Danny. He became a TV writer, supplying a good deal of material to Sid Caesar and Phil Silvers.

On Broadway, Simon contributed sketches to Catch a Star *(1955) and* New Faces of 1956. *His first Broadway play was* Come Blow Your Horn *(1961), followed by the book for the musical* Little Me *(1962). His comedy* Barefoot in the Park *(1963) was selected as a Best Play of its season, as was* The Odd Couple *(1965). Neither of these had closed when the musical* Sweet Charity, *for which Simon wrote the book, came along early in 1966; and none of the three had closed when Simon's* The Star-Spangled Girl *opened the following season in December 1966—so that Simon had the phenomenal total of four hit shows running simultaneously on Broadway during the season of 1966-67. When the last of the four closed the following summer, Simon's hits had played a total of 3,367 performances over four theater seasons.*

Simon immediately began stacking another pile of blue-chip Broadway shows. His Plaza Suite *(1968) was named a Best Play of its year; his book for the musical* Promises, Promises *(1969) was another smash, and* Last of the Red Hot Lovers *(1969) became his fourth Best Play and the third in still another group of Simon shows in grand simultaneous display on Broadway.* Plaza Suite *closed before* The Gingerbread Lady *(1970, also a Best Play) opened, so that Simon's second stack was three plays high. The* Prisoner of

203

Second Avenue *is—let's see, now—Simon's ninth straight success and sixth Best Play.*

Simon lives in the New York City area where he can keep an eye on all this action (he owns the Eugene O'Neill Theater, too). He is married, with two daughters.

Time: The present

Place: An apartment in a modern building in New York's East 80s

ACT I

Scene 1

SYNOPSIS: It is 2:30 a.m. on a hot New York midsummer morning in the living room of the Edisons' 14th-floor apartment *"in one of those prosaic new apartment houses that grow like mushrooms all over New York's overpriced East Side . . . . . What is visible to us is the living room-dining room combination, a small, airless and windowless kitchen off the dining room, a French door that leads to a tiny balcony or terrace off the living room, and a small hallway that leads to two bedrooms and bathrooms."*

The view through the windows and out over the terrace is closed in by other similar but taller high-rise apartment buildings. Mel Edison and his wife Edna have been living here for six years. Now, in the middle of the night, Mel is sitting on a tiny sofa, nervous and wakeful and dressed in pajamas and bathrobe, smoking a cigarette, a caricature of middle-class, early middle-aged anxiety.

Edna joins Mel, pulling a robe over her nightgown, turning on the lights, worrying about her husband, who is calling on God and complaining that the air conditioner isn't modulating properly. Maybe it's just because he's over-tired, but everything seems to irritate him nowadays, especially this apartment. He opens the terrace door and the traffic noises pour in.

MEL: Two-thirty in the morning, there's one car driving around in Jackson Heights and we can hear it . . . Fourteen stories up, I thought it would be quiet. I hear the subway up here better than I hear it in the subway . . . We're like some kind of God damned antenna. All the sound goes up through this apartment and then out to the city.

EDNA: We've lived here six years, it never bothered you before.

MEL: It's worse now. I don't know why. I'm getting older, more sensitive to sounds, to noise. Everything.

He closes door, looks at himself.

You see this? I had that door opened ten seconds, you gotta wash these pajamas now.

EDNA (*anything to please*): Give them to me, I'll get you clean pajamas.

MEL (*paces*): Two-thirty in the morning, can you believe that's still going on next door? (*He points to the wall.*)

EDNA: What's going on?

MEL: What are you trying to be funny? You mean to tell me you don't hear that?

EDNA (*puzzled*): Hear what?

MEL (*closer to wall, still pointing*): That! That! What are you, deaf? You don't hear that?

EDNA: Maybe I'm deaf. I don't hear anything.

MEL: *Listen,* for God's sakes . . . You don't hear Raindrops Falling on His Head? (*Sings.*) "Da dum de dum da dum de da . . . too big for his feet . . ." You don't hear that?

EDNA: Not when you're singing. I don't hear it.

MEL (*stares at wall*): It's those two God damned German airline hostesses. Every night they got someone else in there. Two basketball players, two hockey players, whatever team is in town, win or lose, they wind up in there . . . Every God damned night! Somewhere there's a 747 flying around with people serving themselves because those two broads never leave that apartment.

When Mel forces Edna to place her ear against the wall, she can also hear the music. Mel bangs on the wall, aggravating a crack in the plaster, caused by trouble with the pipes upstairs (the management is going to fix it soon).

Edna cannot go back to sleep with Mel having a bad anxiety attack which even two Valiums cannot relieve. Mel also is suffering from indigestion, complaining "I used to love food. I haven't eaten food since I was thirteen years old." What's more, the air in the apartment is polluted with the smell of the uncollected garbage down on the sidewalk.

Edna advises Mel: "I get hot, I get cold, I smell garbage, I hear noise. You either live with or you get out." But Mel insists on his right to protest. He over-reacts to the barking of a dog somewhere below, going out to the terrace, shouting. Neighbors in an apartment above shout back at him to be quiet.

Edna decides to abandon Mel to his fit of angry protest and starts to leave the room, but Mel begs her to stay: "Talk to me for a few minutes because I think I'm going out of my mind."

EDNA: What is it?

MEL: I'm unraveling . . . I'm losing touch!

EDNA: You haven't been sleeping well lately . . .

MEL: I don't know where I am half the time. I walk down Madison Avenue, I think I'm in a foreign country.

EDNA: I know that feeling, Mel . . .

MEL: It's not just a feeling, something is happening to me . . . I'm losing control. I can't handle things any more. The telephone on my desk rings seven, eight times before I answer it . . . I forgot how to work the water cooler today. I stood there with an empty cup in my hand and water running all over my shoes.

EDNA: It's not just you, Mel, it's everybody. Everybody's feeling the tension these days.

MEL: Tension? If I could just feel tension, I'd give a thousand dollars to charity . . . When you're tense, you're tight, you're holding on to something. I don't know where to grab. Edna, I'm slipping and I'm scared.

Mel's analyst is dead, and he can't face the trouble and expense of starting all over again with another doctor. Edna suggests maybe a vacation would help, but it is Mel's greatest fear that he will soon be on permanent vacation. His firm is losing money, and they are sure to start laying people off. With two girls in college, at 47, with high living expenses symbolized by this apartment, the loss of his job would be a disaster from which he might never recover.

Edna suggests that they could start a new life somewhere else—Spain, maybe—but Mel ridicules this and all other suggestions of escape to places where there would be very little need for the services of an unemployed advertising account executive.

The phone rings, and they stare at it uneasily; finally Mel answers it. It's the stewardesses next door complaining about the noise of the Edisons' raised voices, sending Mel off into a fit of fury. The stewardesses bang on the wall to emphasize their point, and Mel insists that Edna bang back.

The banging contest continues as the lights fade and the curtain falls. In the darkness, a News Logo is flashed onto a screen above the proscenium, and we hear the voice of Roger Keating with the Six O'Clock Report.

VOICE OF ROGER KEATING: . . . This is Roger Keating and the Six O'Clock Report . . . New York was hit with its third strike of the week, this time the city employees of thirty-seven New York hospitals walked out at 3 p.m. this afternoon . . . The Mayor's office has been flooded with calls as hundreds of patients and elderly sick people have complained of lack of food, clean sheets and medicines. One seventy-nine-year-old patient in Lenox Hill Hospital fell in the corridor, broke his leg and was treated by a seventy-three-year-old patient who just recovered from a gall bladder operation . . . Two of the most cold blooded robbers in the city's history today made off with four thousand dollars, stolen from the New York City Home for the Blind . . . Police believe it may have been the same men who got away with thirty-six hundred dollars on Tuesday from the New York Cat and Dog Hospital . . . Water may be shut off tomorrow, says New York Commissioner of Health, because of an anonymous phone call made to the Bureau this morning, threatening to dump fifty pounds of chemical pollutants in the city's reservoirs—the unidentified caller, after making his threat, concluded with, "It's gonna be dry tomorrow,

LEE GRANT AND PETER FALK IN "THE PRISONER OF SECOND AVENUE"

baby." . . . And from the office of Police Commissioner Murphy, a report that apartment house burglaries have risen 7 point 2 percent in August.

Scene 2

A few days later in late afternoon, the room is a shambles, with many objects missing. It is obvious that the apartment has been burgled, and Edna is on the phone, trembling with the shock of just having discovered the crime, stammering out her report to the police.

Following the phone call, Edna decides she needs a drink and gets a glass with some ice—but of course the burglars have taken all the liquor. She decides to settle for a Valium and goes to the medicine cabinet—but everything has been taken from that, too. Edna disappears into the bedroom.

> *The front door opens with a key and Mel enters. He carries his suit jacket and the New York* Post *in his arm. His shirt sleeves are*

rolled up and he looks hot. He closes the door and hangs his jacket in closet. He doesn't seem to even notice the room, consumed with his own thoughts. He crosses to chair and falls into it exhausted, tilts his head back and sighs . . . His eyes open, then he looks at the room, for almost the first time. He looks around the room, be-wildered.

EDNA'S VOICE (*from inside*): Mel? . . . Is that you, Mel?

Mel is still looking at the room, puzzled. Edna appears cautiously from the bedroom. She comes in, holding a vase by the thin end, and looks at Mel.

MEL: . . . Didn't Mildred come in to clean today?

EDNA (*puts vase down*): Not today . . . Mondays and Thursdays.

MEL: What happened here? Why is this place such a mess?

EDNA: . . . We've been robbed . . .

Mel looks at her in a state of shock . . . He slowly rises and then looks at the room, in a new perspective.

MEL: . . . What do you mean, robbed?

EDNA (*starts to cry*): *Robbed! Robbed!* What does robbed mean? They come in, they take things out! *They robbed us ! ! !*

Mel keeps turning, looking at the room in disbelief . . . not know-ing where to look first.

MEL: . . . I don't understand . . . What do you mean, someone just walked in and robbed us?

EDNA: What do you think? . . . They called up and made an appointment? *We've been robbed!*

Mel is beginning to understand, as Edna gives him the details. She went out shopping for food for only five minutes, and when she came back the apartment had been ransacked of everything movable, the color TV, the Scotch. When Mel finds out that they've taken his Chivas Regal, he opens the terrace door and shouts out "Sons of bitches!"

Mel reaches another peak of anger when he finds that they've cleaned out the medicine chest too—"How much are they going to get for a roll of dental floss?" Edna, who has lost her hidden kitchen money along with everything else, drives home the point: "Nobody steals dental floss and mouth wash. Only sick people. Only that's who live in the world today. SICK, SICK, SICK PEOPLE!"

The lock to the front door wasn't broken because Edna had left the door unlocked when she went out (she has lost her key). She didn't think burglars would have time to try the door during the few minutes she was out shopping.

Edna starts to straighten the place up a little, so she can see more easily what is missing. Mel discovers that they have taken his suits, his sports clothes and even his dinner jacket just back from the cleaner's. He throws a tantrum.

. . . . . *He picks up ashtrays from the sideboard and throws them to the floor of the kitchen . . . uncontrollably until all his energy and his vitriol have been exhausted . . . He stands there panting.*

EDNA: . . . It's just things, Mel. Just some old suits and coats, we can re-place them. We'll buy new ones. Can't we, Mel?

MEL: With what? . . . *With what?* They *fired* me.

He sits, back to wall.

EDNA: Oh, my God. Don't tell me.

MEL: Well, I'm telling you. *They fired me!* . . . Me, Hal Chesterman, Mike Ambrozi, Dave Polichek, Arnold Strauss . . . Two others, I can't even remem-ber their names . . . Seven of us, in one fell swoop. *Fired!*

EDNA (*she is so distraught, she can't even stir in her chair*): Oh, Mel, I'm so sorry . . .

MEL: They called us into the office one at a time. They didn't even have to say it, we knew. We saw it coming. Even the secretaries knew. They couldn't look at you when you said "Good morning" . . . Eighty-five dollar a week girls were bringing me coffee and danish and not charging me for it. I knew right away.

EDNA: Oh, Mel, Mel, Mel . . .

MEL: They said they had no choice. They had to make cuts right down the line . . . Seven executives, twelve salesmen, twenty-four in office help . . . Forty-three people in one afternoon . . . It took three elevators two trips to get rid of all the losers . . . Wait'll the coffee and danish man comes in to-morrow, he'll throw himself out the window . . .

EDNA: And then you come home to this. To get fired and then to come home and find your house has been robbed.

MEL: It didn't happen today. It happened Monday.

EDNA: Monday? You mean you've known for four days and you haven't said a word to me?

MEL: I didn't know how to tell you, I couldn't work up the courage . . . I thought maybe another job would turn up, a miracle would happen . . . Mir-acles don't happen when you're 47 . . . When Moses saw the burning bush he must have been 23, 24, the most. Never 47.

Mel goes into the kitchen to get a beer, comes back and tells Edna what he's been doing since Monday: phone calls for jobs in the mornings, museums, auctions and a Central Park bench to kill time in the afternoons. Edna comes over to comfort him, and he holds her desperately while reassuring her, "I'll be all right."

Mel played a game of softball with the kids the day before and lost the game for his side. Edna tries to cheer him up by reminding him that they are in-sured for the robbery loss, but Mel is obsessed with anxiety about how he will pay for the girls in college, this apartment, their living expenses, etc. He begins to go through the useless things they can cut down on: gym and mu-seum memberships, magazine subscriptions. Suddenly, a novelty on the bar, a musical whisky pourer, becomes a symbol of all the costly junk that has cluttered their lives and smothered them.

Mel gets shooting pains in the chest and cries out against his fate—no job, no suit, no pills even to ease his breaking nerves—so loudly the neighbors upstairs shout their complaints about his language, protesting that their children can hear him. Mel goes out onto the terrace and begins shouting back.

VOICE: Don't you have any respect for anyone else?

MEL (*screaming up*): Respect? I got respect for my ass, that's what I got respect for! That's all anybody respects . . .

> *And suddenly Mel gets hit with a torrent of water, obviously from a large bucket. He is drenched, soaked through, completely, devastatingly and humiliatingly . . . He comes back into the room. He is too stunned and shocked to be able to say a word.*

EDNA: Oh, God. Oh God, Mel.

MEL (*very calmly and quietly, almost like a child who has been hurt*): . . . That's a terrible thing to do . . . That's a mean, terrible thing to do . . .

> *And he sits down on a chair and begins to sob, quietly sitting there and sobbing. Edna runs out to the terrace and yells up.*

EDNA: . . . God will punish you for that . . . I apologize for my husband's language . . . but God will punish you for that.

> *She is crying. She runs back to Mel and she picks up some linens from the floor and begins to dry his face and his head.*

It's alright, Mel. It's alright, baby.

MEL: . . . That's a terrible thing to do to a person . . . I would never do that to anyone . . .

EDNA (*wiping him*): Never. You're too good, Mel, too decent . . . You would never do that . . . It's going to be alright, Mel, I promise . . . You'll get another job, you'll see . . . And we'll move away from here. Someplace far away . . . You know what we could do? You're so good with kids, you love being with them, we could start a summer camp . . . You would be the head of the camp and I would do the cooking and the girls can be the riding instructors and the swimming instructors. You would like that, wouldn't you, Mel? We'll just have to save some money, that's all. And if you don't get another job right away, I can always be a secretary again. I can work, I'm strong, Mel . . . But you mustn't get sick. You mustn't get sick and die because I don't want to live in this world without you . . . I don't like it here! . . . I don't want you to leave me alone here . . . We'll show them, Mel . . . We'll show them all . . .

> *She continues to wipe his ears as the curtain slowly falls.*

ACT II

Scene 1

Six weeks later in mid-September, in the afternoon, Mel appears from the bedroom wearing slacks, pajama top, loosely tied bathrobe, slippers and a baseball mitt into which he is pounding a ball. *"Six weeks of unemployment have turned Mel into a different man. His eyes seem to be sunken into his sockets, he has rings under his eyes and only seems to shave sporadically. There is also a grimness about him, an anger, a hostility, the look of a man who is suffering from a deep depression coupled with a tendency to paranoia."*

Mel's movements are aimless. He drifts into the kitchen as a key turns in the door and Edna enters, dressed smartly and carrying groceries in a brown paper bag. She is now the family breadwinner and has come home from the office on her lunch hour to prepare Mel's lunch. Mel drifts around the room, hardly listening to Edna as she makes a steady stream of small talk about goings-on in the city (including a kidnapping of the Police Commissioner).

Edna sits down eagerly to her lunch; Mel just stares into his tomato juice. Mel can hardly bear to talk about his own boring day: looking out the window three times and listening to daytime radio talk shows. Edna urges him to get out, take a walk in the park, join a softball game. Mel replies, "I'm seven years older than the father of the pitcher. I am not going to wait for the kids to get out of school so I can have someone to play with."

Today's paper advertised no jobs suitable for an account executive; it has been a wasted day, and Mel is exceptionally irritable. He even resents Edna's coming home to be with him for lunch.

MEL: Don't you see how humiliating it is? Everyone in the building knows you come home to make me lunches. The only ones here who get lunches cooked for them every day is me and the six-year-old girl on the fourth floor.

EDNA: I don't care what people in this building think.

MEL: I care! I CARE! . . . They probably think you make me take a nap too . . . I can make my own lunches. I can go out to eat.

EDNA: I was just trying to save us money.

MEL: What are you going to do in the winter when it snows, come home to put on my galoshes?

EDNA: Is this what you do all morning? Walk around the edges of the apartment thinking of things like that. Torturing yourself?

MEL: I don't have to torture *myself*. I got dogs, flushing toilets and the Red Baron's two sisters in there.

EDNA: Alright, what did they do today, Mel? Tell me.

MEL: No, listen, I don't want to bother you. I know you've got your own problems at the office. You've got a living to make, don't worry about the house. That's my concern.

EDNA: I thought we agreed about my working. I thought we agreed it was alright for me to take this job until something came through for you.

MEL: I'm not complaining. You've been very nice to me. You pay the rent, buy the food, bought me a nice new sport jacket . . . Maybe next year you'll take me to Hawaii on United Airlines.

EDNA: Do you want me to quit, Mel? Do you want me to leave the job? I'll leave the minute you say so, you know I will.

MEL: Not this week. Margaret Truman has Bess Myerson on this Friday. I don't want to miss it.

Edna gets up and storms into the kitchen. She stands there over the stove and bangs her fist on it in desperation.

Mel assures her that he tries (though she's not accusing him), he stole the paper from next door, but it lists no jobs for him. In this state, Mel even suspects that Edna isn't really working until 7 p.m. every night as she claims, she's probably enjoying herself in some bar.

Exasperated, Edna advises Mel: "I suggest you either get a very tight grip on yourself . . . or you look for someone to help you . . . . . Medical help. A doctor. Some doctor who can talk to you and straighten you out because I am *running out of energy and patience!*"

There is nothing wrong with his mind, Mel assures her, or his capabilities. In reality he is the victim of a vicious plot that he has deduced from listening to the radio. Edna of course wonders what he is talking about, and, with each attempt to explain, Mel's thoughts become more and more confused. "They" are taking over everything, Mel confides to Edna. It is a very sophisticated scheme, and *very* secret, "a plot to change the system. To destroy the status quo. It's not just me they're after, Edna. They're after you. They're after our kids, my sisters, every one of our friends. They're after the cops, they're after the hippies, they're after the government, they're after the anarchists, they're after Women's Lib, the fags, the blacks, the whole military complex. That's who they're after, Edna."

Mel has mentioned everybody, Edna tells him, so there isn't anybody left to plot; but Mel assures her there is. As she tries to soothe him, he denies hotly that he is suffering from paranoia. He offers to give Edna absolute proof that a conspiracy, not a recession, is responsible for all the people being laid off at the agency. When Edna offers to listen to his proof, Mel shouts: "I CAN'T GIVE YOU ANY PROOF ! ! ! . . . *What kind of proof do I have?* I'm out of work, that's my proof . . . They won't let me work."

Mel finally reveals that the whole human race is the instigator of the plot, by allowing the human spirit to deteriorate. Mel enumerates his humiliations at the unemployment office, etc., and is reminded of the humiliation inflicted on him by his neighbor above. Mel will avenge the insult. He is waiting till it snows, then he will watch for his neighbor to appear below, and "they won't find him until the spring."

Edna makes up her mind: it is time to get in touch with a doctor, Mel needs professional help. She prepares to phone the doctor, but Mel ignores her. He is dreaming of his revenge: "They can get your clothes, your Valium, your television, your Red Label whisky, your job, they can get everything. But they can't get your brains . . . That's my secret weapon . . . That and the snow . . . I pray to God it snows tomorrow. I'll wait for him. I bought a shovel today. Oh, yeah . . ."

Edna is determined to take Mel to the doctor that very afternoon if possible. She gets Doctor Frankel on the phone, while Mel dreams about the impact of two pounds of snow falling 14 floors—"And if it doesn't snow this winter, I'll wait till next winter . . . I'm in no hurry, smart ass . . . (*Yelling up.*) I've got nothing but time . . . Nothing but time, baby . . ."

The curtain falls, the News Logo appears, and the scene ends with another direful Six O'Clock Report announcing a judges' strike and the "unsolved mugging and robbing late last night of New York State Governor Nelson Rockefeller on Sixth Avenue and 48th Street."

Scene 2

Two weeks later, Mel's older brother Harry and his three older sisters, all in their fifties, have come to the apartment to visit Mel, and possibly to help him. They are well, even expensively, dressed. They haven't been invited to the apartment for nine years, but now they have all gathered to consult about the crisis in the life of their baby brother. At curtain rise, Edna is in the other room and they sit there silently for a moment or two.

JESSIE: He was always nervous.

PEARL: Always.

JESSIE: As far back as I can remember, he was nervous. Never sat still for a minute, always jumping up and down. Am I lying, Pearl?

PEARL: We're his own sisters, who should know better? Up and down, up and down . . . You want some coffee Harry? Take some coffee.

HARRY: I don't drink coffee.

JESSIE: He always used to fidget. Talked a mile a minute . . . He even chewed fast . . . remember how fast he used to chew?

PEARL: Wasn't I there? Didn't I see him chew? I remember . . . Harry, why don't you take some coffee?

HARRY: When did you ever see me drink coffee? You're my sister fifty-three years, you never saw me drink coffee. Why would I drink coffee now?

PEARL: What do I see you, two times a year? I thought maybe you took up coffee.

PAULINE: He wasn't nervous, he was high strung. Melvin was high strung.

PEARL: I call it nervous. As a baby he was nervous, as a boy he was nervous, in the Army he was nervous. How long did he last in the Army, anyway?

JESSIE: Two weeks.

PEARL: There you are. He was nervous.

PAULINE: Where do you think nerves come from? From being high strung.

PEARL: Then why weren't any of us high strung? We all had the same parents. He was nervous, he was fidgety, he chewed fast . . . I never saw him swallow.

JESSIE: No one could talk to him. Poppa could never talk to him, I remember.

PAULINE: How could Poppa talk to him? Mel was three years old when Poppa died.

PEARL: If he wasn't so nervous, Poppa could have talked to him.

HARRY: I never drank coffee in my life. It's poison. Goes right through the system. (*Looks towards bedroom.*) Who's she on the phone with in there anyway?

PEARL: He had the same thing in high school. A nervous breakdown. Remember when he had the nervous breakdown in high school?

HARRY (*turns to her*): Who you talking about?

PEARL: Mel! He had a nervous breakdown in high school. You don't remember?

HARRY: What are you talking about? He didn't have a nervous breakdown, he had a broken arm. He fell in the gym and broke his arm.

PEARL: I'm not talking about that time.

HARRY: And once on his bicycle he broke his tooth.

PEARL: I'm not talking about that time.

HARRY: Then when are you talking about?

PEARL: I'm talking about the time he had a nervous breakdown in high school. I remember it like it was yesterday, don't tell me. Pauline, tell him.

PAULINE: Mel never had a nervous breakdown.

PEARL: Isn't that funny, I thought he had a nervous breakdown. Maybe I'm thinking of somebody else.

HARRY: You can't even remember that I don't drink coffee.

PAULINE: He must have had some terrible experiences in the Army.

HARRY: In two weeks? He wasn't there long enough to get a uniform. None of you know what you're talking about. There was never anything wrong with Mel. Never. His trouble was you babied him too much. All of you.

JESSIE: Why shouldn't we baby him? He was the baby, wasn't he?

HARRY: You babied him, that's his trouble. He never had the responsibilities as a child like I did. That's why he can't handle problems. That's why he flares up. He's a child, an infant.

PEARL: What if I put some milk in the coffee?

HARRY: I DON'T WANT ANY COFFEE ! !

JESSIE: He doesn't want any coffee, leave him alone.

PAULINE: Correct me if I'm wrong, but when Mel was a tiny baby, didn't you think his head was too large for his body?

PEARL: Mel? Mel had a beautiful head.

PAULINE: I didn't say his head wasn't beautiful. I said it was too large for his body. It always kept falling over to one side. (*She demonstrates.*)

PEARL: *All* babies' heads fall to one side. (*She demonstrates.*)

PAULINE: I know that, but he had trouble getting his up again. (*She demonstrates.*)

HARRY: . . . I was never babied. Poppa wouldn't allow it . . . I was never kissed from the time I was seven years old . . .

JESSIE: Certainly you were kissed.

HARRY: Never kissed . . . I didn't need kissing. The whole world kissed Mel, look where he is today . . . . .

They continue talking about Mel in this special family-circle vein, deciding along the way that maybe Pauline is crazy too. Harry brings them back to the main purpose of this family gathering, for which Jessie has traveled all the way from Lakewood. Harry reviews the facts: Mel is having a breakdown, he is jobless and he is penniless.

HARRY: . . . . . I don't want to pass any comments on how a man and a woman mishandled their money for twenty-seven years, it's none of my business how a man squandered a life's savings on bad investments for which he never asked my advice once, the kind of advice which has given me solvency, security and a beautiful summer place in the country, thank God, *I'll* never have a nervous breakdown . . . none of that is my business. My business is what are we going to do for Mel? How much are we going to give? Somebody make a suggestion.

> *The silence is deafening. No one speaks. No one looks at each other. There is a lot of coffee drinking, but no offers of how much they're going to give . . . After an hour of silence, Harry speaks again.*

Well?

PEARL: You're a businessman, Harry. You make a suggestion. You tell us how much we should all give.

HARRY (*thinks a moment*): . . . Let me have some coffee.

> *Pearl pours him a cup of coffee.*

So let's face the facts . . . The man needs help. Who else can he turn to but us? This is my suggestion . . . We make Mel a loan. We all chip in X number of dollars a week, and then when he gets back on his feet, when he gets straightened out, gets a job again, then he can pay us all back. That's my suggestion. What do you all think?

> *There is a moment's silence. Pauline whispers to Pearl. Pearl nods.*

PEARL: Pauline has a question.

HARRY: What's the question?

PAULINE: How much is X number of dollars?

That's what they're here to decide, Harry tells Pauline, who immediately pleads that she has limited capital. Harry reviews the situation: Mel is sick, he needs a doctor, it is the responsibility of his relatives to see him through financially, even if it takes as long as five years.

There is a stony silence, after which Pauline mutters something about the poorhouse. They try to fix a time limit for Mel's cure, but they have gotten nowhere when Edna comes into the room. Edna repeats to them all that Mel has had a nervous breakdown, he needs rest and care, and there's no telling how long his convalescence may take—maybe as long as two years. Pauline objects: "No, two years is out of the question. I refuse to go along with two years."

Harry tells Edna that he and his sisters have decided to put up the money for the medical treatment. Edna is overwhelmed by this generous offer and mentions that the bills might even run as high as $25,000. At this mention of the potential value of X, the sisters begin to protest, but Harry declares nobly: "I don't care what it's going to cost. The three of you can contribute whatever you think you can afford, *I'll* make up the deficit."

Edna is grateful for Harry's generosity but feels that she and Mel could possibly scrape up money for the treatments by selling all their valuables—it's the future that worries Edna. She feels that Mel should start a new life out of the city after he is cured, and she asks that they lend the $25,000 not for the doctor, but as a down payment to buy a summer camp offered for $100,000.

Harry reacts violently against this suggestion. A man with a nervous breakdown is in no position to take responsibility for children in a camp; he could be sued, he could go broke. They won't even give money for a doctor if he insists on buying a camp when he's cured, because running a camp could drive him crazy and he might need money for a doctor all over again.

Edna pleads, but Harry is adamant, and the sisters are no help. Edna's manner turns icy.

EDNA (*she starts for bedroom*): . . . Will you please excuse me? I've got to make some calls before I go back to the office . . . Just in case I don't see any of you for another nine years—(*Points to tray.*)—have some cookies—
          She storms into the bedroom, slamming the door behind her. They all look at each other, stunned.
HARRY: What did I say that was wrong? You're my witnesses, what did I say that was wrong?
PEARL: You said nothing wrong. I'm a witness.
PAULINE: The truth is, she doesn't *want* us to help him. She's jealous. And I was willing to give him *anything*.
JESSIE (*to Pearl*): Does that mean we're not giving for the doctor either?
PEARL (*to Jessie*): Why don't you pay attention? You never pay attention.
HARRY: A man in his condition running a summer camp. I spoke to him on the phone Thursday, he could hardly say hello.
PAULINE: Why does she hate us? What did we ever do to her? It's jealousy, that's what it is.
PEARL: That's all it is.
PAULINE: Jealousy . . . I'd like to get him out of here. He could move in with me, I'd love to take care of him.
HARRY: A man in his condition running a summer camp. It would take him until August to figure out how to blow up the volley ball.
JESSIE: If nothing is settled yet, can I give my vote to Pauline? I've got shopping to do.
HARRY: *Sit down! Nothing has been settled!* We'll have to settle it with Mel.
PEARL: With Mel? How can Mel make a decision in his condition?
HARRY: Him I can reason with. He's only had a nervous breakdown. *That* woman is crazy! Let me have some more coffee.

A key turns in the front door and Mel enters. "*He looks aged. Perhaps aged isn't the right word. Distant might describe it better. His eyes are ringed, his hair slightly unkempt with a glazed expression on his face . . . . .*" The others are put off by his not seeming to notice them, as he goes to the kitchen and pours a glass of water to take a pill. When he comes back into the room and speaks, *"his voice lacks emotion."* He just had a nice walk, he tells them; yes, he knows who they are (he kisses Pauline and Jessie but cannot seem to see Pearl until his attention is pointed directly toward her).

They all try to pretend that everything is fine, that Mel is feeling fine. Mel himself reassures them.

MEL: Am I feeling alright? . . . Yes . . . Yes, I just had a very nice walk.
PAULINE: Oh, that's nice, dear.
MEL (*looks around*): Where's Pearl? Did Pearl go home?
PEARL (*at window behind him*): Here I am, Mel. I didn't go home.
MEL (*turns*): There she is. Hiding again . . . She always used to hide from me.
HARRY (*pacing*): Mel . . .
MEL: Yes, Harry?
HARRY (*stops*): . . . Mel . . .
PEARL: Harry wants to say something to you, Mel.
MEL: What is it, Harry?
HARRY: . . . Nothing, Mel . . . Nothing . . .
MEL: You don't look well to me, Harry. You're working too hard . . . Don't work so hard, Harry.
HARRY: I won't, Mel.
MEL: You have to relax more. Three things I learned at the doctor's, Harry. You have to relax, you mustn't take the world too seriously . . . and you have to be very careful of what you say when you go out on the terrace.
            Curtain.

The News Logo comes on with another direful Six O'Clock Report, with "Stan Jennings sitting in for Roger Keating who was beaten and mugged last night outside our studio following the Six O'Clock Report . . . . ."

Scene 3

Six weeks later, on a mid-December late afternoon, Edna has just come in and is on the phone trying to find out from the building management why there's no water or electricity in the apartment (they are fixing the pipes and have turned everything off).

Mel complains about his psychiatrist, who never asks him a question but leaves Mel to talk out his troubles in monologue. "I'm curing myself, I'm telling you." The doctor isn't worth the $40 an hour Edna is slaving to pay him.

Edna reassures Mel ironically that he doesn't have to worry about her working too hard any more. Her firm has gone out of business and her job has disappeared. Edna starts to cry.

EDNA: . . . . . What's happening, Mel? Is the whole world going out of business?

MEL (*goes to her*):Okay. It's alright, Edna, it's alright.

EDNA (*sobbing*): I thought we were such a strong country, Mel. If you can't depend on America, who can you depend on?

MEL: Ourselves, Edna. We have to depend on each other.

EDNA: I don't understand how a big place like that can just go out of business. It's not a little candy store. It's a big building. It's got stone and marble with gargoyles on the roof. Beautifully hand-chiseled gargoyles, Mel. A hundred years old. They'll come tomorrow with a sledge hammer and kill the gargoyles.

MEL: It's just a job, Edna. It's not your whole life.

EDNA: You know what I thought about on the way home? One thing. I only had one thing on my mind . . . A bath. A nice, hot bath . . . (*Sobs again.*) And now the water went out of business.

MEL: It'll come back on. Everything is going to come back on, Edna. They're not going to shut us off forever.

EDNA (*she yells*): I want my bath! I want my water! Tell them I want my bath, Mel!

MEL: It's off, Edna. What can I do? There's nothing I can do.

EDNA (*yells*): Bang on the pipes. Tell them there's a woman upstairs who needs an emergency bath. If I don't sit in some water, Mel, I'm going to go crazy. Bang on the pipes.

MEL: Edna, be reasonable . . .

EDNA (*screams*): *I banged for you, why won't you bang for me?*

MEL: Ssh, it's alright, baby. It's alright.

EDNA (*still sobbing*): It's *not*. It's *not* alright. Why are you saying it's alright? Are you out of your mind? Oh, God, Mel, I'm sorry. I didn't mean that. Please forgive me, Mel.

MEL: It's alright, Edna . . . Please calm down.

As Edna begins to quiet down after her outburst, she sees more clearly than ever that they must get away from all the city problems. The doorbell rings, and as Mel goes to answer it Edna goes into the bedroom.

It's Harry, overly solicitous of Mel's condition, carrying an attache case full of apples from the country, a gift for his brother. Edna stays in the bedroom, and Harry, not understanding that she is upset, misinterprets her absence as a sign that she dislikes him. In any case, he has brought something else for Mel and Edna—a check for $25,000 as a down payment on a summer camp: "Your sisters and I contributed equally, fifty-fifty. I'm telling them about it tomorrow."

Mel appreciates Harry's generous gesture but doesn't feel he can accept such a gift from his family. Harry's feelings are hurt by Mel's refusal. Harry begins to feel sorry for himself because he was never the family favorite, as Mel was: "I had to work when I was thirteen years old. I didn't have time to be the favorite." Harry also remembers mournfully that although he was given several childhood birthday parties, no one ever sang "Happy Birthday" to him.

Harry grew up so fast that he missed being babied. "Did you ever see Pearl's family album?" he asks Mel. "There are no pictures of me as a boy. I skipped right over it. Thousands of pictures of you on bicycles, on ponies, in barber chairs . . . one picture of me in a 1938 Buick. I looked like Herbert Hoover."

There are times when Harry would be willing to change places with Mel, to trade advantages, to exchange his own business acumen for just one hour of feeling what it's like to be a family favorite. Harry finally emerges from his sulk and decides good-naturedly: "I don't want to be the favorite. Not if I have to be kissed by Jessie and Pauline."

Harry tries to offer Mel at least $12,500, but again Mel refuses and Harry takes his leave, convinced that Mel is still crazy.

Mel calls for Edna, who comes in in her bathrobe. He reproaches Edna for humiliating him by asking the family for money. Edna objects, telling Mel that she didn't ask, the family offered the money of their own accord, the day they called and Mel was tranquilized to the point of sedation. Edna, on the contrary, felt she was humiliated by Mel's family. Now Edna and Mel are raising their voices, shouting at one another.

WOMAN'S VOICE (*from above*): Will you shut up down there, you hoodlums!

EDNA (*rushes out to terrace, yells up*): Who are you calling hoodlums?

WOMAN'S VOICE: You and your loud-mouthed husband.

EDNA (*yells up*): Don't you call us names. Your husband isn't half the man my husband is. We haven't forgotten the water. We remember the water.

Mel goes out to terrace.

WOMAN'S VOICE: My husband'll be home in an hour. If you don't shut up down there, you're gonna get more of the same.

EDNA: Ha! With what? Where you gonna get the water? Where's your water, big mouth!?

MEL (*pulling her away*): Edna, get away from there. (*He is out on terrace now and calls up.*) I'm sorry. My wife didn't mean to yell. We were just discus—

He gets hit with the pail of water. He re-enters the room drenched. They did it again.

He sits.

EDNA: Where did they get the water? . . . Where did they get the water?

MEL: People like that always have water . . . They save it so that people like us can always get it.

They are both seated . . . It is silent for a few moments.

EDNA (*looks at him*): . . . I think you're behaving very well, Mel . . . I think you're taking it beautifully this time . . . That shows real progress, Mel . . . I think you've *grown* through this experience, Mel, I really do.

And suddenly, behind them on the terrace, we see it begin to snow.

. . . Maybe you're right. Maybe you really *don't* have to go back to the doctor any more . . . I'm so proud of you, Mel . . . so proud . . . because you're
better than them . . . Better than all of them, Mel . . .

> *Snow falls slowly at first but steadily increasing . . . Mel, sensing
> something, turns and looks behind him. Edna looks at Mel, then
> turns to look at the terrace to see what Mel is looking at . . . She
> sees the snow. They look at each other, then turn back and look at
> the snow again. Mel looks at his watch . . . He looks at the snow
> once more, then turns and slowly gets up and crosses to the closet
> . . . Edna watches him . . . He opens closet, and gets out his shovel
> . . . He looks at snow once more, looks at his watch, then crosses
> back and sits in his chair, one hand holding his shovel, the other
> around Edna's shoulder, a contemporary "American Gothic." Then
> we hear the voice of Roger Keating.*

ROGER KEATING: . . . This is Roger Keating and the Six O'Clock Report.
Heavy snow warnings have been posted along the Eastern seaboard tonight
and here in New York a record forty-three inches have been forecast . . .
Snow plows were ordered out on the streets and city residents were asked to
get out their shovels in a joint effort to show how New Yorkers can live together and work together in a common cause . . .

> *The curtain falls.*

OLD TIMES

A Play in Two Acts

BY HAROLD PINTER

Cast and credits appear on page 324

HAROLD PINTER was born in London October 10, 1930. He spent his childhood in Hackney, where his father had a ladies' tailor shop and young Pinter attended grammar school. He entered the Royal Academy of Dramatic Arts but left after three months to begin his theater career as an actor in Anew McMaster's company in Ireland; thence to Donald Wolfit's company in England. In 1957 he wrote his first short play, The Room. *He soon completed two other short plays,* The Dumbwaiter *and* The Birthday Party. *The latter was Pinter's first London production. His next play, the full-length* The Caretaker, *was an award-winning production of the 1960 London season. Since 1962, the year of* The Collection *which he co-directed with Peter Hall, Pinter's major work has been produced by the Royal Shakespeare Company.*

The first Pinter play produced on Broadway was The Caretaker *(1961), a Best Play of its season. This has been followed by* The Homecoming *(1967), also a Best Play and the winner of the New York Drama Critics Circle citation as the year's best,* The Birthday Party *(1967) and now* Old Times. *Pinter also directed Robert Shaw's Best Play* The Man in the Glass Booth *for both London and Broadway.*

Pinter's off-Broadway productions have taken place as follows: The Dumbwaiter *and* The Collection *(originally written for TV, a Best Play of its season), 1962;* The Lover *(originally written for TV, later produced on the London stage) 1964;* The Room *and* A Slight Ache, *1964;* Tea Party *and* The

Basement, *1968; a program of seven playlets, 1969; and* Landscape *and* Silence *at the Lincoln Center Forum Theater, 1970. Several of his scripts have also been produced in revival on and off Broadway.*

Pinter is the author of a number of screen plays including The Servant, The Quiller Memorandum, The Pumpkin Eater, Accident *and* The Go-Between. *Recent directorial assignments in the theater were James Joyce's* Exiles *at the Mermaid Theater in 1970 and the 1971 West End hit* Butley.

Pinter is married to Vivien Merchant, with one son, Daniel. They live in London.

Time: The present, autumn, night

Place: A converted farmhouse

ACT I

SYNOPSIS: The white-on-white living room of a converted farmhouse somewhere near the coast in England is sparsely furnished in modern, almost futuristic, style, comfortably including two sofas and an armchair. A big window takes up most of one wall. The front door is up left and the bedroom door up right.

Three people, *"all in their early 40s"* are motionless in their places, Deeley slumped in an armchair, his wife Kate curled up on a sofa and their house guest Anna standing looking out of the window.

Anna is present in space but not in time; she hasn't arrived yet, and Deeley and Kate discuss her imminent visit, smoking cigarettes, remembering that Kate and Anna were friends many years ago and haven't seen each other in so long that Kate scarcely remembers what Anna looked like.

DEELEY: Did you *think* of her as your best friend?
KATE: She was my only friend.
DEELEY: Your best and only.
KATE: My one and only.
    Pause.
If you have only one of something you can't say it's the best of anything.
DEELEY: Because you have nothing to compare it with?
KATE: Mmnn.
    Pause.
DEELEY (*smiling*): She was incomparable.
KATE: Oh, I'm sure she wasn't.
    Pause.
DEELEY: I didn't know you had so few friends.
KATE: I had none. None at all. Except her.

DEELEY: Why her?

KATE: I don't know.

> *Pause.*

She was a thief. She used to steal things.

DEELEY: Who from?

KATE: Me.

DEELEY: What things?

KATE: Bits and pieces. Underwear.

> *Deeley chuckles.*

DEELEY: Will you remind her?

KATE: Oh . . . I don't think so.

> *Pause.*

DEELEY: Is that what attracted you to her?

KATE: What?

DEELEY: The fact that she was a thief.

KATE: No.

> *Pause.*

DEELEY: Are you looking forward to seeing her?

KATE: No.

DEELEY: I am. I shall be very interested.

KATE: In what?

DEELEY: In you. I'll be watching you.

KATE: Me? Why?

DEELEY: To see if she's the same person.

KATE: You think you'll find that out through me?

DEELEY: Definitely.

Kate has already made her casserole for the weekend, so if Anna turns out to be a vegetarian it'll just be too bad. Anna is married but said nothing in her letter about bringing her husband along; in any event, the casserole is big enough for four.

Kate and Anna shared a flat in the old days, "lived together" as Deeley expresses it. Anna may have been Kate's only friend, but Anna had many friends, many visitors. Deeley doubts that any of these past events matter very much any more.

> *Anna turns from the window, speaking, and moves down to them, eventually sitting on the second sofa.*

ANNA: Queuing all night, the rain, do you remember? my goodness, the Albert Hall, Covent Garden, what did we eat? to look back, half the night, to do things we loved, we were young then of course, but what stamina, and to work in the morning, and to a concert, or the opera, or the ballet, that night, you haven't forgotten? and then riding on top of the bus down Kensington High Street, and the bus conductors, and then dashing for the matches for the gasfire and then I suppose scrambled eggs, or did we? who cooked? both giggling and chattering, both huddling to the heat, then bed and sleeping, and all the hustle and bustle in the morning, rushing for the bus again for work, lunchtimes in Green Park, exchanging all our news . . . . .

Anna has now joined them for the weekend visit. It is evening, after dinner, as Anna continues her reminiscence of their youthful days in London, when they would spend hours drinking coffee and listening to the conversation around them in artists' cafes.

Kate pours coffee for the three of them. Deeley informs Anna "We rarely get to London," then brings brandy for all.

Anna congratulates them on choosing this place for a retreat but confesses she would miss London. Deeley's work takes him away a lot, and Kate enjoys her walks to the sea. Anna makes small talk with Deeley about Kate's good cooking; about her own home near a quite different sort of seacoast.

Finally they get around to the subject of Kate, who seldom interrupts them. Kate (Deeley informs Anna) makes very few friends even here ("She lacks curiosity") and likes long walks alone; at times her face seems to float when he holds it between his hands and then releases it. Kate is a dreamer (Anna informs Deeley) who once actually forgot what day it was, "but she was always a charming companion."

Anna's use of words like "lest" and "gaze" is admired by Deeley. Deeley and Anna begin to communicate to each other in the rich language of the lyrics from popular love-song standards like "Lovely to Look At," "Blue Moon," "All the Things You Are," "I Get a Kick Out of You," "Smoke Gets in Your Eyes" and "These Foolish Things," taking turns singing lines or phrases at each other. The song lyrics serve as both a challenge and a recognition signal.

Deeley launches into a reminiscence of going to see *Odd Man Out* in some remote neighborhood.

DEELEY: . . . . . There were two usherettes standing in the foyer and one of them was stroking her breasts and the other one was saying "dirty bitch" and the one stroking her breasts was saying "mmnnn" with a very sensual relish and smiling at her fellow usherette, so I marched in on this excruciatingly hot summer afternoon in the middle of nowhere and watched *Odd Man Out* and thought Robert Newton was fantastic. And I still think he was fantastic. And I would commit murder for him, even now. And there was only one other person in the cinema, one other person in the whole of the whole cinema, and there she is. And there she was, very dim, very still, placed more or less I would say at the dead center of the auditorium. I was off center and have remained so. And I left when the film was over, noticing, even though James Mason was dead, that the first usherette appeared to be utterly exhausted, and I stood for a moment in the sun, thinking I suppose about something and then this girl came out and I think looked about her and I said wasn't Robert Newton fantastic, and she said something or other, Christ knows what, but looked at me, and I thought Jesus this is it, I've made a catch, this is a trueblue pickup, and when we had sat down in the cafe with tea she looked into her cup and then up at me and told me she thought Robert Newton was remarkable. So it was Robert Newton who brought us together and it is only Robert Newton who can tear us apart.

> *Pause.*

ANNA: F.J. McCormick was good too.

DEELEY: I know F.J. McCormick was good too. But he didn't bring us together.

> *Pause.*

You've seen the film, then?

ANNA: Yes.

DEELEY: When?

ANNA: Oh . . . long ago.

> *Pause.*

DEELEY (*to Kate*): Remember that film?

KATE: Oh yes. Very well.

> *Pause.*

DEELEY: I think I am right in saying the next time we met we held hands. I held her cool hand, as she walked by me, and I said something which made her smile, and she looked at me, didn't you, flicking her hair back, and I thought she was even more fantastic than Robert Newton.

> *Pause.*

And then at a slightly later stage our naked bodies met, hers cool, warm, highly agreeable, and I wondered what Robert Newton would think of this. What would he think of this I wondered as I touched her profoundly all over. (*To Anna.*) What do you think he'd think?

ANNA: I never met Robert Newton but I do know I know what you mean. There are some things one remembers even though they may never have happened. There are things I remember which may never have happened but as I recall them so they take place.

DEELEY: *What?*

ANNA: This man crying in our room . . . . .

Anna remembers coming home one evening and finding a man sitting in the armchair, sobbing, while Kate was sitting on the bed, silent, drinking coffee. Anna went to bed without a word to either of them (she recalls), and later the sobbing stopped and the man approached Anna's bed and looked down at her. "But I would have nothing to do with him, absolutely nothing." After a while the man went out, but he came back, because later that night Anna awoke and saw the man lying across Kate's lap in the bed. In the morning he was gone.

Anna and Deeley remember how animated Kate was years ago, as Kate reproaches them for talking about her here in this room as though she were dead. Kate stands up and offers Anna a cigarette. A subtle wave of warmth flows into Anna's manner toward Kate. Deeley orders, "Stop that!"

Anna tells Deeley how delighted she was to hear the news of Kate's marriage 20 years ago; she knew that Kate would be deeply in love before deciding to get married, and she assumed that Deeley would be the kind of a man who would make a similar commitment. Also, Anna felt that Deeley would be the right sort of man for Kate because Kate had always been interested in the arts. (Deeley's occupation is thus far unidentified, but we will learn that he makes movies.) Anna and Kate used to spend hours together at the Tate, or exploring London for old churches, or at various performances. "For example," Anna concludes, "I remember one Sunday she said to me, looking up from the paper, come quick, quick, come with me quickly, and we seized our handbags and went, on a bus, to some totally obscure, some totally unfamiliar district and, almost alone, saw a wonderful film called *Odd Man Out*."

Deeley makes no response to this statement; instead, he tells Anna how enormously he enjoys his job, which takes him all over the world. Anna observes that he must leave Kate alone by herself for long intervals, and perhaps Anna could come and keep Kate company at such times—Anna's husband wouldn't mind.

With an edge of sarcasm, Deeley observes that he has probably seen Anna's and her husband's villa high in the hills outside Taormina when he visited Sicily for a movie he wrote and directed. Deeley wonders about Anna's yacht, but Kate wonders about the villa's marble floors—does Anna walk on them barefoot? Yes, but not on the terrace, where the stones are too hot.

Deeley speaks rather disparagingly of his talent, his fame, his profession, and even of Sicily. Kate interrupts with a polite question.

KATE (*to Anna*): Do you like the Sicilian people?
    Anna stares at her. Silence.
ANNA (*quietly*): Don't let's go out tonight, don't let's go anywhere tonight, let's stay in. I'll cook something, you can wash your hair, you can relax, we'll put on some records.
KATE: Oh, I don't know. We could go out.
ANNA: Why do you want to go out?
KATE: We could walk across the park.
ANNA: The park is dirty at night, all sorts of horrible people, men hiding behind trees and women with terrible voices, they scream at you as you go past, and people come out suddenly from behind trees and bushes and there are shadows everywhere and there are policemen, and you'll have a horrible walk, and you'll see all the traffic and the noise of the traffic and you'll see all the hotels, and you know you hate looking through all those swing doors, you hate it, to see all that, all those people in the lights in the lobbies all talking and moving . . . and all the chandeliers . . .
    Pause.
You'll only want to come home if you go out. You'll want to run home . . . and into your room . . .
    Pause.
KATE: What shall we do then?

ANNA: Stay in. Shall I read to you? Would you like that?
KATE: I don't know.
        Pause.
ANNA: Are you hungry?
KATE: No.
DEELEY: Hungry? After that casserole?

But Deeley's remark doesn't succeed in bringing the two women back to the present. They continue living in the past, London roommates of 20 years before.

ANNA: Would you like to ask someone over?
KATE: Who?
ANNA: Charley . . . or Jake?
KATE: I don't like Jake.
ANNA: Well, Charley . . . or . . .
KATE: Who?
ANNA: McCabe.
        Pause.
KATE: I'll think about it in the bath.
ANNA: Shall I run your bath for you?
KATE (*standing*): No. I'll run it myself tonight.
        Kate slowly walks to the bedroom door, goes out, closes it. Deeley stands looking at Anna. Anna turns her head towards him. They look at each other. Fade.

ACT II

The bedroom of this converted farmhouse is very much like the living room —white-on-white, one large window, doors to the bathroom at left and sitting room at right, furnished with two divans and an armchair which are placed as were sofas and chair in the living room, but in reversed positions.

Anna is sitting on a divan. A glow in the bathroom door's glass panel signifies that Kate is still in her bath. Deeley enters with the coffee tray.

Deeley informs Anna that he remembers her well from the old days in The Wayfarers Tavern. Anna's reaction is not so much a denial as disbelief. But Deeley is sure he remembers her, the darling of a saloon bar full of "poets, stunt men, jockeys, stand-up comedians" and a man with ginger hair named Luke. "Never," Anna replies, But Deeley insists.

DEELEY: I've bought you drinks.
        Pause.
Twenty years ago . . . or so.
ANNA: You're saying we've met before?

DEELEY: Of course we've met before.
Pause.
We've talked before. In that pub, for example. In the corner. Luke didn't like it much but we ignored him. Later we all went to a party. Someone's flat, somewhere in Westbourne Grove. You sat on a very low sofa, I sat opposite and looked up your skirt. Your black stockings were very black because your thighs were so white. That's something that's all over now, of course, isn't it, nothing like the same palpable profit in it now, it's all over. But it was worth-while then. It was worthwhile that night. I simply sat sipping my light ale and gazed . . . gazed up your skirt. You didn't object, you found my gaze perfectly acceptable.
ANNA: I was aware of your gaze, was I?
DEELEY: There was a great argument going on, about China or something, or death, or China *and* death, I can't remember which, but nobody but I had a thigh-kissing view, nobody but you had the thighs which kissed. And here you are. Same woman. Same thighs.
Pause.
Yes. Then a friend of yours came in, a girl, a girl friend. She sat on the sofa with you, you both chatted and chuckled, sitting together, and I settled lower to gaze at you both, at both your thighs, squealing and hissing, you aware, she unaware, but then a great multitude of men surrounded me, and de-manded my opinion about death, or about China, or whatever it was, and they would not let me be but bent down over me, so that what with their stinking breath and their broken teeth and the hair in their noses and China and death and their arses on the arms of my chair I was forced to get up and plunge my way through them, followed by them with ferocity, as if I were the cause of their argument, looking back through smoke, rushing to the table with the linoleum cover to look for one more full bottle of light ale, looking back through smoke, glimpsing two girls on the sofa, one of them you, heads close, whispering, no longer able to see anything, no longer able to see stocking or thigh, and then you were gone. I wandered over to the sofa. There was no one on it. I gazed at the indentations of four buttocks. Two of which were yours.
Pause.
ANNA: I've rarely heard a sadder story.
DEELEY: I agree.
ANNA: I'm terribly sorry.
DEELEY: That's all right.

Deeley never saw her in The Wayfarers, or in the neighborhood, again.
Anna changes the subject, remarks at the length of time Kate is taking over her bath, which she always relishes. Deeley comments on how carefully Kate soaps herself, how clean she emerges. Anna adds, "She floats from the bath. Like a dream. Unaware of anyone standing, with her towel, waiting for her, waiting to wrap it round her . . . . ."
They discuss the possibilities of each of them in turn drying and powdering

Kate after her bath. Deeley suggests finally that he dry and powder Kate while Anna watches and gives advice. But Kate comes out of the bathroom in her robe, already dry, enjoying her after-bath feeling, just as Deeley comments that he wouldn't have recognized Anna if he'd happened to meet her at The Wayfarers today.

Watching Kate in her bathrobe walk across the room first to the window and then to a divan, Anna and Deeley express their feelings by singing alternate lines of "They Can't Take That Away From Me." They seem to be fencing with each other using lines of the song as weapons, as symbols of their memories of Kate, thrust and riposte as line follows line of the song.

Anna and Deeley finish by commenting on how beautiful Kate looks. Kate admits that she feels fresh after her bath in the country-soft water: "That's one reason I like living in the country. Everything's softer. The water, the light, the shapes, the sounds. There aren't such edges here." She would like to live somewhere with a very hot, lazy climate some day. The only thing nice about a big city, Kate concludes, is the blurring effect of "rain on your lashes."

It's also nice, Anna observes, to have a cozy room to stay home in; she pours Kate a cup of coffee. Deeley expresses concern about whether Kate has dried herself thoroughly, and this brings to Kate's face a special smile like the one Deeley noticed after the showing of *Odd Man Out*.

Kate returns to the pretense that she and Anna are at home in London 20 years before; she wants to know if Charley and McCabe are coming over. They decide they both like two others named Duncan and Christy better.

Deeley deliberately breaks the spell. Anna reminisces about how shy Kate used to be, perhaps still is, bringing to mind a parson's daughter like a Brontë: "But if I thought Brontë I did not think she was Brontë in passion but only in secrecy, in being so stubbornly private."

What's more, Anna can remember Kate's first blush.

DEELEY: What? What was it? I mean why was it?

ANNA: I had borrowed some of her underwear, to go to a party. Later that night I confessed. It was naughty of me. She stared at me, nonplussed, perhaps, is the word. But I told her that in fact I had been punished for my sin, for a man at the party had spent the whole evening looking up my skirt.

Pause.

DEELEY: She blushed at that?

ANNA: Deeply.

DEELEY: Looking up *your* skirt in *her* underwear.

ANNA: But from that night she insisted, from time to time, that I borrow her underwear—she had more of it than I, and a far greater range—and each time she proposed this she would blush, but propose it she did, nevertheless. And when there was anything to tell her, when I got back, anything of interest to tell her, I told her.

Kate liked to turn out the light and listen to Anna's tales in the dark—an

intimate form of communication which sounds to Deeley like a marriage relationship.

DEELEY: You say she was Brontë in secrecy but not in passion. What was
she in passion?

ANNA: I feel that is your province.

DEELEY: You feel it's my province? Well, you're damn right. It is my
province. I'm glad someone's showing a bit of taste at last. Of course it's my
bloody province. I'm her husband.

     Pause.

I mean I'd like to ask a question. Am I alone in beginning to find all this distasteful?

Anna sees nothing distasteful in the situation; she has merely come to visit
an old friend and meet her husband. Deeley pretends that he is concerned
about Anna's husband being left alone in Sicily. Kate comes to life and warns
Deeley: "If you don't like it go," go off to China, Sicily, anywhere.

Anna assures them that she has come "not to disrupt but to celebrate" a
valued friendship. As in the old days, Anna insists, all that concerns her is
Kate's happiness.

Deeley reveals to Kate in a rough, slangy, staccato style of expression—
quite different from the fluid, almost poetic style in which he recounted the incident to Anna—that he and Anna have indeed met before, at The Wayfarers. It almost seemed that Anna was pretending to be Kate; and, wearing
Kate's underwear, she allowed Deeley to gaze at her thighs.

Kate decides that probably Anna fell in love with Deeley's face and wanted
to comfort him "in the only way a woman can." Kate remembers that in
those days they regarded most men as crass and brutish compared to Deeley.
Deeley judges that his own behavior in looking up Anna's skirt was fairly
crass—"If it was her skirt. If it was her."

Anna assures him coldly, "Oh, it was my skirt. It was me. I remember your
look . . . very well. I remember you well."

At this, Kate turns on Anna with "I remember you dead." Kate remembers standing and looking down upon Anna as a corpse with a face that was
somehow begrimed, lying in immaculate sheets.

KATE: . . . . . When you woke my eyes were above you, staring down at
you. You tried to do my little trick, one of my tricks you had borrowed, my
little slow smile, my little slow shy smile, my bend of the head, my half closing
of the eyes, that we knew so well, but it didn't work, the grin only split the
dirt at the sides of your mouth and stuck. You stuck in your grin. I looked for
tears but could see none. Your pupils weren't in your eyes. Your bones were
breaking through your face. But all was serene. There was no suffering. It had
all happened elsewhere. Last rites I did not feel necessary. Or any celebration. I felt the time and season appropriate and that by dying alone and dirty
you had acted with proper decorum. It was time for my bath. I had quite a

lengthy bath, got out, walked about the room, glistening, drew up a chair, sat naked beside you and watched you.

Pause.

When I brought him into the room your body of course had gone. What a relief it was to have a different body in my room, a male body behaving quite differently, doing all those things they do and which they think are good, like sitting with one leg over the arm of an armchair. We had a choice of two beds. Your bed or my bed. To lie in, or on. To grind noses together, in or on. He liked your bed, and thought he was different in it because he was a man. But one night I said let me do something, a little thing, a little trick. He lay there in your bed. He looked up at me with great expectation. He was gratified. He thought I had profited from his teaching. He thought I was going to be sexually forthcoming, that I was about to take a long promised initiative. I dug about in the windowbox, where you had planted our pretty pansies, scooped, filled the bowl, and plastered his face with dirt. He resisted . . . with force. He would not let me dirty his face, or smudge it, he wouldn't let me. He suggested a wedding instead, and a change of environment. (*Slight pause.*) Neither mattered.

Pause.

He asked me once, about that time, who had slept in that bed before him. I told him no one. No one at all.

> *Long silence. Anna stands, walks towards the door, stops, her back to them. Silence. Deeley starts to sob, very quietly. Anna stands still. Anna turns, switches off the lamps, sits on her divan, and lies down. The sobbing stops. Silence.*
>
> *Deeley stands. He walks a few paces, looks at both divans. He goes to Anna's divan, looks down at her. She is still. Silence. Deeley moves towards the door, stops, his back to them. Silence. Deeley turns. He goes towards Kate's divan. He sits on her divan, lies across her lap. Long silence.*
>
> *Deeley very slowly sits up. He gets off the divan. He walks slowly to the armchair. He sits, slumped. Silence.*
>
> *Lights up full very sharply. Very bright. Deeley in armchair. Anna lying on divan, Kate sitting on divan.*
>
> *Curtain.*

VIVAT! VIVAT REGINA!

A Play in Two Acts

BY ROBERT BOLT

Cast and credits appear on page 330

ROBERT BOLT was born in England, at Sale in Cheshire, on Aug. 15, 1924. After his graduation from Manchester University, where he majored in history, he became a school teacher. He wrote a Nativity play for his children to act at Christmas time and soon after decided to concentrate on playwriting. His first play for adults was The Last of the Wine, *about the atomic bomb, and his second,* The Critic and the Heart, *was performed at Oxford. He made his London debut with* Flowering Cherry, *which ran there for more than a year but lasted only 5 performances when brought to Broadway in 1959. Another script,* The Tiger and the Horse, *never crossed the Atlantic.*

Bolt's first international hit was A Man for All Seasons, *about Sir Thomas More, which was acclaimed on Broadway when it opened on Nov. 22, 1961, was named a Best Play of its season and won the Critics Award for best foreign play, ran for 637 performances into June 1963 and was promptly revived in January 1964 by ANTA for 17 more performances.* Vivat! Vivat Regina! *is the second historical play by Bolt to make the Best Plays list and score a hit with Broadway audiences. Among the playwright's other works are a children's play* The Thwarting of Baron Bolligrew *and the movies* Lawrence of Arabia, Ryan's Daughter, Dr. Zhivago *and his own* A Man for All Seasons, *the last two of which won Academy Awards. He is married to Sara Miles, the actress.*

Time: The second part of the 16th century

Place: France, England and Scotland

ACT I

SYNOPSIS: Outdoors at a royal chateau in France, two ladies are accompanying Claud Nau, *"an elderly bachelor; gentle, learned, anxious, utterly upright, deeply affectionate."* Nau is waiting to meet the French queen, Mary of Scotland, married to young Francois II. Nau, who was once Mary's teacher, faintly disapproves of a "mucky tale" the ladies are telling about a Cardinal's love life.

A Chamberlain heralds Mary's entrance. The Queen of France and Scotland is *"overbred, refined and passionate; sympathetic, beautiful, intelligent and brave. But sensual and subjective. Born a queen, deferred to from the cradle, it is a tribute to her nature that she is not simply spoiled. But she mistakes her public office for a private attribute."* Today Mary is not in the mood for mucky tales, she in her turn is looking for Claud Nau, who has ridden hard from Scotland. Mary dismisses the ladies and is surprisingly haughty with her good old teacher, rebuffing him when he calls her by the old pet name "Mignon." Stiffly, Mary asks after her mother.

NAU: Before all else I am to tell you that your mother loves you well, Your Grace.

MARY: My mother does not know me, sir.

NAU: That is her sorrow too. The ruling of your Scottish kingdom in your name has kept your mother from you. And that is love and not the lack of it.

MARY: A kind of love.

NAU: The hardest kind.

MARY: Aye. And granite too is hard. But I have yet to hear it is a good material to make a cradle of. I tell you sir, no care of state would keep me from my child . . . Come, let me know your charges.

NAU: Your Grace has in a manner touched upon my first. Your Grace, your mother wonders if Your Grace may presently, in probability, expect a child.

MARY: She wonders that?

NAU: Your Grace.

MARY: I wonder much that she should wonder that. I wonder you should ask . . . Have you not waited on my husband, Claud?

NAU: But now, Your Grace.

MARY: Did you not see his face? They sometimes draw the curtains, to spare his visitors his face.

NAU: I saw, Your Grace.

MARY: And having seen his face—And having seen the suppurating sores that batten on his poor young mouth—and having seen his ancient eyes—sir, do you ask—do you of all men dare to ask if presently in probability I may expect a child?

NAU (*kneeling*): Pardon.

MARY: No! You shall not have my pardon now . . . (*But seeing the pathetic kneeling figure, on a sudden note of lament and reproach.*) Oh Claud, I was a little girl; and you were all the father and the mother that I had; you taught me how to read and write; and when I got my lessons well—Good God, you sat me on your knee and said I was your best of little girls! And when I got my lessons ill my sharpest punishment was your displeasure! . . . And you stood by and said no word and let them marry me to syphilis! No—!—You shall not have my pardon now!

Nau did speak against the marriage, he tells Mary, but he was threatened with the axe if he persevered in opposing it. Mary's mother made the marriage because, as Nau explains, "Your husband is the King of France. You are the Queen of Scots. And France and Scotland joined might get your English kingdom too."

But Mary wouldn't kiss her husband on the mouth for any kingdom on earth. She prays for him to die so that she may get a husband she can love.

The second part of Nau's commission is a treaty requested by the English Queen Elizabeth, negotiated by Mary's mother. One of its conditions is that Mary stop exhibiting the British leopard on her Cloth of State but show the Scottish lion only. In exchange, Elizabeth will withdraw her English troops from Scotland. Mary considers Elizabeth "a bastard and a heretic" who has no real right to a throne. She is reluctant to sign, but Nau argues that Elizabeth's army is living off Mary's suffering people.

MARY (*shrugs*): Well I will sign it. And she is Queen indeed.

NAU: In this you show more Queen than she.

MARY: Aye anything that makes me less makes me more Queen, Claud, does it not?

NAU: There is much truth in that.

MARY: There is no truth at all in that. And I am sick of hearing that. Diminish me, the Queen's diminished. Starve me and the Queen will fail. If I am sickly, she is pale. I am the Queen and more the Queen the *more* I am myself. (*It is a credo, passionate . . . . .*)

Nau informs Mary that Elizabeth is going through a similar identity crisis, a choice between being more of a woman or more of a queen. She has fixed her affections on a commoner, Robert Dudley, and means to marry him. Dudley is married, and Nau believes the lovers are planning to murder his wife. ("Let them do it!" exclaims Mary, convinced that such a marriage would weaken Elizabeth's hold on the throne).

Finally Nau tells Mary her mother is dying but her final words of advice to

CLAIRE BLOOM AND EILEEN ATKINS IN "VIVAT! VIVAT REGINA!"

Mary were: "Our daughter must think first upon these high affairs of state, not discomposed by any grief she may be pleased to feel, upon our dying." Mary's heart is touched by the pathos and selflessness of this statement and she suffers a few moments of genuine grief, wishing she had known her mother better. There is a fanfare and Nau cries "Ho there—the Queen!"

The leaves and flowers of the outdoor French setting disappear, and the lights change to a cold interior. (A note by the playwright addressed to the scene designer reads in part as follows: "You will see that the stage serves at one moment for the Court of England and at the next for the Court of Scotland. I hope the properties will be solid and pleasurable in themselves to look at, but that the lighting, not the properties, will create the changes of time and place and mood. I hope the costumes will convey the extravagances and extremes of the period, yet not distract the audience nor tie up the actors. I have assumed: one, a flat-topped pyramid or flight of shallow steps, supporting a screen or curtain in the first act and the throne in the second act; two, a table with stools; three, a 'pulpit' though this could be a mere lecturn; four, a hanging or revolving Cloth of State. My intention is to maintain a smoothly continuous narrative to which changes of time and place will seem incidental.")

After servants place a table and throne, William Cecil enters echoing Nau's cry of "Ho there—the Queen!" Cecil is *"a top flight civil servant, reasonable, courteous, ruthless."* Elizabeth his Queen enters and sits on the throne. She is *"personable, willful, highly strung. But schooled to clear sight and tuned to self-discipline by a dangerous and lonely childhood. Commencing her reign as a natural, perhaps just faintly neurotic, young woman, her strength of character is such that she meets the unnatural demands of Queenship with increasing brilliance, in an increasing rage of undisclosed resentment."*

Cecil tells the Queen flatly that her marriage to Dudley is impossible; "He must to prison," pending an inquiry into the sudden, violent death of his wife. Elizabeth is stubborn, but when she hears that Mary cried "Let them do it!" she reflects. Cecil argues that whether Dudley is innocent or guilty he must go to prison and await the inquiry that will clear him in either case; and in neither case can Elizabeth marry him.

Dudley is summoned to be interrogated. He strides in carrying rapier and belt, glances at Cecil, drops to one knee before the Queen. He is *"a tall, hard, virile animal; unintellectual but nobody's fool."* Elizabeth commands him to rise and tell them the facts of his wife's death. Dudley testifies that his wife sent all the servants away to a fair in Abingdon. She was alone in the house; Dudley was away in London. Apparently she was killed in a fall, because when the servants came home they found her lying in the hall at the foot of the stairs with her neck broken.

Dudley admits he had been spreading false rumors that his wife was failing, and even that he received the news of her death "right gladly" (Elizabeth admits she shared this feeling too). She couldn't have fallen by accident (Elizabeth observes) because her body was lying fifteen feet from the stairs. She was thrown, Dudley admits, not by any murderer but by herself, in a defiant suicide. That is all Dudley knows or will say—Elizabeth must decide whether he is guilty or innocent. The Queen is ready to judge Dudley innocent and expects Cecil to agree with her.

CECIL (*shrugs*): Then I say, with Mary Stuart: "Let them do it."
DUDLEY: What's this?
CECIL: Sir, the Queen believes you innocent—and I am ready to believe you innocent—but the Queen, alas, is not the country, nor am I—and you must understand—
DUDLEY: I understand no word you say. Can't you speak like a man?

CECIL: To speak like a "man," sir—If the Queen takes you to bed she will lie down Elizabeth the First and rise the second Mrs. Dudley.

DUDLEY: . . .*Zounds!*—

He lunges for his sword.

ELIZABETH: Put that up!

She gets up, goes and stands below the Cloth of State.

You may withdraw.

DUDLEY: I?

ELIZABETH: . . . Yes Robin.

DUDLEY: And he stays?

ELIZABETH: Yes Robin.

Dudley stares one moment; snatches up his rapier.

DUDLEY (*to Cecil*): Cecil, you have ruined me, and I will not forget it.

CECIL: You are wrong sir, I have saved you. And belike I have made your fortune. And you will forget it.

Dudley snatches a bow at Elizabeth, goes.

ELIZABETH: Cecil, were the summers better than they are now, when you were a child?

CECIL: Your Grace—? . . . Yes, Your Grace, I share that common illusion. The summers then were nothing but sunshine. I and the weather have declined together.

ELIZABETH: Who raised you, Cecil?

CECIL: My father and my mother, Madam.

ELIZABETH: It is not sunshine you remember; it is love. My father killed my mother and disowned me, and I can't remember a summer when it was not raining after that. I was raised by cautious strangers in the shadows, between prisons. I was taught: mathematics, Latin, Greek and caution, too well; and saw too soon where love could lead. Prisons were familiar, and so I put my heart into protective custody. But Cecil, I mislaid the key, and it has lain in darkness, cold and calcifying these twenty years. And Cecil, Robin had a magic word, which opened doors for me . . . You said that you would be my servant and my friend, and will you be my jailer?

CECIL (*moved, but*—): Something of each, Your Grace. Your Grace's Councillor.

ELIZABETH (*looks at him*): Aye. Well then. To Council.

CECIL: And . . . the gentleman?

ELIZABETH: To prison. (*Going.*)

CECIL: Your Grace.

She hears the discreet satisfaction in his voice and turns.

ELIZABETH: But Cecil, we believe him innocent. And if from now until your dying day you whisper one word to the contrary, we will punish you.

The lights and the scene change to St. Andrew's Kirk in Scotland where John Knox (*"a pedant and a demagogue, a nasty combination. But palpably, frighteningly sincere"*) is declaiming against the trappings of the more ornate Catholic ceremonies. He is also analyzing the status of women, deciding that "woman is a lesser thing than man" and therefore her dominion as ruler is "monstrous." Knox calls Mary Stuart a she-cat whose young royal French husband's death was "mysterious"—"He was, they say, unable to supply her raging appetite."

The lights change and a bagpiper enters followed by Mary, ladies in attendance, Nau and Mary's close friend and companion Rizzio, *"a likeable hedonist, affectionate and skeptical; but a lightweight; precarious."*

Mary is dressed in crimson, her entourage in *"grey silk aflutter with white favors."* Scots lords wearing black and somber plaids stand in a grim-faced line behind the piper.

Morton, the leader of the Scots, notices that Mary and her following are faintly amused at the noise of the bagpipes, so he signals the piper to cease playing. Mary apologizes for her lack of appreciation of this music and rebukes Rizzio for strumming a mocking chord on his small beribboned lute.

Mary signals out Lord Bothwell (*"shrewd, coarse-natured, irresponsible; but uncomplaining as unpitying, genuinely a law unto himself; a dangerous vortex to dependent natures"*) and thanks him for conducting her safely from France to Scotland. A half-turned personal compliment from Bothwell momentarily warms Mary, but she soon returns to formalities when Bothwell mentions his position as Lord Lieutenant of the Border.

MARY: They tell me you steal sheep across the Border, Bothwell.
BOTHWELL: Aye, Madam, English sheep.
MARY: We would not have our cousin Elizabeth provoked.
BOTHWELL: Oh, they're not her sheep. They're Harry Percy's.
MARY: Lord Bothwell, we have come here to rule.
BOTHWELL: And welcome to Your Grace's bonny face.
    He goes out.
MARY: Morton, this Border raiding must be stopped.
MORTON: It can't be stopped, Your Grace. Lord Bothwell is the head of the Clan Hepburn.
MARY: So?
MORTON: The Border is Hepburn country.
MARY: All Scotland is my country, my lord.
MORTON: But Your Grace has no men.
MARY: But haven't my Lords in Council men?
MORTON: Aye, Madam. *We* have.
MARY: Well, no doubt we will attune ourselves to both your music and your manners. Now, we will to supper.
MORTON: Now we must to Kirk, Madam.
MARY: "Must" we?
NAU (*quick confidential warning*): Yes.
MARY (*swallows her anger, shrugs*): Well, then, to Kirk.

The lights change to a church interior, where Knox makes a pointed Biblical reference to a great whore dressed in scarlet and sitting on a throne.

Mary takes this as a lapse of tact, if not an insult, and Knox explains that he is referring not to her but to the Church of Rome, which Mary hotly defends. Its priests may be fallible (Mary argues) yet the holy church remain perfect. Insolently, Knox disputes Catholic dogma with Mary; he resents the priest's intrusive presence between Christ himself and his worshipers in the Catholic Mass: "Christ's sacrifice is a cold spring, put here for my soul to drink at freely—which else must perish in this *desert* of a world! But now the Church has led this spring into a tank, and on this tank the priest has put a tap—the Mass—by which he turns Christ's mercy on and off and sells it by the dram!"

Insulted, Mary threatens Knox with royal anger, her temper mounting, naming the Kirk "a market—where a scurrilous low peasant brings his dirty produce! And buys treason from disloyal lords!" She departs for her own chapel to hear Mass, but not before Knox has added the insult of condescension to the injury of insolence.

The scene changes to a ceremony conducted by a Church of England Bishop, blessing the whole Establishment and its authoritative individuals, "steering our course between the Scylla of Rome and the Carybdis of Geneva."

The scene changes to the English Court; Dudley, now out of prison and a Councillor, is trying on his new robe. He is grateful to Cecil for the rise in his fortunes, and he is ready to abide by Cecil's instructions in a matter concerning the Queen, who enters with another Councillor, Walsingham.

The Queen and her Council make much ado about the appointment of a new Dean for Durham, close to the Border in the North. They select a Dr. Boze, who leans toward Geneva, in favor of a Dr. Glover, whom Walsingham calls "three parts Catholic." The Bishop protests the appointment and recommends his own nephew, a Dr. Culpepper, as a compromise, but Elizabeth stands firm on her Council's decision.

The next matter of state is the news from Scotland. Apparently the King of Spain is negotiating to marry his son to Mary. To Elizabeth's irritation, Cecil advises that "Spain would not marry his son to Scotland if he could marry him here." If, on the other hand, Spain were to marry Scotland and make war by land coming down from the north, England would be lost.

ELIZABETH: And the Prince of Spain is a dribbling dwarf! A diminutive monster who foams at the mouth!
    CECIL: I cannot answer for his person, Majesty; I will answer for my policy.
        Dudley shifts.
    ELIZABETH: Aye, what do you think, Councillor Robin?
    DUDLEY: Too much to speak, Your Grace.
    ELIZABETH: Then quit my Council.
    DUDLEY: Robin thinks, war rather, death rather, let England go. Your Grace's Councillor thinks no, let love go; Your Majesty must keep England.
        Elizabeth shifts, looks away.
    ELIZABETH (*harshly*): Love? Who spoke of love? . . .

Cecil has prepared a suitably wooing letter to be signed by Elizabeth and sent to Madrid at once. Almost casually, the Queen rewards Dudley's combination of personal devotion and self-sacrifice by making him Earl of Leicester, on Cecil's recommendation.

While the Queen and Walsingham "freeze," denoting a change of scene, Dudley confides to Cecil that he did not relish this episode. Cecil observes, "We dig for gold because we relish gold, sir. Not because we relish digging."

When Dudley and Cecil turn to speak to Elizabeth once again they are all at Hampton receiving the visit of the Spanish ambassador, De Quadra, who reports the Spanish prince "transported" with delight at Elizabeth's offer of marriage. De Quadra hands the terms of the Spanish King's dowry to Cecil; to the Queen he presents a locket with a likeness of the prince. Elizabeth finds him "well-favored" but learns from De Quadra that he is nowhere near as tall as Dudley, indeed of rather small stature.

Cecil and Walsingham balk at the dowry terms which include Spanish galleys in English ports to use against the Netherlands, England's best trade customer. De Quadra agrees that the galleys are negotiable; not so the marriage form, however. There must be a Catholic ceremony, if not before the Protestant one, then immediately after.

WALSINGHAM: Why immediately?

DE QUADRA (*shrugs*): The same day.

WALSINGHAM: Why the same day?

DE QUADRA (*testy*): Before the *night,* good Master Walsingham . . . In Catholic eyes your English form of marriage would be—(*Spreads his hands, delicately.*)—a form.

WALSINGHAM: As would the Catholic form in English eyes.

DE QUADRA: *Some* English eyes.

He says it significantly and looks at Cecil.

CECIL: Immediately after.

DE QUADRA: Excellent. The—er—form of the form is important too. Your Grace must know—for I alas am told to tell Your Grace—my master will not have his son's soul jeopardized by any form which makes a mock of God.

ELIZABETH: Then tell your master that we think ourselves as careful of our soul as any king in Christendom and would permit no form which mocked at God!

DE QUADRA: Your English Church is, er, flexible, Your Grace. Here it is one thing, there another. Here a priest who is almost a Catholic, there a priest who is no one knows what. There have lately been some church appointments, as that of Doctor Boze at Durham, which have much dismayed my master.

ELIZABETH: Zounds sir, will you make our church appointments now?

DE QUADRA: Oh dear. Of course these vexatious questions would not be, if His Highness were to wed some Catholic queen.

He lets it hang. Cecil and Dudley look at Elizabeth. She sighs.

Soon Elizabeth is writing a letter to the Bishop at Durham instructing him to appoint Dr. Glover instead of Dr. Boze, causing the Bishop to believe "The woman's mad!"

De Quadra having departed satisfied, Elizabeth wonders if this policy will do; Cecil advises candidly that perhaps it won't, but it must *seem* to until Queen Mary marries. Elizabeth thinks maybe they ought to help Mary find a husband, and Cecil agrees. Privately, he suggests to Dudley that since he can never marry Elizabeth (although "You have her heart and always will") it would be a master-stroke of policy to offer marriage to Mary. Very reluctantly, Dudley agrees.

Elizabeth's envoy to Scotland, a young man named Davison, enters and reports that the Spanish embassy has left Scotland and gone home. Their departure has enraged the Queen of Scots.

ELIZABETH (*a grunt of satisfaction*): Ha. And does her rage become her?

DAVISON: Yes, Your Grace. All moods become her. (*He says it defiantly.*)

ELIZABETH (*stares*): God's death, send no more *young* ambassadors to Scotland, Cecil.

> She gets up, goes and examines Davison as an object of deep, half-amused interest.

Describe her then.

DAVISON: Your Grace, I cannot.

ELIZABETH: Cannot? Is she tall?

DAVISON: As Your Grace.

ELIZABETH: Thin?

DAVISON: As Your Grace.

ELIZABETH: We are twins?

DAVISON: No, Your Grace.

ELIZABETH: What color is her hair?

DAVISON: Your Grace, her hair is shadow colored.

ELIZABETH: God's death, he's written poetry. Her eyes?

DAVISON: Her eyes change color with her moods, Your Grace.

ELIZABETH: You seem much taken with her moods. Has she many?

DAVISON: Yes, Your Grace.

ELIZABETH: Aye, sometimes she is right childish, is she not?

DAVISON: Yes, Your Grace. And sometimes—(*Breaks off.*)

ELIZABETH: Well?

DAVISON: Right royal, Your Grace.

ELIZABETH: Hoo! And sometimes, as we hear, she is sportive, hey? Gallante, hey? Wanton?

DAVISON: Yes, Your Grace. And cruel and wilful and unfair. But then there come such sudden sinkings, such declension into soft submission, as sets a man on a high horse.

> His voice vibrates with an emotion too serious to laugh away. She leaves him, on a shaky laugh.

ELIZABETH: God's death it ought not to be hard to find a suitor for the lady, Cecil.

She turns to find Cecil and Dudley making furious faces at Davison.

Elizabeth questions Davison about Rizzio. Davison suggests that Mary could never love Rizzio, he is too small; and Elizabeth sees that the forlorn Davison is small too, hence rejected. While the Queen comforts Davison, she mentions that they must find a tall suitor; then, looking at Cecil and Dudley, she understands their scheme to offer Dudley in marriage to Mary, suddenly and all at once. She lets an "O-o-o-oh" escape. At last she agrees, though it nearly breaks her heart. She dismisses Cecil and the stammering Dudley on their errand of hard, unfeeling policy.

Left alone with the Queen, Walsingham tells her of a Catholic plot against her life in Durham. Once more Elizabeth writes to the Bishop and orders him to install his non-controversial nephew after all. The Bishop pleads that his nephew has now gone to Bristol, and Elizabeth draws herself up and commands: "Lord Bishop! Do as we command or by God we will unfrock you! (*She takes a great gasp of air and almost shouts.*) Elizabeth! Queen!"

The scene changes to the Court of Scotland, where Cecil has offered Robert Dudley, Earl of Leicester, in marriage to Queen Mary. Mary feels herself insulted by the offer. She wants none of Elizabeth's rejects and has chosen a husband for herself: the Englishman Lord Darnley. Cecil is appalled; he calls Darnley "a ladyfaced horseman, empty and idle." He reminds Mary that Elizabeth has forbidden this marriage.

MARY: I do not study Elizabeth's reasons. But can guess them. Lord Darnley is a Catholic.

CECIL: Yes madam.

MARY: And bears the Tudor blood.

CECIL: Yes Madam.

MARY: Aye—and better blood than hers because it is legitimate—

CECIL: Madam, you forget yourself—

MARY: And Europe knows that any child of mine by Darnley would be heir to the English throne. These are Elizabeth's reasons. And mine.

CECIL: Well Madam, I council you to put them from your mind. Lord Darnley is forbidden to quit England and will not come if you call him.

MARY: Call him.

NAU: Lord Darnley.

Darnley enters. Cecil aghast.

Mary insists that she loves Darnley (*"a tall, athletic, good looking aristocrat; too young, too merely pleasant to withstand the heavy personal and public pressures bearing on him"*). Cecil sounds a stern warning to Mary and Darnley, then departs. Darnley can't help observing that much of the world agrees with Cecil that he is unfit to be Mary's husband. Mary disagrees; she tells

Darnley he has aroused her love as well as her interest. Darnley makes the same pledge in return.

MARY: Be careless then, not thoughtful. You know that I love you.

DARNLEY: I know that you would.

MARY: Harry, I have told you, and I swear before the Saints: I'll have a husband I can love, or else I will have none at all.

DARNLEY: Would you have loved the Prince of Spain?

MARY: Nay, do not shame me, love. That was to have been a stroke of State. Yet Harry, even him I would have tried to love.

DARNLEY: And now you are trying to love me.

MARY: My lord, we were so born that we must choose fit marriage mates politically. It is God's generosity that we have found fit mates we naturally love. We are not to scrutinize His generosity, we are to love. If we attend to love, my lord, both dignity and reputation will come begging at our door.

Uplifted, he goes to her. They kiss.

Oh come my love—and let's be married!

The Scottish lords disapprove of Mary's marrying a Catholic. Morton, as their spokesman, makes it clear to Darnley that he is not to be accepted as their ruler. He will rule only Mary's person, not her kingdom.

The scene changes to the court of England, where Elizabeth is informed by Cecil that the Commons wishes her to marry, since Mary is expecting Darnley's child. Morton is visiting the English court, and he tells Elizabeth the news from Scotland. At first Mary adored Darnley so that "she hung upon him like a peddler's bag." He proved useless in Council, however, which incited Mary's anger and contempt. Finally Darnley took to frequenting whores, but not before Mary became pregnant; she is now three months along and praying for a son.

Nevertheless Elizabeth will not marry now; she will take her time. She leaves Morton and Cecil to probe each other's thoughts. Neither penetrates the other's intentions and Cecil goes off as the scene reverts to Scotland—Mary, accompanied by her ladies, Rizzio and Nau, is announcing her pregnancy to the Scots lords. She expects them to rejoice, but they do not.

MARY: If God grants me a son, you'll have a Scottish King.

MORTON: His mother for a start is French.

MARY: My father bore the blood of Bruce. And I was born at Lithgow Castle. When I was five years old I do confess I went away to France and got my breeding there—forgive me, it was an error of my youth. If my manner is offensive, sobeit and good night, I can no more. My child, on whose behalf I do demand your loyalty, will be both born and bred in Edinburgh—and fully Scots as you.

MORTON: And will he so?

MARY: I do not think I understand you, sir.

MORTON: I think you do. This child, my lords, will have a little French on one side, on the other—(*Glares at Rizzio.*)—half Italian!

> *Mary raises a hand as though to strike him, controls herself, turns away.*

Rizzio protests his innocence. Mary dismisses Morton and the lords, but Bothwell remains behind, requesting a private audience, assuring Mary she has nothing to fear from him. Mary sends away her entourage. Bothwell speaks most solicitously of Mary's confinement but contemptuously of Darnley. When Mary flares to anger, Bothwell mimics her "If my manner is offensive, sobeit and good night." Actually, Bothwell appreciates Mary's temper and tells her so.

BOTHWELL: I like your manner fine.
> *She looks at him.*

It's very pretty.

MARY: Good heavens, my lord, that is the second compliment within these same four years.

BOTHWELL: Now fancy you rememberin' the first.

MARY: Remember it—? How not? A compliment in Scotland is a memorable thing. It stands out like a lily on a heap of dung.

BOTHWELL: That's no' a bad description of yourself in Scotland.
> *She looks at him cautiously. They exchange a little mocking bow.*

MARY: I'll hear your matter.

BOTHWELL: It's men and means you want I think?

MARY: It is.

BOTHWELL: You do not mean to meddle with the Kirk?

MARY: The Kirk, sir? Are you pious?

BOTHWELL: When the Kirk threw down the Catholic Church I got some fine broad meadow land that used to belong to the Catholic Church. I'm awfu' pious about those meadows.

MARY: If I got men and means from you, I could not meddle with your meadows.

BOTHWELL: That's true enough. What terms are you offerin'?

MARY: No terms. I have taken out an option on the future, Bothwell; and you have wit enough to see it.

BOTHWELL (*smiling approval*): You're no fool, are you?

MARY: No sir; did you think I was?

BOTHWELL: You married Darnley.

MARY: . . . What is it in me, Bothwell, that provokes you and your fellow lords at every turn and all the time to strip me of my dignity? Is it merely that I am a woman?

BOTHWELL: A bonny woman.

MARY: So?

BOTHWELL: Worth strippin'.

Another compliment, Mary recognizes, though hardly one fit for a queen. Bothwell sees that Mary is somewhat fascinated by his masculinity and insolently he ventures into familiarity. Mary holds him at arm's length but offers him the post of Lord Protector of her child. Bothwell refuses the post because he would have to turn Catholic and "if our ways are different and you would like our ways to match—you must change your ways! To mine!"

Infuriated, Mary calls Bothwell "a tyrant and a sodomist, an enemy to innocence, a vampire and a demonist" and orders him to depart, never to look upon her again. Bothwell, still amused at Mary's passion, departs as Nau and Rizzio enter.

Since the news of her forthcoming childbirth had no power to bring the Scottish lords into line, Mary will look for help elsewhere, she tells her friends. She will write in Latin to the Pope in Rome for money to buy mercenaries in Milan. As she writes, Darnley enters and Nau and Rizzio tactfully withdraw. Darnley approaches Mary tentatively, pathetically, but Mary treats him rudely, accuses him of becoming maudlin from drink, is exasperated when Darnley tries to attract her attention.

> *She blows out an angry sigh, throws down pen and raises her glowering face. But seeing him, her expression alters. She rises, staring, backs away. Rizzio and Nau come forward, alarmed. Darnley averts his face from them.*

NAU: Your Grace.

MARY: There are sores on his mouth . . . Harry, look at me—What are those sores on your mouth?

> *Her reaction has appalled him. He rises, stares wildly at Rizzio and Nau.*

DARNLEY (*defiantly*): It's the frost! I—

MARY: By God I know that frost—Stand off—!

DARNLEY (*has approached*): Mary—

MARY: Sir, will you not stand off? You are unclean—!

DARNLEY (*almost runs to exit, turns, and in a voice shaking with feeling*): . . . God save me from a loving woman.

> *He goes. She starts after him.*

MARY: Harry . . . (*She checks.*) Oh Jesus—the child . . . !

Rizzio assures Mary that according to the timing of the pregnancy her child is safe from the father's disease. Mary is comforted and wishes to be comforted still further; she orders Rizzio to bring his lute and follow to her quarters. Nau warns Rizzio not to go after her, but to no avail.

Morton comes in with the lords and finds the letter to Rome. They all have acquired Church lands and are in danger of losing them if Mary brings Catholic mercenaries to Scotland. Morton hatches a plan to thwart Mary by making an ally of Darnley.

When Darnley comes in, the lords flatter him and defer to him. Morton lifts Darnley's spirits by telling him: "We think the husband of the Queen should be a King." They excite Darnley's jealousy by hinting that the sounds of lute and laughter signify too close a familiarity between Mary and Rizzio. They induce Darnley to sign the articles of conspiracy to put the adulterer to death, hinting that this murder will clear Darnley's way to a crown.

Once signed and sealed, Rizzio's death is delivered. The lords tear away the curtain masking Mary's quarters. Before the Queen can utter a cry, the lords fall upon Rizzio and kill him with a dozen dagger wounds. Morton commands Darnley to strike in his turn, and when Darnley stands paralized one of the lords seizes Darnley's dagger and throws it to Morton, who plunges it into the already mangled corpse.

> *Bothwell and Nau enter at the run, check as lords present daggers, crouching. Bothwell spreads his empty hands, approaches and looks at corpse.*

BOTHWELL: God's death, my lords, you're very thorough. Lord Darnley, I think this is yours.

> *Tosses dagger to Darnley.*

DARNLEY (*piteously*): Mary, I—

> *He dashes from the stage.*

MORTON: Now, Lord Bothwell, are you here to hinder or to help?

BOTHWELL: Neither, Lord Morton.

MORTON: Then you're in my road.

BOTHWELL: Then may I get out of it?

MORTON: Right out of it, Bothwell, out of Edinburgh now.

BOTHWELL: Your Grace.

> *Mary raises her head and looks at him.*

It seems that I must leave you to God's care. I'm for Dunbar.

> *He goes.*

MORTON: Now Madam, though this was rough yet it was justice.

MARY: No my lord, your pardon, but this was not justice.

> *She descends unsteadily, Nau hovering anxiously at her side. She crouches at the corpse and sees the wounds.*

Oh God . . .

> *She rises, bewildered.*

He was my friend.

NAU: Good God my lord—What have you done?

MORTON: Our duty. Naething more.

> *Going. Lords following. He snarls at them.*

Shift it!

> *Morton and lords go, dragging corpse. Mary watches covertly.*

MARY (*when they have gone*): Morton, Ruthven, Lindsay, Douglas, Glencairn, Falconside and Kerr—

NAU (*startled*): Madam?

MARY: Remember them! . . . Remind me every day that they must die.

NAU: Oh, Madam, this is wild—!—The castle is full of their men!

> *She looks about, rises from her knees.*

MARY: So we must quit it.

NAU: There is a guard on every door!

MARY: There will be no guard on the kitchen door. Come.

He follows her, shaken, bewildered.

NAU: But Madam, where?

MARY: Where? To the Border—Dunbar!

They go. Curtain.

ACT II

A throne is at the top of the pyramid, and an ornate golden casket—a Christening font—is placed at the bottom. John Knox complains that although the murder of Rizzio seemed to be a "Godly deed," things have gone badly with Darnley's and Morton's affairs ever since.

Elizabeth enters with Walsingham, Dudley, Cecil and Morton discussing the killing. Morton maintains they had a royal warrant for Rizzio's execution, signed by Darnley. Mary has fled and joined the powerful Bothwell, so that Morton's faction needs Elizabeth's help. She cannot make a policy of supporting disloyalty, but after they have gone she orders Walsingham to give Morton's lords some money, "As little as will keep them rebellious."

Elizabeth sends the others away and stands before the font—which she has sent Mary as a token of support against the rebels—and muses to herself on the subject of her Scottish rival: "She escapes . . . down little stairs and greasy passages, she escapes, through the kitchens. I do not know where the kitchens are . . . And then in the dark, in the sweet smelling stables, she saddles her own horse; he knows her, he is quiet . . . *I* cannot saddle a horse. And then she rides, down rocky screes, through mountain rivers, two days and nights two hundred miles, she must have ridden without sleep . . . . . And then this Bothwell raises men—half-naked men whose whole wealth is a sword—and drives her enemies from Edinburgh—and for what? Why, for herself . . . And now she returns, but easily now, easily. (*Harsh.*) For she is big with child. And that child is my heir, for I am a barren stock!"

Elizabeth ascends to the throne. At her feet—and a nation away—at the golden font which was Elizabeth's gift, Mary's child is baptized "James Stuart, Prince of Scotland, Ireland and England."

Elizabeth exits and Mary, rejoicing, takes her infant from the Archbishop. Nau reminds her that the time has come to appoint a Lord Protector; Bothwell confidently assures him the job is spoken for. To Bothwell's astonishment, Mary calls upon one of the nobles present, Lord Mor, to take charge of the child as Lord Protector. Lord Mor carries the child off and the others exit, leaving Bothwell and Mary alone.

BOTHWELL (*quietly*): So you don't trust me.

MARY (*frightened, placating*): With myself I trust you.

BOTHWELL (*looking away from her, gloomily grunts*): Mebbe.

MARY: I have no choice but trust you, being your slave.

BOTHWELL: Don't you know yourself better than that? You're nobody's slave.

MARY: It is you who do not know me. See.

She kneels, clasping his legs, abased.

BOTHWELL: That's just extravagance. Let go my legs. You want it both ways, Mary. Like—you'll feed me food on a fork. But I must eat it whether I've a mind to it or not, or you'll sling the plate across the room. You've a bluidy awful temper, d'you know that?

MARY: Yes.

BOTHWELL: An you were my wife, I'd have taken a whip to you before this.

MARY: Well, I would be your wife in anything I can.

Bothwell disagrees. Mary likes having her cake and eating it too, the husband Darnley in Glasgow and the lover Bothwell in Edinburgh. Bothwell challenges Mary to bring her husband here. Mary accepts. She departs, and Bothwell summons his kinsman Ormiston to make plans to collect enough kegs of powder to blow the house known as Kirk o' Fields off its foundations.

Bothwell receives a letter from Mary. Darnley is very sick and she feels sorry for him. But they are on their way to Edinburgh. Bothwell orders another hundred pounds of powder for Kirk o' Fields.

Mary enters with her husband; Darnley is a ghost shape wearing *"a weird white mask, white gloves and slippers, a fanciful white dressing gown"* hiding the ravages of his disease. Mary is protective of Darnley, who thinks himself reconciled with the Queen. Bothwell has prepared quarters for Darnley, not at the castle, but at Kirk o' Fields, Mary means to go with him. She cannot (Bothwell tells her), they are committed to attend a dance.

Darnley is sent away, and Mary and Bothwell join hands and go into the motion of the Pavane. Then *"the stage rocks in blinding light. A distant explosion bellows. Uproar, dancers scattering . . . . ."*

When the lights come up, Mary is seated on the throne with Bothwell beside her. Elizabeth and her court are now the dancers; together with other characters they are not actually in Mary's presence but symbolize the people of her time. Mary tries to placate an accusing John Knox, while Elizabeth suggests that Bothwell be brought to trial for Darnley's murder.

MARY: We thank Your Grace, but this gentleman has stood his trial and is found innocent.

KNOX: We know the manner of that trial, and if he's innocent, why so is Satan!

MARY: The law stands over all of us, and we think as the law does, that the gentleman is innocent. In proof of which know all the world that we are married.

POPE: A Protestant pantomime my child, no marriage. Repudiate him.

MARY: Your Holiness, although the form was empty yet our hearts were in it; I account us married in the eyes of God.

PHILIP: Poor fool, poor *fool!*

KNOX: Oh my what sympathy these Catholics show for their own kind. The King of Spain thinks himself a verra pious man. Well here we have adultery, and bigamy, and murder—! And what says His Pious Majesty? Why, not a word.

PHILIP: We nothing doubt but that the lady was involved against her will and merits leniency.

KNOX: The woman is a common criminal and merits death.

The dancers go.

MARY: Lord Mor—Give me my child.

She half descends to meet Mor who moves to meet her; but . . .

MORTON: Give her the child and you give it to Lord Bothwell, Mor. Is that how you'll discharge your trust?

Mor hesitates.

MARY: Lord Mor—!

MOR: I cannot, Madam, while that man is by your side.

Mary will lose even her child by clinging to Bothwell. The lords mean business; they have already hanged Ormiston and threaten Bothwell until Mary offers herself as a hostage for him. Bothwell leaves, promising to return for Mary: "I only met one woman in my life; d'you think I'll no come back for her?"

Morton tries to bargain with the Queen—she must repudiate Bothwell and all will be as it was before. Mary refuses; she chooses to go to prison instead, promising to escape and join Bothwell to take her revenge.

At Elizabeth's court, Morton reports that he and the lords are in control of Scotland, with Mary safely and surely locked up at Loch Leven. Elizabeth gives him some more money to support his cause. No sooner has he reassured the Queen, however, than Cecil enters to report that Mary has escaped, with the help of the jailer Black Douglas's "impressionable" son. To Elizabeth's great embarrassment, Mary has taken refuge in England with the Earl of Westmoreland at Carlisle and has written a letter to Elizabeth throwing herself upon the Queen's mercy and requesting an audience.

ELIZABETH: Why me . . . ? Why my mercy . . . ? We are enemies.

Cecil is watching her carefully.

CECIL (*carefully*): If you see her, Your Grace, you will seem to condone the murder of Lord Darnley.

WALSINGHAM: That woman alive in England is a Trojan Horse. Execute her!

ELIZABETH: It would not be seen as the execution of a murderess, good Francis, it would be seen as the elimination of a rival.

CECIL: Yes . . . It would *be* the elimination of a rival of course.

ELIZABETH: No.

CECIL: I wonder if the matter is not Scottish domestic . . .

ELIZABETH: Good . . . (*Smiling.*) Lord Morton, you may take our sister back to Scotland and—(*Smile goes flat and expressionless.*)—do with her what you will.

    MORTON (*reproving grin*): Oh no, Your Grace. She's yours. An' Your Grace is welcome.

          Takes money, going.

Where she is, there is no safety.

          He goes. They look after him.

    WALSINGHAM: There is no safety for Your Grace's person *while* she is. She has connived at murder once and will again.

Cecil wishes for proof of Mary's complicity in Darnley's murder. Walsingham supplies a letter written by Mary to Bothwell when Mary was away in Glasgow to fetch Darnley. A marked portion reads "Alas my lord, you have sent me here to do a work I much detest," and "Certainly he fears the thing you know of and for his life." Most of the letter is an expression of deeply-felt passion for Bothwell; its obvious sincerity strikes Elizabeth to the heart as well as convinces her that it is genuine and no forgery. Bothwell did not burn it as requested at the end, he kept it, and now it exists as evidence against the Queen of Scots sufficient to cause Elizabeth to order Mary imprisoned at Sheffield, but treated as a Queen.

    WALSINGHAM: She may correspond?

    ELIZABETH: She may do anything a Queen may do. Except leave Sheffield Castle.

    WALSINGHAM: It is not wise, Your Grace.

    ELIZABETH: It is our will! (*Turns at exit, speaks unconvincingly.*) We fear the French connection. (*She goes.*)

    WALSINGHAM (*severely*): Her Grace is too merciful!

    CECIL: I do not think that this is altogether mercy. I think our Queen sees Mary in the mirror.

    WALSINGHAM: You are grown so subtle, Master Cecil, you will shortly be invisible.

In confinement, Mary tells Nau she has learned that Bothwell no longer intends to return for her. He has taken service in Denmark with its King, and has even found another woman. Mary realizes that she should have staked all of her fortunes not on Bothwell but on one little man—her child—and she misses him so much that she has imaginary conversations with the boy every night before she goes to sleep.

    Mary is a restive prisoner. She stalks restlessly around her room, where she has insisted against her jailer's wishes that a Cloth of State be hung. She is permitted to ride horseback in the castle park and (she tells Nau) she has met a man there who has promised to carry letters secretly. Nau warns his mistress that her very life will be in jeopardy if she is caught in a secret correspondence. Mary replies *"quietly and with a wealth of inner suffering which rebukes him"* to Nau: "God gives each one of us a different life to live. And if we live it well he gives us everlasting life in Heaven. And if we live it ill, as surely I have lived right ill, yet still may Heaven be merciful. But if we live it not at all, nay then I think Heaven has no mercy—and God made me a queen! I did not beg to be so born. And maybe I was not equipped to be so born. But since I was so born, by Heaven I will so live!"

As the scene changes, a prisoner is dragged by jailers into the presence of Walsingham and Cecil. As a result of correspondence with Mary, the Pope has issued an edict which almost forces English Catholics to choose between Church and Queen, to regard Elizabeth even as a target for possible assassination.

The prisoner is a priest in disguise and has been plotting to murder the Queen and give over the port of Norwich to Catholic forces including Spanish troops. They offer the priest death by the axe instead of by fire if he will confess that Mary—whom the priest considers Queen of England by divine right—knew about these treasonous plans. The priest refuses their offer and is dragged off, as Elizabeth enters. Like Cecil and Walsingham, she has aged (*"Her face, framed in an extravagantly flaring collar, is more obviously painted"*). They tell her of the priest's plot to shoot her down and bring in Spanish troops; but without proof that Mary is implicated Elizabeth will take no action against the Queen of Scots.

The Duke of Parma is in the Netherlands with 50,000 men, a strong threat just when England's loyalty is divided between two Queens. Elizabeth must take some action, and Cecil advises her to recall Dudley because he is a strong military leader. Elizabeth reacts in anger; Dudley is in disgrace because he has "betrayed" her by getting married and keeping it a secret from Elizabeth for many months.

Finally Elizabeth agrees, and Dudley is recalled. He enters—like the rest, he has grown no younger with the passing years. His manner toward Elizabeth is devoted but formal. He informs her that his wife is expecting a child. Elizabeth replies by calling the Council meeting to order, asking for Dudley's advice on what action to take in regard to Parma's forces in the Netherlands.

DUDLEY: I think if we had time to muster, and if the country were united, we might shock them.

ELIZABETH: . . . And what do you think might unite the country?

DUDLEY: The death of Mary Stuart.

ELIZABETH (*softly*): By God, time was you had other plans for Mary Stuart.

DUDLEY (*uncomfortable*): Time has changed, Your Grace.

ELIZABETH: And you with it. I hope you will prove a constant soldier Robin; for Heaven knows you're an unsteady swain.

    Silence. She throws it off.

(*Brisk.*) How long to muster?

DUDLEY: Three to muster, three to train.

ELIZABETH: Six months in all. And Parma's veterans have not been out of iron for sixteen years—And he will shock them. Cecil, this fifty thousand—will they come overland?

>*She sits bolt upright and expressionless during what follows, a political computer gathering information.*

CECIL: They will if France will let them through, Your Grace.

ELIZABETH: And will France let them through?

CECIL: Not if Your Grace will make the French alliance.

ELIZABETH: Meaning the French marriage.

CECIL: Yes, Your Grace.

ELIZABETH: Walsingham, has Spain sufficient ships to carry fifty thousand?

WALSINGHAM: Your Grace, there is such hammering in the Spanish shipyards that Spain shakes.

ELIZABETH: Have we sufficient ships to sink them?

CECIL: Not yet, Your Grace.

ELIZABETH: And you require six months to muster.

DUDLEY: Yes, Your Grace.

De Quadra seeks an audience, which Elizabeth refuses. She makes up her mind to tell the French Prince she'll marry him, without really intending to do so; besides, he is a Catholic, and her people might not approve. She orders Cecil to send the Prince 100,000 crowns to stimulate his interest in her. She sends orders to Sir Francis Drake to build ten ships quickly, out of green wood if necessary, they need to be used only once to stop an Armada. She orders Dudley to raise troops and engage Parma in the Netherlands, remembering to tell Dudley finally, "Robin, I am glad to see you."

Cecil much admires his Queen's resolution and policy, telling her, "You are a greater monarch than your father, and he was a man among men, Your Grace."

The others gone, Elizabeth finally grants De Quadra an audience. The Spanish ambassador wants to know why the English shipyards are suddenly so busy, why so many volunteers are arming, why such a large sum was presented in France. These moves are more likely to provoke enmity than foster amity with the Spanish King, De Quadra declares.

In reply, Elizabeth hands De Quadra Walsingham's dossiers detailing the conspiracies raised against her with the help of Spain, including one by Anthony Babington who planned to poison England's Queen, with De Quadra's complicity. Elizabeth permits the ambassador to return to his homeland and considers herself lenient in not arresting him on the spot.

Walsingham has proof of Mary's involvement in these conspiracies, but not what he calls "proof *pedantic.*" He must have this sort of proof before she will act, Elizabeth tells him; meanwhile she will take Cecil's advice and hint to Scotland that their boy king might rule England some day, a hint designed to keep the Scots pacified.

The scene changes to the castle prison of Mary Queen of Scots. Nau has found a conspiratorial letter smuggled in a keg of beer and signed by Babington, mentioning a conspiracy and naming names and asking for Mary's signature as the final authority to act. Even Mary is suspicious of this letter as "something too ingenious."

Walsingham enters. Mary, still suspicious, taunts him with the keg of beer but can get no rise out of him. Walsingham has brought other letters for Mary, compromising letters which he has opened before delivery. To prevent her from conspiring (Walsingham tells Mary), she is henceforth to lose much of her freedom of movement—no more going for walks or rides, no large retinue, no visitors. Adding insult to injury, Walsingham also demands that Mary take down her Cloth of State, the very emblem of her royalty.

Mary is furious. When Walsingham leaves the room, she recklessly contemplates the letter which both she and Nau suppose may have been planted in the keg of beer by her enemies. Mary is almost willing to take the risk and sign the call for action—"It could be my release and *her* death-warrant." Nau persuades her against it by invoking the safety of her son.

Walsingham comes back into the room with a basket.

MARY: Another thing?
> *Walsingham lifts the lid of the basket. Mary goes and her face changes, as she takes from the basket a selection of child's toys. Her voice wavers.*

These are the presents I have sent to my son.

WALSINGHAM: And your letters.
> *Takes out and dumps down a wad of letters, taped.*

MARY: He—?—He has kept them?

WALSINGHAM: He has never received them.
> *Tilts basket. Mary takes out two more packets like the first.*

MARY: Never received . . . ? Small wonder that he never wrote to me!

WALSINGHAM: He has no wish to. Nor to see you. He knows you.

MARY: He—?

WALSINGHAM: He has been instructed, Madam, in the manner of your life; and in the manner of his father's death.

MARY (*whispering, incredulous*): You have blackened me?

WALSINGHAM: How blacken black?

MARY: Nay I think this is some practise Master Walsingham; you would provoke—
> *She fawns on him.*

WALSINGHAM: —Upon my soul it is the truth!

MARY (*incredulous, pleading*): But of all my letters . . . not one?

WALSINGHAM: Madam, you have had no communication! . . . It is my mistress who has played the mother's part.
> *He goes. Nau watches in horror and pity as Mary, motionless, slides helplessly into tears which she makes no attempt to hide.*

MARY (*her face darkening and her voice shaking with passion*): Oh she . . . She-ee! . . . Shee-ee! . . . Elizabeth!
> *She speeds to the table and snatches up the pen.*

As Walsingham has hoped, Mary signs the fatal letter over all Nau's warnings and protests. Mary calls in the brewer who smuggled it into her prison and gives him the signed letter to take to the conspirators. Candidly, Mary tells the brewer that she knows he may be a traitor and mean to take the letter to Elizabeth, ". . . . . we only ask that you should tell our sister that before we die we'd have one day—nay one half day of conversation with our son. Ask this of her in charity."

The brewer protests, but of course the letter is soon placed before Elizabeth by Walsingham as the "proof pedantic" she required. At the same time Cecil places before Elizabeth the order for Mary's execution. There is no escape for Elizabeth; she must sign it. She does so and gives it to Davison to carry out, warning him at the same time that after the execution, officially, she will pretend he had no true authority and will put him in the Tower for awhile. Davison, somewhat resentful, doubts the world will be deceived by this lie.

ELIZABETH (*looks at him fathomlessly then*): The world is deceived by nothing. The world must be given something by which to seem to be deceived . . . Well sir, do it.
She mounts toward the throne. Davison picks up warrant.
DAVISON: I think you burden me too much, Your Grace. Your Grace must tell me what to do.
ELIZABETH: Why, man—your office!
Drums. Enter Mary, attendants, Nau, Priest, all in black. Mary stands at the head of the carpet and looks along it, head high but held sideways as though unable to look directly at what is at the end of it, off stage.
MARY (*to Nau*): Love, you have stayed with me long. Spare yourself this last?
NAU: An' it please Your Grace, I'll stay a little longer yet. (*He breaks down.*)
MARY: Hush now!
DAVISON: Are you ready, Madam?
MARY (*formal*): I claim God's fatherly protection for my son; and Christ's incomprehensible compassion for my soul.
ALL: Amen.
MARY: I'm ready now sir.
She moves but Davison kneels quickly before her.
DAVISON: Pardon.
MARY: For what?
DAVISON: Your Grace, I brought the warrant.
He looks up at her. She frowns.
MARY: Be comfortable, sir. The thing you brought was nothing much. A death-warrant requires a royal signature. And I signed my own.
She moves, looks off again at the axe and block, isolated.
And if your great and Virgin Queen should wonder why I signed it, you are

to tell her this: There is more living in a death that is embraced than in a life that is avoided across three score years and ten. And I embrace it—thus!

> *She throws off the black, revealing scarlet head to foot.*

Sir!

DAVISON: Madam?

MARY: Now.

> *Plunges off along the carpet. They tumble after, taken by surprise. Drum beat. Stops convulsively. Cecil enters. Looks at Elizabeth, cautiously.*

ELIZABETH: She was an adulterous, disorderly, lecherous strumpet!

CECIL: Yes, Your Grace.

ELIZABETH: She was a *fool!*

CECIL: Yes, Your Grace.

ELIZABETH: She was—Nay there are no words for saying what she was. Only words for saying what she was not.

> *Cecil approaches the foot of the throne.*

CECIL (*seriously, persuasively*): As—worthy; thoughtful; self-denying; diligent; prepared.

> *She looks at him, attentive, mistrustful.*

Your Grace, next year or the next, Spain sends against us his Invincible Armada. And we shall astonish them! And as their great ships founder and they drown they will cry out: "How? How is this possible?" And our cannon will tell them: "Elizabeth! Elizabeth made it possible!" And they will hear it across Europe in Madrid—!—Aye Madam, they will hear it across Europe— and down centuries.

> *In the ringing silence left by his rhetoric her voice comes hard and dead.*

ELIZABETH: Very like, Master Cecil; very like . . . (*She almost snarls.*) And then?

> *She rises painfully and makes toward exit. A triumphant fanfare. She ignores it. The curtain falls.*

MOONCHILDREN

A Comic Play in Two Acts

BY MICHAEL WELLER

Cast and credits appear on page 333

MICHAEL WELLER was born in New York City in 1942. He was educated at Stockbridge School, Windham College and Brandeis University, where he studied music composition with Arthur Berger, Harold Shapiro and the late Irving Fine and received his B.A. in music in 1965. Meanwhile, during his senior year at Brandeis he began writing plays and skits for his college musi-cal society, and after graduation he went to Manchester in England to study drama. A Weller play entitled How Hoho Rose and Fell in Seven Scenes *was done in England at an Exeter festival in 1968, and in the same year his* The Making of Theodore Thomas; Citizen *received a student production at Toyn-bee School of Drama, where he was teaching playwriting.*

Moonchildren was produced under the title Cancer *last season in London for 36 performances by the Royal Court Theater, which had commissioned it. It was produced as* Moonchildren *by Washington, D.C.'s Arena Stage for 40 more performances this season in Weller's American professional theater de-but, before moving on to his New York theater debut in the Broadway pro-duction which won him his first Best Play citation.*

Weller has completed another Royal Court-commissioned script, The Great-est Little Show on Earth, *about President Kennedy and Lee Harvey Oswald. He is married and lives in London.*

Time: Around 1965-66

Place: A student apartment in an American university town

ACT I

Scene 1: Early evening, fall

SYNOPSIS: The stage is pitch black dark and remains that way through the beginning of the scene, as we hear one young female and two young male voices (Ruth, Mike and Cootie) discussing a cat, who is going to have kittens any minute.

COOTIE: What I want to know is how are we gonna see her when she starts giving birth?

RUTH: Jesus, how stupid can you get? We'll turn on the light.

COOTIE: Yeah, but the whole thing is how do we know when to turn on the light? Like, what if we're too early?

MIKE: Or too late?

COOTIE: Yeah, what if we're too late?

MIKE: Or right in the middle . . .

COOTIE: Holy shit, yeah, what if we flip on the old lights when she's halfway through a severe uterine contraction? She'll go apeshit and clamp up and kill a kitten. And if the kitty gets really lucky and wiggles free it'll grow up into a pretty fucked-up animal.

MIKE: We're sowing the seeds of a neurotic adult cathood . . .

COOTIE: . . . doo-wah, doo-wah . . .

RUTH: Hey, shut up, you guys, willya? Willya shut up?

COOTIE: We're just pointing out that's a shitty way to start life.

RUTH: I know the noise, all right?

MIKE: I think there's probably a more scientific way to watch a cat give birth.

RUTH: Everybody shut the fuck up.

> *A long pause.*

NORMAN: How much longer are you guys gonna have the lights out?

COOTIE: Jesus Christ, Norman, why do you have to go creeping up like that? We forgot you were even in here.

NORMAN: I'm not creeping up, I'm just sitting here. Maybe you didn't notice when you came in, but I was reading this book. I mean, I thought you were only gonna have the lights out for maybe a few minutes or something, but you've already been in here for about an hour and . . . and I really can't read very well with the lights off. I mean . . . you know . . .

COOTIE: Norman, you can't rush a cat when it's giving birth. You try to rush a cat in those circumstances and you come smack up against nature.

MIKE: Norman . . .
NORMAN: What?
MIKE: Don't fight nature, Norman.
NORMAN: I'm not. I'm just trying to read this book.
COOTIE (*pause*): Is it a good book?
RUTH: For chrissakes, what's the matter with everyone?
NORMAN: I don't know. It's a pretty good book. I don't follow all of it. It's written in a funny kind of way so you forget a lot of it right after you've read it. A lot of guys in the mathematics department say it's pretty good. I don't know though.

Norman won't take the book into his own room to read it, even though the cat business could take all night.

The hall door up right opens, letting a little light in, by which can be seen Norman sitting at the round kitchen table with his book, and Ruth, Mike and Cootie crouched over a cardboard box with a hole in it. Dick is standing in the doorway trying to make out what is going on in the room, which seems to be a combination living room-kitchen, the common room as it were, of a group of students who have rented this apartment.

Dick is urged by the others to close the door, which he does, returning the room to total darkness. But it is soon lit up again because Dick opens the icebox door and the automatic light inside goes on. *"You can see the kitchen pretty clearly now. The icebox is very old, dating from the time when electricity was replacing the iceman. It's just a box on legs with one of those barrel-shaped coolers with vents on top. You maybe can't see it yet, but on the door of the icebox there's a large inscription that reads GOD IS COOL. Stacked neatly against one wall are 816 empty two-quart milk bottles, layer upon layer with planks between each level. It's a deliberate construction. There's a huge copper stack heater in one corner by the sink, and it has a safety valve at the top with a copper tube coming out of it and snaking into the sink. The floor is vinyl, in imitation cork, alternating light and dark, but the conspicuous thing about this floor is that it's only half-finished. Where the cork tiles end there is a border of black tar, by now hard, and then wooden floor in broad plank. Around the kitchen table are six chairs, all from different sets. Various posters on the wall, but none as conspicuous as a map of Europe on the wall where the telephone hangs. The sink is full of dirty dishes. There is a pad hanging by the icebox, and a pencil. Everyone uses the kitchen in a special way."*

Dick complains that some of the four dozen hamburgers he's stored in the icebox are mysteriously missing. He turns on the light to enter his missing hamburgers on the "common stock" list on the pad.

Kathy comes in by the front door down left, carrying books in a green canvas waterproof bag. Kathy warns them all that another of the roommates, Bob, is in a foul mood from brooding over a "cosmic equation" which was a subject of classroom discussion. Cootie would rather believe for some reason that Bob must be suffering from an attack of scistosomiasis brought on by contact with snails.

Bob comes in the front door, greeting everybody tersely, wondering about the mail. Cootie informs him that indeed something came for him: "this really big package from Beirut. It took four guys to get it up the stairs." Mike suggests that it might be a harp. The truth is, of course, that Bob has received one small letter, and he goes through the hall door toward his room to get it, with Kathy tagging after him.

They toss around the notion that something is troubling Bob, they bounce it and worry at it. They figure maybe Bob is concerned about his future after graduation, as well they all might be, Mike insists: "You watch what happens at the graduation ceremony. There's gonna be this line of green military buses two miles long parked on the road outside and they're gonna pick us up and take us to Vietnam and we'll be walking around one day in the depths of the rain forest looking out for wily enemy snipers and carnivorous insects and tropical snakes that can eat a whole moose in one gulp and earthworms sixteen feet long and then one day when we least expect it this wily sniper'll leap out from behind a blade of grass and powie. Right in the head."

They agree that the war is bad and ought to be stopped, but Ruth brings the subject back to Bob and his troubled appearance. Maybe there's something wrong between Bob and Kathy, Ruth suggests, but Dick disagrees: Bob doesn't really care about Kathy. Norman suggests that maybe the best way to discover what's eating Bob is to have Ruth ask him.

Mike has been kneeling by the cat box and peering into it.

MIKE: Jesus Christ. Jesus H. fucking Christ.

NORMAN: What's wrong?

MIKE: She wasn't even in there.

COOTIE: What! All that time we were looking at an empty box and she wasn't even in there?

MIKE: She must have slipped out while we had our backs turned.

COOTIE: Sneaky little beastie.

MIKE: Cootie, you don't understand. She might be out there in the road right now.

COOTIE: Right now.

MIKE: With all the traffic.

COOTIE: Oh, Christ, and all those architects driving home drunk from seeing their mistresses . . .

MIKE: And trying to figure out what to tell the little woman. I mean, she's been waiting up all night in a chartreuse quilted sleeping gown with curlers in her hair.

COOTIE: Worrying about the kiddies. Three boys, twenty-seven girls. They got appendicitis.

MIKE: Simultaneously. And when she called the kindly family doctor he was away in Cuba . . .

COOTIE: Doing research for his forthcoming book . . . . .

When not otherwise occupied, they play this game continuously—the imaginative ad libbing of embellishments onto any fact, any situation, the more improbable the better. Mike and Cootie rush down the hall in search of the cat. The three who are left keep on playing the game, of course, it never stops when two or three are gathered together. When Norman and Dick wonder whether Ruth likes Philosophy 720, Ruth informs them, "Nope. Professor Quinn is an albino dwarf queer with halitosis and he smokes too much."

Norman tries to read his book, though Dick keeps interrupting. Mike and Cootie come in dressed in parkas and go out the front door still searching for the cat. Dick lords it over Norman, a graduate mathematics student, for studying irrelevancies whereas Dick is pursuing Far Eastern studies. Dick eats a banana and is reproached by Norman for throwing the peel into the cat's box. Dick enlightens Norman: "Have you ever seen a cat around here? . . . . . Norman, there is no fucking cat. We haven't got a cat. Boy, for a graduate student you got a lot to learn."

Dick disappears down the hall just as Kathy comes in through the kitchen dressed in a man's bathrobe. Down the hall, Bob is fingering a piano, and the music can be heard as Kathy instructs Norman not to let anyone fiddle with the heater while she's taking a shower. She also asks him to put on some coffee. But Norman has decided that he'd like to borrow one of her books on Vietnam, and he is so obsessed with this thought that he follows Kathy right into the bathroom. She throws him out and Norman returns to making the coffee, still juggling his one thought, talking to Kathy through the bathroom door: "I'll just make the coffee first, and when you're finished in there I'll come down to your room with you and get the book. Hey, listen, if you decide to have your coffee in here, could you go down to your room first and bring the book in with you? Yes, that's probably better. Hey is that O.K.? (*Pause.*) Hey, is that O.K.? (*No answer. Norman is left baffled, as the lights dim and Bob's piano chords keep going and going. Curtain.*)

Scene 2: A few weeks later, morning

The group is preparing to take part in a demonstration, getting a banner ready, debating the necessity for taking sandwiches. Bob and Kathy are not quite ready and the others are waiting. Cootie senses that Norman is suffering from pent-up hostility, for some unknown reason.

NORMAN: I'm not feeling hostile . . .
COOTIE: You're not only feeling it, you're dying to tell us about it. That's a basic axiom of hostility.
NORMAN: Oh, boy, you guys.
DICK: Leave him alone.
COOTIE: Dick, that's the worst thing you can do. I know you think you're being a good shit and everything, but if the guy is riddled with hostility and he doesn't get it out of his system it's gonna go haywire and zing all around inside his body till he's twenty-eight years old and then he'll get cancer.

RUTH: You know, we're gonna be really late if those guys don't hurry up . . .

MIKE: That reminds me of a guy I was reading about. He got so pent up with hostility his head fell right down inside his body, no shit, that's what I was reading, right down between his shoulders.

COOTIE: Fell?

MIKE: Yeah, straight down till all you could see was these two little eye-balls peering out over his collarbone.

COOTIE: Mike.

MIKE: What, Mel?

COOTIE (*pause*): Fell?

MIKE (*pause*): Sank?

COOTIE: Subsided.

MIKE: Right.

COOTIE: In fact, as I remember it, his head eventually disappeared completely.

Mike takes this invention and runs with it to incredible lengths, going so far as to describe the miraculous cure: "He was just walking along, you know, and when he got to this corner to stop for a red light a dog peed on his leg, and when he bent forward to see what was making his pants wet a guy up on some scaffolding right behind dropped a pipe wrench on his back, and the impact of this wrench, plus the slightly inclined position of the guy's upper body, knocked his head back into place."

Bob and Kathy appear, ready for the march. Bob has something on his mind he wants to tell his friends, but he has difficulty getting their attention. He speaks haltingly; he makes Norman close his book for once and listen. He tries to communicate.

BOB: . . . . . I just had this stupid thought the other day in humanities. Johnson was saying something idiotic, as usual, and I just started to watch him carefully for the first time talking to us, you know, thirty kids who think he's a prick, and I realized that he probably thinks all of us are pricks . . . and I just started to wonder what the fuck we're all doing. You know what I mean? What the fuck are we all doing, seriously, tell me, I'd really like to know . . . in twenty-five words or less . . . No, no, sorry, come on, carnival time. Let's go marching.

KATHY: I found the letter, Bob.

BOB: What letter?

Kathy takes an official letter out of her bag.

Kathy, where the hell did you get that? Come on, give it here.

KATHY: We're supposed to be like all together in here. If you can't say it yourself, I'll say it for you.

> *Bob is momentarily confused, then realizes that Kathy thinks he was trying to tell everyone about the letter. He finds the situation absurd, annoying and funny.*

BOB: Kathy, that letter has nothing to do with anything and it's none of your business and would you please give it back.

Kathy hands the letter to Ruth. Ruth reads.

RUTH: Oh, fuck.

Ruth hands the letter on. Each reads in turn. It ends in Mike's hands. Bob waits impatiently as the letter makes its round. He's embarrassed and then begins to find it funny that everyone, especially Kathy, has construed the letter as his problem. Mike is by now looking quite seriously at him.

BOB (*laughing it off*): It's just for the physical. I mean, I'm not dead yet.

As Bob says this, something amusing passes through his mind and he stops talking. He turns the thought over in his mind. Mike is looking at the letter again. The others watch Bob.

MIKE: They misspelled your name?

BOB (*comes out of his brief daydream*): Huh?

MIKE: Jobert.

BOB (*amused*): Oh, yeah.

MIKE: Jobert Rettie. Dear Jobert Rettie. Hi, Jobert.

BOB: Hi, Jike.

MIKE: Good old Jobert.

They keep playing around with this letter substitution, "Jel, Jorman, Jathy, Jick," until a young man interrupts them by knocking on the door and then entering, carrying an attache case. His name is Ralph and he is doing some kind of survey for a university, he says. Since the young people are living in this apartment and not on campus, he takes them for government employees, not students.

The group begins putting Ralph on as hard as they know how, but Ralph is too square—or too persistent—to take notice. It soon turns out that Ralph is selling encyclopedias. All but Norman and Dick take up the banner and go out to their march. Ralph explains to Norman—somewhat pathetically—that he is selling the books to put himself through law school, but he's not very good at it.

Dick comes in from the hall dressed in pea jacket and jeans and wearing a day-glo peace button. He departs with Norman for the march, leaving Ralph in the apartment, alone and baffled.

Scene 3: That afternoon

A few hours later, Ruth enters the apartment where Kathy is sitting alone in the kitchen, crying. Ruth missed Kathy and Bob at the rally.

RUTH: I thought you and Bob were coming. You were on the bus and everything. I got lost when the cops charged. Boy, they really got some of those guys. Fucking pigs.

KATHY: When we got there he said he didn't feel like marching.

RUTH: Why not?

KATHY: Oh, Ruthie, I don't know. I don't know anything any more. You devote two years to a guy and what does he give you? He never even told me about that letter. Drafted, and he didn't even tell me.

RUTH: He's not drafted. That letter's for the physical. All he has to do is act queer. They're not gonna take a queer musician.

KATHY: That's what I told him on the bus. He wouldn't even listen until I called him Job.

RUTH: What?

KATHY: He said he was dead. "Bob is dead."

RUTH: Bullshit, he's putting you on.

KATHY: That's what I mean. Me. He's even putting me on. Ungrateful bastard. The things I've done for him, Ruthie. Shit, I sound just like my mother. You know what I mean. I'm not complaining, but you know, you get tired of giving all the time and nothing's coming back. You know what I told him? I said he was the first guy I ever had an orgasm with. I mean, it really made him feel good. Now I gotta live with it. How can you explain something like that?

RUTH: Hey, no shitting around, did he really say he was gonna join?

KATHY: Ruthie, I'm telling you, he's serious. You know what he told me? He thinks the whole antiwar movement is a Goddamn farce. I mean, Jesus, I really thought we were relating on that one. It's not like I'm asking the guy to go burn himself or anything but, I mean, he knows how I feel about the war and he's just doing it to be shitty. There's something behind it, I know that. He's like reaching out, trying to relate to me on the personal level by rejecting me but, like, I don't know how to break through. He says he's gonna study engineering in the army and then when he gets out he's gonna get some kind of plastic job and marry a plastic wife and live in a plastic house in some fucking plastic suburb and have two point seven children. Oh shit, Ruth, it's all too much. He went to a cowboy film.

RUTH: Well, you know, that's how it is.

Kathy is afraid Bob really means to take on a plastic existence. (On her part Ruth, who is Mike's girl, isn't troubled because Mike, despite his love for physics, will probably settle down in his father's lumber business—she sees it as inevitable.) Kathy wants more than a plastic job for Bob, she hopes he'll keep at his music. But at the moment Kathy feels alienated from Bob, yet is still certain that Bob needs her as much as ever.

Mike runs in looking for Ruth, reporting that Cootie has been wounded by the police and arrested—but Cootie strolls in unharmed a few beats later. Mike and Cootie (whom Mike calls Mel) refuse to be upset by Kathy's news that Bob isn't ardently anti-war, and Kathy stamps off down the hall in a fit of anger. Cootie does a snarling takeoff of the song "We Shall Overcome," and Mike silences him as Dick comes in, raving at Norman for carrying and brandishing a gun at the rally (for once, this is not one of their pipe dreams but happens to be true). When Dick discovers that Bob isn't in the apartment, he wants to know where Kathy is.

RUTH: Leave her alone. She's upset.

COOTIE: Yeah, I wouldn't try to lay her just yet, 'cause she's still going with Bob.

> *Dick walks out down the hall.*

MIKE: That was a pretty stupid thing to say.

COOTIE: Just came out.

RUTH: Who cares? Everyone knows what Dirty Dicky's up to. Except maybe Bob.

MIKE: And maybe Kathy.

RUTH: Kathy knows.

A knock on the door closes off this promising avenue of discussion. It's the landlord, Willis, with a tenant, Lucky, who has been complaining about the noise. But Willis's sympathies lie with the students, not with his other tenants. They get rid of Lucky with promises and Willis stays on to have a cup of coffee and overstate his allegiance.

WILLIS: . . . . . You know, I'd give ten'a my other tenants for any one of you guys. You kids are the future of America, I mean that deeply, not too much milk, beautiful. Yeah, you kids live a great life up here. I got tenants complaining all the time about the way you kids carry on, and I'll tell ya something, you wanna know why they complain? 'Cause they'd give the last piece of hair on their heads to live like you kids are living.

RUTH: How's Mrs. Willis?

WILLIS: Huh? Oh, yeah, great, just great. Well, just between you and me and the wall she's gettin' to be a pain in the ass. She wants me to get rid of you, too. Why? I ask her. She don't like the way you live. O.K., I say, if you know so much, how do they live? She don't know and she don't wanna know. I try to tell her, you know, about the wild parties and stuff and taking drugs to have all new sensations in the body and the orgies with six or seven of you all at once. You should see her eyes light up. Same thing with all the tenants. When they hear what it's really like up here they go all funny. They'd pay me a hunnerd dollars to hear more, but they ain't got the nerve to ask. Get rid of them. That's all I hear. Wamme to tell you something?

MIKE: If you got something to say you didn't ought to hold back.

WILLIS: Tremendous. You kids are tremendous. Listen. When the neighbors try to tellya about when they was young, don't believe it. It's a lotta bull, and I should know. When we was young it was so boring you fell asleep when you was twenty and you never woke up again . . . . .

Willis tells the group about his dreams, B-picture sexual fantasies about being a king of the jungle. The young people pretend to believe that Willis's imagined vulgarities are poetic. They send him away believing that he has inspired them.

Dick and Kathy come in from the hall, seemingly fresh from lovemaking and half-wanting the others to notice. They do. Dick reacts by exiting down the hall again, and Kathy tells them all to mind their own business.

The doorbell rings. Mike opens the door to find a strange young girl, Shelly, standing there.

SHELLY: Hi. Does Norman live here?

MIKE: Does anyone here know a Norman?

SHELLY: He said he lived here. I met him at the march today. He said to come here and wait for him. I been standing out in the hall 'cause, like, I heard someone talking and I didn't want to disturb anyone and then this guy just came out so I figured, well, it's now or never kind of thing. I'm Shelly.

RUTH: Come on in. I'm Ruth.

SHELLY: Oh, good, then Norman does live here because I wasn't sure when he gave me the address. Sometimes you meet a guy at a march and he'll like give you an address and you end up waiting for a few days and he never shows. Did that ever happen to you? It's happened to me a lot of times.

KATHY: Listen, everyone, I'm serious, I don't want him to know. I'll tell him when the time's right.

RUTH: It's your scene.

> *Kathy exits down the hall. Shelly, meanwhile, goes under the table and sits down on the floor.*

SHELLY: I'm sorry about this. If you want to laugh go ahead. I'm used to it. It's just I've got this thing at the moment where I keep sitting under tables and I figured I'd better do it right away instead of pretending for a while I didn't sit under tables. I mean, sitting under the table is "me" at the moment, so why hide it? Have you ever done it?

RUTH: Want some coffee, Shelly?

SHELLY: I'm a vegetarian.

MIKE: Coffee's made from vegetables.

SHELLY: I don't drink coffee, thanks. I'll just wait for Norman.

COOTIE: Where's Norman?

SHELLY: Well, he was arrested for carrying a concealed weapon, but he said it's O.K. because he has a permit. He's really a total-action freak, and he's very committed to the whole peace thing.

COOTIE: Oh.

MIKE: Well now . . .

COOTIE: How about that.

> *Fade out.*

Scene 4: Early evening, before Christmas

Shelly is installed under her table, blowing bubbles; Norman as usual is reading; Mike and Cootie are playing chess. Norman accuses the others of having put him on about the cat, but the others counter-argue that this is paranoia.

When Norman tells them his father is a policeman, Mike and Cootie, who call themselves brothers, insist on their right to have a cop in the family too, an uncle.

Norman has been expelled from college after the revolver incident at the rally. He is staying on in the apartment, washing dishes by night and reading about Vietnam by day. Shelly likes it here and has become one of the group. She urges Norman to tell the others about an idea he is turning over in his mind.

NORMAN: Well, you see . . . (*Pause.*) I'm gonna set myself on fire as a protest against the war.
> *Cootie and Mike look at him and exchange brief glances.*

I've thought about it a lot. I mean, I've read I guess about a hundred books about the war and the more you read the more you see it's no one thing you can put your finger on. It's right in the middle of the whole system, like Dick said. I shouldn't've tried to kill those policemen, but I didn't know then they were part of the system like everything else. No one's got the right to take anyone else's life, that's what I've decided. But I've still got the right to take my own life for something I believe in.

SHELLY: I'm gonna burn with Norman. We're gonna burn together. We've thought it all through and, like, if he burns himself alone that's just one person. Everyone'll say he's insane, but if two of us do it . . . wow. Two people. What are they gonna say if two of us do it?

MIKE (*pause*): Three of us.

COOTIE: Four of us.

MIKE: You too, huh?

COOTIE: It's the only way.

Mike and Cootie carry the thought to extremes, as a sort of charm against it really happening. They inform Norman they'd have done it themselves more than a year ago, except they were afraid the press would distort their sacrifice: "Hippie Brothers in Suicide Pact." They'll study hard, graduate with honors and then immolate themselves.

MIKE: . . . . . I'd like to see them say we're insane when two Phi Beta Kappas go up in flames with the son of a policeman and the daughter of a . . . Hey, what does your father do?

SHELLY: Well, it's kind of funny. I mean, he's a pretty weird head in his way. He's got, like, six or seven jobs at any one time.

MIKE: That's okay . . . Daughter of a weird head with six or seven jobs at any given time. That covers the whole spectrum.

NORMAN: What does your father do? I mean, I know your uncle's a policeman because I trust you, but you never said what your father did. I was curious. Like, if they bring our fathers into it what'll they say about you?

COOTIE: He's a trapper.

SHELLY: Wow, that's really something else. Like a fur trapper?

COOTIE: Furs and hides, you know. Rabbit and mink and muskrat and beaver and elk and reindeer and seal. Some otter. Penguin.

SHELLY: Wow, penguin.

COOTIE: Well, you know, he works the Great Northwest Territory up to the mouth of the St. Lawrence seaway and over to the Aleutians.

SHELLY: Boy, this'll really blow everybody's mind.

A knock on the door signals the arrival of two policemen, Bream and Effing, who have come in response to a neighbor's complaint. They seem interested in the fact that there are girls living here in the apartment with the boys, but they decide to overlook it. Norman insists on knowing what the trouble is, and Bream, the elder of the two policemen, tells him someone has complained about seeing naked people walking around the apartment.

Bream seems sympathetic to the students, however, and they sense his basic good nature and inform him they have policemen in their families. Effing, a young policeman, is obviously overzealous and a threat to the general tranquility. Bream readily grants Cootie permission to leave the room to go to the bathroom, though Effing suspects he may be planning to dispose of evidence (and he may be right, because Cootie leaves the room by the front door).

EFFING: Look at that, Bream, the girl keeps sitting under there . . .

BREAM: Goddamnit, Effing, who's in charge around here?

EFFING: But she's sitting under there . . .

BREAM: Did we come here to investigate a complaint about a girl sitting under the table?

EFFING: No sir, but . . .

BREAM: The girl happens to be well within her rights as a taxpaying citizen of the community to sit under any table she wants, and until we get complaints about her sitting under there we leave her alone. Understand?

EFFING: Yeah, yeah, yeah . . .

SHELLY: Thanks.

BREAM: That's okay, lady. The kid's a rookie. They give us pros a bad name. Now let me tell you something about the people complaining about you. They look in here and see you guys bare-assed and they're complaining because they're so sick of looking at each other they gotta go spying on you. We know about them people. They're strict Roman Catholics. Twelve kids in four rooms. The old man can't keep it in his pants for ten minutes running. So they got troubles, right, and everyone that's got troubles wants to give troubles to someone else. So they make a complaint, and that's well within their rights as law-abiding citizens of the community. I got enough troubles without their Goddamn complaints. I got enough to do watching the Vietnam freaks and the niggers and the loonies going up on buildings with high-power rifles picking off everyone down below. Let me give you some good advice. Get curtains . . . . .

Bream even tells them how to make curtains and how to hang them in the window, writing instructions so they won't forget. Effing is nervous about Cootie being gone so long, but Bream brushes him aside.

BREAM (*writing*): So, what are you kids gonna do with yourselves? (*Pause.*) Am I being nosy or something?

MIKE: No, I mean, there's a lot of opportunities all over the place. We're not jumping into anything without we've looked the whole thing over.

BREAM: Smart kids. Boy, that's really something. Cop sending his kid to college. They must pay him pretty good, huh?

NORMAN: I guess so.

BREAM: Yeah, what's he, a sergeant . . . lieutenant or something?

NORMAN: He's Chief of Police for Buffalo County.

BREAM (*whistles*): Whew! Pretty good. That shut me up O.K. Chief of Police. Oh boy, that's really something.

NORMAN: It's just his job, you know.

BREAM: Look, ah, here's your instructions. I want them up by Wednesday. Any complaints after that and all of you guys'll be in court, father or no father, you understand me? This ain't Buffalo.

MIKE: Yes, sir.

NORMAN: O.K.

    Cootie returns and stands in the door. There's a pause.

COOTIE: That's better.

    Curtain.

ACT II

Scene 1: An afternoon after Christmas

Ruth places some cat food in a bowl, and indeed a cat does come in and eat it. Meanwhile, Kathy is worried about how she is going to tell Bob about Dick, though maintaining that she hasn't yet slept with Dick no matter what the others think.

Ruth warns Kathy against Dick, telling her the whole school knows that Dick is staying in his homosexual tutor's good graces by keeping the tutor's wife satisfied while the tutor amuses himself elsewhere. Dick's schoolwide nickname has become "Dirty Dick."

Bob comes in and deliberately ignores Kathy, sitting with Ruth and telling her a story about an incident in music class. Kathy tries to get Bob's attention, but Bob rambles on to Ruth. Finally Ruth takes the situation in hand, tells Bob point-blank that "Kathy wants to talk to you about sleeping with Dick" and runs out the front door.

BOB (*pause*): Meanwhile, back at the ranch . . . You'll never believe this, but when I came in just now, I didn't expect that. Bedbugs, maybe. Thermonuclear war . . .

KATHY: She had no right.

BOB: I'm trying to think of something appropriate to say, like "Name the first one after me." That's Job. J-O-B. Job.

KATHY: Please Bob, can I say something . . .

BOB: Do you have trouble pronouncing the name Job?

KATHY: Jesus Christ, you're impossible.

BOB: Ah, yes, but I exist, nonetheless.

KATHY: You've just cut me right out. You're not even trying to relate to me any more. (*Pause.*) Well, you're not.

BOB: No, Kathy. The fact is, I like you a lot. I, um, sort of love you, if you know what I mean.

KATHY: I don't really want to sleep with Dick.

BOB: Then don't.

KATHY: It's just, he tried to get me that night after the demonstration.

BOB: I know. He told me.

KATHY: That shit.

BOB: I thought it was pretty good of him.

Kathy is trying to create a reaction in Bob, to determine where their relationship stands now, but Bob will not be moved. He suggests that they study together and reminds Kathy: "I'm Job. Bob's dead." Kathy exits down the hall in a huff.

Bob is thinking about finishing the work of covering the floor with tiles, when there is a knock at the outer door; it's Bob's Uncle Murry, *"a middle aged man. He's swaying a little and carrying a bottle of rye."* He has come a couple of hundred miles to see Bob, though he mildly disapproves of his nephew's lifestyle. They discuss the family, especially Bob's mother who lives in New York—she doesn't hear from Bob as often as she'd like to. Murry has something to tell Bob but doesn't quite know how to go about it.

Their conversation is interrupted by a call from the telephone company inquiring about the service. Bob gets embroiled in a tangled telephone argument with phone company personnel about their right to pry into his affairs . . . but just as it becomes heated, Murry takes the receiver and cuts off the conversation. As he stares at his nephew, Bob guesses what he has to say.

BOB (*long pause*): Cancer.

     Murry nods. Bob doesn't see him.

How long's she got?

MURRY: A week. Two weeks. I don't know. Any time now.

BOB: Those operations . . . kidney trouble. Oh, shit, why didn't someone tell me?

MURRY: You got your studies, we should worry you to death?

BOB (*flat*): Fuck you all.

MURRY: I thought . . . I thought maybe you and me fly to New York tonight.

BOB: Yeah, get in there quick for the payoff. That'll be just great.

MURRY: She don't know yet.

BOB: Yeah. "Hi, Mom, I just came flying in with Murry a couple of weeks before Christmas vacation to see you for no good reason." You think she won't guess?

MURRY: She doesn't have to. We can always tell her something.

BOB: You planning to keep it from her, too? I bet it's the first thing she thought of. Two years, She had that first operation two years ago. She's been dying for two years and I didn't even fucking know it.

MURRY: That's it, Bobby. (*Pause.*) Life is full of shit.

BOB (*pause*): I'll pack some stuff. No, you stay here. I want to be alone.

Bob exits down the hall. Murry sits, just as Mike and Cootie come in laden with Christmas presents. They determine that Murry is probably Bob's uncle —in reality—and exit down the hall. Shelly comes in looking for Norman. She pesters Murry, who is now tearful, with questions. Bob comes back into the room, and he and Murry depart just as Dick returns to the apartment.

The point is that in all this milling around Bob has left without telling Kathy where he's going or why. She feels abandoned and she takes it out on Dick. Ruth enters and tries to tell them all about a fantastic experience, but she can hardly make herself heard above Mike and Cootie singing "We Wish You a Merry Christmas."

Ruth tries to tell them that she went to see her "albino dwarf" teacher about homework, and when the two of them stood there looking out of his office window at the snow he said an "incredibly beautiful thing." Ruth is just about to tell them what it was, when Kathy comes in wearing a coat, carrying a hastily packed suitcase. Without a word to the others, Kathy leaves the apartment. Dick follows her.

The others pick up the conversation where they left off, as though nothing were happening, but the curtain falls before Ruth can tell them what her teacher said.

Scene 2: Before graduation

The apartment now has a bare feeling, with most of the posters gone. Letters informing the students of their grades are piled on the table. Ruth and Dick are the only ones home—Ruth finds that she has made graduate school, and Dick has just barely graduated.

Kathy's grades have been sent here even though she long since left the apartment for good. Ruth is curious to know whether Dick made it with Kathy that day she stormed out, and whether Kathy then told him "you were the first guy that ever turned her on," but Dick won't say. He is angry at Kathy for spreading the story about the professor's wife—it got back to the professor and caused Dick a lot of trouble.

Bob comes in and looks at his grades—they're okay, he tells the others. He opens Kathy's envelope and finds her straight As marred by a B minus in Poetry 210 and hopes she hasn't gone to pieces.

Lucky comes in to throw his questionable weight around now that the students are departing, but they manage to get rid of him. Ruth reports that Mike and Cootie have made magna cum laude and have gone to the movies with Shelly and Norman.

Ruth goes out to pack. The two men discuss the future—Bob is going into the army and Dick has a summer job as a milkman. Dick seizes the opportunity for frankness.

DICK: You know something, Bob? You know what's wrong with you?

BOB: I been waiting all this time for someone to tell me. What's wrong with me, Dick?

DICK: You let her get your balls, Bob.

BOB: That was pretty careless, wasn't it?

DICK: No shit, Bob. I remember when you got stung by that bee in the humanities quadrangle. I always wondered about that. I mean, you're supposed to yell when something like that happens. You don't stand there wondering if you should say something. You're really dead, you know.

BOB: Yeah, well, that's what I was trying to tell everyone right before Christmas. I thought I might just try it out, you know, being dead. Didn't feel any different.

DICK: I don't get it.

BOB: No, it's a pretty weird thing.

DICK: I gotta pack.

BOB: Yeah.

Dick goes down the hall as Mike and Cootie burst in the front door, and Ruth comes in from the hall with a suitcase. Mike and Cootie have come home to tell them that they didn't all go to the movies after all; they went to the common, where Norman carried out his suicidal intention of immolation for the cause.

MIKE: . . . . . He had this plan. Honest to shit, we didn't know he was serious. Him and Shelly. We thought he's just . . . we went to the common and he just took all his clothes off and poured gasoline all over himself.

COOTIE: We were just shitting around, Ruth. Honest. If we thought he was serious we'd've stopped him, you know.

MIKE: It was that fucking Shelly.

RUTH: You fucking stupid . . .

MIKE: I'm telling you, it wasn't our fault. He wouldn't have lit the match. I know he poured the gasoline, but he'd never've lit the match.

BOB: He's . . .

MIKE: Oh shit, it was awful. He just sat there turning black. I didn't want to look, but I couldn't turn away. His skin just, Christ, it just fell away from his face and his blood . . . (*Puts head in hand.*)

RUTH: Stupid fucking guys. You should've known. Where's Shelly?

COOTIE: She went crazy, Ruth. She just cracked up. We had to practically knock her out. She's okay now.

> *Shelly comes in the front door. Her eyes are closed and her fists clenched. Ruth runs to her, doesn't know what to do.*

RUTH: Shelly, oh, Shelly, Jesus . . .

SHELLY (*teeth clenched*): Fucking guys.

> *Norman comes in. He's soaking wet and carries a gasoline can. Mike and Cootie rise.*

MIKE: See, everything's cool now. Everybody trusts each other. That's what it's all about.

> *Mike smiles oddly at the others.*

COOTIE (*registering it all*): Holy shit!

> *Mike and Cootie leave the room.*

SHELLY (*yells*): Creeps! (*To Ruth.*) You got any first-aid stuff?

RUTH: Yeah.

> *Ruth gets a box from the pantry. It's a huge white box with a red cross on it, obviously stolen.*

BOB: Hey, what happened?

NORMAN (*sits*): I'm all right.

SHELLY: Don't talk, Norman. Would you make him some coffee?

RUTH: Yeah. Those guys said you burned yourself.

NORMAN: No, I'm okay.

> *Ruth makes coffee while Shelly ties a bandage around Norman's wrist.*

SHELLY: Sorry if this hurts. Hey, Ruth, those guys are really bastards. They gotta learn you don't joke around sometimes.

BOB: Hey, were you really gonna burn yourself?

NORMAN: Well, you know . . .

SHELLY: We were all supposed to do it. All four of us. We waited all this time for them to graduate with good grades and everything. Six months almost. I mean, like, the war could've ended. Fucking creeps. They went and put water in the gasoline can.

NORMAN: I think I might be getting a cold.

Norman has a burn on his wrist from trying to light himself with a match. Ruth reminds them all they have to get out of the apartment tomorrow, and this disturbs Norman, who had no plans beyond today. He decides that he will stay with Shelly and maybe try to get back into graduate school. He is kind of glad to be alive after all, he admits.

They are discussing various possibilities of visiting Europe (Bob is taking down his map) when Willis comes in. He orders them all into his presence and tells them how he wants the apartment left: milk bottles gone, floor finished with the tiles he paid good money for. Bob agrees to finish the floor by tomorrow, and Willis moves on down the hall with most of the others, to inspect the place.

Norman has forgiven Mike and Cootie for pulling the water substitution on him (though Shelly scarcely has) and wants to share rooms with them next year when they return to graduate school. They can write to Norman care of his father at the Buffalo Police Headquarters. Mike in turn assures Norman that he and Cootie can be reached in care of their trapper father in the Northwest Territory. Mike of course believes that Norman is putting him on.

Willis comes back in with the others and informs them he'll keep their $50 deposit to cover minor damage, but he doesn't want to be thought a bad guy on this account; he tells the young people again how much he admires them and hopes for their future. They give Willis an ironic chorus of "For he's a jolly good fellow" as the curtain falls.

Scene 3: The afternoon after graduation

The kitchen is bare; even the icebox is gone, along with most of the milk bottles. There is one chair left in the bare room, where Bob is laying the vinyl tiles.

Cootie comes in with his father, says goodbye to Bob. Mike comes in and meets Cootie's father before they depart (obviously Mike and Cootie are not really brothers after all). But Norman really drove off in a police car with his father, Bob informs Mike, Norman's father really is what Norman said he was.

Dick and the milkman come in with empty cartons to load the last of the milk bottles. The milkman can't resist commenting: "I don't understand you guys. You're supposed to be college graduates. Eight hundred and fifty-seven two-quart milk bottles. That's not the kind of thing a grown up person does. You're supposed to be grownups. I don't get it . . . . . I just hope you guys don't think you can go through life hoarding milk bottles." Dick and the milkman exit with their burden.

The phone rings and Bob answers it (meanwhile waving goodbye to Mike and Ruth, who go off together). The phone call is for Dick, from the professor's wife; but Dick, when he comes back for his suitcases, merely shrugs off the call, says goodbye to Bob and goes.

A plumber enters to replace the stack heater which, he tells Bob, is an extremely dangerous antique. It could have blown all their heads off at any time. The plumber demonstrates and sends a huge jet of steam into the sink, as Kathy comes in.

The plumber goes out to get a pipe wrench, leaving Bob and Kathy together in this apartment from which everyone else has now gone. Kathy picks up the letter with her grades, apologizes to Bob for the upset she feels she has caused him. Ruth has told Kathy that Bob has been feeling low this semester, and Kathy assumes it was because he missed her. Kathy wishes that Bob had been able to express his feelings, she would have come back to him.

Bob's replies to Kathy are monosyllabic; there is hardly any reaction even when Kathy asks him about his mother.

BOB: She's okay. Sort of dead.
KATHY: I like her, Bob. You're lucky. She's, you know, she's a real person.

BOB: No, she's, you know, a real corpse.

KATHY: All right, have it your way.

BOB: No, it's not what I wanted particularly. No, taken all in all, from various different angles, I'd've preferred it if she lived. I'm pretty sure of that.

KATHY (*pause*): She's not really.

BOB: School's over.

KATHY: Bob, do you know what you're saying?

BOB: Kathy, please get the fuck out of here.

KATHY: But, I mean, Ruth never told me . . . Didn't you tell anyone?

BOB: Yeah, I just told you.

KATHY: But, I mean . . . when . . . when did . . .

BOB: Christmas. No, no, it was the day after.

> *Kathy sits.*

KATHY: Jesus, Bob, why didn't you tell anyone? I mean, how could you live for six months without telling someone?

BOB (*with no emotion*): Oh, I don't know. A little perseverence. A little cunning. A little fortitude.

> *Long pause.*

They put her in this room, I don't know what you call it. They bring everyone there just before they kick the bucket. They just sort of lie around looking at each other, wondering what they got in common to talk about. I saw her for fifteen days running. She knew. I'm sure of that. I couldn't believe it. Not the last time anyway. I couldn't believe that thing in bed was alive. It was just a yellow thing. No eyes. Anyway, they drugged her up so heavily she couldn't see anything. I think she was trying to say something, I'm not sure . . . . .

Bob tells Kathy of his disgust, his revulsion at his mother's increasingly repulsive physical deterioration. He was glad when she died. He missed her well-attended burial because his car broke down on the Merritt Parkway.

KATHY: Bob . . .

BOB: Anyway, I, um, I didn't feel like talking about it. I mean, I wasn't all that upset. I was a little upset, mostly because I thought I ought to be more upset, but as for your actual grief, well . . .

> *Kathy has risen.*

Going?

> *Kathy starts out the door.*

Give my regards to that guy you're rescuing at the moment. What's his name.

> *Kathy is gone. Bob shrugs. He sits. The cat comes in.*

Hey, cat, what the fuck do you think you're doing hanging around here? All the human beings are heading west. Everyone done gone, puss-puss.

> *Bob picks up the cat and sets it outside, closing the door. He returns to his tiling; stops and looks around; goes to the hall door and looks down for a while, then turns back to the kitchen.*

O.K. Announcement. This really incredible thing happened to me. Hey, every-one, let me tell you about this really incredible thing that happened to me . . .

His body is doing something he doesn't want it to.

Oh fuck, come on. Shit, no, no . . .

But he is. He's crying, first with just his face, then with his whole body. His mother's death has nothing to do with it. Curtain.

SMALL CRAFT WARNINGS

A Play in Two Acts

BY TENNESSEE WILLIAMS

Cast and credits appear on page 375

TENNESSEE WILLIAMS was born Thomas Lanier Williams in Columbus, Miss. on March 26, 1911. He attended the Universities of Missouri, Washington and Iowa (B.A. 1938) and worked as shoe clerk, elevator operator, waiter, movie usher, etc. He was drawn into the theater through the St. Louis, Mo., Mummers, for whom he wrote his first produced plays: Candles in the Sun *(1936, presented as a curtain raiser) and* The Fugitive Kind *(1937). The University of Iowa put on his* Spring Song *in 1938, and his* Not About Nightingales *was done in St. Louis in 1939. In 1940 the Theater Guild produced* Battle of Angeles *in tryout but never brought it to New York. His* Stairs to the Roof *was produced by the Pasadena, Calif. Playbox during the 1944-45 season.*

Then, with the opening of The Glass Menagerie *(Best Play, Critics Award) March 31, 1945 on Broadway began one of the most distinguished careers of the American theater. The list of major Tennessee Williams plays and prizes is as follows:* You Touched Me! *(1945, in collaboration with Donald Windham),* A Streetcar Named Desire *(1947, Best Play, Critics Award, Pulitzer Prize),* Summer and Smoke *(1948),* The Rose Tattoo *(1951, Best Play),* Camino Real *(1953),* Cat on a Hot Tin Roof *(1955, Best Play, Critics Award, Pulitzer Prize),* Orpheus Descending *(1957, Best Play),* Garden District *(1958, a program of one-acters including* Suddenly Last Summer*),* Sweet Bird of Youth *(1959, Best Play),* Period of Adjustment *(1960, Best Play),* The Night of The Iguana *(1961, Best Play, Critics Award),* The Milk Train Doesn't

276

Stop Here Anymore *(1963, Best Play)*, Slapstick Tragedy *(1966)*, The Seven Descents of Myrtle *1968) and* In the Bar of a Tokyo Hotel *(1969)*. *Small Craft Warnings is his tenth Best Play, tying him with Philip Barry in the all-time list of Best Play citation winners. Only Maxwell Anderson (19), George S. Kaufman (18), Eugene O'Neill (12) and Moss Hart (11) have more.*

Tennessee Williams is also the author of such short plays as This Property Is Condemned, Portrait of a Madonna, 27 Wagons Full of Cotton, Three Players of a Summer Game, Something Unspoken, Talk to Me Like the Rain, I Rise in Flame, Cried the Phoenix *and* The Purification. *Among his screen plays are those for his own* Suddenly Last Summer *and* The Fugitive Kind, *and his published works include collections of poetry and* The Roman Spring of Mrs. Stone. *He is a member of The Dramatists Guild and ASCAP. In 1965 he was the recipient of the Brandeis University Creative Arts Medal in theater and in 1969 of the National Institute of Arts and Letters Gold Medal for Drama.*

Time: The present

Place: A bar along the Southern California coast

ACT I

SYNOPSIS: The sound of the ocean and its winds can sometimes be heard, and the presence of fog all around almost felt, in the dimly-lit barroom of "Monk's Place." The bar is at left, the doors to the lavatories and stairs leading up to Monk's living quarters are at right. There is a door upstage in the glass front, through which is visible a blue neon sign. Inside are a juke box, battered chairs and tables, and a stuffed and varnished sailfish hangs over the bottles behind the bar. This is a seedy dive which *"attracts a group of regular patrons who are nearly all so well known to each other that it is like a community club, and most of these regulars spend the whole evening."*

Monk the bartender and owner—middle-aged, moderately tolerant—is serving a drink to Doc, an aging physician who has lost his license but still practises secretly. Sitting at one of the tables beside her rope-bound suitcase is a youngish woman named Violet—*"Her eyes are too large for her face and they are usually moist; her appearance suggests a derelict kind of existence; still, she has about her a pale, bizarre sort of beauty . . . . . she's like a water plant."*

Bill enters, a large, heavily-muscled man *"with an over-relaxed amiability like a loser putting up a bold front,"* priding himself on being a stud whether or not he is in reality a successful one. Automatically, Monk takes from the refrigerator a can of Bill's favorite brand of beer, without pausing in his conversation with Doc. They have noticed Violet's suitcase.

MONK: What I'm running here is a tavern licensed to dispense spirits, not a dormitory. I don't want nobody checking in here with luggage.

VIOLET (*much aware of him*): Bill?

BILL (*waiting for his beer which is still unopened in Monk's hand*): Hi, Vi'let.

MONK (*pointing to the narrow staircase*): They see those stairs. They know I live up there.

DOC: Yep, they see those stairs to the living quarters above and it gives them the notion you might need companionship up there, the solace of their companionship up those stairs some nights when it suits their convenience to offer you that solace, and I don't have to tell you that this comfort they offer when convenient to them is not the least expensive item, it's not by a long shot the lowest-priced commodity on the shelves of the fucking supermarket that a man of my age spends what's left of his life in . . .

> *Through its booze-filter, his voice has risen to the pitch of a very personal and deep-rooted exigency of his own life. Monk is still holding Bill's beer can, unopened.*

BILL: Hey, Monk, how big a tab has Leona run up here?

MONK (*still holding the unopened can*): Oh, Leona's, her tab, I don't run it through a computer, I don't sweat about hers. (*He now looks at Bill.*) Let me put it this way. I might sweat your tab, if it was yours, not hers, but since it's on hers, added on it, I don't.

BILL: . . . Well, how about opening that can of Miller's and . . .

VIOLET (*overlapping above*): Bill, why don't you come here, I'm lonesome sitting alone, and, and . . . bring a beer, huh, Bill? Oh, and a pepperoni. I'm famished!

Bill obliges. He takes the beers and pepperoni over to Violet's table, greeting her with his *"hustler's smile, the smile of the professional stud—now aging a bit but still with considerable memorabilia of his young charm."*

A radio behind the bar warns of a coming storm. Small craft warnings have been posted. Doc remarks to Monk, "You're running a place of refuge for vulnerable human vessels."

Tonight Bill has deserted Leona, his usual companion (he lives in her trailer), because she seems to be having one of her spells, she has "got her knickers in a twist." Suddenly Leona bursts in the front door *"like a small bull making his charge into the ring. Leona, a large, ungainly woman, is wearing white clam-digger slacks and a woolly pink sweater. On her head of dyed corkscrew curls is a sailor's hat which she occasionally whips off her head to slap something with it—the bar, a table-top, somebody's back—to emphasize a point."*

Leona is furious at Bill for walking out on her while her back was turned. She was fixing an extra special dinner for them, with the table decorated, when Bill just walked out without a word—he says it was to get a bottle because Leona had drunk up everything in the place. Now Leona finds him sitting with Violet who, by the looks of her suitcase, has been thrown out into the street.

Gradually Leona cools off and sits with Bill and Violet, noticing that Violet's nails are dirty under the chipped polish, handing her an orange stick. When Leona gets up to play her favorite number on the juke box, Violet's hand strays and begins to fondle Bill under the table, almost as a reflex action of which she is scarcely aware. Bill settles back to enjoy himself. But Leona notices and explodes at Violet in a jealous assault. Bill holds Leona back while Violet flees to the ladies' room and locks herself in. Struggling, Leona stamps on Bill's foot and kicks Monk's shin. Monk insists that Leona calm down; he will allow no violence in his place.

Seeing that Violet has for the moment escaped her, Leona contents herself with verbal abuse. Violet, Leona insists, is no lady, she has no self-respect: "What could she possibly find to respect in herself? She lives like an animal in a room with no bath that's directly over the amusement arcade at the foot of the pier, yeah, right over the billiards, the pinball games and the bowling alleys at the amusement arcade, it's bang, bang, bang, loud as a TV Western all day and all night, and then bang, bang again at eight A.M. It would drive a sane person crazy but she couldn't care less. She don't have a closet, she didn't have a bureau so she hangs her dresses on a piece of rope that hangs across a corner between two nails, and her other possessions she keeps on the floor in boxes."

Once when Violet was sick, Leona brought her some chicken and found that Violet had to eat it "like a dog," having no plates or implements in her room. Leona brought Violet all the household items she needed and visited her every day, until the day came when Leona arrived and Violet wasn't there.

LEONA: . . . . . I thought my God she's died or they put her away. I run downstairs, and I heard her screaming with joy in the amusement arcade. She was having herself a ball with a shipload of drunk sailor-boys; she hardly had time to speak to me.

BILL: Maybe she'd gotten sick of you. That's a possible reason.

LEONA: It's a possible reason I was sick of her, too, but I'd thought that the bitch was dying of malnutrition, and I thought she was human and a human life is worth saving or what the shit *is* worth saving. But is she human? She's just a parasite creature, not even made out of flesh but out of wet biscuit dough, she always looks like the bones are dissolving in her.

BILL (*banging his beer bottle on the table*): DO YOU THINK I BELONG TO YOU? I BELONG TO MYSELF, I JUST BELONG TO MYSELF.

LEONA: Aw, you pitiful piece of . . . worthless . . . conceit! (*She addresses the bar.*) . . . Never done a lick of work in his life . . . He has a name for his thing. He calls it Junior. He says he takes care of Junior and Junior takes care of him. How long is that gonna last? How long does he figure Junior is going to continue to provide for him, huh? HUH! . . . Forever or *less* than forever? . . . Thinks the sun rises and sets between his legs and that's the reason I put him in my trailer, feed him, give him beer-money, pretend I don't notice there's five or ten bucks less in my pocket book in the morning than my pocketbook had in it when I fell to sleep, night before.

BILL: Go out on the beach and tell that to the seagulls, they'd be more interested in it.

Meanwhile, in the ladies' room Violet is howling, calling for the police. Monk is trying to persuade Leona to settle down.

Steve comes into the bar *"wearing a floral-patterned sports shirt under a tan jacket and greasy white trousers of a short order cook."* Steve is looking for Violet and can hear her complaining behind the locked door while Leona storms around the room, boasting that she hit Violet and threatening to hit her again. Leona orders a bourbon, but Monk tells her, "Leona, you're on a mean drunk, and I don't serve liquor to no one on a mean drunk."

Persistently and somewhat dim-wittedly, Steve wants to know why Leona hit Violet. It wasn't because of her dirty hands, Leona tells him, but because of her fondling Bill under the table. "You should have hit her yourself instead of making me do it," Leona tells Steve, but Steve doesn't feel injured, he isn't married to Violet and never will be, he just wanted to know what was going on.

All at once Leona begins to feel sorry for Violet in her degraded state; she tells herself that she won't hit Violet again.

A man and a boy come into the barroom and sit together at one of the tables, while Leona is muttering to herself: "When I leave here tonight, none of you will ever see me again. I'm going to stop by the shop, let myself in with my passkey and collect my own equipment, which is enough to open a shop of my own, write a goodbye note to Flo, she isn't a bad old bitch, I doubled her trade since I been there, she's going to miss me, poor Flo, then leave my passkey and cut back to my trailer and pack like lightning and move on to . . ." But Leona stops because she doesn't want Bill to know where she intends to head next.

Leona's attention has been attracted by the two newcomers, isolated at their table. *"The boy, Bobby, wears faded jeans and a sweatshirt on the back of which is lettered 'Iowa to Mexico.' The young man, Quentin, is dressed effetely in a yachting jacket, maroon linen slacks and a silk neck-scarf. Despite this costume he has a quality of sexlessness, not effeminacy. Some years ago he must have been remarkably handsome. Now his face seems to have been burned thin by a fever that is not of the flesh . . . . . Bill is grinning and chuckling. Violet's weeping in the ladies' room no longer seems to interest anyone in the bar."*

Leona greets the two amiably, finds that Bobby lives near Dubuque. Leona goes to the juke box to put on her favorite record but drops her coins. Instead of bothering to pick them up she goes over to Monk asking for change for a dollar bill.

QUENTIN: Barman? . . . Barman? . . . What's necessary to get the barman's attention here, I wonder.

Leona crosses back to the juke box. Bobby hands Leona the change
he's picked up off the floor. She looks for a number on the juke box.

MONK: I heard you. You've come in the wrong place. You're looking for
the Jungle Bar, half a mile up the beach.

QUENTIN: Does that mean you'd rather not serve us?

MONK: Let me see the kid's draft card.

BOBBY: I just want a coke.

QUENTIN: He wants a plain Coca-Cola, I'd like a vodka and tonic.

Leona lights up the juke box with a coin and selects a violin num-
ber, "Souvenir." A look of ineffable sweetness appears on her
face at the first note of music.

BILL: Y' can't insult 'em, there's no way to bring 'em down except to beat
'em and roll 'em.

The bar starts to dim and a special spot comes up on Bill. The
violin music on the juke box plays softly under.

I noticed him stop at the door before he come in. He was about to go right
back out when he caught sight of me. Then he decided to stay. A piss-elegant
one like that is asking for it. After a while, say about fifteen minutes, I'll go
in the gents' and he'll follow me in there for a look at Junior. Then I'll have
him hooked. He'll ask me to meet him outside by his car or at the White
Castle. It'll be a short wait and I don't think I'll have t'do more than scare
him a little. I don't like beating 'em up. They can't help the way they are.
Who can? Not me. Left home at fifteen, and like Leona says, I've never done
a lick of work in my life and I never plan to, not as long as Junior keeps
batting on the home team, but my time with Leona's run out. She means to
pull out of here and I mean to stay . . .

The lights come back up in the bar. Leona is listening to the music dreamily,
now completely pacified. Monk goes over to the ladies' room and calls to
Violet that she can come out now.

The bar dims again. This time the special spot comes up on Steve, who
admits to himself that he is one of those unfortunates who must be satisfied
with the scraps of life, must make do with such as Violet, even though he
once caught a disease from her. He drinks beer from a bottle while telling
himself sadly, "Oh my life, my miserable, cheap life! It's like a bone thrown
to a dog! I'm the dog, she's the bone. Hell, I know her habits. She's always
down there in that amusement arcade when I go to pick her up, she's down
there as close as she can get to some navy kid, playing a pinball game, and
one hand is out of sight. Hustling? I reckon that's it. I know I don't provide
for her, just buy her a few beers here, and a hot dog on the way home. But
Bill, why's he let her mess around with him? One night he was braggin' about
the size of his tool, he said all he had to do to make a living was wear tight
pants on the street. Life! . . . Throw it to a dog. I'm not a dog, I don't want
it. I think I'll sit at the bar and pay no attention to her when she comes out."

The lights come up as Violet exits from the ladies' room and goes to the
bar, where Monk gives her a beer. She is playing the martyr; Steve glares at

her. Leona ignores her at first, then ridicules her. Steve, finally the peace-maker, helps Violet from the bar to his table, but not before Violet has man-aged to grab Monk's drink and take it with her.

The phone rings and Monk answers it—it's for Doc. Leona, a thunderstorm that has not yet quite passed over, mutters about Doc's drinking, then turns on Bill. She informs Bill that she let him come live in her trailer because some-times she was lonely, but she won't make that mistake again. Now she wants him out—she throws Bill cab fare and tells him to go remove all his stuff from the trailer. Monk suggests that maybe it's time for Leona to go home now, but she refuses, she wants to hear "Souvenir" some more.

Bill prides himself that he has satisfied Leona for six months, but Leona assures him: "You never satisfied nothing but my mother complex." Besides, Leona tells him, Bill has no appreciation of beauty like God's sky or this violin music (she punches her number on the juke box three more times).

Doc turns away from the phone—he needs a shot of brandy, he has a baby to deliver.

LEONA (*returning to Bill's table*): It wouldn't be sad if you didn't know what you missed by coming into this world and going out of it some day without ever having a sense of, experience of and memory of, a beautiful thing in your life such as I have in mine when I remember the violin of and the face of my young brother . . .

BILL: You told me your brother was a fruit.

LEONA: I told you privately something you're repeating in public with words as cheap as yourself. My brother who played this number had pernicious anemia from the age of thirteen and any fool knows a disease, a condition, like that would make any boy too weak to go with a woman, but he was so full of love he had to give it to someone like his music. And in my work, my profession as a beautician, I never seen skin or hair or eyes that could touch my brother's. His hair was a natural blond as soft as silk and his eyes were two pieces of heaven in a human face, and he played on the violin like he was making love to it . . . . .

Her brother would play soft music during the collection in church, looking like an angel (Leona continues). She would shampoo his golden hair until it looked like a halo. One day he collapsed and soon died of his disease. "He was too beautiful to live," Leona says, "and so he died. Otherwise we'd be living together in my trailer. I'd train him to be a beautician . . . . . to lay his hands on the heads of the homely and lonely and bring some beauty out of them, at least for one night or one day or at least for an hour . . . . ." In which case, Leona finishes, she would not need the companionship of the likes of Bill.

Violet is hungry and wants a hot dog, but Steve is now resentful of her behavior with Bill. Doc makes ready to depart for the trailer park on Treasure Island, where he is to deliver a baby (as he does so, the bar dims again and the spotlight turns on him as he reflects on the eternal miracles and mysteries of life and death).

Leona objects violently to Doc tending a patient in his condition. Doc washes down a benzedrine with yet another brandy. Leona snatches Doc's bag of instruments, which Monk keeps for him behind the bar and resists all the others' efforts to get it back. Finally Bill taunts Leona into attacking him, trying to slap him with her cap, so that Doc is able to recover his bag and escape.

Leona is furious: "All of you are responsible! . . . If he murders a baby tonight and the baby's mother! Is life worth nothing in here?" She storms out to make a phone call. They can't stop her, though they are sure she means to warn the office at Treasure Island, where she parks her own trailer, about Doc. Monk goes to his own telephone, calls Treasure Island and advises them to pay no attention to anything Leona might say if she calls—"She's on a crazy mean drunk."

The lights dim and now the spotlight is on Violet, who protests that her room over the amusement arcade is not as Leona described it. Violet has made it "clean and attractive" and she uses the bathroom facilities downstairs in the arcade.

Leona comes back into the bar and receives the silent treatment from her friends, so she goes over to Quentin and Bobby's table.

LEONA: Well, boys, what went wrong?

QUENTIN: I'm afraid I don't know what you mean.

LEONA: Sure you know what I mean. You're not talking to each other, you don't even look at each other. There's some kind of tension between you. What is it? Is it guilt feelings? Embarrassment with guilt feelings?

BOBBY: I still don't know what you mean, but, uh . . .

LEONA: "But, uh" what?

QUENTIN: Don't you think you're being a little presumptuous?

LEONA: Naw, I know the gay scene. I learned it from my kid brother. He came out early, younger than this boy here. I know the gay scene and I know the language of it and I know how full it is of sickness and sadness; it's so full of sadness and sickness, I could almost be glad that my little brother died before he had time to be infected with all that sadness and sickness in the heart of a gay boy. This kid from Iowa, here, reminds me a little of how my brother was, and you, you remind me of how he might have become if he'd lived.

QUENTIN: Yes, you should be relieved he's dead, then.

Leona flops into a chair without an invitation and asks Quentin to order her a drink because Monk won't serve her one. Quentin tries, but Monk refuses. Leona insists that she is practically "a faggot's moll" and wants Quentin to tell her what has gone wrong between himself and Bobby. Quentin tells her only that he was driving along in his car and passed Bobby on his bicycle and asked Bobby to come home with him to dinner. Quentin also tells Leona that he is a script writer who specializes in making "blue movies bluer with . . . you know, touches of special . . . erotica." Leona confides to Quentin that she is behaving as she is because "it's the death day of my brother." Again, she asks Quentin what the trouble is.

QUENTIN: I only go for straight trade. But this boy . . . look at him! Would you guess he was gay? . . . I didn't, I thought he was straight. But I had an unpleasant surprise when he responded to my hand on his knee by putting his hand on mine.

BOBBY: I don't dig the word *"gay."* To me they mean nothing, those words.

LEONA: Aw, you've got plenty of time to learn the meanings of words and cynical attitudes. Why he's got eyes like my brother's! Have you paid him?

QUENTIN: For disappointment?

LEONA: Don't be a mean-minded mother. Give him a five, a ten. If you picked up what you don't want, it's your mistake and pay for it.

BOBBY: I don't want money from him. I thought he was nice, I liked him.

LEONA: Your mistake, too (*She turns to Quentin.*) Gimme your wallet.

Quentin hands her his wallet.

BOBBY: He's disappointed. I don't want anything from him.

LEONA: Don't be a fool. Fools aren't respected, you fool.

She removes a bill from the wallet and stuffs it in the pocket of Bobby's shirt. Bobby starts to return it.

O.K., I'll hold it for you till he cuts out of here to make another pickup and remind me to give it back to you when he goes. He wants to pay you, it's part of his sad routine. It's like doing penance . . . penitance.

BILL (*loudly*): Monk, where's the head?

MONK: None of that here, Bill.

QUENTIN (*with a twist of a smile toward Bill*): Pity.

Quentin asks Leona to imagine how she would react if she found that fish over the bar swimming around in the air of her bedroom. Impossible? Perhaps, but then so many impossible things do happen. Leona would tell the fish to get the hell out of her bedroom, but not Quentin; Quentin would merely say "Oh, well" and go back to sleep. Quentin has lost the only thing one must never lose in this life, he admits to Leona: "I've lost the capacity for being surprised, so completely lost it, that if I woke up in my bedroom late some night and saw that fantastic fish swimming right over my head, I wouldn't be really surprised."

The bar lights dim and the spotlight comes up on Quentin, who reflects: "There's a coarseness, a deadening coarseness, in the experience of most homosexuals. The experiences are quick, and hard, and brutal, and the pattern of them is practically unchanging. Their act of love is like the jabbing of a hypodermic needle to which they're addicted but which is more and more empty of real interest and surprise . . . . ."

Quentin can remember that once he felt alive, tingling with the surprises of life, experiencing seizures of self-realization. He envies his young friend Bobby's round-eyed wonder at seeing the Pacific Ocean for the first time. But, "I've asked all the questions, shouted them at deaf heaven, till I was hoarse in the voice box and blue in the face, and gotten no answer, not the whisper of one, nothing at all, you see, but the sun coming up each morning and going down that night, and the galaxies of the night sky trooping onstage like chorines, robot chorines: one, two, three, kick, one, two, three, kick . . . Repeat any question too often and what do you get, what's given? . . . A big carved rock by the desert, a . . . monumental symbol of worn out passion and bewilderment in you, a stupid stone paralyzed Sphinx that knows no answers that you don't but comes on like the oracle of all time, waiting on her belly to give out some outcries of universal wisdom, and if she woke up some midnight at the edge of the desert and saw that fantastic fish swimming over her head . . . y'know what she'd say, too? She'd say, 'Oh, well' . . . and go back to sleep for another five thousand years."

The lights come up as Quentin finishes. He wants no more of Bobby; he exits, promising to leave Bobby's bicycle by the door. Leona warns Bobby of the dangers of the road and offers him a place in her trailer. (*"Bill grunts contemptuously but with the knowledge that he is now truly evicted"*). Bobby hesitates, and Leona assures him he has nothing to fear from her; she will handle him with a very, very light touch, unlike Quentin.

Bobby remembers the outrage that was caused back home in Iowa by a man who had a picture of Michelangelo's David and other naked forms in the back room of his flower shop. The bar lights dim, the spot comes onto Bobby, and he remembers how it has been on his journey: "Dreams . . . images . . . night . . . On the plains of Nebraska I passed a night with a group of runaway kids my age and it got cold after sunset. A lovely wild young girl invited me under a blanket with just a smile, and then a boy, me between, and both of them kept saying 'love,' one of 'em in one ear and one in the other, till I didn't know which was which, which 'love' in which ear or which . . . touch . . . The plain was high and the night air . . . exhilarating and the touches not heavy . . ."

The bar is relighted, and Bobby decides to decline Leona's offer. He leaves, forgetting to take his ten dollars, and Leona runs after him to give him the money. Bill sits at the table with Violet and Steve. Monk moves around clearing up glasses and ash trays, while explaining: "I've got no moral objections to them as a part of humanity, but I don't encourage them here. One comes in, others follow. First thing you know you're operating what they call a gay bar and it sounds like a bird cage, they're standing three deep at the bar and lining up at the men's room. Business is terrific for a few months. Then in comes the law. The place is raided, the boys hauled off in the wagon, and your place is padlocked . . . . ."

The next step is to buy protection either from gangsters or from the police, Monk continues, and he wants no part of an operation like that. "I want a small, steady place that I can handle alone, that brings in a small, steady profit. No buddy-buddy association with gangsters and the police. I want to know the people that come in my place so well I can serve them their brand of liquor or beer before they name it, soon as they come in the door. And all their personal problems, I want to know that, too."

The bar lights dim, and Monk is in the spotlight, telling of mutual affection between him and his customers—one of them who died recently in Mexico

City left Monk his $250 savings account. Monk enjoys running the place, and taking a beer upstairs to his bedroom after closing, thinking about everything he's heard that evening. He has heart trouble, he will die some night upstairs, he hopes in his sleep.

>*Leona has returned. The light in the bar comes up but remains at a low level.*

LEONA: . . . Is there a steam engine in here? Did somebody drive in here on a steam engine while I was out?

MONK (*returning from his meditation*): . . . Did what?

LEONA: I hear something going huff-huff like an old locomotive pulling into a station.

>*She is referring to a sound like a panting dog. It comes from Bill at the unlighted table where Violet is seated between him and Steve.*

. . . Oh, well, my home is on wheels . . . Bourbon sweet, Monk.

MONK: Leona, you don't need another.

LEONA: Monk, it's after midnight, my brother's death-day is over, I'll be all right, don't worry.

>*She goes to the bar.*

. . . It was selfish of me to wish he was still alive.

>*A pin-spot of light picks up Violet's tear-stained and tranced face at the otherwise dark table.*

. . . She's got some form of religion in her hands . . .

>*Curtain.*

ACT II

An hour later, Leona is sitting alone at the bar while the others are singing songs. Bill comes to the bar to get another beer. Leona assures him she's serious about leaving town. Wherever she goes she can always find work as a beautician.

Leona admits to Bill that she loved him. He is "special but not superior," and she is going to worry about him because he refuses to grow up. Violet begins to weep for Leona because Leona will be lonely in a new town, "without a soul in the world."

LEONA: . . . . . As for being lonely, listen, ducks, that applies to every mother's son and daughter of us alive, we were given warning of that before we were born almost, and yet . . . when I come to a new place, it takes me two or three weeks, that's all it takes me, to find somebody to live with in my home on wheels and to find a night spot to hang out in. Those first two or three weeks are rough, sometimes I wish I'd stayed where I was before, but I know from experience that I'll find somebody and locate a night spot to booze in, and get acquainted with . . . friends . . .

>*The light has focused on her. She moves downstage with her hands*

*in her pockets, her face and voice very grave as if she were less
confident that things will be as she says.*
And then, all at once, something wonderful happens. All the past disappoint-
ments in people I left behind me just disappear, evaporate from my mind, and
I just remember the good things, such as their sleeping faces, and . . . Life!
Life! I never just said, "Oh, well," I've always said "Life!" to life, like a
song to God, too, because I've lived in my lifetime and not been afraid of . . .
changes . . .
   She goes back to the bar.
. . . However, y'see, I've got this pride in my nature. When I live with a
person I love and care for in my life, I expect his respect, and when I see
I've lost it, I GO, GO! . . . So a home on wheels is the only right home for me.

Violet joins Leona at the bar and smothers her with maudlin sympathy
and affection. Leona warns her that next time she gets sick there will be no
one to take care of her, no one to bring her delicacies, but she advises Violet:
"When you die you should feel a relief from the conditions you lived in."
   Doc comes back, upset, needing a drink. Leona starts in on him, calling
him a quack, demanding to see his license. Since Leona is still in her hostile
mood, Monk suggests that Bill take her home. Leona refuses angrily to have
anything more to do with Bill and slaps the bar with her sailor cap as though
warding off enemies.
   Violet pleads with Steve for something to eat. She is hungry, but Steve is
still half-annoyed at Violet for behaving as she did with Bill. Leona and Doc
are at the bar deep in private thoughts.
   Violet offers to go off with Bill, but Steve objects. The three decide to leave
together, to visit the hamburger stand. Leona tries to stop Violet, but the two
men usher her out the door. Leona runs out after them, and soon Violet's
shrill cries are heard.
   Monk notices that Violet has left her suitcase and so is probably coming
back. Doc agrees: ". . . . . She's going to provide you with the solace of her
companionship up those stairs to the living quarters. Y'know, that narrow
flight of stairs is like the uterine passage to life and I'd say that strange, that
amorphous-looking creature is expecting to enter the world up the uterine
passage to your living quarters above. (*He rises, chuckling darkly.*) Did you
know that I was a poet, a poet-physician whose office is here? No shit. But
the uterine passage to life is down not up, so the image wasn't much good . . .
and neither was my experience at Treasure Island tonight . . . . ."
   Doc lumbers off to the men's room, as Bill rushes into the bar to report on
the fracas outside. They are going to have to call for help in restraining Leona,
he believes. Violet comes into the bar, announces that the police are coming
for Leona, and hides once again in the ladies' room. Monk bolts the street
door but reopens it long enough to let in Steve carrying hot dogs for Violet.
But not even for these will Violet come out of her hiding place.
   Monk offers to buy Doc a nightcap, as Bill broods over his own situation—
no one has ever thrown him out before. Doc tells Monk what happened this
evening: he was called to deliver a three-months premature baby who was

born dead. Doc disposed of the body in the sea, but then the mother began to bleed to death. "I could have told the man to call an ambulance for her," Doc remembers, "but I thought of the probable consequences to me, and while I thought about that, the woman died." Doc gave the father $50 he'd received that day for performing an abortion "in return for his promise not to remember my name."

Monk warns Doc that Leona called Treasure Island earlier that evening and gave them Doc's name, so Doc may be in real trouble. They both agree that Doc should leave town at once.

MONK (*stands to shake*): G'bye, Doc. Keep in touch.

DOC: G'bye, Monk. Thanks for all and the warning.

MONK: Take care, Doc.

STEVE: Yeh, Doc, you got to take care. Bye, Doc.

BILL: No sweat, Doc, g'bye.

> *The Doc exits.*

MONK: That old son of a bitch's paid his dues . . .

> *Approach of a squad car siren is heard at a distance.*

Yep, coming the law!

BILL: I don't want in on this.

STEVE: Not me neither.

> *They rush out. Squad car screeches to a stop. Leona appears at the door, shouting and pounding.*

LEONA: MONK! THE PADDY WAGON IS SINGING MY SONG!

> *Monk lets her in and locks the door.*

MONK: Go upstairs. Can you make it?

> *She clambers up the steps, slips, nearly falls. A policeman, Tony, knocks at the door. Monk admits him.*

Hi, Tony.

TONY: Hi, Monk. What's this about a fight going on here, Monk?

MONK: Fight? Not here. It's been very peaceful tonight. The bar is closed. I'm sitting here having a nightcap with . . .

TONY: Who's that bawling back there?

MONK (*pouring a drink for Tony*): Some dame disappointed in love, the usual thing. Try this and if it suits you, take the bottle.

TONY (*he drinks*): . . . O.K. Good.

MONK: Take the bottle. Drop in more often. I miss you.

TONY: Thanks, g'night.

> *He goes out.*

MONK: Coast is clear, Leona.

> *As Monk puts another bottle on the table, Leona comes awkwardly back down the stairs.*

LEONA: Monk? Thanks, Monk.

> *She and Monk sit at the table. Violet comes out of the ladies' room.*

VIOLET: Steve? . . . Bill?

> *She sees Leona at the table and starts to retreat.*

LEONA: Aw, hell, Violet. Come over and sit down with us, we're having a nightcap, all of us, my brother's death-day is over.

VIOLET: Why does everyone hate me?

> She sits at the table; drinks are poured from the bottle. Violet hitches her chair close to Monk's. In a few moments she will deliberately drop a matchbook under the table, bend to retrieve it and the hand on Monk's side will not return to the table surface.

As her final act of friendship for Violet, Leona advises her that she needs "medical help in the mental department." She likens Violet to a water plant, rootless, drifting here and there with every current. Leona challenges Violet to explain how or why or when she moved into the amusement arcade, and Violet can't remember—her memory is hazy.

Leona rises and goes to play her favorite record again. She plans to leave town this very night, drink or no drink, fog or no fog, but she has a few things to say about Violet before she goes: ". . . . . I don't think she's sure where she was before she came here, any more sure than she is where she'll go when she leaves here. She don't dare remember and she don't dare look forward, neither. Her mind floats on a cloud and her body floats on water. And her dirty fingernail hands reach out to hold on to something she hopes can hold her together. (*She starts back toward the table, stops; the bar dims and light is focused on her.*) . . . Oh, my God, she's at it again, she's got a hand under the table. (*Leona laughs sadly.*) Well, I guess she can't help it. It's sad, though. It's a pitiful thing to have to reach under a table to find some reason to live. You know, she's worshipping her idea of God Almighty in her personal church. Why the hell should I care she done it to a nowhere person that I put up in my trailer for a few months? I wish that kid from I-oh-a with eyes like my lost brother had been willing to travel with me, but I guess I scared him. What I think I'll do is turn back to a faggot's moll when I haul up to Sausalito or San Francisco. You always find one in the gay bars that needs a big sister with him, to camp with and laugh and cry with, and I hope I'll find one soon . . . it scares me to be home alone in my home on wheels built for two . . ."

Leona pulls herself together as the lights come up and pays her final tab at Monk's. Monk and Violet hardly hear her as Leona departs quoting as her exit line the Italian proverb "Meglior solo que mal accompanata"—better alone than in bad company.

Alone with Violet, Monk voices his suspicions that she has brought her suitcase because she expects to spend the night, although his tavern is not licensed for rooms.

VIOLET (*with a tone and gesture of such ultimate supplication that it would break the heart of a stone*): I just meant . . . let's go upstairs. Huh? Monk?

> Monk stares at her reflectively for a while, considering all the portential complications of her taking up semi- or permanent residence up there.

Why're you look at me that way? I just want a temporary, a night, a . . .

MONK: . . . Yeah, go on up and make yourself at home. Take a shower up there while I lock up the bar.

VIOLET: God love you, Monk.

> *She crosses, with a touch of "labyrinthitis," to the stairs and mounts two steps.*

Monk! . . . I'm scared of these stairs, they're almost steep as a ladder. I better take off my slippers. Take my slippers off for me.

> *There is a tone in her voice that implies she has already "moved in" . . . She holds out one leg from the steps, then the other. Monk removes her slippers and she goes on up.*

(*Calling down to him.*) Bring up some beer, sweetheart.

MONK: Yeh, I'll bring some beer up. Don't forget your shower.

> *Alone in the bar, Monk crosses downstage.*

I'm going to stay down here till I hear that shower running, I'm not going up there till she's took a shower.

> *He sniffs the ratty slipper.*

Dirty, worn-out slipper still being worn, sour-smelling with sweat from being worn too long, but still set by the bed to be worn again the next day, walked on here and there on pointless errands till the sole's worn through, and even then not thrown away, just padded with cardboard till the cardboard's worn through and still not thrown away, still put on to walk on till it's . . . past all repair.

> *During this, he has been turning out lamps in the bar.*

Hey, Violet, will you for Chrissake take a . . .

> *This shouted appeal breaks off with a disgusted laugh. He drops the slipper, then grins sadly.*

She probably thinks she'd dissolve in water. I shouldn't of let her stay here. Well, I won't touch her, I'll have no contact with her, maybe I won't even go up there tonight.

> *He crosses to open the door. We hear the boom of the ocean outside.*

I always leave the door open for a few minutes to clear the smoke and liquor smell out of the place, the human odors, and to hear the ocean. Y'know, it sounds different this late than it does with the crowd on the beach-front. It has a private sound to it, a sound that's just for itself and for me.

> *Monk switches off the blue neon sign. It goes dark outside. He closes door. Sound of water running above. He slowly looks toward the sound.*

That ain't rain.

> *Tired from the hectic night, maybe feeling a stitch of pain in his heart (but he's used to that), Monk starts to the stairs. In the spill of light beneath them, he glances up with a slow smile, wry, but not bitter. A smile that's old too early, but it grows a bit warmer as he starts up the stairs. Curtain.*

A GRAPHIC GLANCE

LARRY BLYDEN AND PHIL SILVERS IN THE REVIVAL OF "

"FUNNY THING HAPPENED ON THE WAY TO THE FORUM"

JOAN HACKETT AND LEN CARIOU IN "NIGHT WATCH"

LOU GOSSETT AND JEAN-PIERRE AUMONT IN "MURDEROUS ANGELS"

JEFF FENHOLT AS JESUS OF NAZARETH

"JESUS CHRIST SUPERSTAR"

RAUL JULIA AND DIANA DAVILA (FOREGROUND) AND CLIFTON DAVIS
AND JONELLE ALLEN IN "TWO GENTLEMEN OF VERONA"

RICHARD KILEY AND CLIVE REVILL IN "THE INCOMPARABLE MAX"

TONY ROBERTS, ELAINE JOYCE
AND ROBERT MORSE IN "SUGAR"

MAUREEN STAPLETON, JASON ROBARDS AND GEORGE GRIZZARD
IN THE REVIVAL OF "THE COUNTRY GIRL"

INGRID BERGMAN IN THE REVIVAL OF SHAW'S "CAPTAIN
BRASSBOUND'S CONVERSION"

RON HUSMANN, PHYLLIS NEWMAN, REMAK RAMSEY, DONNA MCKECHNIE, J

HARDS AND BERNADETTE PETERS IN THE REVIVAL OF "ON THE TOWN"

"FIDDLER ON THE ROOF" (WITH PEG MURRAY AS GOLDE AND PAU
STICKNEY AND HOWARD LINDSAY) AND "TOBACCO ROAD" (WIT

...SON AS TEVYE) PULLS AHEAD OF "LIFE WITH FATHER" (DOROTHY
...NRY HULL) TO BECOME BROADWAY'S LONGEST RUNNING SHOW

GEORGE ROSE, BUD CORT, DONALD PLEASENCE AND LAUREN JONES IN "WISE CHILD"

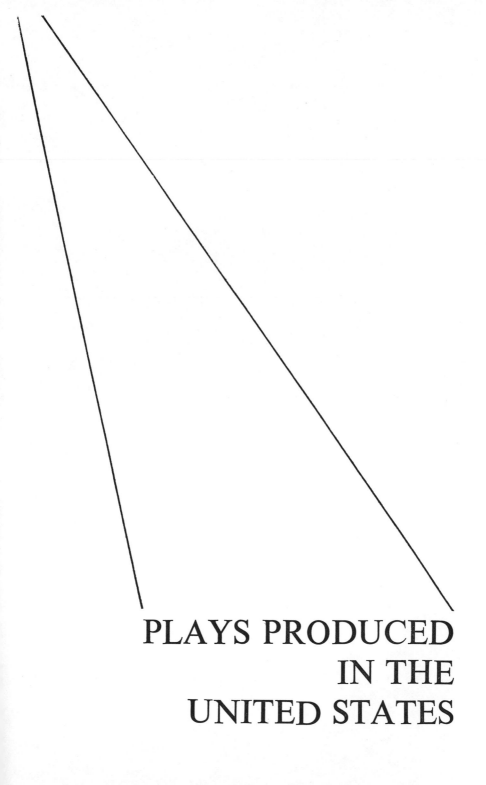

PLAYS PRODUCED
IN THE
UNITED STATES

PLAYS PRODUCED ON BROADWAY

Figures in parentheses following a play's title indicate number of performances. The figures are acquired directly from the production office in each case and do not include previews or extra non-profit performances.

Plays marked with an asterisk (*) were still running on June 1, 1972. Their number of performances is figured from opening night through May 31, 1972.

Shows presented under contracts technically classified as "Middle Broadway" or "Limited Gross Broadway Theater Agreement" are included in this listing of Broadway productions, with a notation (Limited Broadway) or (Middle) following the name of the theater in each such entry.

In a listing of a show's numbers—dances, sketches, musical scenes, etc.— the titles of songs are identified by their appearance in quotation marks (").

HOLDOVERS FROM PREVIOUS SEASONS

Plays which were running on June 1, 1971 are listed below. More detailed information about them appears in previous *Best Plays* volumes of appropriate years. Important cast changes are recorded in a section of this volume.

* **Fiddler on the Roof** (3,205; longest musical run in Broadway history). Musical based on Sholom Aleichem's stories; book by Joseph Stein; music by Jerry Bock; lyrics by Sheldon Harnick. Opened September 22, 1964.

Man of La Mancha (2,328). Musical suggested by the life and works of Miguel de Cervantes y Saavedra; book by Dale Wasserman; music by Mitch Leigh; lyrics by Joe Darion. Opened November 22, 1965. (Closed June 26, 1971)

* **Hair** (1,712). Musical with book and lyrics by Gerome Ragni and James Rado; music by Galt MacDermot. Opened April 29, 1968.

Promises, Promises (1,281). Musical based on the screen play *The Apartment* by Billy Wilder and I.A.L. Diamond; book by Neil Simon; music by Burt Bacharach; lyrics by Hal David. Opened December 1, 1968. (Closed January 1, 1972)

1776 (1,217). Musical based on a conception of Sherman Edwards; book by Peter Stone; music and lyrics by Sherman Edwards. Opened March 16, 1969. (Closed February 13, 1972)

* **Oh! Calcutta!** (1,331). Musical revue devised by Kenneth Tynan; with contributions by Samuel Beckett, Jules Feiffer, Dan Greenburg, John Lennon, Jacques Levy, Leonard Melfi, David Newman and Robert Benton, Sam Shepard, Clovis Trouille, Kenneth Tynan and Sherman Yellen; music and lyrics by The Open Window. Opened June 17, 1969 (originally classified off Broadway; reclassified Middle Broadway; moved to Belasco Theater February 26, 1971 after 704 performances at the Eden Theater through February 21, 1971).

311

* **Butterflies Are Free** (1,090). By Leonard Gershe. Opened October 21, 1969.

Last of the Red Hot Lovers (706). By Neil Simon. Opened December 28, 1969. (Closed September 4, 1971)

Purlie (688). Musical based on the play *Purlie Victorious* by Ossie Davis; book by Ossie Davis, Philip Rose and Peter Udell; music by Gary Geld; lyrics by Peter Udell. Opened March 15, 1970. (Closed November 7, 1971)

Applause (896). Musical based on the film *All About Eve* and the original story by Mary Orr; book by Betty Comden and Adolph Green; music by Charles Strouse; lyrics by Lee Adams. Opened March 30, 1970. (Closed May 27, 1972)

Company (705). Musical with book by George Furth; music and lyrics by Stephen Sondheim. Opened April 26, 1970. (Closed January 1, 1972)

The Rothschilds (507). Musical based on *The Rothschilds* by Frederic Morton; book by Sherman Yellen; music by Jerry Bock; lyrics by Sheldon Harnick. Opened October 19, 1970. (Closed January 2, 1972)

Paul Sills' Story Theater. Repertory of two programs. **Story Theater** (243). Adapted by Paul Sills. Opened October 26, 1970. (Closed July 3, 1971) **Ovid's Metamorphoses** (35). Created by Paul Sills; adapted and translated by Arnold Weinstein; lyrics by Arnold Weinstein. Opened April 22, 1971. (Closed July 3, 1971)

Two by Two (351). Musical based on the play *The Flowering Peach* by Clifford Odets; book by Peter Stone; music by Richard Rodgers; lyrics by Martin Charnin. Opened November 10, 1970. (Closed September 11, 1971)

* **Sleuth** (650). By Anthony Shaffer. Opened November 12, 1970.

The Me Nobody Knows (586). Musical with book by Stephen M. Joseph; edited from the book *The Me Nobody Knows* and adapted by Robert H. Livingston and Herb Schapiro; music by Gary William Friedman; lyrics by Will Holt; original idea by Herb Schapiro. Opened off Broadway May 18, 1970 and played 208 performances; transferred to Broadway December 18, 1970 and played 378 more performances. (Closed November 28, 1971)

Two by Ibsen. Repertory of two revivals by Henrik Ibsen; new adaptations by Christopher Hampton. **A Doll's House** (111). Opened January 13, 1971. (Closed June 26, 1971) **Hedda Gabler** (56). Opened February 17, 1971. (Closed June 19, 1971)

* **No, No, Nanette** (580). Musical revival with book by Otto Harbach and Frank Mandel; music by Vincent Youmans; lyrics by Irving Caesar and Otto Harbach. Opened January 19, 1971.

How the Other Half Loves (104). By Alan Ayckbourn. Opened March 29, 1971. (Closed June 26, 1971)

* **Follies** (485). Musical with book by James Goldman; music and lyrics by Stephen Sondheim. Opened April 4, 1971.

The Repertory Theater of Lincoln Center. 1970-71 schedule of four revivals ended with **Antigone** (46). By Sophocles; English version by Dudley Fitts and Robert Fitzgerald. Opened May 13, 1971. (Closed June 20, 1971)

* **Lenny** (426). By Julian Barry; music by Tom O'Horgan; based on the life and words of Lenny Bruce. Opened May 26, 1971.

PLAYS PRODUCED JUNE 1, 1971—MAY 31, 1972

You're a Good Man, Charlie Brown (32). Musical revival based on the comic strip "Peanuts" by Charles M. Schulz; book, music and lyrics by Clark Gesner (book under the nom de plume John Gordon). Produced by Arthur Whitelaw and Gene Persson at the John Golden Theater. Opened June 1, 1971. (Closed June 27, 1971).

Linus	Stephen Fenning	Schroeder	Carter Cole
Charlie Brown	Dean Stolber	Snoopy	Grant Cowan
Patty	Lee Wilson	Lucy	Liz O'Neal

Understudies: Messrs. Fenning, Stolber, Cole, Cowan—Jason Holt; Misses Wilson, O'Neal—Merry Flershem.

Directed by Joseph Hardy; musical direction, Jack Holmes; scenery and costumes, Alan Kimmel; lighting, Jules Fisher; musical staging, Patricia Birch; musical supervision, arrangements and additional material, Joseph Raposo; associate producer, Warren Lockhart; stage manager, Barbara Tuttle; press, Max Eisen, Warren Pincus.

Time and place: An average day in the life of Charlie Brown. The play was presented in two acts.

You're a Good Man Charlie Brown (minus a comma in its off-Broadway title but using it in its title song) was first produced off Broadway 3/7/67 for 1,597 performances and was named a Best Play of its season.

The list of musical numbers in *You're a Good Man Charlie Brown* appears on pages 415-6 of *The Best Plays of 1966-67*.

The Trial of the Catonsville Nine (29). Transfer from off Broadway of the 1970-71 production of the play by Daniel Berrigan S.J.; text prepared for New York production by Saul Levitt. Produced by the Phoenix Theater, T. Edward Hambleton managing director, and Leland Hayward at the Lyceum Theater. Opened June 2, 1971. (Closed June 26, 1971)

Daniel Berrigan	Colgate Salisbury	George Mische	Michael Moriarty
Philip Berrigan	Biff McGuire	Mary Moylan	Ronnie Claire Edwards
David Darst	James Woods	Defense	Josef Sommer
John Hogan	Barton Heyman	Judge	Mason Adams
Thomas Lewis	Sam Waterston	Witness	Helen Stenborg
Marjorie Melville	Jacqueline Coslow	Prosecution	Davis Roberts
Thomas Melville	Joe Ponazecki		

Marshals: Peter Gorwin, James O'Connell, Gerry Murphy.

Understudies: Messrs. Salisbury, Roberts, Sommer—Jake Dengel; Messrs. McGuire, Heyman, Adams, Ponazecki—Arlen Snyder; Misses Edwards, Coslow, Stenborg—Nancy Franklin; Messrs. Moriarty, Waterston, Woods—Peter Gorwin.

Directed by Gordon Davidson; scenery, Peter Wexler; costumes, Albert Wolsky; lighting, Tharon Musser; production stage manager, Daniel Freudenberger; press, Sol Jacobson, Lewis Harmon.

Time: Monday, October 7, 1968. Place: United States District Court for the District of Maryland. The play was presented without intermission.

The Trial of the Catonsville Nine appeared off Broadway in this production for 130 performances beginning 2/7/71 (see its entry in the "Plays Produced off Broadway" section of the 1970-71 *Best Plays* volume) and was named a Best Play of its season.

No Place to Be Somebody (39). Revival of the play by Charles Gordone. Produced by Ashton Springer and Jeanne Warner at the Morosco Theater. Opened September 9, 1971. (Closed October 10, 1971)

Gabe Gabriel	Philip Thomas	Mary Lou Bolton	Terry Lumley
Shanty Mulligan	Ian Sander	Sweets Crane	Julius W. Harris
Johnny Williams	Terry Alexander	Mike Maffucci	Nick Lewis
Dee Jacobson	Elaine Kerr	Judge Bolton	Ed Van Nuys
Evie Ames	Paulette Ellen Jones	Louis	Jim Jacobs
Cora Beasley	Mary Alice	Sergeant Cappaletti	Peter Savage
Melvin Smeltz	Henry Baker	Harry	Malcolm Hurd

Directed by Charles Gordone; scenery, John Retsek; lighting, Conrad Penrod; stage managers, Garland Lee Thompson, Malcolm Hurd; press, Howard Attlee, David Roggensack, Ellen Levene.

No Place to Be Somebody was first produced off Broadway at the Public Theater 5/4/69 for 250 performances and was named a Best Play of its season and received the 1969-70 Pulitzer Prize. It was produced off Broadway in a return engagement of 312 performances 1/20/70 and on Broadway for 16 performances 12/30/69.

The Black Light Theater of Prague (10). Musical novelty with libretto by Jiri Srnec and Frantisek Kratochvil; music by Jiri Srnec. Produced by Pacific World Artists, Inc., in association with City Center of Music and Drama at the New York City Center. Opened September 27, 1971. (Closed October 3, 1971)

F. Kratochvil	J. Rybova
V. Kubicek	M. Cechova
J. Lutovsky	E. Srncova
M. Matejcek	J. Kozeluhova
F. Spergr	M. Rychlikova
J. Mateickova	

Technicians: Z. Benes, Ing. R. Ledvina, M. Srnec, J. Schroeder, B. Zemlicka, M. Blahova. Directed by Jiri Srnec; scenery, Jiri Srnec and Frantisek Kratochvil; stage manager, Ing. P. Postrehovsky; production manager, Richard Berg; press, Bill Doll & Co., Dick Williams, Cindy Reagan.

ACT I, Scene 1: Introduction. Scene 2: Washwoman. Scene 3: Horse. Scene 4: Dialogue. Scene 5: Ghosts. Scene 6: *Fair of Hands,* Part 1. Act II: *Fair of Hands,* Part II.

Series of black cabinet "magic" illusions, with actors and objects in black with luminous paint moving against a black background. The major sequence, *Fair of Hands,* is a mimed allegory about individuality and freedom symbolized in the action of a street fair. A foreign play previously produced in Prague and at the Edinburgh Festival.

Solitaire/Double Solitaire (36). Program of two one-act plays by Robert Anderson. Produced by Gilbert Cates, Roy N. Nevans and Albert J. Schiff at the John Golden Theater (Limited Broadway). Opened September 30, 1971. (Closed October 31, 1971)

SOLITAIRE

Sam Bradley	Richard Venture	Wife	Joyce Ebert
Madam	Ruth Nelson	Father	John Cromwell
Daughter	Patricia Pearcy	Captain	William Swetland
Brother	Will Fenno		

DOUBLE SOLITAIRE

Charley	Richard Venture	Sylvia	Martha Schlamme
Barbara	Joyce Ebert	George	William Swetland
Mrs. Potter	Ruth Nelson	Peter	Will Fenno
Mr. Potter	John Cromwell		

Standbys: Misses Ebert, Nelson, Schlamme—Alice Hirson; Messrs. Cromwell, Swetland, Venture—William Countryman. Understudies: Mr. Fenno—Stephen Conrad; Miss Pearcy—Jean Weigel.

Directed by Arvin Brown; scenery, Kert Lundel; costumes, Lewis Rampino; lighting, Ronald

Wallace; production stage manager, Martin Gold; press, Harvey B. Sabinson, Lee Solters, Sandra Manley.

In *Solitaire*, a man of the future is nearly dehumanized by computerization and other regimentation. In *Double Solitaire*, the emotional pretenses of a middle-aged married couple of the present day are exposed and examined. Previously produced at the Long Wharf Theater, New Haven, Conn. and at the Edinburgh Festival in Scotland.

Dianne Wiest replaced Patricia Pearcy and William Countryman replaced William Swetland 10/19/71.

* **Jesus Christ Superstar** (268). Musical based on the last seven days in the life of Jesus of Nazareth; conceived for the stage by Tom O'Horgan; music by Andrew Lloyd Webber; lyrics by Tim Rice. Produced by Robert Stigwood in association with MCA, Inc., by arrangement with David Land at the Mark Hellinger Theater. Opened October 12, 1971.

Judas Iscariot	Ben Vereen	Simon Zealotes; Merchant;	
Jesus of Nazareth	Jeff Fenholt	Leper	Dennis Buckley
Mary Magdalene	Yvonne Elliman	Pontius Pilate	Barry Dennen
1st Priest	Alan Braunstein	Peter; Merchant; Leper	Michael Jason
2nd Priest	Michael Meadows	Maid by the Fire; Leper	Linda Rios
Caiaphas	Bob Bingham	Old Man; Apostle; Leper	Peter Schlosser
Annas	Phil Jethro	King Herod; Merchant; Leper	Paul Ainsley
3d Priest	Steven Bell		

Soldiers: Tom Stovall, Paul Sylvan, Edward Barton, Tony Gardner. Judas's Tormentors: Tom Stovall, Paul Sylvan, Edward Barton, Tony Gardner. Tormentors (Judas's Death): James Sbano, Clifford Lipson, Dennis Cooley, Doug Lucas. Cured Lepers: Robin Grean, James Sbano, Laura Michaels, Clifford Lipson, Bonnie Schon, Pi Douglass, Celia Brin, Dennis Cooley. Temple Ladies: Robin Grean, Laura Michaels, Bonnie Schon, Celia Brin, Anita Morris, Kay Cole, Ferne Bork, Denise Delapenha. Apostles: James Sbano, Clifford Lipson, Pi Douglass, Dennis Cooley, Willie Windsor, Samuel E. Wright, Robalee Barnes, Doug Lucas. Merchants: James Sbano, Clifford Lipson, Robalee Barnes. Reporters: Bonnie Schon, Pi Douglass, Anita Morris, Ted Neeley, Kay Cole, Kurt Yaghjian, Margaret Warncke, Willie Windsor, Ferne Bork, Samuel E. Wright, Robalee Barnes, Dough Lucas. Apostle Women: Celia Brin, Anita Morris, Kay Cole, Ferne Bork, Denice Delapenha. Lepers: Anita Morris, Kay Cole, Kurt Yaghjian, Margaret Warncke, Willie Windsor, Ferne Bork, Samuel E. Wright, Denise Delapenha, Robalee Barnes, Doug Lucas, Charlotte Crossley, Cecelia Norfleet, Janet Powell. Soul Girls: Charlotte Crossley, Cecelia Norfleet, Janet Powell. And various Palm Sunday Attendants, Alabaster Monsters, the Mob and Members of the Crowd.

Understudies: Mr. Vereen—Kurt Yaghjian; Mr. Fenholt—Ted Neeley, Dennis Cooley; Miss Elliman—Denise Delapenha; Mr. Bingham—Peter Schlosser; Mr. Dennen—Phil Jethro; Mr. Ainsley—Michael Meadows; Mr. Jethro—Michael Jason; Mr. Buckley—Robalee Barnes—Mr. Jason—Willie Windsor; Messrs. Meadows, Braunstein—Clifford Lipson; Mr. Bell—Doug Lucas; Swing Girl—Marsha Faye; Swing Boy—Nat Morris.

Directed by Tom O'Horgan; musical direction, Marc Pressel; scenery, Robin Wagner; costumes, Randy Barcelo; lighting, Jules Fisher; sound, Abe Jacob; orchestrations, Andrew Lloyd Webber; production supervisor, Charles Gray; associate producers, Gatchell and Neufeld; stage manager, Galen McKinley; press, Merle Debuskey, Leo Stern.

The final chapter in the story of Jesus Christ presented as a rock opera, with the Biblical narrative transposed into contemporary language and imagery. The score was previously published in a record album by Decca.

Marta Heflin replaced Yvonne Elliman 4/17/72. Seth Allen replaced Barry Dennen 1/24/72.

ACT I

Overture ....Company
"Heaven on Their Minds" ....Judas
Bethany, Friday night
   "What's the Buzz" ....Jesus, Mary, Apostles, Their Women
"Strange Thing Mystifying" ....Judas, Jesus, Apostles, Their Women
"Everything's Alright" ....Mary, Judas, Jesus, Apostles, Their Women
Jerusalem, Sunday
   "This Jesus Must Die" ....Caiaphas, Annas, Priests, Company

"Hosanna" ....Caiaphas, Jesus, Company
"Simon Zealotes" ....Simon, Company
"Poor Jerusalem" ....Jesus
Pontius Pilate's house, Monday
  "Pilate's Dream" ....Pilate
"The Temple" ....Jesus, Company
"I Don't Know How to Love Him" ....Mary, Jesus
Tuesday
  "Damned for All Time" ....Judas, Annas, Caiaphas, Priests

ACT II

Thursday Night
  "The Last Supper" ....Jesus, Judas, Apostles
The Garden
  "Gethsemane" ....Jesus
"The Arrest" ....Peter, Jesus, Apostles, Reporters, Caiaphas, Annas
"Peter's Denial" ....Maid, Peter, Soldier, Old Man, Mary
Pilate's palace, Friday
  "Pilate and Christ" ....Pilate, Soldier, Jesus, Company
House of Herod
  "King Herod's Song" ....Herod
"Could We Start Again, Please" ....Mary, Peter
"Judas' Death" ....Judas, Annas, Caiaphas
Pilate's palace
  "Trial Before Pilate" ....Pilate, Caiaphas, Jesus, Mob
"Superstar" ....Voice of Judas, Company
Golgotha
  "The Crucifixion" ....Jesus, Company
"John 19:41" ....Orchestra

The Incomparable Max (23). By Jerome Lawrence and Robert E. Lee; based on stories by Max Beerbohm. Produced by Michael Abbott, Rocky H. Aoki and Jerry Hammer at the Royale Theater. Opened October 19, 1971. (Closed November 6, 1971)

Max Beerbohm ....Clive Revill
Usher; Girl-in-a-Hurry;
  Maid ....Christina Gillespie
William Rothenstein ....Michael Egan
Lewis, a Waiter;
  A Frenchman ....Louis Turenne
Enoch Soames; A.V. Laider ...Richard Kiley
The Man; Col. Elbourne .....Martyn Green

Library Clerk; Young Man ..John Fitzgibbon
Girl Library Attendant; Usher;
  Mrs. Blake ....Fionnuala Flanagan
Theatergoer ....Claude Horton
Theatergoer's Wife ....Betty Sinclair
Hotel Clerk; Uncle Sydney ...Donald Marye
Mrs. Elbourne ....Constance Carpenter
Mr. Blake ....Rex Thompson

Standbys: Messrs. Kiley, Revill—Robert Stattel. Principal understudies: Messers. Green, Egan—Louis Turenne; Mr. Fitzgibbon—Rex Thompson; Mr. Thompson—John Fitzgibbon; Miss Gillespie— Fionnuala Flanagan; Mr. Turenne—Stephen Schnetzer.
    Directed by Gerald Freedman; scenery, David Mitchell; costumes, Theoni V. Aldredge; lighting, Martin Aronstein; special sound, James Reichert; associate producer, Donald Sheff; production stage manager, Alan Hall; stage manager, Mary Porter Hall; press, David Powers.
    The play was divided into two acts. The first, entitled *Max . . . and Enoch Soames,* was based on Beerbohm's story about a failed poet whose dreams that posterity will admire him are shattered when the Devil grants him a glimpse into the future. The second, *Max . . . and A.V. Laider,* is a cliffhanger about fortune-telling and a predicted train wreck.

* Ain't Supposed to Die a Natural Death (256). Musical subtitled *Tunes From Blackness* with book, music and words by Melvin Van Peebles. Produced by Eugene V. Wolsk, Charles Blackwell, Emanuel Azenberg and Robert Malina at the Ethel Barrymore Theater. Opened October 20, 1971.

Gloria Edwards	Clebert Ford
Dick Williams	Sati Jamal
Ralph Wilcox	Jimmy Hayeson
Barbara Alston	Toney Brealond
Joe Fields	Beatrice Winde
Marilyn B. Coleman	Albert Hall
Arthur French	Garrett Morris
Carl Gordon	Bill Duke
Madge Wells	Minnie Gentry
Lauren Jones	

Musicians: Harold Wheeler, Arthur Jenkins, Richard Pratt, Bill Salter, Lloyd Davis, Charles Sullivan, Robert Corten.

Directed by Gilbert Moses; musical direction and supervision, Harold Wheeler; scenery, Kert Lundell; costumes, Bernard Johnson; lighting, Martin Aronstein; sound, Jack Shearing; associate producer, Howard Friedman; production stage manager, Nate Barnett; stage manager, Helaine Head; press, Merle Debuskey, Faith Geer.

Time: Now. Place: Here. The play was presented in two parts.

Series of vignettes, presented in poetic recitatives with musical accompaniment (rather than songs) adding up to a somber portrait of the black ghetto today. Previously produced at Sacramento, Calif. State College.

Cecelia Norfleet replaced Lauren Jones 1/4/72. Lauren Jones replaced Gloria Edwards and Charles Adu replaced Dick Williams 5/9/72.

A Best Play; see page 179

NUMBERS: Just Don't Make No Sense—Arthur French; Coolest Place in Town—Gloria Edwards; You Can Get Up Before Noon Without Being a Square—Ralph Wilcox; Mirror Mirror on the Wall—Joe Fields. Come Raising Your Leg on Me—Marilyn B. Coleman; You Gotta Be Holdin Out Five Dollars on Me—Carl Gordon, Madge Wells; Sera Sera Jim—Lauren Jones; Catch That on the Corner—Clebert Ford; The Dozens—Jimmy Hayeson; Funky Girl on Motherless Broadway—Toney Brealond; Tenth and Greenwich—Beatrice Winde; Heh Heh (Chuckle) Good Mornin' Sunshine—Arthur French; You Ain't No Astronaut—Jimmy Hayeson; Three Boxes of Longs Please—Albert Hall; Lily Done the Zampoughi Every Time I Pulled Her Coattail—Garrett Morris, Barbara Alston; I Got the Blood—Bill Duke; Salamaggi's Birthday—Dick Williams; Come on Feet Do Your Thing—Sati Jamal; Put a Curse on You—Minnie Gentry.

To Live Another Summer, To Pass Another Winter (173). Musical revue from Israel, in the English language, written by Hayim Hefer; music by Dov Seltzer; additional music by David Krivoshei, Alexander Argov and Naomi Shemer; additional lyric by Naomi Shemer. Produced by Leonard Soloway at the Helen Hayes Theater. Opened October 21, 1971. (Closed March 19, 1972)

Rivka Raz	Ili Gorlizki
Aric Lavie	Hanan Goldblatt
Yona Atari	

Singers: Abigail Atarri, Lisa Butbul, David Devon, Rafi Ginat, Sarah Golan, Ronit Goldblatt, Moses Goldstein, Lenore Grant, Mordecai Hamer, Yochai Hazani, Judith Rosenberg, Tslila Steren, Hillik Zadok. Dancers: Zvulum Cohen, Constantin Dolgicer, Katya Dror, David Glazer, Nava Harari, Yuval Harat, Mina Kiviti, Ruth Lerman, Joseph Maimon, Ita Oren, Adam Pasternak, Hadassa Shachar, Ofira Tishler, Tuvia Tishler, Efraim Zamir, Miriam Zamir.

Directed and choreographed by Jonaton Karmon; designed by Neil Peter Jampolis; costumes, Lydia Pincus Gany; music arranged & conducted by David Krivoshei; lyrics translated by David Paulsen; musical supervisor, Gary McFarland; sound design, Anthony Alloy; production stage manager, Moshe Raz; press, Betty Lee Hunt, Henry Luhrman, Harriett Trachtenberg, Maria Pucci.

Songs, episodes and stories mostly about Israel's emergence as a nation, with some Biblical incidents, performed by an all-Israeli cast. A foreign play previously produced in Tel Aviv.

ACT I

"Son of Man" ....Rivka Raz, Aric Lavie, Company
Translated by David Axelrod

"The Sacrifice" ....Lavie, Yochai Hazani, Company
"What Are the Basic Things?" ....Ili Gorlizki, Company
  Translated by Lillian Burstein
"The Grove of Eucalyptus" ....Miss Raz, Company
  Music and lyrics by Naomi Shemer; translated by George Sherman
"The Tradition That Was Destroyed:" Hasidic Medley ....Hanan Goldblatt, Gorlizki,
                                                      Miss Raz, Yona Atari, Company
  Music by Sarah and Ehud Zweig, David Weinkranz, Rabbi Carlibach
"The Boy With the Fiddle" ....Lavie
  Music by Alexander Argov
"Can You Hear My Voice?" ....Miss Atari, Company
  Lyrics by Rachel, music by Samuel Kraus; translated by George Sherman
"Mediteranee" ....Company
"When My Man Returns" ....Miss Raz
  Music by George Moustaki
"Better Days" ....Miss Atari, Company
Tha'am Haze ....Company

ACT II

"To Live Another Summer, To Pass Another Winter" ....Goldblatt, Lavie, Misses Atari,
                                                                  Raz, Company
"Hora Nora" ....Company
  Music by Alexander Argov
"Noah's Ark" ....Gorlizki
  Music by Naomi Shemer
"Don't Destroy the World" ....Lavie
  Lyrics in collaboration with Hayim Guri
"Give Shalom and Sabbath to Jerusalem" ....Company
"Sorry We Won" ....Gorlizki, Goldblatt, Miss Atari
  Music by David Krivoshei
"I'm Alive" ....Rivka Raz, Company
  Music by David Krivoshei
"Give Me a Star" ....Miss Raz, Lavie, Company
  Music by David Krivoshei
Finale ....Company
  "I Wanted to Be a Hero," with music by David Krivoshei, sung by Goldblatt and David
Devon, was added to the show midway in its run.

Unlikely Heroes: 3 Philip Roth Stories (23). Program of three one-act plays *Defender of the Faith, Epstein* and *Eli, the Fanatic* adapted by Larry Arrick from stories by Philip Roth. Produced by Robert L. Livingston at the Plymouth Theater. Opened October 26, 1971. (Closed November 13, 1971)

PERFORMER	"DEFENDER OF THE FAITH"	"EPSTEIN"	"ELI, THE FANATIC"
David Ackroyd	Sgt. Nathan Marx		The Man
Rose Arrick		Ida	Miriam
George Bartenieff	Maj. Leo Ben Ezra		Artie
Anna Berger		Goldie	
Dori Brenner	Cpl. Shulman	Sheila	Nurse
Lou Jacobi		Epstein	Tzuref
Jon Korkes	Pvt. Sheldon Grossbart	Doctor	
Alvin Kupperman	Pvt. Michael Halpern	Michael	Deliveryman
Josh Mostel	Pvt. Larry Fishbein	Folk Singer	1st Intern
Lucille Patton		Mrs. Katz	Shirley
Tom Rosqui	Capt. Paul Barrett		Harry
Michael Tolan			Eli
Lee Wallace			Ted
Stephen van Benschoten	LaHill; Sgt. Philips	Ambulance Driver	2d Intern

Directed by Larry Arrick; scenery, Robert U. Taylor; costumes, Frank Thompson; lighting, Roger Morgan; music researched and edited by Barbara Damashek; production stage manager Randall Brooks; press, Merle Debuskey, Leo Stern.

Defender of the Faith is about a veteran army sergeant who is forced to concern himself with the social and religious needs of a group of recruits who are fellow Jews. In *Epstein*, the father of a family is humiliated by a suspicious rash which develops following a love affair with an attractive widow. *Eli, the Fanatic* is a suburban lawyer assigned to evict a Hebrew school under his community's zoning regulations but he becomes a staunch champion of these so-called "undesirables."

On the Town (73). Musical revival with book and lyrics by Betty Comden and Adolph Green; music by Leonard Bernstein; based on an idea by Jerome Robbins. Produced by Jerry Schlossberg-Vista Productions in the Ron Field Production at the Imperial Theater. Opened October 31, 1971. (Closed January 1, 1972)

Workman; S. Uperman	David Wilder	Claire	Phyllis Newman
Chip	Jess Richards	Maude P. Dilly	Fran Stevens
Ozzie	Remak Ramsay	Pitkin	Tom Avera
Gabey	Ron Husmann	Lucy Schmeeler	Marilyn Cooper
Flossie	Carol Petri	Gina Henie	Gina Paglia
Flossie's Friend	Marybeth Kurdock	MC at Diamond Eddie's	Dennis Roth
Bill Poster;		Diana Dream	Sandra Dorsey
MC at Congacabana	Don Croll	Senorita Dolores	Laura Kenyon
Little Old Lady	Zoya Leporska	Bimmy	Larry Merritt
Announcer; Figment	Orrin Reiley	Coney Island Zoot Suit	
Ivy Smith	Donna McKechnie	Dancers	Charles Goeddertz, Tony Stevens
Hildy	Bernadette Peters		

Singers: Martha Danielle, Sandra Dorsey, Bobbi Franklin, Laura Kenyon, Gail Nelson, Marie Santell, Don Croll, Richard Marr, Orrin Reiley, Dennis Roth, Luke Stover, David Wilder, Craig Yates.

Dancers: Carole Bishop, Jill Cook, Nancy Dalton, Marybeth Kurdock, Bruce Lea, Nancy Lynch, Gina Paglia, Pamela Peadon, Carol Petri, Andy Bew, Paul Charles, Larry Merritt, Charles Goeddertz, Ken Scalice, Tony Stevens, Chester Walker.

Understudies: Misses Newman, Cooper—Laura Kenyon; Miss Peters—Marilyn Cooper; Miss McKechnie—Pamela Peadon; Messrs. Husmann, Ramsay—Orrin Reiley; Mr. Richards—Andy Bew; Mr. Avera—Richard Marr; Miss Stevens—Bobbi Franklin; Miss Leporska—Nancy Lynch.

Directed and choreographed by Ron Field; musical director, Milton Rosenstock; scenery, James Trittipo; costumes, Ray Aghayan, Bob Mackie; lighting, Tharon Musser; orchestrations, Leonard Bernstein, Hershy Kay; assistant choreographer, Michael Shawn; musical coordinator, Dorothea Freitag; associate producers, Rick Mandell, Allen Litke; production stage manager, Lee Murray; stage manager, Robert Corpora; press, Betty Lee Hunt Associates, Henry Luhrman, Harriett Trachtenberg.

Time: June 1944. Place: New York City. Act I, Scene 1: Brooklyn Navy Yard. Scene 2: Subway train. Scene 3: New York street. Scene 4: Miss Turnstiles. Scene 5: Taxi cab. Scene 6: Museum of Natural History. Scene 7: New York street. Scene 8: Carnegie Hall. Scene 9: Claire's apartment. Scene 10: Hildy's apartment. Scene 11: Times Square. Act II, Scene 1a: Diamond Eddie's Manhattan Roof. Scene 1b: Congacabana. Scene 1c: Slam bang. Scene 2: Subway train. Scene 3: Imaginary Coney Island. Scene 4: Coney Island express. Scene 5: Coney Island. Scene 6: Brooklyn Navy Yard.

On the Town was first produced 12/28/44 at the Adelphi Theater for 463 performances. It was revived off Broadway in the 1958-59 season.

ACT I

Overture
"I Feel Like I'm Not Out of Bed Yet" .... Workmen
"New York, New York" .... Chip, Ozzie, Gabey
Miss Turnstiles Ballet .... Contestants, Ivy, Manhattanites
"Come Up to My Place" .... Hildy, Chip
"Carried Away" .... Claire, Ozzie

"Lonely Town" ....Gabey, New Yorkers
"Do-Do-Re-Do" ....Ivy, Mme. Dilly, Teachers, Students
"I Can Cook Too" ....Hildy, Chip
"Lucky to Be Me" ....Gabey, New Yorkers
Times Square Ballet ....Entire Company

ACT II

So Long Baby Ice Revue ....Gina, Skaters
"Nightclub Song" ....Diana
"Nightclub Song" (Spanish) ....Senorita Dolores
"You Got Me" ....Claire, Ozzie, Hildy, Chip
"I Understand" ....Pitkin, Lucy
Playground of the Rich Ballet ....Gabey, Ivy, High Society Dancers
"Some Other Time" ....Claire, Hildy, Chip, Ozzie
"Coney Island Hep Cats" ....Flossie, Friend, Zoot Suit Dancers
"New York, New York" (Reprise) ....Entire Company

The Grass Harp (7). Musical based on the novel by Truman Capote; book and lyrics by Kenward Elmslie; music by Claibe Richardson. Produced by Theater 1972 (Richard Barr, Charles Woodward, Michael Harvey) at the Martin Beck Theater. Opened November 2, 1971. (Closed November 6, 1971)

Dolly Talbo ....Barbara Cook
Collin Talbo ....Russ Thacker
Catherine Creek ....Carol Brice
Verena Talbo ....Ruth Ford
Maude Riordan ....Christine Stabile

Dr. Morris Ritz ....Max Showalter
Judge Cool ....John Baragrey
Babylove ....Karen Morrow
Sheriff Amos Legrand ......Harvey Vernon

The Heavenly Pride and Joys: Kelly Boa, Trudy Bordoff, Colin Duffy, Eva Grant, David Craig Moskin.
Standbys: Misses Cook, Ford—Laurie Franks; Miss Brice—Alyce Webb; Miss Morrow—Travis Hudson; Mr. Thacker—Walter Bobbie; Mr. Showalter—Willian Larsen. Understudies: Mr. Vernon—Allen Williams; Mr. Baragrey—Harvey Vernon; Miss Stabile—Ann Hodapp.
Directed by Ellis Rabb; choreography, Rhoda Levine; musical direction, Theodore Saidenberg; scenery and lighting, James Tilton; costumes, Nancy Potts; musical arrangements, J. (Billy) Ver Planck; additional orchestrations, Jonathan Tunick, Robert Russell Bennett; dance and incidental music, John Berkman; associate producer, Michael Kasdan; production stage manager, Bruce A. Hoover; stage manager, Charles Kindl; press, Betty Lee Hunt Associates, Henry Luhrman, Harriett Trachtenberg, Maria Pucci.
Time: The past. Place: At the Talbo House, in Joy City, and in River Woods. The play was presented without intermission.
Sentimental pastorale of the good old days, with the heroine guarding her secret gypsy elixir (and her innocence) from all her friends and neighbors. A straight-play version by Truman Capote of his novel was produced on Broadway 3/27/52 for 36 performances and was revived off Broadway the following season and in 1960-61.

MUSICAL NUMBERS

Scene 1: The Talbo backyard
"Dropsy Cure Weather" ....Dolly, Catherine, Collin
"This One Day" ....Collin
"This One Day" Dance ....Collin, Maude
Scene 2: The Talbo house
"Think Big Rich" ....Dr. Ritz
"If There's Love Enough" ....Catherine
"Yellow Drum" ....Dolly, Catherine, Collin
Scene 3: The tree-house in River Woods
"Marry With Me" ....Catherine
"I'll Always Be in Love" ....Dolly
"Floozies" ....Collin

The Babylove Miracle Show
"Call Me Babylove" ....Babylove
"Walk Into Heaven" ....Babylove
"Hang a Little Moolah on the Washline" ....Babylove, Pride'n Joys
"Talkin' in Tongues" ....Babylove
"Whooshin' Through My Flesh" ....Babylove, Catherine, Dolly, Collin, Company
"Walk Into Heaven" ....Babylove
"Something for Nothing" ....Dr. Ritz
Scene 4: The jail
"Indian Blues" ....Catherine, Company
"Take a Little Sip" ....Collin, Dolly, Catherine, Maude, Company
Scene 5: Joy City
"Yellow Drum" ....Company
"What Do I Do Now?" ....Verena
Scene 6: The tree-house
"Pick Yourself a Flower" ....Babylove, Company
The Flower Fortune Dance ....Company
"Reach Out" ....Dolly, Company

* **The Prisoner of Second Avenue** (229). By Neil Simon. Produced by Saint-Subber at the Eugene O'Neill Theater. Opened November 11, 1971.

Mel Edison	Peter Falk	Pearl	Florence Stanley
Edna Edison	Lee Grant	Jessie	Tresa Hughes
Harry Edison	Vincent Gardenia	Pauline	Dena Dietrich

Standbys: Mr. Gardenia—Mitchell Jason; Misses Stanley, Hughes, Dietrich—Carol Morley.
Directed by Mike Nichols; scenery, Richard Sylbert; lighting, Tharon Musser; costumes, Anthea Sylbert; stage manager, Wisner Washam; press, Harvey B. Sabinson, Lee Solters, Cheryl Sue Dolby.
Time: The present. Place: An apartment in a modern building in New York's East 80s. The play was presented in two acts.
Comedy of contemporary manners as a member of the high-rise set succumbs to big-city pressures, loses his well-paying job and goes through a nervous breakdown.
Jack Somack replaced Vincent Gardenia 5/22/72. Art Carney replaced Peter Falk and Barbara Barrie replaced Lee Grant 6/5/72.
A Best Play; see page 203

* **The Repertory Theater of Lincoln Center.** Schedule of four programs. **Mary Stuart** (44). Revival of the play by Friedrich Schiller; freely translated and adapted by Stephen Spender. Opened November 11, 1971. (Closed December 18, 1971) **Narrow Road to the Deep North** (44). By Edward Bond. Opened January 6, 1972. (Closed February 12, 1972) **Twelfth Night** (44). Revival of the play by William Shakespeare. Opened March 2, 1972. (Closed April 8, 1972) * **The Crucible** (40) Revival of the play by Arthur Miller. Opened April 27, 1972. Produced by The Repertory Theater of Lincoln Center under the direction of Jules Irving, Robert Symonds associate director, at the Vivian Beaumont Theater.

MARY STUART

Hannah Kennedy	Aline MacMahon	Earl of Kent	Ray Stewart
Sir Amias Paulet	Robert Symonds	Page	Mark Woods
Sir Drue Drury	Seth Allen	Count Aubespine	Ray Fry
Mary Stuart	Salome Jens	Bellievre	Adolph Caesar
Sir Edward Mortimer	Robert Phalen	Officer	James Tolkan
Lord Burleigh	Stephen Elliott	O'Kelly	Richard Greene
Sir William Davison	Andy Robinson	Serving Girl	Crickett Coan
Talbot	Sydney Walker	Sir Andrew Melvil	Joseph Maher
Queen Elizabeth	Nancy Marchand	Sheriff of Northampton	Stuart Pankin
Robert Dudley	Philip Bosco		

Guards, Courtiers, Gentlewomen: Robert Christian, Crickett Coan, Kathleen Doyle, Richard Kline, Marilyn Meyers, Ronald Roston, Peter Weil.

Principal understudies: Misses Jens, Marchand—Frances Sternhagen; Mr. Bosco—Richard Greene; Mr. Elliott—Ray Fry; Messrs. Phalen, Woods—Richard Kline; Messrs. Walker, Maher—Ray Stewart.

Directed by Jules Irving; scenery, Douglas W. Schmidt; lighting, James Gleason; costumes, Malcolm McCormick; music composed by Stanley Silverman; production stage manager, Barbara-Mae Phillips; stage manager, Craig Anderson; press, Susan Bloch, William Schelble, Sedgwick Clark.

Time: 1587. Act I, Scene 1: A chamber in Fotheringay Castle. Scene 2: Royal Palace at Westminster. Scene 3: Neighborhood of a park at Fotheringay. Act II, Scene 1: Palace antechamber. Scene 2: Chamber in the Queen's apartment. Scene 3: A chamber in Fotheringay Castle. Scene 4: Chamber in the Queen's apartment.

Schiller's *Mary (Maria) Stuart* was last performed in New York in German at the City Center for 6 performances by the Vienna Burgtheater 3/26/68. An excerpt from the play was done off Broadway 9/9/63, and the Phoenix Theater presented the Jean Stock Goldstone-John Reich adaptation for 56 performances 10/8/57. This production was the American premiere of the Stephen Spender translation.

NARROW ROAD TO THE DEEP NORTH

Basho	Robert Symonds	Georgina	Martha Henry
Kiro	Andy Robinson	1st Peasant	Harold Miller
Argi	James Cahill	Peasant Woman	Marilyn Meyers
Tola	James Tolkan	Man in the Sack	Ray Fry
Heigoo	Robert Christian	Nun; Peasant Wife	Susan Sharkey
Breebree	Lawrence Wolf	Gunner Tar	Richard Greene
Shogo	Cleavon Little	Gunner Tar's Mate	Robert Phalen
Prime Minister	Philip Bosco	2d Peasant	Stuart Pankin
Commodore	Sydney Walker	Man From River	Richard Kline

Peasants, Soldiers, Tribesmen, etc.: Richard Greene, Richard Kline, Marilyn Meyers, Harold Miller, Stuart Pankin, Ronald Roston, Susan Sharkey, Ray Stewart, Peter Weil, Mark Woods.

Musicians: Thomas Kaye flute; Richard Fitz, Roy Pennington percussion.

Stage Managers: Luis Avalos, Crickett Coan, James Cook.

Principal understudies: Mr. Symonds—Richard Greene; Mr. Robinson—Richard Kline; Mr. Little—Robert Christian; Mr. Bosco, Ronald Roston; Messrs. Walker, Miller—Ray Stewart; Misses Henry, Meyers—Susan Sharkey.

Directed by Dan Sullivan; scenery, Douglas W. Schmidt; lighting, John Gleason; costumes, Carrie Fishbein Robbins; music, Stanley Silverman; production stage manager, Patrick Horrigan; stage manager, Barbara-Mae Phillips.

Time: About the 17th, 18th or 19th Centuries. Place: Japan. Introduction: The river bank (based on an incident in Matsuo Basho's *The Records of a Weather-Exposed Skeleton*). Part I, Scene 1: The same place. Scene 2: Basho's Garden. Scene 3: A road. Scene 4: Shogo's court. Scene 5: The deep North. Scene 6: The river bank. Part II, Scene 1: The court. Scene 2: The deep North. Scene 3: The river bank. Scene 4: The same place.

Symbolic personifications of the poetic dreamer, the war lord, the simple peasant, the interfering British Empire, etc., opposing each other in black comedy episodes. A foreign play previously produced in London and at the Charles Playhouse in Boston.

TWELFTH NIGHT

Orsino	Moses Gunn	Feste	George Pentecost
Curio	Crickett Coan	Olivia	Martha Henry
Valentine	Robert Christian	Malvolio	Rene Auberjonois
Viola	Blythe Danner	Antonio	Philip Bosco
Sea Captain	Richard Greene	Sebastian	Stephen McHattie
Sir Toby Belch	Sydney Walker	Fabian	Harold Miller
Maria	Cynthia Belgrave	Priest	Ray Fry
Sir Andrew Aguecheek	Leonard Frey	Sailor	Richard Kline

Soldiers of Orsino: Charles Turner, Richard Kline. Attendants to Olivia: Kathleen Doyle, Marilyn Meyers. Attendants to Orsino: Stuart Pankin, Robert Phalen, Peter Weil, Mark Woods.

Principal understudies: Mr. Gunn—Robert Christian; Misses Belgrave, Coan—Kathleen Doyle; Miss Henry—Marilyn Meyers; Mr. Auberjonois—Robert Phalen; Mr. Walker—Richard Greene; Messrs. Frey, McHattie—Richard Kline.

Directed by Ellis Rabb; music, Cathy MacDonald; scenery, Douglas W. Schmidt; lighting, John Gleason; costumes, Ann Roth; vocal director, Roland Gagnon; production stage manager, Barbara-Mae Phillips; stage manager, Craig Anderson.

Place: Illyria. The play was presented in two parts.

Twelfth Night has been produced in New York more than two dozen times in the 20th century, including musical versions. Its last major production was by the New York Shakespeare Festival outdoors in Central Park 8/6/69 for 20 performances.

Stuart Pankin replaced Ray Fry 3/7/72. Charles Turner replaced Robert Christian 4/5/72.

THE CRUCIBLE

Reverend Parris	Jerome Dempsey	Giles Corey	Sydney Walker
Betty Parris	Alexandra Stoddart	Reverend John Hale	Philip Bosco
Tituba	Theresa Merritt	Elizabeth Proctor	Martha Henry
Abigail Williams	Pamela Payton-Wright	Francis Nurse	Wendell Phillips
Susanna Walcott	Crickett Coan	Ezekiel Cheever	Richard Greene
Mrs. Ann Putnam	Pauline Flanagan	Marshal Herrick	Richard Kline
Thomas Putnam	Ben Hammer	Judge Hathorne	Robert Phalen
Mercy Lewis	Kathleen Doyle	Deputy Gov. Danforth	Stephen Elliott
Mary Warren	Nora Heflin	Sarah Good	Doris Rich
John Proctor	Robert Foxworth	Hopkins	Stuart Pankin
Rebecca Nurse	Aline MacMahon	Deputy	Mark Woods

Principal understudies: Mr. Foxworth—Richard Greene; Misses Henry, Flanagan, Rich— Barbara Tarbuck; Miss Payton-Wright—Crickett Coan; Miss Merritt—Louise Stubbs; Miss Heflin—Kathleen Doyle; Messrs. Elliott, Walker, Phillips—John Newton; Mr. Bosco—Robert Phalen; Messrs. Dempsey, Hammer—Stuart Pankin.

Directed by John Berry; scenery and lighting, Jo Mielziner; costumes, Carrie Fishbein Robbins; vocal director, Roland Gagnon; production stage manager, Patrick Horrigan; stage manager, Barbara-Mae Phillips.

Time: 1692. Place: Salem, Mass. Act I: An upper bedroom in the house of Rev. Samuel Parris in the spring of the year. Act II: The common room of Proctor's house, eight days later. Act III: The vestry room of the Salem meeting house, now serving as the anteroom of the General Court. Act IV: A cell in Salem jail, that fall. The play was presented in two parts with the intermission following Act II.

Miller's drama of early American witch-hunting and its consequences was first produced 1/22/53 on Broadway for 197 performances and was named a Best Play of its season. A successful off-Broadway revival opened during the season of 1957-58 and ran for 571 performances. It also appeared on Broadway in a National Repertory Theater touring version 4/6/64 for 16 performances.

John Newton replaced Richard Greene 5/16/62.

* **Twigs** (228). Program of four one-act plays by George Furth: *Emily, Celia, Dorothy* and *Ma*. Produced by Frederick Brisson in association with Plum Productions, Inc. at the Broadhurst Theater. Opened November 14, 1971.

EMILY

Emily	Sada Thompson	Frank	Nicolas Coster

CELIA

Celia	Sada Thompson	Swede	Conrad Bain
Phil	Simon Oakland		

DOROTHY

Lou	A. Larry Haines	Ned	Walter Klavun
Dorothy	Sada Thompson		

MA

Pa	Robert Donley	Priest	MacIntyre Dixon
Ma	Sada Thompson		

Standbys: Miss Thompson—Bobo Lewis; Messrs. Haines, Oakland, Coster, Bain—Rod Colbin; Messrs. Donley, Klavun—Jon Richards. Understudy: Mr. Dixon—Ned Farster.

Directed by Michael Bennett; scenery, Peter Larkin; costumes, Sara Brook; lighting, David F. Segal; assistant to the producers, Fred Hebert; production assistant, Bob Avian; production stage manager, Jeff Chambers; press, Harvey Sabinson, Lee Solters, Marilynn LeVine.

Time: The day before Thanksgiving in continuous time sequence going from 9 in the morning until 9 in the evening. Place: A variety of kitchens on the outskirts of a major city. Act I, Scene 1: Emily—9 a.m. the day before Thanksgiving. Scene 2: Celia—1 p.m. on the same day. Act II, Scene 1: Dorothy—6 p.m. that evening. Scene 2: Ma—9 p.m. that evening.

In *Emily,* a lonely but attractive divorcee is aided in fixing up her new kitchen by a moving man who finally asks her to dinner. *Celia* is a housewife who once played a bit part in a Hollywood movie but is now submerged in the boring vulgarities of her husband and his dreary friend drinking beer and discussing sports. *Dorothy* is a suburban housewife whose holiday tete-a-tete with her husband is interrupted by a visit from his aging father. *Ma* is the mother of the above three heroines, an aged, failing but still crusty crone who dreads her daughters' sentimental holiday phone calls but decides to legitimize them at last by marrying their father before she dies. All four playlets are comedies, with all the title roles played by the same actress, Sada Thompson, in this production.

Mark Dawson replaced Simon Oakland 5/31/72.

Old Times (119). By Harold Pinter. Produced by Roger L. Stevens in association with the Royal Shakespeare Company at the Billy Rose Theater. Opened November 16, 1971. (Closed February 26, 1972)

Deeley	Robert Shaw	Kate	Mary Ure
Anna	Rosemary Harris		

Directed by Peter Hall; scenery and lighting, John Bury; costumes, Beatrice Dawson; a Dowling-Whitehead-Stevens production; production stage manager, Frederic de Wilde; stage manager, Wayne Carson; press, Seymour Krawitz, Patricia Krawitz.

Time: Autumn; night. Place: A converted farmhouse. The play was presented in two parts.

A movie director, his wife and his wife's former roommate spend an evening of strange reminiscences, desires and mixed emotions in a country house by the sea. A foreign play previously produced in London by the Royal Shakespeare Company.

A Best Play; see page 221

Only Fools Are Sad (144). Israeli musical in English translation, based on old Hassidic stories and parables; book by Dan Almagor; music derived from Hassidic songs. Produced under the patronage of the prime minister of Israel, Mrs. Golda Meir, by Yaacov Agmon at the Edison Theater. Opened November 22, 1971. (Closed March 26, 1972)

Galia Ishay	Shlomo Nitzan
Danny Litanny	Michal Noy
Don Maseng	Aviva Schwarz

Understudies: Yael Yaacov, David Zakai.

Directed by Yossi Yzraely; music arranged by Yohanan Zarai and Gil Aldema; book translated by Shimon Wincelberg and Valerie Arnon; lyrics translated by Robert Friend; scenery, Dani Karavan; lighting, Yehiel Orgal; American production scenery supervised by Herbert Senn, costumes by Helen Pond, lighting by Robert Brand; musical instructor and advisor, Hanna Hakohen; production manager, Naomi Schilo; production stage manager, Marko Bechar; stage manager, Boaz Ben-Zion; press, David Lipsky.

Anthology of songs and stories of the Hassidic movement, founded in the 18th Century in Europe and stressing the simple, pious life with its pleasures and happiness. A foreign play previously produced in Tel Aviv in Hebrew under the title *Ish Hassid Haya* (Once There Was a Hassid).

PART I—"Once There Was a Melody," entire company; Isaac, the Baker (The Treasure), Danny Litanny and Michael Noy (Narrators), Galia Ishay (Isaac); A Merry Melody, entire company; Berl, the Tailor (Opening a New Account), Don Maseng (Berl), Shlomo Nitzan (Rabbi Levy Itzhak); The Promise That Was Kept, Litanny (Narrator); "Don't Suck the Bones," Nitzan (Narrator); "Eat, Lord, and Enjoy," Michal Noy (Narrator); "Tell Me What the Rain Is Saying," Aviva Schwartz (Soloist); "Don't Sell It Cheap," Nitzan (Narrator); A Drinking Song, Maseng (Soloist); The Ten Ruble Note, Nitzan (Narrator); "Kol Rinah Vishu'ah," entire company; Gedaliah, the Tar Maker, Miss Schwartz (Narrator), Nitzan (Rabbi Israel Ba'al Shem Tov), Litanny (Gedaliah).

PART II—The Goat, Maseng, Michal Noy (Narrators), Miss Ishay (The Son); "Forest, Forest," Miss Noy (Soloist); Smoking on the Sabbath, Nitzan (Narrator); "Bim-Bam-Bom," entire company; Waiting for the Messiah, Miss Noy (narrator), Maseng (Rabbi Moshe Teitelbaum); Haim, the Goose-Herder, Miss Ishay; Getzl, the Shoemaker (Aleph . . . Beth), Litanny; The Rabbi Who Promised to Wait, Nitzan (Narrator); A Letter to the Rabbi, Maseng Soloist); "Angel, Angel . . ." Miss Ishay; "Only Fools Are Sad," Miss Schwarz (Soloist); Avreymele Melamed, Litanny, Nitzan, Maseng (Soloists); A Sabbath Song, Nitzan (Soloist), "And God Said Unto Jacob," Litanny (Soloist).

* Two Gentlemen of Verona (209). Musical based on the play by William Shakespeare (see note); adapted by John Guare and Mel Shapiro; music by Galt MacDermot; lyrics by John Guare. Produced by the New York Shakespeare Festival, Joseph Papp producer, at the St. James Theater. Opened December 1, 1971.

Thurio	Frank O'Brien	Crab	Phineas
Speed	Jose Perez	Duke of Milan	Norman Matlock
Valentine	Clifton Davis	Silvia	Jonelle Allen
Proteus	Raul Julia	Eglamour	Alvin Lum
Julia	Diana Davila	Vissi D'Amore	Frank O'Brien
Lucetta	Alix Elias		Georgyn Geetlein
Launce	John Bottoms	Milkmaid	Sheila Gibbs
Antonio; Tavern Host	Frederic Warriner		

Citizens of Verona and Milan: Loretta Abbott, Christopher Alden, Roger Briant, Douglas Brickhouse, Stockard Channing, Paul DeJohn, Nancy Denning, Richard De Russo, Arthur Erickson, Georgyn Geetlein, Sheila Gibbs, Jeff Goldblum, Edward Henkel, Albert Insinnia, Jane Jaffe, Signa Joy, Kenneth Lowry, Sakinah Mahammud, Otis Sallid, Madeleine Swift.

Quartet (Black Passion): Sheila Gibbs, Signa Joy, Kenneth Lowry, Sakinah Mahammud.

Understudies: Miss Allen—Signa Joy; Miss Elias—Stockard Channing; Mr. Matlock—Don Jay; Mr. Lum—Jeff Goldblum.

Directed by Mel Shapiro; choreography, Jean Erdman; scenery, Ming Cho Lee; costumes, Theoni V. Aldredge; lighting, Lawrence Metzler; musical supervision, Harold Wheeler; additional musical staging, Dennis Nahat; sound, Jack Shearing; associate producer, Bernard Gersten; production stage manager, R. Derek Swire; stage manager, D.W. Koehler; press, Merle Debuskey, Faith Geer.

Place: Verona, Milan and the forest. The play was presented in two acts.

Musicalization of Shakespeare's comedy about the love of Valentine and Proteus for Silvia and Julia, which was previously produced by the New York Shakespeare Festival in the summer of 1971 at the Delacorte Theater in Central Park and on the Mobile Theater circuit (see its entry in the "Plays Produced off Broadway" section of this volume).

NOTE: This show was originally presented in Central Park under Shakespeare's title *The Two Gentlemen of Verona* but dropped the definite article from the title for its Broadway billing.

Elwoodson Williams replaced Norman Matlock 4/4/72.

ACT I

"Summer, Summer"	Ensemble
"I Love My Father"	Ensemble
"That's a Very Interesting Question"	Proteus, Valentine
"I'd Like to Be a Rose"	Proteus, Valentine
"Thou, Julia, Thou Hast Metamorphosed Me"	Proteus
"Symphony"	Proteus, Ensemble
"I Am Not Interested in Love"	Julia
"Love, Is That You?"	Vissi D'Amore
"Thou, Proteus, Thou Hast Metamorphosed Me"	Julia
"What Does a Lover Pack?"	Julia, Proteus, Ensemble
"Pearls"	Launce
"I Love My Father" (Reprise)	Proteus

"Two Gentlemen of Verona" ....Julia, Lucetta, Ensemble
"Follow the Rainbow" ....Valentine, Speed, Proteus, Launce, Julia, Lucetta
"Where's North?" ....Valentine, Speed, Duke of Milan, Silvia, Thurio, Ensemble
"Bring All the Boys Back Home" ....Duke of Milan, Thurio, Ensemble
"Love's Revenge" ....Valentine
"To Whom It May Concern Me" ....Silvia, Valentine
"Night Letter" ....Silvia, Valentine
"Love's Revenge" (Reprise) ....Valentine, Proteus, Speed, Launce
"Calla Lily Lady" ....Proteus

ACT II

"Land of Betrayal" ....Lucetta
"Thurio's Samba" ....Thurio, Duke of Milan, Ensemble
"Hot Lover" ....Launce, Speed
"What a Nice Idea" ....Julia
"Who Is Sylvia" ....Proteus, Host, Ensemble
"Love Me" ....Silvia, Ensemble
"Eglamour" ....Eglamour, Sylvia
"Kidnapped" ....Julia, Duke of Milan, Proteus, Thurio, Ensemble
"Mansion" ....Valentine
"Eglamour" (Reprise) ....Silvia, Eglamour
"What's a Nice Girl Like Her" ....Proteus
"Dragon Fight" ....Dragon, Eglamour, Proteus, Valentine
"Don't Have the Baby" ....Julia, Lucetta, Speed, Launce
"Love, Is That You?" (Reprise) ....Thurio, Lucetta
"Milkmaid" ....Launce, Milkmaid
Finale
  "I Love My Father" (Reprise) ....Full Company
  "Love Has Driven Me Sane" ....Full Company

Wild and Wonderful (1). Musical with book by Phil Phillips; music and lyrics by Bob Goodman; from an original work by Bob Brotherton and Bob Miller. Produced by Rick Hobard in association with Raymonde Weil at the Lyceum Theater. Opened and closed at the evening performance, December 7, 1971.

Jenny	Laura McDuffie	Brother John	Larry Small
Charlie	Walter Willison	Father Desmond	Ted Thurston
Lionel Masters	Robert Burr		

Ensemble: Yveline Baudez, Pam Blair, Mary Ann Bruning, Carol Conte, Bob Daley, Anna Maria Fanizzi, Marcelo Gamboa, Adam Grammis, Patti Haine, Ann Reinking, Jimmy Roddy, Steven Vincent, Eddie Wright Jr.
  Directed by Burry Fredrik; dances and musical numbers staged by Ronn Forella; musical direction, vocal arrangements, dance music composition and arrangement, Thom Janusz; scenery, Stephen Hendrickson; costumes, Frank Thompson; lighting, Neil Peter Jampolis; orchestrations, Luther Henderson; associate producer, John C. O'Regan; production stage manager, Robert Keegan; stage manager, Louis Pulvino; press, Max Eisen, Jeanne Gibson Merrick, Milly Schoenbaum.
  Time: The present. Place: The big city.
  Subtitled A "Big City Fable, the show's book is about an ex-West Pointer assigned by the CIA to infiltrate a metropolis's youth movement.

ACT I

"Wild and Wonderful" ....Company
"My First Moment" ....Jenny
"I Spy" ....Charlie
"Desmond's Dilemma" ....Desmond, Brother John
"Moment Is Now" ....Ensemble
"Something Wonderful" ....Jenny
"Chances" ....Jenny, Models

"She Should Have Me" ....Lionel
"Jenny" ....Charlie
"Fallen Angels" ....Brother John, Company
Dance ....Company

ACT II

"Petty Crime" ....Jenny, Judge, Company
"Come a Little Closer" ....Jenny, Charlie
"Little Bits and Pieces" ....Lionel, Models
"Is This My Town" ....Jenny
"You Can Reach the Sun" ....Brother John, Company
"Wild and Wonderful" (Reprise) ....Company

Inner City (97). Musical based on the book *The Inner City Mother Goose* by Eve Merriam; conceived by Tom O'Horgan; music by Helen Miller; lyrics by Eve Merriam. Produced by Joseph Kipness, Lawrence Kasha and Tom O'Horgan in association with RCA Records at the Ethel Barrymore Theater. Opened December 19, 1971. (Closed March 11, 1972)

Joy Garrett	Paulette Ellen Jones
Carl Hall	Larry Marshall
Delores Hall	Allan Nicholls
Fluffer Hirsch	Florence Tarlow
Linda Hopkins	

Directed by Tom O'Horgan; musical direction, Clay Fullum; scenery, Robin Wagner; costumes, Joseph G. Aulisi; lighting, John Dodd in association with Jane Reisman; orchestrations and arrangements, Gordon Harrell; vocal arrangements, Helen Miller; sound, Gary Harris; associate producers, Harvey Milk, John M. Nagel; production stage manager, Nicholas Russiyan; stage manager, Daniel Landau; press, Bill Doll & Co., Dick Williams, Virginia Holden, Cindy Reagan.

Subtitled *A Street Cantata,* a musical pot pourri of nursery-rhyme parodies taking off on the ironies and miseries of life in our decaying central cities.

MUSICAL NUMBERS

ACT I—Scene 1, Nub of the Nation: "Fee Fi Fo Fum," Linda Hopkins; "Now I Lay Me," Carl Hall, Delores Hall, Allan Nicholls; "Locks," "I Had a Little Teevee," Fluffer Hirsch; "Hushabye Baby," "My Mother Said," Paulette Ellen Jones; "Diddle Diddle Dumpling," "Rub a Dub Dub," Larry Marshall; "You'll Find Mice," Miss Hopkins; "Ding Dong Bell," Hall, Cast; "The Brave Old City of New York," Joy Garrett; "Urban Renewal," Miss Hopkins; "The Nub of the Nation," Cast. Scene 2, Urban Mary: "Mary, Mary," Cast; "City Life," Florence Tarlow; "One Misty Moisty Morning," Marshall; "Jack Be Nimble," Hall, Hirsch, Marshall; "If Wishes Were Horses," Miss Hall. Scene 3, Deep in the Night: "One Man," "Deep in the Night," Miss Hopkins. Scene 4, Take-a-Tour, Congressman: "Statistics," "Twelve Rooftops Leaping," "Take-a-Tour, Congressman," Cast; "Simple Simon," Marshall, Nicholls, Cast; "Poverty Program," Cast; "One, Two," Hall, Cast; "Tom, Tom," Nicholls; "Hickety, Pickety," Cast; "Half Alice," Miss Hall. Scene 5, The Spirit of Education: "This Is the Way We Go to School," Cast; "The Spirit of Education," Miss Tarlow; "Little Jack Horner," Cast; "Subway Dream," Marshall; "Christmas Is Coming," Hirsch; "I'm Sorry Says the Machine," Marshall, Cast; "Jeremiah Obadiah," Marshall; "Riddle Song," "Shadow of the Sun," Cast.

ACT II—Scene 1, Wisdom: "Boys and Girls Come Out to Play," Cast; "Summer Nights," Misses Garrett, Hall, Jones; "Lucy Locket," Hirsch; "Winter Nights," Misses Hopkins, Tarlow; "Wisdom," Marshall; "The Hooker," Miss Garrett. Scene 2, Starlight: "Wino Will," "Man in the Doorway," Miss Jones; "Starlight Starbright," Miss Hall; "The Cow Jumped Over the Moon," Marshall; "The Dealer," Nicholls. Scene 3, Crooked Man: "Taffy," Hall, Hirsch, Cast; "Numbers," Marshall, Cast; "The Pickpocket," Hall; "Law and Order," Miss Hall, Cast. Scene 4, Kindness: "Kindness," Nicholls, Cast; "As I Went Over," Nicholls; "There Was a Little Man," "Who Killed Nobody," Cast. Scene 5, If: "It's My Belief," Miss Hopkins; "Street Sermon," "The Great If," Hall; "On This Rock," "The Great If" (Reprise), Cast.

Murderous Angels (24). By Conor Cruise O'Brien. Produced by the Phoenix Theater, T. Edward Hambleton managing director, by arrangement with Elliot Martin and George W. George at the Playhouse Theater. Opened December 20, 1971. (Closed January 9, 1972)

Baron d'Auge ....Richard Venture	Ambassador of
Viscount Tamworth ....Neil Fitzgerald	United States ....John Baragrey
James Bonham ....Richard Easton	U.N. Sergeant ....Jack Landron
Mr. Ainsworth ....Donald Symington	White Settler;
Mr. Calvin ....Humbert Allen Astredo	British Consul ....John Clarkson
Dag Hammarskjold .....Jean-Pierre Aumont	Congolese Singer;
Diallo Dop ....Herbert Jefferson Jr.	Mme. Pauline Lumumba .....Ula Walker
Monsignor Polycarpe ....William Larsen	Congolese Woman ....Mabel Robinson
Father Boniface ....Les Roberts	U.N. Attendant ....Sharon Laughlin
Patrice Lumumba ....Lou Gossett	Rajat Asdal ....Gilbert Green
Mme. Rose Rose ....Barbara Colby	Col. Alcibiade Zbyre ....Joseph Mascolo
Ambassador of	Moise Tshombe ....Leonard Jackson
Soviet Union ....Ben Hammer	

U.N. Soldiers, Congolese Men and Women: Tyrone Brown, Stephen Goff, Gerry Murphy, Lynda Westcott, Elwoodson Williams, Stephen Zulick.

Alternate: Mr. Aumont—Humbert Allen Astredo. Stanby: Messrs. Gossett, Green—J.A. Preston. Principal Understudies: Mr. Easton—John Clarkson; Miss Colby—Sharon Laughlin; Messrs. Jefferson, Roberts—Jack Landron; Messrs. Astredo, Larsen—Gilbert Green.

Directed by Gordon Davidson; scenery, Peter Wexler; costumes, Frank Thompson; lighting, Gilbert Hemsley Jr.; sound score, Pia Gilbert; film sequences, Sterling Johnson (Group One Productions), Jack Coddington; production stage manager, Daniel Freudenberger; stage managers, David Barber, James S. Lucas Jr.; press, Sol Jacobson, Lewis Harmon, Ruth D. Smuckler.

Time: June 30, 1960 through Sept. 17, 1961. Place: New York, Brussels, London, the Province of Katanga and the Republic of the Congo. Act I, Scene 1: June 30, 1960, prelude. Scene 2: Late July 1960, New York, the Secretary-General's conference room, 38th floor, United Nations. Scene 3: Aug. 1960, Elizabethville, residence of Monsignor Polycarpe. Scene 4: Aug. 12, 1960, Elizabethville airport. Scene 5: Immediately following. Scene 6: Late afternoon of the same day, Leopoldville, residence of the Prime Minister of the Republic of the Congo, Patrice Lumumba. Scene 7: Later the same evening, Leopoldville, the Secretary-General's suite at the Hotel Royale. Scene 8: Leopoldville, Sept. 10-14, 1960.

ACT II, Scene 1: Nov. 1960, New York, Dag Hammarskjold's office, 38th floor, United Nations. Scene 2: Two days later, Leopoldville, Lumumba's residence. Scene 3: Leopoldville, Dec. 1960-Jan. 1961 Scene 4: Brussels, early Feb. 1961. Scene 5: New York, Feb. 13, 1961, Hammarskjold's office at the U.N. Scene 6: July-Sept. 1961.

Fictionalized dramatization of international events and personalities at the time of the deaths of Lumumba and Hammarskjold, written by one who was the Secretary-General's special representative in Katanga while these events were taking place. A foreign play previously produced at the Mark Taper Forum in Los Angeles.

Anne of Green Gables (16). Musical adapted by Donald Harron from the novel by L.M. Montgomery; music by Norman Campbell; lyrics by Donald Harron and Norman Campbell. Produced by City Center of Music and Drama, Inc., Norman Singer executive director, in association with The Charlottetown Festival, Prince Edward Island, Canada, in the Canadian National Musical Theater production at the City Center 55th Street Theater (formerly the New York City Center). Opened December 21, 1971. (Closed January 2, 1972)

Mrs. Rachel Lynde ....Maud Whitmore	Earl; Stationmaster ....Bill Hosie
Mrs. MacPherson; Lucilla ...Cleone Duncan	Cecil ....George Merner
Mrs. Barry ....Nancy Kerr	Marilla Cuthbert ....Elizabeth Mawson
Mrs. Sloane;	Matthew Cuthbert ....Peter Mews
Mrs. Spencer ....Flora MacKenzie	Anne Shirley ....Gracie Finley
Mrs. Pye ....Kathryn Watt	Mrs. Blewett; Miss Stacy .....Roma Hearn
Minister ....Lloyd Malenfant	Diana Barry ....Glenda Landry
Rev. Smythe Hankinson;	Young Ladies at Avonlea School
Mr. Philips ....Jack Northmore	Prissy Andrews ....Sharlene McLean

Josie Pye ....Barbara Barsky
Ruby Gillis ....Patti Toms
Tillie Boulter ....Lynn Marsh
Gertie Pye ....Deborah Millar
Boys at Avonlea School
Gilbert Blythe ....Jeff Hyslop

Charlie Sloane ....George Juriga
Moody MacPherson ....Dan Costain
Gerry Buote ....Andre Denis
Tommy Sloane ....John Powell
Malcolm Andrews ....Calvin McRae

Directed and choreographed by Alan Lund; musical direction and orchestration, John Fenwick; production design, Murray Laufer; costumes, Marie Day; lighting, Ronald Montgomery; associate musical director, Fen Watkin; additional lyrics, Mavor Moore, Elaine Campbell; associate lighting designer, Gary Craswell; production stage manager, David Loynd; stage managers, J.P. Regan, Ernie Abugov; press, Jack McAndrew, Meg Gordean, Ellen Levene.

Time: The turn of the century. Place: Avonlea, a tiny village on Prince Edward Island, Canada's smallest province.

Sentimental stage treatment of the sentimental novel about the growing up of an orphan girl. A foreign play previously produced at Prince Edward Island, in London and elsewhere.

ACT I

"Great Workers for the Cause" ....Rachel, Ladies
"Where Is Matthew Going?" ....Townspeople
"Gee I'm Glad I'm No One Else But Me" ....Anne
"We Clearly Requested" (Trio) ....Marilla, Anne, Matthew
"The Facts" ....Anne, Mrs. Spencer, Mrs. Blewett, Marilla
"Where'd Marilla Come From?" (Reprise) ....Mailman, Farmer, Ladies
"Humble Pie" ....Matthew, Anne
"Oh Mrs. Lynde!" ....Anne
Back to School Ballet ....Pupils
"Avonlea We Love Thee" ....Mr. Philips, Pupils
"Wondrin' " ....Gilbert
"Did You Hear?" ....Josie, Mrs. Pye, Lucilla, Mrs. Barry, Mailman, Farmer, Rachel
"Ice Cream" ....Diana, Company
"The Picnic" ....Company

ACT II

"Where Did the Summer Go To?" ....Pupils
"Kindred Spirits" ....Anne, Diana
"Open the Window!" ....Miss Stacy, Pupils
"The Words" ....Matthew
"Open the Window!" (Reprise) ....Miss Stacy, Pupils
Nature Hunt Ballet ....Pupils
"I'll Show Him" ....Anne, Gilbert
"General Store" ....Lucilla, Matthew, Townspeople
"Pageant Song" ....Pupils
"If It Hadn't Been for Me" ....Company
"Where Did the Summer Go To?" (Reprise) ....Anne, Gilbert, Pupils
"Anne of Green Gables" ....Matthew
"The Words" (Reprise) ....Marilla
"Wondrin' " (Reprise) ....Anne, Gilbert

Fun City (9). By Lester Colodny, Joan Rivers and Edgar Rosenberg. Produced by Alexander H. Cohen and Rocky H. Aoki at the Morosco Theater. Opened January 2, 1972. (Closed January 8, 1972)

Fritzie Ziroka ....Renee Lippin
Paul Martino ....Gabriel Dell
Jill Fairchild ....Joan Rivers
Jose Rodriguez ....Pierre Epstein
Mailman ....Paul Ford
Hilly Martino ....Victor Arnold

Mr. Ziroka ....Louis Zorich
Estelle Fogelman ....Rose Marie
Ptl. Toomey ....Howard Storm
Ptl. McCarthy ..................J.J. Barry
Man ....Noel Young

Standbys: Misses Rivers, Lippin—Laura May Lewis; Miss Marie—Thelma Lee. Understudies: Messrs. Epstein, Zorich, Ford—Gene Varrone; Messrs. Storm, Barry—Noel Young.

Directed by Jerry Adler; scenery, Ralph Alswang; costumes, Ann Roth; lighting, Jules Fisher; production associate, Hildy Parks; associate producer, Roy Somlyo; production stage manager, Robert L. Borod; stage manager, Gene Varrone; press, James D. Proctor, Richard Hummler.

Time and place: Fun City in the immediate probable future. Act I: Christmas Eve, early evening. Act II: Christmas Day, early evening.

Comedy about life and love in the disintegrating, problematical but always exciting community of New York City as it will soon be if things go on as they are.

There's One in Every Marriage (16). By Georges Feydeau; adapted by Suzanne Grossmann and Paxton Whitehead. Produced by David Merrick in association with Byron Goldman in The Stratford National Theater of Canada's production at the Royale Theater. Opened January 3, 1972. (Closed January 15, 1972)

Lucienne	Roberta Maxwell	Victor	Robin Marshall
Pontagnac	Peter Donat	Hotel Manager	John Cutts
Vatelin	Richard Curnock	Clara	Jeanette Landis
Jean; 2d Commissioner	Wyman Pendleton	Pinchard	Tony Van Bridge
Roubillon	Jack Creley	Mme. Pinchard	Helen Burns
Mme. Pontignac	Tudi Wiggins	2d Bellboy Asst. Commissioner	Tom Alway
Ulla	Marilyn Gardner	Commissioner	Hamish Robertson
Soldignac	Donald Ewer	Gerome	Joseph Maher
Armandine	Patricia Gage		

Hotel Guests: Stewart Robinson, Barbara Lester, Carol Jenkins, Luke Wymes, Eugene Brezany.

Principal understudies: Misses Maxwell, Gage, Gardner—Jeanette Landis; Messrs. Donat, Creely—John Cutts; Mr. Curnock—Hamish Robertson.

Directed by Jean Gascon; design, Alan Barlow; lighting, Gil Wechsler; stage manager, Elspeth Gaylor; press, Lee Solters, Harvey B. Sabinson, Marilynn LeVine.

Time: The beginning of this century, Place: Paris. Act I: Salon of the Vatelin house. Act II: Room 39, Hotel Ultimus. Act III: Roubillon's study.

Farcical Feydeau treatment of an amorous romp in which friends chase after various women including each others' wives. The first New York professional production of this turn-of-the-century French play, adapted for the Stratford, Canada company.

Vivat! Vivat Regina! (116). By Robert Bolt. Produced by David Merrick and Arthur Cantor by arrangement with H.M. Tennent Ltd. at the Broadhurst Theater. Opened January 20, 1972. (Closed April 29, 1972)

Catherine de Medici;		David Rizzio; Pope	Gaetano Bongiovanni
1st Court Lady	Diana Kirkwood	Lord Morton	Stephen Scott
Mary Queen of Scots	Claire Bloom	Lord Bothwell	Lee Richardson
Francois II; Cleric;		Bishop of Durham;	
Ormiston	Norman Allen	Lord Mor	Don McHenry
Cardinal of Lorraine;		de Quadra	Dillon Evans
Sir Francis Walsingham	John Devlin	Davison	Noel Craig
William Cecil	Douglas Rain	Lord Darnley	Peter Coffield
Elizabeth I	Eileen Atkins	Ruthven	Ian Sullivan
Robert Dudley	Robert Elston	Lindsey	Joseph Hill
John Knox	Alexander Scourby	Scots Archbishop; Doctor	Theodore Tenley
Claud Nau	Ralph Clanton	Tala; Prisoner	Ralph Drischell
2d Court Lady	Jane Singer	Philip II	Brian Sturdivant
Bagpiper; Jailer	Randy Levey	Jailer; Brewer	Stephen Macht

Courtiers, Lairds, Clerks, Servants, etc.: Ian Sullivan, Theodore Tenley, Stephen Macht, Brian Sturdivant, Randy Levey.

Understudies: Miss Bloom—Jane Singer; Miss Atkins—Diana Kirkwood; Messrs. Rain, Scourby—Ralph Drischell; Mr. Scott—Joseph Hill; Mr. Devlin—Stephen Macht; Mr. Clanton —Don McHenry; Messrs. Elston, Coffield—Brian Sturdivant; Messrs. Bongiovanni, Allen—John

Handy; Mr. Richardson—Ian Sullivan; Mr. Evans—Norman Allen; Mr. Allen—Randy Levey.
Directed by Peter Dews; lighting, Lloyd Burlingame; design, Carl Toms; associate producer, Samuel Liff; production stage manager, Mitchell Erickson; stage manager, John Handy; press, Arthur Cantor Associates, Ellen Levene.

Time: The second part of the 16th century. Place: France, England and Scotland. The play was presented in two parts.

Historical conflict between Elizabeth I and Mary Queen of Scots, emphasizing in both cases the individual's choice between being a woman or being a queen, with Elizabeth seen as chosing the latter and Mary the former. A foreign play previously produced at the Chichester Festival and in London.

John Cullum replaced Lee Richardson 3/25/72.

A Best Play; see page 232

The Sign in Sidney Brustein's Window (5). Revival of the play by Lorraine Hansberry; adapted by Robert Nemiroff and Charlotte Zaltzburg; music by Gary William Friedman; lyrics by Ray Errol Fox. Produced by Robert Renfield at the Longacre Theater. Opened January 26, 1972. (Closed January 29, 1972)

Sidney Brustein	Hal Linden	Max	Dolph Sweet
Alton Scales	John Danelle	Mavis Parodus Bryson	Frances Sternhagen
Iris Parodus Brustein	Zohra Lampert	David Ragin	William Atherton
Wally O'Hara	Mason Adams	Gloria Parodus	Kelly Wood

Singers: Pendleton Brown, Richard Cox, John Lansing, Arnetia Walker.

Standbys: Mr. Linden—Mark Gordon; Misses Lampert, Wood—Kay Tornborgh; Messrs. Atherton, Danelle—Gus Fleming; Messrs. Sweet, Adams—Walt Wanderman.

Directed by Alan Schneider; scenery, William Ritman; costumes, Theoni V. Aldredge; lighting, Richard Nelson; musical staging, Rhoda Levine; musical direction, Mack Schlefer; music orchestrated and arranged by Gary William Friedman; associate producer, Robert Nemiroff; production manager, Bruce Hoover; stage manager, Richard Foltz; press, Max Eisen, Milly Schoenbaum.

Time: The early 1960s. Place: In the Brusteins' apartment and adjoining courtyard in Greenwich Village, New York City. Act I, Scene 1: Early evening, the late spring. Scene 2: Dusk, the following week. Act II, Scene 1: Just before daybreak, the following day. Scene 2: Evening, late summer. Scene 3: Later that evening, Scene 4: Election night, early fall. Act III: Scene 1: Several hours later. Scene 2: Early the next morning.

The Sign in Sidney Brustein's Window, about pressures on an idealistic young publisher, was first produced on Broadway 10/15/64 for 101 performances. For this production, it was adapted to include songs presented as a comment on the action by a chorus.

MUSICAL NUMBERS: "Can a Flower Think?", "In Another Life," "Mountain Girl," "To the People," "While There's Still Time," "Things as They Are," "Sweet Evenin' ".

Wise Child (4). By Simon Gray. Produced by Paul Alter at the Helen Hayes Theater. Opened January 27, 1972. (Closed January 29, 1972)

Mrs. Artminster	Donald Pleasence	Mr. Booker	George Rose
Jerry	Bud Cort	Janice	Lauren Jones

Standby: Messrs. Pleasence, Rose—Richard Neilson. Understudies: Mr. Cort—Tobias Haller; Miss Jones—Peggy Kirkpatrick.

Directed by James Hammerstein; scenery, Peter Larkin; lighting, Neil Peter Jampolis; costumes, Jane Greenwood; production stage manager, Robert Vandergriff; press, Max Eisen, Milly Schoenbaum.

Time: The present. Place: The Southern Hotel, Reading, England. Act I, Scene 1: Late afternoon. Scene 2: The next morning. Act II: The same evening.

Identity conflicts surrounding a fugitive from the law disguised as a woman and hiding out in a provincial hotel. A foreign play previously produced in London.

The Love Suicide at Schofield Barracks (5). By Romulus Linney. Produced by Cheryl Crawford, Konrad Matthaei, Hale Matthews and Robert Weinstein in association with The American National Theater and Academy. Opened February 9, 1972. (Closed February 12, 1972)

Commanding General ....Robert Burr	Lt. Gen. Evans ....John Berry
Capt. Martin ....Earl Hindman	Sgt. Maj. Ruggles ....Alan Mixon
Maj. Cassidy ....John P. Ryan	Lucy Lake ....Mercedes McCambridge
Pfc. Bowers ....Mark Lamos	Mrs. Norvel Bates ....Del Green
Master Sgt. Bates ....Ralph Roberts	Col. Moore ....William Redfield
Patricia Bates ....Katherine DeHetre	Judith Borden ....Lisa Richards
Katherine Nomura ....Tina Chen	Friend ....David Stock
Warrant Officer Levandre ...Matthew Tobin	Edward Roundhouse ......Jerome Dempsey

Voices: Lucille Patton, Michael Landrum. Mime: Frank Geraci, Michael Landrum. Military Police: Frank Geraci, Michael Landrum, John Straub, Edmund Williams.

Principal understudies: Misses McCambridge, Green—Lucille Patton; Messrs. Berry, Burr, Redfield—John Straub; Messrs. Dempsey, Mixon, Roberts—Edmund Williams; Messrs. Hindman, Lamos—David Yanowitz.

Directed by John Berry; scenery and costumes, Douglas W. Schmidt; lighting, John Gleason; electronic sound, Paul Earls; production stage manager, Larry Whiteley; press, Max Eisen, Milly Schoenbaum.

Time: Just after Halloween 1970. Place: The Officers' Club, Schofield Barracks, Hawaii. The play was presented in two parts.

Military investigation, courtroom-style, of the ritual suicide of a commanding general and his wife, intended as a dramatic protest against war. Previously produced by the HB Playwrights' Foundation.

* **Grease** (122). Musical with book, music and lyrics by Jim Jacobs and Warren Casey. Produced by Kenneth Waissman and Maxine Fox in association with Anthony D'Amato at the Eden Theater (see note). Opened February 14, 1972.

Miss Lynch ....Dorothy Leon	Kenickie ....Timothy Meyers
Patty Simcox ....Ilene Kristen	Sonny LaTierri ....Jim Borrelli
Eugene Florczyk ....Tom Harris	Frenchy ....Marya Small
Jan ....Garn Stephens	Sandy Dumbrowski ....Carole Demas
Marty ....Katie Hanley	Danny Zuko ....Barry Bostwick
Betty Rizzo ....Adrienne Barbeau	Vince Fontaine ....Don Billett
Doody ....James Canning	Johnny Casino; Teen Angel ......Alan Paul
Roger ....Walter Bobbie	Cha-Cha Di Gregorio ....Kathi Moss

Understudies: Female roles—Joy Rinaldi; male roles—Jeff Conaway.

Directed by Tom Moore; musical numbers and dances staged by Patricia Birch; musical supervision and orchestrations, Michael Leonard; musical direction and vocal & dance arrangements, Louis St. Louis; scenery, Douglas W. Schmidt; costumes, Carrie F. Robbins; lighting, Karl Eigsti; sound, Bill Merrill; production stage manager, Joe Calvan; stage manager, A. Robert Altshuler; press, Betty Lee Hunt Associates, Henry Luhrman, Harriett Trachtenberg.

Nostalgic parody of the Elvis Presley era, the early stages of rock 'n' roll in the late 1950s.

NOTE: Though *Grease* opened geographically off Broadway, it did so under first class Broadway contracts. On 6/7/72 it moved uptown to the Broadhurst Theater.

ACT I

Scene 1: Reunion
   "Alma Mater" ....Miss Lynch, Patty, Eugene
   "Alma Mater" Parody ....Pink Ladies, Burger Palace Boys
Scene 2: Cafeteria and school steps
   "Summer Nights" ....Sandy, Danny, Pink Ladies, Burger Palace Boys
   "Those Magic Changes" ....Doody, Burger Palace Boys, Pink Ladies
Scene 3: Pajama party
   "Freddy, My Love" ....Marty, Jan, Frenchy, Rizzo
Scene 4: Street corner
   "Greased Lightnin' " ....Kenickie, Burger Palace Boys
Scene 5: Schoolyard
Scene 6: Park
   "Mooning" ....Roger, Jan
   "Look at Me, I'm Sandra Dee" ....Rizzo
   "We Go Together" ....Pink Ladies, Burger Palace Boys

ACT II

Scene 1: Kids' homes
    "Shakin at the High School Hop" ....Entire Company
    "It's Raining on Prom Night" ....Sandy
        (Radio Voice, Kathi Moss)
Scene 2: School gym
    "Shakin at the High School Hop" (Reprise) ....Entire Company
    "Born to Hand-Jive" ....Johnny Casino, Company
Scene 3: Front of Burger Palace
    "Beauty School Dropout" ....Teen Angel, Frenchy, Choir
Scene 4: Drive-in movie
    "Alone at a Drive-in Movie" ....Danny, Burger Palace Boys
Scene 5: Jan's party
    "Rock 'n' Roll Party Queen" ....Doody, Roger
    "There Are Worse Things I Could Do" ....Rizzo
    "Look at Me, I'm Sandra Dee" (Reprise) ....Sandy
Scene 6: Burger Palace
    "All Choked Up" ....Sandy, Danny, Company
Finale: "We Go Together" (Reprise) ....Entire Company

Moonchildren (16). By Michael Weller. Produced by David Merrick in association with Byron Goldman and Max Brown by arrangement with Martin Rosen, in
the Washington Arena Stage Production, at the Royale Theater. Opened February
21, 1972. (Closed March 4, 1972)

The Students		The Others	
Mike	Kevin Conway	Ralph	Donegan Smith
Ruth	Maureen Anderman	Mr. Willis	Robert Prosky
Cootie (Mel)	Edward Herrmann	Lucky	Ronald McLarty
Norman	Christopher Guest	Bream	Louis Zorich
Dick	Stephen Collins	Effing	Peter Alzado
Kathy	Jill Eikenberry	Uncly Murry	Salem Ludwig
Bob Rettie (Job)	James Woods	Cootie's Father	George Curley
Shelly	Cara Duff-MacCormick	Milkman	Michael Tucker

Understudies: Messrs. Collins, Herrmann, Alzado—Donegan Smith; Messrs. Woods, Tucker
—Peter Alzado; Messrs. Guest, Conway, Curley—Michael Tucker; Misses Eikenberry, Ander-
man, Duff-MacCormick—Gretchen Corbett; Messrs. Zorich, Smith, Prosky—Ronald McLarty;
Messrs. Ludwig, McLarty—George Curley.
    Directed by Alan Schneider; scenery, William Ritman; costumes, Marjorie Slaiman; lighting,
Martin Aronstein; associate producer, Samuel Liff; production stage manager, Alan Hall; stage
manager, George Curley; press, Lee Solters, Harvey B. Sabinson, Marilynn LeVine.
    Time: Around 1965-66. Place: A student apartment in an American university town. Act I,
Scene 1: Early evening, fall. Scene 2: A few weeks later, morning. Scene 3: That afternoon.
Scene 4: Early evening, before Christmas. Act II, Scene 1: An afternoon after Christmas. Scene
2: Before graduation. Scene 3: An afternoon after graduation.
    Sardonic comedy of student attitudes, fears, longings in the 1960s with very thin lines of
demarcation between laughter and tragedy, reality and fantasy. An American play previously
produced in an earlier version under the title *Cancer* at the Royal Court Theater, London, and
in this version at the Arena Stage in Washington, D.C.
    A Best Play; see page 256

* **Night Watch** (108). By Lucille Fletcher. Produced by George W. George and
Barnard S. Straus at the Morosco Theater. Opened February 28, 1972.

Elaine Wheeler	Joan Hackett	Blanche Cooke	Elaine Kerr
John Wheeler	Len Cariou	Lieutenant Walker	William Kiehl
Helga	Jeanne Hepple	Dr. Tracey Lake	Barbara Cason
Vanelli	Martin Shakar	Sam Hoke	Rudy Bond
Curtis Appleby	Keene Curtis		

Standbys: Miss Hackett—Linda Selman; Messrs. Cariou, Curtis—William Kiehl; Mr. Shakar —Frank Hartenstein.

Directed by Fred Coe; scenery, George Jenkins; costumes, Donald Brooks; lighting, Tharon Musser; stage manager, Frank Hartenstein; press, Harvey B. Sabinson, Lee Solters, Cheryl Sue Dolby.

Time: The present. Place: A townhouse in the East 30s, New York City. Act I, Scene 1: A winter morning, 5 a.m. Scene 2: The same day, 5 p.m. Act II, Scene 1: 20 minutes later. Scene 2: Three days later, 9 p.m.

Cat-and-mouse game of murder played by a domineering husband and his patiently long-suffering wife.

Edward Winter replaced Len Cariou 5/2/72.

* Sticks and Bones (104; see note). By David Rabe. Produced by the New York Shakespeare Festival, Joseph Papp producer, at the John Golden Theater. Opened March 1, 1972; see note.

The Family		
Ozzie ....Tom Aldredge	Rick ....Cliff DeYoung	
Harriet ....Elizabeth Wilson	The Sgt. Major ....Hector Elias	
David ....Drew Snyder	The Priest ....Charles Siebert	
	The Girl ....Asa Gim	

Standbys: Messrs. Aldredge, Siebert—Tom Rosqui; Miss Wilson—Ruth Manning; Mr. Snyder —Peter Weller; Mr. DeYoung—Nathan Young; Mr. Elias—Walter McGinn; Miss Gim—Lani Miyazaki.

Directed by Jeff Bleckner; scenery, Santo Loquasto; costumes, Theoni V. Aldredge; lighting, Ian Calderon; song "Baby When I Find You" Music by Galt MacDermot, lyrics by David Rabe; associate producer, Bernard Gersten; production stage manager, David Eidenberg; press, Merle Debuskey, Leo Stern.

Time: Autumn 1968. Place: The family home. The play was presented in two parts.

Returning wounded Vietnam veteran brings much of the spiritual horror and some of the violence of the Indochina war back with him to his apple-pie American home and family.

NOTE: This production of *Sticks and Bones* was presented off Broadway at the Anspacher Theater 11/7/71 for 121 performances before being transferred to Broadway; see its entry in the "Plays Produced off Broadway" section of this volume.

A Best Play; see page 181

Children! Children! (1). By Jack Horrigan. Produced by Arthur Whitelaw and Seth Harrison in association with Ben Gerard at the Ritz Theater. Opened and closed at the evening performance March 7, 1972.

Philip Collins ....Dennis Patrick	Helen Giles ....Gwen Verdon	
Evelyn Collins ....Elizabeth Hubbard	Mark Collins ....Shawn Campbell	
Peg Yaeger ....Elaine Hyman	Susan Collins ....Ariane Munker	
Dr. Karl Yaeger ....Josef Sommer	Bobby Collins ....Johnny Doran	

Directed by Joseph Hardy; scenery and lighting, Jo Mielziner; costumes, Ann Roth; production stage manager, Victor Straus; stage manager, Philip Cusack; press, Max Eisen, Milly Schoenbaum.

Time: Ten o'clock New Year's Eve. Place: The Collins's duplex apartment off Gramercy Park in New York City. The play was presented without intermission.

Thriller about a baby sitter threatened by three malevolent children.

The Country Girl (61). Revival of the play by Clifford Odets. Produced by The John F. Kennedy Center for the Performing Arts, Roger L. Stevens producer in association with Hugh O'Brian, at the Billy Rose Theater. Opened March 15, 1972. (Closed May 6, 1972)

Bernie Dodd ....George Grizzard	Nancy Stoddard ....Eda Zahl	
Larry ....James Karen	Frank Elgin ....Jason Robards	
Phil Cook ....Roland Winters	Georgie Elgin ....Maureen Stapleton	
Paul Unger ....Joe Ponazecki	Ralph ....William Shust	

Standby: Miss Stapleton—Jan Farrand. Understudies: Mr. Robards—James Karen; Messrs. Grizzard, Karen, Winters, Penazecki—William Shust; Mr. Shust—Frank Hartenstein; Miss Zahl—Julia Fremon.

Directed by John Houseman; scenery and lighting, Douglas W. Schmidt; costumes, Frank Thompson; production supervised by Max Allentuck; stage manager, Allen Leicht; press, Michael Sean O'Shea, Leonard Traube.

Act I, Scene 1: The stage of a New York Theater. Scene 2: A furnished room, later the same day. Scene 3: The stage, ten days later. Scene 4: The furnished room, a week later. Scene 5: A dressing room in a Boston theater, after midnight, a week later. Act II, Scene 1: The Boston dressing room, a few nights later. Scene 2: The same, the next day. Scene 3: A dressing room in a New York theater, evening, some weeks later.

Clifford Odets's play about an aging star and his ever-present wife was originally produced on Broadway 11/10/50 for 235 performances. It was revived by The City Center Drama Company 9/29/66 for 22 performances and off Broadway by the Equity Library Theater in the season of 1960-61 and under the title *Winter Journey* 3/12/68 for 15 performances. This production was first staged at the Eisenhower Theater, John F. Kennedy Center in Washington, D.C.

The Selling of the President (5). Musical based on the book by Joe McGinniss; book by Jack O'Brien and Stuart Hample; music by Bob James; lyrics by Jack O'Brien. Produced by John Flaxman in association with Harold Hastings and Franklin Roberts at the Shubert Theater. Opened March 22, 1972. (Closed March 25, 1972)

Sen. George W. Mason ....Pat Hingle	TV Studio Singers and Dancers:
Grace Mason ....Barbara Barrie	Van Denisovich ....Rick Atwell
Sen. Hiram Robinson ....Richard Goode	Casey Steele ....Jamie Carr
Sydney Wales ....Robert Fitzsimmons	Franklin Douglass Pierce .....Pi Douglass
Irene Jantzen ....Karen Morrow	Bonnie Sue Taylor ....Suellen Estey
Ted Bacon ....Robert Darnell	Linda Allington ....Pamela Myers
Johnny Olson ....Johnny Olson	Ralph Reeder ....Tim Noble
Arthur Hayes ....John Bentley	Burgundy Moore ....Trina Parks
Minister ....Ralph Reeder	Molly Kilgallen ....Sheilah Rae
Capt. Terror ....Barney Zawicki	Inga Brand ....Deborah St. Darr
Timmy ....Molly Kilgallen	Barney Zawicki ....Steve Shochet
Creepy ....Randall Phillips	Randall Phillips ....Philip M. Thomas
Ghoulie ....Franklin Douglass Pierce	Gloria Miller ....Tasha Thomas
Dr. Lloyd Blenheim ....Bill Rienecke	Fleetwing Horn ....Vilma Vaccaro
Mrs. Pearline Gibbons ....Lurlu Lindsay	Julia Milano ....Pam Zarit
Mr. Warren Stevenson ......Peter Grounds	

Directed by Robert H. Livingston; musical direction, Harold Hastings; scenery, Tom John; costumes, Nancy Potts; lighting, Thomas Skelton; orchestrations, Jonathan Tunick; multimedia design, William Claxton, Mort Kasman, Gary Youngman, Jim Sant'Andrea; production stage manager, Martha Knight; stage manager, Jason Travis; press, Gifford/Wallace Inc., Violet Welles.

Time and place: Unspecified.

Based on the book by Joe McGinnis about promoting the candidacy of President Nixon in the 1968 campaign, the show is about a group of media experts and young people who turn a Senator into a hot Presidential candidate by means of product-advertising techniques, virtually confining the whole campaign to a TV studio.

ACT I

"Something Holy" ....Gloria, Ensemble
"If You Like People"
    Duet ....Bonnie Sue, Ralph
    Quintet ....Burgundy, Randall, Gloria, Isaac, Julie
    Soloists ....Casey, Franklin, Linda
    Sextette ....Inga, Van, Barney, Molly, Fleetwing, unspecified
"Sunset" ....Van, Ralph, Franklin, Barney
"Mason Cares" ....Julie, Molly, Bonnie Sue

"Little Moon"	Casey, Fleetwing
"Come-on-a-Good-Life"	Franklin
"Accupressure"	Ensemble
"On the Winning Side"	Linda
"Captain Terror"	Terror, Creepie, Ghoulie
"Gap Game"	Casey
"He's a Man"	Burgundy, Julie, Gloria

ACT II

"Stars of Glory"	Ralph
"Terminex"	Barney, Bonnie Sue, Linda, Inga
"Take My Hand"	Casey, Gloria, Ralph, Fleetwing
"A Passacaglia"	Ensemble
"We're Gonna Live It Together"	Ensemble
"Minority Ticket"	Randall
"America"	Ensemble

* A Funny Thing Happened on the Way to the Forum (72). Musical revival based on the plays of Plautus; book by Burt Shevelove and Larry Gelbart; music and lyrics by Stephen Sondheim. Produced by David Black in association with Seymour Vall and Henry Honeckman, in the Larry Blyden production at the Lunt-Fontanne Theater. Opened March 30, 1972.

Prologus; Pseudolus	Phil Silvers	Tintinabula	Lauren Lucas
Senex	Lew Parker	Panacea	Gloria Mills
Domina	Lizabeth Pritchett	The Geminae	Trish Mahoney, Sonja Haney
Hero	John Hansen	Vibrata	Keita Keita
Hysterium	Larry Blyden	Gymnasia	Charlene Ryan
Lycus	Carl Ballantine	Philia	Pamela Hall
Erronius	Reginald Owen	The Proteans	Joe Ross, Bill Starr,
Miles Gloriosus	Carl Lindstrom		Chad Block

Understudies: Mr. Blyden—Joe Ross; Misses Pritchett, Lucas, Mahoney, Haney, Keita, Ryan—Patti Karr; Mr. Hansen—Bill Starr; Mr. Lindstrom—Chad Block; Messrs. Ross, Starr, Block—Patrick Spohn.

Directed by Burt Shevelove; choreography, Ralph Beaumont; musical and vocal direction, Milton Rosenstock; scenery, James Trittipo; costumes, Noel Taylor; lighting, H.R. Poindexter; production associate, Jose Vega; orchestrations, Irwin Kostal, Sid Ramin; dance music arrangement, Hal Schaefer; additional dance music, Richard De Benidictis; stage manager, Scott Jackson; press, Betty Lee Hunt Associates, Henry Luhrman, Harriett Trachtenberg.

Time: 200 years before the Christian era, a day in spring. Place: A street in Rome in front of the houses of Lycus, Senex and Erronius. The play was presented in two acts.

This musical was originally produced on Broadway 5/8/62 for 964 performances. The present revival was previously produced at the Ahmanson Theater, Los Angeles.

The list of musical numbers in *A Funny Thing Happened on the Way to the Forum* appears on page 297 of *The Best Plays of 1961-62*. For this revival, the number "Pretty Little Picture" was dropped from Act I and "Farewell" (Domina) added; the number "That'll Show Him" was dropped from Act II and "Echo Song" (Philia and Hero) added.

Voices (8). By Richard Lortz. Produced by Jerry Schlossberg, Jerry Hammer and Adela Holzer at the Ethel Barrymore Theater. Opened April 3, 1972. (Closed April 8, 1972)

Robert	Richard Kiley	Claire	Julie Harris

The Others: Patrick Wheel, Lisa Essary, Scott Firestone.
Standbys: Miss Harris—Laurie Franks; Mr. Kiley—Robert Stattel.
Directed by Gilbert Cates; scenery and lighting, Jo Mielziner; costumes, Theoni V. Aldredge; original music, Peggy Stuart Coolidge; sound, Teiji Ito; production associate, Seymour Gendal; production stage manager, Martin Gold; stage manager, Jean Weigel; press, Gifford/Wallace Inc., Michael Gifford.

Act I, The Appearance. Scene 1. A late afternoon, mid-winter. Scene 2: A few hours later. Scene 3: The following morning. Act II, The Reality. Scene 1: Twilight, the same day. Scene 2: Later that evening. Scene 3: Late afternoon, the following day.

Ghost story about a couple taking refuge from a snowstorm in a deserted Maine house and finding the place haunted.

Elizabeth I (5) By Paul Foster; music by David Sheridan Spangler. Produced by Edgar Lansbury, Stuart Duncan and Joseph Beruh at the Lyceum Theater. Opened April 5, 1972. (Closed April 8, 1972)

King Philip; God; Headsman;	Bowyer; Stubbes; Walsingham; Sun;
Pipesmoker ....Jeff Chandler	Lazarus Tucker ....Charles Haid
Burghley; Nostradamus; Adelantade-Admiral;	Queen Catherine,
Cambridge Dean;	Queen Elizabeth I ....Jeanette Landis
Muscovite ....Jerry Cunliffe	Mary of Scotland; Sky; Laundress;
Hatton; Feria; Dauphin; Earth; Paulet;	Pipesmoker ....Ruby Lynn Reyner
Martin-Admiral; Crest Keeper; Cambridge	Witch; Moon; Mousorsky;
Don ....Tom Everett	Pipesmoker ....Dawn Siebel
Francis Bacon; Pope Gregory XIII;	Cecil; Dwarf; Warsavite;
Whitgift-Archbishop of	Spanish Cardinal ....Herve Villechaize
Canterbury ....Donald Forrest	Elizabeth the Player
Leicester; Lord Mayor; Pipesmoker;	Queen ....Penelope Windust
d'Aubigny ....Jerry Glover	(Parts in *Elizabeth I* are interchangeable)

Standby: James Richardson.

Musicians: David Sheridan Spangler, Michael Myers, Charles Macety, Tom Everett.

Directed by John-Michael Tebelak; scenery, Robert Anton; costumes, Susan Tsu; lighting, Roger Morgan; sound, Jack Shearing; associate producers, Edwin and Michael Gifford; production stage manager, Gail Bell; press, Max Eisen, Milly Schoenbaum.

Time: Late 1500s, the apogee of Elizabeth's reign. Place: A touring company of Elizabethan players performing their version of *Elizabeth I* on a street platform in Shoreditch, London. They are thrown out of London, then perform in a farm town on the back roads of England, and then at Cambridge University. The play was presented in two acts.

Impressionistic, cartoon-like play-within-a-play dealing with some of the events and ideas of the Elizabethan era.

* Sugar (61). Musical based on the screen play *Some Like It Hot* by Billy Wilder and I.A.L. Diamond (based on a story by Robert Thoeren); book by Peter Stone; music by Jule Styne; lyrics by Bob Merrill. Produced by David Merrick at the Majestic Theater. Opened April 9, 1972.

Sweet Sue ....Sheila Smith	Jerry ....Robert Morse
Society Syncopaters:	Spats Palazzo ....Steve Condos
Piano ....Harriett Conrad	Dude ....Gerard Brentte
Drums ....Linda Gandell	Knuckles Norton ....Dick Bonelle
Bass ....Nicole Barth	1st Poker Player ....Igors Gavon
Trumpets ..Leslie Latham, Marylou Sirinek	Sugar Kane ....Elaine Joyce
Trombones .Terry Cullen, Kathleen Witmer	Cabdriver ....Ken Ayers
Saxophones ......Pam Blair, Eileen Casey,	Olga ....Eileen Casey
Debra Lyman, Sally Neal, Mary Zahn	Train Conductor ....George Blackwell
Bienstock ....Alan Kass	Bellboy ....Andy Bew
Joe ....Tony Roberts	Osgood Fielding Jr. ....Cyril Ritchard

Spats's Gang: Andy Bew, Roger Bigelow, Gene Cooper, Arthur Faria, Gene GeBauer, John Mineo, Don Percassi. Knuckles's Gang: Ken Ayers, Richard Maxon, Dale Muchmore, Alexander Orfaly. Sunbathers: Nicole Barth, Pam Blair, Eileen Casey, Robin Hoctor, Debra Lyman, Peggy Lyman, Sally Neal, Pamela Sousa. "Chicago" Singers: Ken Ayers, George Blackwell, Dick Bonelle, Igors Gavon, Hal Norman.

Swing Dancers: Sandra Brewer, Denny Martin Finn.

Directed and choreographed by Gower Champion; musical direction and vocal arrangements, Elliot Lawrence; scenery, Robin Wagner; costumes, Alvin Colt; lighting, Martin Aronstein; orchestrations, Philip J. Lang; dance music arrangements, John Berkman; associate choreog-

rapher, Bert Michaels; stage manager, Bob St. Clair; press, Harvey B. Sabinson, Sandra Manley.
Time: 1931. Place: Chicago, Miami and in between.
Two Prohibition-era jazz musicians dress up in women's clothes and join an all-girl orchestra in order to hide from pursuing gangsters, as in the story of the movie *Some Like It Hot*.

ACT I

Overture	The Orchestra
"Windy City Marmelade"	Sweet Sue, All-Girl Band
"Penniless Bums"	Jerry, Joe, Unemployed Musicians
"Tear the Town Apart"	Spats and Gang
"The Beauty That Drives Men Mad"	Jerry, Joe
"We Could Be Close"	Jerry, Sugar
"Sun on My Face"	Jerry, Joe, Sugar, Sweet Sue, Bienstock, Ensemble
"November Song"	Osgood, Millionaires
"Sugar"	Jerry, Joe

ACT II

Entr'acte	The Orchestra
"Hey, Why Not!"	Sugar, Ensemble
"Beautiful Through and Through"	Osgood, Jerry
"What Do You Give to a Man Who's Had Everything?"	Joe, Sugar
"Magic Nights"	Jerry
"It's Always Love"	Joe
"When You Meet a Man in Chicago"	Jerry, Joe, Sugar, Sweet Sue, All-Girl Band, Chorus Line

That's Entertainment (4). Musical revue with lyrics and music by Howard Dietz and Arthur Schwartz. Produced by Gordon Crowe in association with J. Robert Breton at the Edison Theater (Middle). Opened April 14, 1972. (Closed April 16, 1972)

Greg	David Chaney	Jack	Scott Salmon
Richard	Jered Holmes	Lucille	Bonnie Schon
Carol	Judith Knaiz	Donald	Michael Vita
Adele	Michon Peacock	Sam	Alan Weeks
Lena	Vivian Reed		

Standbys: Misses Peacock, Knaiz, Reed, Schon—Sharron Miller; Messrs. Vita, Chaney, Salmon, Holmes, Weeks—Ken Ploss.
Directed by Paul Aaron; choreography, Larry Fuller; musical direction, orchestrations and arrangements, Luther Henderson; scenery and lighting, David F. Segal; costumes, Jane Greenwood; sound, Anthony Alloy; production stage manager, May Muth; assistant choreographer, Merry Lynn Katis; stage manager, Herman Magidson; press, Samuel J. Friedman, Louise Ment.
Though its performers have character names, this is a bookless, revue-type anthology of Dietz-Schwartz songs from past shows, many of them all-time favorites.

ACT I

Overture	Company
Medley	Adele, Lucille, Jack, Greg
"We Won't Take It Back," "Hammacher Schlemmer, I Love You," "Come, oh, Come"	
"I'm Glad I'm Single"	Richard
"You're Not the Type," "Miserable With You"	Carol, Richard
"Something to Remember You By"	Carol
"Hottentot Potentate"	Lena, Sam
"Day After Day," "Fly by Night"	Company
"Everything"	Richard
"Blue Grass"	Sam
"Fatal Fascination," "White Heat"	Lucille
"Right at the Start of It"	Sam
"Confession"	Carol, Donald

"Smoking Reefers" .....Lena
"How High Can a Little Bird Fly?" .....Jack
"Keep Off the Grass" .....Greg
"I See Your Face Before Me" .....Donald, Adele
"Experience" .....Greg
"Two Faced Woman" .....Sam
"Foolish Face" .....Jack
"By Myself" .....Lena
"That's Entertainment" .....Donald

ACT II

Dance medley .....Company
  "You and the Night and the Music," "Louisiana Hayride," "Dancing in the Dark"
"Triplets" .....Lucille, Greg, Richard
"High and Low" .....Jack
"How Low Can a Little Worm Go?" .....Carol
"Absent Minded" .....Richard
"High Is Better Than Low" .....Carol, Jack
"If There Is Someone Lovelier Than You" .....Greg
"I've Made a Habit of You" .....Lucille
"I Guess I'll Have to Change My Plan" .....Sam
"New Sun in the Sky" .....Lena
"Farewell My Lovely" .....Adele
"Alone Together" .....Donald
"Shine on Your Shoes" .....Company

Promenade, All! (48). By David V. Robison. Produced by Fred Coe, Arthur Cantor and Charles Taubman in association with Larc, Inc., at the Alvin Theater. Opened April 16, 1972. (Closed May 27, 1972)

1895

Willie .....Richard Backus   Ollie H .....Eli Wallach
Mother H .....Anne Jackson   Grandfather Huntziger .....Hume Cronyn

1920

Wesley .....Richard Backus   Grandmother H .....Anne Jackson
Willie .....Hume Cronyn   Ollie H .....Eli Wallach

1945

Walter .....Richard Backus   Doris .....Anne Jackson
Wesley .....Eli Wallach   Willie .....Hume Cronyn

APPROXIMATELY NOW

Wendell .....Richard Backus   Doris; Joan .....Anne Jackson
Wesley .....Eli Wallach   Willie .....Hume Cronyn

Standbys: Messrs. Cronyn, Wallach—Ben Kapen; Miss Jackson—Virginia Kiser; young men—James Staley.

Directed by Arthur Storch; scenery, David Chapman; costumes, James Berton Harris; lighting, Martin Aronstein; assistant to the producers, Rose Teed; production stage manager, Ben Janney; stage manager, James Staley; press, Arthur Cantor, Fred Weterick

Time: 1895 to the present. Place: Home and offices of the Huntziger, later Hunt, family. The play was presented in two parts of two episodes each.

Comedy about six generations of an American family, some greedily ambitious and some pleasure-loving, in family conflicts reflecting the mores and issues of four different periods of the recent American past.

Captain Brassbound's Conversion (16). Revival of the play by George Bernard Shaw. Produced by Roger L. Stevens and Arthur Cantor by arrangement with

H.M. Tennent Ltd. for a limited engagement at the Ethel Barrymore Theater. Opened April 17, 1972. (Closed April 29, 1972)

Rankin	Leo Leydon	Johnson	Jack Davidson
Drinkwater	Geoff Garland	Osman	Leroy Lessane
Hassan	Yusef Bulos	Sidi El Assif	Manu Tupou
Lady Cicely Waynflete	Ingrid Bergman	The Cadi	Louis Guss
Sir Howard Hallam	Eric Berry	American Bluejacket	Ben Masters
Marzo	Zito Kozan	Capt. Kearney, U.S.N.	Jay Garner
Captain Brassbound	Pernell Roberts	American Armed Guard	Calvin Culver
Redbrook	Richard Cox		

Captain Brassbound's Men, Sidi El Assif's Retinue, Cadi's Retinue, American Officers: Michael Diamond, John Pavelko, Steven Rosenthal, Joe Zaloom, Yusef Bulos, Richard Bowden, Calvin Culver, George Emch, Albert Sanders, John Scanlan.

Principal understudies: Mr. Roberts—Michael Diamond; Messrs. Leyden, Garner—John Scanlan; Messrs. Garland, Bulos—Louis Guss; Messrs. Guss, Lessane—Joe Zaloom; Mr. Tupou —Steven Rosenthal.

Directed by Stephen Porter; scenery, Michael Annals; costumes, Sara Brook; Miss Bergman's costumes, Beatrice Dawson; lighting, William H. Batchelder; production stage manager, Bert Wood; stage manager, David Taylor; press, Arthur Cantor Associates, Ellen Levene.

Time: The turn of the century. Place: Morocco. Act I: Mogador, Mr. Rankin's garden, evening. Act II: A room in a castle in the Atlas Mountains, mid-day. Act III: A room in Mr. Rankin's house, morning.

The only modern professional revival of this Shaw play about an indomitable woman was 12/27/50 for 15 performances at the City Center, with Edna Best in the leading role. This production starring Ingrid Bergman originated in London and played at the John F. Kennedy Center in Washington before coming to New York on its American tour.

Lost in the Stars (39). Musical revival based on Alan Paton's novel *Cry, the Beloved Country;* words by Maxwell Anderson; music by Kurt Weill. Produced by Roger L. Stevens and Diana Shumlin for the John F. Kennedy Center for the Performing Arts at the Imperial Theater. Opened April 18, 1972. (Closed May 21, 1972)

Answerer	Lee Hooper	Alex	Giancarlo Esposito
Dancer; William	Harold Pierson	Foreman; 1st Policeman	Mark Dempsey
Leader	Rod Perry	Mrs. MKize	Alyce Elizabeth Webb
Drummer	Babafumi Akunyun	Hlabeni	Garrett Saunders
Stephen Kumalo	Brock Peters	Eland	Peter Bailey-Britton
Grace Kumalo	Rosetta Le Noire	Linda	Marki Bey
Stationmaster	Adam Petroski	Johannes Pafuri	Autris Paige
Young Man	Sid Marshall	Matthew Kumalo	Damon Evans
Woman	Ruby Greene Aspinall	Absalom Kumalo	Gilbert Price
Arthur Jarvis	Don Fenwick	Rose	Judy Gibson
James Jarvis	Jack Gwillim	Irina	Margaret Cowie
Edward Jarvis	David Jay	2d Policeman; Guard	Roy Hausen
Mrs. Jarvis	Karen Ford	Servant	Richard Triggs
John Kumalo	Leonard Jackson	Burton	Alexander Reed
Paulus; McRae	Leonard Hayward	Judge	Staats Cotsworth

Singers: Lana Caradimas, Suzanne Cogan, Karen Ford, Aleesaa Foster, Ruby Greene Aspinall, Amelia Haas, Edna Husband, Urylee Leonardos, Rona Leslie Pervil, Therman Bailey, Donald Coleman, Raymond Frith, Leonard Hayward, Autris Paige, Mandingo Shaka, Richard Triggs.

Dancers: Michael Harrison, Wayne Stevenson Hayes, Oba-Ya, Michael Oiwake.

Standbys: Mr. Esposito—Douglas Grant; Mr. Jay—Riley Mills. Understudies: Messrs. Peters, Perry—Clyde Walker; Messrs. Fenwick, Gwillim—Mark Dempsey; Mr. Price—Harold Pierson; Misses Cowie, Bey—Judy Gibson; Mr. Jackson—Leonard Hayward; Miss Le Noire—Lee Hooper; Messrs. Paige, Evans—Sid Marshall; Mr. Cotsworth—Adam Petroski; Miss Hooper— Edna Husband; Mr. Bailey-Britton—Alex Reed.

Directed by Gene Frankel; choreography and musical staging, Louis Johnson; musical direction, Karen Gustafson; scenery, Oliver Smith; costumes, Patricia Quinn Stuart; lighting, Paul

Sullivan; musical arrangements and orchestrations, Kurt Weill; production stage manager, Frank Hamilton; stage manager, Robert Keegan; press, Seymour Krawitz, Martin Shwartz, Patricia Krawitz.

Lost in the Stars, a "musical tragedy" about two South African families, one black and one white, was first produced 10/30/49 for 273 performances. It was revived 3/22/68 for 15 Equity Library Theater performances.

ACT I

Place: Ndotsheni, a small village in South Africa
Opening: "The Hills of Ixopo" ....Leader, Answerer, Singers
Scene 1: Stephen Kumalo's home
"Thousands of Miles" ....Stephen
Scene 2: The railroad station
"Train to Johannesburg" ....Leader, Singers
Place: Johannesburg
Scene 3: John Kumalo's tobacco shop
Scene 4: The search—(1) The factory office, (2) Mrs. MKize's house, (3) Hlabeni's house, (4) Parole Office
"The Search" ....Stephen, Leader, Singers
Scene 5: Stephen's Shantytown lodging
"The Little Grey House" ....Stephen, Singers
Scene 6: A dive in Shantytown
Scene 7: A street in Shantytown
"Stay Well" ....Absolom
Scene 8: Irina's hut in Shantytown
"Trouble Man" ....Irina
Scene 9: Arthur Jarvis's home
"Murder in Parkwold" ....Singers
Scene 10: A street in Shantytown
"Fear" ....Singers
Scene 11: Prison
Scene 12: A street in Shantytown
"Lost in the Stars" ....Stephen, Singers

ACT II

Place: Johannesburg
Scene 1: Stephen's Shantytown lodging
Opening: "The Wild Justice" ....Leader, Singers
Stephen's Prayer: "O Tixo, Tixo, Help Me" ....Stephen
Scene 2: Arthur Jarvis's doorway
Scene 3: The courtroom
Scene 4: Prison cell
"Cry, the Beloved Country" ....Leader, Singers
Place: Ndotsheni
Scene 5: Stephen's chapel
"Big Mole" ....Alex
Scene 6: Stephen Kumalo's home
"Thousands of Miles" (Reprise) ....Singers

* Don't Bother Me, I Can't Cope (50). Musical revue by Micki Grant. Produced by Edward Padula and Arch Lustberg in Vinnette Carroll's Urban Arts Corps production at the Playhouse Theater (Middle). Opened April 19, 1972.

Alex Bradford   Bobby Hill
Hope Clarke   Arnold Wilkerson
Micki Grant

Singers: Alberta Bradford, Charles Campbell, Marie Thomas. Dancers: Thommie Bush, Gerald G. Francis, Ben Harney, Leona Johnson. Musicians: Danny Holgate, Herb Lovell (drums), Rudy Stevenson (guitar, flute), John Lucien (bass).

Conceived and directed by Vinnette Carroll; choreography, George Faison; musical direction and arrangements, Danny Holgate; scenery, Richard A. Miller, supervised by Neil Peter Jampolis; costumes, Edna Watson, supervised by Sara Brook; lighting, B.J. Sammler, supervised by Ken Billington; associate producer, Gordon Gray Jr.; presented in association with Ford's Theater Society, Washington, D.C.; production supervisor, Sam Ellie; stage manager, Robert Moeser; press, Betty Lee Hunt, Harriett Trachtenberg, Henry Luhrman, Maria C. Pucci.

Collection of songs and dances with some musical themes borrowed from ballads, calypso, Gospel music, etc. Previously produced in a slightly different version by the Urban Arts Corps in Washington, D.C., in small theaters around New York and elsewhere.

ACT I—"I Gotta Keep Movin'" Alex Bradford, Alberta Bradford, Charles Campbell, Bobby Hill, danced by Ben Harney; Harlem Streets, Dancers; "Lookin' Over From Your Side," Hill; "Don't Bother Me, I Can't Cope," Company; "When I Feel Like Moving," Hope Clarke, Dancers; "Help," Miss Clarke, Dancers; "Fighting for Pharoah," Bradford, Hill, Campbell, Miss Bradford; "Good Vibrations," Bradford, Company; "Love Power," Hill, Miss Clarke, Company; You Think I got Rhythm?, Dancers; "They Keep Coming," Company; "My Name Is Man," Arnold Wilkerson.

Act II—"Questions," Micki Grant; "It Takes a Whole Lot of Human Feeling," Miss Grant; "You Think I got Rhythm?, Wilkerson, Miss Grant; "Time Brings About a Change," Thommie Bush, Harney, Wilkerson, Miss Grant, Leona Johnson, Marie Thomas; "So Little Time," Miss Grant; "Thank Heaven for You," Hill, Miss Grant; "So Long Sammy," Hill, Miss Clarke, Dancers; "All I Need," Miss Bradford, Company; "I Gotta Keep Movin'" (Reprise), Miss Grant, Bradford, Company.

All the Girls Came Out to Play (4). By Richard T. Johnson and Daniel Hollywood. Produced by Richard T. Johnson and Daniel Hollywood at the Cort Theater. Opened April 20, 1972. (Closed April 22, 1972)

Barbara Duryea	Bette Marshall	Joe Ryals	Fred Nassif
Claude Duryea	Michael (M.P.) Murphy	Fred Richards	Bill Britten
Betty Ryals	Peg Shirley	Ronnie Ames	Dennis Cole
Jean Fowler	Susan Bjurman	Angel Rodriguez	Jay Barney
Mary Lou Richards	Charlotte Fairchild	Susan	Christine Jones
Ken Fowler	Conard Fowkes	Bruce	Don Simms

Standbys: Mr. Cole—Donn Whyte; Mr. Britten—Jack Aaron. Understudies: Messrs. Nassif, Fowkes, Murphy—Don Simms; Misses Marshall, Bjurman—Claire Malis, Christine Jones.

Directed by John Gerstad; scenery & lighting, Leo B. Meyer; costumes, Joseph G. Aulisi; production supervisor, Wally Peterson; stage manager, Don Simms; press, Mary Bryant, Stanley F. Kaminsky.

Time: The present. Place: Pleasant Valley, a typically middle class suburban community some 70 miles from New York City. Act I, Scene 1: A morning in July, the patio of the home of Barbara and Claude Duryea. Scene 2: Later that morning, the new neighbor's house. Act II, Scene 1: A week later, the patio. Scene 2: Immediately following, the garage. Scene 3: shortly after, the neighbor's house. Scene 4: Later, the neighbor's house.

Comedy about an author and his agent in suburbia, living together to get some work done and mistakenly identified in the community as homosexuals.

The Little Black Book (7). By Jean-Claude Carriere; American version by Jerome Kilty. Produced by Arthur Cantor at the Helen Hayes Theater. Opened April 25, 1972. (Closed April 29, 1972)

A Man ....Richard Benjamin   A Woman ....Delphine Seyrig

Standbys: Mr. Benjamin—Dean Santoro; Miss Seyrig—Kathleen Miller.

Directed by Milos Forman; scenery, Oliver Smith; costumes, Sara Brook; lighting, Martin Aronstein; stage manager, Robert L. Borod; press, Arthur Cantor Associates, Ellen Levene.

Time: Today. Place: A bachelor's apartment on West 12th Street, New York City. Act I Scene 1: Morning. Scene 2: Early evening. Scene 3: The next morning. Scene 4: Late that night. Act II, Scene 1: Early afternoon. Scene 2: That evening.

Comedy about an attractive young woman intruding into a bachelor's apartment and remaining to weave her spell. A French play previously produced in Paris as L'Aide-Memoire.

Ring Round the Bathtub (1). By Jane Trahey. Produced by Jacqueline Babbin and Jay Wolf at the Martin Beck Theater. Opened and closed at the evening performance April 29, 1972.

Darcy Train ....Eileen Kearney	Louis Rockosy ....Louis Turenne
Mrs. Hanlon (Gran) ......Carmen Mathews	Cousin Esther ....Margaret Linn
Maggie Train ....Elizabeth Ashley	Mr. Enright ....Alek Primrose
Dan Train ....Richard Mulligan	Capt. Harfeather ....James Greene
Esme Train ....Carol Kane	Nurse Samson ....Kate Wilkinson
Bea Rockosy ....Kathleen Maguire	Radio Commentator ....John Cannon

Directed by Harold Stone; scenery, Ed Wittstein; costumes, Joseph G. Aulisi; lighting, Roger Morgan; sound, Gary Harris; production stage manager, Steven Zweigbaum; stage manager, Joel Wolfe; press, Shirley Herz.

Time: Between October and Christmas of a year in the 1930s when the Depression was in full swing. Place: The Train home in Chicago, Ill. Act I, Scene 1: A late afternoon in October. Scene 2: The last Sunday in October. Act II, Scene 1: The morning of Election Day. Scene 2: The evening of Election Day. Act III, Scene 1: Afternoon of Dec. 24. Scene 2: That night.

Nostalgic view of an Irish-American family overcoming hard times in Chicago. Previously produced at the Alley Theater, Houston.

An Evening With Richard Nixon And . . . (16). By Gore Vidal. Produced by Hillard Elkins at the Sam S. Shubert Theater. Opened April 30, 1972. (Closed May 13, 1972)

Pro ....Gene Rupert	Jessamyn West; Harriet Palmer Hudspeth;
Con ....Humbert Allen Astredo	Splendid Girl; Interpreter; Martha Mitchell;
George Washington ....Stephen D. Newman	Tricia Nixon ....Susan Sarandon
Colonial; Eisenhower Aide & Caddie;	Football Coach; Nixon Aide; Sen. Knowland;
Soldier ....Robert Christian	Sam Rayburn; Gov. Pat Brown; Lyndon B.
Dwight D. Eisenhower ......Philip Sterling	Johnson; Spiro Agnew ..Robert Blackburn
John F. Kennedy ....Robert King	Student; Franklin D. Roosevelt; Jerry Voorhis;
Hannah Nixon;	Dana Smith; Thomas E. Dewey; Frank
Pat Nixon ....Dorothy Dorian James	Waters; Kennedy (mask) ......Alex Wipf
Richard M. Nixon ....George S. Irving	Don Nixon; Nikita S. Khrushchev; Pres.
Henrietta Shockney; Evelyn Dorn; Gloria	Diem; Southern Senator; Hubert Humph-
Steinem; Interviewer ..Maureen Anderman	rey; Pvt. Meadlo ....Chet Carlin
Reporter; Frank Nixon; Campaign Worker;	Drama Coach; Harry S. Truman; Adlai E.
Campaign Manager; Eisenhower (mask);	Stevenson; Eisenhower Caddie; Noah Diet-
Lt. Calley; Herbert	trich; Barry Goldwater; Dr. Hutschnecker;
Klein ....William Knight	Howard K. Smith ....George Hall

American People, Reporters, Military Officers, Photographers, Aides, Students, Campaign Workers, Soldiers, Advisors, Policemen, Cadets, Party Workers, Hippies, Demonstrators, etc.: Maureen Anderman, Robert Blackburn, Chet Carlin, Robert Christian, George Hall, Dorothy Dorian James, William Knight, Susan Sarandon, Alex Wipf.

Directed by Edwin Sherin; scenery, William Ritman; costumes, Joseph G. Aulisi; lighting, H.R. Poindexter; makeup, Bob O'Bradovich; masks, Jane Stein; visuals, Marjorie Morris; music arranged and conducted by Charles Gross; sound, Jack Shearing; projection consultant, William Batchelder; production supervisor, Michael Thoma; associate producer, George Platt; stage manager, John Actman; press, Samuel J. Friedman.

Political satire based on the President's public statements, depicting Nixon as the opportunistic but logical heir of past American imperialistic policies. The play was presented in two parts.

Different Times (24). Musical with book, music and lyrics by Michael Brown. Produced by Bowman Productions, Inc. in association with William L. Witt and William J. Gumperz at the ANTA Theater. Opened May 1, 1972. (Closed May 20, 1972)

Stephen Adams Levy ......Sam Stoneburner	Mrs. Callahan; Josie .....Mary Jo Catlett
Margaret Adams ....Barbara Williams	Mrs. Hepplewhite's Mother;
Gregory Adams ....Jamie Ross	Kimberly Langley ....Patti Karr
Mrs. Daniel Webster Hepplewhite; The	Nelle Harper ....Joyce Nolen
Kaiser; Hazel Hughes; Lady Ffenger;	Larry Lawrence Levy; Stan ......Joe Masiell

Angela Adams ....Candace Cooke	Joe ....Terry Nicholson
Officer; Bobby; Frank;	Don ....David K. Thome
Frank Gonzales ....Ronald Young	Mel ....Ronnie DeMarco
Marianne; Marilyn; Linda ...Dorothy Frank	Hattie, Pauline & Mae Verne .Dorothy Frank,
Columbia ....Karin Baker	Candace Cooke, Karin Baker
Elsie; Abigail ....Mary Bracken Phillips	

Doughboys: Terry Nicholson, Ronnie DeMarco, David K. Thome; The Hazelnuts: Candace Cooke, Dorothy Frank, Karin Baker, Joyce Nolen; The Keynoters: Terry Nicholson, Mary Bracken Phillips, David K. Thome, Ronald Young.

Principal understudies: Miss Frank—Karin Baker; Miss Phillips—Candace Cooke; Miss Catlett—Patti Karr; Miss Karr—Dorothy Frank; Mr. Young—Terry Nicholson.

Directed by Michael Brown; dances and musical numbers staged by Tod Jackson; musical direction, dance and vocal arrangements, Rene Wiegert; scenery and costumes, David Guthrie; lighting, Martin Aronstein; orchestrations, Norman Paris, Arthur Harris, Ted Simons; audio, Jack Shearing; production stage manager, Jack Timmers; stage manager, Mary Porter Hall; press, David Powers, Michael Ewell.

Prologue: 1970. Act I, Scene 1: 1905, the fair in Portland, Ore. Scene 2: 1905, a hotel room in Portland. Scene 3: 1915, a street in Boston. Scene 4: 1917, a hotel room in Boston. Scene 5: 1917, a theater stage. Scene 6: 1924-1929, a speakeasy in Boston. Scene 7: 1929, the Gregory Adams house in Boston. Scene 8: 1933, the Bijou Ballroom in Bayonne. Act II, Scene 1: 1942, Ffenger Hall, London. Scene 2: 1942, a street in London. Scene 3: 1942, the Gregory Adams house in Boston. Scene 4: 1963, the Stephen Adams house in Mt. Kisco and Stephen's office in Manhattan. Scene 5: 1965, Abigail's room in Manhattan. Scene 6: 1968, an art gallery. Scene 7: 1970, Central Park. Epilogue: 1970.

Episodes spread over several generations of a troubled American family, from 1905 through the Prohibition Era to World War II and the present.

ACT I

"Different Times" ....Stephen
"Seeing the Sights" ....People of 1905
"The Spirit Is Moving" ....Margaret, People of 1905
"Here's Momma" ....Margaret
"Everything in the World Has a Place" ....Gregory, Margaret
"I Wish I Didn't Love Him" ....Margaret
"Forward Into Tomorrow" ....Mrs. Hepplewhite, Suffragettes
"You're Perfect" ....Angela
"Marianne" ....Officer, Doughboys, Marianne, Columbia, Kaiser
"Daddy, Daddy" ....Hazelnuts
"I Feel Grand" ....Hazel Hughes, Hazelnuts
"Sock Life in the Eye" ....Larry
"I'm Not Through" ....Larry, Marathon Dancers

ACT II

"I Miss Him" ....Hattie, Pauline, Mae Verne
"One More Time" ....Kim, Keynoters
"Here's Momma" (Reprise) ....Stephen
"I Dreamed About Roses" ....Stephen, Kim, USO Guests
"I Wish I Didn't Love Her" (Reprise) ....Gregory
"The Words I Never Said" ....Stephen, Kim
"The Life of a Woman" ....Kim
"Here's Momma" (Reprise) ....Kim, Momma's Poppas
"Genuine Plastic" ....Stephen, Gallery Guests
"Thanks a Lot" ....Frank, Abigail, Friends
"When They Start Again" ....Abigail, Frank
"Different Times" (Reprise) ....Stephen
"The Spirit Is Moving" (Reprise) ....Company

Tough to Get Help (1). By Steve Gordon. Produced by Sandy Farber and Stanley Barnett in association with Jules Love and Roy Rubin at the Royale Theater. Opened and closed at the evening performance, May 4, 1972.

Luther Jackson ....John Amos	Carlotta; Young Beulah ....Chip Fields
Beulah Jackson ....Lillian Hayman	Abe Lincoln ....Abe Vigoda
Elaine Grant ....Billie Lou Watt	Pee Wee ....Jimmy Pelham
Clifford Grant ....Dick O'Neill	Mr. Charlie ....Anthony Palmer
Leroy Jackson;	Boy Ghost ....Ralph Carter
Young Luther ....John Danelle	

Directed by Carl Reiner; scenery, Ed Wittstein; costumes, Joseph G. Aulisi; lighting, John Gleason; associate producer, Larry Rosen; stage managers, Lee Murray, Stephen P. Pokart; press, Seymour Krawitz, Martin Shwartz.

Time: The present. Place: The Grants' home in suburban Larchmont. The play was presented in two parts.

Comedy about the relationship between a liberal advertising man and the black couple who work for him.

Hard Job Being God (6). Musical based on the Old Testament; music and lyrics by Tom Martel; book uncredited. Produced by Bob Yde in association with Andy Wiswell at the Edison Theater (Middle). Opened May 15, 1972. (Closed May 20, 1972)

Sarah; Jacob's Wife; Slave; Pharaoh's	God ....Tom Martel
Soldier; Moabite; Judean;	Slave; Pharaoh's Soldier; Ruth; Judean;
Susanna ....Gini Eastwood	Shepherd ....Anne Sarofeen
Jacob's Son; Moses; Moabite;	Abraham; Jacob; Pharaoh; Moabite;
David ....Stu Freeman	Judean; Amos ....John Twomey

Band: Roy Bittan keyboard, Pete Gries bass, Steve Merola drums, Harry Rumpf guitar.

Directed by Bob Yde; musical staging, Lee Theodore; musical direction, Roy Bittan; scenery, Ray Wilke; costumes, Mary Whitehead; lighting, Patrika Brown; audio, Bill Sandreuter; stage manager, Ray Wilke; press, Sol Jacobson, Lewis Harmon, Ruth D. Smuckler.

Rock musical based on Genesis and other books of the Old Testament.

MUSICAL NUMBERS

Scene 1: Anytime, anywhere
"Hard Job Being God" ....God, Company
Scene 2: Canaan c. 1935 B.C.
"Wherever You Go" ....Sara, Abraham
Scene 3: Canaan c. 1700 B.C.
"Famine" ....Jacob, Jacob's Wife, Sons
Scene 4: Slave camp in Egypt c. 1240 B.C.
"Buy a Slave" ....Egyptian Slave Merchants
"Prayer" ....Hebrew Slaves
Scene 5: Court of Rameses II, Pharoah of Egypt, same day c. 1240 B.C.
"Moses's Song" ....Moses, Pharaoh
"The Ten Plagues" ....Pharaoh, Soldiers, Moses
"Passover" ....Soldiers, Pharaoh, Moses, Slaves
Scene 6: The foot of Mt. Sinai three months later
"The Eleven Commandments" ....Moses, Freed Slaves
Scene 7: The land of Moab 1110 B.C.
"Tribes" ....Hebrew Women, Tribes
"Ruth" ....Moabites, Ruth
Scene 8: Jerusalem 1005 B.C.
"Festival" ....Judeans
"Hail, David" ....Judeans, David
"A Very Lonely King" ....David
Scene 9: Israel c. 812 B.C.—"Battle"
Scene 10: Israel c. 780 B.C.
"You're on Your Own" ....Hebrews, God
Scene 11: On the banks of the Jordan River, 760 B.C.
"A Psalm of Peace" ....Susanna, Hebrews

Scene 12: A pasture in Judah 750 B.C.
  "I'm Countin' on You" ....God, Amos
Scene 13: Feast Day, royal shrine of Bethel in Israel 749 B.C.
  "Shalom L'chaim!" ....Hebrews
  "Amos Gonna Give You Hell" ....Shepherd
Scene 14: Anytime, anywhere
  "What Do I Have to Do?" ....God, Company

* **Don't Play Us Cheap!** (18). Musical with book, music and lyrics by Melvin Van Peebles. Produced by Melvin Van Peebles at the Ethel Barrymore Theater. Opened May 16, 1972.

Mr. Percy	Thomas Anderson	Trinity	Joe Keyes Jr.
Mrs. Washington	Joshie Jo Armstead	Mrs. Bowser	Mabel King
Harold Johnson; Rat	Nate Barnett	David	Avon Long
Mr. Johnson; Cockroach	Frank Carey	Mr. Washington	Geo. "Oopee" McCurn
Mr. Bowser	Robert Dunn	Miss Maybell	Esther Rolle
Earnestine	Rhetta Hughes	Mrs. Johnson	Jay Vanleer

Directed by Melvin Van Peebles; musical supervision, Harold Wheeler; scenery, Kert Lundell; costumes, Bernard Johnson; lighting, Martin Aronstein; production stage manager, Charles Blackwell; stage manager, Charles Briggs; press, Michael Alpert, Arthur Rubine.
Time: A coupla days before tomorrow. Place: Here.
A musical fantasy, all in fun, about a pair of inefficient demons intruding into a Saturday night Harlem family party.

ACT I

"Some Days It Seems That It Just Don't Even Pay to Get Out of Bed" ......Rat, Cockroach
"Break That Party" ....David, Trinity
"8 Day Week" ....Mr. Percy, Company
"Saturday Night" ....Company
"I'm a Bad Character" ....Trinity, Company
"You Cut Up the Clothes in the Closet of My Dreams" ....Mrs. Washington
"It Makes No Difference" ....Miss Maybell, Company
"Quittin Time" ....Mr. Washington, Company

ACT II

"Ain't Love Grand" ....Earnestine, Company
"The Book of Life" ....Mr. Bowser, Company
Quartet:
  "Ain't Love Grand" ....Earnestine
  "Know Your Business" ....Miss Maybell
  "Big Future" ....The Johnsons
  "Break That Party" ....David, Trinity
"Feast on Me" ....Mrs. Bowser, Company
"The Phoney Game" ....David, Company
"Smash Him" ....Company

Heathen! (1). Musical with book by Robert Helpmann and Eaton Magoon Jr.; music and lyrics by Eaton Magoon Jr. Produced by Leonard J. Goldberg and Ken Gaston in association with R. Paul Woodville at the Billy Rose Theater. Opened and closed at the evening performance May 21, 1972.

Rev. Jonathan Beacon;		Kaha Kai; The Chanter	Dennis Dennehy
Jonathan	Russ Thacker	Alika	Mokihana
Kalialani; Kalia	Yolande Bavan	Hawaiian Boy	Charles Goeddertz
Mano'ula; Mano	Edward Rambeau	Policeman	Christopher Barrett
Rev. Hiram Burnham;		Pueo	Honey Sanders
Tourist	Dan Merriman	Momona-Nui	Tina Santiago
Hepsibah Burnham;			
Tourist	Ann Hodges		

The Muggers: Dennis Dennehy, Justis Skae, Sal Pernice. Church Elders: Christopher Barrett, Mary Walling, Michael Serrecchia. Boys in Jail: Charles Goeddertz, Michael Serrecchia, Quitman Fludd. The Girls and Boys of Past and Present: Nancy Dafgek, Jaclynn Villamil, Mary Walling, Karen Kristin, Dennis Dennehy, Randy DiGrazio, Quitman Fludd, Charles Goeddertz, Sal Pernice, Michael Serrecchia, Justis Skae.

Directed by Lucia Victor; choreography, Sammy Bayes; musical direction, Clay Fullum; music supervisor, vocal, dance and incidental music by Mel Marvin; scenery, Jack Brown; lighting, Paul Sullivan; costumes, Bruce Harrow; orchestrations, Larry Fallon; associate choreographer, Dan Siretta; production stage manager, Alan Hall; stage manager, Jack B. Craig; press, Max Eisen, Milly Schoenbaum.

Time: 1819 and 1972. Place: Hawaii.

Basic needs, beliefs and desires of two eras compared and found similar.

ACT I

The present: A beach by a sea wall, Waikiki
  "Paradise" ....Jonathan, Beach People
The past: A church in Boston
  "The Word of the Lord" ....Hiram, Hepsibah, Elders
The past: Aboard a ship at sea
  "My Sweet Tomorrow" ....Rev. Jonathan
Mano'ula's canoe at sea
  "A Man Among Men" ....Mano'ula, Rowers
The Kona shore
  "Aloha" ....Company
  "Kalialani" ....Kalialani
The present: The beach, Waikiki.
The past: A grove near Jonathan's hut
  "No Way in Hell" ....Rev. Jonathan, Kalialani, Mano'ula
The present: Jail in Honolulu
The past: On the edge of the village
  "Battle Cry" ....Kalialani
The past: The Heiau, a council meeting
  "This Is Someone I Could Love" ....Mano'ula
The past: Mano'ula's compound
  "House of Grass" ....Mano'ula
Past and present blend
  "Kava Ceremony" ....Company

ACT II

The present: Jail in Honolulu
  "For You Brother" ....Jonathan, Boys in Jail
The past: The church grounds, dedication ceremony
  "Spear Games" ....Company
  "Christianity" ....Company
The present: Waikiki Beach bar
  "This Is Someone I Could Love" (Reprise) ....Kalia
The past: Mano'ula's compound
  "Heathen" ....Rev. Jonathan
The past: Riding the breakers
  "Heathen" (Reprise) ....Rev. Jonathan, Mano'ula
The past: A corner of the compound
  "More Better Go Easy" ....Alika
The past: Kalialani's hut
The past: The village under the eruption of Mauna Loa
Past and present blend
  "Eighth Day" ....Company

PLAY WHICH CLOSED
PRIOR TO BROADWAY OPENING

A play which was organized in New York for Broadway presentation, but which closed during its tryout performances, is listed below.

Keep Off the Grass. By Ronald Alexander. Produced by Shepard Traube and Edwin S. Lowe in a pre-Broadway (middle theater) tryout at the Maurice Mechanic Theater in Baltimore. Opened April 3, 1972. (Closed at the Hanna Theater in Cleveland April 22, 1972)

Billie Malone ....Rita Gardner	Mike Balter ....Steven Gilborn
Dan Shaw ....Richard Morse	Gladys Wagner ....Margaret Phillips
Poon ....Kim Chan	Detective ....Jess Osuna
Consuela Manning ....Julie Newmar	

Directed by Shepard Traube; scenery, Peter Harvey; costumes, Zoe Brown; stage managers, Perry Bruskin, Barbara Logan; press, Lenny Traube.

Comedy about a woman with two jobs—department store detective by day, divorce investigator by night—set in her apartment. The play was presented in two acts.

PLAYS PRODUCED
OFF BROADWAY

Some distinctions between off-Broadway and Broadway productions at one end of the scale and off-off-Broadway productions at the other end were beginning to blur in the New York theater of the 1970s. For the purposes of this *Best Plays* listing, the term "off Broadway" signifies a show which opened for general audiences in a mid-Manhattan theater seating 299 or less during the time period covered by this volume and 1) employed an Equity cast, 2) planned a regular schedule of 7 or 8 performances a week and 3) offered itself to public comment by critics at opening performances.

Occasional exceptions of inclusion (never of exclusion) are made to take in visiting troupes and a few non-qualifying productions which readers might expect to find in this list because they appear under an off-Broadway heading in other major sources of record.

Figures in parentheses following a play's title indicate number of performances. These figures are acquired directly from the production office in each case and do not include previews or extra non-profit performances.

Plays marked with an asterisk (*) were still running on June 1, 1972. Their number of performances is figured from opening night through May 31, 1972.

In a listing of a show's numbers—dances, sketches, musical scenes, etc.— the titles of songs are identified by their appearance in quotation marks (").

Most entries of off-Broadway productions that ran fewer than 20 performances are somewhat abbreviated.

HOLDOVERS FROM PREVIOUS SEASONS

Plays which were running on June 1, 1971 are listed below. More detailed information about them appears in previous *Best Plays* volumes of appropriate years. Important cast changes are recorded in a section of this volume.

* **The Fantasticks** (5,026; longest continuous run of record in the American theater). Musical suggested by the play *Les Romantiques* by Edmond Rostand; book and lyrics by Tom Jones; music by Harvey Schmidt. Opened May 3, 1960.

* **Jacques Brel Is Alive and Well and Living in Paris** (1,809). Cabaret revue with music by Jacques Brel; production conception, English lyrics, additional material by Eric Blau and Mort Shuman; based on lyrics and commentary by Jacques Brel. Opened January 22, 1968.

The Effect of Gamma Rays on Man-in-the-Moon Marigolds (819). By Paul Zindel. Opened April 7, 1970. (Closed May 14, 1972)

The Dirtiest Show in Town (509). By Tom Eyen. Opened June 27, 1970. (Closed September 19, 1971)

Touch (422). Musical with Book by Kenn Long and Amy Saltz; music by Kenn Long and Jim Crozier; lyrics by Kenn Long. Opened November 8, 1970. (Closed October 3, 1971)

Waiting for Godot (277). Revival of the play by Samuel Beckett. Opened February 3, 1971. (Closed October 3, 1971)

The House of Blue Leaves (337). By John Guare. Opened February 10, 1971. (Closed December 3, 1971)

* One Flew Over the Cuckoo's Nest (490). Revival of the play by Dale Wasserman. Opened March 23, 1971.

* The Proposition (513). Improvisational revue conceived by Allan Albert. Opened March 4, 1971 (order and method of presentation somewhat rearranged for "new" edition beginning September 16, 1971).

Long Day's Journey Into Night (121). Revival of the play by Eugene O'Neill. Opened April 21, 1971. (Closed August 22, 1971)

* Godspell (434). Musical based on the Gospel according to St. Matthew; conceived by John-Michael Tebelak; music and lyrics by Stephen Schwartz. Opened May 17, 1971.

The Homecoming (32). Revival of the play by Harold Pinter. Opened May 18, 1971. (Closed June 13, 1971)

New York Shakespeare Festival Public Theater. 1970-71 schedule of programs included **The Basic Training of Pavlo Hummel** (363). By David Rabe. Opened May 20, 1971. (Closed April 1, 1972)

The Negro Ensemble Company. 1970-71 schedule of four programs concluded with **Ride a Black Horse** (32). By John Scott. Opened May 25, 1971. (Closed June 20, 1971)

PLAYS PRODUCED JUNE 1, 1971—MAY 31, 1972

The Justice Box (7). By Michael Robert David; music by Basheer Quasar. Produced by C.K. Alexander by special arrangement with Lucille Lortel Productions. Opened June 2, 1971. (Closed June 6, 1971)

Directed by Arthur Alan Seidelman; scenery and lighting, John Doepp; costumes, Patrice Alexander; production stage manager, Larry Spiegel; press, Saul Richman. With Michael Lipton, C.K. Alexander, Tally Brown, Michael Proccacino, Richard Alfieri, Gretchen Corbett, Jayme Daniel, Sally Kirkland. Jerome Dempsey.

Mystery play about a substitute executioner, set in France in the shadow of the guillotine.

The Repertory Theater of Lincoln Center. 1971 schedule of five off-Broadway programs ended with Play Strindberg (65). By Friedrich Duerrenmatt; based on August Strindberg's *The Dance of Death;* translated by James Kirkup. Produced by The Repertory Theater of Lincoln Center under the direction of Jules Irving, Robert Symonds associate director, at the Forum Theater. Opened June 3, 1971. (Closed October 23, 1971; see note)

Alice	Priscilla Pointer	The Band:	
Edgar	Robert Symonds	Trumpet	Robert Harley
Kurt	Conrad Bain	Tuba	Robert Ricci
Stage Manager	Jean-Daniel Noland		

Directed by Dan Sullivan; scenery, Douglas W. Schmidt; lighting, John Gleason; costumes, James Berton Harris; musical direction, Roland Gagnon; production stage manager, Patrick Horrigan; stage manager, Jean-Daniel Noland; press, Susan Bloch, William Schelble.

The play was presented as a contest of 12 "rounds" in two parts.

A free black comedy version, not an adaptation, of the Strindberg play by the Swiss playwright Duerrenmatt. A foreign play previously produced on German-speaking stages throughout Europe.

NOTE: *Play Strindberg* suspended 7/3/71 after 36 performances and resumed 9/29/71 for 29 additional performances through 10/23/71.

Ray Fry replaced Conrad Bain 6/29/71. Richard Greene replaced Jean-Daniel Noland for the return engagement 9/29/71.

Charlie Was Here and Now He's Gone (17). By Dennis Turner. Produced by Art James, Cary Sawyer and Ted Rado at the Eastside Playhouse. Opened June 6, 1971. (Closed June 20, 1971)

Directed by Jerry Adler; scenery, David Chapman; lighting, Martin Aronstein; costumes, Jeanne Button; production stage manager, Nate Barnett; press, Gifford/Wallace Inc., Tom Trenkle. With Joe Morton, Philip Williamson, Robert Guillaume, Rosalind Cash, Robert LuPone, Jerome Anello, Norman Thomas Marshall, David Friedman.

The life of a young man in the black ghetto turns into melodrama through drug addiction.

New York Shakespeare Festival Public Theater. 1971 schedule of programs concluded with **Dance Wi' Me** (53). By Greg Antonacci; music by Greg Antonacci. Produced by the New York Shakespeare Festival, Joseph Papp producer, Bernard Gersten associate producer, at the Florence S. Anspacher Theater of the Public Theater. Opened June 10, 1971. (Closed July 18, 1971)

Honey Boy	Greg Antonacci	Pepper Pot	Sarah Venable
Jimmy Dick	Johnny Bottoms	Sailor Avocado	Peter Alzado
Judy Jeanine	Judy Allen	Dr. Sincere	Tommy St. Cyr
Professor Alan	Alan Wynroth	Jane Trinculo	Jane Margaret Whitehill
Venerable Zwish	Joel Zwick	The Band	Peter Frumkin

Directed by Joel Zwick; lighting, Laura Rambaldi; production manager, Andrew Mihok; press, Merle Debuskey.

Comedy with music in one act, free-wheeling fantasies of a young and engaging urban loser, subtitled *The Fatal Twitch* and set in the 1950s. Previously produced by the La Mama Experimental Theater Club.

Black Girl (234). By J.E. Franklin. Produced by Henry Street Settlement's New Federal Theater, Woodie King and Dick Williams, at the Theater de Lys. Opened June 16, 1971. (Closed January 16, 1972)

Billie Jean	Kishasha	Mama Rosie	Louise Stubbs
Little Earl	Arthur W. French III	Mu'Dear	Minnie Gentry
Sheryl	Lorraine Ryder	Mr. Herbert	Jimmy Hayeson
Norma	Gloria Edwards	Earl	Arthur French
Ruth Ann	Loretta Green	Netta	Saundra Sharp

Directed by Shauneille Perry; scenery, Charles Mills; lighting, Buddy; costumes, Femi; presented by special arrangement with Lucille Lortel Productions, Inc.; production stage manager, Horacena J. Taylor; press, Howard Atlee, David Roggensack, Irene Gandy.

Time: The present. Place: A small town in Texas. The play was presented without intermission.

A black family is distressed but emergent, with two of the most persistent and gifted members finally making their escape to a better way of life. Previously produced for 6 performances at the New Federal Theater.

Sandra McClain replaced Gloria Edwards, Esther Rolle replaced Minnie Gentry and Leonard Parker replaced Arthur W. French III 10/5/72.

The Last Analysis (46). Revival of the play by Saul Bellow. Produced by Circle in the Square (Theodore Mann, Paul Libin, Paul Jacobson) in association with Howard A. Schwartz and Jack T. Schwartz at the Circle in the Square. Opened June 23, 1971. (Closed August 1, 1971)

Bummidge	Joseph Wiseman	Aufschnitt	Shimen Ruskin
Imogen	Diana Davila	Bella	Louise Troy
Winkleman	David Brooks	Gallupo	Hansford Rowe
Louie Mott	Martin Garner	Tante Frumkah	Jane Hoffman
TV Technician	Joseph Stern	Western Union	
Madge	Grayson Hall	Messenger	Daniel Kreitzberg
Max	Edward Zang	Fiddleman	Humphrey Davis
Bertram	David Margulies	Kalbfuss	Martin Silbersher
Pamela	Lucille Patton		

Directed by Theodore Mann; scenery, Marsha L. Eck; lighting, Roger Morgan; costumes, Joseph G. Aulisi; production manager, Charles Hamilton; press, Merle Debuskey, Bob Ullman.

Revised version of Saul Bellows's comedy about a man trying to conduct his own psychoanalysis, first produced on Broadway 10/1/64 for 28 performances.

New York Shakespeare Festival. Summer schedule of outdoor productions of two revivals and one new musical adaptation of plays by William Shakespeare. **Timon of Athens** (19). Opened June 25, 1971; see note. (Closed July 18, 1971) **The Two Gentlemen of Verona** (14). Musical adapted from Shakespeare's play by John Guare and Mel Shapiro; music by Galt MacDermot; lyrics by John Guare. Opened July 22, 1971; see note. (Closed August 8, 1971) **The Tale of Cymbeline** (15). Opened August 12, 1971. (Closed August 29, 1971). Produced by New York Shakespeare Festival Public Theater, Joseph Papp producer, Bernard Gersten associate producer, in cooperation with the City of New York, Hon. John V. Lindsay Mayor, Hon. August Heckscher Commissioner of Parks, and the New York State Council on the Arts and the National Endowment for the Arts at the Delacorte Theater in Central Park.

ALL PLAYS: Scenery, Ming Cho Lee; costumes, Theoni V. Aldredge; production stage manager, R. Derek Swire; stage manager, John Beven; press, Merle Debuskey, Faith Geer, M.J. Boyer.

TIMON OF ATHENS

Lucius	Albert Stratton	Flavius	Reno Roop
Apemantus	Michael Dunn	Ventidius	Robert Reilly
Lucullus	Louis Galterio	Cupid; Whore's Page	Sam Tsoutsouvas
Sempronius	Louis Turenne	Lucius Servant	Michael Richardson
Poet	Robert Ronan	Philotus	Nathan Young
Painter	Geoff Garland	1st Senator	James Cahill
Merchant; Courier	Norman Snow	2d Senator	Brooks Rogers
Jeweller	Stuart Pankin	Caphis; 1st Bandit	Jeff Eagle
Timon of Athens	Shepperd Strudwick	Varro Servant; 2d Bandit	Peter Weil
Hortensius; Messenger	John Nichols	Isidore Servant; 3d Bandit	Ernest Gray
Old Athenian	Ron Peer	Flaminius	Carl M. Franklin
Lucilius	Mark Zeray	3d Senator	Charles Randall
Alcibiades	Marco St. John	4th Senator	Stephen P. Schnetzer
Servilius	W.K. Stratton	Titus	William Strohmeier

Ladies of the Masque: Nedra Marlin, Peggy Myers, Debbie Zalkind, Christina Zompakos. Citizens, Servants, Soldiers: Jeff Eagle, Carl M. Franklin, Ernest Gray, Nedra Marlin, Peggy Myers, John Nichols, Stuart Pankin, Ron Peer, Robert Reilly, Michael Richardson, Stephen P. Schnetzer, Norman Snow, W.K. Stratton, William Strohmeier, Sam Tsoutsouvas, Peter Weil, Nathan Young, Debbie Zalkind, Mark Zeray, Christina Zompakos.

Directed by Gerald Freedman; music, Jonathan Tunick; lighting, Martin Aronstein; choreography, Joyce Trisler.

Place: Athens—Timon's house, the Senate, the streets and a desolate area on the outskirts. The play was presented in two parts.

This is the first and only professional New York production of record since 1894 of *Timon of Athens*, a drama about a rich man who—somewhat like King Lear—tries to buy friendship and finds himself abandoned when he runs out of wealth.

THE TWO GENTLEMEN OF VERONA

Julia	Carla Pinza	Speed	Jose Perez
Lucetta	Alix Elias	Duke of Milan	Norman Matlock
Proteus	Raul Julia	Thurio	Frank O'Brien
Valentine	Clifton Davis	Silvia	Jonelle Allen
Antonio; Tavern Host	Frederic Warriner	Eglamour	Alvin Lum
Launce	Jerry Stiller		

Street Urchins: Anthony Cuascut, Ralph Cuascut, Alex Velez. Citizens: Christopher Alden, Paul De John, Richard DeRusso, Richard Erickson, Brenda Feliciano, Sheila Gibbs, Jeff Goldblum, Albert Insinnia, Elizabeth Lage, Ken Lowrie, Gale McNeeley, Douglass Riddick, Madeleine Swift.

Orchestra: The P.P. Mavens (Bernard Purdie, Adolphus Anthony Cheatham, Ted Dunbar, Gordon Edwards, Billy Nichols, Jerry Thomas).

Directed by Mel Shapiro; choreography, Jean Erdman; musical direction, Margaret Harris; lighting, Lawrence Metzler.

Place: Verona, Milan and the forest. The play was presented in two acts.

Musicalization of Shakespeare's comedy about the love of Valentine and Proteus for Silvia and Julia. This production played 23 performances on the New York Shakespeare Festival Mobile Theater tour of the five boroughs of New York City 8/11/71 through 9/5/71. It was brought to Broadway, where it opened 12/1/71.

A list of musical numbers in *The Two Gentlemen of Verona* appears in its entry in the "Plays Produced on Broadway" section of this volume.

THE TALE OF CYMBELINE

Cymbeline	Tom Aldredge	2d Lord	Joseph Stern
Imogen	Karen Grassle	1st Lord	Stephen P. Schnetzer
Cloten	Sam Waterston	Dorothy	Diana Kirkwood
Queen	Jane White	Iachimo	William Devane
Posthumus Leonatus	Christopher Walken	Philario	Norman Snow
Arviragus (Cadwal)	Sam Tsoutsouvas	The Frenchman	Carl Mikal Franklin
Guiderius (Polydore)	Bruce Cobb	Cornelius	Joseph Ragno
Belarius (Morgan)	Mark Hammer	Caius Lucius	Alexander Panas
Pisanio	Don Plumley	Messenger	William Strohmeier

Ensemble—Birds: Hornbill, Carl Mikal Franklin; Cockatoo, Ernest Gray; Crowned Crane, Dennis Klein; Egret, W.K. Stratton; Hoatzin, Nathan Young; Crown Pigeon, Mark Zeray. Beats: Elephant, Stuart Pankin; Walrus, Ronald Peer; Boar, Michael Richardson; Frog, Robert Reilly; Alligator, Norman Snow; Armadillo, Peter Weil.

Directed by A.J. Antoon; music, Galt MacDermot; lighting, Martin Aronstein; animal battles, Diane Adler.

Time: Once upon a . . . Place: Two kingdoms and a forest. The play was presented in two parts.

Shakespeare's tale of the near-tragic consequences of a husband's wager on his wife's fidelity. Usually entitled merely *Cymbeline*, it was first produced in New York before the turn of the century. It was last produced by Lee Shubert as a vehicle for E.H. Sothern at the Jolson Theater on Broadway 10/2/23.

NOTE: In this volume, the programs of off-Broadway companies like the New York Shakespeare Festival are sometimes exceptions to our rule of counting the number of performances from the date of the press coverage. When the press opening night takes place late in the run of a play's paid public performances (after previews), we count the first performance of record, not the press date, as opening night. Press date for *Timon of Athens* was 6/30/71, for *The Two Gentlemen of Verona* 7/27/71, for *Cymbeline* its opening performance.

Georgie Porgie (73). By George Birimisa. Produced by Robert Weinstein and George Grec (Georgetown Productions) at the Village Arena. Opened August 10, 1971. (Closed October 10, 1971)

Georgie ....Claude Barbazon	The Man; Jack ....John P. McGowan
Ina; Mom; Grace ....Stacy Alden Giles	Judge's Voice ....David Sullivan
The Statue ....Sam Wright	Grover ....J Pearson Gant
Marv; The Stroller;	Finley; Skylar ....Paul Rosson
Rufus ....Geoff Springer	Tony ....Richie Broche
Steve; Jim ....Barry Kael	

Directed by George Birimisa; scenery, Joseph DiGiorgio; lighting, John Dodd; music supervision, John Herbert McDowell; associate producer, Jack R. Compton; production stage manager, David Sullivan; press, Saul Richman.

A homosexual's relationship with his mother, wife, lovers, etc. The play was presented without intermission. Previously produced off off Broadway at the Cooper Square Arts Theater.

Out of Control and **The Marriage of the Telephone Company Man** (6). Program of two one-act plays by Martin Craft. Produced by Marlow Ferguson at the Actors Playhouse. Opened September 9, 1971. (Closed September 12, 1971)

Directed by Frank Bara; scenery, Albert Carrier; press, Max Eisen. With Alexander Duncan, Duane Morris, Blainie Logan, J.C. Barrett, Dianne Trulock, Kricker James, Glenn Peters, Mary Carr Taylor, Mary Magone.

Out of Control is a farcical treatment of a lawyer-guilty client relationship. *The Marriage of the Telephone Company Man* is a curtain-raiser characterizing the phone company as part of the omnipotent Establishment.

Leaves of Grass (49). Musical based on the writings of Walt Whitman; adaptation and music by Stan Harte Jr. Produced by New Era Productions at Theater Four. Opened September 12, 1971. (Closed October 4, 1971)

Yolande Bavan	Scott Jarvis
Lynn Gerb	Joe Masiell

Directed by Stan Harte Jr. and Bert Michaels; musical staging, Bert Michaels; musical direction, Karen Gustafson; design, David Chapman; score arranged by Bill Brohn; production stage manager, Jan Moerel; press, Seymour Krawitz, Patricia Krawitz.

Anthology of Whitman's works arranged as lyrics and set to music.

ACT I—"Come Said My Soul," Joe Masiell; "There Is That in Me," Scott Jarvis; "Song of the Open Road," Masiell, Ensemble; "Give Me," Yolande Bavan, Lynn Gerb; "Who Makes Much of a Miracle?", Miss Gerb, Ensemble; "Tears," Miss Gerb; "Twenty-eight Men," Jarvis, Ensemble; "A Woman Waits for Me," Masiell; "As Adam," Miss Bavan, Ensemble; "Do You Suppose," Jarvis, Ensemble. "Enough," Masiell; "Dirge for Two Veterans," Jarvis; "How Solemn," Miss Gerb, Ensemble; "Oh Captain! My Captain!", Miss Bavan, Ensemble.

ACT II—Entracte, The Orchestra; "Pioneers," Ensemble; "Song of Myself," Ensemble; "Excelsior," Miss Bavan; "In the Prison," Miss Bavan; "Twenty Years," Masiell, Ensemble; "Unseen Buds," Masiell, Ensemble; "Goodbye, My Fancy," Miss Gerb; "Thanks," Masiell; "I Hear America Singing," Ensemble.

Look Me Up (406). Musical cabaret revue conceived by Laurence Taylor; book by Laurence Taylor. Produced by Costas Omero in association with Rio Plaza Productions Ltd., by special arrangement with Cafe Chantant Ent., at Plaza 9 Music Hall. Opened October 6, 1971. (Closed May 28, 1972)

Ted Agress	Linda Gerard
Zan Charisse	Mary Lynn Kolas
Kevin Christopher	Linda Kurtz
Murphy Cross	Don Liberto
Connie Day	Jeff Richards
Robin Field	Geoffrey Webb

Directed by Costas Omero; musical direction and arrangements, Horace Diaz; choreography, Bob Tucker; scenery, James Steward Morcum; costumes, Rosemary Heyer; lighting, Augusto Martinez; vocal and dance arrangements, Gene Casey; production stage manager, Robert Tucker; press, Harvey B. Sabinson, Lee Solters, Sandra Manley.

Collection of song and dance numbers with music written during and near the 1920s, with the accent on happy nostalgia.

ACT I—Scene 1: The Forerunners. "Runnin' Wild" (by Clifford Grey, Cyrus Wood & Gibbs), Ted Agress, Kevin Christopher, Don Liberto, Jeff Richards, Geoffrey Webb; A Song and Dance Man (medley), Robin Field; "Hallelujah" (by Vincent Youmans, Leo Robin & Clifford Grey), Company; "Get Happy" (by Harold Arlen & Ted Koehler), Company; "Happy Feet" (by Jack Yellen & Milton Ager), Liberto; "Someone to Watch Over Me" (by George & Ira Gershwin), Richards, Linda Gerard; "Making Whoopee" (by Gus Kahn & Walter Donaldson), Webb; "Button Up Your Overcoat (by B.G. DeSylva, Lew Brown & Ray Henderson), Zan Charisse, Linda Kurtz, Mary Lynn Kolas, Murphy Cross. Scene 2: In the Park. "You Made Me Love You" (by James Monaco & Joseph McCarthy), Connie Day, Field; "Bidin' My Time" (by George & Ira Gershwin), Agress, Christopher, Richards, Webb; "Can't Help Lovin' That Man" (by Jerome Kern & Oscar Hammerstein II), Miss Gerard; "Strike Up the Band" (by George & Ira Gershwin), Company.

INTERMISSION—Sing Along With Sam Bixby and His Cousins: Sam Bixby—Don Liberto; Bixby—Robin Field; Frank Bixby—Kevin Christopher.

ACT II—"Drums in My Heart" (by Vincent Youmans & Heyman), Company; "It Had to Be You" (by S. Jones & Gus Kahn), Richards, Miss Gerard; "If You Knew Susie" (by Joseph Meyer & B.G. DeSylva), Webb, Miss Day, Company; "Thinking of You," (by Walter Donaldson & Harry Akst), Richards; "The Best Things in Life Are Free" (by B.G. DeSylva, Lew Brown & Ray Henderson), Miss Gerard, Richards, Company; "Glad Rag Doll" (by Milton Ager, Jack Yellen & Dougherty), Miss Day; "Yes Sir, That's My Baby" (by Gus Kahn & Walter Donaldson), Misses Charisse, Kurtz, Kolas, Cross; "Baby Face" (by Benny Davis & Harry Akst), Agress, Girls; "Aba Daba Honeymoon" (by Fields & Donovan), Agress; "Manhattan" (by Richard Rodgers & Lorenz Hart), Liberto, Company; "How Long Has This Been Going On" (by George & Ira Gershwin), Miss Gerard; "Great Day" (by Vincent Youmans, William Rose & Elisco), Company.

Where Has Tommy Flowers Gone? (78). By Terrence McNally. Produced by Richard Scanga and Adela Holzer at the Eastside Playhouse. Opened October 7, 1971. (Closed December 12, 1971)

Tommy Flowers	Robert Drivas	The Girls	Barbara Worthington
Ben Delight	Wallace Rooney	The Men	F. Murray Abraham
Nedda Lemon	Kathleen Dabney	The Women	Marion Paone

Directed by Jacques Levy; scenery, David Chapman; lighting, Marc B. Weiss; costumes, James Berton Harris; visuals, Ed Bowes, Bernadette Mayer; production stage manager, Nicholas Russiyan; stage manager, Kate M. Pollock; press, Alan Eichler, James J. O'Rourke.

Time: Now. Place: New York City; here, there and everywhere. The play was presented in two acts.

Sketches, mostly farcical, of a young dropout living in the big city by his wits and charm and radical lifestyle (and just in case, he is perfecting a home-made bomb). Previously produced by the Yale Repertory Company and the 1971 Berkshire Drama Festival.

Sally Kirkland replaced Kathleen Dabney 10/16/21.

A Best Play; see page 131

The James Joyce Memorial Liquid Theater (189). Audience-participation revue conceived by Steven Kent; music by Jack Rowe, Robert Walker and Lance Larsen. Produced by Brooke Lappin and Bruce Bassman in association with Michael Edlin in the Company Theater of Los Angeles production at the Solomon R. Guggenheim Museum. Opened October 11, 1971. (Closed March 15, 1972)

Cast: Arthur Allen, Gar Campbell, Gladys Carmichael, William Dannevik, Barbara Grover, Donald Harris, Nancy Hickey, Larry Hoffman, William Hunt, Steven Kent, Lance Larsen, Candace Laughlin, Polita Marks, Sandra Morgan, Marcina Motter, Barry Opper, Michael Carlin Pierce, Roxanne Pyle, Russell Pyle, Dennis Redfield, Wiley Rinaldi, Jack Rowe, Richard Serpe, Trish Siodik, Michael Stefani, Robert Walker, Tobin Barbato, Bruce Bouchard, Joseph

Capone, Carotte, Doug Carfrae, Richard Cassese, Bob Cohen, Tony Giambrone, Virginia Glynn, Jenny Gooch, Margaret Goodenow, Scott Gruher, Oleta Hale, Nancy Hart, Amy Hass, Michael Haynes, Sandy Helberg, Nancy Heikin, Jonathan Hunter, Janis Jablecki, Kathleen Joyce, Lee Lanzet, John Livosi, Constance Mellors, Vincent J. Millard, Roger Nelson, Steve Nisbet, Ellen Parker, Cara Robin, John Roddick, Eileen Roehm, Susan Saltz, Ervin Stiggs, Michael Thayer, Gary White, Fritzi Winnick.

Directed by Steven Kent; musical director, Jack Rowe; scenery and lighting, Donald Harris; projections, William Dannevik, Steven Kent; maze created by the Company Theater of Los Angeles; production manager, Bruce Bassman; press, Gifford/Wallace Inc., Howard Newman.

Liquid in the sense that audience and entertainment run together, the show begins with concerts and games; then the audience passes, eyes closed, through a maze while being offered demonstrations of affection and other physical sensations; appeals are made to the senses in various encounter stunts and finally in a period of dancing. Previously produced in Los Angeles.

Friends and **Relations** (5). Program of two one-act plays by Eugene Yanni. Produced by Tom Millott at the Provincetown Playhouse. Opened October 14, 1971. (Closed October 17, 1971)

Directed by Tom Millott; assistant directors, Marilyn Fried, Elizabeth Stearns; scenery, Steve Askinazy; press, Samuel Lurie. With Grayson Hall, Madeleine Sherwood.

Friends is conversation about a friend who has just died. *Relations* is a mother's rejection of her movie-star daughter.

The Roundabout Repertory Company. Schedule of four programs. **The Master Builder** (64). Revival of the play by Henrik Ibsen; translated by Michael Meyer. Opened October 17, 1971. (Closed December 19, 1971) **The Taming of the Shrew** (29). Revival of the play by William Shakespeare. Opened January 30, 1972. (Closed February 20, 1972) **Misalliance** (46). Revival of the play by George Bernard Shaw. Opened March 28, 1972. (Closed April 30, 1972) **Conditions of Agreement** (1). By John Whiting. Opened and closed at the evening performance May 29, 1972. Produced by The Roundabout Repertory Company, Gene Feist producing director, at the Roundabout Theater.

THE MASTER BUILDER

Halvard Solness	Paul Sparer	Ragnar Brovik	Gene Galusha
Aline Solness	Elizabeth Owens	Kaia Fosli	Eren Ozker
Dr. Herdal	Sterling Jensen	Hilde Wagnel	Jill O'Hara
Knut Brovik	Fred Stuthman		

Directed by Gene Feist; original score by Philip Campanella; scenery, Holmes Easley; costumes, Mimi Maxmen; lighting, Robert Murphy; stage manager, William Stiegel; press, Michael Fried.

The most recent professional New York production of *The Master Builder* was the Phoenix Theater's for 40 performances 3/1/55. This is the first such production of this translation.

THE TAMING OF THE SHREW

Baptista	Sterling Jensen	Lucentio	David Hendricks
Katharina	Joan Bassie	Tranio; Tailor	Louis G. Trapani
Bianca	Judith Sullivan	Biondello	Robert Zay
Hortensio; Pedant	Philip Campanella	Petruchio	Michael Wager
Gremio	Fred Stuthman	Grumio	Gui Andrisano
Vicentio; Curtis	Lyle J. Lorentz	Widow	Nancy Sondag

Directed by Gene Feist and Gui Andrisano; score by Philip Campanella; scenery, Holmes Easley; costumes, Mimi Maxmen; masks, Jean Held; lighting, Robert Murphy; stage manager, Lauren Weiner.

The Taming of the Shrew was last presented in New York by the New York Shakespeare Festival Mobile Theater 6/27/65 for 26 performances (N.Y. Shakespeare had previously presented it in Central Park during the summer of 1960). Since its musicalization as the long-run *Kiss Me Kate* 12/30/48, it has been produced at the City Center 4/25/51 for 15 performances, by American Shakespeare Festival 2/20/57 for 23 performances and by the Phoenix Theater 3/6/63 for 39 performances.

MISALLIANCE

Johnny Tarleton	Ian Stuart	John Tarleton	Hugh Franklin
Bentley Summerhays	Lou Trapani	Joey Percival	Tom V.V. Tammi
Mrs. John Tarleton	Ruth Warrick	Lina Sczcepanowska	Elizabeth Owens
Hypatia Tarleton	Christine Sumerfield	Gunner	Philip Campanella
Lord Summerhays	Fred Stuthman		

Directed by Gene Feist; scenery, Holmes Easley; costumes, Mimi Maxmen; musical supervision, Philip Campanella; lighting, Robert Murphy; stage manager, Lauren Weiner.

Shaw's comedy was first produced in New York before 1920. Its only Broadway revival of record was by the City Center Drama Company, 2/18/53 for 114 performances. It was revived by Equity Library theater the season of 1950-51 and again off Broadway 9/25/61 for 156 performances.

CONDITIONS OF AGREEMENT

Emily Doon	Ruth Warrick	Nicolas Doon	Tom V.V. Tammi
Peter Bembo	Fred Stuthman	Patience Doon	Christine Sumerfield
A.G.	Humphrey Davis		

Directed by Gene Feist; scenery, Holmes Easley; costumes, Mimi Maxmen; lighting, Robert Murphy; original score, Philip Campanella; stage manager, Robert De Martino.

Time: September, 1948. Place: The living room of Emily Doon's house in a small town near Oxford, England. Act I, Scene 1: Thursday afternoon. Scene 2: Sunday morning. Act II, Scene 1: Sunday afternoon. Scene 2: That evening.

Sense of omnipresent evil built out of sinister memories of an accidental death and the menace of cruel practical joking; a mood play which stops short of action. American premiere of a foreign play previously produced in England.

Drat! (1). Musical conceived by Fred Bluth; book and lyrics by Fred Bluth; music by Steven Metcalf. Produced by Theater 1972 (Richard Barr and Charles Woodward; Michael Kasdan associate producer) at the McAlpin Rooftop Theater. Opened and closed at the evening performance, October 18, 1971.

Directed by Fred Bluth; design supervision, Christian Thee; lighting, Richard Nelson; costume supervision, Tomianne Wiley; musical director, Steven Metcalf; arrangements, Don Pippin; production stage manager, Murray Gitlin; press, Betty Lee Hunt. With Bonnie Franklin, Jane Connell, Gary Gage, Walter Bobbie, James (Red) Wilcher, Carol Swarbrick, Donna Sands.

Musical spoof of Victorian melodrama. Previously produced at Goodspeed Opera House, East Haddam, Conn.

A Song for the First of May (5). By Ted Pezzulo. Produced by James J. Thesing and Fredric V. Ralston at the Actors Playhouse. Opened October 22, 1971. (Closed October 24, 1971)

Directed by Anthony Wiles; scenery, Hal Tine; costumes, Fran Brassard; lighting, John Urban; stage manager, Doug Ellis; press, Betty Lee Hunt. With Max Gulack, William Robertson, Jean Bruno, Sheila Coonan, Colin Hamilton.

Conversation in an Upper West Side barroom.

A Gun Play (23). By Yale M. Udoff. Produced by Ken Gaston, Leonard Goldberg and A.I. Baron in association with Steven Beckler and Jon Delon, William Gumperz associate producer, at the Cherry Lane Theater. Opened October 24, 1971. (Closed November 14, 1971)

Stan	Eugene Troobnik	Motorcycle Officers	John Doherty,
Orlando	Arny Freeman		Ralph Maurer
Wallace	Tony Musante	George	Robert Moberly
Lita	Lara Parker	Melinda	Kelly Wood
Linden	William Bogert	Fashion Model	Pat Evans
Norma	M'el Dowd	Young Girl	Cheryl Houser
Jack	Jim Weston	Johnni	Shane Ousey

Directed by Gene Frankel; costumes, Sara Brook; scenery, Ralph Funicello, Marjorie Kellogg; lighting, Paul Sullivan: sound, Tony Barbetta; stage manager, Peter B. Mumford; press, Betty Lee Hunt.

Declining once-chic restaurant becomes an arena for violence, symbolizing our life and times. The play was presented in one act. Previously produced by the Hartford, Conn. Stage Company.

In the Time of Harry Harass (1). By Carolyn Rossi. Produced by Harrass Productions, Inc. at the Players Theater. Opened and closed at the evening performance, October 25, 1971.

Directed by Janet Bruders; scenery, Andy Dobrivich, Bill Balint; lighting, Edward Goetz; costumes, Annie Borys; stage manager, Regina Lynn; press, Sol Jacobson, Lewis Harmon. With Warren Pincus, Bernard Erhard, Heather Haven, Les Shenkel, Alice Elliott.

Comedy about a day in the life of a contemporary Everyman.

F. Jasmine Addams (6). Musical based on Carson McCullers's *The Member of the Wedding;* book by Carson McCullers, G. Wood and Theodore Mann; music and lyrics by G. Wood. Produced by Circle in the Square (Theodore Mann, Paul Libin, David J. Seltzer) at Circle in the Square. Opened October 27, 1971. (Closed October 31, 1971)

Directed by Theodore Mann; musical direction, Liza Redfield; musical arrangements, Luther Henderson; scenery, Marsha Louis Eck; lighting, Roger Morgan; costumes, Joseph G. Aulisi; musical numbers staged by Patricia Birch; production stage manager, Suzanne Egan; press, M.J. Boyer. With Theresa Merritt, Neva Small, Johnny Doran, Northern J. Calloway, Robert Kya-Hill, William LeMassena, Alicia Marcelo, Bill Biskup, Ericka Petersen, Edmund Gaynes, Carol Anne Ziske, Page Miller, Merry Flershem.

The play on which this musical is based, about a lonely 12-year-old Southern girl whose older sister is getting married, was originally produced on Broadway 1/5/50 for 501 performances, when it was named a Best Play of its season and won the Critics Award.

Bil Baird's Marionettes. Schedule of two marionette programs. **The Wizard of Oz** (65). Revival based on L. Frank Baum's stories; book by Arthur Cantor and Bil Baird; music by Harold Arlen; lyrics by E.Y. Harburg. And **Bil Baird's Variety.** Opened October 30, 1971. (Closed December 5, 1971) Reopened April 28, 1972. (Closed May 21, 1972) **Peter and the Wolf** (131). Book by A.J. Russell; music by Serge Prokofiev; lyrics by Ogden Nash. And **Bil Baird's Variety.** Opened December 18, 1971. (Closed April 23, 1972). Produced by the American Puppet Arts Council, Arthur Cantor executive producer, in the Bil Baird's Marionettes production at the Bil Baird Theater.

PERFORMER	"THE WIZARD OF OZ"	"PETER AND THE WOLF"
Peter Baird	Apparitions, Trees, Monkeys	Duck; Crow; Turtle
Pady Blackwood	Aunt Em; Glinda; Tin Woodman	Beaver; Crow; Wolf (in story); Hunter
Olga Felgemacher	Dorothy	Rabbit; Peter
Merry Flershem		Person in Forest
George S. Irving		Wolf's Singing Voice
John O'Malley	Toto; Oz	Owl; Crow
Frank Sullivan	Uncle Henry; Scarecrow	Mouse; Weasel; Grandpa; Hunter

PERFORMER	"THE WIZARD OF OZ"	"PETER AND THE WOLF"
Bill Tost	Tanglefoot; Cowardly Lion	Wolf; Bird; Squirrel; Humphrey's Singing Voice
Byron Whiting	Kalidah; Guardian; Witch of West	Humphrey; Crow; Cat; Hunter

BOTH PROGRAMS—Executive producers, Bil and Pat Baird; artistic associate, Frank Sullivan; directed by Gordon Hunt; production manager, Carl Harms.

THE WIZARD OF OZ—Musical director, Alvy West. Place: In and around Kansas. U.S.A. and the Land of Oz. The play was presented in two parts. Last produced in New York 11/27/68 for 118 performances.

PETER AND THE WOLF—Music adapted and arranged by Paul Weston; incidental music by Paul Weston; musical direction and special arrangements, Alvy West; assistant to Messrs. Nash and Weston, Sheldon Harnick; scenery, Howard Mandel; original production conceived by Bil and Cora Baird and Burt Shevelove. The play was presented in two parts; a puppet visualization of the Prokofiev musical work.

BIL BAIRD'S VARIETY—Finale conceived by Pady Blackwood. Billed as "a selection of puppet virtuosity embodying many styles and types."

Szene 71. Program of two plays in the German language. **Kabale und Liebe** (Cabals and Loves) (7). By Friedrich Schiller. Opened November 2, 1971. (Closed November 7, 1971). **Der Prozess** (The Trial) (7). Dramatized by Jan Grossman from the book by Franz Kafka. Opened November 9, 1971. (Closed November 14, 1971). Produced by the Gert von Gontard Foundation in the Szene 71 Productions, Oscar Fritz Schuh founding director, at Barbizon-Plaza Theater.

PERFORMER	"KABALE UND LIEBE"	"DER PROZESS"
Alwy Becker	Lady Milford's Maid	Leni
Kaspar Brüninghaus	Pres. von Walter	Supervisor; Thrasher; Manufacturer; Priest
Wolfgang Dörich	Miller	Lawyer
Axel Klingenberg	Servant	Student; Asst. Director
Ilse Laux	Miller's Wife	Frau Grubach
Klaus Münster	Wurm	1st Guard; Judge; Head Clerk
Esther Carola Regnier	Luise	Laundress
Albert Rueprecht	Ferdinand	Titorelli
Gerhard Soor	Valet	2d Guard; Court Attendant; Uncle
Hans von Borsody	von Kalb	Josef K
Renate Völkner	Lady Milford	Fraülein Bürstner

Directed by Oscar Fritz Schuh; scenery and costumes, Ursula Schuh; *Der Prozess* music, Eckart Ihlenfeld, sound master, Günter Hübner; assistant director, Axel Klingenberg; technical direction and lighting, Heinz Kraile, Friedrich Schoberth; stage manager, Günther Seufert; press, Philip C. Rogerson.

Visiting foreign troupe from Schweinfurt, Germany, in two of its productions. The Schiller play, *Kabale und Liebe,* is a social comment on morality and class conflict first produced in 1794; this is its first New York professional performance of record in any language. *Der Prozess* was the American premiere of this new stage version of Kafka's novel about the mysterious victimization of Josef K, last presented here in the Gide-Barrault version on Broadway for 4 performances in the 1952-53 season, and by Equity Library Theater in the 1964-65 season. Both plays were presented in two parts.

Love Me, Love My Children (187). Musical with book, music and lyrics by Robert Swerdlow. Produced by Joel W. Schenker and Edward F. Kook at the Mercer-O'Casey Theater. Opened November 3, 1971. (Closed April 23, 1972)

Don Atkinson	Matthew Diamond
Mark Baker	Ed Evanko
Salome Bey	Sharron Miller
Jacqueline Britt	Michon Peacock

Patsy Rahn	Rose Mary Taylor
Chapman Roberts	Suzanne Walker
Myrna Strom	

Directed by Paul Aaron; dances and musical numbers staged by Elizabeth Swerdlow; musical direction and arrangements, Michael Alterman; scenery, Jo Mielziner; costumes, Patricia Quinn Stuart; lighting, Dahl Delu; vocal arrangements, Robert DeCormier; production stage manager, David Taylor; press, Sol Jacobson, Lewis Harmon, Ruth D. Smuckler.

Runaway girl joins the youth culture in the big city and is disillusioned by it. The play was presented without intermission. A foreign play previously produced in Toronto.

Margaret Castleman replaced Patsy Rahn 11/30/71.

MUSICAL NUMBERS—"Don't Twist My Mind," Company; "Reflections," Chapman Roberts, Patsy Rahn; "Don't Twist Her Mind," Rose Mary Taylor, Company; "See," Salome Bey, Patsy Rahn, Matthew Diamond, Company; "Fat City," Company; "Deca Dance," Sharron Miller, Company; "Leave the World Behind," Myrna Strom, Ed Evanko, Suzanne Walker, Roberts, Miss Taylor, Company; "Don't Be a Miracle," Company; "Face to Face," Jacqueline Britt, Company; "Journey Home," Misses Bey, Rahn, Michon Peacock; "Critics," Don Atkinson, Mark Baker, Company; "Let Me Down," Evanko, Diamond, Miss Rahn; "Walking in the World," Miss Bey, Company; "North American Shmear," Company; "Gingerbread Girl," Roberts, Company; "Plot and Counterplot," Company; "Do the Least You Can," Evanko, Roberts, Misses Taylor, Peacock, Company; "You're Dreaming," Evanko, Company; "Running Down the Sun," Diamond, Misses Bey, Rahn; "Love Me, Love My Children," Company; "Don't Twist My Mind" (Reprise), Company.

* New York Shakespeare Festival Public Theater. Schedule of seven programs. **Sticks and Bones** (121). By David Rabe. Opened November 7, 1971. (Closed February 20, 1972; see note) **The Black Terror** (180). By Richard Wesley. Opened November 10, 1971. Closed March 26, 1972) **The Wedding of Iphigenia** and **Iphigenia in Concert** (139). Musical adaptation from Euripides by Doug Dyer, Peter Link and Gretchen Cryer; music by Peter Link; lyrics from Euripides. Opened December 16, 1971. (Closed March 8, 1972) **Black Visions** (64). Program of four one-act plays: *Sister Son/ji* by Sonia Sanchez, *Players Inn* and *Cop and Blow* by Neil Harris and *Gettin' It Together* by Richard Wesley. Opened April 4, 1972. (Closed April 30, 1972) *** That Championship Season** (34). By Jason Miller. Opened May 2, 1972. *** Older People** (29). By John Ford Noonan. Opened May 14, 1972. **The Hunter** (10). By Murray Mednick. Opened May 23, 1972. Produced by New York Shakespeare Festival Public Theater, Joseph Papp producer, Bernard Gersten associate producer, at the Public Theater.

STICKS AND BONES

The Family:		Rick	Cliff DeYoung
Ozzie	Tom Aldredge	The Sgt. Major	Hector Elias
Harriet	Elizabeth Wilson	The Priest	Charles Siebert
David	David Selby	The Girl	Asa Gim

Directed by Jeff Bleckner; scenery, Santo Loquasto; costumes, Theoni V. Aldredge; lighting, Ian Calderon; song "Baby When I Find You" music by Galt MacDermot, lyrics by David Rabe; stage manager, David Eidenberg; press, Merle Debuskey, Bob Ullman.

Time: Autumn 1968. Place: The family home. The play was presented in two parts.

Returning wounded Vietnam veteran brings much of the spiritual horror and some of the violence of the Indochina war back with him to his apple-pie American home and family.

NOTE: This production of *Sticks and Bones* was transferred to Broadway for an additional run 3/1/72; see its enry in the "Plays Produced on Broadway" section of this volume.

A Best Play; see page 181

THE BLACK TERROR

Ahmed	Kirk Young	Geronimo	Don Blakely
Keusi	Kain	Radcliffe	Earl Sydnor
M'Bahlia	Susan Batson	Dancer	Dolores Vanison
Antar	Paul Benjamin		

Brothers: Niger O. Akoni, Preston Bradley, James Buckley 3d, Dudley Lloyd, Kim Sullivan. Sisters: Sylvia Soares, Dolores Vanison, Freda Vanterpool. Drummers: Babafemi Akinlana, Ladji Camara, Ralph Dorsey. Radio Voices: Ron Dozier, William Mooney, Dolores Vanison, Ed VanNuys.

Directed by Nathan George; scenery, Marjorie Kellogg; costumes, Edna Watson; lighting, Buddy; Kuumba Dance, Bob Johnson; stage manager, Ron Dozier.

Time: The very near future, given the nature of American society. Scene 1: Terrorist H.Q. Scene 2: A tenement apartment, a few days later. Scene 3: Terrorist H.Q., the same day. Scene 4: A tenement apartment, a few days later. Scene 5: A tenement apartment, the following day. (Intermission) Scene 6: Terrorist H.Q., the next day. Scene 7: A tenement apartment, the same day. Scene 8: Radcliffe's home, some time later. The play was presented in two parts.

Executioner for a group of black terrorists has his doubts about the efficacy of these violent methods in bringing about an improvement in the black condition. Previously produced by the W.A.S.T.S.A. Theater Group at Howard University.

IPHIGENIA

Agamemnon . . . . .Manu Tupou   Iphigenia (in alphabetical order):
Clytemnestra . . . . .Madge Sinclair

Nell Carter	Lynda Lee Lawley
Margaret Dorn	Andrea Marcovicci
Leata Galloway	Julienne Marshall
Bonnie Guidry	Pamela Pentony
Patricia Hawkins	Marion Ramsey
Marta Heflin	Sharon Redd

Music: Goatleg (Henry "Bootsie Normand lead guitar, Chip McDonald rhythm guitar, Leon Medica bass guitar, steel guitar, Robert Patriquin, percussion, Fred Sherry cello, Peter Link acoustic guitar)

Directed and staged by Gerald Freedman; music arranged by Peter Link and Goatleg; scenery, Douglas Schmidt; costumes, Theoni V. Aldredge; lighting, Laura Rambladi; production stage manager, Michael Turque; stage manager, John Beven; press, Merle Debuskey, Robert Ullman.

The story of Iphigenia freely adapted as a rock musical. The first part, *The Wedding of Iphigenia*, deals with the sacrifice of Iphigenia by Agamemnon in Aulis. The second part, *Iphigenia in Concert* (her character is fragmented and performed by a rock chorus of 12 women), deals with the rituals of her life in Tauris before her escape.

ACT I—Opening, Madge Sinclair, Chorus; "What Has Your Tongue to Tell?", Andrea Marcovicci, Julienne Marshall, Chorus; "On a Ship With Fifty Oars," Miss Marshall, Marion Ramsey, Chorus; "Ride on to Highest Destiny," Madge Sinclair, Chorus; "The Line Is Unbroken," Chorus; "Who Will Lay Hands?" Margaret Dorn, Chorus; "Oh What Bridal Song," Chorus; "All Hail the King," Chorus; "I Was First to Call You Father," Chorus; "This New Land," Miss Dorn, Chorus; "Lead Me On," Nell Carter, Chorus; "I Was First to Call You Father" (Reprise), Marta Heflin; "They Sing My Marriage Song at Home," Miss Carter, Chorus; "Can't Stand in the Way of My Country," Misses Marcovicci, Ramsey, Linda Lee Lawley, Leata Galloway; "All Greece," Miss Galloway; "To Greece I Gave This Body of Mine," Sharon Redd, Chorus; "Who Will Lay Hands," Miss Dorn; "Lead Me On" (Reprise), Pamela Pentony; "Come Let Us Dance," Patricia Hawkins, Chorus; Finale, Miss Heflin, Chorus.

ACT II—"Lead Me On" (Reprise), Miss Carter, Chorus; "And Now," Part I solos Misses Marshall, Lawley, Marcovicci, Hawkins, Chorus; Part II solos Misses Carter, Heflin, Lawley, Hawkins, Galloway, Marshall, Chorus; "Only Stone," Miss Galloway, Chorus; "Last Night in a Dream," Bonnie Guidry, Manu Tupou, Miss Sinclair, Chorus; "Your Turn Has Come," Miss Redd, Chorus; "I Wonder," Miss Pentony with Misses Carter, Dorn, Redd, Marshall, Guidry; "How Can I Tell My Joy," Miss Marcovicci, Chorus; "Gate Tender," Misses Ramsey, Carter, Heflin, Galloway; "Unhappiness Remembering Happiness," Misses Dorn, Guidry, Chorus; "On a Ship With Fifty Oars" (Reprise), Henry "Bootsie" Normand, Chorus; "Crown Us With the Truth," Miss Lawley, Chorus.

BLACK VISIONS

Sister Son/ji
Sister Son/ji ....Gloria Foster

Players Inn
Barmaid ....Juanita Clark
Customer ....Bill Cobbs
Tittylip ....Berk Costello
Johnny ....Walter Cotton
Spabby ....Tommy Lane
Deadeye ....Hank Frazier
Numberman ....Sylvester Vonner
1st Junkie ....Jeffrey Miller
2d Junkie ....Jojo Kokayi
White Detective ....Norman Beim
Black Detective ....Tucker Smallwood
Drop Man ....Lou Rogers III

Cop and Blow
Tex ....Bill Cobbs
Nosegut ....Robert Judd
Barmaid ....Barbara Montgomery
Frank ......................J.A. Preston
Knowledge ....Jojo Kokayi
Tittylip ....Berk Costello
Zulu ....Tommy Lane
Hitman ....Tucker Smallwood
Policeman ....Sylvester Vonner
1st White Detective ....Frank Bara
2d White Detective ....Rick Petrucelli
Black Detective ....John Henry Redwood

Gettin' It Together
Nate ....Morgan Freeman
Coretta ....Beverly Todd
Radio D.J. ....Lou Rogers III

Sister Son/ji directed by Novella Nelson; other plays directed by Kris Keiser; scenery, Ademola Olugebefola; costumes, Grasanne Driskell; lighting, Ernest Baxter; choreography, Hope Clark; production stage manager, Garland Lee Thompson.

Sister Son/ji is a review of a woman's past, in monologue; *Players Inn* and *Cop and Blow* are Harlem barroom dramas by the same author. *Gettin' It Together* is a closeup of a problematical love affair.

THAT CHAMPIONSHIP SEASON

Tom Daley ....Walter McGinn
George Sikowski ....Charles Durning
James Daley ....Michael McGuire

Phil Romano ....Paul Sorvino
Coach ....Richard A. Dysart

Understudy: Messrs. McGinn, Sorvino—Jason Miller.

Directed by A.J. Antoon; scenery, Santo Loquasto; costumes, Theoni V. Aldredge; lighting, Ian Calderon; production manager, Andrew Mihok.

Time: The present. Place: The Coach's house, somewhere in the Lackawanna Valley.

At their annual reunion, middle aged ex-basketball champs discover that the qualities which won them the prize 20 years before may have led them into becoming losers in life.

A Best Play; see page 169

OLDER PEOPLE

Roger; Dubufay; Man;
  Felix Devine ....Will Hare
Clarice; Wendy; Fay; Woman;
  Mary ....Bette Henritze
Sam Beckman; Dubufay; Gastoni; Francis;
  Hooch; Harry; Stanley ...Bernard Hughes

Stella Beckman; Kay;
  Zelda ....Polly Rowles
Dubufay; Dunbar; Bubber; Sidney; Bob;
  Howardina's Brother ......Stefan Schnabel
May; Maggie; Geraldine;
  Howardina ....Madeleine Sherwood

Musicians: Margaret Dorn, Henry "Bootsie" Normand, Peter Link.

Directed by Mel Shapiro; scenery, Ming Cho Lee; costumes, Theoni V. Aldredge; lighting, Roger Morgan; music, Peter Link; lyrics, John Ford Noonan; production stage manager, John Margulis.

Vignettes, mostly comic, of middle to old age, most of them involving sex or the longing for it.

The roles of Sam Beckman, Stella Beckman, Clarice, Mary and Bob were deleted shortly after the opening. The roles of Penny Arcade (Bette Henritze) and Candy Concession (Polly Rowles) were added.

THE HUNTER

Lee ....Michael Hadge
Harry ....Robert Glaudini

Hunter ....Douglass Watson
Marianne ....Kathleen Cramer

Directed by Kent Paul; scenery, Ralph Funicello; costumes, Theoni V. Aldredge; lighting, Spencer Mosse; music, Peter Link; stage manager, Jeff Hamlin.

Symbolic drama of two soldiers in Civil War uniforms who crucify and then kill a hunter. The play was presented in three acts.

NOTE: In Joseph Papp's Public Theater there are many separate auditoriums. *The Black Terror* played the Other Stage, *Sticks and Bones* and *Older People* played the Florence S. Anspacher Theater, *Iphigenia* played Martinson Hall, *Black Visions* and *The Hunter* played the Public Theater Annex, *That Championship Season* played the Estelle R. Newman Theater.

In addition to its regular schedule of off-Broadway productions open to the public and reviewed by the critics, there were many special and experimental projects staged during the season at the Public Theater including *Four for One*, a work-in-progress program of four one-act plays at the Other Stage 5/16/72. It consisted of *The Corner* directed by S.J. Gaines and *You Gonna Let Me Take You Out Tonight, Baby?* directed by Carl Taylor, both by Ed Bullins; *His First Step* by Oyamo, directed by Kris Keiser; and *One: The Two of US* written and directed by Ulunga Adell.

Kumquats (53). Puppet revue with book and lyrics by Cosmo Richard Falcon; music by Gustavo Motta. Produced by Cosmo Richard Falcon and Wayland Flowers in association with Art and Bert D'Lugoff. Opened November 15, 1971. (Closed January 2, 1972)

| Michael Alogna | James Racioppi |
| Wayland Flowers | Gregory Smith |

Directed by Nicholas Coppola; production created and designed by Wayland Flowers; musical direction and arrangements, Michael Leonard; lighting, Ken Moses; stage manager, Margaret Peckham; press, Harvey B. Sabinson, Lee Solters, Cheryl Sue Dolby.

Billed as "The World's First Erotic Puppet Show," a puppet lampoon of erotica.

ACT I—Madame, "In the Name of Love;" "Kumquats;" "At the Library;" Old Hat Joke; "American Dream Girl;" Legs!; The Evil Fairy and the Hippie; The Wee Scotsman; A Day at the Sexual Research Institute; The Wee Scotsman (Repeat); *Hello!* Dolly; "The Dirty Word Waltz."

ACT II—"Irma's Candy Heaven;" Old Hat Joke (Repeat); Adam and Eve, "This Is Paradise;" "The Evil Fairy and the Hard Hat; Madame Meets a Midget; Legs! (Repeat); Mao Tse Tongue; Madame, "The Sensuous Woman;" The Wee Scotsman (Repeat); Legs! (Repeat); "The Story of Oooh!"; Finale, "In the Name of Love" (Reprise).

Richard Farina: Long Time Coming and a Long Time Gone (7). Musical adapted from the works of Richard Farina by Nancy Greenwald. Produced by Free Flow Productions and Jay K. Hoffman at the Fortune Theater. Opened November 17, 1971. (Closed November 21, 1971)

Directed by Robert Greenwald; musical direction and arrangements, Arthur Miller; scenery and collage, Richard Hammer, Patrick Sullivan; lighting, John Dodd; costumes, Joyce and Jerry Marcel; stage manager, Daniel Adams; press, Lindsay Maracotta. With Richard Gere, Vicki Sue Robinson, Penelope Milford, Charles Weldon, Jessica Harper, Brendan Hanion, Michael Lewis.

Collection of stories, poems and songs of the late folk singer Richard Farina.

The Repertory Theater of Lincoln Center. Schedule of four programs. **People Are Living There** (20). By Athol Fugard. Opened November 18, 1971. (Closed December 4, 1971) **The Ride Across Lake Constance** (20). By Peter Handke; translated by Michael Roloff. Opened January 13, 1972. (Closed January 29, 1972) **The Duplex** (28). By Ed Bullins. Opened March 9, 1972. (Closed April 1, 1972) **Suggs** (20). By David Wiltse. Opened May 4, 1972. (Closed May 20, 1972) Produced by The Repertory Theater of Lincoln Center under the direction of Jules Irving, Robert Symonds associate director, at the Forum Theater.

PEOPLE ARE LIVING THERE

Milly .... Estelle Parsons   Shorty .... Peter Rogan
Don .... Leonard Frey   Sissy .... Diana Davila

Directed by John Berry; scenery, Douglas W. Schmidt; costumes, Jeanne Button; lighting, John Gleason; production stage manager, Patrick Horrigan; stage manager, Brian Meister; press, Susan Bloch, William Schelble, Sedgwick Clark.

Place: The kitchen of an old two-storied house in Braamfontein, Johnnesburg, South Africa. The play was presented in two parts.

Conversation in a run-down kitchen adds up to an image of futility, intended to represent life itself. A foreign play previously produced in South Africa.

Susan Sharkey replaced Diana Davila 11/23/71.

THE RIDE ACROSS LAKE CONSTANCE

Kathleen Doyle   Priscilla Pointer
Stephen Elliott   Keene Curtis
Paul Hecht   Margaret Howell
Salome Jens   Kathryn Howell

Directed by Carl Weber; scenery and costumes, Dahl Delu; lighting, John Gleason; production stage manager, Paul Bengston; stage manager, Brian Meister.

Controversial, storyless, non-linear collage of words and phrases in an experimental script by an Austrian playwright previously produced in Germany and elsewhere. The play was presented without intermission. At the direction of the author, "When the play is staged the characters should bear the names of the actors playing the roles: the actors are and play themselves at one and the same time."

THE DUPLEX

Velma Best .... Mary Alice   Sister Sukie .... Phylicia Ayers-Allen
Montgomery Henderson .... Johnny Hartman   Pops .... Joseph Attles
Tootsie Franklin .... Albert Hall   O.D. Best .... Frank Adu
Marco Polo Henderson .Carl Mikal Franklin   Crook .... Kirk Kirksey
Steve Benson .... Les Roberts   Marie Horton .... Norma Donaldson
Mama .... Clarice Taylor   Wanda .... Marie Thomas

Directed by Gilbert Moses; scenery, Kert Lundell; lighting, John Gleason; costumes, Bernard Johnson; music, Gilbert Moses; lyrics, Ed Bullins; music arranged and directed by Coleridge-Taylor Perkinson; production stage manager, Patrick Horrigan; stage manager, Brian Meister.

Time: Early 1960s. Place: A Southern California duplex. Act I, 1st Movement: You Gotta Be Mah Man, Man. 2d Movement: Party Killer. Act II, 3d Movement: Save Me, Save Me, Baby. 4th Movement: Cool Blowin'.

James Hainesworth replaced Frank Adu 3/26/72. J. Herbert Kerr Jr. replaced Carl Mikal Franklin and Charles Weldon replaced Albert Hall. 3/29/72.

Orgiastic slice of black life taking off from a party as in Bullins's previous play *The Pig Pen*, with episodes of drinking, card playing, love making, etc., subtitled "A Black Love Fable in Four Movements," with musical introductions to each scene. Previously produced at the New Lafayette Theater.

SUGGS

Bum .... Charles Turner   Suggs .... William Atherton
Talker .... Robert Levine   Goff .... Ralph Bell
Crone .... Joan Pape   Jo Ann .... Lee Lawson

Directed by Dan Sullivan; scenery, Douglas W. Schmidt; costumes, Jeanne Button; lighting, John Gleason; production stage manager, Craig Anderson; stage manager, Robert Lowe.

Wide-eyed Western youth eagerly embraces life in the big city, is gradually disillusioned.

In addition to its regularly-scheduled productions, the Repertory Theater of Lincoln Center presented a series of workshop programs entitled "Explorations in the Forum" at the Forum Theater, as follows: *Kool Aid,* two one-act plays by Merle Molofsky, directed by Jack Gelber, 5 performances 11/3/71-11/6/71; *Delicate Champions* written and directed by Stephen Varble, 6 performances 12/29/71-1/1/72; Anna Sokolow's Players Project repertory of four works—*Magritte Magritte,* Samuel Beckett's *Act Without Words No. 1, A Short Lecture and Demonstration of the Evolution of Ragtime as Presented by Jelly Roll Morton* and *Rooms*— 6 performances, 2/23/72-2/26/72.

JFK (9). One-man program based on the records of the John F. Kennedy administration; performed by Jeremiah Collins; adapted by Jeremiah Collins and Mark Williams. Produced by Walt DeFaria at the Circle in the Square. Opened November 21, 1971. (Closed November 28, 1971)

Directed by Mark Williams and Walt DeFaria; scenery and lighting, David F. Segal; still photography, Ken Howard; associate producer, Phil McLaughlin; press, Frank Goodman, Les Schecter. With Jeremiah Collins, Frank Baginski, John Cain, Jane Loeb.

Portrayal of Pres. John F. Kennedy mostly from his on-the-record speeches and replies to questions by reporters (actors planted at the show as members of the audience). Previously produced at the National Press Club, Washington, D.C.

* The Negro Ensemble Company. Schedule of three programs. **The Sty of the Blind Pig** (64). By Phillip Hayes Dean. Opened November 16, 1971; see note. (Closed January 9, 1972) **A Ballet Behind the Bridge** (48). By Lennox Brown. Opened March 7, 1972; see note. (Closed April 16, 1972) *** Frederick Douglass ... Through His Own Words** (26). Program based on the play by Arthur Burghardt and Michael Egan; adapted from the writings of Frederick Douglass. Opened May 9, 1972. Produced by The Negro Ensemble Company, Douglas Turner Ward artistic director, Robert Hooks executive director, Frederick Garrett administrative director, at St. Marks Playhouse.

THE STY OF THE BLIND PIG

Weedy	Clarice Taylor	Alberta Warren	Frances Foster
Doc	Adolph Caesar	Blind Jordan	Moses Gunn

Directed by Shauneille Perry; scenery, Edward Burbridge; lighting, Ernest Baxter; sound, Chuck Vincent; costume supervision, Steve Carter; production stage manager, Horacena J. Taylor; press, Howard Atlee, David Roggensack.

Time: The 1950s, just before the beginning of the civil rights movement. Place: The Warren apartment on the South Side of Chicago. Act I, Scene 1: Dusk, late summer. Scene 2: Several days later. Scene 3: A week later. Scene 4: A week later, midday. Act II, Scene 1: Two weeks later, early fall. Scene 2: Later. Act III, Scene 1: Several days later. Scene 2: One hour later. Scene 3: Several hours later.

The personal generation gap between a black Southern mother and daughter who have moved to Chicago and are sharing an apartment. Previously presented in a staged reading by the Playwrights Unit of the Actors Studio.

Julius Harris replaced Moses Gunn for 8 performances during the play's run.

A BALLET BEHIND THE BRIDGE

Joseph Drayton	David Downing	Mano Drayton; King	Gilbert Lewis
Vain Woman	Michle Shay	European King; Mahon	C. David Colson
Nat'l Guard Commander	Duane Jones	European Queen	Carolen Ross
Maraval	Neville Richen	Priest	Howland Chamberlain
Borbon	David Connell	Mahal	Larry Desmond
Lalsingh	Adolph Caesar	Shouter Woman	Esther Rolle
Achong	Stephen Cheng	African Queen; Prostitute	Lauren Jones
Alcoholic	Jack Landron	Jesus Monkey	Norman L. Jacob
Mrs. Drayton	Frances Foster	Head Teacher	Robert Stocking

Soldiers of the National Guard: Tom Jenkins, Cary Barnes, Ron Hines, Bernard Wyatt. Off Stage Four: Sonny Morgan, Nathaniel Bettis, Eliebank Crichlow, Richard Pablo Landrum.

Directed by Douglas Turner Ward; scenery, Edward Burbridge; lighting, Jennifer Tipton; costumes, Bernard Johnson; choreography, Louis Johnson; "Cannes Brulees" composed by Joseph Brown; arrangements, Sonny Morgan; sound, Chuck Vincent; production stage manager, Horacena J. Taylor; press assistant, Clarence Allsopp.

Time: The recent past. Place: Port-of-Spain, Trinidad. Act I: Night, East Dry River, popularly called Behind the Bridge, a ghetto in Port-of-Spain. Scenes alternate between the "Bridge" locale, the home of the Draytons and flashbacks to 15th century European and African palaces. Act II: Later, the same night to the next morning.

Ballet in the sense that it is a ceremonial drama of opposing family, racial and cultural forces. A foreign (Canadian) play in its first production.

FREDERICK DOUGLASS . . . THROUGH HIS OWN WORDS

Frederick Douglass . . . . .Douglas Turner Ward, Adolph Caesar, Duane Jones

Scenery, Edward Burbridge; production stage manager, Horacena J. Taylor; assistant production manager, Coral Hawthorne.

Act I: Retrospective views, visions and prophecies. Bondage and thoughts of freedom. Act II: Abolition and editorship. The Civil War and afterwards orations supreme.

The 19th century ex-slave and black leader Frederick Douglass presented onstage in a program compiled from his own writings. Previously produced at the Triangle Theater and on television.

WORKS IN PROGRESS

In addition to its professional programs of record, The Negro Ensemble Company presented a series of informal programs entitled "Works in Progress" 1/12/71-2/7/71, with press invited for observation but not for review. The series was coordinated by Michael Schultz; sound by Chuck Vincent; basic lighting by Shirley Prendergast; basic scenery by Edward Burbridge.

Programs were as follows: 1/12-1/13—*Top Hat* by Paul Harrison and *Home Cooking* by Clay Goss, both directed by Paul Harrison; 1/14-1/15—*The One* by Oliver Pitcher, directed by Norman Bush, and *Sisyphus and the Blue-Eyed Cyclops* written and directed by Garland Thompson, with Al Freeman Jr.; 1/16-1/17—*Sister Son/ji* by Sonja Sanchez, *Where We At* by Martie Charles, *Perfection in Black* by China Clark, all directed by Novella Nelson; 1/19-1/20—*Black Magic Anyone?* by Leatrice El, directed by Buddy Butler; 1/21-1/22—*An Evening With Max Roach* directed by Louis Johnson, with the J.C. White Choir; 1/26-1/27—Staged readings of new plays; 1/28-1/29—*The Corner* by Ed Bullins and *His First Step* by Oyamo, both directed by Kris Keiser, and *Andrew,* a showcase by NYU students; 1/30-1/31—*An Adaptation: Dream* written and directed by Bill Duke and *Terraced Apartment* by Steve Carter, directed by Shauneille Perry, with Denise Nicholas; 2/2-2/3—*Us Versus Nobody* written and directed by Hal de Windt; 2/4-2/7—Staged readings of new plays.

NOTE: In this volume, the programs of off-Broadway subscription companies like The Negro Ensemble Company are sometimes exceptions to our rule of counting the number of performances from the date of the press coverage. When the press opening night takes place late in the run of a play's paid public performances (after previews) for the subscription audience, we count the first subscription performance, not the press date, as opening night. Press date for *The Sty of the Blind Pig was* 11/23/71, for *A Ballet Behind the Bridge* 3/16/72.

Masquerade (1). By Gertrude Gayle. Produced by The Masquerade Company at Theater Four. Opened and closed at the evening performance, November 28, 1971.

Directed by Don Toner; scenery and lighting, James T. Singelis; costumes, Domingo A. Rodriguez; production stage manager, David Godbold; press, Alan Eichler. With John Svar, Carl Strano, Kay Williams, Barry Corbin, C. David Colson, Kathleen Moore, Rex Brown, Jean Toner, Adam Kimmelman, McCoy Baugham, Susan Berger, Don Chafey, Fred Stone, Becki Davis, Brian Farrell.

Drama of a love affair between Queen Elizabeth I and the Earl of Oxford. Previously produced at the Theater Center of Mississippi, Jackson.

El Hajj Malik (40). By N.R. Davidson Jr. Produced by Afro-American Studio at the Martinique Theater. Opened November 29, 1971. (Closed January 9, 1972)

Joan Bailey	Deborah Howard
Cindy Burroughs	Augustus Keith
Norman Butler	James Lee
Woody Carter	Jim Mallette
Lee Cooper	Joan Seale
James Harris	

Directed by Ernie McClintock; music composed and arranged by William Saltar; choreography, Milo Timmons; designed by Ron Walker; costumes, Augustus Keith; associate producer, Marc Primus; stage manager, John Hines; press, Bill Doll & Co.

Subtitled *The Dramatic Life and Death of Malcolm X,* this is a series of episodes, some symbolic, some realistic, in the life and career of the noted black leader, using many of his own words. The play was presented in two acts.

* **The Chelsea Theater Center of Brooklyn.** Schedule of four programs. **The Screens** (28). By Jean Genet; translated by Minos Volanakis. Opened November 30, 1971; see note. (Closed December 26, 1971) **Kaddish** (100). Based on a poem by Allen Ginsberg. Opened February 1, 1972; see note. (Closed February 20, 1972). Reopened at Circle in the Square, March 7, 1972. (Closed May 14, 1972) * **The Beggar's Opera** (31). Revival of the musical by John Gay; musical score newly realized by Ryan Edwards. Opened March 21, 1972; see note. (Closed April 16, 1972) Reopened at the McAlpin Roof Theater May 30, 1972. **The Water Hen** (21). By Stanislaw Ignacy Witkiewicz; translated by Daniel C. Gerould. Opened May 9, 1972; see note. (Closed May 28, 1972). Produced by The Chelsea Theater Center of Brooklyn, Robert Kalfin artistic director, Michael David executive director, at the Brooklyn Academy of Music.

THE SCREENS

Said	Robert Jackson	Scribe	Gerald Finnigan
Mother	Julie Bovasso	Cadi	Martin Garner
Mustapha	John Capodice	Madani; Habiba's Husband	James Cahill
Brahim; Azuz	Henry Smith	Gendarme; Si Slimane;	
Ahmed; Condemned Man	David Pendleton	Missionary	Kurt Garfield
Warda	Grayson Hall	Mr. Blankensee	Richard Ramos
Maid; Srira	Reah Smith	Malik; Salem	Jeff Druce
Malika	Joan Harris	Abdil; Kaddur	Matt Greene
Legionnaire	Greg Macosko	Nasser; Kuider	Darcy Hollingsworth
Leila	Janet League	Lieutenant	John Granger
Sir Harold	Charles Bartlett	Sergeant	Barry Bostwick
Habib; Guard; Old Man	Joseph Della Sorte	Mrs. Blankensee; Aziza	Dorothy Chace
Taleb	John Coe	Arab Dignitary	Greg Etchison
Kadidja	Despo	Lassen	Thomas Barrett
Nedjma	Marilyn Diane	Old Woman; Djemila	Marilyn Sokol
Chigha; Mme. Bonneuil	Marilyn Chris	Sir Harold's Son	Tobias Haller
Habiba	Linda Rubinoff	M'Barek; Abdesselem;	
Policeman; M. Bonneuil	Robert Einenkel	Grocer	Stephen Billias
Flute Player	Jerrold Ziman	Ommu	Osceola Archer
Man Who Pissed	Gene Elman	Grocer's Boy	Valcour Lavizzo
Woman; Aicha	Vira Colorado		

Arabs: Tom Barrett, Stephen Billias, John Capodice, Gerald Finnigan, Dwight Schultz, Henry Smith. Europeans: Gerald Finnigan (Photographer), Sasha von Scherler (Vamp), Jerrold Ziman (Academician), Richard Ramos (General), Dwight Schultz (Soldier), Gene Elman (Banker), John Capodice (Judge), Diana Bero (Little Girl). Combatants (sic): John Capodice, Joseph Della Sorte, Wayne Mitchell, David Pendleton.

Legionnaires: Greg Macosko (Preston, Felton, Roland), Dwight Schultz (Walter, Helmut, Roger), Henry Smith (Hernandez, Morales, Jojo), Robert Einenkel (Brandineschi, Nestor), John FitzGibbon (Pierre).

Directed by Minos Volanakis; scenery, Robert Mitchell; costumes, Willa Kim; lighting,

Bennet Averyt; production manager, Burl Hash; stage manager, Stephen McCorkle; press, Ron Christopher, Monica Frakes.

Scene 1: On the road. Scene 2: The brothel. Scene 3: At home. Scene 4: Sir Harold's field. Scene 5: The prison gate. Scene 6: The square of an Arab village. Scene 7: In court. Scene 8: The cemetery. Scene 9: At home. Scene 10: Sir Harold's orange grove. Scene 11: The night of the revolution. Scene 12: The day of the revolution. (Intermission) Scene 13: On the road. Scene 14: The village square. Scene 15: Among the dead. Scene 16: Warda's murderer. Scene 17: After the revolution.

Doomed antihero, doomed civilization, in an epic stage treatment with a background in Algeria at the time of the crisis of the 1950s. A foreign (French) play previously produced in Germany, England and finally France in 1966. This production was its American premiere.

A Best Play; see page 150

KADDISH

Allen	Michael Hardstark	Football Hero	John Nichols
Naomi	Marilyn Chris	Louis	Michael Vale
Young Allen	Glenn Weitzman	Nurse Attendant; Bus Clark; Woman;	
School Boy	Valcour Lavizzo	Nurse (Greystone); Art Teacher; Nurse	
Bus Driver; 2d Attendant;		(Pilgrim State)	Jani Brenn
2d Policeman	Gregory Etchison	3d Attendant; Pharmacist	David Elyah
1st Attendant; Voice; Dr. Mabuse;		Eugene	Jerrold Ziman
Evangelist; Crapp; Dr. Luria;		Man	Tim Warnet
1st Policeman	Bernie Passeltiner	Eleanor	Ronica Stern

Directed by Robert Kalfin; video by Arthur Ginsberg and Video Free America; scenery and costumes, John Scheffler; lighting, Bennet Averyt; production manager, Burl Hash; stage manager, Virginia Friedman.

Time: The late 1930s to the mid 1950s. Part I: Poison Germs (locations are Paterson, Lakewood, the Hoboken ferry, a footmall field). 1—Poison Germs; 2—Louis in Pyjamas Listening to Phone; 3—Barefoot in the Pharmacy. Part II: Eugene's Face of Pain (locations are Paterson, Newark, Greystone Hospital). Part III: Beautiful Thoughts All Day. 1—The Homecoming. (Intermission) Part III (continued): Beautiful Thoughts All Day (locations are 18th Street in Manhattan, National Maritime Union Clinic). 2—Beautiful Thoughts All Day; 3—Working for Dr. Luria. Part IV: Late Naomi in the Bronx. 1—Late Naomi in the Bronx; 2—Naomi Expresses Herself; 3—Naomi Bothers Eleanor; 4—One Mythological Cousinesque Room; 5—She Waved, Tears in Her Eyes. Part V: Last Visit to Hospital. 1—Last Visit to Pilgrim State.

A second Chelsea Theater Center experiment with integrated use of TV and live action (first was last season's AC/DC), framed in a stage presentation of Allen Ginsberg's poetry about his mother Naomi.

When Kaddish moved to Circle in the Square 3/7/72 there were some cast changes and augmenting of other credits, as follows: Chip Zien replaced Michael Hardstark and several Greg Etchison roles; Paul Nevens replaced some of the Bernie Passeltiner roles; Virginia Friedman was stage manager; The Circle in the Square and Charles R. Rothschild, associate producer William Matthews, cooperated in the production. Kaddish played 79 performances at Circle in the Square in addition to its original 21 performances at the Academy of Music.

THE BEGGAR'S OPERA

Jemmy Twitcher	Joseph Palmieri	Crook-Fingered Jack	Neil Hunt
Mr. Peachum	Gordon Connell	Diana Trapes	Connie Van Ess
Filch	John Long	Dolly Trull	Joan Nelson
Mrs. Peachum	Jeanne Arnold	Mrs, Coaxer	Lynn Ann Leveridge
Polly Peachum	Kathleen Widdoes	Jenny Diver	Tanny McDonald
Macheath	Stephen D. Newman	Suky Tawdry	Irene Frances Kling
Ben Budge	Roy Brocksmith	Lockit	Reid Shelton
Matt of the Mint	William Newman	Lucy Lockit	Marilyn Sokol

Musicians: Roland Gagnon keyboard, Zizi Mueller flute, David Taylor violin, Dean Kelso cello, Tony Perfetti trumpet, Garrett List trombone.

Directed by Gene Lesser; musical director, Roland Gagnon; scenery, Robert U. Taylor; costumes, Carrie F. Robbins; lighting, William Mintzer; dances arranged by Elizabeth Keen;

production manager, Burl Hash; production stage manager, James Doolan.

Time: Early 18th century. Place: London. Act I: In and around the Peachum's house and a tavern near Newgate. Act II: In and around Newgate Prison.

John Gay's popular 18th century hit has been seen in New York in many versions from 1920 to the present. The most recent included a marionette version in 1966, a Richard Baldridge version at the City Center 3/13/57 for 15 performances and the famous Bertolt Brecht-Kurt Weill off-Broadway version *The Threepenny Opera* which opened at the Theater de Lys in the season of 1953-54 and played 2,611 performances, the second-longest running off-Broadway production of record.

When *The Beggar's Opera* reopened 5/30/72 at the McAlpin Rooftop Theater, Timothy Jerome replaced Stephen D. Newman in the role of Macheath, Ralston Hill replaced Reid Shelton, Jill Eikenberry replaced Joan Nelson, and the roles of Crook-Fingered Jack and Diana Trapes were omitted. It had played 29 performances at the Academy of Music before resuming its run at the McAlpin Rooftop.

THE WATER HEN

Elizabeth Gutzie-Virgeling ....Garn Stephens	Richard (Hoozy) ....Joseph Della Sorte
Edgar Valpor ....James Cahill	Ephermer Typowicz ....Joseph Leon
Tadeuz Gutzie-Virgeling ......Mickey Finn	Isaak Specter ....Joey Fitter
Lamplighter ....Vincent Schiavelli	Alfred Evader ....Martin Meyers
Albert Valpor ....Paul Sparer	Jan Parblichenko ....Ronnie Newman
Alice ....Patricia Elliott	Afrosia Yupupova ....Elaine Grollman
	Adolph Orsin ....Wil Albert

Footmen: James Banick, Hank Botwinik, James Donnellan, Anthony Werner. Detectives: James Himelsbach, John Stravinsky.

Directed by Carl Weber; scenery, Fred Kolouch; costumes, Theodora Skipitares; lighting, Richard M. Devin; music, William Bolcom; production manager, Burl Hash; production stage manager, Stephen McCorkle.

Act I: An open field, then a barracks courtyard. Act II: A salon, Nevermore Castle. Act III: Ten years later; a salon, Nevermore Castle.

Symbolic comedy of the ridiculous about an enchantress who captivates three generations of a family. American premiere of a foreign (Polish) play written in 1921.

BROWN BAG PROJECTS

The following special "Brown Bag" projects to introduce new forms, ideas and writers were produced by The Chelsea Theater Center on a limited budget and offered in a limited schedule of performances.

FOUR AMERICANS. Repertory of two bills of two one-act plays. First bill (6): *Now There's Just the Three of Us* by Michael Weller, directed by Roger Hendricks Simon, and *The Reliquary of Mr. and Mrs. Potterfield* by Stephen H. Foreman, directed by Dennis Rosa. Opened October 19, 1971. Design, John Scheffler; lighting, Bennet Averyt. With Tobias Haller, Stephen McHattie, Tony Travis, Linda Rubinoff, Michael Vale, Edward Zang, Jeanne Hepple. Second bill (6): *Tall and Rex* by David Wiltse, directed by Roger Hendricks Simon, and *Things* by David Kranes, directed by Dennis Rosa. Opened October 26, 1971. Design, John Scheffler; lighting, Bennet Averyt, With Margaret Winn, Michael Vale, Drout Miller, Ruth Baker, Alice Beardsley, Edward Zang. (Repertory closed November 6, 1971)

INTERROGATION OF HAVANA (14). Translated by Peter Mayer from the German of Hans Magnus Enzensberger. Opened December 27, 1971. (Closed January 15, 1972) Direction, Louis Criss; scenery, John Scheffler; lighting, Bennet Averyt. With Rocko Cinelli, Andre Pavon, Roland F. Sanchez, Robert Baines, Martin Shakar, Ben Slack, Brad Sullivan, Donald Warfield, Roger Robinson, Joseph Leon, Jeff David, Joseph Ragno, Dwight Schultz, David Margulies, Nicholas Kepros, Andrew Jarkowsky, Koula Antoniadou.

EROS AND PSYCHE (18). Dance drama-mime by John Argue. Opened April 26, 1972. (Closed May 14, 1972). Direction, John Argue; music, James Fulkerson. With Anna Brennan, Diane Salinger, Andrew Potter, Cassandra Case, Sheila Kotkin, Billie Jo Williams, John Guerrasio, Susan Brickell, Gillian Gordon, Charlotte Linzer, Angelita Reyes, Donald Larkin, Kenneth Weiss, Anthony White.

NOTE: In this volume, the programs of off-Broadway subscription companies like The Chelsea Theater Center of Brooklyn are sometimes exceptions to our rule of counting the number of performances from the date of the press coverage. When the press opening night takes place late in the run of a play's paid public performances (after previews) for the subscription audience, we count the first subscription performance, not the press date, as opening night. Press date for *The Screens* was 12/10/71, for *Kaddish* 2/10/72, for *The Beggar's Opera* 3/29/72 and for *The Water Hen* 5/18/72.

* **The American Place Theater.** Schedule of three programs. **Fingernails Blue as Flowers** by Ronald Ribman and **Lake of the Woods** by Steve Tesich (33). Program of two one-act plays. Opened December 6, 1971; see note. (Closed January 8, 1972) **Sleep** (32). By Jack Gelber. Opened February 10, 1972; see note. (Closed March 11, 1972) * **The Chickencoop Chinaman** (5). By Frank Chin. Opened May 27, 1972; see note. Produced by The American Place Theater, Wynn Handman director, Julia Miles associate director, at The American Place Theater.

FINGERNAILS BLUE AS FLOWERS

Eugene Naville	Albert Paulsen	Jesse	Larry Block
Waiter	Zakes Mokae	Rosemary	Karli Dwyer
Estelle Singer	Pamela Shaw		

Directed by Martin Fried; scenery, Kert Lundell; costumes, Patricia McGourty; lighting, Roger Morgan; production stage manager, Franklin Keysar; stage manager, Grania M. Hoskins; press, Howard Atlee, David Roggensack.
   Time: 1971. Place: A resort hotel in Jamaica.
   A tense, paranoid vacationer symbolizes our maladjustment to modern living.

LAKE OF THE WOODS

Winnebago	Hal Holbrook	Forest Ranger	Will Hussung
Christo	Armand Assante	Musician	Ron Panvini
Juanita	Esther Benson		

Directed by Jack Gelber; scenery, John Wulp; costumes, Willa Kim; lighting, Roger Morgan; music and lyrics, Ron Panvini.
   Time: Now. Place: Great Outdoors. Scene 1: Afternoon. Scene 2: Night and the following morning.
   Man coping with the outdoors is a symbol of our effort to survive in a disintegrating society.

SLEEP

The Subject:		The Dream Figures:	
Gil	David Spielberg	Black Actress	Verona Barnes
The Sleep Scientists:		Black Actor	Norman Bush
Dr. Morphy	Don Fellows	White Actor	Barton Heyman
Dr. Merck	Conard Fowkes	White Actress	Dorrie Kavanaugh

Directed by Jacques Levy; scenery, Kert Lundell; costumes, Willa Kim; lighting, Roger Morgan; production stage manager, Franklin Keysar; stage manager, Grania M. Hoskins.
   Time: The present. Place: An experimental sleep lab. The play was presented in two parts.
   Mr. Average Guy is the subject of a scientific sleep experiment, during which his dreams are acted out.

THE CHICKENCOOP CHINAMAN

Tam Lum	Randy Kim	Robbie	Anthony Marciona
Hong Kong Dream Girl	Joanna Pang	Tonto; Tom	Calvin Jung
Kenji	Sab Shimono	Lone Ranger	Merwin Goldsmith
Lee	Sally Kirkland	Charley Popcorn	Leonard Lackson

Directed by Jack Gelber; scenery, John Wulp; costumes, Willa Kim; lighting, Roger Morgan; production stage manager, Franklin Keysar; stage manager, Grania M. Hoskins.

Act I, Scene 1: Tam's Hong Kong Dream Girl dream: screaming into Pittsburgh. Scene 2: Kenji's apartment, early evening. Act II, Scene 1: Tam's Dream Lone Ranger: The legendary radio childhood. Scene 2: Charley Popcorn's Pornie House, Pittsburgh, night. Scene 3: Tam in limbo. Scene 4: Kenji's apartment, later that night.

Identity problems of the Chinese American in our race-conscious, stereotype-loving society. Previously produced as the prizewinner of a Los Angeles playwriting contest.

NOTE: In this volume, the programs of off-Broadway subscription companies like The American Place Theater are sometimes exceptions to our rule of counting the number of performances from the date of the press coverage. When the press opening night takes place late in the run of a play's paid public performances (after previews) for the subscription audience, we count the first subscription performance, not the press date, as opening night. Press date for *Fingernails Blue as Flowers* and *Lake of the Woods* was 12/23/71, for *Sleep* 2/22/72 and for *The Chickencoop Chinaman* 6/12/72.

In addition to its regular schedule, American Place produced *The Metamorphosis* by Charles Dizenzo, adapted from Franz Kafka short stories, for subscription audiences 4/8/72 through 5/6/72, not submitted for public review.

Nightride (94). By Lee Barton. Produced by Bill Shirley at the Vandam Theater. Opened December 9, 1971. (Closed February 27, 1972)

Erik Fenstrom	Philip Larson	Jab Humble	Chandler Hill Harben
Marcus Sternberg	Don Draper	Peter Duchos	Jeremy Stockwell
Jon Bristow	Lester Rawlins		

Directed by Milton Lyon; scenery, Alan Kimmel; lighting, Ken Billington; costumes, Katrin; production stage manager, Charles Roden; press, Betty Lee Hunt Associates, Henry Luhrman.

Time: The present. Place: A beach house in Puerto Rico. Act I: 10 p.m. Act II: 5 a.m. the following morning.

Famous playwright, a closet homosexual, makes a painful adjustment to the new atmosphere of sexual openness.

Memphis Store-Bought Teeth (1). Musical with book by E. Don Alldredge; music by William Fisher; lyrics by D. Brian Wallach. Produced by D. Brian Wallach at the Orpheum Theater. Opened and closed at the evening performance, December 29, 1971.

Directed by Marvin Gordon; musical supervision and arrangements, Ted Simons; scenery, Robert O'Hearn; costumes, William Pitkin; lighting, George Vaughn Lowther; conductor, Rene Weigert; stage manager, Doug Laidlaw; press, Frank Goodman, Les Schecter. With Jerry Lanning, J.J. Jepson, Alice Cannon, Travis Hudson, Evelyn Brooks, Lloyd Harris, Sherill Price, Hal Robinson.

Traveler returns home and helps reenact an amorous incident that took place 15 years before.

22 Years (16). By Robert Sickinger. Produced by Jeff Britton in association with the Manhattan Theater Club at Stage 73. Opened January 4, 1972. (Closed January 16, 1972)

Directed by Robert Sickinger; scenery, Robert King; lighting, Gary Marec; production stage manager, Ralph Carideo; press, M.J. Boyer. With King Morton, Joan Grove, Frank Girardeau, Marc Handler, Diane Jayne, Barbara Marchant, Julie Burgher, Gail Hayden, Kristin Marle, Louise Garone, Robert Corwin, Molly Larson, Curly Hurley, Nikki Ana Dominguez, Dennis Kear, Ron Osborne, O.B. Lewis, Chaz Palminteri, Loree Gold, Emanuel Kaufman, David Walker, Jeanette Arnone, Tony Bruni, Tad Lathrop, Rita Ballard.

Billed as a "rockumentary" about the life of multiple murderer Charles Manson and his "family," presenting Manson as an an innocent victim and interpolating several songs, two of them written by Manson himself.

Rosebloom (23). By Harvey Perr. Produced by Harlan Kleiman and Peter Goldfarb at the Eastside Playhouse. Opened January 5, 1972. (Closed January 23, 1972)

Sylvie	Sylvia Miles	Mark	Ron Rifkin
Enola Gay	Regina Baff	Harry Rosebloom	Harold Gary

Directed by Jered Barclay; scenery, Merrill Sindler; lighting, Thomas Skelton; costumes, Ann Roth; production stage manager, Murray Gitlin; press, David Powers.

Time: The present. Place: The living room of Mark and Enola Gay Rosebloom. The play was presented in two acts.

Crippled son, his wife and his mother await the father's return home from prison. Previously produced at the Mark Taper Forum in Los Angeles.

Wanted (79). Musical with book by David Epstein; music and lyrics by Al Carmines. Produced by Arthur D. Zinberg at the Cherry Lane Theater. Opened January 19, 1972. (Closed March 26, 1972)

Starr Faithful Brown ....Andra Akers	Ma Barker ....Lee Guilliatt
Billy the Kid ....Reathel Bean	Deafy; Jelly Barker ....John Kuhner
Babycakes ....Jerry Clark	Jesse James ....Peter Lombard
Opal ....Cecelia Cooper	Sheriff Sweet; Doc Barker .....Stuart Silver
John Dillinger ....Frank Coppola	Miss Susannah Figgit;
Shorty ....June Gable	Sister Powhatan Lace ..Gretchen Van Aken
Jacob Hooper ....Merwin Goldsmith	

Directed by Lawrence Kornfeld; musical direction, Susan Romann; scenery, Paul Zalon; costumes, Linda Giese; lighting, Roger Morgan; stage manager, Jimmy Cuomo; press, M.J. Boyer.

Comic reversal of attitude towards the supposed good guys and bad guys, in episodes from the history of American outlawry.

ACT I

"I Am the Man" ....Jesse
"Where Have You Been Up to Now?" ....Billy, Starr Faithful
"Outlaw Man" ....Miss Susannah
"Who's on Our Side?" ....Hooper, Babycakes, Shorty
   (Lyrics by Al Carmines and David Epstein)
"Parasol Lady" ....Hooper
"Jailhouse Blues" ....Ma
"I Want to Ride With You" ....Starr Faithful, Billy
   (Lyrics by Al Carmines and David Epstein)
"You Do This" ....Johnny, Shorty, Deafy
"Guns Are Fun" ....Johnny

ACT II

"I Do the Best I Can" ....Ma, Doc
   (Lyrics by Al Carmines and David Epstein)
"Wahoo!" ....Doc, Jelly, Ma
"Whispering to You" ....Babycakes, Hooper
"I Want to Blow Up the World" ....Shorty
"The Indian Benefit Ball" ....Sister Powhatan Lace, Shorty, Ma, Doc, Jelly, Johnny
"The Lord Is My Light" ....Jessie, Sister Powhatan Lace, Shorty, Ma, Doc, Jelly, Johnny
   (Lyrics by Al Carmines and David Epstein)
"It's Love" ....Hooper
"As I'm Growing Older" ....Ma, Hooper

Two if by Sea (1). Musical with book by Priscilla B. Dewey and Charles Werner Moore; music by Tony Hutchins; lyrics by Priscilla B. Dewey. Produced by The Tea Party Company at Circle in the Square. Opened and closed at the evening performance, February 6, 1972.

Directed by Charles Werner Moore; musical numbers staged by Edward Roll; musical direction, Jeff Lass; scenery, John Doepp; costumes, Julie Weiss; lighting, Roger Morgan; orchestrations and additional music, Jeff Lass and John Nagy; production stage manager, Alan Fox; press, Saul Richman. With Kay Cole, Jack Gardner, Judy Gibson, Rod Loomis, Joe Morton, Rick Podell, Jan Ross, John Stratton, John Witham.

Parallels between contemporary youth rebellion and the American Revolution.

Dylan (48). Revival of the play by Sidney Michaels. Produced by Joseph Rhodes, Marty Richards and Martin Edelman at the Mercer O'Casey Theater. Opened February 7, 1972. (Closed March 19, 1972)

Caitlin ....Rue McClanahan	Annabelle; Miss Wonderland ..Karen Gorney
Dylan ....Will Hare	Mattock ....Kurt Garfield
Brinnin ....Carleton Carpenter	Bartender; Stagehand;
Angus ....John Coe	Deck Officer ....Jeff Eagle
Clubwoman; Elena ....Delphi Lawrence	Minister; Jay Henry ....Ed Crowley
Meg ....Joanna Miles	

Reporters: Karen Gorney, Ed Crowley, Michael Wieben, Jeff Eagle.
Directed by Lee D. Sankowich; scenery, John Scheffler; costumes and lighting, Andrew Greenhut; associate producer, Nina Goodman; stage manager, Dan Hild; press, Betty Lee Hunt Associates, Henry Luhrman, Abner B. Klipstein, Harriett Trachtenberg.
Time: The early 1950s. Place: America and Wales. The play was presented in two acts.
This biographical play about the life and death of the Welsh poet Dylan Thomas was first produced on Broadway 1/18/64 for 273 performances and was named a Best Play of its season. It was revived last season in an off-off-Broadway production.

Brothers (1). By Stephen White. Produced by Whitecaps Productions at Theater Four. Opened and closed at the evening performance, February 13, 1972.

Directed by David Williams; scenery and lighting, C. Murawski; costumes, Jeanne Button; stage manager, Robert J. Bruyr; press, David Lipsky. With Everett McGill, Brian Farrell, Tisa Chang, Jim Mallette, Evelyn Page, Brendan Fay, Paul Barry, Diane Gardner, Elaine Sulka, Rodney Cleghorne, James J. Mapes, Tim Moses.
In a middle class American family, one son goes to war and the other joins the peace movement.

The Shadow of a Gunman (72). Revival of the play by Sean O'Casey. Produced by Norman Kean and John Heffernan at the Sheridan Square Playhouse, Opened February 29, 1972. (Closed April 30, 1972)

Donal Davoren ....Leon Russom	Tommy Owens ....Bruce French
Seumas Shields ....John Heffernan	Mrs. Henderson ....Paddy Croft
Mr. Maguire;	Mr. Gallogher ....Bernard Frawley
An Auxilary ....Joseph Daly	Mrs. Grigson ....Estelle Omens
Mr. Mulligan ....James Carruthers	Adolphus Grigson ....James Gallery
Minnie Powell ....Jacqueline Coslow	

Directed by Philip Minor; scenery, Lloyd Burlingame; costume supervision, Margaret M. Mohr; lighting, Fred Allison; production stage manager, Dean Compton; press, Bob Ganshaw.
O'Casey's 50-year-old drama of violence in Dublin in the 1920s had its first New York production of record off Broadway during the 1951-52 season. It was revived on Broadway 11/20/58 for 52 performances.

Alice in Wonderland (50). Revival of the play adapted from the writings of Lewis Carroll by the Manhattan Project; "translator," Kenneth Cavander. Produced by Lyn Austin and Oliver Smith in the Manhattan Project (An N.Y.U.S.O.A. Theater Company) production at the Performing Garage (off off Broadway). Opened March 1, 1972. (Closed May 7, 1972)

Gerry Bamman	Jerry Mayer
Tom Costello	Angela Pietropinto
John Ferraro	Larry Pine
Saskia Noordhoek Hegt	Kathleen Tolan
John P. Holms	

Directed by Andre Gregory; designers, Eugene Lee, Franne Newman; press, Lisa Stam.
This production of *Alice* was first produced 10/8/70 for 119 performances at The Extension.

374   THE BEST PLAYS OF 1971-1972

* **Walk Together Children** (67). One-woman show arranged, adapted and performed by Vinie Burrows. Produced by Ananse Productions at the Mercer Brecht Theater. Opened March 16, 1972.

Production stage manager, Ken Starrett; taped music, Brother Ahh (Robert Northern); gowns, Arthur McGee; press, Bill Doll and Company, Inc.
Selections of poetry, songs and various other writings, subtitled "the black journey from auction block to new nation time."
PART I—Membrances, by Jenny Proctor; Speech, by Sojourner Truth; Runagate Runagate, by Robert Hayden; Slave Song (anonymous); The Party, by Paul Laurence Dunbar; Life Cycle in the Delta, by George Houston Bass; When My Uncle Willie Saw, by Carol Freeman; I Know Jesus Heard Me, by Charles Anderson; Scarlet Woman, by Fenton Johnson; W.E.B. to Booker T., by Dudley Randall; Between the World and Me, by Richard Wright.
PART II—Alberta K. Johnson, by Langston Hughes; Two Jazz Poems, by Carl Wendell Hines Jr.; U Name This One, by Carolyn Rodgers; Benediction, by Bob Kaufman; Conversation (anonymous); Jitterbugging in the Streets, by Calvin Hernton; Brother Harlem Bedford Watts Tells Mr. Charlie Where It's At, by Bobb Hamilton; Three Movements and a Coda, by Imamu Amiri Baraka (LeRoi Jones); When I Heard Dat White Man Say, by Zack Gilbert; Poem of Angela Yvonne Davis, by Nikki Giovanni; Poem to Complement Other Poems, by Don L. Lee.

The Web and the Rock (9). By Dolores Sutton; based on Thomas Wolfe's novel. Produced by Cheryl Crawford and Jean Dalrymple, in association with Robert S. Mankin and Jim Wise, by special arrangement with Lucille Lortel Production, Inc. at the Theater de Lys. Opened March 19, 1972. (Closed March 26, 1972)

Directed by José Ferrer; scenery, Peter Wexler; costumes, Edith Lutyens Bel Geddes; lighting, Roger Morgan; sound, Gary Harris; production stage manager, Maxine S. Taylor; press, Jean Dalrymple. With Sal Carollo, Dolores Sutton, Elsa Raven, James Naughton, Peter Jason, Carolyn Groves, Darlene Parks, David Kerman, Eugene Stuckman.
Stage adaptation of Thomas Wolfe's posthumously published novel, about a love affair between a young writer and an older woman.

Uhuruh (8). Musical revue with book, music and lyrics by Danny Duncan. Produced by Franklin Fried and Bert Wainer in association with City Center of Music and Drama Inc., at the City Center Downstairs. Opened March 20, 1972. (Closed March 25, 1972)

Directed and choreographed by Danny Duncan; musical direction, Rick Appling; production coordinator, Alice Alexander; lighting, Kueleza Furaha; costumes, Richmond Curry; press, Howard Atlee, David Roggensack, Clarence Allsopp. With Danny Duncan, Blondell Breed, Gregory Burrell, Pasy Cain, Alice Alexander, Raymond Wade, Ebony Wright, David Gardner, Cyril Tyrone Hanna II, Walterine Ross, Pamela Swedon, Victor Willis, Earl Young, Samaki 'Zuri.
Topical musical cabaret revue-type show, originally produced in San Francisco.

Rain (7). Revival of the play by John Colton and Clemence Randolph; based on W. Somerset Maugham's *Miss Thompson*. Produced by Bruce Mailman by special arrangement with Sheldon Abend at the Astor Place Theater. Opened March 23, 1972. (Closed March 28, 1972).

Directed by Michael Flanagan; scenery, Stuart Wurtzel; costumes, Raoul Pene du Bois; lighting, Barry Arnold; production stage manager, Robert Vandergriff; press, Saul Richman. With Antonia Rey, John Travolta, Richard Ryder, Beeson Carroll, Paul Milikin, Elizabeth Farley, Bernie Passeltiner, Madeleine Le Roux, James Cahill, Bob Parlan, Ben Stack, Patricia O'Connell.
This play was first produced on Broadway 11/7/22 by Sam H. Harris, with Jeanne Eagles and Robert Kelly in the leading roles. The same production was revived 9/1/24, and Mr. Harris revived it again for Tallulah Bankhead for 47 performances 2/12/35. It was last revived on Broadway in a musical version entitled *Sadie Thompson,* 11/16/44 for 60 performances.

Theater: Fair of Opinion (15). Limited engagement of a program of Latin-American theater in English. Produced by Theater of Latin America at St. Clement's Church. Opened March 23, 1972. (Closed April 9, 1972).

Directed by Augusto Boal; press, Sol Jacobson, Lewis Harmon. With Patric Epstein, Joyce Roth, Jake Dengel, Scott Cunningham, Arthur Rosen, Robert Burgos.
A kaleidoscope of Latin-American theater and music.

Whitsuntide (1). By Tom LaBar. Produced by Bert Steinberg and Howard Champion-Smith at the Martinique Theater. Opened and closed at the evening performance March 26, 1972.

Directed by Russell Treyz; costumes, A.E. Kohout; lighting, John Dodd; vocal arrangements and direction, Peter Schlosser; production stage manager, Jeff Hamlin; press, Seymour Krawitz. With Michael Miller, Joyce Elliott, George DiCenzo, Susanne Wasson, Grace Carney, Dallas Alinder, Celia Howard, Elizabeth George, Robert Molnar, Alan Howard.
A Connecticut town suffers an epidemic of glossolalia (speaking in tongues).

In Case of Accident (8). By Peter Simon. Produced by William Craver at the Eastside Playhouse. Opened March 27, 1972. (Closed April 2, 1972)

Directed by Ted Cornell; scenery, John Scheffler; lighting, Marc B. Weiss; costumes, David James; production stage manager, Kate M. Pollock; press, Gifford/Wallace Inc. With Michael Shannon, Fay Sappington, Joseph Boley, Patricia Elliott, Terry Kiser, Henderson Forsythe.
Young painter living in an upstate New York farmhouse receives a late-night visit from three enigmatic friends.

* Small Craft Warnings (67). By Tennessee Williams. Produced by Ecco Productions (Robert Currie, Mario De Maria, William Orton) at the Truck and Warehouse Theater. Opened April 2, 1972.

Violet	Cherry Davis	Steve	William Hickey
Doc	David Hooks	Quentin	Alan Mixon
Monk	Gene Fanning	Bobby	David Huffman
Bill McCorkle	Brad Sullivan	Tony the cop	John David Kees
Leona Dawson	Helena Carroll		

Directed by Richard Altman; production design, Fred Voelpel; lighting, John Gleason; production stage manager, Robert Currie; stage manager, John David Kees; press, Gifford/Wallace Inc.
Time: The present. Act I: A bar along the Southern California coast. Act II: An hour or two later.
Life viewed from the underside in an evening among the sad, defeated clients of a third-rate barroom.
Tennessee Williams replaced David Hooks at the performances of 6/6/72 and 6/7/72.
A Best Play; see page 276

The Soft Core Pornographer (1). By Martin Stone and John Heller. Produced by Ivan Mars at Stage 73. Opened and closed at the evening performance April 11, 1972.

Directed by Word Baker; scenery, Ed Wittstein; lighting, David F. Segal; costumes, Caley Summers; production stage manager, T.L. Boston; press, Dorothy Ross. With Dorrie Kavanaugh, Frank Raiter, Richard Latessa.
Comedy about a pornography writer whose wife envisions a more ambitious use of his talents.

God Says There Is No Peter Ott (8). By Bill Hare. Produced by Square Root Productions at the McAlpin Rooftop Theater. Opened April 17, 1972. (Closed April 23, 1972)

Directed by Leland Ball; incidental music, Arthur B. Rubinstein; scenery, David Chapman; lighting, Judy Rasmuson; costumes, Pamela Scofield; production stage manager, Bud Coffey; press, Seymour Krawitz. With Rue McClanahan, Ann Sweeny, Tom Ligon, Alice Drummond, Hansford Rowe.

Family situations in a run-down Cape Cod guest house.

* And They Put Handcuffs on the Flowers (44). By Fernando Arrabal; English translation by Charles Marowitz; revised by Lois Messerman. Produced by Ted Menten at the O'Casey Theater (Mercer Arts Center). Opened April 21, 1972.

Amiel	George Shannon	Drima	Muriel Miguel
Katar	Peter Maloney	Lelia	Patricia Gaul
Pronos	Ron Faber	Falidia	Ellen Schindler
Tosan	Baruk Levi	Apparition	Riley Kellogg

Directed by Fernando Arrabal; design, Fernando Arrabal and Duane Mazey; production director and asst. to Arrabal, James Denton; stage manager, Lawrence Sellars; press, Alan Eichler, James J. O'Rourke.

Brutalization of political prisoners in a dictatorship, and their physical and moral degradation brought on by their imprisonment (Arrabal was thrown into a Franco prison for a short time in 1966). A foreign (French) play previously produced off off Broadway.

* The Real Inspector Hound and **After Magritte** (43). Program of two one-act plays by Tom Stoppard. Produced by Susan Richardson, Lawrence Goossen and Seth Schapiro at Theater Four. Opened April 23, 1972.

AFTER MAGRITTE

Harris	Konrad Matthaei	Foot	Remak Ramsay
Thelma	Carrie Nye	Holmes	Edmond Genest
Mother	Jane Connell		

Time: Early evening. Place: A room. Married couple, a ballroom dancing team, quarrel with each other and with his mother who lives with them and plays the tuba—all much to the farcical confusion of a suspicious but inept inspector from Scotland Yard.

THE REAL INSPECTOR HOUND

Moon	David Rounds	Cynthia	Carrie Nye
Birdboot	Tom Lacy	Magnus	Remak Ramsay
Mrs. Drudge	Jane Connell	Inspector Hound	Edmond Genest
Simon	Konrad Matthaei	BBC Voice	Brian Murray
Felicity	Boni Enten		

Time: Opening night. Place: A theater. Parody of a mystery play with all the cliches, and with the added zest of mixing a pair of drama critics into the impossibly complicated plot.

BOTH PLAYS—Directed by Joseph Hardy; scenery, William Ritman; costumes, Joseph G. Aulisti; lighting, Richard Nelson; incidental choreography, Patricia Birch; stage manager, Suzanne Egan; press, Alan Eichler, James J. O'Rourke.

British plays previously produced in London.

Cold Feet (1). By Marvin Pletzke. Produced by D. Frederick Baker, Stuart Goodman, Frank M. Celecia and FM Productions at the Players Theater. Opened and closed at the evening performance April 24, 1972.

Directed by Stuart Goodman; scenery and lighting, Kay L. Coughenour; costumes, Kathleen Sacchi; production stage manager, John Bernabel; press, Saul Richman. With Frank Vohs, Joe Kottler, Catherine Bacon, Jeri Archer, Aurelia de Felice, Sally De May.

Comedy about a shoe salesman as the target of various attempted seductions.

The Divorce of Judy and Jane (7). By Arthur Whitney. Produced by Dudley Field Malone and Van Rapoport at the Bijou Theater. Opened April 26, 1972. (Closed April 30, 1972)

Directed by Roderick Cook; scenery, Helen Pond, Herbert Senn; costumes, Edith Lutyens Bel Geddes; lighting, Gilbert Hemsley; production stage manager, Mark Healy; press, Sol Jacobson, Lewis Harmon, Ruth D. Smuckler. With Louise Troy, Parker McCormick, Delphi Lawrence, Estelle Gettleman, Lois de Banzie, Constance Forslund, Ruth Manning.

An abrasive gathering of Lesbian types.

God Bless Coney (3). Musical with book, music and lyrics by John Glines. Produced by Paul B. Reynolds at the Orpheum Theater. Opened May 3, 1972. (Closed May 5, 1972)

Directed by Bob Schwartz; musical direction, orchestrations and arrangements, Robert Rogers; scenery, Don Tirrell; lighting, William Mintzer; costumes, Margaretta Maganini; production stage manager, Brooks Fountain; press, M.J. Boyer. With Bill Hinnant, Ann Hodapp, Marcia Lewis, William Francis, Liz Sheridan, Johnny La Motta.

Coney Island lifeguard plans to commit suicide during a fireworks display.

* **Anna K.** (26). Variations of Tolstoy's *Anna Karenina* conceived by Eugenie Leontovich. Produced by Rick Hobard at the Actors Playhouse. Opened May 7, 1972.

Anna ....Catherine Ellis	Serpuhovsky; Nikolai; Prince Scherbatsky;
Dolly; Betsy; Hostess ....Ann Mitchell	Vronsky's Footman; Karenin's Valet;
Princess Scherbatsky; Princess Maykoff;	Tartar Waiter; Trainman ...Richard Ooms
Masha; Ambassador's Wife;	Levin; Ambassador;
Seriozha ....Cam Kornman	Trainman ....George Bamford
Kitty; Sappho ....Lanna Saunders	Vronsky ....Mark MacCauley
Countess Lydia; Annushka; Countess	Tuskevich; Landau; Kuzma; Matvey;
Vronsky ....Eugenie Leontovich	Vronsky's Footman; Karenin's Valet;
Karenin ....Arthur Roberts	Tartar Waiter ....Dick Fuchs
Stiva; Vladimir; Kritsky ...Rudolph Willrich	

Directed by Eugenie Leontovich; lighting, Richard Nelson; movement, Elizabeth Keen; sound, Port-o-Vox; production associate, Michele Bejarano; music for Act II prologue, George Bamford; production stage manager, Michael J. Frank; press, Max Eisen, Milly Schoenbaum.

Act 1, Prologue: A rehearsal studio, New York City. Scene 1: Oblonsky's home, Moscow. Scene 2: A fashionable Moscow restaurant. Scene 3: Moscow train station. Scene 4: Oblonsky home, Moscow. Scene 5: Scherbatsky's house, Moscow. Scene 6: Hotel room, Moscow. Scene 7: Grand ballroom, Moscow. Scene 8: Train station, Petersburg. Scene 9: Princess Betsy's, Petersburg. Scene 10: Karenin's home, Petersburg. Scene 11: A gypsy camp. Scene 12: A rehearsal studio, New York City. Scene 13: Karenin's summer villa. Scene 14: A box at the race track. Scene 15: A military barracks. Scene 16: Karenin's summer villa. Scene 17: Karenin's home, Petersburg. Scene 18: The same, later. Scene 19: Oblonsky's home, Moscow. Scene 20: The same, later. Scene 21: Karenin's hotel room, Moscow. Scene 22: Karenin's home, Petersburg. Scene 23: Vronsky's home, Moscow.

Act II, Prologue: A rehearsal studio, New York City. Scene 1: Karenin's home, Petersburg. Scene 2: The same, later. Scene 3: Anna's bedroom, Karenin's home. Scene 4: Levin's country house. Scene 5: Nikolai's hotel, Moscow. Scene 6: A street in Italy. Scene 7: Karenin's home, Petersburg. Scene 8: The same, later. Scene 9: The Vronsky estate. Scene 10: The same. Scene 11: The same. Scene 12: Karenin's home, Petersburg. Scene 13: Princess Betsy's, Petersburg. Scene 14: Countess Lydia's, Petersburg. Scene 15: Vronsky's hotel, Moscow. Scene 16: The same. Scene 17: Train station, Moscow. Scene 18: Levin's estate.

Play-within-a-play flashing back and forth between actors rehearsing the *Anna Karenina* drama and the characters in the drama itself.

The Silent Partner (12). By Clifford Odets. Produced by the Actors Studio, Lee Strasberg supervisor, in a limited engagement of a special showcase production at the Actors Studio (off off Broadway). Opened May 11, 1972. (Closed May 21, 1972)

Directed by Martin Fried; press, Alan Eichler. With Sally Kirkland, William Prince, Viveca Lindfors, Peter Masterson.

World premiere of an unproduced 1937 Odets drama about the shift of power from bosses to workers in a factory town during the Depression, in a showcase production with both readings and staged sections.

* Jamimma (18). By Martie Evans-Charles. Produced by Woodie King Jr. and Dick Williams at the New Federal Theater (formerly the Ellen Stewart). Opened May 15, 1972.

Jameena Caine	Marcella Lowery	Tyrone Jackson	Charles Weldon
Omar Butler I	Dick Williams	Gil Washington	Aston S. Young
Vivian Williams	Lucretia R. Collins	Hussein	Lester Forte
Viola Caine Robinson	Roxie Roker	Radio Lady (WLIB)	Vi Higgins
Crazy Man Johnson	Arnold Johnson		

Directed by Shauneille Perry; scenery, C. Richard Mills; lighting, Shirley Prindergast; costumes, Edna Watson; production coordinator, Mayme Mitcham; production stage manager, Fred Seagraves; press, Howard Atlee, David Roggensack.

Time: Dawn of the 1970s. Place: Jameena's apartment. Act I, Scene 1: Early evening. Scene 2: Evening. Scene 3: Immediately following. Act II, Scene 1: Two months later. Scene 2: Immediately following. Scene 3: A few hours later. Scene 4: Still later that evening. Act III, Scene 1: Afternoon. Scene 2: late evening. Scene 3: Some hours later.

Problems of a modern young woman living in the Harlem of today. Previously produced by the New Federal Theater in a workshop production 3/16/72 for 8 performances.

* Hark! (10). Musical revue with music by Dan Goggin and Marvin Solley; lyrics by Robert Lorick. Produced by Robert Lissauer at the Mercer O'Casey Theater. Opened May 22, 1972.

Jack Blackton	Sharron Miller
Dan Goggin	Elaine Petricoff
Danny Guerrero	Marvin Solley

Directed by Darwin Knight; vocal arrangements and musical direction, Sande Campbell; scenery and lighting, Chenault Spence; costumes, Danny Morgan; musical arrangements and orchestrations, John Lissauer; sound, Bill Merrill; production stage manager, John Toland; press, Betty Lee Hunt Associates, Henry Luhrman, Harriett Trachtenberg, Maria C. Pucci.

Series of songs about youth, love and other more specific phenomena of the present day.

PROLOGUE—"Hark!", Company; "Take a Look," Company; "George," Company; "Hip Hooray for America," Company. PART I: THE CYCLE BEGINS—"Smart People," Company; "What D'Ya Wanna Be?", Elaine Petricoff, Danny Guerrero, Company; "Six Little Kids," Dan Goggin, Marvin Solley; "Icarus," Solley, Miss Petricoff, Company; "Sun Down," Sharron Miller; "Conversation Piece," Jack Blackton, Guerrero, Misses Petricoff, Miller; "The Outstanding Member," Guerrero, Company; "How Am I Doin', Dad?", Company; "All Good Things," Guerrero; "Molly," Goggin, Solley; "Smart People" (Reprise), Company; "In a Hundred Years," Company.

PART II: THE CYCLE CONTINUES—"It's Funny About Love," Company; "Coffee Morning," Blackton; "Suburbia Square Dance," Goggin, Solley, Company; "I See the People," Blackton, Goggin, Solley; "Pretty Jack," Miss Miller; "Big Day Tomorrow," Guerrero; "Lullaby," Miss Petricoff; "Here's to You, Mrs. Rodriguez," Goggin, Solley; "Early Sunday," Blackton, Company; "I See the People" (Reprise), Company; "What's Your Sun Sign, Mr. Simpson?", Misses Petricoff, Miller; "All Good Things (Reprise), Goggin; "A Dying Business," Guerrero, Company; "Waltz With Me, Lady," Solley. EPILOGUE—Company.

* One for the Money (8). Revival of selected excerpts from musical revues with sketches and lyrics by Nancy Hamilton; music by Morgan Lewis. Produced by Charles Forsythe at the Eastside Playhouse. Opened May 24, 1972.

Pamela Adams	Pat Lysinger
Georgia Engel	Charles Murphy
Joy Garrett	Liz Otto
Douglas Houston	Edward Penn
Geoff Leon	Jess Richards

Directed and choreographed by Tom Panko; musical direction and arrangements, Peter Howard; scenery and costumes, Fred Voelpel; lighting, Judy Rasmuson; production stage manager, Bud Coffey; press, Sol Jacobson, Lewis Harmon, Ruth D. Smuckler.

A compilation of highlights from Nancy Hamilton-Morgan Lewis revues of 1939, 1940 and 1946.

ACT I—"An Ordinary Family:" Maid, Georgia Engel; Mother, Liz Otto; Father, Ed Penn; Sister, Pamela Adams; Brother, Douglas Houston; Guests, Geoff Leon, Joy Garrett, Jess Richards, Pat Lysinger, Charles Murphy. Post-Mortem: He, Ed Penn; She, Liz Otto; Alexandra, Charles Murphy; Press Agent, Jess Richards; Bellboy, Douglas Houston. "Teeter Totter Tessie:" Joy Garrett. "I Only Know:" Officer, Charles Murphy; Woman, Pat Lysinger; Man, Jess Richards. The Guess It Hour: Announcer, Geoff Leon; Asst. Announcer, Charles Murphy; Bessie, Pamela Adams; Mr. Barnswallow, Ed Penn; Mrs. Higgins, Georgia Engel. "Born for Better Things:" Sylvia, Joy Garrett; Offstage Voice, Ed Penn. "Wisconsin," or Kenosha Canoe: Announcer, Boy, Judge, Ed Penn; Auntie Plum, Liz Otto; Clyde, Geoff Leon; Spook, Girl, Whore, Pat Lysinger; Spook, Mr. Snow White, Jess Richards; Girl, Ido Wanny, Georgia Engel; Girl, June Alden, Whore, Joy Garrett; Roberta, Pamela Adams; Boy, Douglas Houston; Yellow Belly, Charles Murphy.

ACT II—"If It's Love:" Company. The Russian Lesson: Mrs. Buttrous, Joy Garrett; Mrs. Budge, Pat Lysinger; Mrs. Pellobie, Georgia Engel; Miss Umstedder, Liz Otto. "The Old Soft Shoe:" Douglas Houston, Jess Richards, Geoff Leon. The Christmas Tree Bauble: Pat Lysinger. "A House With a Little Red Barn:" Company. "How High the Moon:" Jess Richards. The Story of the Opera: Marilyn, Pat Lysinger, Waiter, Ed Penn; Lucy, Georgia Engel. "Goodnight Mrs. Astor:" Company.

Sweet Feet (6). Musical with book by Dan Graham; music and lyrics by Don Brockett. Produced by Proscenium Productions, Inc. at the New Theater. Opened May 25, 1972. (Closed May 28, 1972)

Directed by Don Brockett; scenery and lighting, James French; costumes, Tom Fallon; production stage manager, Kate Pollock; press, Gifford/Wallace Inc., Tom Trenkle. With Marty Goetz, Lenora Nemetz, Dan Graham, Scott Burns, John Dorish, Bert Lloyd, Florence Lacey, Barney McKenna.

Satire on Hollywood in the 1940s.

Some Additional Productions And Off Off Broadway

Here is a selected listing of off-off-Broadway and other experimental or peripheral New York stage productions. Producing groups are identified in alphabetical order in **bold face type** and examples of their outstanding 1971-72 programs are listed with play titles in capital letters. In many cases these are works in progress with changing scripts and casts, often without an engagement of record (but if a premiere took place its date appears in the show's entry).

American Center for Stanislavski Theater Art. Sonia Moore's acting ensemble in the Stanislavski tradiion.

DESIRE UNDER THE ELMS by Eugene O'Neill, directed by Sonia Moore. THE MAN WITH THE FLOWER IN HIS MOUTH by Luigi Pirandello, THE STRONGER by August Strindberg and THE SLAVE by Imamu Amiri Baraka (LeRoi Jones), directed by Sonia Moore.

American Theater Company. This East 14th Street group specializes in works of early American theater, with some new ones included.

FOUND OBJECTS by Marjorie Taubenhaus and THE CONTRAST (excerpts) by Royall Tyler, directed by Thomas Connolly. THE BATTLE OF BROOKLYN, directed by Richard Kuss. THE PRICE OF LIFE by David Korr. HOTEL UNIVERSE by Philip Barry, directed by Ellis Santone. A BETTER PLACE by Robert Hogan, directed by Thomas Connolly. THE BROKEN SWING by Naomi Rubel, directed by Richard Kuss.

Bed-Stuy Theater. Group specializing in the production of black-oriented theater for neighborhood audiences. Its director, Delano Stewart, is first president of Black Theater Alliance, an organization formed to institutionalize New York's major black production outlets.

BLACK EVOLUTION conceived by Delano Stewart, directed and choreographed by Eleo Pomare.

Circle Theater Company. Repertory troupe presenting programs annually in an upper-Broadway loft, under Marshall W. Mason's artistic directorship.

THE ELEPHANT IN THE HOUSE, February 20, 1972, by Berrilla Kerr, directed by Marshall W. Mason, with Jane Cronin. In repertory with GHOST SONATA by August Strindberg. TIME SHADOWS, April 9, 1972, by Helen Duberstein, directed by Marshall Ogelsby, design Ronald Radice. THE GREAT NEBULA IN ORION; IKKE, IKKE, NYE, NYE, NYE & THE FAMILY CONTINUES, May 21, 1972, program of three one-act plays by Lanford Wilson, directed by Marshall W. Mason, with Stephanie Gordon, Tanya Berezin, Rob Thirkield, Lucy Silvay.

CSC Repertory. This troupe's repertory of usually classical or standard plays in its Greenwich Village theater included in the 1971-72 schedule:

TITUS ANDRONICUS, January 29, 1972, by William Shakespeare, adapted and directed by Christopher Martin, scenery and lighting Christopher Martin, costumes Evelyn Thompson, with Harris Laskawy, Thomas Francis, Lawrence McGlade, Ronald Klein, Daniel Landon, Kathryn Wyman. PURLY by David Mowat, directed by David Villaire, presented by Hamm and Clov Stage Company. MARAT/ SADE by Peter Weiss, directed by Christopher Martin. JULIUS CAESAR by William Shakespeare, directed by Christopher Martin. THE INSPECTOR GENERAL by Nikolai Gogol, directed by Robert Bielecki. CAR by McCrea Imbrie and Neil Seldon, presented by Hamm and Clov Stage Company. ZUBER writted and directed by Eric Krebs, based on *Woyzeck*, presented by Hamm and Clov Stage Company.

The Cubiculo. This small but well-equipped midtown (414 W. 51st St.) experimental theater houses more than 100 programs a season in many media. Some of its stage attractions were:

THE WHORES OF BROADWAY by Gregor Rozakis, directed by Ron Link. EXILES by James Joyce and DRACULA based on the novel by Bram Stoker, presented by the Intense Family. CONFESSIONS OF A SPENT YOUTH, January 15, 1972, by and with Vance Bourjaily, directed by John Pearson. ALLIGATOR MAN by Jack Kaplan directed by Nancy Rubin, in repertory with THE PARTY by Slawomir Mrozek, directed by Peter Weil. UNDER MACDOUGAL STREET by James Prideaux, directed by Bolen High. THE DEATH OF JFK by W. Nicholas Knight, directed by Maria Piscator. ONTOLOGICAL PROOF OF MY EXISTENCE by Joyce Carol Oates, music by George Prideaux, directed by Maurice Edwards. MEDEA by Jean Anouilh, directed by Paul Bengston.

The Dove Company. St. Peter's Church on West 20th Street is the home of this well-established performance group. 1971-72 programs included:

FLO UNDER THE FLAG, THE WINNER & THE ROSE FESTIVAL, two plays and a pageant by Arthur Williams, music and direction by John Herbert McDowell. MILDRED by Robert Martin, directed by Natalie Rogers; CRY IN THE NIGHT FROM A NICE JEWISH BOY IN TROUBLE by Robert Kerner, directed by Lou Furman; and CHOCK FULL by Nan Jesse, directed by Michael Douglas. DISCOVER AMERICA,

TIMBERLINES & MEATLOAF SURPRISE, three plays by Jeannine O'Reilly, directed by Joseph Siracuse. COFFEE STAND by Sharon Thie, directed by Donald Kvares. HARDCORE SOFT SHOE by Annabelle Johnson, directed by Barry Preston, TOY LAND by Annabelle Johnson, directed by Jon Surgal, and MAGIC TIME by Bill Kushner, directed by Penny Peck.

Equity Library Theater. Actors Equity produces a series of revivals each season at the 300-seat Master Theater as showcases for the work of its actor-members. The 1971-72 series under the managing directorship of George Wojtasik included:

JUNE MOON, October 21, 1971, by Ring Lardner and George S. Kaufman, directed by Gordon Hunt, scenery and costumes Danny Morgan. PARK, November 11, 1971, musical by Paul Cherry and Lance Mulcahy, directed by Bick Goss, musical director John De Main, scenery Billy Puzzo, costumes Paulette Olson. MIDDLE OF THE NIGHT, December 9, 1971, by Paddy Chayefsky, directed by Nick Havinga, scenery Boyd Demrose, costumes Evelyn Thompson, lighting John Nathan. OEDIPUS AT COLONOS, February 10, 1972, by Sophocles, translated by Theodore Howard Banks, directed by David Bamberger, musical direction William Boswell, scenery Ernie Smith, costumes, Dina Harris. NO STRINGS, March 9, 1972, musical with book by Samuel Taylor, music and lyrics by Richard Rodgers, directed by Ric Michaels, musical director Don Sturrock, dances Lynn Gann-

away, scenery Billy Puzzo, costumes Sally Krell, lighting Cammie Caroline Lavine, with Mary Louise, Robert Tananis, Ann Hodges, Richard Stack, Martha Greenhouse. THE SERVANT OF TWO MASTERS, April 6, 1972, by Carlo Goldoni, translated by Edward J. Bent, directed by Clint Anderson, scenery Otis Seezey, costumes Howard Aller, lighting Arlee Stephen, with James Sutorius, Nancy Weems, Robert Sevra, Carolyn Mignini, Randy Kim. DU BARRY WAS A LADY, May 4, 1972, musical by Cole Porter, Herbert Fields and B.G. DeSylva, directed by Marvin Gordon, musical director William Boswell, tap choreographer Jack Dyville, scenery Donald Padgett, costumes Danny Morgan, lighting Cheryl Thacker, with Diane Lindlay, Bill Linton, Katie Anders, Danny De Vitro, Paul Eichel.

Ethical Culture Society. The organization's facility at 2 W. 64th St. housed a limited engagement of a rock opera. Produced by the Everyman Street Theater Company.

EVERYMAN AND ROACH, October 4, 1961, rock opera by Brother Jonathan and Geraldine Fitzgerald, music by John Orlando,

directed by Brother John, with Geraldine Fitzgerald, Eugene Washington, Ernest Alton Andrews.

The Extension. Small, arena-style theater in a chapel on lower Park Avenue is identified with avant-garde production styling.

FIRST DEATH by Walter Leyden Brown, directed by William M. Hoffman. ELECTRA by Sophocles, directed by Joel Stone, pre-

sented by Theater Asylum. AND THEY PUT HANDCUFFS ON THE FLOWERS written and directed by Fernando Arrabal.

Greenwich Mews Spanish Theater. This group specializes in presenting Spanish-language stage works in both Spanish and English performances.

WHEN A GIRL SAYS YES by Moratin, directed by Norberto Kerner. HOUSE OF FOOLS by Joseph de Valdivielso. LIFE IS A

DREAM by Calderon de la Barca, directed by Rene Buch.

Jones Beach Marine Theater. A full-scale musical production is mounted each summer in the Long Island recreation area's outdoor amphitheater. Produced by Guy Lombardo.

THE SOUND OF MUSIC, July 8, 1971, musical with book and lyrics by Oscar Hammerstein II, music by Richard Rodgers, directed by John Fearnley, scenery Peter Wolf, costumes Winn Morton, lighting Peggy Clark, with Constance Towers, John Michael King, Christopher Hewitt, Maggie Task, Nancy Eaton, Helen Noyes.

The Judson Poets' Theater. The Judson Arts Program at the Judson Memorial Church is directed by Al Carmines and it includes stage productions annually. Here are the 1971-72 programs:

WANTED musical with book by David Epstein, lyrics by David Epstein and Al Carmines, music by Al Carmines, directed by Lawrence Kornfeld. JOAN musical written and directed by Al Carmines. CHRISTMAS RAPPINGS oratorio with music and direction by Al Carmines. A LOOK AT THE FIFTIES musical written and directed by Al Carmines.

La Mama Experimental Theater Club. This is the Cafe La Mama facility at 74A E. 4th St., of which Ellen Stewart is executive director, sometimes mounting its own experimental productions, sometimes booking in packages. This season's multi-faceted activity included:

Eight-week program of rotating repertory, January 9, 1972, comprising GERTRUDE collage of Gertrude Stein memorabilia & DEMON derived from the Noh play *The Damask Drum;* CARMILLA, January 16, 1972, based on a 19th century novel by LeFanu, music by Ben Johnston; THE ONLY JEALOUSY OF EMER, January 23, 1972, by William Butler Yeats, adapted by John Braswell and Wilford Leach, music by Barbara Benary; all direction, design, lighting, choreography by John Braswell and Wilford Leach. SISTER SADIE, March 17, 1972, by Clifford Mason, directed by Allie Woods, with Louise Stubbs. PERSIA, A DESERT CHEAPIE, April 9, 1972, by John Vaccaro and Bernard Roth, a Playhouse of the Ridiculous audience-participation production, music by the Dark Ages.

Light Opera of Manhattan. Operetta productions under the producership of William Mount-Burke, presented in repertory at Jan Hus.

IOLANTHE, December 8, 1971, THE MIKADO and H.M.S. PINAFORE, librettos by W.S. Gilbert, music by Arthur Sullivan, directed by William Mount-Burke, scenery, costumes and lighting William Duke, with Raymond Allen.

Manhattan Theater Club. This is the Stage 73 facility uptown with a new name and status as a theater club, whose varied 1971-72 attractions included visiting productions of the New York Theater of the Americas. Here were some of the other programs this season:

THE DIARY OF ANNE FRANK by Frances Goodrich and Albert Hackett, directed by June Plager. THE ELEPHANT CALF by Bertolt Brecht and THE BALD SOPRANO by Eugene Ionesco, directed by Mary Tiffany, presented by Theater Movement. THE FIELD by Michael Parriott, directed by Terry Walker. THE ROOMMATES by M.J. Bevans, directed by Ken Golden. JOHN BROWN'S BODY by Stephen Vincent Benet, adapted by James Secrest, directed by Ted Tiller. THE RETURN by Guy Parker, directed by Sara Van Horn. SLEEPING DOGS by David Libman and THE POSTMAN by Ed Gold, both directed by Nancy Rubin. SOON JACK NOVEMBER by Sharon Thie, directed by Donald Kvares. ALL THROUGH THE HOUSE by Anthony Scully, directed by Lynne Meadow. LET ME MAKE ONE THING PERFECTLY CLEAR by Michael Kortchmar, directed by Michael Lentsch. MILDRED by Joe Ponce, directed by Richard Jordan. A SANDBURG ODYSSEY selected and staged by David O. Glazer.

Masterworks Laboratory Theater. Weekend productions at the Madison Avenue Baptist Church, supervised by Richard J. Hughes.

MARRIAGE, February 12, 1972, by Nikolai Gogol, adapted by Eric Bentley, directed by Walt Witcover, musical direction Elise Bretton.

Matinee Theater Series. Two matinee performances of each production in whatever set is current at the Theater de Lys, under the artistic directorship of Lucille Lortel.

A BIO IN SONG, December 6, 1971, with Irving Caesar. SALLY, GEORGE AND MARTHA, December 20, 1971, by Sam Dann, directed by David Brooks, with Michael Higgins, Gloria Maddox, Kathryn

Walker. A PLACE WITHOUT MORNINGS, January 10, 1972, by Robert Koesis, directed by Josef Warik, with Leora Dana, Staats Cotsworth.

New Federal Theater. Producers of plays of special interest to the black audience, under the supervision of Woodie King and Dick Williams, first at Henry Street Playhouse, later at the Ellen Stewart Theater (renamed the New Federal Theater). Some of their productions were full-fledged off-Broadway shows. Their experimenal activity included:

DON'T LET IT GO TO YOUR HEAD, January 17, 1972, by J.E. Gaines, directed by Gilbert Moses. JAMIMMA, March 16, 1972 (later produced off Broadway), by Martie Evans-Charles, directed by Shaunelle Perry, with Dick Williams, Marcella Lowery, Lu-

cretia Collins, Lester Forte, Arnold Johnson. ABDALA—JOSE MARTI directed by Ivan Acosta. HOMECOOKIN' directed by Sati Jamal, ANDREW directed by Carl Taylor and OURSIDES directed by Eric Hughes, program of three plays by Clay Goss.

New Lafayette Theater of Harlem. Specializes in plays of special interest to its black community audience.

THE PSYCHIC PRETENDERS, December 24, 1971, author and director unspecified, scenery and lighting James Macbeth, Tobias

Macbeth, Alfred Smith, with Sonny Jim (J.E. Gaines).

New Old Reliable Theater. This Lower East Side, back room of a tavern theater, once merely the Old but now the New Old Reliable, has at times operated in liaison with Columbia University theater factions. Its programs this season included:

THE DAY THEY GAVE BABIES AWAY by David Gaard, directed by Bill Lentsch. THE ZOO STORY by Edward Albee. HOO-

HAH! by Stanley Kaplan, directed by Frank Miazga. THE MASTER PSYCHOANALYST by Stanley Nelson, directed by Bill Lentsch.

New York Theater Ensemble. Prolific off-off-Broadway organization oriented to the production of new plays in a small but almost continuously active facility. This season's programs included:

FINAL COMMITMENT by Rose Sher, directed by Ossie Daljord. AN HONEST ANSWER by Irving Glusack, directed by Barry Bruns, THE LOGICAL ROOM by John Crennan, directed by Craig Barrish, "SMASH!" by Tony Barsha, directed by Donald Warfield. ARRANGEMENT FOR CHILDREN by Robert C. Herron, directed by Ossie Daljord. POOF! by Gerald Schoenewolf, directed by Paul Pierog, THREE'S PLAY by Stanley Kaplan, directed by Carla Joseph, and ILONA AND THE EVIL EYE PEOPLE by Florence Miller, directed by Rae Taftenbaum. TRIPPING by Donald Kvares, directed by Ossie Daljord and CONFESSIONAL FOR STREET PEOPLE by Paul Pierog, directed by Rory Gerstle. REFUGEES by Donald Kvares, directed by Ossie Daljord, and THE ROBERTA FLACK FAN CLUB

by Hal Craven, directed by Rory Gerstle. SLIP INTO THE STREET by Carla Joseph, directed by Mark Jessurun-Lobo. ISLAND written and directed by Anthony J. Ingrassia. HELEN'S HAND by Raymond Platt, directed by Denis Geisel, THE CUP by Nancy Wynn and Jane Dunlap, directed by Harve Brosten, and THE SUPREME COMMANDER by Murray Moltner, directed by Mark Jessurun-Lobo. RELATIONSHIPS AND OTHER MISTAKES by Paul Pierog, directed by Dennis Brite. FRIENDS REVISITED by Stan Zawatski, directed by Denis Geisel, RE-UNION AMONG RUINS BY David Kerry Heefner, directed by Scott Robinson, and THE PROGERIAN by Dallys Mayr, directed by Barry Burns. THE SOFTNESS OF DAMON'S UNDERWEAR written and directed by Robert C. Herron, MOTHER MARY'S

HONOR STUDENT by James Shannon, directed by Anthony de Vito, LOVE IS A TUNA CASSEROLE by Gloria Gonzalez, directed by Jack Sims. ROGER AND ARLENE —A PREMARITAL FARCE by Bruce Berkow, directed by Denis Geisel, THE PICK-POCKET by Ron Radice, directed by Ossie Daljord, and GARBAGE WINE by Michael Hardstock, directed by Mark Jessurun-Lobo. WE AGREE, CROSS-COUNTRY & AUSTRALIA PLAY by Sally Ordway, directed by Frederick Bailey.

New York Theater of the Americas. Programs in English and Spanish produced by Miguel Ponce and Oreste Marachena, many of them at the Manhattan Theater Club facility at Stage 73. Some of the 1971-72 offerings were:

THE TERRIBLE ANGELS, November 1, 1971, by Roman Chalbaud, directed by Juan Carlos Uviedo. THREE GROTESCAS written and directed by Rafael Bunuel. JOURNEY TO BAHIA, December 21, 1971, by Alfredo Dias Gomes, adapted by Stanley Richards, directed by Miguel Ponce. ONE MORE FOOL written and directed by Peter Muller. THE HANDS OF GOD by Carlos Solorzano, directed by Delfor Peralta. TALES TO BE TOLD by Oswaldo Dragun, music by Dan Padnos with Martin Siegel, directed by Miguel Ponce. THE MAID FROM HUE by Andres Monreal, directed by John Grimaldi.

Omni Theater Club. Produces original scripts written, acted and directed by its own membership under Viktor Allen's artistic directorship.

APRIL by John Wolfson and THE TEAM by Stuart Oderman, directed by Viktor Allen and Gladys Farrow Smith. AFTERNOON FOR A GAY DEATH by Gene Land, directed by John T. Dudich, and LET'S HEAR IT FOR MISS AMERICA by Gloria Gonzalez, directed by Peter Reigert. A TOUCH OF ORPHEUS by Wallace Hamilton, directed by Gladys Farrow Smith, choreography by Tray Christopher. NEWPORT AIRLINES: FLIGHT 901 by John Wolfson, directed by Gladys Farrow Smith. SEASON OF THE CARNIVAL by Stuart Oderman, directed by Gladys Farrow Smith. A WILD RIDE TO A SPECIAL MOON by Chad Henderson and OPERATION THWACK by Betzie Parker, directed by Viktor Allen.

The Open Theater. Under Joseph Chaikin's direction, with the participation of writers as well as actors, this group is a major contemporary effort of collaborative theater.

TERMINAL created by the Open Theater Ensemble under the direction of Joseph Chaikin and Roberta Sklar, texts by Susan Yankowitz, with the participation of Mark Kaminski, Nancy Martin and Sam Shepard, writers, and Dick Peaslee and Stanley Walden, composers. THE MUTATION SHOW created and performed by the Open Theater Ensemble (the 1972 Obie Award winner), directed by Joseph Chaikin and Roberta Sklar.

The Performing Garage. This is the made-over garage which houses The Performance Group, founded by Richard Schechner as a spinoff from Jerzy Grotowski's seminar at N.Y.U., in the genre of collaborative, non-literary theater. Here are the 1971-72 offerings of the home team and visitors.

THE THIRD COMMUNE with the ensemble of The Performance Group. EUNUCHS OF THE FORBIDDEN CITY written and directed by Charles Ludlam, presented by the Ridiculous Theater Company. CHRISTOPHER AT SHERIDAN SQUARED by H.M. Koutoukas, directed by Donald L. Brooks.

The Playbox. A small off-off-Broadway house at 94 St. Mark's Place, but one of the busiest in town. Its 1971-72 schedule included:

CLUTTERED by Shaunee Lawrence, directed by Frederick Bailey. 30 YEARS PAST, program of two one-act plays by Robert Bailey. COMFORT, JOY AND TIDINGS by Joseph Gath, Edna Schappert and Gloria Gonzales, directed by Jack Sims. HERE YOU ARE written and directed by Paul Pierog and MAGIC TIME by William Kushner, directed by Ted Mornell. WALK ME HOME by William Kushner, PORT AUTHORITY directed by Judy Zimmerman, THE VOICE IS COMING written and directed by Guy Gauthier and LA CHEVALE NOIR written and directed by John Francis Quinn. THE HOODED GNOME written and directed by Frederick Bailey, A CERTAIN KIND OF WOMAN by Ray Banacki, directed by Frederick Bailey and MANITOBA written and directed by Guy Gauthier. AN INTERVIEW WITH F. SCOTT FITZGERALD by Paul Hunter, directed by Eduardo Gorbe, THE PIG AND THE SPY by Jerry Ingram, ENCOUNTER IN A BEACH COTTAGE by John Shinn, directed by Lucille St. Peter, and IMPROMPTU, directed by Bruce Michael.

MISS GEORGE ALLIANCE by Edward Gallardo, directed by Ned Leavitt. LOVE GAME by Tom Coble. THE WORLD TIPPED OVER AND LAYING ON ITS SIDE by Mary Feldhaus Weber, directed by Will Lieberson, and GOLDEN OLDIES, AND LOVED written and directed by William Derringer. MATINEE by Wallace Hamilton, directed by Ron Frazier, TRICK OF THE EYE by Chad Henderson, directed by Anthony Osnato, and EVE AND ADAM by Joan Durant, directed by Chaim Sprei.

Puerto Rican Traveling Theater. Production for citywide tour, Miriam Colon executive producer.

THE PASSION OF ANTIGONA PEREZ, May 18, 1972, directed by Pablo Cabera, with Miriam Colon.

St. Clement's. Upstairs in the auditorium and downstairs in the basement (St. Clement's Space) the former home of the American Place Theater on West 46th Street is as hospitable as ever to experimental theater production. Here are some of the programs housed at St. Clements Church this season:

THE EROTIC TALE OF A TALL GIRL by Frank Spiering, directed by Russell L. Treyz. DON'T WALK ON THE CLOUDS, musical with book by Marvin Gordon, music and lyrics by John Aman. UBU ROI by Alfred Jarry, directed by Lynne Meadow. THE SOUND OF A WOMAN by Frank Spiering.

MEDICINE SHOW directed by Barbara Vann. PLOT COUNTER PLOT by Michael Procaccino, directed by Charles Briggs. A HATRACK NAMED GEORGE by Susan Sherman and MAN IN A BUCKET by Richard V. Benner.

Theater at Noon. Equity showcase productions at St. Peter's Gate, 123 East 64th St., Mondays through Fridays at lunch time, two performances each day. Miriam Fond is artistic director and directed all shows.

TWO BY LARDNER, November 8, 1971, program of two short stories by Ring Lardner Jr: *Haircut* adapted and performed by Herbert Du Val and *Golden Honeymoon* adapted and performed by Chet Carlin. THE BREAD TREE, November 15, 1971, by Kit Jones, with Chet Carlin, Lucy Lee Flippin. A LADY NAMED JOE, December 6, 1971, musical by Ben Finn, based on *Little Women*. LET'S HEAR IT FOR MISS AMERICA, January 17, 1972, by Gloria Gonzalez, with Patricia Bryant, Valerie Ogden. RED EYE

OF LOVE, January 24, 1972, by Arnold Weinstein, with Tony Lang, Frank A. Admirati, Carol Nadell. THE MARRIAGE BROKER, February 7, 1972, musical with book by Tom Tippett, music and lyrics by Robert Hold and Theo Carus, with Susan Lehman, Joe Vaccarella, Jay Bonnell. TELEMACHUS, FRIEND, April 17, 1972, musical by Sally Dixon Wiener, based on the O. Henry short story, musical direction & arrangements William Foster McDaniel.

Theater for the New City. This Bank Street-based organization specializes in the production of new works, sometimes in the workshop stage of development.

CROSSLOTS by Lyon Phelps, directed (in reading) by George Bartenieff. THE CELEBRATION: JOOZ, GUNS, MOVIES, THE ABYSS by Arthur Sainer, directed by Crystal Field. EVIDENCE presented by Richard

Foreman's Ontological Hysteric Theater. THE KING OF THE UNITED STATES, work in progress by Jean-Claude van Itallie, music by Richard Peaslee, directed by Jean-Claude van Itallie and Michael Smith.

Theater Genesis. Off-off-Broadway group based in a loft above St. Mark's Church in the Bowery.

MUTILATIONS, May 28, 1972, surreal play with multimedia by Walter Hadler, directed by Gaby Rodgers, scenery Robert Lavigne, film by David Rosenberg, with Richard Bright, Georgia Lee, Joe Hardy, Ann Hennessey.

CARTOON by Murray Mednick, directed by Walter Blood. COUNTRY MUSIC written and directed by Michael Smith. BORROWED TIME by Robert Glaudini. JIMTOWN by Kathleen Kimball, directed by Andrea Clarke.

Urban Arts Corps. Vinnette Carroll's experimental theater group, whose production of *Don't Bother Me, I Can't Cope* appeared this season on Broadway.

CROESUS AND THE WITCH, August 24, 1971, musical based on a fable with music and lyrics by Micki Grant, directed by Vinnette Carroll, choreography Talley Beatty, scenery Richard A. Miller, lighting Ben Sammler, with George Turner, Marie Thomas,

Eric Kilpatrick, Chapman Roberts, Joanna Mendl. BLACK NATIVITY, December 21, 1971, narrated and directed by Vinnette Carroll, costumes Edna Watson, choreography Hope Clarke, With Alex Bradford, Bradford Singers, Leona Johnson.

Workshop of the Players' Art. This Bowery-based group is one of the oldest and busiest of the off-off-Broadway organizations. Its 1971-72 list of programs included:

CYBELE musical by Mario Fratti based on *Sundays and Cybele,* music and lyrics by Paul Dick, directed by Amy Saltz. THE RIDICULOUS YOUNG LADIES and THE INTELLIGENT YOUNG LADIES by Molière, translated and adapted by Josef Bush. NAXOS BOUND by Josef Bush, directed by Hugh Gittens. PLACEBO written and directed by Jeannine O'Reilly and WHALE: A PLAY by Kent Jarratt, directed by Harry Orzello. DOG DAYS by Walter Corwin, directed by Nor-

man Thomas Marshall, and THE BABS AND JUDY SHOW by Stephen Holt, directed by Bob Plunket. GOIN' A BUFFALO by Ed Bullins. WALDEN POND written and directed by Joseph Renard. CHARLATANS three one-act plays based on Cervantes's interlude plays, translated by Linda Lashbrook, adapted and directed by Paul Meacham, music by Joseph Smith. A TOUCH OF THE POET by Eugene O'Neill, directed by Betsy Shevey.

CAST REPLACEMENTS AND TOURING COMPANIES

Compiled by Stanley Green

The following is a list of the more important cast replacements in productions which opened in previous years, but were still playing in New York during a substantial part of the 1971-72 season; or were still on a first class tour in 1971-72 (casts of first class touring companies of previous seasons which were no longer playing in 1971-72 appear in previous *Best Plays* volumes of appropriate years).

The name of each major role is listed in *italics* beneath the title of the play in the first column. In the second column directly opposite appears the name of the actor who created the role in the original New York production (whose opening date appears in *italics* at the top of the column). Indented immediately beneath the original actor's name are the names of subsequent New York replacements, together with the date of replacement when available.

The third column gives information about first-class touring companies, including London companies (produced under the auspices of their original Broadway managements). When there is more than one roadshow company, #1, #2, #3, etc., appear before the name of the performer who created the role in each company (and the city and date of each company's first performance appears in *italics* at the top of the column). Their subsequent replacements are also listed beneath their names, with dates when available.

A note on bus-truck touring companies appears at the end of this section.

AND MISS REARDON DRINKS A LITTLE

	New York 2/25/71	*Baltimore 9/6/71*
Anna Reardon	Julie Harris	Julie Harris
Catherine Reardon	Estelle Parsons	Kim Hunter
Ceil Adams	Nancy Marchand	DeAnn Mears
Fleur Stein	Rae Allen	Jo Flores Chase
Bob Stein	Bill Macy	Bill Macy

APPLAUSE

	New York 3/30/70	*Toronto 11/29/71*
Margo Channing	Lauren Bacall Anne Baxter 7/19/71 Arlene Dahl 5/1/72	Lauren Bacall
Bill Sampson	Len Cariou Keith Charles 5/3/71 John Gabriel 5/1/72	Don Chastain
Eve Harrington	Penny Fuller Patti Davis 4/16/71 Penny Fuller 5/3/71 Janice Lynde 11/22/71	Virginia Sandifur Penny Fuller 4/25/72
Howard Benedict	Robert Mandan Lawrence Weber 4/19/71 Franklin Cover 1/17/72	Norwood Smith
Karen Richards	Ann Williams Gwyda Donhowe 8/24/70 Peggy Hagan 12/13/71 (name changed to Phebe Hagan 5/1/72)	Beverly Dixon
Buzz Richards	Brandon Maggart	Ted Pritchard
Duane Fox	Lee Roy Reams Tom Rolla 11/22/71 Larry Merritt 4/24/72	Lee Roy Reams
Bonnie *	Bonnie Franklin Carol Petrie 4/29/71 Bonnie Franklin 6/21/71 Leland Palmer 9/6/71 Bonnie Franklin 11/22/71	Leland Palmer

* Name of character changed to Nancy during Bonnie Franklin's absences in New York. On road, character known as Leland.

THE BASIC TRAINING OF PAVLO HUMMEL

	New York 5/20/71
Pavlo Hummel	William Atherton Bob Balaban 11/27/71

BUTTERFLIES ARE FREE

	New York 10/21/69	#1 Los Angeles 5/19/70 #2 London 11/4/70

Don Baker	Keir Dullea
	    Kipp Osborne 10/13/70
	    David Huffman 9/7/71
	    Dirk Benedict 2/8/72
		#1 Wendell Burton
		    Kipp Osborne 9/70
		    David Huffman 10/12/70
		#2 Keir Dullea

Mrs. Baker	Eileen Heckart
	    Patricia Wheel 9/28/70
	    Rosemary Murphy 10/13/70
	    Gloria Swanson 9/7/71
		#1 Eve Arden
		    Gloria Swanson 10/12/70
		#2 Eileen Heckart

Jill Tanner	Blythe Danner
	    Kathleen Miller 8/31/70
	    Pamella Bellwood 7/19/71
	    Karen Grassle 4/24/72
	    Pamela * Bellwood 5/1/72
		#1 Ellen Endicott-Jones
		    Kristina Callahan 10/12/70
		#2 Barbara Ferris

* Billing changed from Pamella to Pamela

COMPANY

	New York 4/26/70	#1 Los Angeles 5/20/71 #2 London 1/18/72

Robert	Dean Jones
	    Larry Kert 5/29/70
	    Kenneth Cory
	    Larry Kert 8/23/71
	    Gary Krawford 12/27/71
		#1 George Chakiris
		    Allen Case 1/10/72
		#2 Larry Kert

Joanne	Elaine Stritch
	    Jane Russell 5/13/71
	    Vivian Blaine 11/1/71
		#1 Elaine Stritch
		    Julie Wilson 12/28/71
		#2 Elaine Stritch

Sarah	Barbara Barrie
	    Audrey Johnson 7/1/71
	    Cynthia Harris 7/12/71
		#1 Marti Stevens
		    Barbara Broughton 12/71
		#2 Marti Stevens

Harry	Charles Kimbrough
	    Charles Braswell 3/29/71
	    Kenneth Kimmins 5/13/71
		#1 Charles Braswell
		    Bernie McInerney
		#2 Kenneth Kimmins
		    Robert Colman 4/10/72

Susan	Merle Louise
	    Alice Cannon 10/5/70
	    Charlotte Frazier 3/29/71
		#1 Milly Ericson
		    Ann Johnson
		#2 Joy Franz
		    Connie Booth 4/10/72

Peter	John Cunningham
	    Kenneth Cory 4/26/71
		#1 Gary Krawford
		    Johnny Stewart
		#2 J. T. Cromwell
		    Phillip Hinton 4/10/72

Jenny	Teri Ralston
	    Jane A. Johnston 5/13/71
	    Teri Ralston 10/25/71
		#1 Teri Ralston
		    Jane A. Johnston 10/25/71
		#2 Teri Ralston
		    Barbara Tracey 4/10/72

David	George Coe
	    Lee Goodman 3/29/71
	    George Wallace 5/13/71
	    Lee Goodman 10/25/71
		#1 Lee Goodman
		    George Wallace 10/25/71
		#2 Lee Goodman
		    Paul Tracey 4/10/72

Amy	Beth Howland Marian Hailey 5/13/71 Beth Howland 10/25/71	#1 Beth Howland Marian Hailey 10/25/71 Tandy Cronyn #2 Beth Howland Dilys Watling 4/10/72
Paul	Steve Elmore	#1 Don Hinkley #2 Steve Elmore Richard Owens 4/10/72
Larry	Charles Braswell Stanley Grover 3/29/71	#1 Robert Goss Nolan Van Way 12/71 #2 Robert Goss Eric Flynn 4/10/72
Marta	Pamela Myers Annie McGreevey 5/13/71	#1 Pamela Myers Louisa Flaningam #2 Annie McGreevey Julia Sutton 4/10/72
Kathy	Donna McKechnie Brenda Thomson 5/13/71 Priscilla Lopez 10/25/71	#1 Donna McKechnie Susan Plantt 8/71 #2 Donna McKechnie Antonia Ellis 4/10/72
April	Susan Browning Carol Richards 12/71	#1 Bobbi Jordan Rolly Fanton #2 Carol Richards Julia McKenzie 3/6/72

THE EFFECT OF GAMMA RAYS ON MAN-IN-THE-MOON MARIGOLDS

	New York 4/7/70	*#1 Boston 4/20/71* *#2 Detroit 10/26/71*
Beatrice	Sada Thompson Cathryn Damon 2/16/71 Mary Hara 6/8/71 Carolyn Coates 6/28/71 Joan Blondell 9/28/71 Carolyn Coates 1/4/72	#1 Eileen Heckart Betty Field 7/5/71 #2 Dorothy Loudon
Tillie	Pamela Payton-Wright Swoosie Kurtz 2/16/71	#1 Marcia Jean Kurtz #2 Kathryn Baumann

THE FANTASTICKS

	New York 5/3/60	
El Gallo	Jerry Orbach Gene Rupert Bert Convy John Cunningham Don Stewart 1/63 David Cryer Keith Charles 10/63 John Boni 1/13/65 Jack Mette 9/14/65 George Ogee Keith Charles	Tom Urich 8/30/66 John Boni 10/5/66 Jack Crowder 6/13/67 Nils Hedrick 9/19/67 Keith Charles 10/9/67 Robert Goss 11/7/67 Joe Bellomo 3/11/68 Michael Tartel 7/8/69 Joe Bellomo 2/15/72 David Cryer 5/2/72

Luisa	Rita Gardner	Leta Anderson 8/7/67
	Carla Huston	Carole Demas 9/4/67
	Liza Stuart 12/61	Anne Kaye 1/23/68
	Eileen Fulton	Carole Demas 2/13/68
	Alice Cannon 9/62	Anne Kaye 5/28/68
	Royce Lenelle	Carolyn Mignini 7/29/69
	B.J. Ward 12/1/64	Virginia Gregory 7/27/70
	Leta Anderson 7/13/65	Marty Morris 3/7/72
	Carole Demas 11/22/66	
Matt	Kenneth Nelson	Gary Krawford 12/12/67
	Gino Conforti	Steve Skiles 2/6/68
	Jack Blackton 10/63	Craig Carnelia 1/69
	Paul Giovanni	Erik Howell 7/18/69
	Ty McConnell	Samuel D. Ratcliffe 8/5/69
	Richard Rothbard	Michael Glenn-Smith 5/26/70
	Gary Krawford	Jimmy Dodge 9/20/70
	Bob Spencer 9/5/64	Geoffrey Taylor 8/31/71
	Erik Howell 6/28/66	Erik Howell 3/14/72

FIDDLER ON THE ROOF

New York 9/22/64

Tevya	Zero Mostel	Jerry Jarrett 1/5/70
	Luther Adler 8/15/65	Paul Lipson 1/19/70
	Herschel Bernardi 11/8/65	Jerry Jarrett 10/12/70
	Harry Goz 8/14/67	Paul Lipson 10/19/70
	Herschel Bernardi 9/18/67	Jerry Jarrett 10/11/71
	Harry Goz 11/6/67	Paul Lipson 10/18/71
	Jerry Jarrett 5/12/69	Jan Peerce 12/14/71
	Harry Goz 9/8/69	Paul Lipson 5/2/72
Golde	Maria Karnilova	Peg Murray 9/14/70
	Martha Schlamme 4/9/68	Laura Stuart 12/21/70
	Dolores Wilson 7/1/68	Peg Murray 2/1/71
	Rae Allen 7/15/68	Laura Stuart 10/71
	Peg Murray 6/30/69	Mimi Randolph
	Mimi Randolph 8/3/70	Peg Murray 5/22/72
Yente	Beatrice Arthur	
	Florence Stanley 6/65	
	Ruth Jaroslow 8/19/71	
Tzeitel	Joanna Merlin	Rosalind Harris 2/70
	Ann Marisse 5/65	Judith Smiley 5/5/70
	Joanna Merlin 10/66	Mimi Turque 11/9/70
	Bette Midler 2/67	
Motel	Austin Pendleton	
	Leonard Frey 8/65	
	David Garfield 3/67	
	Peter Marklin 6/2/70	
Perchik	Bert Convy	Richard Morse
	Leonard Frey	Michael Zaslow 4/71
	Gordon Gray 8/65	
Hodel	Julia Migenes	
	Mimi Turque 4/67	
	Adrienne Barbeau 10/68	
	Susan Hufford 11/2/70	

Lazar Wolf	Michael Granger	Harry Goz 7/67
	Paul Lipson 8/65	Boris Aplon 8/67
	Paul Marin	
Chava	Tanya Everett	
	Peggy Longo 6/69	
	(name changed to	
	Peggy Atkinson)	
Bookseller	Paul Lipson	Jerry Jarrett
	Joe Cusanelli	Mitchell Jason
	David Masters 8/67	Ronald C. Moore
Shprintze	Marilyn Rodgers	Leslie Silvia
	Peggy Longo 9/66	Jill Harmon 2/8/72
	Faye Menken 6/69	

FOLLIES

New York 4/4/71

Phyllis Stone	Alexis Smith
Sally Plummer	Dorothy Collins
Buddy Plummer	Gene Nelson
Benjamin Stone	John McMartin
Christine Crane	Ethel Barrymore Colt
	Terry Saunders 7//7/71
	Jan Clayton 2/27/72
Meredith Lane	Sheila Smith
	Marion Marlowe 1/29/72
	Terry Saunders 4/24/72
	Marion Marlowe 5/16/72
Young Ben	Kurt Peterson
	John Johann 8/23/71

THE GINGERBREAD LADY

	New York 12/13/70	Hartford 10/18/71
Evy Meara	Maureen Stapleton	Nancy Kelly
Toby Landau	Betsy von Furstenberg	Betsy von Furstenberg

GODSPELL

	New York 5/17/71	#1 Boston 12/11/71 #2 Washington 4/7/72
Jesus	Stephen Nathan	#1 Dan Stone
	Andy Rohrer 5/72	#2 Dean Pitchford
Judas	David Haskell	#1 Lloyd Bremseth
	Andy Rohrer	#2 Irving Lee
	Bart Braverman 5/72	

HAIR

(Owing to the multiplicity of regional productions and of cast changes and exchanging of "tribe" members among the road companies—there were two *Hair* companies on tour during 1971-72—we list only the actors who played the major roles for a length of time in the New York companies)

New York: off Broadway 10/29/67; Broadway 4/29/68

Berger	Gerome Ragni	Oatis Stevens
	(off Broadway)	Allan Nicholls
	Steve Curry 12/22/67	Oatis Stevens 2/70
	Gerome Ragni	Larry Marshall
	(on Broadway)	Red Sheppard 12/17/70
	Steve Curry 11/22/68	Oatis Stevens 2/71
	Barry McGuire 1/69	Allan Nicholls 4/71
	Peter Link	Gregory V. Karliss
Claude	Walker Daniels	Eric Robinson
	(off Broadway)	Robin McNamara 8/69
	James Rado	Keith Carradine 10/69
	(on Broadway)	Allan Nicholls 2/70
	Barry McGuire 11/22/68	Robin McNamara 4/71
	Joseph Campbell Butler 1/69	Willie Windsor
	Kim Milford	
Sheila	Jill O'Hara	Melba Moore 10/69
	(off Broadway)	Victoria Medlin 12/69
	Lynn Kellogg	Heather MacRae 6/70
	(on Broadway)	Victoria Medlin 8/70
	Diane Keaton 7/68	Marta Heflin 3/71
	Heather MacRae 1/69	Beverly Bremers

THE HOUSE OF BLUE LEAVES

New York 2/10/71

Artie Shaughnessy	Harold Gould
	Lee Allen 6/71
	Ralph Meeker 7/6/71
	Joseph Bova 11/17/71
Bunny Flingus	Anne Meara
	Peggy Pope 6/22/71
	Jacqueline Brookes 11/17/71
Bananas Shaughnessy	Katherine Helmond
Billy Einhorn	Frank Converse
	Jeremiah Sullivan 4/20/71
	Jered Mickey 5/71
Ronnie Shaughnessy	William Atherton
	John Glover 4/20/71

JACQUES BREL IS ALIVE AND WELL AND LIVING IN PARIS

(Alternate casts at almost every performance; dates following names refer to when performers first joined company, though some later rejoined.)

New York 1/22/68

Original cast	Elly Stone
	Mort Shuman
	Shawn Elliott
	Alice Whitfield

Replacements & alternates	Robert Guillaume 1/22/68	Sally Cooke 5/11/69
	June Gable 1/22/68	J.T. Cromwell 5/20/69
	Betty Rhodes 5/28/68	Dominic Chianese 5/27/69
	Chevi Colton 6/22/68	Michael Johnson 5/27/69
	Joe Masiell 6/22/68	Teri Ralston 5/27/69
	Juanita Franklin 7/68	Joe Silver 6/3/69
	Adam Stevens 7/68	Norman Atkins 3/3/70
	Wayne Sherwood 7/16/68	Margery Cohen 3/10/70
	Fleury Dantonakis 7/24/68	Howard Ross 6/16/70
	Amelia Haas 7/30/68	Joy Franz 6/23/70
	Stan Porter 8/1/68	Henrietta Valor 6/23/70
	John C. Attle 8/13/68	Michael Vita 6/23/70
	George Ball 8/20/68	Barbara Gutterman 11/24/70
	Denise LeBrun 8/20/68	George Lee Andrews 12/26/70
	Aileen Fitzpatrick 8/20/68	Ben Bryant 1/9/71
	Jack Eddleman 9/17/68	Fran Uditsky 5/4/71
	Jack Blackton 10/8/68	Amanda Bruce 6/3/71
	Elinor Ellsworth 1/25/69	Ted Lawrie 1/11/72
	Rita Gardner 4/1/69	Janet McCall 5/13/72

LAST OF THE RED HOT LOVERS

New York 12/28/69

Barney Cashman	James Coco
	A. Larry Haines 7/6/70
	James Coco 7/20/70
	Tom Lacy 6/1/71
	Dom DeLuise 6/7/71

Elaine Navazio	Linda Lavin
	Rita Moreno 7/27/70
	Cathryn Damon 11/9/70
	Rita Moreno 11/16/70
	Cathryn Damon 6/7/71

Bobbi Michele	Marcia Rodd
	Barbara Sharma 3/8/71
	Carol Richards 7/7/71

Jeanette Fisher	Doris Roberts

LENNY

New York 5/26/71

Lenny Bruce	Cliff Gorman
	Sandy Barron 6/12/72

Judges, etc.	Joe Silver

LONG DAY'S JOURNEY INTO NIGHT

New York 4/21/71

James Tyrone	Robert Ryan
	John Beal 7/20/71

Mary Cavan Tyrone	Geraldine Fitzgerald
	Carole Teitel 7/20/71

James Tyrone, Jr.	Stacy Keach
	Tom Atkins 5/25/71
	Donald Gantry 7/20/71

Edmund Tyrone	James Naughton
	Dan Hamilton 7/20/71

NO, NO, NANETTE

	New York 1/19/71	*Cleveland 12/27/71*
Sue Smith	Ruby Keeler Penny Singleton 8/16/71 Ruby Keeler 8/31/71 Ruth Maitland 3/27/72 Ruby Keeler 4/4/72	June Allyson
Jimmy Smith	Jack Gilford Ted Tiller 1/3/72 Benny Baker 1/10/72	Dennis Day
Billy Early	Bobby Van Anthony S. Teague 4/10/72	Jerry Antes
Lucille Early	Helen Gallagher	Sandra Deel
Pauline	Patsy Kelly	Judy Canova
Nanette	Susan Watson Barbara Heuman 12/72	Dana Swenson
Tom Trainor	Roger Rathburn	Bill Biskup
Flora Latham	K.C. Townsend Sandra O'Neill 3/17/71 Sally Cooke 8/71	Laura Waterbury
Betty Brown	Loni Zoe Ackerman Jill Jaress	Connie Danese
Winnie Winslow	Pat Lysinger Judy Knaiz 5/1/72	Gwen Hiller

ONE FLEW OVER THE CUCKOO'S NEST

	New York 3/23/71
Randle Patrick McMurphy	William Devane Lane Smith 6/71
Nurse Ratched	Janet Ward Jane Curtin 6/1/72

PROMISES, PROMISES

	New York 12/1/68
Chuck Baxter	Jerry Orbach Gene Rupert 8/3/70 Jerry Orbach 8/17/70 Tony Roberts 10/26/70 Gene Rupert 4/12/71 Bill Gerber 11/8/71
Fran Kubelik	Jill O'Hara Patti Davis 8/17/70 Jill O'Hara 8/31/70 Jenny O'Hara 12/7/70 Lorna Luft 10/18/71
J.D. Sheldrake	Edward Winter James Congdon 12/7/70
Dr. Dreyfuss	A. Larry Haines Norman Shelly 11/69

Marge MacDougall   Marian Mercer
                      Pam Zarit 12/1/69
                      Mary Louise Wilson 7/20/70
                      Marilyn Child 5/71

PURLIE

	New York 3/15/70	*Philadelphia 11/19/71*
Purlie	Cleavon Little Robert Guillaume 10/4/71	Robert Guillaume
Lutiebelle	Melba Moore Patti Jo 3/30/71	Patti Jo
Missy	Novella Nelson Carol Jean Lewis 3/30/71	Carol Jean Lewis
Ol' Cap'n	John Heffernan Art Wallace 10/20/71	Art Wallace
Gitlow	Sherman Hemsley	Sherman Hemsley

THE ROTHSCHILDS

	New York 10/19/70	*San Francisco 5/9/72*
Mayer Rothschild	Hal Linden Howard Honig 8/17/71 Hal Linden 8/31/71	Hal Linden
Nathan Rothschild	Paul Hecht Timothy Jerome 6/7/71	C. David Colson
Gutele Rothschild	Leila Martin	Carol Fox Prescott
Prince William; Fouche; Herries; Metternich	Keene Curtis Reid Shelton 7/12/71	Reid Shelton
Hannah Cohen	Jill Clayburgh Caroline McWilliams 2/28/71 Prairie Dern 8/71 Caroline McWilliams 10/18/71	Sandra Thornton

SLEUTH

	New York 11/12/70	*Toronto 10/6/71*
Andrew Wyke	Anthony Quayle Paul Rogers 9/27/71	Michael Allinson
Milo Tindle	Keith Baxter Donal Donnelly 8/16/71 Keith Baxter 9/20/71 Brian Murray 3/27/72	Donal Donnelly

STORY THEATER

(Because cast members often exchanged roles, only the original cast plus replacements and alternates are listed below.)

New York 10/26/70

Peter Bonerz   Valerie Harper
Hamid Hamilton Camp   Richard Libertini
Melinda Dillon   Paul Sand
Mary Frann   Richard Schaal

Replacements & *alternates*	Lewis Arquette 10/26/70 Molly McKasson 10/26/70 Charles Bartlett 12/70 Peter Boyle 12/70 Linda Lavin 12/70	Regina Baff 2/71 MacIntyre Dixon 2/71 Paula Kelly 4/71 Avery Schreiber 4/71 Penny White 4/71

1776

	New York 3/16/69	*San Francisco 4/23/70*
John Adams	William Daniels John Cunningham 5/4/71	Patrick Bedford
Benjamin Franklin	Howard Da Silva Jay Garner 7/12/71	Rex Everhart
John Dickinson	Paul Hecht David Ford 7/70 George Hearn 8/30/71	George Hearn
Edward Rutledge	Clifford David John Cryer 5/30/69 John Cullum 5/19/70 Paul David Richards 9/13/71	Jack Blackton Michael Davis 11/16/70
Stephen Hopkins	Roy Poole Edmund Lyndeck 1/70 Truman Gaige 9/6/71	Truman Gaige
Thomas Jefferson	Ken Howard John Fink 5/30/69 Jon Cypher 9/16/69 Peter Lombard 11/24/69 Brian Foley 1/15/71	Jon Cypher Robert Elston George Backman 11/16/70
Abigail Adams	Virginia Vestoff Ellen Hanley 12/69 Virginia Vestoff 2/16/70 Rita Gardner 10/19/71	Barbara Lang
Richard Henry Lee	Ronald Holgate Gary Oakes 2/9/71 Ronald Holgate 5/11/71 Jon Peck 8/30/71	Gary Oakes Virgil Curry 12/7/70
Martha Jefferson	Betty Buckley Mary Bracken Phillips 8/28/69 Betty Buckley 10/5/70 Pamela Hall 4/13/71 Chris Callan 7/4/71	Pamela Hall Kirsten Banfield 4/71

THE TRIAL OF THE CATONSVILLE NINE

	New York 2/7/71
Philip Berrigan	Michael Kane Biff McGuire 6/8/71
Defense	David Spielberg Josef Sommer 6/8/71
David Darst	Leon Russom James Woods 6/8/71

TWO BY TWO

New York 11/10/70

Noah   Danny Kaye
                  Harry Goz 2/5/71
                  Danny Kaye 2/18/71

Shem   Harry Goz
                  Stephen Pearlman 2/5/71
                  Harry Goz 2/18/71
                  Jack Davison 9/5/71

Goldie   Madeline Kahn
                  Caroline Tenney 8/16/71

Japheth   Walter Willison
                  John Stewart 8/16/71

WAITING FOR GODOT

New York 2/3/71

Vladimir (Didi)   Henderson Forsythe
                      Warren Pincus
                      Jordan Charnay 5/4/71
                      David Byrd 5/18/71
                      Tom Ewell 6/29/71
                      Henderson Forsythe 9/20/71

Estragon (Gogo)   Paul B. Price
                      Oliver Clark 4/6/71
                      Joey Faye 6/29/71
                      Warren Pincus 7/20/71
                      Geoff Garland 9/10/71

Pozzo   Edward Winter
                      Larry Bryggman 5/11/71
                      Ed Bordo

Lucky   Anthony Holland
                      Tom Rosqui
                      Dan Stone

BUS-TRUCK TOURS

These are touring productions designed for maximum mobility and ease of handling in one-night and split-week stands (with occasional engagements of a week or more). Among Broadway shows on tour in the season of 1970-71 were the following bus-truck troupes:

Butterflies Are Free with Jan Sterling, John Spencer and Pamela Gilbreath, 98 cities, 10/8/71-3/26/72
Carousel with John Raitt, 70 cities, 1/27/72-5/27/72
Company with George Chakiris and Elaine Stritch, 86 cities, 5/20/71-5/20/72
Hair, 86 cities, 1/6/71-3/23/72
Last of the Red Hot Lovers with Stubby Kaye, 89 cities, 10/15/71-3/25/72
Promises, Promises with Will Mackenzie and Sydnee Balaber, 119 cities, 5/20/71-5/20/72
The Me Nobody Knows, 24 cities, 11/1/71-12/11/71
You're a Good Man, Charlie Brown, 47 cities, 9/24/71-12/11/71

FACTS AND
FIGURES

LONG RUNS ON BROADWAY

The following shows have run 500 or more continuous performances in a single production, usually the first, not including previews or extra non-profit performances, allowing for vacation layoffs and special one-booking engagements, but not including return engagements after a show has gone on tour. Where there are title similarities, the production is identified as follows: (p) straight play version, (m) musical version, (r) revival.

THROUGH MAY 31, 1972

(PLAYS MARKED WITH ASTERISK WERE STILL PLAYING JUNE 1, 1972)

Plays	Number Performances	Plays	Number Performances
Life With Father	3,224	Lightnin'	1,291
*Fiddler on the Roof †	3,205	Promises, Promises	1,281
Tobacco Road	3,182	The King and I	1,246
Hello, Dolly!	2,844	Cactus Flower	1,234
My Fair Lady	2,717	1776	1,217
Man of La Mancha	2,328	Guys and Dolls	1,200
Abie's Irish Rose	2,327	Cabaret	1,165
Oklahoma!	2,212	Mister Roberts	1,157
South Pacific	1,925	Annie Get Your Gun	1,147
Harvey	1,775	The Seven Year Itch	1,141
*Hair	1,712	Pins and Needles	1,108
Born Yesterday	1,642	Plaza Suite	1,097
Mary, Mary	1,572	*Butterflies Are Free	1,090
The Voice of the Turtle	1,557	Kiss Me, Kate	1,070
Barefoot in the Park	1,530	The Pajama Game	1,063
Mame (m)	1,508	The Teahouse of the August	
Arsenic and Old Lace	1,444	Moon	1,027
The Sound of Music	1,443	Damn Yankees	1,019
How To Succeed in Business		Never Too Late	1,007
Without Really Trying	1,417	Any Wednesday	982
Hellzapoppin	1,404	A Funny Thing Happened on	
The Music Man	1,375	the Way to the Forum	964
Funny Girl	1,348	The Odd Couple	964
*Oh! Calcutta! ††	1,331	Anna Lucasta	957
Angel Street	1,295	Kiss and Tell	956

† On June 17, 1972, after this volume's cutoff date, *Fiddler on the Roof* played its 3,225th performance and became the longest-running production in Broadway history. On July 2, 1972 it closed after its all-time record 3,242d performance.

†† First 704 performances were played off Broadway.

Plays	Number Performances	Plays	Number Performances
The Moon Is Blue	924	Seventh Heaven	704
Bells Are Ringing	924	Gypsy (m)	702
Luv	901	The Miracle Worker	700
Applause	896	Cat on a Hot Tin Roof	694
Can-Can	892	Li'l Abner	693
Carousel	890	Peg o' My Heart	692
Hats Off to Ice	889	The Children's Hour	691
Fanny	888	Purlie	688
Follow the Girls	882	Dead End	687
Camelot	873	The Lion and the Mouse	686
The Bat	867	White Cargo	686
My Sister Eileen	864	Dear Ruth	683
Song of Norway	860	East Is West	680
A Streetcar Named Desire	855	Come Blow Your Horn	677
Comedy in Music	849	The Most Happy Fella	676
You Can't Take It With You	837	The Doughgirls	671
La Plume de Ma Tante	835	The Impossible Years	670
Three Men on a Horse	835	Irene	670
The Subject Was Roses	832	Boy Meets Girl	669
Inherit the Wind	806	Beyond the Fringe	667
No Time for Sergeants	796	Who's Afraid of Virginia Woolf?	664
Fiorello!	795	Blithe Spirit	657
Where's Charley?	792	A Trip to Chinatown	657
The Ladder	789	The Women	657
Forty Carats	780	Bloomer Girl	654
Oliver	774	The Fifth Season	654
State of the Union	765	*Sleuth	650
The First Year	760	Rain	648
You Know I Can't Hear You When the Water's Running	755	Witness for the Prosecution	645
Two for the Seesaw	750	Call Me Madam	644
Death of a Salesman	742	Janie	642
Sons o' Fun	742	The Green Pastures	640
Gentlemen Prefer Blondes	740	Auntie Mame (p)	639
The Man Who Came to Dinner	739	A Man for All Seasons	637
Call Me Mister	734	The Fourposter	632
West Side Story	732	The Tenth Man	623
High Button Shoes	727	Is Zat So?	618
Finian's Rainbow	725	Anniversary Waltz	615
Claudia	722	The Happy Time (p)	614
The Gold Diggers	720	Separate Rooms	613
Carnival	719	Affairs of State	610
The Diary of Anne Frank	717	Star and Garter	609
I Remember Mama	714	The Student Prince	608
Tea and Sympathy	712	Sweet Charity	608
Junior Miss	710	Bye Bye Birdie	607
Last of the Red Hot Lovers	706	Broadway	603
Company	705	Adonis	603
		Street Scene (p)	601

Plays	Number Performances	Plays	Number Performances
Kiki	600	Good News	551
Flower Drum Song	600	Let's Face It	547
Don't Drink the Water	598	Milk and Honey	543
Wish You Were Here	598	Within the Law	541
A Society Circus	596	The Music Master	540
Blossom Time	592	Pal Joey (r)	540
The Me Nobody Knows	586	What Makes Sammy Run?	540
The Two Mrs. Carrolls	585	What a Life	538
Kismet	583	The Unsinkable Molly Brown	532
Detective Story	581	The Red Mill (r)	531
Brigadoon	581	A Raisin in the Sun	530
*No, No, Nanette (r)	580	The Solid Gold Cadillac	526
No Strings	580	Irma La Douce	524
Brother Rat	577	The Boomerang	522
Show Boat	572	Rosalinda	521
The Show-Off	571	The Best Man	520
Sally	570	Chauve-Souris	520
Golden Boy (m)	568	Blackbirds of 1928	518
One Touch of Venus	567	Sunny	517
Happy Birthday	564	Victoria Regina	517
Look Homeward, Angel	564	Half a Sixpence	511
The Glass Menagerie	561	The Vagabond King	511
I Do! I Do!	560	The New Moon	509
Wonderful Town	559	The World of Suzie Wong	508
Rose Marie	557	The Rothschilds	507
Strictly Dishonorable	557	Shuffle Along	504
A Majority of One	556	Up in Central Park	504
The Great White Hope	556	Carmen Jones	503
Toys in the Attic	556	The Member of the Wedding	501
Sunrise at Campobello	556	Panama Hattie	501
Jamaica	555	Personal Appearance	501
Stop the World—I Want to Get Off	555	Bird in Hand	500
Floradora	553	Room Service	500
Ziegfeld Follies (1943)	553	Sailor, Beware!	500
Dial "M" for Murder	552	Tomorrow the World	500

LONG RUNS OFF BROADWAY

Plays	Number Performances	Plays	Number Performances
*The Fantasticks	5,026	You're a Good Man Charlie Brown	1,597
The Threepenny Opera	2,611	The Blacks	1,408
*Jacques Brel Is Alive and Well and Living in Paris	1,809	Little Mary Sunshine	1,143

Plays	Number Performances	Plays	Number Performances
The Boys in the Band	1,000	Hogan's Goat	607
Your Own Thing	933	The Trojan Women (r)	600
Curley McDimple	931	Krapp's Last Tape and	
Leave It to Jane (r)	928	The Zoo Story	582
The Mad Show	871	The Dumbwaiter and	
The Effect of Gamma Rays on		The Collection	578
Man-in-the-Moon Marigolds	819	Dames at Sea	575
A View From the Bridge (r)	780	The Crucible (r)	571
The Boy Friend (r)	763	The Iceman Cometh (r)	565
The Pocket Watch	725	The Hostage (r)	545
The Connection	722	Six Characters in Search of an	
Adaptation and Next	707	Author (r)	529
Oh! Calcutta!	704	*The Proposition	513
Scuba Duba	692	The Dirtiest Show in Town	509
The Knack	685	Happy Ending and Day of	
The Balcony	672	Absence	504
America Hurrah	634	The Boys From Syracuse (r)	500

DRAMA CRITICS CIRCLE VOTING, 1971-72

The New York Drama Critics Circle voted *That Championship Season* the best play of the season by a plurality of 37 points on a weighted second ballot, after no play won a majority of first choices (11 of the 21 critics present) on the first ballot. *Sticks and Bones* was the runner-up with 36 points and was voted a special citation by the Critics Circle members (it had at first been declared the winner after a mathematical error, but the mistake was soon discovered). Other best-play points on the weighted ballot (counting 3 for each critic's first choice, 2 for his second and 1 for his third) were distributed as follows: *The Screens* 18, *Old Times* 13, *Moonchildren* 10, *Vivat! Vivat Regina!* 5, *Kaddish* 2, *The Prisoner of Second Avenue* 2, *The Sty of the Blind Pig* 1, *Twigs* 1, *The Basic Training of Pavlo Hummel* 1.

Having named an American play best, the critics decided to vote on a best foreign play. By the same weighted scoring method as above after the first ballot, *The Screens* won a one-point victory over *Old Times* 35-34 and the citation as best foreign play of 1971-72; *Old Times* was then voted a special citation. Other points in the category of best foreign play were distributed as follows: *The Real Inspector Hound* and *After Magritte* 17, *Vivat! Vivat Regina!* 11 (and this play was the first choice on the first ballot of Jack Gaver and Ted Kalem, who both abstained on the second weighted ballot), *The Ride Across Lake Constance* 2, *And They Put Handcuffs on the Flowers* 1, *There's One in Every Marriage* 1, *Wise Child* 1.

Two Gentlemen of Verona won the Critics Award for best musical of the year by a majority of 13 first choices on the first ballot in this category. Musical revivals which had been in the running for a Critics Award in other years—such as *A Funny Thing Happened on the Way to the Forum* and *Lost in the Stars*—were ineligible under the rules of the Circle voting. Here's how the votes of the 21 critics present and voting were distributed on this first-choice musical ballot: *Two Gentlemen of Verona* (13)—Clive Barnes and Walter Kerr of the New York *Times,* John Beaufort of *Christian Science Monitor,* Harold Clurman of *The Nation,* Brendan Gill of *The New Yorker,* William Glover of AP, Henry Hewes of *The Saturday Review,* Edward S. Hipp of the Newark *News,* Emory Lewis of the Bergen *Record,* Leo Mishkin of *Racing Form,* George Oppenheimer of *Newsday,* Douglas Watt of the New York *Daily News* and Richard Watts Jr. of the New York *Post; Ain't Supposed to Die a Natural Death* (3)—Martin Gottfried of *Women's Wear Daily,* Jack Kroll of *Newsweek* and Marilyn Stasio of *Cue; Godspell* (1)—John Simon of *New York;* abstained (4)—Jack Gaver of UPI, Ted Kalem of *Time,* John Lahr of the *Village Voice* and William Raidy of the Newhouse papers.

Here's the way the Circle members' votes were distributed on the weighted second ballots for best play and best foreign play (first-ballot choices are indicated by first choices in this list except in the two cases noted above):

SECOND BALLOT FOR BEST PLAY

Critic	*1st Choice (3 pts.)*	*2d Choice (2 pts.)*	*3d Choice (1 pt.)*
Clive Barnes	Sticks and Bones	Old Times	That Championship Season
John Beaufort	Championship	Sticks and Bones	The Screens
Harold Clurman	The Screens	Old Times	Sticks and Bones
Jack Gaver	Vivat! Vivat Regina!	Championship	Moonchildren
Brendan Gill	Sticks and Bones	Championship	Old Times
William Glover	Championship	Sticks and Bones	The Prisoner of Second Avenue
Martin Gottfried	Sticks and Bones	Kaddish	The Sty of the Blind Pig
Henry Hewes	The Screens	Old Times	Sticks and Bones
Edward S. Hipp	Championship	Moonchildren	Sticks and Bones
Ted Kalem	Sticks and Bones	Championship	Prisoner
Walter Kerr	Moonchildren	Championship	Twigs
Jack Kroll	The Screens	Sticks and Bones	Moonchildren
John Lahr	Moonchildren	Old Times	Championship
Emory Lewis	Sticks and Bones	Championship	The Basic Training of Pavlo Hummel
Leo Mishkin	Championship	Sticks and Bones	Vivat!
George Oppenheimer	Sticks and Bones	Championship	The Screens
William Raidy	The Screens	Championship	Old Times
John Simon	Sticks and Bones	Championship	The Screens
Marilyn Stasio	Sticks and Bones	Championship	The Screens
Douglas Watt	Old Times	Championship	Sticks and Bones
Richard Watts Jr.	Championship	The Screens	Vivat!

SECOND BALLOT FOR BEST FOREIGN PLAY

Critic	*1st Choice (3 pts.)*	*2d Choice (2 pts.)*	*3d Choice (1 pt.)*
Clive Barnes	Old Times	The Real Inspector Hound and After Magritte	The Screens
John Beaufort	Old Times	Vivat!	The Screens
Harold Clurman	The Screens	Old Times	And They Put Handcuffs on the Flowers

Jack Gaver	Abstain	Abstain	Abstain
Brendan Gill	Old Times	The Screens	Vivat!
William Glover	Old Times	Inspector Hound	Vivat!
Martin Gottfried	Inspector Hound	The Screens	The Ride Across Lake Constance
Henry Hewes	The Screens	Old Times	There's One in Every Marriage
Edward S. Hipp	Old Times	Vivat!	The Screens
Ted Kalem	Abstain	Abstain	Abstain
Walter Kerr	Abstain	Abstain	Abstain
Jack Kroll	The Screens	Inspector Hound	Lake Constance
John Lahr	Old Times	Inspector Hound	The Screens
Emory Lewis	Old Times	The Screens	Inspector Hound
Leo Mishkin	Abstain	Abstain	Abstain
George Oppenheimer	The Screens	Vivat!	Old Times
William Raidy	The Screens	Inspector Hound	Old Times
John Simon	The Screens	Inspector Hound	Vivat!
Marilyn Stasio	Old Times	The Screens	Inspector Hound
Douglas Watt	Old Times	The Screens	Wise Child
Richard Watts Jr.	The Screens	Vivat!	Old Times

Choices of some other critics:

Critic	Best Play	Best Musical
Judith Crist "Today"	Championship	A Funny Thing Happened on the Way to the Forum
Norman Nadel Scripps-Howard	Sticks and Bones	Abstain
Tom Prideaux Life	Pavlo Hummel	Verona
Hobe Morrison Variety	Championship	Abstain
Leonard Harris WCBS-TV	Old Times	Verona
Alvin Klein WNYC Radio	Sticks and Bones	Verona
Kevin Sanders ABC-TV	Championship	Op

NEW YORK DRAMA CRITICS CIRCLE AWARDS

Listed below are the New York Drama Critics Circle Awards from 1935-36 through 1971-72, classified as follows: (1) Best American Play, (2) Best Foreign Play, (3) Best Musical, (4) Best, regardless of category (this category was established by new voting rules in 1962-63 and did not exist prior to that year).

1935-36—(1) Winterset
1936-37—(1) High Tor
1937-38—(1) Of Mice and Men, (2) Shadow and Substance
1938-39—(1) No award, (2) The White Steed
1939-40—(1) The Time of Your Life
1940-41—(1) Watch on the Rhine, (2) The Corn Is Green
1941-42(1) No award, (2) Blithe Spirit
1942-43—(1) The Patriots
1943-44—(2) Jacobowsky and the Colonel
1944-45—(1) The Glass Menagerie
1945-46—(3) Carousel

1946-47—(1) All My Sons, (2) No Exit, (3) Brigadoon
1947-48—(1) A Streetcar Named Desire, (2) The Winslow Boy
1948-49—(1) Death of a Salesman, (2) The Madwoman of Chaillot, (3) South Pacific
1949-50—(1) The Member of the Wedding, (2) The Cocktail Party, (3) The Consul
1950-51—(1) Darkness at Noon, (2) The Lady's Not for Burning, (3) Guys and Dolls

1951-52—(1) I Am a Camera, (2) Venus Observed, (3) Pal Joey (Special citation to Don Juan in Hell)

1952-53—(1) Picnic, (2) The Love of Four Colonels, (3) Wonderful Town

1953-54—(1) Teahouse of the August Moon, (2) Ondine, (3) The Golden Apple

1954-55—(1) Cat on a Hot Tin Roof, (2) Witness for the Prosecution, (3) The Saint of Bleecker Street

1955-56—(1) The Diary of Ann Frank, (2) Tiger at the Gates, (3) My Fair Lady

1956-57—(1) Long Day's Journey Into Night, (2) The Waltz of the Toreadors, (3) The Most Happy Fella

1957-58—(1) Look Homeward, Angel, (2) Look Back in Anger, (3) The Music Man

1958-59—(1) A Raisin in the Sun, (2) The Visit, (3) La Plume de Ma Tante

1959-60—(1) Toys in the Attic, (2) Five Finger Exercise, (3) Fiorello!

1960-61—(1) All the Way Home, (2) A Taste of Honey, (3) Carnival

1961-62—(1) The Night of the Iguana, (2) A Man for All Seasons, (3) How to Succeed in Business Without Really Trying

1962-63—(4) Who's Afraid of Virginia Woolf? (Special citation to Beyond the Fringe)

1963-64—(4) Luther, (3) Hello, Dolly! (Special citation to The Trojan Women)

1964-65—(4) The Subject Was Roses, (3) Fiddler on the Roof

1965-66—(4) The Persecution and Assassination of Marat as Performed by the Inmates of the Asylum of Charenton Under the Direction of the Marquis de Sade, (3) Man of La Mancha

1966-67—(4) The Homecoming, (3) Cabaret

1967-68—(4) Rosencrantz and Guildenstern Are Dead, (3) Your Own Thing

1968-69—(4) The Great White Hope, (3) 1776

1969-70—(4) Borstal Boy, (1) The Effect of Gamma Rays on Man-in-the-Moon Marigolds, (3) Company

1970-71—(4) Home, (1) The House of Blue Leaves, (3) Follies

1971-72—(4) That Championship Season, (2) The Screens, (3) Two Gentlemen of Verona (Special citations to Sticks and Bones and Old Times)

PULITZER PRIZE WINNERS, 1916-17 TO 1971-72

1916-17—No award

1917-18—Why Marry?, by Jesse Lynch Williams

1918-19—No award

1919-20—Beyond the Horizon, by Eugene O'Neill

1920-21—Miss Lulu Bett, by Zona Gale

1921-22—Anna Christie, by Eugene O'Neill

1922-23—Icebound, by Owen Davis

1923-24—Hell-Bent fer Heaven, by Hatcher Hughes

1924-25—They Knew What They Wanted, by Sidney Howard

1925-26—Craig's Wife, by George Kelly

1926-27—In Abraham's Bosom, by Paul Green

1927-28—Strange Interlude, by Eugene O'Neill

1928-29—Street Scene, by Elmer Rice

1929-30—The Green Pastures, by Marc Connelly

1930-31—Alison's House, by Susan Glaspell

1931-32—Of Thee I Sing, by George S. Kaufman, Morrie Ryskind, Ira and George Gershwin

1932-33—Both Your Houses, by Maxwell Anderson

1933-34—Men in White, by Sidney Kingsley

1934-35—The Old Maid, by Zoë Akins

1935-36—Idiot's Delight, by Robert E. Sherwood

1936-37—You Can't Take It With You, by Moss Hart and George S. Kaufman

1937-38—Our Town, by Thornton Wilder

1938-39—Abe Lincoln in Illinois, by Robert E. Sherwood

1939-40—The Time of Your Life, by William Saroyan

1940-41—There Shall Be No Night, by Robert E. Sherwood

1941-42—No award

1942-43—The Skin of Our Teeth, by Thornton Wilder

1943-44—No award

1944-45—Harvey, by Mary Chase

1945-46—State of the Union, by Howard Lindsay and Russel Crouse

1946-47—No award.

1947-48—A Streetcar Named Desire, by Tennessee Williams

1948-49—Death of a Salesman, by Arthur Miller

1949-50—South Pacific, by Richard Rodgers, Oscar Hammerstein II and Joshua Logan

1950-51—No award

1951-52—The Shrike, by Joseph Kramm
1952-53—Picnic, by William Inge
1953-54—The Teahouse of the August Moon, by John Patrick
1954-55—Cat on a Hot Tin Roof, by Tennessee Williams
1955-56—The Diary of Anne Frank, by Frances Goodrich and Albert Hackett
1956-57—Long Day's Journey Into Night, by Eugene O'Neill
1957-58—Look Homeward, Angel, by Ketti Frings
1958-59—J. B., by Archibald MacLeish
1959-60—Fiorello!, by Jerome Weidman, George Abbott, Sheldon Harnick and Jerry Bock
1960-61—All the Way Home, by Tad Mosel
1961-62—How to Succeed in Business Without Really Trying, by Abe Burrows, Willie Gilbert, Jack Weinstock and Frank Loesser
1962-63—No award
1963-64—No award
1964-65—The Subject Was Roses, by Frank D. Gilroy
1965-66—No award
1966-67—A Delicate Balance, by Edward Albee
1967-68—No award
1968-69—The Great White Hope, by Howard Sackler
1969-70—No Place to Be Somebody, by Charles Gordone
1970-71—The Effect of Gamma Rays on Man-in-the-Moon Marigolds, by Paul Zindel
1971-72—No award

ADDITIONAL PRIZES AND AWARDS, 1971-72

The following is a list of major prizes and awards for theatrical achievement. In all cases the names of winners—persons, productions or organizations—appear in **bold face type.**

MARGO JONES AWARD (for encouraging production of new playwrights). **Zelda Fichandler** of the Arena Stage, Washington, D.C.

JOSEPH MAHARAM FOUNDATION AWARDS (for distinguished New York theatrical design. Outstanding scenic design for a new production, **Kert Lundell** for *Ain't Supposed to Die a Natural Death;* for a revival, **Robert U. Taylor** for *The Beggar's Opera*. Costume design, **Willa Kim** for *The Screens.*

ELIZABETH HULL-KATE WARRINER AWARD (to the playwright whose work produced within each year dealt with controversial subjects involving the fields of political, religious or social mores of the time, selected by the Dramatists Guild Council). **David Rabe** for *The Basic Training of Pavlo Hummel.*

GEORGE JEAN NATHAN AWARD (for criticism). **Richard Gilman.**

VILLAGE VOICE OFF-BROADWAY (OBIE) AWARDS for off-Broadway excellence, selected by a committee of judges whose members were Dick Brukenfeld, Michael Feingold, John Lahr, Julius Novick, Arthur Sainer, Michael Smith and Martin Washburn, all of the *Village Voice* staff). Best theater piece, The Open Theater's *The Mutation Show.* Distinguished performances, **Salome Bey** in *Love Me, Love My Children,* **Maurice Blanc** in *The Celebration: Jooz/Guns/ Movies/ The Abyss,* **Alex Bradford** in *Don't Bother Me, I Can't Cope,* **Marilyn Chris** in *Kaddish,* **Ron Faber** in *And They Put Handcuffs on the Flowers,* **Jeanne Hepple** and **Ed Zang** in *The Reliquary of Mr. and Mrs. Potterfield,* **Danny Sewell** in *The Homecoming,* **Marilyn Sokol** in *The Beggar's Opera,* **Elizabeth Wilson** in *Sticks and Bones.* Distinguished direction, **Wilford Leach** and **John Braswell** for *The Only Jealousy of Emer,* **Mel Shapiro** for *Two Gentlemen of Verona,* **Michael Smith** for *Country Music,* **Tom Sydorick** for *20th Century Tar.* Best music and lyrics, **Micki Grant** for *Don't Bother Me, I Can't Cope.* Best composer, **Liz Swados** for *Medea.* Best visual effects, **Video Free America** for *Kaddish.* Special citations to **Charles Stanley** as actor, dancer, choreographer and costume designer, **Meredith Monk** for *Vessel,* **Theater of Latin America** for *Latin American Fair of Opinion,* **Free the Army.**

NOTE: The name of **Donald Ewer** was inadvertently omitted from the list of 1970-71 Obie Award winners in last year's *Best Plays* volume. He won an Obie for a distinguished performance together with his colleagues Margaret Braidwood and James Woods in *Saved.*

THEATER WORLD AWARDS (for outstanding new acting talent on and off Broadway). **Jonelle Allen** in *Two Gentlemen o*

Verona, Maureen Anderman, Cara Duff-McCormick and James Woods in *Moonchildren,* William Atherton in *Suggs,* Richard Backus in *Promenade, All!,* Adrienne Barbeau in *Grease,* Robert Foxworth in *The Crucible,* Elaine Joyce in *Sugar,* Jess Richards in *On the Town,* Ben Vereen in *Jesus Christ Superstar,* Beatrice Winde in *Ain't Supposed to Die a Natural Death.*

STRAWHAT AWARDS (for excellence during the 1971 summer theater season). Best actor, Allan Jones. Best actress, Sandy Dennis. Best director, Charles Maryan. Best supporting actor, Rex Thompson. Best supporting actress, Salome Jens. Most promising newcomers, Richard Backus, Tracy Brooks Swope. Author of best new play, David V. Robison for *Promenade, All!* Strawhat Achievement Award to a graduate of stock companies "who has contributed significantly to the American Theater and peripheral avenues in the world of arts," Peggy Wood.

NEW YORK STATE COUNCIL ON THE ARTS 1972 AWARD to Joseph Papp for "undaunted spirit, unflagging energy and uncompromising dedication to quality in pursuit of a public theater."

BRANDEIS UNIVERSITY CREATIVE ARTS AWARDS. Theater medal to Alfred Lunt and Lynn Fontanne as "the first couple of the American theater." Citation to the New Dramatists for theater arts.

AMERICAN ACADEMY OF DRAMATIC ARTS/PACE COLLEGE PLAYWRIGHTS AWARD. Murray Schisgal for "contribution to comedy in the American theater."

ANTA NATIONAL ARTIST AWARD. Alfred Lunt and Lynn Fontanne for "contribution to the American theater and to the nation."

CLARENCE DERWENT AWARDS (for best male and female non-featured performances in the dramatic field). Pamela Bellwood in *Butterflies Are Free,* Richard Backus in *Promenade, All!*

OUTER CIRCLE AWARDS (voted by critics of out-of-town periodicals for distinctive achievement in the New York Theater. John Gassner Playwriting Medallion to Jason Miller for *That Championship Season* and David Rabe for *Sticks and Bones.* Outstanding musical, *Don't Bother Me, I Can't Cope.*

VERNON RICE AWARD (for outstanding contribution to the off-Broadway season). Chelsea Theater Center.

ANNUAL *VARIETY* POLL OF LONDON THEATER CRITICS (bests of the 1970-71 season in London, published in autumn 1971). New British play, *Forget-Me-Not-Lane.* New British musical, *Catch My Soul.* New foreign play, *Butterflies Are Free.* New foreign musical, *1776.* Male leading performances, Alan Badel in *Kean* and Paul Scofield in *Captain of Koepenick* (straight plays, tie), Lance Le Gault in *Catch My Soul* (musical). Female leading performances, Eileen Atkins in *Vivat! Vivat Regina!* (straight play), no choice (musical). Male supporting performances, Michael Bates in *Forget-Me-Not-Lane* (straight play), no choice (musical). Female supporting performances, Annette Crosbie in *The Winslow Boy* (straight play), no choice (musical). Most promising new actor, Anthony Hopkins in *A Woman Killed With Kindness* and no choice (tie). Most promising new actress, Felicity Kendal in *Kean.* Decor, Christopher Morley for *The Winter's Tale,* Malcom Pride for *Catch My Soul,* Oliver Smith for *The Great Waltz* (tie). Director, Michael Blakemore for *Forget-Me-Not-Lane,* Trevor Nunn for *The Winter's Tale* (tie). Most promising playwright, David Hare for *Slag.*

THE DRAMA DESK AWARDS

The Drama Desk Awards for outstanding contributions to the theater season are voted by the critics, editors and reporters who are members of the Drama Desk, a New York organization of theater journalists in all media. Selections are made from a long list of nominees covering Broadway, repertory theater, off Broadway and off off Broadway. In order that work in productions seen by only a portion of the voters can compete fairly with that seen by almost all, the ballots ask each voter to check only those candidates whose work they actually saw. This makes it possible to compute the proportion of those who voted for the show to those who saw the show, determining winners by percentages rather than total votes received.

Winners of Drama Desk Awards for 1971-72 are listed below in the order of percentages received. The actual percentage figure is given for those who scored highest in each category. Except for the most promising playwright category, which does list the playwrights in the order of percentage votes received, no percentage figure is given for those who won the most promising citations because they were chosen by a committee of the Drama Desk (previous winners of most promising awards are not eligible).

OUTSTANDING PERFORMANCES (chosen from 69 nominees). **Marilyn Chris** (80 per cent) in *Kaddish*, **Sada Thompson** in *Twigs*, **Eileen Atkins** in *Vivat! Vivat Regina!*, **Raul Julia** in *Two Gentlemen of Verona*, **Julie Bovasso** in *The Screens*, **Richard A. Dysart** in *That Championship Season*, **Robert Morse** in *Sugar*, **Jonelle Allen** in *Two Gentlemen of Verona*, **Paul Sorvino** in *That Championship Season*, **George S. Irving** in *An Evening With Richard Nixon*, **Charles Durning, Walter McGinn** and **Michael McGuire** in *That Championship Season*, **Kain** in *The Black Terror*, **Rosemary Harris** in *Old Times*, **Ron Faber** in *And They Put Handcuffs on the Flowers*, **William Atherton** in *Suggs*, **Linda Hopkins** in *Inner City*, **Micki Grant** in *Don't Bother Me, I Can't Cope*, **Brock Peters** in *Lost in the Stars*, **Lester Rawlins** in *Nightride*, **Tom Aldredge** in *Sticks and Bones*.

OUTSTANDING DIRECTORS (chosen from 13 nominees). **A.J. Antoon** (89.9 per cent) for *That Championship Season*, **Mel Shapiro** for *Two Gentlemen of Verona* and *Older People*, **Jeff Bleckner** for *Sticks and Bones*, **Andrei Serban** for *Medea*, **Peter Hall** for *Old Times*.

OUTSTANDING SCENE DESIGNERS (chosen from 19 nominees). **Santo Loquasto** (60.8 per cent) for *Sticks and Bones* and *That Championship Season*, **Robert U. Taylor** for *The Beggar's Opera*, **Kert Lundell** for *Ain't Supposed to Die a Natural Death*.

OUTSTANDING COSTUME DESIGNERS (chosen from 5 nominees). **Willa Kim** (68.7 per cent) for *The Screens*, **Theoni V. Aldredge** for *Two Gentlemen of Verona*.

OUTSTANDING COMPOSER (chosen from 9 nominees). **Galt MacDermot** (48.5 per cent) for *Two Gentlemen of Verona*.

OUTSTANDING LYRICIST (chosen from 8 nominees). **John Guare** (74.1 per cent) for *Two Gentlemen of Verona*.

OUTSTANDING CHOREOGRAPHERS (chosen from 3 nominees, **Patricia Birch** for *Grease* (39.2 per cent), **Jean Erdman** for *Two Gentlemen of Verona*.

OUTSTANDING BOOK WRITERS (chosen from 5 nominees). **John Guare** and **Mel Shapiro** (59.5 per cent) for *Two Gentlemen of Verona*.

MOST PROMISING PLAYWRIGHTS (chosen from 12 nominees). **Jason Miller** (100 per cent) for *That Championship Season*, **Michael Weller** for *Moonchildren*, **David Wiltse** for *Suggs*, **J.E. Franklin** for *Black Girl*, **Richard Wesley** for *The Black Terror*, **Philip Hayes Dean** for *The Sty of the Blind Pig*, **J.E. Gaines** for *Don't Let It Go to Your Head*.

MOST PROMISING DIRECTORS. **Dan Sullivan** for *Suggs*, **Gilbert Moses** for *Ain't Supposed to Die a Natural Death*.

MOST PROMISING SCENE DESIGNER **Video Free America** for *Kaddish*.

MOST PROMISING COSTUME DESIGNER. **Carrie F. Robbins** for *Grease* and *The Beggar's Opera*.

MOST PROMISING COMPOSER. **Andrew Lloyd Webber** for *Jesus Christ Superstar*.

MOST PROMISING LYRICIST. **Micki Grant** for *Don't Bother Me, I Can't Cope*

MOST PROMISING BOOK WRITER. **Melvin Van Peebles** for *Ain't Supposed to Die a Natural Death*.

THE TONY AWARDS

The Antoinette Perry (Tony) Awards are voted by members of the League of New York Theaters, the governing bodies of the Dramatists Guild, Actors Equity, the American Theater Wing, the Society of Stage Directors and Choreographers, the United Scenic Artists Union and the first and second night press, from a list of three or four nominees in each category. Nominations are made by a committee serving at the invitation of the League of New York Theaters, which is in charge of Tony Awards procedure. The personnel of the nominating committee changes every year. The 1971-72 committee was composed of John Beaufort, Harold Clurman, William Glover, Otis L. Guernsey Jr., Ted Kalem, Leo Lerman, Rebecca Morehouse, Marilyn Stasio, Isabelle Stevenson and Douglas Watt. Their list of nominees follows, with winners listed in **bold face type.**

BEST PLAY. *Old Times* by Harold Pinter, produced by Roger L. Stevens. *The Prisoner of Second Avenue* by Neil Simon, produced by Saint-Subber. **Sticks and Bones** by David Rabe, produced by Joseph Papp. *Vivat! Vivat Regina!* by Robert Bolt, produced by David Merrick and Arthur Cantor.

BEST MUSICAL. *Ain't Supposed to Die a Natural Death* produced by Eugene V. Wolsk, Charles Blackwell, Emanuel Azenberg and Robert Malina. *Follies* produced by Harold Prince. *Grease* produced by Kenneth Waissman and Maxine Fox. **Two Gentlemen of Verona** produced by Joseph Papp.

BEST BOOK OF A MUSICAL. *Ain't Supposed to Die a Natural Death* by Melvin Van Peebles, *Follies* by James Goldman, *Grease* by Jim Jacobs and Warren Casey, **Two Gentlemen of Verona** by John Guare and Mel Shapiro.

BEST SCORE. *Ain't Supposed to Die a Natural Death*, music and lyrics by Melvin Van Peebles. **Follies,** music and lyrics by Stephen Sondheim. *Jesus Christ Superstar*, music by Andrew Lloyd Webber, lyrics by Tim Rice. *Two Gentlemen of Verona*, music by Galt MacDermot, lyrics by John Guare.

BEST ACTOR—PLAY. Tom Aldredge in *Sticks and Bones*, **Cliff Gorman** in *Lenny*, Donald Pleasence in *Wise Child*, Jason Robards in *The Country Girl*.

BEST ACTRESS—PLAY. Eileen Atkins in *Vivat! Vivat Regina!*, Colleen Dewhurst in *All Over*, Rosemary Harris in *Old Times*, **Sada Thompson** in *Twigs*.

BEST ACTOR—MUSICAL. Barry Bostwick in *Grease*, Clifton Davis and Raul Julia in *Two Gentlemen of Verona*, **Phil Silvers** in *A Funny Thing Happened on the Way to the Forum*.

BEST ACTRESS—MUSICAL. Jonelle Allen in *Two Gentlemen of Verona*, Dorothy Collins and **Alexis Smith** in *Follies*, Mildred Natwick in *70 Girls 70*.

BEST SUPPORTING ACTOR—PLAY. Vincent Gardenia in *The Prisoner of Second Avenue*, Lee Richardson and Douglas Rain in *Vivat! Vivat Regina!*, Joe Silver in *Lenny*.

BEST SUPPORTING ACTRESS—PLAY. Mercedes McCambridge in *The Love Suicide at Schofield Barracks*, Cara Duff-MacCormick in *Moonchildren*, Frances Sternhagen in *The Sign in Sidney Brustein's Window*, **Elizabeth Wilson** in *Sticks and Bones*.

BEST SUPPORTING ACTOR—MUSICAL. Larry Blyden in *A Funny Thing Happened on the Way to the Forum*, Timothy Meyers in *Grease*, Gene Nelson in *Follies*, Ben Vereen in *Jesus Christ Superstar*.

BEST SUPPORTING ACTRESS—MUSICAL. Adrienne Barbeau in *Grease*, **Linda Hopkins** in *Inner City*, Bernadette Peters in *On the Town*, Beatrice Winde in *Ain't Supposed to Die a Natural Death*.

BEST DIRECTOR—PLAY. Jeff Bleckner for *Sticks and Bones*, Gordon Davidson for *The Trial of the Catonsville Nine*, Peter Hall for *Old Times*, **Mike Nichols** for *The Prisoner of Second Avenue*.

412   THE BEST PLAYS OF 1971-1972

BEST DIRECTOR—MUSICAL. Gilbert Moses for *Ain't Supposed to Die a Natural Death*, **Harold Prince** and **Michael Bennett** for *Follies*, Mel Shapiro for *Two Gentlemen of Verona*, Burt Shevelove for *A Funny Thing Happened on the Way to the Forum*.

BEST SCENIC DESIGNER. **Boris Aronson** for *Follies*, John Bury for *Old Times*, Kert Lundell for *Ain't Supposed to Die a Natural Death*, Robin Wagner for *Jesus Christ Superstar*.

BEST COSTUME DESIGNER. Theoni V. Aldredge for *Two Gentlemen of Verona*. Randy Barcelo for *Jesus Christ Superstar*, **Florence Klotz** for *Follies*, Carrie F. Robbins for *Grease*.

BEST LIGHTING DESIGNER. Martin Aronstein for *Ain't Supposed to Die a Natural Death*, John Bury for *Old Times*, Jules Fisher for *Jesus Christ Superstar*, **Tharon Musser** for *Follies*.

BEST CHOREOGRAPHER. **Michael Bennett** for *Follies*, Patricia Birch for *Grease*, Jean Erdman for *Two Gentlemen of Verona*.

VARIETY'S POLL OF NEW YORK DRAMA CRITICS
1971-72 BROADWAY SEASON

Each year, representative New York drama critics are polled by *Variety* to determine their choices for Broadway's bests other than best play and musical. In 1971-72, 24 critics participated: Clive Barnes, Martin Bookspan, Casper Citron, Harold Clurman, William Glover, Martin Gottfried, Henry Hewes, Ted Kalem, Walter Kerr, Alvin Klein, Stuart Klein, Emory Lewis, Leo Mishkin, Norman Nadel, Julius Novick, George Oppenheimer, Leonard Probst, William Raidy, Peggy Stockton, John Simon, Marilyn Stasio, Allan Wallach, Douglas Watt and Virginia Woodruff. Names of those cited in the various categories appear below, together with the number of critics' votes received (in parentheses). Winners are listed in **bold face type.**

MALE LEAD, STRAIGHT PLAY. **Jason Robards** in *The Country Girl* (5), Tom Aldredge in *Sticks and Bones* (4), Hume Cronyn in *Promenade, All!* (2), Cliff Gorman in *Lenny* (2), Michael Tolan (2) and Lou Jacobi (1) in *Unlikely Heroes*, James Woods in *Moonchildren* (2), Peter Falk in *The Prisoner of Second Avenue* (1), George S. Irving in *An Evening With Richard Nixon And . . .* (1), Richard Kiley in *The Incomparable Max* (1), Donald Pleasence in *Wise Child* (1), Paul Sorvino in *That Championship Season* (1), No choice (1).

FEMALE LEAD, STRAIGHT PLAY. **Sada Thompson** in *Twigs* (10), Eileen Atkins in *Vivat! Vivat Regina!* (8), Rosemary Harris (2) and Mare Ure (1) in *Old Times*, Lee Grant in *The Prisoner of Second Avenue* (1), Maureen Stapleton in *The Country Girl* (1), Elizabeth Wilson in *Sticks and Bones* (1).

MALE LEAD, MUSICAL. **Phil Silvers** in *A Funny Thing Happened on the Way to the Forum* (9), Raul Julia in *Two Gentlemen of Verona* (7), Robert Morse in *Sugar* (5),

Brock Peters in *Lost in the Stars* (2), No choice (1).

FEMALE LEAD, MUSICAL. **Jonelle Allen** in *Two Gentlemen of Verona* (18), Micki Grant in *Don't Bother Me, I Can't Cope* (2), Carol Demas in *Grease* (1) Pamela Hall in *A Funny Thing Happened on the Way to the Forum* (1), Alexis Smith in *Follies* (1), No choice (1).

ACTOR, SUPPORTING ROLE. **Vincent Gardenia** in *The Prisoner of Second Avenue* (7), Larry Blyden in *A Funny Thing Happened on the Way to the Forum* (2), George Grizzard in *The Country Girl* (2), Lou Jacobi (2) and Michael Tolan (1) in *Unlikely Heroes*, Ben Vereen in *Jesus Christ Superstar* (2) Rene Auberjonois in *Twelfth Night* (1), Alex Bradford in *Don't Bother Me, I Can't Cope* (1), Hume Cronyn in *Promenade, All!* (1), Edward Herrmann in *Moonchildren* (1), Raul Julia (1) and Jerry Stiller (1) in *Two Gentlemen of Verona*, Avon Long in *Don't Play Us Cheap* (1), Lee Richardson in *Vivat! Vivat Regina!* (1).

ACTRESS, SUPPORTING ROLE. **Frances Sternhagen** in *The Sign in Sidney Brustein's Window* (5), **Elizabeth Wilson** in *Sticks and Bones* (5), Linda Hopkins in *Inner City* (2½), Bernadette Peters in *On the Town* (2½), Martha Henry in *Twelfth Night* and *Narrow Road to the Deep North* (2), Mercedes McCambridge in *The Love Suicide at Schofield Barracks* (2), Eileen Atkins in *Vivat! Vivat Regina!* (1), Blythe Danner in *Twelth Night* (1), Diana Davila in *Two Gentlemen of Verona* (1), Cara Duff-MacCormick in *Moonchildren* (1), No choice (1).

MOST PROMISING NEW BROADWAY ACTOR. **Richard Backus** in *Promenade, All!* (9), Edward Herrmann in *Moonchildren* (4), William Atherton in *The Sign in Sidney Brustein's Window* (2), Robert Foxworth in *The Crucible* (2), Nicholas Coster in *Twigs* (1), George S. Irving in *An Evening With Richard Nixon And . . .* (1), No choice (5).

MOST PROMISING NEW BROADWAY ACTRESS. Cara Duff-MacCormick in *Moonchildren* (3), Joyce Ebert in *Solitaire/Double Solitaire* (3), Delphine Seyrig in *The Little Black Book* (3), Rhetta Hughes in *Don't Play Us Cheap* (2), Margaret Cowie in *Lost in the Stars* (1), Roberta Maxwell in *There's One in Every Marriage* (1), **No choice 11.**

BEST DIRECTOR. **Jeff Bleckner** for *Sticks and Bones* (6), Peter Hall for *Old Times* (5), John Houseman for *The Country Girl* (3), Mel Shapiro for *Two Gentlemen of Verona* (3), Gilbert Moses for *Ain't Supposed to Die a Natural Death* (2), Tom O'Horgan for *Jesus Christ Superstar* (2), Alan Schneider for *Moonchildren* (2), A.J. Antoon for *That Championship Season* (1).

BEST SET DESIGNER. **John Bury** for *Old Times* (5), Ming Cho Lee for *Two Gentlemen of Verona* (4), Kert Lundell for *Solitaire/Double Solitaire* and *Ain't Supposed to Die a Natural Death* (4), Santo Loquasto for *Sticks and Bones* and *That Championship Season* (3), Douglas W. Schmidt for *The Country Girl* and *Twelfth Night* (2), Robin Wagner for *Jesus Christ Superstar* (2), Boris Aronson for *Follies* (1) Jo Mielziner for *The Crucible* (1), Oliver Smith for *Lost in the Stars* (1), Richard Sylbert for *The Prisoner of Second Avenue* (1).

BEST COSTUME DESIGNER. **Theoni V. Aldredge** for *Two Gentlemen of Verona* (12), Randy Barcelo for *Jesus Christ Superstar* (2), Alvin Colt for *Sugar* (2), Malcolm McCormick for *Mary Stuart* (2), James Burton Harris for *Promenade, All!* (1), Bernard Johnson for *Ain't Supposed to Die a Natural Death* (1), Florence Klotz for *Follies* (1), Carrie Robbins for *Grease* (1), Carl Toms for *Vivat! Vivat Regina!* (1), No choice (1).

BEST COMPOSER. **Galt MacDermot** for *Two Gentlemen of Verona* (11), Kurt Weill for *Lost in the Stars* (3), Andrew Lloyd Webber for *Jesus Christ Superstar* (3), Leonard Bernstein for *On the Town* (1), Micki Grant for *Don't Bother Me, I Can't Cope* (1), Stephen Sondheim for *Follies* (1), Melvin Van Peebles for *Ain't Supposed to Die a Natural Death* (1), No choice (3).

BEST LYRICIST. **John Guare** for *Two Gentlemen of Verona* (12), Stephen Sondheim for *Follies* and *A Funny Thing Happened on the Way to the Forum* (3), Micki Grant for *Don't Bother Me, I Can't Cope* (2), Melvin Van Peebles for *Ain't Supposed to Die a Natural Death* (2), Warren Casey and Jim Jacobs for *Grease* (1), Tim Rice for *Jesus Christ Superstar* (1), No choice (3).

MOST PROMISING NEW PLAYWRIGHT. **David Rabe** for *Sticks and Bones* (13½), Michael Weller for *Moonchildren* (5), Jason Miller for *That Championship Season* (2½), Melvin Van Peebles for *Ain't Supposed to Die a Natural Death* (1½), John Guare for *Two Gentlemen of Verona* (½), No choice (1).

BEST PRODUCER. **Joseph Papp** (*Sticks and Bones, Two Gentlemen of Verona, That Championship Season*, etc.) (20), Roger Stevens (*Old Times, The Country Girl, Lost in the Stars*) (1), Harold Prince (*Follies*) (1), No choice (2).

1971-72 OFF-BROADWAY SEASON

Each year in recent seasons, representative New York drama critics are polled by *Variety* to learn their choices for off Broadway's best other than best play and musical. In 1971-72, 20 critics participated: Clive Barnes, Martin Bookspan, Harold Clurman, William Glover, Martin Gottfried, Henry Hewes,

Ted Kalem, Walter Kerr, Alan Klein, Emory Lewis, Leo Mishkin, Julius Novick, Edith Oliver, George Oppenheimer, Leonard Probst, John Simon, Marilyn Stasio, Peggy Stockton, Allan Wallach and Douglas Watt. Names of those cited in the various categories appear below, together with the number of critics' votes received (in parentheses). Winners are listed in **bold face type.**

MALE LEAD, STRAIGHT PLAY. **Ensemble** (Charles Durning, Richard A. Dysart, Walter McGinn, Michael McGuire, Paul Sorvino) (6), Richard A. Dysart (2), Walter McGinn (1), Paul Sorvino (1) in *That Championship Season*, Hal Holbrook in *Lake of the Woods* (3), William Atherton in *Suggs* (2), Lester Rawlins in *Nightride* (2), Will Hare in *Dylan* (1), Kain in *The Black Terror* (1), David Rounds in *The Real Inspector Hound* (1).

FEMALE LEAD, STRAIGHT PLAY. **Marilyn Chris** in *Kaddish* (5), Julie Bovasso in *The Screens* (4), Frances Foster in *The Sty of the Blind Pig* (2), Gloria Foster in *Black Visions* (2), Vinie Burrows in *Walk Together Children* (1), Rosalind Cash in *Charlie Was Here and Now He's Gone* (1), Rue McClanahan in *Dylan* (1), Carrie Nye in *The Real Inspector Hound* (1), Dolores Sutton in *The Web and the Rock* (1), No choice (2).

MALE LEAD, MUSICAL. **Stephen D. Newman** (4) and Gordon Connell (1) in *The Beggar's Opera*, Jack Blackton in *Hark!* (2), Barry Bostwick in *Grease* (1), Robert Drivas in *Where Has Tommy Flowers Gone?* (1), Merwin Goldsmith in *Wanted* (1), Raul Julia in *Two Gentlemen of Verona* (1), Chapman Roberts in *Love Me, Love My Children* (1), No choice (8).

FEMALE LEAD, MUSICAL. **Kathleen Widdoes** (4), Marilyn Sokol (3) and Jeanne Arnold (1) in *The Beggar's Opera*, Sharron Miller in *Hark!* (2), Hope Clark (1) and Micki Grant (1) in *Don't Bother Me, I Can't Cope*, Carole Demas in *Grease* (1), Lee Guilliatt in *Wanted* (1), Gisela May in *German Theater Songs* (1), Ensemble of *The Wedding of Iphigenia* and *Iphigenia in Concert* (1), Ensemble of *Love Me, Love My Children* (1), No choice (3).

ACTOR, SUPPORTING ROLE. **Paul Sorvino** (5¼), Michael McGuire (1½) and Richard A. Dysart (1¼) in *That Championship Season*, Philip Campanella in *Misalliance* (2), "Arnold" in *Where Has Tommy Flowers Gone?* (1), Stephen Elliott in *The Crucible* (1), William Hickey in *Small Craft Warnings* (1), Kain in *The Black Terror* (1), Terry Kiser in *In Case of Accident* (1), John Long in *The Beggar's Opera* (1), David Selby in *Sticks and Bones* (1), No choice (3).

ACTRESS, SUPPORTING ROLE. **Julie Bovasso** in *The Screens* (2), Mary Alice (1) and Norma Donaldson (1) in *The Duplex*, Regina Baff in *Rosebloom* (1), Susan Batson in *The Black Terror* (1), Salome Bey in *Love Me, Love My Children* (1), Jane Connell (1) and Carrie Nye (1) in *The Real Inspector Hound*, Paddy Croft in *Shadow of a Gunman* (1), Diana Davila in *People Are Living There* (1), Frances Foster in *A Ballet Behind the Bridge* (1), Natalie Gray in *Medea* (1), Rue McClanahan in *Dylan* (1), Clarice Taylor in *The Sty of the Blind Pig* (1), Kathleen Widdoes in *The Beggar's Opera* (1), Elizabeth Wilson in *Sticks and Bones* (1), No choice (3).

MOST PROMISING NEW OFF-BROADWAY ACTOR. **Kain** in *The Black Terror* (3), John Bottoms in *Dance Wi' Me* (2), William Atherton in *Suggs* (1), Cliff DeYoung in *Sticks and Bones* (1), Gene Fanning in *Small Craft Warnings* (1), Hank Frazier in *Black Visions* (1), Timothy Jerome in *The Beggar's Opera* (1), Robert Moberly in *A Gun Play* (1), David Rounds in *The Real Inspector Hound* (1), Ben Slack in *Rain* (1), Paul Sorvino in *That Championship Season* (1), No choice (6).

MOST PROMISING NEW OFF-BROADWAY ACTRESS. **Kishasha** (2) and Louise Stubbs (1) in *Black Girl*, Beverly Todd in *Black Visions* (2), Mary Alice in *The Duplex* (1), Salome Bey (1) and Patsy Rahn (1) in *Love Me, Love My Children*, Marilyn Chris in *Kaddish* (1), Kay Cole in *Two if by Sea* (1), Diana Davila in *People Are Living There* (1), Despo in *The Screens* (1), Priscilla Smith in *Medea* (1), No Choice (7).

BEST DIRECTOR. **A.J. Antoon** for *That Championship Season* (15½), Steven Kent for *James Joyce Memorial Liquid Theater* (1), Andrei Serban for *Medea* (1), Robert Kalfin for *Kaddish* (½), No choice (2).

BEST SET DESIGNER. **Santo Loquasto** for *That Championship Season* (9), Robert U. Taylor for *The Beggar's Opera* (5), Video Free America, John Scheffler for *Kaddish* (2), Edward Burbridge for *The Sty of the Blind Pig* (1), No choice (3).

BEST COSTUME DESIGNER. **Willa Kim** for *The Screens* (7), Carrie F. Robbins for *The Beggar's Opera* and *Grease* (5), Joseph G. Aulisi for *The Real Inspector Hound* and *After Magritte* (1), No choice (7).

BEST COMPOSER. Al Carmines for *Wanted* (5), Peter Link for *The Wedding of Iphigenia* and *Iphigenia in Concert* (4), Robert Swerdlow for *Love Me, Love My Children* (2), Warren Casey and Jim Jacobs for *Grease* (1), Micki Grant for *Don't Bother Me, I Can't Cope* (1), Dr. Pepusch, Ryan Edwards for *The Beggar's Opera* (1), **No choice** (6).

BEST LYRICIST. Al Carmines for *Wanted* (5), John Gay for *The Beggar's Opera* (2),

Micki Grant for *Don't Bother Me, I Can't Cope* (2), Robert Loric for *Hark!* (2), Peter Link for *The Wedding of Iphigenia* and *Iphigenia in Concert* (1), Warren Casey and Jim Jacobs for *Grease* (1), **No choice** (7).

MOST PROMISING NEW PLAYWRIGHT. **Jason Miller** for *That Championship Season* (17), J.E. Gaines for *Don't Let It Go to Your Head* (1), Allen Ginsberg for *Kaddish* (1), Richard Wesley for *The Black Terror* (1).

BEST PRODUCER. **Joseph Papp** (N.Y. Shakespeare Festival) (14), Robert Kalfin, Michael David (Chelsea Theater Center) (4), Company Theater of Los Angeles (1), No choice (1).

1971-1972 PUBLICATION
OF RECENTLY-PRODUCED PLAYS

AC/DC. Heathcote Williams. Calders & Boyars. (Also paperback.)
After Magritte. Tom Stoppard. Faber & Faber. (Paperback.)
All Over. Edward Albee. Atheneum.
And Miss Reardon Drinks a Little. Paul Zindel. Random House.
Borstal Boy. Frank McMahon. Random House.
Deer Kill, The. Murray Mednick. Bobbs-Merrill. (Also paperback.)
Effect of Gamma Rays on Man-in-the-Moon Marigolds, The. Paul Zindel. Bantam. (Paperback.)
Evening With Richard Nixon, An. Gore Vidal. Random House.
Follies. James Goldman and Stephen Sondheim. Random House.
Gingerbread Lady, The. Neil Simon. Random House.
Happy Birthday, Wanda June. Kurt Vonnegut Jr. Delacorte Press. (Also paperback.)
Home. David Storey. Random House.
House of Blue Leaves, The. John Guare. Viking.
Indians. Arthur Kopit. Bantam. (Paperback.)
Jacques Brel Is Alive and Well and Living in Paris. Eric Blau. Dutton. (Also paperback.)
Mary Stuart. Stephen Spender's translation and adaptation of Schiller's play. Faber & Faber.
Moonchildren. Michael Weller. Delacorte Press. *Cancer* (original title of same play when done in England). Faber & Faber. (Also paperback.)
Night Thoreau Spent in Jail, The. Jerome Lawrence and Robert E. Lee. Bantam. (Paperback.)
Old Times. Harold Pinter. Grove. (Paperback.)
Paradise Now. Judith Malina and Julian Beck. Random House.
Rabelais. Jean-Louis Barrault. Hill & Wang. (Also paperback.)
Scratch. Archibald MacLeish. Houghton Mifflin.
Scripts 1. Collections of playscripts published by New York Shakespeare Festival and Joseph Papp. (Paperback; contents of first six issues are listed here.) *The Legacy of Cain* by The Living Theater, *Terminal* by The Open Theater Ensemble and Susan Yankowitz, *Dirty Hearts* by Sonia Sanchez, *Sun* by Adrienne Kennedy, *The Basic Training of Pavlo Hummel* by David Rabe.
Scripts 2. Edited by Erica Munk, William Coco and Sandy MacDonald. *Kontraption* by Rochelle Owens, *The Tommy Allen Show* by Megan Terry, *The Black Terror* by Richard Wesley, *Crabs, Cross-Country* by Sally Ordway, *Intersections 7* by Paul Epstein.
Scripts 3. Edited by Erica Munk, William Coco and Sandy MacDonald. *The Citizens Correction Committee* by Ronal Tavel, *The Rock Garden* by Sam Shepard, *Mary Stuart* by Wolfgang Hildesheimer.
Scripts 4. Edited by Erica Munk, William Coco and Sandy MacDonald. *Subject to Fits* by Robert Montgomery, *Audioplay 1: Voices* by Jacov Lind, *Three Short Plays* by Roger Howard, *The Fabulous Miss Marie* by Ed Bullins.

Scripts 5. Edited by Erica Munk. *Larry Parks's Day in Court* by Eric Bentley, *Four Infiltration Pieces* by Marc Estrin, *The Ride Across Lake Constance* by Peter Handke, *The Wax Engine* by Robert Nichols.
Scripts 6. Edited by Erica Munk. *The Life and Times of J. Walter Smintheus* by Edgar White, *Eunuchs of the Forbidden City* by Charles Ludlam, *Free This Day: A Trial in Seven Exhibits* by Himilce Novas, *Jazznite* by Walter Jones.
Slag. David Hare. Faber & Faber.
Steambath. Bruce Jay Friedman. Bantam. (Paperback.)
Vivat! Vivat Regina! Robert Bolt. Random House.

A SELECTED LIST OF OTHER PLAYS PUBLISHED IN 1971-1972

Bertolt Brecht: Collected Plays. Vol. 5. Edited by Ralph Manheim and John Willett. Vintage. (Paperback.)
Best Short Plays 1971, The. Stanley Richards, editor. Chilton.
Black Drama Anthology. Woodie King and Ron Milner, editors. New American Library. (Paperback.)
Black Theater—A 20th Century Collection of the Work of Its Best Playwrights. Compiled by Lindsay Patterson. Dodd, Mead.
Collected Plays of Lillian Hellman, The. Little, Brown.
Come and Be Killed and *Dear Janet Rosenberg, Dear Mr. Kooning.* Stanley Eveling. Calder & Boyars.
Comedy of Neil Simon, The. Random House.
Complete Plays of Vladimir Mayakovsky, The. Translated by Guy Daniels. Simon & Schuster.
Dear Antoine. Jean Anouilh. Hill & Wang.
Forget-Me-Not Lane. Peter Nichols. Faber & Faber.
Four Dynamite Plays. Ed Bullins. *It Bees Dat Way, Death List, The Pig Pen, Night of the Beat.* Murrow.
Friends, The. Arnold Wesker. Jonathan Cape.
Max. Gunter Grass. Harcourt, Brace.
Plays of Christopher Marlowe, The. Edited by Roma Gill. Oxford. (Paperback.)
Portable Arthur Miller, The. Viking. (Also paperback.)
Straight Up. Syd Cheatle. Methuen.
Theater of Tennessee Williams, The. Three volumes. New Directions.
Trotsky in Exile. Peter Weiss. Atheneum.
West of Suez. John Osborne. Faber & Faber. (Also paperback.)
Why Tuesday Never Has a Blue Monday. Robert Heide. Breakthrough. (Paperback.)

MUSICAL AND DRAMATIC RECORDINGS OF NEW YORK SHOWS

Title and publishing company are listed below. Each record is an original New York cast album unless otherwise indicated. An asterisk (*) indicates recording is also available on cassettes. Two asterisks (**) indicate it is available on eight-track cartridges.

Ain't Supposed to Die a Natural Death. A & M.
Boy Friend, The (movie sound track). MGM.
Cabaret (movie sound track). ABC.
Don't Bother Me, I Can't Cope. Polydor.
Don't Play Us Cheap. Stax (two records).
Fiddler on the Roof (orig. London cast). Columbia (*)(**).
Fiddler on the Roof (movie sound track). United Artists (two records).
Fiddler on the Roof (Bernardi). Harmony.
Fiddler on the Roof (Picon, Merrill, Black, London Festival Orchestra and Chorus). London.
Fiddler on the Roof (Topol, London production). Columbia.
Godspell. Bell (*)(**).

Grass Harp, The. Painted Smiles.
Grease. MGM.
Hair (orig. London cast). Atco (*)(**).
I Never Sang for My Father (movie sound track). Bell (*)(**).
Inner City, A Street Cantata. TCA (*)(**).
Iphigenia. ABC (*)(**).
Jesus Christ Superstar. Decca (*)(**) (two records).
Lenny. Blue Thumb (two records).
The Music Man (orig. London cast). Stanyan.
On the Town. Columbia.
Sail Away. (orig. London cast). Stanyan.
70, Girls, 70. Columbia.
Show Boat. (orig. London cast). Stanyan.
Sugar. United Artists.
Tarot. United Artists.
To Live Another Summer, To Pass Another Winter. Buddah (two records).
Touch. Ampex (*)(**).
Two Gentlemen of Verona. ABC (*)(**) (two records).
Will Rogers's U.S.A. Columbia (**) (two records).

THE BEST PLAYS, 1894-1971

Listed in alphabetical order below are all those works selected as Best Plays in previous volumes in the *Best Plays* series. Opposite each title is given the volume in which the play appears, its opening date and its total number of performances. Those plays marked with an asterisk (*) were still playing on June 1, 1972 and their number of performances was figured through May 31, 1972. Adaptors and translators are indicated by (ad) and (tr), and the symbols (b), (m) and (l) stand for the author of the book, music and lyrics in the case of musicals.

NOTE: A season-by-season listing, rather than an alphabetical one, of the 500 Best Plays in the first 50 volumes, starting with the yearbook for the season of 1919-20, appears in *The Best Plays of 1968-69.*

PLAY	VOLUME	OPENED	PERFS.
ABE LINCOLN IN ILLINOIS—Robert E. Sherwood	38-39	Oct. 15, 1938	472
ABRAHAM LINCOLN—John Drinkwater	19-20	Dec. 15, 1919	193
ACCENT ON YOUTH—Samson Raphaelson	34-35	Dec. 25, 1934	229
ADAM AND EVA—Guy Bolton, George Middleton	19-20	Sept. 13, 1919	312
ADAPTATION—Elaine May; and NEXT—Terrence McNally	68-69	Feb. 10, 1969	707
AFFAIRS OF STATE—Louis Verneuil	50-51	Sept. 25, 1950	610
AFTER THE FALL—Arthur Miller	63-64	Jan. 23, 1964	208
AFTER THE RAIN—John Bowen	67-68	Oct. 9, 1967	64
AH, WILDERNESS!—Eugene O'Neill	33-34	Oct. 2, 1933	289
ALIEN CORN—Sidney Howard	32-33	Feb. 20, 1933	98
ALISON'S HOUSE—Susan Glaspell	30-31	Dec. 1, 1930	41
ALL MY SONS—Arthur Miller	46-47	Jan. 29, 1947	328
ALL THE WAY HOME—Tad Mosel, based on James Agee's novel *A Death in the Family*	60-61	Nov. 30, 1960	333
ALLEGRO—(b, l) Oscar Hammerstein II, (m) Richard Rodgers	47-48	Oct. 10, 1947	315
AMBUSH—Arthur Richman	21-22	Oct. 10, 1921	98
AMERICA HURRAH—Jean-Claude van Itallie	66-67	Nov. 6, 1966	634
AMERICAN WAY, THE—George S. Kaufman, Moss Hart	38-39	Jan. 21, 1939	164
AMPHITRYON 38—Jean Giraudoux, (ad) S. N. Behrman	37-38	Nov. 1, 1937	153
ANDERSONVILLE TRIAL, THE—Saul Levitt	59-60	Dec. 29, 1959	179

NECROLOGY

MAY 1971—JUNE 1972

PERFORMERS

Ackerman, Al (90)—November 4, 1971
Aitken, Kate (81)—December 11, 1971
Angeli, Pier (39)—September 10, 1971
Angold, Edith (76)—October 4, 1971
Antoine, Josephine (64)—October 30, 1971
Atkins, Robert (85)—February 9, 1972
Austin, Gene (71)—January 24, 1972
Ayed, Aly Ben (40)—February 15, 1972
Baird, Leah (60)—October 3, 1971
Baker, Elsie (78)—August 16, 1971
Baker, Jane King (75)—May 23, 1971
Basse, Joe (71)—February 4, 1972
Baxter, Gladys—January 20, 1972
Beatty, George (76)—August 6, 1971
Beers, Robert (51)—May 26, 1972
Bernardi, Helen (89)—May 22, 1971
Blagoi, George (73)—June 23, 1971
Blanchfield, Charles E. (Charley) (83)—July 23, 1971
Blocker, Dan (43)—May 13, 1972
Blythe, Betty (72)—April 7, 1972
Boardman, Virginia True (82)—June 10, 1971
Boesen, William (48)—March 25, 1972
Bourbon, Rae (78)—July 19, 1971
Brady, Pat (57)—February 27, 1972
Britton, Ethel (57)—February 26, 1972
Bronson, Betty (64)—October 21, 1971
Burke, Bonnie (71)—September 24, 1971
Byington, Spring (77)—September 7, 1971
Cabot, Bruce (67)—May 3, 1972
Cadwalader, Jessica (Mrs. Robert Ryan) (57) —May 15, 1972
Carr, Georgia (46)—July 4, 1971
Carroll, Gene (74)—March 5, 1972
Carver, Robert—January 25, 1971
Chalif, Frances Robinson—August 15, 1971
Chevalier, Maurice (83)—January 1, 1972
Clarke, Gordon B. (65)—January 11, 1972
Cleary, Peggy (80)—January 10, 1972
Comingore, Dorothy—December 30, 1971
Conroy, Thom (60)—November 16, 1971
Coogran, Gene B.—January 26, 1972
Cooper, Gladys (82)—November 17, 1971
Corley, Robert A.—November 18, 1971
Costello, William A. (73)—October 9, 1971
Cowan, Jerome (74)—January 24, 1972
Craig, May (83)—February 8, 1972
Dale, Charlie (90)—November 16, 1971
Dale, Margaret (96)—March 23, 1972

Dalton, Dorothy (78)—April 13, 1972
Dark, Christopher—October 8, 1971
Darvi, Bella (44)—September 17, 1971
Date, Keshavrao (32)—September 13, 1971
Davis, Rev. Gary (76)—May 5, 1972
De Blasio, Gene (30)—November 3, 1971
De Marney, Terrance (62)—May 25, 1971
DeWharton, Barbara Lee (48)—March 1972
Dilligh, Avni (62)—Summer 1971
Donlevy, Brian (69)—April 6, 1972
Dubas, Marie (78)—March 1972
Duel, Peter (31)—December 31, 1971
Dugan, Johnny (50)—May 17, 1972
Dunca, Kenney (69)—February 5, 1972
D'Usseau, Ottola Nesmith (83)—February 7, 1972
Eberg, Victor (47)—February 26, 1972
Edwards, Cliff (Ukulele Ike) (76)—July 18, 1971
Ellsworth, Arley B. (74)—May 27, 1971
Elvey, Gwladys—February 3, 1972
Evans, Renee (63)—December 22, 1971
Fadel, Yvan (78)—August 2, 1971
Fairbanks, Albert L. (65)—November 5, 1971
Farrell, Eve—January 31, 1972
Farrell, Josephine (87)—April 9, 1972
Fealy, Maude (90)—November 9, 1971
Field, Alexander (79)—September 1971
Fife, Bobby (70)—January 17, 1972
Flack, Nannette—December 13, 1971
Fox, Phil—April 26, 1972
Fuqua, Charles (60)—December 21, 1971
Gaudschmidt, Max (83)—February 28, 1972
Gerrard, Gene (81)—June 1971
Getty, Talitha Pol—July 10, 1971
Gilbert, Billy (77)—September 23, 1971
Gillian, Maurice (80)—December 13, 1971
Gomez, Thomas (65)—June 19, 1971
Goode, Jack (63)—June 24, 1971
Goodman, Lillian Rosedale (84)—January 23, 1972
Gordon, Robert (76)—October 26, 1971
Gorman, Eric (85)—November 24, 1971
Gorman, Frederick E. (89)—November 25, 1972
Gorman, Tom (63)—October 2, 1971
Goulding, Alfred (76)—April 25, 1972
Greener, Dorothy (54)—December 6, 1971
Griebling, Otto (75)—April 19, 1972
Hallor, Edith (75)—May 21, 1971
Hammond, Virginia (78)—April 6, 1972

429

Hassett, Michael—January 29, 1972
Hatton, Raymond (84)—October 21, 1971
Haynes, Henry D. (51)—August 7, 1971
Heflin, Van (60)—July 23, 1971
Helton, Percy (77)—September 11, 1971
Henry, Jo-Ann (49)—May 6, 1972
Herman, Tom (63)—March 26, 1972
Hicks, Leonard M. (53)—August 8, 1971
Hilliard, Hazel (83)—August 1, 1971
Hoffmann, Hermine H. (47)—December 7, 1971
Holbrook, William (70s)—August 6, 1971
Holman, Libby (65)—June 19, 1971
Holmes, Stuart (87)—December 29, 1971
Howes, Bobby (76)—April 27, 1972
Hudson, Rochelle (57)—January 17, 1972
Ihnat, Steve (37)—May 12, 1972
Ishii, Kan (71)—April 29, 1972
Jackson, Mahalia (61)—January 27, 1972
Jacobson, Barbara Scott (57)—April 4, 1972
Jewell, Isabel (62)—April 5, 1972
Johnson, Edna (83)—July 4, 1971
Johnson, Florence Osbeck (63)—September 21, 1971
Jones, T. C. (50)—September 26, 1971
Kane, Irving (Chick) (68)—April 14, 1972
Kaye, Sparky (65)—August 23, 1971
Kchessinska, Mathilde (99)—December 7, 1971
Kearns, Red (64)—December 7, 1971
Kedrov, Mikhail N. (78)—March 22, 1972
Keith, Sherwood (59)—February 21, 1972
Kelety, Julia (85)—January 1, 1972
Kenneally, Michael (80)—April 3, 1972
Kershaw, Elinor (86)—September 12, 1971
Kikume, Al (78)—March 27, 1972
Kinney, Ray (71)—January 28, 1972
Kirkland, Muriel (68)—September 26, 1971
Korris, Harry (79)—June 4, 1971
Kowal, Mitchell (56)—May 1, 1971
Kramer, Phil (72)—March 31, 1972
Kumari, Meena (40)—March 31, 1972
Kuscher, Marion North (54)—July 14, 1971
Laine, Vicki (41)—February 23, 1972
Landick, Olin (77)—March 26, 1972
Landis, Jessie Royce (67)—February 2, 1972
Lang, Alois (80)—December 23, 1971
Lang, Gertrude (73)—July 14, 1971
Lawrence, Bert (47)—May 25, 1971
Lewis, Joe E. (69)—June 4, 1971
Litel, John (77)—February 3, 1972
Litonius, Marian (62)—September 7, 1971
Lloyd, Harold Jr. (39)—June 8, 1971
Lowery, Robert (57)—December 26, 1971
Lukas, Paul (76)—August 15, 1971
Lynn, Diana (45)—December 18, 1971
McComb, H. (90)—November 5, 1971
McDermott, Hugh (63)—January 30, 1972
McGowan, Oliver F. (64)—August 23, 1971
McGrath, William P. (45)—August 10, 1971
McGuinn, Joseph Ford (67)—September 22, 1971

McGuire, Lavinia (56)—October 31, 1971
McMahon, David (63)—January 27, 1972
McMahon, Horace (64)—August 17, 1971
MacCormack, Franklyn (63)—June 12, 1971
Madeira, Humberto (50)—July 15, 1971
Manna, Charlie (51)—November 9, 1971
Marinoff, Fania (81)—November 16, 1971
Martin, Cye (56)—March 21, 1972
Maskova, Hana—March 31, 1972
Maxwell, Marilyn (49)—March 20, 1972
Meyn, Robert (76)—March 3, 1972
Miller, Barbara (Wicker) (86)—May 6, 1972
Miller, Flournoy (84)—June 6, 1971
Mistral, Jorge (49)—April 20, 1972
Mitchell, George (67)—January 18, 1972
Mondose, Alex (78)—January 18, 1972
Monterosso, Emily Jan Madson (29)—August 15, 1971
Moody, Ralph (84)—September 16, 1971
Moorey, Stefa (38)—February 3, 1972
Morgan, Jane (91)—January 1, 1972
Morrison, Jim (27)—July 3, 1971
Moseley, Thomas W. (93)—August 17, 1971
Muir, Gavin (62)—May 24, 1972
Neary, Sime (77)—June 17, 1971
Nehrer, John W. (61)—March 16, 1972
Nelson, John (74)—April 13, 1972
Nirdlinger, Jane Nixon (80)—May 15, 1971
O'Connor, Harry M. (98)—July 10, 1971
Offenbach, Joseph (66)—October 15, 1971
Oldaker, Max (64)—February 2, 1972
Operti, Le Roi (75)—June 22, 1971
O'Sullivan, Michael (37)—July 24, 1972
Parlo, Dita (65)—January 1972
Pennington, Ann (77)—November 4, 1971
Pol, Talitha (31)—July 13, 1971
Pray, Anna M. (80)—June 30, 1971
Preminger, Marion (58)—April 16, 1972
Pully, B. S. (61)—January 6, 1972
Rae, Melba (49)—November 29, 1971
Rambal, Enrique (47)—December 15, 1971
Rathbone, George (77)—May 1972
Raven, David (58)—October 10, 1971
Ravik, Michael (40)—November 25, 1971
Raymon, Rubee (77)—June 21, 1971
Reddick, Walter (65)—May 10, 1971
Rennie, Michael (62)—June 10, 1971
Riano, Renie—July 3, 1971
Robinson, Gladys L. (75)—June 6, 1971
Robson, June (50)—March 16, 1972
Romaine, Doug (56)—May 25, 1971
Rosmer, Milton (89)—December 7, 1971
Russell, Billy—November 25, 1971
Rutherford, Margaret (80)—May 22, 1972
Sadler, Ian (69)—Summer 1971
St. Clair, Yvonne (57)—September 22, 1971
St. Helier, Ivy—November 8, 1971
Sande, Walter (63)—November 22, 1971
Sanders, George (65)—April 25, 1972
Santley, Joseph (81)—August 8, 1971
Scala, Gia (38)—April 30, 1972
Scotti, Joe (57)—May 13, 1972

Sedgwick, Edie (28)—November 16, 1971
Seed, Phil (70)—September 9, 1971
Shawn, Ted (80)—January 9, 1972
Small, Dick (58)—February 21, 1972
Smiley, Red (47)—January 2, 1972
Smith, Charles W. (74)—July 23, 1971
Smith, Maybelle (48)—January 23, 1972
Snow, Amanda (67)—March 15, 1972
Snyder, Glyde—March 21, 1972
Southgate, Howard S. (76)—May 15, 1971
Spivak, Irene Daye (53)—November 1, 1971
Stanley, Mrs. Gladys B.—December 25, 1971
Stantley, Ralph (58)—May 10, 1972
Steel, John (71)—June 25, 1971
Steinke, Hans (78)—June 26, 1971
Styler, Charlotte (75)—May 30, 1971
Sues, Leonard (50)—October 24, 1971
Swan, Paul (88)—February 1, 1972
Tackova, Jarmilla (59)—September 26, 1971
Taggart, Hal (79)—December 12, 1971
Terriss, Ellaline (100)—June 16, 1971
Thompson, William (58)—July 15, 1971
Tollinger, Ned (69)—May 7, 1972
Tsiang, H. T. (72)—July 16, 1971
Turleigh, Veronica (68)—Fall 1971
Tweed, Tommy (64)—October 12, 1971
Tweddell, Frank (76)—December 20, 1971
Tyler, Gladys (79)—April 14, 1972
Vickers, Martha (46)—November 3, 1971
Vincent, Gene (36)—October 12, 1971
Wadkar, Hansa (47)—August 23, 1971
Wainright, Hope (30)—April 1972
Wakefield, Hugh (83)—December 1971
Walsh, Joseph F. (76)—March 15, 1972
Ward, William (62)—May 9, 1972
Warren, C. Denier (82)—August 27, 1971
Warwick, John (67)—January 10, 1972
Watkins, Helen W. (84)—March 24, 1972
Wayne, Thomas (31)—August 15, 1971
Webley, John (24)—Fall 1971
Webster, Marion Litonius (62)—September 5, 1971
Wessels, Florence (72)—July 20, 1971
Weston, Joseph J. (84)—May 1, 1972
Whitney, Peter (55)—March 30, 1972
Wilhelm, Theodore (62)—November 30, 1971
Wilkerson, Guy (70)—July 15, 1971
Wilkinson, Leslie (72)—December 26, 1971
Williams, Rita (51)—November 13, 1971
Wills, Betty Chappele (63)—November 11, 1971
Wilson, Roberta (68)—February 2, 1972
Winik, Edna Mae—July 22, 1971
Winston, Jackie (56)—November 9, 1971
Wolff, Frank (43)—December 12, 1971
Woolf, Barney (95)—February 10, 1972
Woodward, Robert (63)—February 7, 1972
Workman, Gertrude (87)—March 15, 1972
Wright, Hazel (70s)—July 28, 1971
Young, Carleton G. (64)—July 11, 1971
Young, Mary Marsden (92)—June 23, 1971

PLAYWRIGHTS

Arent, Arthur (67)—May 18, 1972
Armstrong, Eunice B. (84)—June 29, 1971
Ashford, Daisy (90)—January 17, 1972
Belaval, Emilio (68)—March 31, 1972
Booth, John H. (85)—November 23, 1971
Colum, Padraic (90)—January 10, 1972
Coppel, Alec—January 22, 1972
Davis, Blevins (68)—July 16, 1971
Ephron, Phoebe (57)—October 13, 1971
Eustace, Edward J.—August 10, 1971
Finn, Jonathan (87)—June 4, 1971
Gehman, Richard (50)—May 13, 1972
Gehri, Alfred (76)—January 8, 1972
Ghrada, Mairead Ni (78)—June 3, 1971
Guynes, Charles (37)—June 4, 1971
Hershey, Burnet (75)—December 13, 1971
Kesselring, Charlotte E.—August 18, 1971
Korneichuk, Aleksandr (66)—May 14, 1972
McCracken, Esther (69)—August 11, 1972
Mannheim, Albert (58)—March 19, 1972
Mills, Hugh Travers—October 27, 1971
O'Dea, John (63)—May 7, 1972
Perl, Arnold (58)—December 11, 1971
Pirandello, Stefano (76)—February 5, 1972
Pohlman, Max Edward—July 31, 1971
Rodale, J. I. (72)—June 7, 1971
Roeburt, John (63)—May 22, 1972
Sifton, Paul F. (74)—April 4, 1972
Sorell, Doris—October 10, 1971
Spencer, Franz—July, 1971
Spewack, Samuel (72)—October 14, 1971
Towber, Chaim (70)—February 26, 1972
Ullman, James Ramsey (63)—June 20, 1971
Washburn, Charles (82)—January 9, 1972
Wilde, Hagar (67)—September 25, 1971
Zoellner, Peter Lee—September 21, 1971

COMPOSERS AND LYRICISTS

Babin, Victor (63)—March 1, 1972
Bagdasarian, Ross S. (52)—January 16, 1972
Ballantine, Edward (84)—July 2, 1971
Bart, Jan (52)—August 12, 1971
Bonds, Margaret (59)—April 26, 1972
Boutnifoff, Ivan (78)—February 17, 1972
Brooks, Jack (59)—November 8, 1971
Carroll, Jimmy (59)—March 19, 1972
Cassel, Irwin (84)—July 22, 1971
Confrey, Zez (76)—November 22, 1971
Cribarai, Joe (51)—August 14, 1971
Cutner, Sidney B. (68)—September 20, 1971
Davis, Uriel (80)—September 18, 1971
Donaldson, Muriel Pollock—May 24, 1971
Drohan, Benjamin V. (77)—April 24, 1972
Feleky, Leslie (59)—August 28, 1971
Gasparre, Dick (72)—October 17, 1971
Grofe, Ferde (80)—April 3, 1972
Hanlon, Bert—January 1, 1972
Henry, Shirley (47)—February 15, 1972
Jordan, Joe (89)—September 11, 1971
Jurmann, Walter (67)—June 24, 1971
Kopp, Rudolph G. (84)—February 20, 1972

432   THE BEST PLAYS OF 1971-1972

McFarland, Gary (38)—November 2, 1971
Miller, Seymour (63)—August 17, 1971
Moore, Douglas—July 25, 1971
Mundy, John (85)—May 29, 1971
Pober, Leon (51)—May 31, 1971
Ruggles, Carl (95)—October 24, 1971
Simon, William J. (80s)—August 3, 1971
Steiner, Max R. (83)—December 28, 1971
Strachey, Jack (78)—May 27, 1972
Tyler, T. Texas (55)—January 23, 1972
Wirges, William (77)—September 28, 1971
Wolpe, Stefan (69)—April 4, 1972

PRODUCERS, DIRECTORS, CHOREOGRAPHERS

Aufricht, Ernst Josef (72)—Summer 1971
Bailey, Frank J. (32)—June 27, 1971
Balloch, George S. (46)—October 21, 1971
Biberman, Herbert (71)—June 30, 1971
Brandt, Lou (56)—October 1, 1971
Brown, Harry Joe (78)—April 28, 1972
Carey, Rev. Thomas (68)—May 9, 1972
Cieplinski, Jan (71)—April 17, 1972
Coghlan, Charles F. (25)—March 16, 1972
Crocker, Emerson (60)—May 21, 1971
Daniels, Harold (68)—December 27, 1971
Deeter, Jasper (78)—May 31, 1972
Earl, Josephine—January 7, 1972
Field, William H. (56)—October 18, 1971
Franks, Jerry (63)—June 19, 1971
Fraser, Eddie (61)—February 21, 1972
Glazer, Maurice (51)—May 19, 1971
Goldin, Elias (59)—April 7, 1972
Hebert, Fred (60)—March 7, 1972
Hoffman, Charles H. (60)—April 8, 1972
Hoyt, Howard (65)—November 27, 1971
Hurdle, Jack (62)—July 12, 1971
James, Hal (58)—August 2, 1971
Jarvis, Robert C. (79)—November 13, 1971
Konstantinov, Vladimir (67)—April 24, 1972
Lander, Harald (66)—September 14, 1971
Lewis, Windsor (53)—May 15, 1972
McCleery, Albert (60)—May 13, 1972
Nagy, Dr. Elmer (65)—January 30, 1972
Nijinska, Bronislava (81)—December 20, 1971
Paumgartner, Bernhard (83)—July 27, 1971
Porterfield, Robert H. (65)—October 28, 1971
Prager, Stanley (54)—January 18, 1972
Randall, Peter (55)—June 14, 1971
Roth, Carl Heins (62)—April 11, 1972
Skinner, Richard (71)—August 3, 1971
Strickland, Cowles (68)—October 22, 1971
Tyson, Ruth M. (58)—September 13, 1971
Wolf, Van (44)—March 22, 1972

CONDUCTORS

Bertolami, J. Albert (73)—December 29, 1971
Cimini, Pietro (97)—October 25, 1971
Faier, Yuri F. (81)—August 4, 1971
Ford, Harry (71)—June 26, 1971
Goodman, Al (81)—January 10, 1972
Hill, Harry L. Ton (60)—December 13, 1971

Lewis, Ted (80)—August 25, 1971
Spann, Robert (Buster (62)—January 18, 1972
Webb, Edward J. (55)—November 26, 1971

DESIGNERS

Dunkel, Eugene (81)—April 10, 1972
Gherardi, Piero (61)—June 7, 1971
Lawrence, Pauline (70)—July 16, 1971
Lee, Tom (61)—July 14, 1971
St. Pierre, Louis (82)—November 17, 1971
Scharf, Erwin (71)—February 8, 1972
Trittipo, James (43)—September 15, 1971

CRITICS

Abelman, Lester (58)—May 27, 1972
Bolton, Edwin L. (53)—July 28, 1971
Bryant, Marshall F. (79)—September 27, 1971
Chapman, John (71)—January 19, 1972
Cowran, Clay (58)—January 27, 1972
Delehanty, Thornton W. (77)—August 13, 1971
Heriat, Philippe (73)—October 10, 1971
Izant, Robert J. (84)—December 8, 1971
Kienzl, Florian (77)—April 1, 1972
Marsh, W. Ward (77)—June 23, 1971
Miller, Llewellyn (72)—September 1, 1971
Sacchi, Filippo (84)—September 7, 1971
Weinstock, Herbert (65)—October 21, 1971
Winchell, Walter (74)—February 20, 1972

MUSICIANS

Allman, Duane (25)—October 29, 1971
Armstrong, Louis (71)—July 6, 1971
Baker, Eustace (32)—August 11, 1971
Barlow, Howard (80)—January 31, 1972
Barraclough, David (42)—May 6, 1971
Beers, Robert (52)—May 26, 1972
Bergman, Edward I. (66)—October 22, 1971
Bergman, Paul M. (67)—November 22, 1971
Boatman, Sidney (44)—May 6, 1971
Bonano, Joseph G. (72)—March 27, 1972
Britt, Gary—December 19, 1971
Clark, Garner (56)—November 21, 1971
Curtis, King (37)—August 13, 1971
Ecton, Nello (78)—March 22, 1972
Fio Rita, Ted (70)—July 22, 1971
Fisher, William H. (58)—April 24, 1972
Guy, Fred (73)—November 22, 1971
Hardin, Lil—August 27, 1971
Harris, Sidney (67)—June 3, 1971
Hayes, Clarence Leonard (63)—February 12, 1972
Hodges, John G. (56)—October 12, 1971
Horner, Anton (94)—December 4, 1971
Howard, Cammie (61)—April 14, 1972
Humphrey, Earl (68)—June 26, 1971
McCallum, David (75)—March 1972
McGarity, Lou (54)—August 28, 1971
Markoe, Mirko (62)—March 17, 1972
Miller, Ernest (75)—December 4, 1971
Morgan, Lee (33)—February 19, 1972
Nyer, Don (69)—April 14, 1972

Parenti, Tony (71)—April 17, 1972
Philburn, Al (69)—February 29, 1972
Pollack, Ben (67)—June 7, 1971
Pulliam, Steve—October 20, 1971
Roberts, Skip (24)—March 3, 1972
Rooney, Dave (38)—October 4, 1971
Shavers, Charlie (53)—July 8, 1971
Shulman, Harry (55)—October 23, 1971
Smith, Tab—August 17, 1971
Stern, Carl (69)—July 12, 1971
Stogel, Steve (23)—February 1, 1972
Sullivan, Joe (61)—October 13, 1971
Tomas, John (69)—November 7, 1971
Unwin, Kenneth C. (56)—February 1, 1972
Voelker, Melvin D. (60)—February 12, 1972
Wright, Johnny (70)—February 7, 1972

OTHERS

Aaron, John A. (51)—February 6, 1972
  TV producer assoc. with Edward R. Murrow
Alberty, Sir Bronson (90)—July 21, 1971
  British theater management
Altier, William B.—July 13, 1971
  Founder of first dinner theater
Amberg, George H. (69)—July 27, 1971
  Curator of dance and theater design, Museum of Modern Art
Anspacher, Mrs. Florence S. (84)—July 21, 1971. Theater benefactor
Anthony, Edward (76)—August 16, 1971
  Author of theatrical biographies
Arlen, Stephen (59)—January 1972
  Director of Sadler's Wells Opera
Barbier, Lawrence H. (69)—November 14, 1971. Film publicist
Barkow, Arthur A. (58)—May 23, 1972
  Stage manager
Barnum, Bush (60)—December 27, 1971
  Publicist
Beech, Mrs. Isabella (77)—January 3, 1972
  Radio commentator
Bellard, Mrs. Marian (70)—February 9, 1972
  Head usher at Town Hall
Blocki, Fritz (71)—May 17, 1972
  Writer and producer of TV Shows
Bochert, Charles G. (92)—June 15, 1971
  Publicist
Bonnheim, Byron A. (54)—March 20, 1972
  Publicist
Bose, Devaki K. (73)—November 17, 1971
  Indian film director
Bourke-White, Margaret (67)—August 27, 1971. Photo-journalist
Brady, Thomas F. (56)—April 4, 1972
  Hollywood correspondent for N. Y. *Times*
Brooks, Maude (92)—September 9, 1971
  Co-owner of Brooks Stock Company
Brown, Fredric (65)—March 11, 1972
  Author of movie scripts, mysteries
Burnside, Col. Mortimer B. (81)—August 23, 1971. Investment banker in show business
Bushman, Bruce (60)—February 12, 1972
  Cartoon and amusement park artist

Cameron, Alan (71)—March 28, 1972
  Screen writer
Carlin, Phillips (77)—August 27, 1971
  Pioneer radio and TV broadcaster
Carlton, Leonard (60)—September 9, 1971
  Radio editor for N. Y. *Post*
Carney, William (73)—March 9, 1972
  N. Y. *Times* theater and talkie movie writer
Case, Ethel L. (87)—November 29, 1971
  One of founders of Long Beach Community Players
Cavanagh, James P. (49)—September 25, 1971
  Film-TV writer
Cerf, Bennett A. (73)—August 27, 1971
  Publisher, humorist, TV personality
Charles, Jacques (89)—October 1971
  Discovered Maurice Chevalier, Mistinguette
Chatin, Marienne (68)—September 13, 1972
  Trustee American Shakespeare Festival
Chavchavadze, Paul (72)—July 9, 1971
  Active in Cape Cod Summer Theater
Clairmont, Ingrid (43)—October 14, 1971
  Hollywood columnist for Swedish papers
Clark, Walter Van Tilburg (62)—November 10, 1971. Author of *The Ox-Bow Incident*
Cohen, Max A. (75)—June 4, 1971
  Theater owner
Colburn, Everett (79)—March 21, 1972
  Operator of World's Championship Rodeo
Comer, Charles A. (73)—November 28, 1971
  Founder of Community Theaters
Conklin, Chester (83)—October 11, 1971
  Pioneer of two-reel Keystone Kop era, Barnum circus clown
Conklin, James (71)—June 17, 1971
  Theater manager
Connelly, Eugene P. (70)—December 1, 1971
  City Council member concerned with New York City cultural affairs
Corbin, Ray (35)—October 26, 1971
  Country Western singer, composer, band leader
Crowley, Mrs. Alice (88)—January 6, 1972
  Co-founder of Neighborhood Playhouse
Dalzell, Allan C. (75)—March 13, 1972
  Newark columnist and theatrical publicist
Davis, Bob (Alabama) (61)—September 22, 1971. Franchot Tone's stand-in
Davis, Charles E. (93)—November 1, 1971
  Circus buff and collector
Dillon, Josephine (87)—November 10, 1971
  Hollywood dramatic coach
Dinin, Samuel (58)—May 3, 1972
  Film photographer
Disney, Roy O. (78)—December 20, 1971
  Chairman of board of Walt Disney productions
Douglass, Kingman (75)—October 8, 1971
  Adele Astaire's husband
Downing, Harry (78)—January 9, 1972
  Actor in first talkie, *Lights of New York*
Drake, Harry (70)—December 10, 1971
  Theatrical booking agent

Dronge, Alfred (60)—May 3, 1972
Director of Avnet, Inc., President of Guild Musical Instruments
Duffield, John M. (62)—February 11, 1972
Fireworks producer for outdoor displays
Dupre, Marcel (85)—May 30, 1972
Master organist and improviser
Edson, Elie (89)—November 21, 1971
Publicist
Elliott, Jack (57)—January 3, 1972
Film-TV producer, reporter for *Variety*
Fairbairn, Ann (70)—February 7, 1972
Novelist, handled tours for George Lewis's band
Falck, Lionel L. (82)—Summer 1971
Manager of Strand Theater in London
Feldman, Erwin (67)—April 20, 1972
Attorney in theater, films, TV.
Fenton, Frank (65)—Summer 1971
Screen writer, novelist
Fineman, Bernard P. (76)—September 26, 1971. Film producer
Fiske, Frank (80)—December 5, 1971
Newspaperman and *Variety* staffer
Fitzpatrick, Thomas J. (89)—June 26, 1971
Publicist
Fleischman, Harvey (65)—March 22, 1972
Vice president Wometco Enterprises, Inc.
Foley, Norman (67)—January 22, 1972
Songplugger and music publisher
Fox, Sam (89)—November 30, 1971
Publisher of film music
Franklin, Sidney (79)—May 18, 1972
Film producer and director
Friendly, Dan (59)—February 1, 1972
Box office treasurer
Gamet, Kenneth (67)—October 13, 1971
Film TV writer
Gates, Nellie (91)—May 1972
Film producer
Geiger, Milton—September 28, 1971
TV writer
Gillis, Thomas C. (58)—February 8, 1972
Director of fund-raising for Lincoln Center
Goldsmith, Clifford (72)—July 11, 1971
Creator of *The Aldrich Family*
Gordon, Maurice (58)—November 5, 1971
Scenic designer for TV commercials
Grace, Jean (85)—February 24, 1972
Theatrical booker
Gray, Irving (66)—January 16, 1972
Personal manager for Milton Berle
Greenberg, Ben (70)—February 27, 1972
Theatrical manager
Greenburger, Sanford (67)—June 9, 1971
Publishers' and writers' agent
Grierson, John (73)—February 19, 1972
Filmmaker who coined word "documentary"
Gross, Mike (49)—April 21, 1972
Music editor of *Variety*
Grossman, George (67)—January 4, 1972
Publicist and former newspaperman

Hamid, Mrs. George A. Sr. (74)—June 19, 1971. Widow of George A. Hamid
Hamid, George A. (75)—June 13, 1971
Showman at Steel Pier, Atlantic City
Hanau, Stella (81)—April 23, 1972
Publicist
Heatter, Gabriel (82)—March 30, 1972
Radio commentator
Heffernan, Harold—October 29, 1971
Hollywood columnist for Detroit *News*
Heflin, Martin—April 1972
Publicist, brother of Van Heflin
Herbert, A. P. (81)—November 11, 1971
British wit, collaborator on musicals, revues
Hohner, Dr. Karl (78)—November 1, 1971
Senior director H. Hohner, Inc. harmonicas
Holt, Nat (78)—August 3, 1971
Theater manager, film producer
Hubbard, Lucien (82)—December 31, 1971
Screen writer, director, producer
Hunt, Mrs. Minabel (79)—June 5, 1971
Mother of Marsha Hunt, played for first radio broadcast in 1920s picked up by ship at sea
Jacobson, Clarence (84)—August 6, 1971
Theatrical company manager
Kaaihue, Johnny (70)—November 29, 1971
Founder of Royal Hawaiians
Karavaeff, Simeon (77)—February 15, 1972
Partner of Pavlova
Kendall, Cricket E. (65)—March 8, 1972
Publicity director
King, Ed (50)—November 18, 1971
TV writer
King, James Joyce (Red) (61)—November 29, 1971. Publicist
Kornheiser, Phil (88)—February 24, 1972
Leo Feist general professional manager
Kramer, Earl (76)—November 29, 1971
Uncle of Stanley Kramer, treasurer of Kramer Productions
Landi, Erberto (63)—October 10, 1971
Producer, publicist
Lang, Walter (73)—February 7, 1972
Film director
Laurence, Jack I. (63)—February 10, 1972
Manager of Glenn Miller orchestra
Lawrence, Harry (74)—September 9, 1971
Radio, TV writer
Levin, Harry (68)—April 15, 1972
Theater ticket broker
Levin, Philip J. (62)—August 3, 1971
President of Madison Square Garden
Levy, Matthew M.—September 4, 1971
Representative of IATSE
Lipton, Elsie Cukor—November 1, 1971
Hollywood agent, sister of George Cukor
Lopez, Eddie (31)—November 26, 1971
Columnist for San Juan *Star,* humorist
McManus, John (58)—September 12, 1972
Film editor
McSorley, Lars Michael (41)—February 16, 1972. Publicist

MacGregor, Jock (56)—November 25, 1971
Variety staffer, British film trade journalist
Majeski, John, Sr. (79)—November 19, 1971
Owner, publisher *Musical America*
Mangel, Ira (61)—December 17, 1971
Publicist and manager for Louis Armstrong
Mann, Hank (84)—October 10, 1971
One of Keystone Kops
Manning, Marty (55)—November 22, 1971
Arranger
Martin, Al (75)—October 10, 1971
Screen writer
Menges, Herbert (69)—February 21, 1972
Director of music for Old Vic
Mills, Win (63)—December 24, 1971
Columnist
Navarro, Albert (57)—December 31, 1971
Head of Navarro Orchestra
Nicoll, Oliver W. (67)—September 30, 1971
Company manager
Norman, Fred (78)—April 17, 1972
Booking agent
O'Haffey, Thom (53)—August 15, 1971
Variety correspondent
O'Riada, Sean (40)—October 3, 1971
Director of music at Abbey Theater
Pearce, Sam (62)—September 12, 1971
Curator of Theater and Music Collection of
the Museum of the City of New York
Peers, Victor (74)—September 18, 1971
Film and TV writer, producer
Peterson, Eloise Kimball Walton (69)—De-
cember 13, 1971. Publicist
Pinanski, Samuel (77)—February 8, 1971
Pioneer in developing theaters
Priteca, B. Marcus (81)—October 1, 1971
Theater architect
Raine, Norman Reilly (76)—July 19, 1971
Creator of "Tugboat Annie"
Ramos, Joao Ortigao (76)—Summer 1971
Portuguese theatrical impresario
Rathvon, N. Peter (81)—May 26, 1972
Film producer
Rau, Neil—November 19, 1971
Hollywood legman, for Louella Parsons
Reed, John (66)—Summer 1971
General counsel for National Association of
Theater Owners of Texas
Reek, Edmund H. (73)—October 24, 1971
Producer, vice president of Fox Movietone
News
Rice, Cy (58)—August 23, 1971
Author of books about show people
Roeburt, John (63)—May 22, 1972
Author of radio and TV dramas
Romm, Mikhail I. (70)—November 1, 1971
Russian film director
Rosen, Jerry M. (60)—February 28, 1972
Theatrical agent
Rousseau, William P. (57)—May 2, 1972
TV, radio producer, writer, director
Rubinstein, Leon J. (83)—February 18, 1972
Publicist

Ruggles, Wesley (82)—January 8, 1972
Film director, brother of Charles Ruggles
Ruland, Bishop (70)—September 10, 1971
Paramount Theater organist, arranger
Saint-Denis, Michel (73)—July 31, 1971
Educator, founding director of Old Vic
Theater School, founder of London Theater
Studio
Sanford, Robert (65)—August 17, 1971
Personal manager
Sarnoff, David (80)—December 12, 1971
Chairman of board of RCA, pioneer in elec-
tronics and broadcasting
Sawyer, Jeannette—November 1, 1971
Publicist, writer, illustrator
Schang, Frederick C., III (44)—July 15, 1971
Vice president Columbia Artists Manage-
ment
Schwartz, Abraham G. (78)—July 19, 1971
Theaterowner from nickelodeon days
Seeburg, N. Marshall (74)—January 29, 1972
Jukebox and vending machine pioneer
Shulman, Thomas—November 29, 1971
Theater man on Boston *Record American*
Skouras, Spyros P. (78)—August 16, 1971
Film pioneer, head of 20th Century Fox
Smith, Betty (75)—January 17, 1972
Author of *A Tree Grows in Brooklyn*
Solomon, Steve (24)—May 6, 1972
Assistant agent at William Morris Agency
Spiegel, Henry (61)—November 22, 1971
Publicity director, Paramount Theater
Stahl, Herman (85)—April 27, 1972
Pioneer of nickelodeon business
Stempel, Frank (75)—December 17, 1971
Hollywood personal manager
Stern, Bill (64)—November 19, 1971
Sports announcer
Stern, George (68)—May 3, 1972
MCA agent
Sternberger, Estelle (85)—December 23, 1971
Radio commentator
Stewart, Rosalie (81)—December 12, 1971
Hollywood literary agent
Stitt, Jesse (67)—November 23, 1971
Pastor who sponsored plays at Greenwich
Mews
Stuart, Donald (52)—May 15, 1972
Partner and co-producer of Originals Only
Sugarman, Harry (72)—May 31, 1972
Theaterowner
Sumner, John S. (94)—June 20, 1971
Executive secretary, Society for Suppression
of Vice
Sumner, Stanley (81)—July 5, 1971
Manager of several Greater Boston theaters
Sunami, Soichi (86)—November 11, 1971
Staff photographer, Museum of Modern Art
Tabor, Ethel F. (70s)—April 16, 1972
Costumer
Taft, James Gordon (42)—November 21, 1971
Theatrical attorney

Tashlin, Frank (59)—May 5, 1972
Movie director, writer
Terry, Paul H. (84)—October 25, 1971
Pioneer animated cartoonist, "Terrytoons"
Tetu, Princess (79)—July 10, 1971
Ringling Brothers "Queen of the High Wire"
Thomas, Sandra—January 20, 1972
Founder of and president of Stage Mothers' Club
Thorne, John N., Jr. (56)—February 7, 1972
Life specialist on entertainment issues
Toscanini, Walter (73)—June 30, 1971
Son of Arturo Toscanini
Trendle, George W. (87)—May 10, 1972
Creator of radio's "The Lone Ranger"
Turner, Terry (79)—November 30, 1971
Publicist
Van Deventer, Fred (68)—December 2, 1971
Originator of "Twenty Questions"
Ward, Edward (73)—September 26, 1971
Composer-conductor at movie studios
Warren, Mrs. Mirian Howell (72)—April 3, 1972. Actor's and author's agent

Weinberg, Myron K. (43)—December 30, 1971. Manager for Broadway plays
Weininger, Lloyd (78)—December 23, 1971
Teacher of scenic design Drama Department, Carnegie Institute of Technology
Weissman, Dr. Philip (61)—February 27, 1972. Psychiatrist specializing in theater
Widner, Randell C. (47)—September 9, 1971
Managing director of Grand Opera House, Macon, Ga.
Williams, Bernie (60)—December 19, 1971
Publicist
Winston, Carl (78)—June 7, 1971
Writer, associate producer
Wylie, Philip (69)—October 25, 1971
Author
Yorker, Emerson (70s)—September 6, 1971
Pioneer producer in radio, TV
Zeitlin, Sally (62)—March 18, 1972
Publicity executive secretary
Zelli, Joe (82)—December 12, 1971
Owner of Parisian nightclub

INDEX

Play titles are in **bold face** and **bold face italic** page numbers refer to pages where cast and credit listings may be found.